BARRON'S

HOW TO PREPARE FOR THE

GRE

PSYCHOLOGY

GRADUATE RECORD EXAMINATION IN PSYCHOLOGY

5th EDITION

Edward L. Palmer, Ph.D.
Watson Professor
Department of Psychology
Davidson College
Davidson, North Carolina

and

Sharon L. Thompson-Schill, Ph.D.
Assistant Professor
Department of Psychology
University of Pennsylvania
Philadelphia, Pennsylvania

BARRON'S

All inquiries should be addressed to:
Barron's Educational Series, Inc.
250 Wireless Boulevard
Hauppauge, New York 11788
http://www.barronseduc.com

Library of Congress Catalog Card No. 00-068886
International Standard Book No. 0-7641-1704-1

Library of Congress Cataloging-in-Publication Data
Palmer, Edward L.
    GRE psychology : how to prepare for the Graduate Record Examination in psychology /
Edward L. Palmer and Sharon L. Thompson-Schill.—5th ed.
     p. cm.
    ISBN 0-7641-1704-1 (alk. paper)
    1. Psychology—Examination—Study guides. 2. Graduate Record Examination—Study
guides. 3. Psychology—Examinations, questions, etc. I. Title: How to prepare for the Graduate
Record Examination in psychology. II. Thompson-Schill, Sharon L. III. Title.

BF78 .P34 2001
150'.76—dc21   00-068886

Contents

Preface

There is no substitute for study in preparing for any examination. *Barron's How to Prepare for the Graduate Record Examination in Psychology* is a study guide, designed to aid you in your test preparation by providing general information on testing purposes and procedures, establishing the areas in psychology on which you should concentrate for best results, and enabling you to become more familiar with the actual test by offering six sample tests with answers to check your progress.

The first chapter gives general information about the test including an explanation of its purpose, directions on how to apply, the format of the test, test-taking strategy, and how the test is scored. There is also a section on test preparation and how to make the best use of this book.

Chapter 2 provides a diagnostic test for your general knowledge assessment. It will help you to identify the areas needing your most concentrated review effort.

Chapter 3, a comprehensive review of the main areas covered on the test, includes discussions of physiological and comparative psychology, sensation and perception, learning, cognition and complex human learning, developmental psychology, motivation and emotion, social psychology, personality, psychopathology, clinical psychology, methodology, and applied psychology. This review, along with the sources for further reading appearing at the end of the chapter, should serve as the basis for your study. By using this information as a starting point, you will be able to touch on all the major areas of psychology, concentrating on those topics with which you are least familiar.

Chapter 4 provides a second diagnostic test for you to assess your progress after reviewing the main areas covered on the test.

Chapter 5 consists of four sample tests, modeled after the actual GRE Subject Test in Psychology, with answers and answer explanations. By simulating the conditions of the real test as you take these sample tests, you can judge how well you will do.

Used properly, *Barron's How to Prepare for the Graduate Record Examination in Psychology* can be very helpful to you in your test preparation. If at the conclusion of your review you have developed confidence in your ability to do well on this test, it will have served its purpose well.

Acknowledgments

We want to express our deep appreciation to our caring families, friends, and colleagues who knew our pressures, gave us distance, balance, generous support, and beautiful understanding. Special thanks to Mrs. Fern Duncan and Ms. Irene Kan who assisted at critical moments throughout the intensive process. And our thanks to you for the privilege of "walking with you" as you pursue your goal and accept its challenge.

CHAPTER 1

The Psychology Test

Purpose

The Graduate Record Examination (GRE) Psychology Test, administered by the Educational Testing Service (ETS), is used by graduate admissions committees to assess and select applicants for graduate programs in psychology, and to determine the recipients of scholarships, fellowships, and various other academic awards.

Due to the large number of applicants for graduate study in psychology, it is often difficult for graduate schools to compare the qualifications of all the candidates for admission to their psychology programs. The Psychology Test, taken by nearly all applicants, serves as a common denominator. Although it seldom is the sole criterion for admission or rejection, the Psychology Test is an important factor in the admissions decision. When considered along with such information as each candidate's undergraduate program and grades, it can give the graduate school a good idea of the individual's capabilities and chances for success in graduate study.

Application Procedure

Students interested in taking the Psychology Test should send for the *GRE Information Bulletin*, published by ETS. The *Bulletin* contains information about application deadlines, examination dates, fee schedules, and testing locations, along with the necessary test registration forms. It can be obtained by writing:

> Graduate Record Examinations
> Educational Testing Service
> P.O. Box 6000
> Princeton, New Jersey 08541-6000

The Psychology Test is usually given in October or November, December, and April. Since the competition for places in graduate psychology programs is intense, you would be wise to take the examination as early as possible to ensure that your scores are reported to the schools of your choice in plenty of time to receive full consideration.

You can get current test dates and general information at *www.gre.org*. You can also purchase a Subject Test practice book that contains an actually administered test, answer sheets, correct answers, and question-by-question analysis of how the students who took that test performed. The book is available from the web site or from 1(800)537-3160 (U.S.) or 1(609)771-7243 (outside U.S.).

Format of the Test

The Psychology Test is a multiple-choice examination consisting of about 200–220 questions, each with five possible answer choices. Some questions involve the interpretation of graphs, diagrams, and reading passages; others directly require you to recall information gathered from your psychology courses. The test runs for 170 minutes, and as there are no separately timed sections, you may set your own pace as you work through the questions.

On the paper form of the test, you can refer to any question throughout the test-taking session. On the computerized form of the test, the level of test question difficulty is determined by the questions you previously have answered correctly and subsequent questions you receive are tailored to your response level. Question scoring is weighted on this difficulty basis.

A Word About "A/E" Questions

ETS recently added to their testing a question format they call A/E (Analysis of Evidence). It's a question type that focuses on methodology/analysis and your ability to spot weaknesses or inconsistencies in a data set, an experiment, a design, or the conclusions drawn from the data. You might be presented with a graph, a data set, or an experimental description followed by, perhaps, two to five questions relating to it. You can expect 6 to 15 questions (meaning 2 or 3 A/E questions) within any given form of the test.

Here's how these questions are described by the current chair and past chair of the ETS committee of faculty members making up questions for the Psychology GRE:

> For these questions, the student reads a paragraph describing a hypothetical research study and its results and then answers two to five questions about proper conclusions to be drawn, potential weaknesses of the study as described, and ways to improve the research design or to follow up with additional research (Kalat, J.W., & Matlin, M.W. (2000). "The GRE Psychology Test: A useful but poorly understood test." *Teaching of Psychology*, 27(1), 24–27).

We haven't seen these actual questions on a test. None of our references or the test booklet sold by ETS contained any, so we're going to drop an item into each of the tests that we bet will be a pretty close approximation to what you'll see.

Within your review you'll become expert analysts, so don't worry. Also remember that the A/E questions form a very small portion of the test.

Test-Taking Strategy

It is important to remember that the Psychology Test has been designed in such a way that even those students who achieve the highest scores will not answer every question correctly. The questions you may find difficult are not worth any more points than those that come easily to you, so make sure that you answer all the questions you are sure about before going back to tackle the harder ones.

Guessing

"Should I guess?" is one of the most common questions asked by students taking standardized tests. In the scoring of the GRE Psychology Test, correct answers count one point, incorrect answers are minus 1/4 point, and unanswered questions neither add to nor detract from the total score:

correct answers — 1/4 # incorrect answers = total score

Since each question has five possible answers, statistically you have a one in five chance of correctly answering a question in which you cannot eliminate even one of the possible answers. The more choices you can eliminate, of course, the better are the odds of your guessing the right answer. So, since you only lose 1/4 point for a wrong answer, guessing will very likely work to your benefit if you can eliminate at least one possible choice. On the other hand, it is very unlikely that guessing will prove detrimental to your total score as long as you refrain from guessing indiscriminately.

Scoring

Each student who takes the Psychology Test will receive three scaled scores: a total score for the entire test, an Experimental Psychology subscore, and a Social Psychology subscore. The total score range varies with each administration of the test, but a score of approximately 530 generally constitutes an average performance. The subscores are reported on a scale of 20 to 99, with a score of approximately 53 constituting the mean. The scores are reported on a scaled basis to enable the ETS and graduate admissions committees to compare directly performances across different administrations of the test. The scale acts as a yardstick by which all scores on the Psychology Test can be compared, regardless of the test date or the form of the test taken. Score interpretation information is contained in the booklet *A Description of the Psychology Test*, which is sent by the ETS to all test applicants. Be sure to retain this booklet so that you may accurately interpret your scores when you receive them.

Preparing for the Test

Psychology is a very broad subject, as you are already aware. This breadth gives the field interest, but at the same time means that preparation for a test such as the Psychology Test will require you to refamiliarize yourself with a wide range of material and concepts. There is no way to determine exactly how much coverage will be given to each of the areas within the discipline. Proportionate area coverage will vary from one examination to the next, although the areas being tested will remain constant. In two recent tests, the percentages of material devoted to the respective area concentrations were as follows:

Physiological and comparative psychology	13.6%	15.4%
Developmental psychology	12.2%	10.8%
Learning and motivation	12.2%	13.8%
Sensation and perception	12.2%	9.7%
Clinical psychology and psychopathology	10.8%	9.2%
Personality and social psychology	10.8%	21.0%
Cognition and complex human learning	10.0%	8.7%
Applied psychology	9.1%	2.2%
Methodology	9.1%	9.2%

While you can definitely see variations in the individual percentage coverages, there is an impressive agreement between the two columns. Physiological/ comparative, learning/motivation, sensation/perception, and cognition/complex human learning make up the area groupings generally known as experimental psychology. Developmental, clinical/psychopathology, personality/ social, and applied make up the area groupings generally known as interpersonal or social. Experimental comprises 48.0% of the questions in the first exam and 47.6% in the second. Interpersonal/social comprises 42.9% of the questions in the first exam and 43.2% in the second. These relative percentage weightings most likely will be consistent in whatever form of the GRE you take.

ETS makes a three-part distinction and estimates that 40% of its questions will fall in the Experimental/Natural Science category 1, 43% in the social/ social science category 2, and the remaining 17% in the general category, which encompasses history, applied research, measurement, research designs, and statistics.

Each of the above topic areas contains a central core of material that will demand your competence. Pay special attention to "theories," "effects," "models," "classic studies," and similar basic terminology. These terms reflect core material that you should know and understand. Also, since psychology is an active research field, major current studies will be of prominent interest to the psychologists who construct the GRE questions. A comprehensive introductory psychology textbook can provide an excellent starting point for your psychology review. These are a few of the many:

Baron, Robert A. *Psychology.* Needham Heights, MA: Allyn and Bacon, 2001.

Bernstein, Douglas A., Alison Clarke-Stewart, Louis A. Penner, Edward J. Roy, and Christopher D. Wickens. *Psychology.* New York: Houghton Mifflin, 2000.

Gleitman, Henry, Alan J. Fridlund, and Daniel Reisberg. *Psychology.* New York: W. W. Norton & Co., 1999.

Myers, David. *Exploring Psychology.* New York: Worth, 2000.

Weiten, Wayne. *Psychology: Themes and Variations.* Pacific Grove, Calif.: Brooks/Cole, 1999.

You likely have one of these books or a comparable book already. If not, virtually any of these will give you a strong, basic review. Where there's a choice, go for recency. *Contemporary Psychology*—a periodical available in most college and university libraries—will keep you abreast of new editions and new works just released. It will be an excellent reference source in every area of your review.

How to Use This Book

Barron's How to Prepare for the Graduate Record Examination in Psychology has been designed to help you review for the GRE Psychology Test while you are at the same time familiarizing yourself with the test format and the types of questions used on the test. Chapter 2 of this book contains a diagnostic test for you to try at the outset; this test will identify the topic areas in which you need the most work. Chapter 3 contains a comprehensive review of the basic areas of knowledge covered by the test. Chapter 4 of this book contains a second diagnostic test for you to try after reviewing the basic areas of knowledge. Chapter 5 consists of four sample tests, including answers and explanations for each of the questions. These tests simulate the actual GRE Psychology Test in number of questions, type of questions, and time allotted. By studying the material in Chapter 3 and testing your knowledge on the four sample tests, you will develop a familiarity with the Psychology Test that will bolster your confidence when taking the test and, most important of all, let you earn the highest score you can.

It should be stressed here that this book is *not* intended to take the place of an extensive review of your college psychology courses. For an examination such as the Psychology Test, in which specific knowledge is tested, it would be impossible to cover all the pertinent review material in a book of this size. *You* must decide what you need to concentrate on most heavily and how much time you will need to complete your review adequately. This book can help by showing you where your weaknesses lie. By taking the Chapter 2 diagnostic test at an early point in your review schedule, you will be able to see which areas give you the most trouble and then devote extra time to strengthening your knowledge of those particular areas.

Here are a few suggestions to help you get the most from this book:

- Don't try to cram your review into a few short evenings—give yourself enough time.
- Utilize as many review sources as you feel are necessary.
- Try to simulate the actual exam as you take each practice test (170 minutes per test, no looking at notes or other study aids).
- Learn from your mistakes. The answers and explanations included in this book are geared toward pointing out your weaknesses so that you may strengthen them.

By using this book throughout your review, in conjunction with other review materials, you will be well on your way to achieving a better score on the GRE Psychology Test.

2 Diagnostic Test 1 for Review Analysis

The purpose of this diagnostic test is to help you spot areas of weakness so that you can focus your review time and effort most efficiently. The test will have a normal GRE Test length and timing, and its area coverages will be representative. In this chapter you will familiarize yourself with the test areas and procedure while discovering where you need to do your most concentrated review.

Preparation for Taking the Diagnostic Test

Now is the time to look at that sacred set of notes you took in your introductory psychology class. Spend some time reviewing them and refreshing your mind on the subject matter. Do the same with your introductory psychology book—if it is of recent vintage. If your book is not recent, do this review with one of the textbooks mentioned in Chapter 1. Your notes and book review will freshen the psychology content you have had. Once you have done this it will be time for your "content check-up."

How to Use the Diagnostic Test

Find a quiet place free of distraction. Take several sharpened pencils and a watch or suitable timer. Put away all your notes and books. Limit yourself to 170 minutes and begin, recording your answer choices on the answer grid sheets. Remember, this test will *assess areas to work on*, so there is no need to panic when you encounter a question you can't answer. That will give you the chance to use your guessing strategy! Later on in your review you will notice that you don't need to guess nearly as much—a beautiful sign of progress. Good luck!

Diagnostic Test 1

Time: 170 minutes

Directions: Each of the following questions contains five possible responses. Read the question carefully and select the response that you feel is most appropriate. Then completely darken the oval on your answer grid that corresponds with your choice.

1. Dysthymic disorders are

   (A) mood disorders
   (B) sexual disorders
   (C) substance-related disorders
   (D) schizophrenic disorders
   (E) somatoform disorders

2. Current trends in mental health do *not* include

   (A) construction of larger state hospitals
   (B) stepped up emphasis on outpatient care
   (C) greater emphasis on community mental health centers
   (D) prominent use of behavior modification
   (E) group therapy

3. "It treats symptom rather than cause!" This is a criticism commonly leveled at

   (A) psychoanalysis
   (B) implosive psychotherapy
   (C) insight-oriented therapy
   (D) behavior therapy
   (E) transactional analysis

4. Among first admissions to public mental hospitals, which one of the following diagnoses is most prevalent?

   (A) schizophrenic reaction
   (B) psychoneurotic disorder
   (C) alcoholic addiction
   (D) involutional psychotic reaction
   (E) cerebral arteriosclerosis

5. The view that neurosis is essentially synonymous with personal immaturity is held by

   (A) Fromm
   (B) Mowrer
   (C) Jung
   (D) Skinner
   (E) Watson

6. The veterans hospital plans to implement a technique known as "flooding." Within this approach the veterans will vividly re-live and re-experience the traumatic events they went through during combat. "Flooding" would be technically described as

   (A) client-centered therapy
   (B) systematic desensitization
   (C) implosive therapy
   (D) counterconditioning
   (E) logotherapy

7. Which form of schizophrenia contains delusions of grandeur or persecution?

   (A) residual   (B) disorganized   (C) catatonic
   (D) paranoid   (E) undifferentiated

8. Which of the following could lead to psychopathology?

   (A) fear of failure
   (B) self-actualization
   (C) self-confidence
   (D) little gap between real and ideal self
   (E) self-direction

Questions 9 and *10* are based on the following passage.

Every profession has its own jargon, and we psychiatrists have ours. But while the strange terms a lawyer or an archeologist uses are harmless enough—the worst they do is mystify outsiders—the terms psychiatrists use can hurt people and sometimes do. Instead of helping to comfort and counsel and heal people—which is the goal of psychiatry—the terms often cause despair. Words like *schizophrenia*, *manic-depressive*, and *psychotic*, for example, frighten patients and worry their anxious relatives and friends. The use of these alarming terms also affects psychiatrists. They lead us back into the pessimism and helplessness of the days when mental illness was thought to be made up of many specific "diseases," and when each "disease" bore a formidable label and a gloomy prognosis. (From Karl Menninger, "Psychiatrists Use Dangerous Words," *Saturday Evening Post*, April 25, 1964.)

9. From reading this well-known position statement, one would expect Menninger to draw which one of the following conclusions?

   (A) The diagnostic, medical model should be used in emotional disturbances.
   (B) Emotional disturbance is an illness in the same sense as any physiological disease.
   (C) Psychiatry should dispense with labels for emotional disturbances.
   (D) Labels, though frightening to patients and their relatives, have a definite role in emotional rehabilitation.
   (E) The nomothetic approach to personality is the only viable approach.

10. Which one of the following persons would you expect to be in most agreement with this stated view of Menninger?

   (A) Szasz   (B) Freud   (C) Sullivan
   (D) Templeton   (E) Hathaway

11. The detective was in constant danger. One day his head was slightly creased by a bullet, and he indicated immediately afterward that he was blind. Hospital observation indicated no physiological cause for the blindness. This is a case of

   (A) paranoid-type schizophrenia
   (B) obsessive-compulsion
   (C) neurasthenia
   (D) anxiety disorder
   (E) conversion disorder

12. A seventeen-year-old girl sits in a corner, weeping continually. This behavior could be

   (A) hypochondria   (B) nomadism   (C) repression
   (D) regression   (E) reaction formation

13. Enuresis

   (A) is most common among adults
   (B) has a poor prognosis
   (C) is more common among women than men
   (D) can result from faulty parental discipline
   (E) is contagious and highly communicable

14. A man walking to work counts the cracks in the sidewalk. Although he is almost to his office, he fears that he has miscounted and so returns to the subway terminal to begin counting again. This behavior is known as

   (A) hypochondriacal reaction
   (B) conversion disorder
   (C) obsessive-compulsive disorder
   (D) sociopathic disorder
   (E) schizophrenic reaction

15. *DSM-IV* refers to

   (A) *Drug and Shock for Mental Depression*, 4th ed.
   (B) *Developmental and Social Manual of Mental Development*, 4th ed.
   (C) *Diagrammatic and Schematic Manual of Mental Deficiencies*, 4th ed.
   (D) *Diagnostic and Statistical Manual of Mental Disorders*, 4th ed.
   (E) *Developmental and Schematic Manual of Mental Disorders*, 4th ed.

16. Using the dynamic model of psychopathology, the theoretical cause of emotional disturbance would be

   (A) faulty learning   (B) lack of responsibility
   (C) faulty morality   (D) unconscious conflicts
   (E) faulty perception

17. *Not* a major criterion upon which to define mental illness is

    (A) statistical deviation
    (B) cultural deviation
    (C) criminal deviation
    (D) behavioral deviation
    (E) clinical deviation

18. Insulin shock therapy

    (A) has a fatality rate of approximately 5 percent
    (B) has been considered most valuable with depressed patients
    (C) was considered most useful with paranoid schizophrenics but is rarely used today
    (D) involves the creation of a dazed state without loss of consciousness
    (E) has had its greatest success in the treatment of problems associated with alcoholism

19. The term most closely associated with the name Eysenck is

    (A) autonomic reactivity
    (B) parapraxes
    (C) reintegration
    (D) shadow
    (E) functional fictionalism

20. The primary problem encountered in treating drug addicts, alcoholics, and sociopaths is

    (A) their preference for their present life style
    (B) the expense of therapy
    (C) the fact that more want help than can be treated
    (D) the side effects of aversive conditioning
    (E) the exclusive posture of Synanon

21. Which one of the following is within the psychotomimetic drug classification?

    (A) aspirin   (B) chlorpromazine   (C) *d*-tubocurarine
    (D) LSD   (E) nicotine

22. Researchers have found correlations between juvenile delinquency and such background aspects as

    (A) broken homes and parental absenteeism
    (B) neurotic, dependent fathers
    (C) father acceptance and mother submissiveness
    (D) strong religious background
    (E) warm, permissive family setting

23. Body metabolism is a key function of the

    (A) pituitary gland   (B) adrenal gland   (C) thyroid gland
    (D) pineal gland   (E) lymph gland

24. *Not* reduced during sleep is the level of

    (A) respiration
    (B) blood pressure
    (C) body temperature
    (D) heart rate
    (E) gastric contractions

25. Which one of the following bodily patterns does *not* accompany dreaming activity?

    (A) a distinctive EEG pattern
    (B) rapid eye movement
    (C) high level of cerebral blood flow
    (D) higher brain temperature
    (E) higher level of general muscle activity

26. Which one of the following best describes the central nervous system?

    (A) autonomic system
    (B) efferent fibers
    (C) the brain and the spinal cord
    (D) the spinal cord and the glandular system
    (E) afferent fibers

27. Which person's work and writing triggered the "psychocivilization versus electroligarchy" debate and discussions?

    (A) Magoun   (B) Mowrer   (C) Sperry
    (D) Fisher   (E) Delgado

28. In some neurons, the axon is insulated by the

    (A) Sylvian sheath   (B) Pacinian sheath   (C) nerve fiber
    (D) ganglion   (E) myelin sheath

29. Comparatively speaking, which one of the following animals has the most prominent cerebral cortex?

    (A) salmon   (B) alligator   (C) pigeon
    (D) rabbit   (E) dog

30. Among animals or humans, which one of the following is *not* a cycle affecting the degree or prominence of sexual behavior?

    (A) life   (B) estrous   (C) androgenous
    (D) menstrual   (E) breeding, seasonal

31. Which of the following is *not* an entry in a sensory grouping based on locus of stimulus source?

    (A) exteroceptors   (B) proprioceptors   (C) interoceptors
    (D) nociceptors   (E) peripheroceptors

32. The sympathetic nervous system

    (A) is a subdivision of the somatic nervous system
    (B) is a subdivision of the autonomic nervous system
    (C) parallels the effects of the parasympathetic nervous system
    (D) preserves the homeostatic model
    (E) promotes syntonic functioning

33. Sensory-motor responses that are rapid and automatic are called

    (A) instincts   (B) reuptakes   (C) permeable
    (D) reflexes   (E) affective

Questions 34 and 35 are based on the following statements.

    (1) The animal eats because it needs certain nutrients.
    (2) The animal eats because it knows it needs food.
    (3) The animal eats because it feels hungry.
    (4) The animal eats because it is aware of its need for nutrition.
    (5) The animal eats because of a change in blood-sugar level.

34. Which one of the preceding would comparative psychologists consider the most purely teleonomic statement?

    (A) 1   (B) 2   (C) 3   (D) 4   (E) 5

35. Which one of the preceding would comparative psychologists consider the most purely mechanistic statement?

    (A) 1   (B) 2   (C) 3   (D) 4   (E) 5

36. Body maintenance of a state of internal physiological balance is described by the term

    (A) innervation   (B) ionization   (C) reflex
    (D) homeostasis   (E) piloerection

37. The corpus callosum of an individual has been sectioned as part of a treatment for epilepsy. On which of the following WAIS subtests could the person be expected to encounter the most postoperative difficulty?

    (A) information
    (B) arithmetic
    (C) similarities
    (D) vocabulary
    (E) block design

38. The cells that respond to changes in their environment and signal these changes to the nervous system are known as
    (A) receptors
    (B) effectors
    (C) striated
    (D) myelin
    (E) affectors

Questions 39–43 are based on the following diagram. Using the drawing below, mark the number corresponding to the primary area for the following functions.

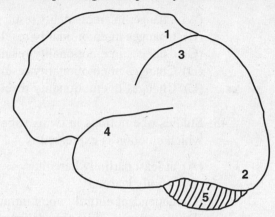

39. Motor functions

    (A) 1   (B) 2   (C) 3   (D) 4   (E) 5

40. Visual functions

    (A) 1   (B) 2   (C) 3   (D) 4   (E) 5

41. Auditory functions

    (A) 1   (B) 2   (C) 3   (D) 4   (E) 5

42. Somatosensory functions

    (A) 1   (B) 2   (C) 3   (D) 4   (E) 5

43. Maintenance of balance and posture

    (A) 1   (B) 2   (C) 3   (D) 4   (E) 5

44. Which one of the following is true of afferent neurons?

    (A) located in the dorsal column of the spinal cord
    (B) located in the ventral column of the spinal cord
    (C) not located in the spinal cord
    (D) equivalent in function to the efferent neurons
    (E) found only in the striated muscles

45. Which one of the following abbreviations is common to discussions of synaptic potential?

    (A) ENSP   (B) APSP   (C) INSP   (D) EPSP   (E) ANSP

46. Ordinary dreaming is

    (A) probably identical to daydreaming
    (B) always in black and white
    (C) selective in the perception and incorporation of the external world into the dreams
    (D) most prevalent in Stage II sleep
    (E) most prevalent in Stage I sleep

47. Which one of the following would be considered an operational definition in GSR lie detection?

    (A) Changes in emotionality result in measurable physiological changes.
    (B) Changes in emotionality result in observable behavioral change.
    (C) Changes in emotionality result in changes of thought.
    (D) Changes in emotionality result in brain-wave changes.
    (E) Changes in emotionality result in attitude changes.

48. Studies of emotions in twins suggest that the intensity and manner in which emotion is expressed is

    (A) at least partially hereditary
    (B) wholly learned
    (C) dependent entirely upon intrauterine environment
    (D) a matter of sibling modeling
    (E) dependent entirely upon "expected value of response"

49. On the basis of McClelland's findings, in which one of the following groups could a person expect to find the lowest achievement need?

    (A) male college graduates with bachelor's degrees
    (B) female college graduates with bachelor's degrees
    (C) male professional students with Ph.D.s
    (D) female professional students with Ph.D.s
    (E) male high-school graduates with vocational training

50. In probability and decision-making settings, EV signifies

    (A) Edward's valence
    (B) energizing variable
    (C) enervating variable
    (D) expected value
    (E) experimental variable

51. The concept of equipotentiality refers to

    (A) the visual learning of synonyms
    (B) bipolar adjectives
    (C) recovery of function within the brain
    (D) performance impairment as a function of phenobarbital
    (E) electroconvulsive shock effects on long-term memory

52. In a well-known study by Barker, Dembo, and Lewin, frustrated children

    (A) engaged in aggression toward their toys
    (B) engaged in aggression toward each other
    (C) regressed to behaviors they had performed at an earlier age
    (D) engaged in cooperative play
    (E) engaged in parallel play

53. The phrase that "the bodily changes follow directly the perception of the exciting fact, and . . . our feeling of the same changes as they occur *is* the emotion" expresses a central aspect of the

    (A) Cannon-Bard theory   (B) Yerkes-Dodson law
    (C) Cannon-Washburn theory   (D) Freudian theory
    (E) James-Lange theory

54. Which one of the following terms is most aptly defined by the words "how behavior gets started, is energized, is sustained, is directed"?

    (A) emotion   (B) motivation   (C) achievement need
    (D) aspiration   (E) osculation

55. What Hull referred to as reaction potential, Spence referred to as

    (A) habit potential   (B) drive potential   (C) incentive
    (D) excitatory potential   (E) summation potential

56. "With Freud, psychology had lost its soul and with [him], psychology was losing its mind."

    Who is the target of this criticism of radical behaviorism?
    (A) Watson   (B) Tolman   (C) McDougall
    (D) Woodworth   (E) Hull

57. Which of the following terms is *least* likely to appear in the formulations of Lewin?

    (A) force field   (B) valence   (C) life space
    (D) tension   (E) interference

58. Which one of the following pairs does *not* contain synonyms?

    (A) classical conditioning—type S
    (B) operant conditioning—instrumental conditioning
    (C) instrumental conditioning—type R
    (D) discriminative stimulus—S(Delta)
    (E) reinforcement—increased likelihood of response repetition

59. You have learned to type and with experience you have reached your peak speed. No matter how much typing you do, your speed will not increase. In learning curve terms you have reached

    (A) plateau   (B) reminiscence   (C) latency
    (D) extinction   (E) asymptote

60. A single-goal object has both desirable and undesirable features in

    (A) approach-approach conflict
    (B) approach-avoidance conflict
    (C) avoidance-avoidance conflict
    (D) double approach-avoidance conflict
    (E) double avoidance-avoidance conflict

61. Responding to a conditioned stimulus in order to avoid electric shock is an example of

(A) punishment   (B) shaping   (C) avoidance conditioning
(D) escape conditioning   (E) successive approximation

62. Hungry rats that do not find food reinforcement at the end of a T-maze learn very slowly in comparison with another group of rats that find such reinforcement. Immediately after the rats in the first group are given food reinforcement, their performance parallels that of the rats in the second group. This is an example of

(A) behavior chaining   (B) law of effect   (C) law of exercise
(D) latent learning   (E) intrinsic learning

63. Under which of the following reinforcement schedules is it most important for an organism to learn to estimate time accurately?

(A) fixed interval   (B) fixed ratio   (C) variable interval
(D) variable ratio   (E) a combination of fixed and variable ratio

64. Which one of the following statements appears to be true of punishment?

(A) It is effective in behavior control without undesirable side effects.
(B) It has a long-range inhibitory effect upon behavior.
(C) Its inhibitory effect is only short-range, and the general behavior tendency remains essentially unchanged.
(D) It is effective as a means of extinction.
(E) It is effective specifically in cases of retroactive inhibition.

65. The pursuit rotor is used in many studies involving

(A) intelligence
(B) memory
(C) motor learning
(D) mechanical aptitude
(E) pilot training

66. The S-shaped curve indicates

(A) prior familiarity with the task
(B) greatest amount of improvement during the last few trials
(C) the representation of the entire learning process
(D) greatest amount of improvement in the first few trials
(E) improvement not dependent on practice

67. Partial reinforcement

(A) enhances classical conditioning speed and efficiency
(B) interferes with classical conditioning
(C) interferes with the maintenance of an operantly conditioned response
(D) is never used in operant conditioning
(E) is never used in type R conditioning

68. The Law of Effect suggests that

(A) practice alone produces learning
(B) in addition to practice there must be reinforcement
(C) in addition to reinforcement there must be reward
(D) neither practice nor reward is important to learning
(E) Skinner's view has been superseded by Hull's

69. Harlow's experiments demonstrate that female infant monkeys raised in isolation with a cloth mother

(A) develop normally in all respects
(B) develop normally, but are totally inadequate as mothers
(C) have unresolved Oedipal conflicts
(D) die at an earlier age than monkeys raised normally
(E) are better adjusted than normally raised monkeys

70. Functional autonomy of motives is associated with the work of

(A) Allport   (B) McClelland   (C) Atkinson
(D) McDougall   (E) Allen

Questions 71–74 are based on the following experiment.

Each subject was given serial presentation of a twelve-item list of nonsense syllables. Following the presentation, the subject was dismissed from the laboratory with instructions to return the following day at the same time. Upon returning, the subject was asked to recall the items on the list presented the preceding day. The number of items correctly recalled was recorded, and the subject then received serial presentation of a second list of nonsense syllables with instructions to return the following day for similar procedures and a new list. The subjects each received a total of nine lists, and the recall data (in percentages) is presented in the following table.

List	Percentage Recall
1	75
2	67
3	56
4	50
5	42
6	33
7	25
8	17
9	8

71. A phenomenon that appears to be operating within this learning procedure is

(A) retroactive inhibition
(B) proactive inhibition
(C) retroactive facilitation
(D) proactive facilitation
(E) von Restorff effect

72. Which one of the following correctly expresses the dependent variable within this experiment?

    (A) nonsense syllable   (B) percentage recall
    (C) number of lists   (D) number of items per list
    (E) serial presentation

73. The results suggest that

    (A) the more lists a person learns, the better he remembers them
    (B) serial anticipation is the best method for use in recall-type studies
    (C) time delay between learning and recall is the single most important factor in forgetting
    (D) longer exposure to individual items within a list enhances recall
    (E) there is a negative correlation between the number of lists learned and the percentage recall

74. In analyzing a study of this type, the statistical design most likely to be used is the

    (A) treatments-by-subjects, repeated-measures design
    (B) Latin Square design
    (C) Kendall Rank-Order Correlation
    (D) Pearson Product-Moment Correlation
    (E) *t*-test for unrelated measures

75. Which one of the following is *not* true of a normal distribution?

    (A) Approximately 68 percent of the scores are within one standard deviation of the mean.
    (B) Approximately 68 percent of the scores are within one standard deviation of the median.
    (C) Approximately 68 percent of the scores are within one standard deviation of the mode.
    (D) Negative skew is equivalent to positive skew.
    (E) Approximately 34 percent of the scores occur between a *z*-score of +1 and the mean.

76. A researcher notes a +0.40 correlation between college grades and income level five years after graduation. It is further noted that leadership aptitude test scores attained while in college correlate +0.80 with income level five years after graduation. Assuming a +1.0 reliability on all measures taken, the relationship between income level and leadership aptitude test scores is

    (A) twice as strong as the relationship between income level and grades
    (B) 80 percent stronger than the relationship between income level and grades
    (C) half as strong as the relationship between income level and grades
    (D) 40 percent stronger than the relationship between income level and grades
    (E) ten times stronger than the relationship between income level and grades

77. Which one of the following would be of primary importance in determining the accuracy of inferences being made about a population?

    (A) size of the population
    (B) sample variance
    (C) sample representativeness
    (D) sample mean
    (E) sample standard deviation

78. On a certain scattergram, the pattern extends from the lower left-hand corner to the upper right-hand corner. From this knowledge it can be determined that the scattergram exhibits

    (A) positive correlation   (B) negative correlation
    (C) no correlation   (D) negative skew   (E) positive skew

79. Which one of the following is central to a frequency polygon?

    (A) scattergram
    (B) bar graph
    (C) histogram
    (D) flow chart
    (E) points connected by lines

Questions 80–83 are based on the following answer choices.

    (1) z
    (2) t
    (3) F
    (4) chi-square
    (5) r

80. This statistic and its corresponding analysis determines whether there is systematic relationship between two sets of variables.

    (A) 1   (B) 2   (C) 3   (D) 4   (E) 5

81. This statistic assumes direct knowledge of a population mean and standard deviation.

    (A) 1   (B) 2   (C) 3   (D) 4   (E) 5

82. This statistic reflects an unknown population mean and inference based on data obtained from a sample. It is assumed that the terms in the population from which the sample is drawn are normally distributed or, at least, do not depart dramatically from normality.

    (A) 1   (B) 2   (C) 3   (D) 4   (E) 5

83. This statistic deals with differences between the terms *expected value* and *obtained value*.

    (A) 1   (B) 2   (C) 3   (D) 4   (E) 5

Questions 84–87 are based on the following statistical information.

Interval	Frequency
67–69	10
64–66	24
61–63	28
58–60	20
55–57	12
52–54	4
49–51	2

84. The median of the score distribution is

   (A) 55.7   (B) 65.2   (C) 61.8   (D) 60   (E) 57.9

85. The mode of the distribution is

   (A) 60   (B) 64   (C) 65   (D) 62   (E) 59

86. The 40th percentile of this distribution would most closely approximate

   (A) 59   (B) 61   (C) 62   (D) 64   (E) 65

87. The mean of this distribution most closely approximates

   (A) 60   (B) 61   (C) 63   (D) 65   (E) 66

Questions 88–91 are based on the following information for five persons who took different IQ tests. (M = Mean, SD = Standard Deviation)

(1)	(2)	(3)	(4)	(5)
IQ = 110	IQ = 115	IQ = 120	IQ = 130	IQ = 110
M = 100	M = 100	M = 100	M = 100	M = 100
SD = 10	SD = 20	SD = 30	SD = 40	SD = 20

88. Comparing them according to percentile rank, which person has the highest IQ?

   (A) 1   (B) 2   (C) 3   (D) 4   (E) 5

89. Using the same comparative framework, which person has the lowest IQ?

   (A) 1   (B) 2   (C) 3   (D) 4   (E) 5

90. Which person would have a *z*-score of +.50?

   (A) 1   (B) 2   (C) 3   (D) 4   (E) 5

91. In which distribution is there evidence of greatest score variability?

   (A) 1   (B) 2   (C) 3   (D) 4   (E) 5

92. A researcher has just developed a new test of intelligence and wants to determine whether it is a valid measure. The new test is given to a large group of children and those same children are given a second, well-established IQ test. Scores children attained on each of the two tests are then compared through correlation. This procedure for determining the validity of the new test is labeled

   (A) content validity
   (B) concurrent validity
   (C) conjoint validity
   (D) test-retest validity
   (E) regressional validity

93. The fact that a person can awaken at a specific hour without alarm clock assistance is attributable to

   (A) correlation of bodily processes with predictable time passage
   (B) predisposed stimulus in the form of external noises heard regularly at a given hour
   (C) predisposed response generalization
   (D) convergence
   (E) configuration

94. Which one of the following is an *incorrect* statement?

   (A) The brains of no two persons are structurally identical.
   (B) Brain lesions sustained in infancy have less incapacitating effect on sensory-motor functions than similar lesions sustained in adulthood.
   (C) Brain lesions sustained in infancy have greater incapacitating effects on intellectual-learning functions than similar lesions sustained in adulthood.
   (D) The cerebral hemisphere dominant in speech is, without exception, the cerebral hemisphere dominant in handedness.
   (E) The right cerebral hemisphere is most often dominant in nonverbal intellectual functions.

95. Dember believes figure reversibility is evidence of the fact that

   (A) the eyes are highly adaptable
   (B) cone vision predominates during bright intensity viewing
   (C) change is essential to the maintenance of perception
   (D) figure-ground is an essentially useless perceptual concept
   (E) texture gradient is not functioning properly

96. Restle's adaptation-level theory

   (A) confirms the existing apparent-distance theory
   (B) seeks to explain the phi phenomenon
   (C) seeks to explain the horizontal-vertical illusion
   (D) seeks to explain the "moon illusion"
   (E) seeks to explain the trapezoidal window phenomenon

97. As a person views a picture one way, he sees craters. When he turns it 180 degrees, the craters become bumps. The perceptual phenomena are due to

(A) linear perspective   (B) convergence   (C) texture
(D) relative position   (E) light and shadow

98. Emmert's law was the forerunner of the

(A) Necker cube illusion
(B) experiments in motion parallax
(C) phi phenomenon
(D) size-distance invariance principle
(E) major studies in altruism

99. Distal stimulus : proximal stimulus : :

(A) right brain : left brain
(B) external object : retinal image
(C) anterior : posterior
(D) primary : secondary
(E) cerebrum : cerebellum

100. Which one of the following name combinations contains two Gestalt psychologists?

(A) Koffka, Kohler, Kelman
(B) Kohler, Cohen, Kelman
(C) Wertheimer, Wundt, Kelman
(D) James, Jensen, Kelman
(E) Wundt, James, Wertheimer

101. Which of the following most accurately defines the function of the middle ear?

(A) synaptic transmission
(B) formation of neural impulse
(C) sound collection
(D) sound-wave amplification
(E) transmission to the brain

102. The fact that hues at the short-wave end of the color spectrum appear bright at nightfall is a function of

(A) light adaptation   (B) Purkinje effect   (C) Zeigarnik effect
(D) Young-Helmholtz effect   (E) Rutherford effect

103. Most sensory information is relayed to the cerebral cortex by the

(A) transducer   (B) medulla   (C) proprioceptors
(D) bipolar cells   (E) thalamus

104. For the experience of taste to occur, a substance must be

    (A) at least slightly soluble in water
    (B) highly soluble in butric acid
    (C) in contact with receptors located in the center of the tongue
    (D) insoluble in butric acid
    (E) slightly above 7 on the pH scale

105. Which one of the following perceptual charts contains several rows of letters of decreasing size?

    (A) Landolt chart   (B) Vernier chart   (C) Snellen chart
    (D) Ricco chart   (E) Talbot chart

106. The perception of distance as one views a two-dimensional picture of a railroad track is due primarily to

    (A) the phi phenomenon   (B) motion parallax
    (C) texture gradient   (D) linear perspective   (E) closure

107. Jastrow illusion involves

    (A) parallel straight lines
    (B) straight lines at right angles
    (C) geometrical curvatures positioned one above the other
    (D) geometrical curvatures positioned at right angles to each other
    (E) straight lines emanating from a center point at forty-five degree angles

108. The "piano" theory holds that

    (A) all nerve fibers fire in all frequency ranges
    (B) specific nerve fibers respond to specific sound frequencies
    (C) specific nerve fibers respond to specific decibel ranges
    (D) all nerve fibers fire in all decibel ranges
    (E) Rutherford's theory was essentially correct but needed elaboration

109. Among monocular cues for depth perception is

    (A) convergence
    (B) retinal disparity
    (C) assimilation
    (D) accommodation
    (E) interposition

110. The condition under which a person experiences the perceptual phenomenon of closure involves

    (A) a circle with approximately one-eighth of its line omitted
    (B) parallel lines
    (C) intersecting lines
    (D) a triangle with a dot in the middle
    (E) a square with diagonal lines going to opposite corners

111. Which one of the following is an *incorrect* statement?

   (A) Ethology attained its peak with the work of Lorenz and Tinbergen.
   (B) Lashley helped revitalize comparative psychology in the post-World War II period.
   (C) Tinbergen's work has relied heavily on the experimental laboratory method.
   (D) Darwin's work had far-reaching effects and influence upon comparative psychology.
   (E) Romanes's work utilized the anecdotal method.

112. The phi phenomenon

   (A) is an integral part of telekinesis
   (B) relates to electrical stimulation of the brain
   (C) deals with experience common to the state of alpha-wave relaxation
   (D) occurs in response to sequentially flashing lights
   (E) occurs in response to a spot of light in a darkened room

113. The fact that a pinpoint down the railroad track is perceived by a person as a diesel engine is an example of

   (A) continuity   (B) closure   (C) size constancy
   (D) motion parallax   (E) accommodation

114. One of the earliest and most important color vision theories was formulated by

   (A) Rutherford and Hayes
   (B) Young and Helson
   (C) Meissner and Middleton
   (D) Rutherford and Young
   (E) Young and Helmholtz

115. Which one of the following sayings would social-attraction research find most generally acceptable?

   (A) "Birds of a feather flock together."
   (B) "Likes repel, opposites attract."
   (C) "Familiarity breeds contempt."
   (D) "Misery loves company."
   (E) "Friends till the end."

116. You could expect Maslow's self-actualized person to be

   (A) id-dominated
   (B) ego-dominated
   (C) relatively independent of his culture and environment
   (D) thanatos-oriented
   (E) highly aggressive

117. Prominent among the persons associated with ego analysis is

   (A) Sullivan   (B) Horney   (C) Fromm
   (D) Erikson   (E) Rank

118. For many of their perceptual differentiations, the phenomenologists are indebted to the

    (A) Gestaltists   (B) psychoanalysts   (C) behaviorists
    (D) trait theorists   (E) ego analysts

119. In the classic Asch experiment

    (A) five individual booths were utilized
    (B) the "critical" subject was less likely to conform to group opinion if one other subject dissented from the group
    (C) the "critical" subject under no circumstances conformed to group opinion
    (D) the "critical" subject was the middle subject in the group
    (E) five individuals at a time were given an attitude test

120. The concept of family constellation is most evident in the works of which one of the following?

    (A) Jung   (B) Freud   (C) Rogers
    (D) Adler   (E) Horney

121. Which one of the following schools constitutes the Lockean view of personality?

    (A) ego analysis   (B) behaviorism   (C) psychoanalysis
    (D) archetypal analysis   (E) trait analysis

122. In the Jungian view of personality, key functions include

    (A) anima, animus, shadow
    (B) sensing, feeling, intuiting
    (C) prototaxic, parataxic, syntaxic
    (D) extroversion, introversion, interposition
    (E) belongingness, love, safety

123. The personality theorist who developed the Internal-External Control Scale was

    (A) B. F. Skinner   (B) Alfred Adler   (C) John Watson
    (D) Sigmund Freud   (E) Julian Rotter

124. Most basic among Freudian defense mechanisms is

    (A) rationalism   (B) reaction formation   (C) identification
    (D) repression   (E) denial

125. The field theorist view is compatible with which one of the following statements?

    (A) Learning is based on specific responses to specific stimuli.
    (B) The phenomenal world and the objective world are in agreement.
    (C) Total experience is "greater than the sum of its parts."
    (D) Reward preserves learning.
    (E) The phenomenal world is, in effect, more accurate than the objective world.

126. ". . . Make up as dramatic a story as you can . . . Tell what has led up to the event shown in the picture, describe what is happening at the moment, what the characters are feeling and thinking; and then give the outcome." This constitutes part of the procedure for

(A) psychoanalytic free association   (B) TAT
(C) MMPI   (D) Rorschach   (E) Blacky

127. Two groups are in devastating conflict with each other—highly competitive and hostile. The challenge you have been given is to convert this hostility to cooperation and friendship (no small order!). Given your recollection of a comparable boys' camp problem study, the approach you recommend will center upon which of the following?

(A) reactance theory
(B) superordinate goal
(C) opponent process theory
(D) simply bringing the two groups together
(E) vulnerability theory

128. In the "experimental dormitory" situation with preassigned roommates

(A) those with similar attitudes were likely to be attracted to one another
(B) those with dissimilar attitudes were likely to be attracted to one another
(C) complete roommate rearrangement occurred within the first two months
(D) proximity proved to be a more significant factor than similarity
(E) sex proved to be a more important factor than proximity

129. If Adorno informed persons that they had just attained high scores on the *F*-scale, they could accurately conclude that

(A) their scores were significant beyond the .05 level
(B) they had scored high on authoritarianism
(C) there was strong likelihood that they were not very superstitious
(D) there was strong likelihood that they had below-average concern in areas involving sex
(E) they had high flexibility and openness in their attitude formation and change

130. An African-American and an Anglo-American in a group have supported the experimental subject's position on several issues; another African-American and Anglo-American have taken positions differing from those of the subject. According to Rokeach the people whose company the experimental subject would later prefer would be

(A) same-race persons, regardless of their beliefs
(B) those persons whose views closely paralleled the subject's, regardless of race
(C) those same-race persons whose views closely paralleled the subject's
(D) persons who were of both the same race and the same sex as the subject
(E) persons who were of the same race, same sex, and same beliefs as the subject

131. Zajonc found that familiarity leads to

    (A) positive reaction
    (B) negative reaction
    (C) contempt
    (D) fear
    (E) failure

132. Lewinson-Zubin scales are associated with

    (A) phrenology   (B) philology   (C) syntonomy
    (D) graphology   (E) physiognomy

133. *Not* among the factors associated with the Crutchfield technique is

    (A) individual booths
    (B) critical subjects
    (C) signal-light panels
    (D) false feedback
    (E) each person involved is a subject

134. In the Acme-Bolt Trucking Game research, it was found that

    (A) cooperation is greatest in the presence of potential threat
    (B) cooperation is greatest when the two parties have direct communication
    (C) cooperation is greatest in the absence of threat
    (D) women are more likely to utilize threat than men
    (E) cooperation reaches its peak when both threat and direct communication are present

135. Modern psychological views most readily reject which one of the following theoretical tenets?

    (A) Fromm's relatedness principle
    (B) Erikson's eight stages
    (C) Jung's collective unconscious
    (D) Dollard and Miller's four types of conflict situations
    (E) Horney's three modes of relating

136. "The role of a given cause in producing a given effect is discounted if other plausible causes are also present." This quote is called the

    (A) discounting rule of Kelley
    (B) covariance rule of McArthur
    (C) effects rule of Milgram
    (D) consistency rule of Sherif
    (E) attribution rule of Schneider

137. In relation to communications, "all are created equal" within which one of the following systems?

    (A) chain   (B) Y   (C) circle   (D) wheel   (E) T-design

138. During dating, which one of the following relationships takes on critical importance for the adolescent?

(A) same-sex parent
(B) opposite-sex parent
(C) both same- and opposite-sex parent relationships
(D) neither same- nor opposite-sex parent relationship
(E) grandparent confidant

139. Identical twins raised separately and found to have similar IQs are cited as examples of the contribution made to intelligence by

(A) environment   (B) infant stimulation   (C) heredity
(D) learning   (E) parental interaction

140. High correlation with premature birth has been found in cases where the mother's behavior included

(A) depression
(B) exposure to radiation
(C) smoking
(D) thalidomide
(E) alcoholic beverages

141. In the early work of Hartshorne and May, designed to assess children's moral behavior, it was found that

(A) moral children always adhere to generally recognized moral standards
(B) children seem to apply situational morality, acting differently in separate situations involving the same moral principle
(C) moral children never cheat
(D) a basic distinction can be made between cheaters and noncheaters and that, invariably, the noncheaters were from religious home environments
(E) boys generally have stronger consciences than girls

142. An expectant mother in her eighth month of pregnancy decides to initiate a sequence involving banging loudly on the side of the bathtub followed by application of a vibrator to her abdomen. The developing fetus

(A) probably will not be classically conditioned by such a procedure
(B) very likely can be classically conditioned by such a procedure
(C) will be operantly conditioned by such a procedure
(D) will be unable to detect either the vibration or the sound
(E) will be permanently damaged by such a procedure

143. Among the following, the *incorrect* pairing is

(A) fetal period—eighth week until birth
(B) germinal period—first two weeks
(C) embryonic period—second week until eighth week
(D) embryonic period—rapid neural development
(E) germinal period—onset of initial heartbeat

144. DNA refers to the

    (A) molecular configuration making up chromosomes
    (B) germ-cell configurations in genes
    (C) atom structure in genes
    (D) neural structure in cell bodies
    (E) dinitroacetic structures

145. Experiments demonstrate that infants register strongest preference for which one of the following visual stimuli?

    (A) plain, solid colors
    (B) bright colors
    (C) patterned triangles
    (D) likenesses of the human face
    (E) likenesses of animals and pets

146. The prenatal period during which X rays and specific drugs can have the most detrimental effect upon development is

    (A) the first eight weeks
    (B) the second to fourth months
    (C) the sixth to eighth months
    (D) just prior to birth
    (E) the fifth to seventh months

147. Which of the following expresses a correct sequence in cognitive development?

    (A) voluntary movement, intuitive thought, object permanence
    (B) concrete operations, mental representation, information processing
    (C) mental representation, symbolic thought, intuitive thought
    (D) conservation, object permanence, intuitive thought
    (E) information processing, intuitive thought, symbolic thought

148. Which one of the following combinations would *not* be possible in a set of triplets?

    (A) three fraternal
    (B) three identical
    (C) three mongoloid
    (D) two identical, one fraternal
    (E) two fraternal, one identical

149. Which one of the following expressions could act as a substitution for "nature-nurture controversy" without changing the basic meaning?

    (A) heredity-maturation controversy
    (B) environment-learning controversy
    (C) achievement-acquisition controversy
    (D) heredity-environment controversy
    (E) evolution-mutation controversy

150. Which one of the following types of acceptance is most critical and pervasive to the long-range emotional health of a child'?

(A) peer   (B) sibling   (C) self
(D) vocational   (E) educational

151. The play pattern most prevalent among three-year-old children is

(A) solitary play   (B) associative play   (C) cooperative play
(D) parallel play   (E) covariant play

152. Sex differences in the area of perception and personality are

(A) apparent before age five
(B) initially detectable at age seven
(C) indistinguishable prior to age eight
(D) essentially mythical
(E) not as apparent as those in the area of cognition

153. Which one of the following accurately describes an aspect of prenatal development?

(A) Heartbeat begins during the second week.
(B) Wastes are absorbed through the placental walls into the mother's blood.
(C) The developing child and the mother have completely intermixing, constantly interchanging blood supplies.
(D) The fetus has immunity to syphilis.
(E) It encompasses a 250-day gestation period.

154. If a mother must be separated from her child for three months during the child's first year, an absence during which one of the following age periods would be *least* detrimental to the child's development?

(A) two to five months
(B) three to six months
(C) one to four months
(D) seven to ten months
(E) birth to three months

155. Which one of the following statements is true of embryonic development?

(A) The development of organs and organ systems varies among embryos in both timing and sequence.
(B) Only one developmental sequence, heart development during the fourth week, is consistent among embryos.
(C) All organ systems essentially develop together.
(D) Universally consistent sequences and sequential timing characterize organ system development.
(E) Fetal growth can compensate for any deficiencies occurring during the embryonic period.

156. Down syndrome is

    (A) synonymous with hydrocephaly
    (B) synonymous with Klinefelter's syndrome
    (C) caused by the presence of an extra chromosome number 21
    (D) caused only by infectious hepatitis during pregnancy
    (E) caused only by x-ray treatment during pregnancy

157. Babies allowed to select their own food for a six-month period would

    (A) eat too many sweets
    (B) eat too many carbohydrates
    (C) develop anemia
    (D) overeat consistently
    (E) maintain a generally balanced diet over the long range

158. Within the human embryo, activity related to the development of hair and nails is centered in the

    (A) mesoderm   (B) endoderm   (C) exoderm
    (D) ectoderm   (E) ochloderm

159. A young child's disobedience generally signifies

    (A) creativity
    (B) intelligence
    (C) unhappiness
    (D) need for punishment
    (E) reinforcement

160. Anoxia is

    (A) a disease of the blood cells
    (B) interruption of the oxygen supply to the brain
    (C) an oversupply of oxygen to the brain
    (D) hyperventilation
    (E) never fatal but a primary cause of retardation

161. The term *circadian* refers to

    (A) the cyclic daily body rhythms of activity and repose
    (B) the circles around the eyes noted in newborns
    (C) the cycle accompanying toilet training
    (D) the babbling between identical twins
    (E) the childhood ability to distinguish circles from squares

162. Strong evidence suggests that the newborn

    (A) sees only blurred shadows
    (B) has visual capacity for pattern discrimination
    (C) sees clearly but not in color
    (D) visually tracks successfully
    (E) smiles in response to the human voice

163. Sternberg's short-term memory research focused on the question of whether memory search processes are

    (A) parallel or serial
    (B) anterograde or retrograde
    (C) primary or secondary
    (D) classical or instrumental
    (E) discriminative or nondiscriminative

164. According to the tenets of the Zeigarnik effect

    (A) a completed task is more likely to be remembered than an interrupted one
    (B) an interrupted task is more likely to be remembered than a completed one
    (C) a task at the beginning of a sequence is more likely to be remembered than a task in the middle of the sequence
    (D) a task in the middle of a sequence is more likely to be remembered than a task at the beginning of the sequence
    (E) a digit is more likely to be remembered when it is part of a word list than when it is part of a list of digits

165. In Guilford's approach to intelligence, the ability to generate a variety of hypotheses in a given problem situation is known as

    (A) cognitive memory
    (B) convergent production
    (C) divergent production
    (D) mediational memory
    (E) intuitive production

166. If you studied Spanish in high school, you might have a hard time learning German in college because of

    (A) retroactive interference
    (B) proactive interference
    (C) generalization
    (D) decay
    (E) dual coding

167. How many stages of cognitive development are associated with Piaget?

    (A) seven stages   (B) four stages   (C) two stages
    (D) six stages   (E) one stage

168. Which one of the following is *not* true of the WAIS?
    (A) used with adults
    (B) separate verbal and performance IQ scores
    (C) block design
    (D) $MA/CA \times 100$
    (E) digit span

169. Retrograde amnesia is a phenomenon in which a person suffering brain injury in an accident loses memory of

(A) early childhood experiences
(B) events immediately after the injury
(C) events immediately prior to the injury, with earlier memory being unimpaired
(D) middle childhood events, then forgets early childhood events
(E) early childhood events, then forgets middle childhood events

170. The Ebbinghaus curve

(A) shows a gradual drop in retention followed by a steep decline
(B) shows a steep initial drop in retention followed by a gradual decline
(C) shows an S-shaped pattern
(D) shows higher retention for rote learning than for concept learning
(E) shows a steady, gradual decline throughout its span

171. Phonemes are

(A) measurements
(B) the smallest units of meaningful sound
(C) syllables
(D) a series of morphemes
(E) the smallest units of sound

172. When a child modifies an existing cognitive schema to make it compatible with the cognitive aspects of an incoming stimulus, the process is called

(A) assimilation   (B) adaptation   (C) conservation
(D) accommodation   (E) mediational clustering

173. That language patterns play a dominant role in shaping a person's thoughts and subsequent behavior is a view advanced in the hypothesis developed by

(A) Gardner   (B) Whorf   (C) Brown
(D) Miller   (E) Dollard

174. The earliest studies of verbal learning and rote memory were conducted by

(A) Thorndike   (B) Pavlov   (C) Miller
(D) Mowrer   (E) Ebbinghaus

175. Forgetting that occurs solely as a function of the passage of time is called

(A) interference   (B) amnesia   (C) inhibition
(D) adaptation   (E) decay

176. Profound anterograde amnesia results from accidental injury or surgical removal of the

(A) hippocampus   (B) hypothalamus   (C) pituitary gland
(D) cerebellum   (E) corpus callosum

177. As a person fills in a number series such as 3, 6, 9, __, __, 18, he is engaging in the thinking process known as

    (A) extrapolation   (B) interpolation   (C) structuring
    (D) modeling   (E) decision making

178. Bruner sees cognitive growth as

    (A) unaffected by the mastery of techniques and skills
    (B) strongly affected by the mastery of techniques and skills
    (C) occurring at essentially the same speed and level in all human infants
    (D) faster for girls than for boys
    (E) faster for rural children than for urban ones

179. The serial position effect in memory refers to the fact that when trying to remember a list of words,

    (A) it is easier to recall the list if it was studied using rote rehearsal than if it was studied using elaborative rehearsal
    (B) it is easier to recall the first and last words on the list than the words in the middle of the list
    (C) it is easier to recall words in the order that they were studied than in a random order
    (D) it is easier to recall unusual or surprising words on the list than it is to recall common words
    (E) it is easier to recall the list if it was studied for short periods distributed over several days than if it was studied for one long period during a single day

180. The process by which a stimulus is attended to, identified, studied, and incorporated into memory is called

    (A) storage   (B) chunking   (C) encoding
    (D) reasoning   (E) retrieval

181. The capacity of the short-term store is best described in terms of the number of meaningful units of information, called

    (A) chunks   (B) features   (C) scripts
    (D) propositions   (E) prototypes

182. A possible neural mechanism for learning is

    (A) dendritic plaques
    (B) long-term potentiation
    (C) spatial summation
    (D) dendritic assimilation
    (E) excitatory potentiation

183. In a corporate hierarchy, a person could expect communications to be initiated most frequently in which of the following patterns?

    (A) lower to higher echelon   (B) higher to lower echelon
    (C) women to women   (D) men to men   (E) women to men

184. A primary function of human engineering is

    (A) vocational testing
    (B) personnel screening
    (C) to modify aspects of a specific job to promote efficiency
    (D) to modify aspects of an employee's behavior to fit a job requirement
    (E) consumer research

185. Industrial psychologists and human engineering personnel employ the term *ET*, which means

    (A) evaluative technique
    (B) effective temperature
    (C) efficiency test
    (D) evaluation and training
    (E) evaluation and testing

186. A key reference source in psychological topic areas of research is

    (A) *Psychological Bulletin*
    (B) *Psychological Review*
    (C) *Contemporary Psychology*
    (D) *Psychological Abstracts*
    (E) *Psychology Today*

187. With a month to go before an English test, a student would be well advised to engage in

    (A) massed practice
    (B) distributed practice
    (C) massed-distributed-massed practice pattern
    (D) distributed-massed-distributed practice pattern
    (E) massed-distributed-distributed practice pattern

188. *Not* included in a Bauer or Shannon diagram of communication is

    (A) source   (B) transmitter   (C) channel
    (D) receiver   (E) translator

189. The foot-in-the-door technique suggests that a person is most likely to gain consumer cooperation on a sizable purchase or a large favor if he or she

    (A) is open about the large purchase or favor in initial contact
    (B) is the first salesman to come to the consumer's door
    (C) represents a reputable company
    (D) can successfully make a small sale or first gain the consumer's cooperation on a small favor
    (E) can associate his company with a famous person familiar to the consumer

190. Conservation mastery in which one of the following dimensions indicates the most advanced level of child cognitive development?

    (A) number   (B) length of a line   (C) volume displacement
    (D) "lemonade stand" demonstration   (E) weight of an object

191. Proximity as a factor in social attraction

    (A) proves least important in apartment-building settings
    (B) is generally unimportant
    (C) proves to be of primary importance
    (D) is less important than occupation
    (E) is less important than family background

192. Because of the rate of a child's physiological development, parents should

    (A) initiate toilet training when the child begins to walk
    (B) initiate toilet training when the child begins to talk
    (C) wait until at least age two for toilet training
    (D) toilet train at the same time as the child is weaned
    (E) begin a form of toilet training almost immediately after birth

193. The setting in which an experimental subject acts as his own control is

    (A) Pearson Product Moment correlation
    (B) point biserial correlation
    (C) *t*-test
    (D) chi-square
    (E) repeated measures

194. To determine representative income level in a neighborhood having mostly lower-middle-class families and a few very rich people, the recommended measure is

    (A) mode   (B) median   (C) mean
    (D) *z*-score   (E) *t*-score

195. In screening for a specific position, the best aptitude test measures

    (A) creativity   (B) intelligence   (C) sociability
    (D) capacity for position-related tasks   (E) mechanical aptitude

196. From a perceptual standpoint, the most dangerous point for commercial pilots during night flight is

    (A) the take off   (B) midflight   (C) a right bank
    (D) a left bank   (E) the runway approach

197. Human engineers have found that the airplane cockpit is a setting in which

    (A) color coding on the dials is extremely important
    (B) shape coding is extremely important
    (C) the phi phenomenon must be carefully counterbalanced
    (D) techniques must be utilized to control autokinetic effect
    (E) the Zeigarnik effect poses a perpetual engineering problem

198. Which one of the following was developed by the Army as the first group-administered test of intelligence?

    (A) Otis   (B) Bender Gestalt   (C) Pintner Patterson
    (D) Alpha   (E) Beta

199. To increase the possibility of behavior change, a person would be well advised to create

    (A) only slight cognitive dissonance
    (B) no cognitive dissonance
    (C) a large amount of cognitive dissonance
    (D) a moderate amount of cognitive dissonance
    (E) a large amount of cognitive irrelevance

200. Among human engineering principles relating to man-machine systems, a control principle states that the direction of movement on any control should be

    (A) to the right
    (B) to the left
    (C) compatible with the effects produced
    (D) the reverse of the effects produced
    (E) clockwise

How did it go? If you find at this point that you were pushed for time and did not finish in the 170 minutes, finish the questions still remaining. The point right now is review and analysis of weak spots. As you refresh your mind on the subject matter and take further sample tests, you will find your speed improving. In the sample tests, you will also find it helpful to answer the questions you know and note those you were not sure about so you can return to them when you have completed a particular test. Even then, spend only a minimal amount of time on each question—eliminating the answer choice or choices you can, making your best guess, and moving on.

After you have completed Diagnostic Test 1, check your responses with the correct answers. (The answer explanations will help you understand any questions you might have missed, and they're a great first step toward your review.) Next, turn to the section at the end of the chapter entitled "Evaluating Your Score." Head for the tally chart and check-mark the item numbers you missed. Then go just below the tally chart and jot down the number of items missed in each question-number range. The page following the tally chart, entitled "Test Score Scaling" will give you a clear set of steps for comparing your performance with the 75th percentile in each topic area. Then you'll know exactly where to focus your review. Concentrate your Chapter 3 review on those areas where you scored below the 75th percentile.

Diagnostic Test 1: Answer Comments

1. (A) Dysthymic disorders are mood disorders, specifically, depression lasting at least two years.

2. (A) Current mental health trends include emphases on outpatient care, community mental health centers, behavior modification, and group therapy, not on construction of large, institution-style buildings.

3. (D) Behavior therapy has been criticized on the grounds that it treats the observable behavior rather than the underlying problem.

4. (A) Schizophrenic reaction is the most prevalent diagnosis among first admissions to public mental health facilities—evidence of the category's breadth and "stretchability."

5. (B) Mowrer has advanced the view that neurosis is a product of personal immaturity.

6. (C) "Flooding" is an expression of implosive therapy. In implosive therapy the person experiences the most traumatic events that were a part of the original setting that triggered the emotional disturbance. The theory is that when the person has gone through the "worst imaginable," there will be a release and the critical beginnings of problem resolution.

7. (D) Paranoid-type schizophrenia involves delusions of grandeur or persecution.

8. (A) Fear of failure is one of the main bases for emotional disturbance. Such fear becomes intricately interwoven with a poor self-concept.

9. (C) Menninger concludes that psychiatry should dispense with labels for emotional disturbances, relying more on a way of behaving than on a disease concept.

10. (A) Szasz—well known for *The Myth of Mental Illness* and *The Age of Madness*—would be in agreement with Menninger.

11. (E) The lack of physiological basis for the blindness is evidence of conversion disorder.

12. (D) The continual weeping could be indicative of regression to a behavior characteristic of an earlier period in her life.

13. (D) Enuresis (bedwetting) has a close relationship to parentally-instilled fears.

14. (C) Such behavior as compulsive counting and recounting on grounds of having miscounted indicates a strong obsessive-compulsive disorder.

15. (D) *DSM-IV* is the *Diagnostic and Statistical Manual of Mental Disorders*, 4th ed. It was published by the American Psychiatric Association in 1994, and contains the basic categories and subcategories used in classifying mental disorders.

16. (D) The dynamic model of psychopathology spotlights unconscious conflict as the basis of emotional disturbance.

17. (C) Statistical, cultural, behavioral, and clinical deviation are four basic models on which to define mental illness. Criminal deviation is not a similar definitional model.

18. (C) When used, insulin shock therapy centered upon the diagnosis of paranoid schizophrenia.

19. (A) Within his mathematical approach to personality theory, Eysenck utilizes the term *autonomic reactivity*.

20. (A) The fact that these people prefer their present life style is a continuing and nagging problem in the treatment of drug addicts, alcoholics, and sociopaths. A sincere desire to be helped is critically important to effective treatment.

21. (D) Psychotomimetic drugs (hallucinogens) produce symptoms in normal subjects resembling those found in psychotic patients—distortions of body image, disorganized thinking, and hallucinations. LSD is a major drug in this category.

22. (A) Significant correlation has been found between juvenile delinquency and the background of a broken home and parental absence.

23. (C) Body metabolism is a key function of the thyroid gland.

24. (E) Although heart rate, blood pressure, respiration, and body temperature are lowered during sleep, gastric contractions are not affected.

25. (E) Dream activity is accompanied by distinctive EEG patterns, rapid eye movement, high-level cerebral blood flow, and higher brain temperature, but it is not characterized by a higher level of general muscle activity.

26. (C) Basic to the central nervous system are the brain and the spinal cord.

27. (E) Delgado's *Physical Control of the Mind: Toward a Psychocivilized Society* triggered much debate and fear of electroligarchy.

28. (E) The myelin sheath carries the function of insulating an axon.

29. (E) Among the entries given, the dog would have the most prominent cerebral cortex, and therefore the most advanced brain.

30. (C) The life, estrous, menstrual, and breeding cycles affect degree or prominence of sexual behavior, but there is no cycle known as the androgenous.

31. (E) Peripheroceptors is a meaningless term not common to any discussion of sensory groupings.

32. (B) The sympathetic and the parasympathetic form the two subdivisions of the autonomic nervous system. The sympathetic nervous system relates to emotion.

33. (D) Reflexes are rapid, automatic responses that are neither conscious nor voluntary. They are centered primarily in the spinal cord.

34. (A) In relation to the Tinbergen areas for study in animal behavior—development, mechanisms, function, evolution—teleonomic questions deal with functions, in this case, the animals' *need* for certain nutrients.

35. (E) Mechanistic questions deal with the relationship between behavior and physiological systems.

36. (D) Homeostasis refers to the body's tendency to maintain a state of internal physiological balance.

37. (E) Persons having had corpus callosum sectioning demonstrate severe problems on the block-design task—the hands, in effect, fighting with each other (one hand "knowing how" and the other hand "ignorant").

38. (A) Receptors are the cells that respond to changes in their environment and signal these changes to the nervous system. Subsequent muscle response would occur as a result of the functioning of effectors.

39. (A) The primary motor area of the cortex is just in front of the fissure of Rolando.

40. (B) The visual area of the cortex is the occipital lobe, located in the back between the parietal lobe and the cerebellum.

41. (D) Audition centers in the temporal lobe of the left cerebral hemisphere, just below the fissure of Sylvius.

42. (C) The somatosensory (sensation from knees, wrists, hands, fingers, face, and so on) center is located just behind the fissure of Rolando.

43. (E) Maintenance of balance and posture is a function of the cerebellum, which adjoins the brain stem and the occipital lobe.

44. (A) Afferent neurons are located in the dorsal column of the spinal cord.

45. (D) EPSP means excitatory postsynaptic potentials. Its often-seen counterpart is IPSP (inhibitory postsynaptic potentials).

46. (C) In ordinary dreaming, the external world gets incorporated selectively. Frequently, a dream contains aspects of the preceding day's activity.

47. (A) Operational definitions deal with specific details relating to the measurement of a behavioral phenomenon. In the case of GSR, measurable physiological changes (here meaning electrical conductance of the skin) would satisfy such operational definition requirements.

48. (A) There is convincing evidence of hereditary elements in emotionality, particularly in studies of twins, where heredity can be viewed as a constant.

49. (E) McClelland finds achievement need positively correlated with amount of formal education.

50. (D) An expression common to motivational studies, the letters stand for expected value.

51. (C) Lashley's concept of equipotentiality refers to a cortical system's capacity to assume functions previously assumed within another portion of the system. The concept has critical importance in cases of brain damage.

52. (C) The Barker-Dembo-Lewin study demonstrated vividly the child response of regression following frustration.

53. (E) This excerpt comes from the James-Lange theory of emotion— that emotion results from behavior rather than vice versa.

54. (B) An apt definition of motivation, and one that Atkinson has used, is how behavior gets started, is energized, is sustained, and is directed.

55. (D) Hull's reaction potential was conceptualized by Spence as excitatory potential.

56. (A) Watson's radical behaviorism was attacked by critics as discounting the importance of an individual's mental processes on learning and behavior. Focus was on stimulus-response exclusively.

57. (E) The terms *force field*, *valence*, *life span*, and *tension* are integral to Lewin's field theory; *interference* is not.

58. (D) S(Delta) refers to the absence of a discriminative stimulus.

59. (E) When your typing speed has reached its all-time peak, the learning-curve expression that covers the situation is asymptote.

60. (B) A combination of desirable and undesirable aspects attached to the same goal object is central to approach-avoidance conflict.

61. (C) In avoidance conditioning, as in this description, UCS is not received.

62. (D) The rats that do not receive reinforcement have been learning nonetheless, which is evident when reinforcement is introduced. Central to Tolman, the concept is known as latent learning.

63. (A) Time estimation is most critical to a fixed-interval reinforcement schedule.

64. (C) The inhibitory effects of punishment appear to be only immediate and short-range.

65. (C) The pursuit rotor is a turntable-style apparatus designed to measure effectiveness in motor tracking.

66. (C) The span of a normal learning process is depicted by the S-shaped curve.

67. (B) Classical conditioning relies upon consistency in CS-UCS pairing—a consistency not maintained by partial reinforcement.

68. (B) Thorndike's Law of Effect points to the central role of reinforcement in learning.

69. (B) Harlow found apparent normal development in the cloth-mother-reared females, but they proved woefully inadequate as mothers, sitting on their young, and so on. The opportunity to interact with peers during early development resolved this problem.

70. (A) Allport speaks of functional autonomy, whereby an activity that initially satisfied a basic need (e.g., hunting) now becomes rewarding simply as an activity itself.

71. (B) The fact that earlier list learning was interfering with recall of subsequent lists is indicative of proactive inhibition or proactive interference.

72. (B) Percentage recall was the dependent variable; number of lists was the independent variable.

73. (E) Results would suggest a negative correlation between the number of lists learned and the percentage of recall. As the number of lists increased, percentage recall decreased.

74. (A) The measure being taken with these subjects is the percentage of recall after each given list is learned. In effect, there are several treatments (recall measures) on each subject, a factor suggesting the treatments-by-subjects, repeated-measures design.

75. (D) A normal distribution is symmetrical, being completely free of either positive or negative skew.

76. (A) The range of possible correlation is 0 (no relationship) to + or −1.00 (perfect relationship). A correlation of +0.80 would express a relationship twice as strong as a correlation of +0.40.

77. (C) To make accurate inferences about a population, a representative sample is essential.

78. (A) Such a scattergram pattern—lower left to upper right—indicates positive correlation.

79. (E) A frequency polygon consists of points connected by lines.

80. (E) An *r* indicates correlation—a systematic relationship between two sets of variables.

81. (A) A *z*-score assumes direct knowledge of a population mean and standard deviation.

82. (B) A *t*-score reflects an unknown population mean and inference based on data obtained through sampling procedures.

83. (D) The extent to which obtained value differs from expected value is a central concern of the chi-square statistic.

84. (C) The median, or 50th percentile, of the score distribution is 61.8 (in effect, 12/28 of the way into the middle interval of 61–63).

85. (D) The mode is the midpoint of the most frequently occuring interval, in this case 62.

86. (B) The 40th percentile—the point in the distribution where forty percent of the scores are less than or equal to that point—is approximately 61.

87. (B) The mean (average score) most closely approximates 61.

88. (A) This person has scored one standard deviation above the mean, at approximately the 84th percentile. None of the others has scored at the level of one standard deviation above the mean.

89. (E) This person has scored only a half standard deviation above the mean, but all the other persons have scored at least a two-thirds standard deviation above the mean.

90. (E) This score of a half standard deviation above the mean would be expressed by a z-score of +.50.

91. (D) The size of the standard deviation is indicative of score variability. The largest standard deviation is 40.

92. (B) A researcher who uses a well-established intelligence scale to test the validity of one just developed is using the approach known as concurrent validity.

93. (A) Cycles in bodily processes are related to this awake-at-a-specific-time phenomenon.

94. (D) Though the cerebral hemisphere dominant in speech is generally the cerebral hemisphere dominant in handedness, there are notable exceptions.

95. (C) Dember sees figure reversibility as evidence that change is essential to the maintenance of perception.

96. (D) Restle's adaptation-level theory relates to the "moon illusion"— the tendency to see the moon as larger when it is on the horizon than when it is overhead.

97. (E) Light and shadow differentiations create such perceptual phenomena as bumps and craters.

98. (D) Emmert (1981) discovered that the size of the visual afterimage differed with the distance of the surface from the person. His experiment was based on focusing upon the middle of a black circle with a white center. When the stimulus had been focused for about a minute and the subject looked at a distant wall, the afterimage circle seemed smaller. When looking at a surface closer than the original one, the afterimage seemed larger. Emmert concluded the size of the afterimage varied systematically with the distance from the object—a convincing argument for size constancy.

99. (B) Distal stimulus is the actual external object. Proximal stimulus is the inverted image on the retina.

100. (A) The principal names in Gestalt psychology were Wertheimer, Koffka, and Kohler.

101. (D) The middle ear provides amplification via a kind of increased "thrust."

102. (B) The Purkinje effect deals with visual phenomena associated with the transition between cone and rod activation. Such effects as a short-wave-length hue appearing bright occur prominently at dusk.

103. (E) The thalamus—located at the top of the reptilian brain—relays inputs from the sensory systems to the cerebrum.

104. (A) Taste is a chemical sense strongly dependent upon liquid (solubility in water) for its sensitivity.

105. (C) The Snellen chart is the familiar rows-of-letters eye chart used in many eye examinations.

106. (D) Distance perception in a two-dimensional representation of a railroad track is primarily a function of linear perspective—the track lines converging as they "move into the distance."

107. (C) The Jastrow illusion contains two geometric curves (ends downward) placed one above the other. The illusion involves seeing the upper curve as smaller than the lower, though they are identical in size.

108. (B) The "piano" theory of hearing (also called place theory) suggests that the specific nerve fibers, in the same manner as piano wires, respond to specific sound frequencies.

109. (E) Interposition refers to objects viewed as standing in front of other objects—a monocular cue to depth perception.

110. (A) Closure is the perceptual tendency to complete a circle or a square where a gap in the needed stimulus line currently exists.

111. (C) Tinbergen's work used the method of naturalistic observation, not the laboratory method.

112. (D) Lights blinking in sequence (as in many neon signs) and perceived as movement are an example of the phi phenomenon.

113. (C) Size constancy is functioning in any setting where a large object far in the distance is perceived as that large object rather than as a tiny speck on the retina.

114. (E) The Young-Helmholtz Trichromatic Theory of color vision was one of the earliest and most important.

115. (A) The saying "Birds of a feather flock together" reflects the social attraction notion of attitude similarity—a dominant characteristic confirmed by research.

116. (C) Maslow's self-actualized person is relatively independent of his culture and environment.

117. (D) Erikson and Hartmann are the two most prominent names in ego-analytic personality theory (a contemporary extension of Freud's theorizing).

118. (A) Phenomenology's perceptual formulations are borrowed mainly from the Gestaltists.

119. (B) In the Asch experimental pattern, the critical (naive) subject was less likely to conform to group opinion if one other subject dissented from group opinion.

120. (D) Adler initiated the personality concept of family constellation, suggesting specific personality characteristics for family members on the basis of their position in the family birth order.

121. (B) The Lockean view underscores the importance of environment in personality, a view held strongly by proponents of behaviorism.

122. (B) Jung's key functions are sensing, feeling, thinking, and intuiting.

123. (E) Rotter developed the Internal-External Control Scale. It measures the extent to which one feels life to be controlled by oneself or by forces and people in the environment.

124. (D) Freud considered repression the grandfather of all other defense mechanisms—in effect, the key to and most basic of all such mechanisms.

125. (C) Field theory and the Gestalt influence suggest that total experience is "greater than the sum of its parts."

126. (B) Instructions to make up a story about a specific picture, describe current events and the thoughts and feelings of the main characters, and conclude with a description of how the situation turns out would be characteristic of the Thematic Apperception Test (TAT).

127. (B) The situation described is similar to that which was produced in Sherif's "Robbers Cave" experiment. Placing boys in two groups at camp, the experimenters quickly found competition fostering hostility. When they attempted to reduce hostility by bringing the groups together in the dining hall, it served only further to compound the problem. Hostility was lowered only with the introduction of a superordinate goal (i.e., a problem that was bigger than either group's capacity to solve alone). Then they were faced with having to work together to solve their common problem.

128. (A) In Newcomb's "experimental dormitory" research, proximity functioned in early associations, but attitude similarity proved to be the more dominant long-range factor.

129. (B) The *F*-scale (Fascism scale) was developed by Adorno to measure authoritarian tendencies.

130. (B) Rokeach and Mezei's work underscored the importance of attitude similarity in social attraction (a much more critical element than racial similarity).

131. (A) Zajonc has found that familiarity leads to positive reactions and liking (rather than to contempt).

132. (D) The Lewinson-Zubin scales are associated with graphology interpretations relating to personality.

133. (B) Critical subjects are present in the Asch, but not in the Crutchfield, technique of conformity research.

134. (C) Deutsch has found that threat is totally ineffective as an incentive for cooperation. Cooperation is most likely in the absence of threat.

135. (C) Jung's collective unconscious and archetypal concepts have been most heavily criticized and rejected by personality theorists.

136. (A) Kelley's discounting rule indicates that ragweed as the cause of our sniffles will be discounted if other possible causes (e.g., someone else in the family with an earlier case of sniffles) also are present.

137. (C) The circle pattern is a democratic, equal-opportunity pattern of communication.

138. (A) At dating age, an adolescent's relationship to the same-sex parent becomes critically important.

139. (C) An identical-twin study involving separate environments for one member of each twin pair would seek to study the effects of heredity.

140. (C) Significant positive correlation has been found between maternal smoking and the incidence of premature birth of offspring.

141. (B) The Hartshorne and May studies found that children seem to apply a situational morality, even in cases where different situations involve the same moral principle. It was impossible for the experimenters to divide the children into groups labeled *cheaters* and *noncheaters*.

142. (B) Experiments identical to the one described have resulted in classical conditioning of the fetus.

143. (E) The germinal period refers to the first two weeks after conception.

144. (A) DNA (deoxyribonucleic acid) is a molecular configuration making up chromosomes.

145. (D) Experiments show that newborns demonstrate a distinct preference for stimuli that contain a likeness of the human face.

146. (A) The prenatal period during which X rays and specific drugs could be most detrimental to development is the first eight weeks, when basic structures are being formed.

147. (C) In cognitive development, the following sequence occurs: voluntary movement, mental representation and object permanence, symbolic thought, intuitive thought, concrete operations and conservation, information processing.

148. (E) There is no such thing as "one identical" member of any group.

149. (D) The nature-nurture controversy deals with the respective influences of heredity and environment upon human development.

150. (C) Self-acceptance has the most critical, long-range effect upon the emotional health of an individual.

151. (D) Three-year-old children normally conduct individual activities side-by-side and close to one another without any evidence of cooperative or associative interaction.

152. (A) Sex differences in personality and perception become well established during the first few years of a child's life.

153. (B) In prenatal development, fetal wastes are absorbed through the placental walls into the mother's blood.

154. (D) The critical social-development period for the infant is the period between six weeks and six months of age.

155. (D) During embryonic development, both a universally consistent sequence and timing characterize organ systems development. Therefore, one embryo could not undergo brain development before heart development while another embryo developed in the reverse order.

156. (C) Down syndrome, or Mongolism, has been associated with an extra chromosome number 21.

157. (E) Research suggests that a child has a tendency to maintain a generally balanced diet, long-range, if placed in a self-selection food situation (the balance not being apparent in any given meal).

158. (D) The ectoderm is the center of activity for development of the hair and nails.

159. (C) Developmental psychology views disobedience of the young child in the context of frustration and unhappiness.

160. (B) Anoxia refers to interruption of the oxygen supply to the brain— a cause of death among newborns.

161. (A) *Circadian* refers to the cyclic daily body rhythms of activity and repose—a special problem for air travelers crossing several different time zones in close succession.

162. (B) Experiments with newborns suggest the presence of pattern discrimination.

163. (A) Sternberg's memory-process research compared serial and parallel search processes and supported the serial search hypothesis.

164. (B) The Zeigarnik effect suggests that an interrupted task is more likely to be remembered than a completed one.

165. (C) Guilford's model describes divergent production as the ability to generate a variety of hypotheses in a given problem situation. This is a central aspect within creativity.

166. (B) The interfering effect of old information (Spanish) on new learning (German) is called proactive interference.

167. (B) Piaget speaks of four major stages of cognitive development— sensorimotor, preoperational, concrete operations, and formal operations.

168. (D) The WAIS standardizes for each age level and does not utilize the $MA/CA \times 100$ formula.

169. (C) In retrograde amnesia resulting from an accident-caused brain injury, a person loses memory of events immediately prior to the injury.

170. (B) The Ebbinghaus curve's steep initial drop followed by a gradual decline is evidence that most forgetting occurs shortly after learning.

171. (E) Phonemes are the smallest units of sound. Morphemes are the smallest units of *meaningful* sound.

172. (D) *Accommodation* is Piaget's term describing a child's modification of an existing cognitive schema to make it compatible with the cognitive aspects of an incoming stimulus.

173. (B) Whorf's well-known position advances the belief that language patterns play a dominant role in shaping a person's thoughts and subsequent behavior.

174. (E) The earliest studies of verbal learning and rote memory were the nonsense-syllable studies of Ebbinghaus.

175. (E) Decay theories of forgetting based purely on the passage of time are contrasted with interference theories of forgetting.

176. (A) Damage to the hippocampus, in the medial temporal lobe, causes an impairment in the ability to learn new information.

177. (B) Establishing a principle on the basis of existing information and then filling in missing information on the basis of the principle is an example of interpolation.

178. (B) Bruner sees a strong relationship between a child's mastery of techniques and skills and his cognitive growth.

179. (B) When asked to recall a list of words in any order, people tend to recall best the words at the beginning and end of the list. The characteristic U-shaped plot of percent recall as a function of position on the list is called the serial position effect.

180. (C) The first memory stage or process, encoding, is the translation of an environmental stimulus, whether a word, a picture, or an event, to a long-term memory representation. Successful encoding requires attention, rehearsal, and elaboration.

181. (A) The capacity of short-term memory is about seven units, or chunks.

182. (B) Long-term potentiation results in synaptic changes dependent on experience for relatively long periods of time.

183. (B) Corporate communication is initiated most frequently in a higher-to-lower-echelon direction.

184. (C) Human engineering seeks to promote efficiency in a specific job setting.

185. (B) In human engineering usage ET refers to effective temperature.

186. (D) A key research reference source in psychology is *Psychological Abstracts*.

187. (B) Given sufficient time to utilize it, the distributed-practice approach will prove most effective in examination preparation.

188. (E)   Source, transmitter, channel, receiver, and audience are Bauer-Shannon entries in communications diagramming.

189. (D)   The foot-in-the-door technique suggests that a person who has agreed to a small favor is more likely to agree later to a larger favor than a person not approached about the initial small favor.

190. (C)   In the Piaget framework, the concept of volume-displacement conservation would be the most advanced and the last to occur developmentally.

191. (C)   Proximity holds prominence and importance in social attraction (e.g., it is important to be a neighbor or friend to the person living next door rather than to the person living "three doors down").

192. (C)   Because of the pace of a child's physiological development—particularly the development of sphincter muscles—it is recommended that parents wait until the child is at least two years old before attempting toilet training.

193. (E)   In the repeated-measures (test-retest) experimental design, a subject acts as his own control.

194. (B)   Because the mean is extremely sensitive to divergent scores, the median is a more representative measure in the situation described.

195. (D)   An aptitude test is best and most timely if it measures the person's capabilities on position-related tasks.

196. (E)   From the standpoint of dependence on perceptual cues, the most dangerous point for commercial pilots during night flight is the moment of runway approach.

197. (B)   Human engineers have found that shape coding is extremely important in airplane cockpit design. A common shape for different-function knobs could cause confusion and possibly fatal accidents.

198. (D)   The Army Alpha was the first group-administered test of intelligence developed by the Army. It was developed by Yerkes in 1921.

199. (C)   There is strong positive correlation between likelihood of behavioral change and amount of cognitive dissonance.

200. (C)   In human engineering, one of the control principles states that the direction of movement on any control should be compatible with the effects produced. Therefore, turning a steering wheel counterclockwise to achieve a right turn would be a case of incompatibility.

Diagnostic Test 1: Evaluating Your Score

Abbreviation Guide for Quick Reference (Translation)

PyCl:	Psychopathology/Clinical
PC:	Physiological/Comparative
LM:	Learning/Motivation/Emotion
M:	Methodology
SnP:	Sensation/Perception
PrS:	Personality/Social
D:	Developmental
CHL:	Cognition/Complex Human Learning
Ap:	Applied

TALLY CHART									
Checkmark to the left of the items you missed.									
1	21	41	61	81	101	121	141	161	181
2	22	42	62	82	102	122	142	162	182
3	23	43	63	83	103	123	143	163	183
4	24	44	64	84	104	124	144	164	184
5	25	45	65	85	105	125	145	165	185
6	26	46	66	86	106	126	146	166	186
7	27	47	67	87	107	127	147	167	187
8	28	48	68	88	108	128	148	168	188
9	29	49	69	89	109	129	149	169	189
10	30	50	70	90	110	130	150	170	190
11	31	51	71	91	111	131	151	171	191
12	32	52	72	92	112	132	152	172	192
13	33	53	73	93	113	133	153	173	193
14	34	54	74	94	114	134	154	174	194
15	35	55	75	95	115	135	155	175	195
16	36	56	76	96	116	136	156	176	196
17	37	57	77	97	117	137	157	177	197
18	38	58	78	98	118	138	158	178	198
19	39	59	79	99	119	139	159	179	199
20	40	60	80	100	120	140	160	180	200

Record the number of questions you missed (checkmarked) in each area.

PyCl (1–22) _____   PC (23–46) _____   LM (47–70) _____

M (71–92) _____   SnP (93–114) _____   PrS (115–137) _____

D (138–162) _____   CHL (163–182) _____   Ap (183–200) _____

Test Score Scaling

Now, see how you "stacked-up" in each of the subject areas. Subtract the number of questions you missed in a given subject area from the total number of questions in that area. Compare the result with the 75th percentile number. If the number is equal to or larger than the 75th percentile number, you know that area pretty well. If the number is smaller than the 75th percentile number, it's an area you will want to review thoroughly. For instance, if you missed 6 questions in the PyCl area, subtract that 6 from 22 (the total number of PyCl questions on the test) and come up with 16. The 75th percentile for PyCl would be 18, so you have some brush-up work ahead of you in that area.

PyCl Area: 22 – _____ (your number missed) = _____ // 18 = 75th percentile
PC Area: 24 – _____ (your number missed) = _____ // 19 = 75th percentile
LM Area: 24 – _____ (your number missed) = _____ // 19 = 75th percentile
M Area: 22 – _____ (your number missed) = _____ // 18 = 75th percentile
SnP Area: 22 – _____ (your number missed) = _____ // 18 = 75th percentile
PrS Area: 23 – _____ (your number missed) = _____ // 18 = 75th percentile
D Area: 25 – _____ (your number missed) = _____ // 20 = 75th percentile
CHL Area: 20 – _____ (your number missed) = _____ // 15 = 75th percentile
Ap Area: 18 – _____ (your number missed) = _____ // 14 = 75th percentile

How did you do? In the review ahead you can focus on those specific areas where you dropped a bit short of the mark. You'll be amazed what a difference the review will make. Take a deep breath and plunge in!

Just a Thought or Two

As we review together we're naturally going to make some observations. We thought we'd pass along a few we've made, which might be of help as you review:

- Even though most of our life span happens after childhood, most of the developmental questions will fall in the child development area. Maybe that is because it has the most extensive research background, but in any case, the emphasis will be on child development. Adolescence will be the next-most-covered, and the rest of the life span, the least covered.
- Within the child development area, make sure you have Piaget "nailed." Both textbook writers and testmakers heap lots of coverage on Piaget— probably due in part to his influence, but also due in part to his concepts lending themselves to specific questions.
- Focus your Methodology review on the concepts and terms. For your life within psychology, a strong methodological base and understanding will be a tool for which you'll be forever grateful.
- The Applied area will be the least covered in testing. This may be due in part to its topically sprawling nature. It's not as self-contained as, for example, a Physiological or a Learning area.
- Remember to answer the questions you know and make note of the ones you're not sure about. You can return to those when you've gotten through the test. Don't spend a lot of time on any one question. Move through steadily.
- When you return to the "unsures," guess! If you can eliminate even one answer option, the odds are in your favor.
- Our questions include proper names like Egbert and Ignatius. We've done it on purpose to add interest to your review. The GRE itself has proper names, too, but NOT Egbert and Ignatius!
- We've topically grouped questions on the diagnostic tests for your ease in scoring. After the two diagnostic tests, we'll "mix it up." The GRE itself will be a mix and blend of topic questions in no special groupings.
- Expect the GRE to use the "I, II, III" format, in which they give you choices I, II, and III and then follow up with (A) I and II only, (B) II and III only, and so on. We know they're not your favorite questions— not ours, either—but don't be thrown by them. Go with what you know and your first answer impulse. Don't second guess. These kinds of questions can twist you in knots on second-guessing. Look for these questions in Diagnostic Test 2 in Chapter 4.

CHAPTER

3 Review of Psychology

About the Review

Now you know how well your introductory psychology notes and the under-lining and notations in your book prepared you for the GRE. Naturally, there is work to be done, and this section is designed to help you in your compre-hensive review.

Start by reading through the entire section, spending more time in the areas that were weak in your Diagnostic Test 1 analysis. Keep a current general psychology book handy (see listings in Chapter 1), and use it frequently as you review. After you have finished reviewing, take Diagnostic Test 2. Evaluate your score using the same procedures you did with Diagnostic Test 1. This will tell you which areas need still more review; return to those sections for addi-tional work. Use the *Sources for Further Reading* at the end of this chapter to find other books dealing with the topics you want to spend more time on.

As stated in Chapter 1, the subject areas covered by the Psychology Test and included in this review are the following:

Physiological and comparative psychology
Sensation and perception
Learning
Cognition and complex human learning
Developmental psychology
Motivation and emotion
Social psychology
Personality
Psychopathology
Clinical psychology
Methodology
Applied psychology

Topics are arranged in a continuum starting with the basic elements of behavior and brain function (physiological aspects of psychology) and moving toward a consideration of the whole person (clinical, social, and applied psy-chology). This arrangement enables you to see the basic interrelationship of all aspects of psychology and points up the need for an overall comprehension of the entire subject area in order to understand the value of each topic. At the onset of your review you will find that you are more familiar with some of the areas than with others; our mutual goal is to have all of them sounding very familiar to you by the time you take the Psychology Test.

A standardized test such as this will not necessarily correspond with the emphasis that you encountered during your studies in the field of psychology. Therefore, if you were trained in the "whole-person-centered" approach you will now need to concentrate on the physiological, basic experimental, and methodological sides of psychology. If, on the other hand, you are thoroughly grounded in experimental design, statistics, and the animal laboratory, you will have to work on the personality, clinical, and developmental aspects of the field. Finally, if you have received a balanced education, a general review to sharpen the knowledge you already have will be your best approach.

During your review, keep in mind that for each subject area you will be expected to exhibit a mastery of basic principles and concepts (theories and laws, if the area has any), names of persons associated with the better-known concepts and research, and primary research findings. By concentrating on these aspects in each review area, you will soon gain a clearer understanding both of the individual areas and of the science of psychology as a whole.

To facilitate your review, each topical section will include a brief, descriptive introduction to the area. An outline of basic principles, concepts, personalities, and terms will follow the introduction. Don't panic when you view an outline and find little or nothing familiar. That's why we're here—to get acquainted with the area. You'll soon be quite familiar with those strange-looking outlines! A comprehensive general psychology text will serve as a helpful reference and for clarification throughout your review.

Think of it this way: The outline is a road map to the area. It tells you the major routes, the cities and towns along the way. The general psychology text resembles a close-up of a particular area on the map as well as an atlas for reference and clarification. Between them, you definitely will know where you're going!

Physiological and Comparative Psychology

When you have completed this section of the review, you should be quite familiar with such names as Gazzaniga, Sperry, Olds, Sherrington, Delgado, Penfield, Thompson, McGaugh, and Kandel, and definitions relating to parts of the brain, the glands, and the nervous system should be as familiar as your best friend's favorite meal. Much is happening in physiological and comparative psychology today, and it is impossible to be in on the excitement unless you know the playing field and the game rules. Mastery of key names and definitions will prepare you to share the action and perhaps even contribute to it—as well as tell the Educational Testing Service that you know what it's all about.

PHYSIOLOGICAL PSYCHOLOGY

Welcome to the incredible "hidden universe," the human brain. Like Mt. Everest, it has challenged the curiosity and inquiry of the brightest people over several centuries. One must admire the brilliance of early "brain explorers." Working with only the crudest of research tools—or, in many instances, no tools at all—they formulated concepts and a legacy for other explorers who would follow. And as the research tools and methods became all the more sophisticated across the centuries, we gained an even deeper respect for the early explorers and their insights. In the seventeenth century, *Descartes* formulated the concept of *reflex action*. In what has become a famous drawing, one can see a kneeling figure with his foot near the fire. Sketched from the brain and extending down the left leg is a nerve tube. The fire's heat begins a process up the nerve tube that opens a cavity in the brain from which animal spirits flow through the nerve tube to the muscles, which pull the foot from the fire. We can smile a bit at all Descartes' assumptions, but his reflex action concept has stood the test of time.

At the turn of the twentieth century, the Spanish medical researcher, Santiago *Ramon y Cajal*, was making histological discoveries destined to be generally recognized and honored throughout the world. In 1906, he was accorded Nobel Prize recognition in medicine and physiology. A marvel of Cajal's work was that given the primitive state of the field he was able to work only with structure, and from it he advanced concepts of neural function. His description of the *structure and function of neurons*, his view of the central nervous system as many separate but communicating nerve cells, and his descriptions of the direction of neural conduction and of neural regeneration all earned him the "father of present-day physiology" title and acknowledgment.

In the early twentieth century, Sir Charles *Sherrington* (British physiologist) corrected a misconception relating to the reflex pathway. Until that point, researchers envisioned nerve tissue as a long, continuous, wire-like design along which the neural impulse traveled. Sherrington introduced the concept of the *synapse*—a gap between neurons across which they had to communicate. Several years later, Otto *Loewi* demonstrated that the basis of communication across the synapse was chemical, thereby paving the way for the discovery of what are now known as neurotransmitters. Like Descarte and Ramon y Cajal before them, the conceptual legacy of Sherrington and Loewi was destined to stand the test of time and technological sophistication. The concept of neural transmission would now be forever envisioned in a new and different way. The synaptic gap concept gave rise to a vast new conceptual landscape, one that would bring with it concepts such as threshold, summation, neurotransmitters, and many more.

There have been many explorers on this challenging expanse of hidden universe, and we haven't the time or space to name them all here. One of the leading researchers into the neuronal substrates of behavioral plasticity has been Richard F. *Thompson*. Best known for his work on the neural mechanisms of habituation and sensitization, he and W. Alden *Spencer* developed the generally accepted *criteria for habituation*, demonstrating that the basic process is a form of synaptic depression that occurs presynaptically. *Thompson* more recently has investigated the *neuronal substrates of associative learning*, identifying two critical systems—the hippocampus and the cerebellum. Eric *Kandel* is among the researchers investigating the *link between proteins, synapses, and the formation of long-term memories*. Specific proteins have demonstrated the capacity to strengthen synaptic connections basic to one's long-term memory storage. It's an exciting field with implications for Alzheimer's sufferers. James L. *McGaugh* has physiologically addressed the question of *why emotionally arousing events are so memorable*. McGaugh concludes that emotionally arousing events stimulate norepinephrine synapses (B-adrenergic), which enhance memory storage. These emotionally arousing events also arouse the sympathetic nervous system, which converts glycogen into glucose and raises the blood-glucose level. Since glucose is the brain's "petrol," increasing levels facilitate brain functioning.

You can readily see the excitement within current explorations of our "hidden universe," and there comes a deep, abiding respect for the many who are contributing to this field and to each of us.

The brain, as "mission control" in the central nervous system, works very closely with muscles and glands. Thus, the function and contribution of each to the total picture is critically important. To familiarize you with mission control, any of the comprehensive introductory textbooks mentioned earlier will be helpful. With so much material to cover, it would be easy to get bogged down in a mountain of names, functions, and small details. You will not, of course, be expected to have a Ph.D.'s competence in physiology in order to pass the Psychology Test, but you should understand the basics and the function of physiology within behavior.

We think, feel, act, enjoy, laugh, cry, and—yes—even write papers and books. At this very moment many elaborate, complex activities are occurring within your body—some in response to incoming stimuli, others to maintain bodily processes and their balance, and so forth. Most of this elaborate functioning is geared toward taking care of you. Psychology, by definition, studies human behavior, so it is essential and natural that a field of psychology (physiological/behavioral neuroscience) is directed toward the behaving organism and the physiological structures and elements that underlie behavior. As we head for this aspect of your review, a helpful sequence will be to read carefully and absorb this outline section and your introductory textbook chapter on the brain and biological bases of behavior. Pay special attention to outline headings, parts, systems, functions, and groupings. The more you can bring meanings and relationships to the material, the easier it will be for you to remember names and groupings. Then check yourself out on the following terms and concepts, so that you will know how prepared you are to move on.

Physiological Psychology Outline

Concepts	Names	Terms
Neurons and basic elements	Descartes Ramon y Cajal	Neuron Glia Cell body (soma) Dendrites Axon Axon terminal Myelin sheath
	Sherrington	Synapse
The nerve impulse		Resting potential Action potential Threshold All-or-none law Node of Ranvier

Concepts	Names	Terms

Synaptic transmission and the function of the synapse	Loewi
	
	McGaugh
		Neurotransmitters
		 Biogenic Amines
		  Acetylcholine
		  Serotonin
		  Catecholamines
		   Dopamine
		   Norepinephrine
		   Epinephrine
		 Amino Acids
		  Glutamate
		  GABA
		 Peptides (Neuromodulators)
		  Substance P
		  Endorphins
		Receptors
		Lock-and-key model
		Excitatory
		Inhibitory
		Breakdown and reuptake

Nervous system and its two major divisions		Central (CNS) Brain and spinal cord Sensory (afferent) neurons Motor (efferent) neurons Peripheral Somatic Autonomic Sympathetic Parasympathetic

Brain divisions and their functions		Brainstem
		 Hindbrain
		  Medulla
		  Pons
		 Midbrain
		 Cranial nerves
		 Reticular formation
		Cerebellum
		Forebrain
		 Thalamus
		 Basal ganglia
		 Limbic system
		  Hypothalamus
		  Amygdala
		  Hippocampus
		Cerebral cortex
		 Sulcus and gyrus
		 Hemispheres
		  Right (nonverbal) and left (verbal)
		  Corpus callosum
		 Lobes
		  Occipital (vision)
		  Temporal (audition, language, Wernicke's area)
		  Parietal (somatosensation, spatial ability)
		  Frontal (motor control, planning, Broca's area)

Concepts	Names	Terms
Endocrine system of glands		Hypothalamus
		Pituitary
		Thyroid
		Parathyroid
		Adrenal cortex
		Adrenal medulla
		Pancreas
		Ovaries and testes
Methods for measuring brain function		Recording techniques
		Electrical
		Single-cell recording
		Electroencephalogram (EEG)
		Event-related potentials (ERP)
		Metabolic, hemodynamic
	Raichle, Petersen	Positron emission tomography (PET)
		Functional magnetic resonance imaging (FMRI)
		Structural
		Computerized axial tomography (CT)
		Magnetic resonance imaging (MRI)
	Olds	Electrical stimulation
	Penfield	Motor and sensory homunculus
		Lesion/brain damage
		Chemical and electrical lesions
	Phineas Gage	Natural injury (stroke, trauma, disease)
	Sperry, Gazzaniga	Surgical ablation, callosotomy (split-brain)
Neural plasticity	Thompson	Synaptic modification
	Kandel	Long-term potentiation
		Collateral sprouting
	Ramachandran	Cortical reorganization
		Interaction of environment/ behavior with brain
Mood/behavior altering drugs (see outline pp. 71–72)		Agonists
		Antagonists
		Blood-brain barrier
		Classification
		Depressants
		Stimulants
		Narcotics/opiates
		Antipsychotics
		Hallucinogens/psychedelics

The next few pages embellish the outline a bit with more detail. From there your work with a strong "intro psych" book will give you the confidence you need to master this outline and move on to the next topic.

Outline Terms Elaborated

➤ **Neurons and basic elements:**

There are two kinds of cells in the nervous system: *Neurons*, or nerve cells, transmit information in the form of electrochemical changes. *Glial* cells perform a variety of other functions but do not transmit information (e.g., one type of glial cell forms the myelin sheath mentioned below). Our nervous systems contain hundreds of billions of neurons varying in size, shape, function, and response speed. The prototypical neuron has three parts—*cell body*, *dendrites*, and *axon*. As you view any drawing of a neuron, you will see branches seeming to grow from what looks like an egg, sunny-side up. The branches are the dendrites (from the Greek for "tree"), which receive signals from other neurons and send them to the cell body. The egg-resembling part is the cell body, or *soma*, which collects and sums these incoming signals to determine whether the neuron should initiate its own signal. The stem-like corridor is the axon, which transmits the neuron's signal to the dendrites of other neurons, and the process begins again. In many neurons, the axon is wrapped in an insulating covering called the *myelin sheath*; deterioration of myelin is seen in a disease called *Multiple Sclerosis (MS)*. There is a tiny gap, called a *synapse*, between the ending of the axon of one neuron (the *axon terminal*) and the dendrites of the next neuron. There are two kinds of communication used by all neurons: electrical and chemical. Electrical changes result in the propagation of a neural signal from the dendrites to the axon terminal. Chemical changes result in the transmission of the signal from one neuron to the next. These two processes are discussed in more detail below.

➤ **The nerve impulse:**

The entire neuron is surrounded by a membrane that carefully regulates the passage of molecules between the inside of the neuron and the outside of the neuron. When a neuron is at rest, this membrane maintains a constant electrical differential between the inside and outside of the neuron; this difference is called the cell's *resting potential*. When a neuron is communicating information, this differential changes, and is referred to as an *action potential*, also known as an impulse, a signal, or firing. When incoming signals to a neuron, pooled by numerous dendrites, reach a certain *threshold*, the cell body initiates an action potential, which then propagates down the axon to the axon terminal. Because the action potential is always of the same magnitude, it is referred to as an *all-or-none* event. However, the speed of an action potential can vary: In axons surrounded by myelin, the action potential reaches the axon terminal quickly because the action potential "jumps" down the axon, from one break in the myelin, called a *node of Ranvier*, to the next. In all neurons, the arrival of the action potential at the axon terminal initiates a chemical reaction that leads to synaptic transmission of the neural signal.

➤ **Synaptic transmission and function of the synapse:**

When an action potential reaches the axon terminal of a neuron, it causes that neuron to release chemicals that fill the synapse. These chemicals are collectively called *neurotransmitters*. These neurotransmitters attach to *receptors* in the membrane of the dendrites of another neuron, in a specific *lock-and-key* fashion. This can result in one of two effects: Binding of an *excitatory* neurotransmitter to a receptor can move that neuron closer to its threshold for having an action potential. Conversely, binding of an *inhibitory* neurotransmitter to a receptor can move that neuron further from its threshold for having an action potential. All of these inputs are summed by the cell body of the neuron, much the way credit and debits are summed on an accountant's ledger sheet, and if the net result is above threshold, the neuron fires an action potential. After a brief period of time, the neurotransmitter is either broken-down (by other chemicals) or taken back up into the neuron that released it. There are dozens of neurotransmitters used by the brain. Three major neurotransmitter categories are biogenic amines (dopamine, norepinephrine, epinephrine, serotonin, and acetylcholine), amino acids (glutamate, GABA), and peptides (substance P, endorphins). Those in the latter group are often considered to be *neuromodulators*, because their effects are in some ways closer to those of hormones than true neurotransmitters. This distinction is not a sharp one.

➤ **Nervous system and its two major divisions:**
Central (CNS), consisting of the brain and the spinal cord (with its sensory [afferent] neurons carrying information into the CNS and its motor [efferent] neurons carrying information away from the CNS); and *peripheral*, consisting of the *somatic* (transmitting information from sense organs to CNS to voluntary, skeletal muscles) and the *autonomic* (controlling the viscera [smooth muscles of the blood vessels, digestive system, and glands] and the cardiac [heart] muscles).

The autonomic has two divisions: the *sympathetic* (activating organs and glands "in sympathy" with emotions, and mobilizing the body's resources for "fight-or-flight" emergencies), and the *parasympathetic* (opposing the sympathetic and conserving body resources and energy).

➤ **Brain divisions and their functions:**
The brain consists of three major divisions—the *hindbrain*, the *midbrain*, and the *forebrain*. The hindbrain begins where the spinal cord ends, and has three structures: the *medulla*, the *pons*, and the *cerebellum*. The medulla and pons contain entry and exit points for most of the twelve cranial nerves and control vital functions such as digestion, heart rate, and respiration. They also contain the *reticular formation*, or reticular activating system (RAS), which controls general arousal (sleep, waking, and attention). The cerebellum controls functions of balance and coordination of motor movement and may also contribute to skill learning. Just above the hindbrain sits the midbrain, which contains more cranial nerves, parts of the reticular formation, and important relay stations for sensory information. The midbrain also contains a group of neurons called the *substantia nigra*, which produce dopamine and which degenerate in *Parkinson's disease*. The midbrain, the pons, and the medulla are collectively known as the *brainstem*. The largest division of the brain in humans is the forebrain, which consists of all of the following structures: The *thalamus* relays sensory information to the cerebral cortex. The *basal ganglia* are involved in move-

ment, speech, and other complex behaviors. Parts of the basal ganglia are damaged in Parkinson's disease and *Huntington's disease*. The *hypothalamus* works with both the central nervous system and the endocrine system and has a key role in motivated behaviors such as eating, drinking, sexual behavior, and aggression. The *hippocampus* is essential for learning and memory. The *amygdala* is involved in emotional expression. The hypothalamus, the amygdala, and the hippocampus, along with a few other structures, are collectively called the *limbic system*. All of the preceding brain structures are termed *subcortical structures*, in contrast to the rest of the forebrain, called the *cerebral cortex*. The cerebral cortex (Latin for "brain bark") is the convoluted surface of hills *(gyri)* and valleys *(sulci)* that you probably picture when you think of the brain. The cerebral cortex is divided into two nearly symmetrical *hemispheres* (with the left processing language and calculation and the right handling spatial and nonverbal functions in most people), which can each be further subdivided into four lobes: the *occipital lobe* in the rear, the *parietal lobe* on top, the *frontal lobe* in the front, and the *temporal lobe* on the bottom. The two hemispheres are connected by a bundle of nerve fibers called the *corpus callosum*. Regions of the cerebral cortex are often functionally subdivided into the *projection areas* that receive sensory input (vision in the occipital lobe, audition in the temporal lobe, somatosensation in the parietal lobe) or initiate motor commands (frontal lobe) and the *association areas* that make up the remaining 80% of cortex and subserve functions like planning and organization (frontal lobe), speech production (*Broca's area* in the frontal lobe), speech comprehension (*Wernicke's area* in the temporal lobe), and spatial organization (parietal lobe).

➤ **Endocrine system of glands:**

Including the *hypothalamus* (which serves as the glandular system "control center" and produces the hormones oxytocin and antidiuretic); the *pituitary* (which stimulates bone growth and produces the hormones: growth (somatotropin), prolactin, thyroid-stimulating, adrenocorticotropic (ACTH), follicle-stimulating, and luteinizing); the *thyroid* (which has a major role in metabolism stimulation/maintenance and produces the hormones thyroxin and calcitonin); the *parathyroid* (which has a calcium-related role and produces the hormone parathyroid); the *adrenal cortex* (which functions in metabolism [carbohydrate, protein, lipid] and in the system's salt/water balance, producing the hormones cortisol and aldosterone); the *adrenal medulla* (which increases heart rate, dilates and constricts blood vessels, and increases blood sugar and produces the hormones epinephrine and norepinephrine); the *pancreas* (which regulates enzyme discharge into the intestines and produces the hormone insulin); the *ovaries/testes* (which affect sex characteristics development/maintenance and produce the hormones estrogen/progesterone [in female, ovaries] and testosterone [in male, testes]).

➤ **Methods for measuring brain function:**

Recording techniques measure changes in neural activity in the functioning brain. The most direct measure of brain activity comes from animal studies, in which a small electrode is placed next to a neuron and is able to record individual action potentials as they occur. So called *single-cell recording* is not possible in humans, because of its invasiveness, although there are a number of techniques that are suitable for use with humans that provide a measure of neural activity. The closest parallel is the *electroencephalogram (EEG)*, which records electrical changes across the brain with electrodes placed on the scalp. The EEG shows you a fluctuating picture of voltage changes. The EEG is known to vary predictably with the arousal level of the individual being recorded: When awake and active, the waveforms have a high frequency and a low amplitude *(beta waves)*; when relaxed, the waveforms have a lower frequency and a higher amplitude *(alpha waves)*; during sleep, the waveforms change with different stages of sleep, from Stage 1 light sleep (some alpha wave activity) to Stage 2 sleep (higher amplitude, lower frequency activity with some evidence of "spikes" called K-complex) to the deeper Stage 3 and Stage 4 sleep ("slow wave" sleep with a prevalence of *delta wave* activity) and finally to *Rapid Eye Movement (REM)* sleep (irregular brain wave pattern). Measurement of these patterns has revealed that the typical sleep pattern includes 4–5 REM cycles, when leaving deep sleep and moving back toward Stage 1 sleep, with each REM stage getting progressively longer as the night goes on. The EEG can also be used diagnostically, to reveal abnormal electrical patterns such as those observed in *epilepsy*. Although these EEGs can look like nothing more than jerky scribbles at first glance, there is a lot more we can learn about brain function by taking a closer look. Buried in these complex waveforms lie hidden treasures—voltage changes that depend on neural responses to stimuli in the environment. The examination of EEGs in relation to an experimental stimulus event goes by the name *event-related potentials* (ERPs) or evoked potentials. ERPs are simply averaged EEGs over many periods of time that are locked to (that is, that immediately follow) a stimulus of interest, such as a flash of light or a spoken word. There are other electrophysiological recording techniques that measure eye movement (EOG—electrooculogram), muscle tension (EMG—electromyogram), heart rate (EKG—electrocardiogram), and respiration. One area of research, which you may know as "biofeedback," enables people to monitor some of their own bodily functions, such as blood pressure and heart rate and control functions that were previously thought to be entirely involuntary. Neal Miller and his associates have had surprising success with experiments in this area.

In recent years a number of indirect measurements of neural activity in humans have been developed. All of these techniques rely on the coupling of neural activity and blood flow: Neurons that are firing lots of action potentials increase their demand for oxygen and glucose found in blood. One such technique is the *positron emission tomography* (PET) scan procedure, which injects a radioactive isotope tracer into the blood. As brain cells take up the tracer, they emit radiation that is recorded by detectors placed around the head. The more active a cell is, the more radiation it will emit. Raichle and Petersen conducted seminal studies of reading and speech processes using PET. A related technique is functional magnetic resonance imaging (FMRI), which makes use of the observation that hemoglobin bound to oxygen has different magnetic properties than hemoglobin not bound to oxygen. In other words, FMRI uses a tracer that is endogenous to our bodies! PET and FMRI scans are both methods for looking at the function of different parts of the brain. These differ from methods that only provide pictures of the structures of the brain. Two such methods are the computerized axial tomography (CAT or CT) scan, which performs multi-angle brain X rays that are then computer-analyzed to produce a picture of each "slice" of the brain; and the magnetic resonance imaging (MRI) scan, which creates magnetic fields and records signals that occur when brain molecules respond to these fields. Remember: CAT and MRI scans depict brain structures while PET and FMRI scans analyze brain functions.

Electrical stimulation is the application of small levels of electrical current to part of the brain via an implanted electrode. Olds and Hess did pioneering work with electrical stimulation in animals, and Delgado and Penfield explored the effects of electrical stimulation in humans. *Olds* investigated pleasure centers in the hypothalamus, finding that a rat will happily self-administer electric current to these centers hour after hour. In humans, Delgado raised the possibility of helping people avert depression or aggressive behavior, for instance, by teaching them to recognize signals that accompany the onset of these problems and to stimulate their own brains via implanted electrodes. Other researchers have used electrical stimulation to examine the control of feeding and drinking, sexual behavior, and emotional responses. Hoebel produced eating behavior in completely satiated animals; similar drinking behavior has been produced by Miller et al. Fisher was able to obtain mating and maternal sexual behaviors in male animals, and Delgado convincingly demonstrated that the dominant animal in a colony can become quite submissive under certain conditions. Among other key researchers, Valenstein has worked with brain stimulation and psychosurgery and Magoun has worked with the reticular formation. Wilder *Penfield* used electrical stimulation to "map the cerebral cortex" in humans prior to brain surgery. Because the brain has no pain receptors, electrical stimulation could be applied to the brain of a fully conscious patient; using this technique, Penfield and his colleagues identified a systematic mapping of the body in motor and sensory cortex (for example, regions that control finger movement are adjacent to regions that control wrist movement) that is sometimes referred to as a *homunculus*. George *Ojemann* used electrical stimulation to map language areas throughout the brain. Clinically, this technique is important in identifying language and motor areas in each patient that can then be avoided during brain surgery.

Lesion and brain damage enables researchers to study how behavior is changed when some part of the brain is removed. The experimental lesion method in animals was pioneered by Charles *Sherrington*, who severed nerve fibers in dogs to study the importance of sensory feedback in motor control. Today, lesions are made with chemical and electrical techniques that allow remarkable precision. Of course, these techniques cannot be used in humans, although scientists do study the effects of naturally occurring brain damage on behavior.

Some patients develop lesions, or tissue damage, following accidental head trauma, stroke, tumors, hemorrhage, infections, or disease. Perhaps the most famous head trauma case ever reported is that of Phineas Gage, the young construction worker who sustained a head injury after dynamite propelled an iron rod through his head. Gage's survival, and subsequent behavior changes, provided the first clues as to the function of the frontal lobes in regulating personality and emotion. Diseases that affect the brain are often tied to disruptions in one or more neurotransmitter systems. *Alzheimer's disease*, a degenerative memory loss resulting from widespread cortical atrophy, has been linked to a deficiency in the neurotransmitter acetylcholine; *Parkinson's disease*, a degenerative loss of motor control, results from the loss of neurons in the substantia nigra that produce the neurotransmitter dopamine; *schizophrenia* symptoms such as hallucinations are hypothesized to result from an excess of dopamine. Other patients are given therapeutic lesions to control neurological disorders, most typically to reduce or eliminate epileptic seizures. For example, to reduce the severity of seizures, the corpus callosum (the communication "link" between the two hemispheres) can be severed, thus providing a fascinating and unique way to study the differential functioning of the left and right hemispheres. *Sperry* pioneered this field first in animals and then in humans, and *Gazzaniga* continues to productively study these so-called *split-brain* patients to understand hemispheric differences.

► **Neural plasticity:**

Plasticity refers to the flexibility that neurons have in their organization, connectivity, and function. In some regards, the brain exhibits remarkable plasticity, both during prenatal development (all neurons start out as the same type of stem cell, and look what happens!) and even into adulthood. For example, learning is thought to reflect the modification of *synaptic connectivity*; one process that has been studied for its relation to learning is called *long-term potentiation* of a synapse. However, in other regards the brain is decidedly non-plastic. The inability of the adult brain to grossly re-organize is the reason why brain damage can have such devastating, permanent effects. However, scientists are studying conditions and limitations on reorganization that could relate to recovery of some types of functions. *Collateral sprouting* is a mechanism whereby neurons make connections to new areas to change their connectivity. *Cortical reorganization* can also be seen in the sensory and motor maps, in response to amputation of limbs or even learning. Changes in the brain have also been observed in certain regions in response to changes in the environment, such as social dominance status in animals.

► **Mood/behavior altering drugs:**

All drugs have their effects at the synapse, by mimicking or changing the amount of neurotransmitter released by a presynaptic neuron or by modulating the effectiveness of a neurotransmitter on the postsynaptic neuron. In general, drugs that enhance a neurotransmitter's effect are called *agonists* while drugs that diminish the effect are called *antagonists*. Not every chemical can have an effect on the brain because not all chemicals have access to the brain and thus to the synapses; the *blood-brain barrier* is a mechanism that controls the passage of chemicals through the capillaries in the brain. The blood-brain barrier regulates which chemicals can enter the brain and how quickly they do.

Mood/behavior altering drugs fall into several major categories. We will give a narrative outline "intro" to drugs and their classification and will then follow with a quick-reference table. With that combination you'll have a strong grasp of the different categories, the characteristics of the category, and properties of specific types of drugs within each given category. Throughout this narrative we will be using the *medical classification* system (drug-effect-based) rather than the *legal classification* system, which is abuse-based. Where some drugs, for example, medically might not be classified as narcotics, a legal classification system might give them this label because they carry high abuse potential. What follows will be a medical classification.

Depressants

Depressants slow the CNS (central nervous system) functioning, reducing heart rate and breathing, and impairing motor functioning (e.g., the drunk person who staggers and would be lethal behind the wheel of a car). A depressant's crowning achievement is to put the person to sleep.

- *Alcohol* (ethanol) is our nation's most frequently used and abused depressant. With its physically addictive characteristics, a person developing a tolerance often will increase intake steadily to get the same "high." It's a vicious circle that compounds itself in many ways, including the person's capacity to function and the family's pain and dysfunction. The common, popular misnomer about alcohol is that it heightens sexual functioning when, in truth, it depresses this functioning and, alas, puts the person to sleep! Because it is addictive, the individual will experience withdrawal symptoms ranging from irritability and sleeplessness to seizures, heart attacks, and death. Its deleterious effects upon the body include destruction of brain cells and destruction of neurons in the CNS, liver damage, and damage to other organs of the body. Individual effects vary. Where one person will be drunk on one beer, another may take four or five before they appear intoxicated. These differences depend upon such factors as body weight, how quickly your body metabolizes and eliminates alcohol, and the level of tolerance developed through previous alcohol use/abuse.

- *Barbiturates* generally carry "al" endings. Phenobarbital, Pentothal, Nembutal, and Seconal are among this cadre of depressants called "downers." Once prescribed as "sleeping pills," this group carries the same risks and dangers inherent to alcohol. When an intoxicated person takes barbiturates, the risks increase dramatically because the effects of taking alcohol and barbiturates together multiply exponentially. The combined user can easily overdose. It literally can be a deadly accident.

- *Anxiolytics*, once called tranquilizers or *anti-anxiety* drugs, function to reduce anxiety feelings, calming and relaxing a person. Like alcohol and barbiturates, they also can produce sleep. Where meprobamate (Miltown) in small doses can reduce anxiety, larger doses can produce sleep or even death. *Benzodiazepine anxiolytics* such as Valium (diazepam class), Librium (chlordiazepoxide class), Xanax (alprazolam class), and Klonapin (clonazepam class) carry anxiety-reducing potential and frequently are used to treat anxiety disorders such as panic disorder and obsessive-compulsive disorder. Benzodiazepines produce less sedation than Miltown. Anxiolytics carry the same risks of psychological and physical dependence present with barbiturates, and the withdrawal process here can be every bit as painful.

Narcotics/Opiates

Narcotics/opiates such as *opium*, its *derivatives* (*codeine, heroin, morphine*), and the *synthetics* (e.g., *methadone*) function as painkillers. Like the depressants, they produce temporary feelings of euphoria, and bring on drowsiness and sleep. Narcotics are very highly addictive and carry a very high death-risk from overdose. Withdrawal also tends to be excruciating in its physical craving, pain, and suffering. AIDS and hepatitis are often transmitted by narcotics users through needle-sharing and blood-contact. Beyond these transmission risks, the bodily damage from narcotics/opiates surprisingly is less than that from alcohol abuse.

- *Opium*, coming from the poppy plant, is the "father or mother opiate." Its "offspring derivatives" are morphine; its derivative, heroin; and codeine. Heroin is three times more powerful than its "parent," morphine, and it brings intensely pleasurable reactions. Because it functions within a narrow range, a user can easily overdose, with devastating consequences including death. All opium derivatives produce euphoria and pain-control, and all are very highly addictive—both physically and psychologically.

- *Methadone*, a synthetic narcotic/opiate, holds a unique place and function within this group. While it has pain-control properties, it produces very little euphoria. With this blend of properties, it is frequently used in narcotics treatment programs (methadone maintenance programs). Because it, too, is very highly addictive, its use in treatment programs has been highly controversial. The recovering narcotics addict is, in effect, trading one addiction for another.

Psychedelics

Psychedelics (*hallucinogens* or *psychotomimetics [mimicking psychosis]*) are perception, emotion, and mood-altering. Body images may become distorted (the user feeling God-like or ant-like), identity may become confused (much like amnesia), and the loss of reality may include dream-like fantasies and hallucinations.

The two "major players" in the psychedelic realm are *LSD* and *marijuana*.

- *LSD (lysergic acid diethylamide)* was synthesized from a rye fungus by a Swiss chemist, Albert Hofmann, in 1938. When he accidentally swallowed a bit of it and "tripped out," he became vividly aware of its bizarre qualities. Timothy Leary became the LSD guru in this country. As a serotonin agonist, LSD enhances the action of serotonin across the synapse. Minds can leave bodies, sounds can become visual, and time can become distorted. Trips are entirely unpredictable. They can be very pleasurable or very, very bad. LSD is not addictive, but its prolonged use has been linked with short-term memory loss, nightmares, paranoia, panic attacks, and flashbacks. Such side effects can prove lasting . . . consequently, the nickname, "acid heads."

- *Marijuana ("pot," "dope," "reefer")* and its active ingredient *(tetra-hydrocannabinol, THC)* is a blend of crushed leaves, flowers, and stems from the hemp plant (*Cannabis sativa*). THC can be inhaled and quickly absorbed by the body and the brain. Senses and sensory experience are enhanced, and the user may feel dreamy, carefree, floating, and blissful. The effect lasts for a few hours. Like alcohol, it can impair muscle movement and coordination, and motor impairment can persist for an extended period after the enhanced state has dissipated. Frequent users can have lasting impairments to reasoning and memory.

"Minor players" include *mescaline*, *psilocybin*, and *PCP (phencyclidene)*.

- *Mescaline* occurs naturally in peyote cactus. The "trip" begins after the cactus buttons are chewed and the juice swallowed. It's a four-to-six-hour trip and, the user hopes, a blissful one.
- *Psilocybin* comes from certain mushrooms. They, too, are chewed and the juice swallowed. The trip resembles that of mescaline.
- *PCP (Phencyclidene, "angel dust")* is a synthetic originally used as an anesthetic. It can be ingested or smoked with trip qualities and dangers similar to those outlined above.

Stimulants

Stimulants literally live up to their name. They increase activity in the CNS, heightening arousal and energy level. More than one student has called upon an aluminum can of their favorite stimulant to "pull an all-nighter" or two . . . not you, of course, but some of your peers! Virtually all stimulants carry the "ine" ending—amphetamines (Benzedrine ["bennies," "speed"], Dexedrine ["uppers"], Methedrine ["ice"]), methamphetamines ("crystal meth") and derivatives (MDMA ["ecstasy" or "X"]), cocaine ("coke" and "crack"), caffeine, nicotine, and convulsants (strychnine).

- *Amphetamines* stimulate the brain and the sympathetic nervous system. Heart rate and blood pressure elevate, blood vessels constrict, mucous membranes shrink, and appetite is reduced. This latter property made amphetamines popular for weight control in the 1950s and 1960s.
- *Methamphetamines ("crystal meth")* and *derivatives (MDMA ["ecstasy" or "X"])* have amphetamine-like properties. "Crystal meth" is a powder that can be "snorted" or injected. For quite obvious reasons, MDMA is short for 3,4-Methylenedioxymethamphetamine (impress your date with that one!). Also known as "Ecstasy" or "X," it produces both stimulant and psychedelic effects. Effects are similar to those produced by amphetamines and cocaine. All is not ecstasy, however, because the user may experience jaw muscle spasms ("lock-jaw") and "day after" muscle aches, depression, and fatigue.
- *Cocaine* has properties and effects similar to amphetamines, increasing norepinephrine and dopamine activity. With its rapid onset and short duration, it is very highly addictive; and "crack," the purified, smokable form is all the more powerful, addictive, and dangerous. While use can temporarily stimulate self-confidence and a sense of well-being, the long-range effects include nausea, hyperactivity, insomnia, hallucinations, depressive "crashes," sexual dysfunction,

and seizures. The "roller-coaster" carries an exceptionally high price tag, and breaking an addiction is exceedingly difficult. A minimum of one year in treatment carries the greatest hope of success and, even then, recidivism runs disturbingly high. Buprenorphine, an opiate antagonist, may hold treatment promise; but all treatment results have been mixed. "Cocaine babies" carry severe and permanent intellectual/behavioral problems that provide no small societal challenge.

- *Caffeine* is, without a doubt, the world's most popular drug. At one time or another we all have encountered it in our chocolates, coffee, tea, and sodas; and a surprising number of us have liked it and continued its use. While it temporarily fights drowsiness, and heightens physical work and problem-solving, it also keeps us headed to the toilet frequently and brings a packet of unwelcome "guests" like anxiety, headaches, craving, fatigue, and the "shakes." Like alcohol, the user can build a tolerance as well as a physical dependence.
- *Nicotine* powerfully stimulates the autonomic nervous system and carries many psychoactive effects such as mood elevation and increased attention. The U.S. Surgeon General equates its physically addictive properties with those of heroin and cocaine, while others make reference to psychological dependence. Mark Twain once said, paraphrased, "Stopping smoking is the easiest thing in the world to do. I've done it many times." Many would-be abstainers from smoking can readily identify with Twain's comment about stopping. Smoking is an exceedingly difficult habit to break. Many women develop the habit for weight control, trying to attain the body image of "Virginia Slim," and weight gain is one of the notable effects for those who stop smoking, along with irritability, craving, and anxiety.
- *Convulsants* (strychnine) are a rough and "one-way-ticket" way to stimulate. Beyond "who done it?" mystery novels, we wouldn't recommend your spending much time on this one.

Now we come to the "anti's"—*antidepressants* (*thymoleptics*), *antimanics* (*thymoleptics*), and *antipsychotics* (*neuroleptics*). Technically, the anxiolytics are "anti's," too, but we covered them earlier within our antianxiety discussion.

Antidepressants

Depression has been called the "common cold" of our generation—highly present and pervasive within our society. Consequently, *antidepressants* are very frequently prescribed mood elevators. There are three major categories—*tricyclics*, *monoamine oxidase (MAO) inhibitors*, and *serotonin reuptake inhibitors*. All three categories prolong the activity of the neurotransmitters dopamine, norepinephrine, and serotonin. This prolonged activity stimulates receptors on the postsynaptic neuron. Tricyclics prevent the reabsorption of dopamine, norepinephrine, or serotonin; MAO inhibitors block the enzyme monoamine oxidase from breaking down neurotransmitter molecules; and serotonin reuptake inhibitors prevent the reabsorption of serotonin. In each instance, more neurotransmitter crosses the synapse to the postsynaptic neuron. Tricyclics and MAO inhibitors were the earlier generation of antidepressants, and serotonin reuptake inhibitors are the exciting "new kids on the block."

- *Tricyclics (TCAs)* are a potent category of antidepressants frequently prescribed for a person suffering from severe depression. Two of the commonly prescribed tricyclics are *imipramine (Tofranil)* and *amitriptyline (Elavil)*. These drugs carry fewer side effects and potential medical complications than MAO inhibitors.
- *MAO inhibitors (or MAOIs)* are less frequently prescribed because of their unwelcome side effects. When mixed with the food substance tyramine (present in sharp cheeses, dinner wines, and chicken livers), severe hypertension results. A newer version of MAOIs have mitigated many of these side effects.
- *Serotonin reuptake inhibitors* are the so-called "second generation" of antidepressants. This is the "land of *Prozac*, *Zoloft*, and *Paxil*." With few side effects, these drugs allow many depression sufferers to function effectively outside the hospital setting. More than 60 percent of current antidepressant prescriptions now come from this category, and one of the current controversies revolves around the risk of overprescribing—something of a "designer drug" use rather than a prescribed use for depression.

Antimanics

Antimanics (*thymoleptics*) relieve the symptoms of bipolar (manic-depressive) disorders. As the name implies, they are especially effective in relieving the manic phase. There is truly only one effective entry in this group, *lithium carbonate*, but several other entries round out the group, including *valproic acid* and *carbamazepine*.

- *Lithium carbonate* is a mineral salt whose calming properties for bipolar disorders were discovered in the early 1970s. Drug company interest was understandably mute because it was a naturally occurring substance. Lithium is effective in approximately 80 percent of manic disorders, and dosage level is critical. While too little produces no effect, too much produces nausea or, in extreme instances, death. Like the antidepressants, time is required to build up the desired blood level before any effective relief is apparent.
- *Valproic acid* and *carbamazepine* are two other entries in this class. From their names you can readily conclude that, unlike lithium, they are manufactured rather than naturally occurring.

Antipsychotics

Antipsychotics (*neuroleptics*) entered the mental health scene in the early 1950s and revolutionized the treatment of mental disorders. With their use the schizophrenic's hallucinations, delusions, mental incoherence, and fragmented thought patterns were notably ameliorated. This was the first wave of drug treatment in the mental health movement. The most frequently prescribed drugs in this group are the following:

- *Phenothiazines (chlorpromazine [Thorazine], trifluoperazine [Stelazine], fluphenazine [Prolixin], and thioridazine [Mellaril]).*

Other entries include the:

- *Butyrophenones (haloperidol [Haldol])* and the
- *Atypicals (clozapine [Clozaril] and risperidone [Risperdal]).*

Like the antidepressants, dosage level is critically important, and prolonged use of antipsychotics can result in irreversible CNS disorders such as involuntary repetitive movements or tics.

Well, you've been thoroughly drugged at this point, and along the way we introduced the terms *agonist* and *antagonist* within our definitions. Let's pause for a moment to understand more fully what this means. Think of a receptor dendrite as though it were your electrical outlet on the wall. When neurotransmitters are functioning normally, they cross the synapse and "plug into" the receptor dendrite much as your plug for the radio or stereo would. When neurotransmitters are abnormally functioning, either too much or too little is crossing the synapse to the receiving dendrite. Where the problem is too little crossing the synapse, an agonist "plugs in" and establishes a normal flow. Where the problem is too much crossing the synapse, an antagonist blocks flow similar to those clever little plastic inserts we place in outlets to keep toddlers from getting toasted. Of necessity the example is oversimplified, but we wanted you to know and understand these terms.

Now let's summarize at-a-glance what we've just been through.

Mood/Behavior Altering Drugs Outline

Function	Class	Chemical and/or Trade and Street Name
Depressants	Alcohol	Ethanol ("booze")
	Barbiturates ("al" endings)	Phenobarbital ("downers" or "sleeping pills")
		Pentothal
		Nembutal
		Seconal
		Tuinal
	Hypnotics	Methaqualone
		Glutethimide
Pleasure/Euphoria/ Pain-relief	Narcotics/Opiates	Opium
		Morphine (Percodan, Demerol)
		Heroin ("junk," "smack")
		Codeine
	Synthetics	Methadone
Psychedelics	Hallucinogens or Psychotomimetics	LSD ("acid")
		Marijuana (cannabis)(THC)("pot," "dope," "reefer," "hashish")
		Mescaline
		Psilocybin
		PCP (phencyclidene, "angel dust")
Stimulants ("ine" endings)	Amphetamines	Benzedrine ("bennies," "speed")
		Dexedrine ("uppers")
		Methedrine ("ice")
	Methamphetamines	"Crystal meth"
	Derivatives	MDMA ("ecstasy," "X")
	Others	Caffeine
		Cocaine ("coke," "crack")
		Convulsants (strychnine)
		Nicotine ("smokes," "weeds," "coffin nails")

Function	Class	Chemical and/or Trade and Street Name
The "Anti's"		
Antianxiety (anxiolytics)	Benzodiazepines	Diazepam (Valium)
		Chlordiazepoxide (Librium)
		Alprazolam (Xanax)
		Clonazepam (Klonapin)
	Other	Buspirone (Buspar)
Antidepressant (thymoleptics)	Tricyclics	Amitriptyline (Elavil)
		Imipramine (Tofranil)
		Nortriptyline (Pamelor)
		Desipramine (Norpramine)
		Doxepin (Sinequan)
		Clomipramine (Anafranil)
	Monoamine oxidase (MAO) inhibitors	Phenelzine (Nardil)
		Tranylcypromine (Parnate)
	Serotonin reuptake inhibitors	Fluoxetine (Prozac)
		Sertaline (Zoloft)
		Paroxetine (Paxil)
		Fluvoxamine (Luvox)
Antimanic (thymoleptics)	Lithium carbonate	Lithium (Eskalith, Lithobid, Lithonate)
	Other	Valproic acid (Depakene)
		Carbamazepine (Tegretol)
Antipsychotic (neuroleptics)	Phenothiazines	Chlorpromazine (Thorazine)
		Trifluoperazine (Stelazine)
		Fluphenazine (Prolixin)
		Thioridazine (Mellaril)
	Butyrophenones	Haloperidol (Haldol)
	Others	Clozapine (Clozaril)
		Risperidone (Risperdal)

Physiological Pyschology Summary

Now that you have thought through your outlines and have thoroughly reviewed your introductory psychology textbook chapter in the biological bases of behavior, check yourself out on the following sample of basic concepts and information. If they feel familiar to you, move on in your review. If they feel very spotty, strengthen your review-grasp before heading on.

- Neuron and its components: dendrites, soma, axon, synapse
- Distinction between central nervous system and peripheral nervous system
- Major neurotransmitters and the distinction between excitatory effects and inhibitory effects
- Distinction between receptors and effectors (and corresponding words such as sensory, afferent fibers and motor, efferent fibers)
- Autonomic nervous system (and its subdivisions into sympathetic and parasympathetic)
- Brain hemispheres and the four lobes within each—frontal, temporal, parietal, and occipital—with knowledge of what general behavioral functions each area encompasses

- Subcortical structures including cerebellum, basal ganglia, medulla, pons, midbrain, thalamus, hypothalamus, amygdala, hippocampus
- Terms such as sulcus, gyrus, corpus callosum, reticular formation, limbic system, acetylcholine, epinephrine, norepinephrine, serotonin, dopamine, blood-brain barrier, action potential, myelin
- Distinction among striated (voluntary), smooth (visceral), and heart muscles
- Location and function of endocrine glands—pineal, anterior and posterior pituitary, thyroid, parathyroid, thymus, adrenal medulla and adrenal cortex, and ovaries/testes
- Relationships between hormonal secretions and behavior
- The neuroendocrine system
- The physiology and neuroanatomy of sexual behavior
- The uses of and differences between EEG, ERP, CAT, PET, MRI

Note—you need not spend time and energy on terms such as brachial plexus, ventral nerve root, and the like. Your time is limited, and your goal is basic understanding.

- Alpha, beta, delta, and theta waves (the types of activity and the general wave frequency associated with each)
- Stages of sleep (their sequence and frequency)
- Dreams (their relationship to sleep stages, their frequency, and bodily functioning, such as REM, that accompanies them)
- Basic brain function activity in relation to sensory input and the effects of hormones and drugs
- Drug categories and their behavioral effects: depressants, stimulants, narcotics/opiates, antipsychotics, hallucinogens/psychedelics
- Neurotransmitters and their implications in depression (norepinephrine and serotonin) and schizophrenia (dopamine) as well as their function in memory trace (see Donald A. Norman's *Learning and Memory* [1995] for an excellent orientation, if needed; Lindsay and Norman's chapter entitled "Neural Basis of Memory" you may find especially helpful).

Within your review you probably sensed the vibrance, pace, and excitement of this pioneering, rapidly moving field. With technological breakthroughs such as the CAT scan (computerized axial tomography), PET scan (positron emission tomography), and the MRI scan (magnetic resonance imaging), *the study of brain structure and activity has taken a quantum leap*. Just sixty years ago, links between brain structure and function were made only by following patients with specific behavioral or cognitive deficits to autopsy and forming crude post-mortem descriptions of their brain damage. Now it is possible to "take a picture" of the brain of a living, healthy volunteer who is speaking, reading, solving problems, remembering, or performing any other complex task under a psychologist's control. This opens an exciting, vast expanse for future research into the intricate inner workings of brain and memory. A related area—the developmental study of neural activity in the brain—also has limitless potentials stemming from these new technologies. As we discover how neurally and chemically active is the brain of the two year old in comparison with the brain of the six year old, for instance, we stand on the threshold of studying the "birth of learning." What we have seen to date is just the tip of the iceberg in these research potentials and the contribution they will make to our lives and our future.

If you need or want more in-depth reading before moving on, refer to one of the recent introductory textbooks mentioned at the end of Chapter 1 and delve into some of the readings recommended there. Strong introduction to the field of physiological psychology can be obtained through a source such as Carlson's *Physiology of Behavior* (Boston: Allyn & Bacon, 1993), Bloom and Lazerson's *Brain, Mind, and Behavior* (San Francisco: W. H. Freeman, 1995), Springer and Deutsch's *Left Brain, Right Brain* (San Francisco: W. H. Freeman, 1995), Ornstein and Thompson's *The Amazing Brain* (Boston: Houghton Mifflin, 1991), and Gazzaniga, Ivry, and Mangun's *Cognitive Neuroscience: The Biology of the Mind* (New York: W. W. Norton, 2000). In the "classics" area, publications you may find helpful are W. Penfield's article "The Interpretive Cortex" (*Science*, 1959, pp. 1719–25) and Gazzaniga and LeDoux's book *The Integrated Mind* (1978). General sources that you will find valuable for tuning in to current developments include *Annual Editions: Readings in Psychology* (Guilford, CT.: Dushkin Publishing) and the monthly issues of *Psychology Today*. Indeed, such sources will be helpful to you throughout your work in the various topic areas covered in this book. *Scientific American* may be an equally valuable source—especially the issue featuring brain research (September, 1979) now available as a paperback book (*The Brain*) from W. H. Freeman Publishing.

COMPARATIVE PSYCHOLOGY

Comparative psychology centers upon the evolution of behavior. Dewsbury and Rethlingshafer indicate its panoramic definition to be "the systematic study of everything every species does or is capable of doing." Through reasonable limitations upon the number of organisms studied, however, it has become "a broad, but manageable, science of behavior." Within this basic definitional framework, researchers attempt to describe and explain species differences and similarities with regard to all aspects of behavior, including communication, sexual and aggressive patterns, learning, social, fixed-action patterns, and so on. An investigator could approach these tasks by grouping muscle-contraction patterns observed, but most researchers in the area prefer a second option—describing behaviors in terms of effects on the environment.

The field had its historic moorings and primary foundation within classical European ethology. Given impetus and direction through the pioneering work of *Tinbergen*, *Lorenz*, and *von Frisch*, ethology focused upon instinctive behavior and its observation within the natural habitat of the species. Comparative psychologists in the American tradition have placed their major emphasis upon observing animal behavior under controlled laboratory conditions. *Lashley* pioneered post-World War II research in this tradition and has inspired *Hebb* and other gifted students to follow his impressive lead. Ethology has had major influence upon the laboratory approach, and communication between those involved in these orientations is frequent and constructive.

As outlined by Tinbergen, the four areas of study in animal behavior are development, mechanisms, function, and evolution. *Development* is concerned with genetic determinants of behavior and their interaction with environmental determinants. *Mechanisms* deals with the interaction between behavior and physiological systems, and *function* places emphasis upon the adaptive and survival capacities of a species. *Evolution* provides the unifying central theme and cohesive focus for all aspects of the field.

Comparative Psychology Outline

Concepts	Names	Terms
Earliest human-tendency fossil		Australopithecus
First to walk upright		*Homo erectus*
First "human" tendencies		*Homo sapiens*
Genetic diversity	Darwin	Natural selection Sexual mating from diverse backgrounds
Eugenics	Tryon	Selective breeding (e.g., "maze-bright" and "maze-dull" rats)
	Weiner	Genes with reproductive advantage spread in frequency across generations
Heredity's chemical basis		Genes DNA (deoxyribonucleic acid) Hereditary "blueprint"

Living cell		Cell nucleus
		  Genes
		  46 chromosomes (23 prs)

Sex determinant		Female—two X chromosomes Male—one X, one Y chromosome
Genetic make-up of cells		Genotype
Trait characteristics developing from genetic make-up		Phenotype
Negative impact on genetic diversity		Physical isolation (inbreeding) Genetic drift
Dominant and recessive genes	Mendel's Law	Dominant characteristic emergence when paired with a recessive; Recessive characteristic emergence when paired with another recessive
Chromosomal abnormalities		Down syndrome (Mongolism) Turner's syndrome
Behaviorial genetics		Heritability
Nature-nurture controversy		Degree to which a given trait is a result of genetics or environment
	Herrnstein & Murray Loehlin Plomin	Their research places the relative weighting toward heritability influence
Intelligence	Scarr, Weinberg, Waldman	Environmentally disadvantaged children adopted into enriched home environments show modest increases in IQ scores

Concepts	Names	Terms
	Bouchard, Capron, Duyme	Heritability continues to have the more major role in adoptive instances
Species-typical behaviors		Fixed-action patterns (triggered by releasing stimuli)
Ethology	Lorenz Tinbergen	Imprinting Aggression/courtship fixed-action patterns in stickleback (fish species)
Evolution	Darwin	Theory of natural selection and "survival of the fittest"
Phylogenetic scale		Brain weight-to-body weight in different species (humans and porpoises to birds and moles)
Sociobiology	Wilson	Evolution and biological bases of social behavior

Outline Terms Elaborated

➤ *Australopithecus* was the earliest fossil with human tendencies, dated approximately 14 million years ago in Africa and India.

➤ A general sense of time-ranking on the evolutionary scale proceeds from *Australopithecus* (earliest), to *Homo erectus* (first to walk upright), Neanderthal, and Cro Magnon, to *Homo sapiens*.

➤ The concept of *genetic diversity*, in which members of a species who adapt to their environments especially well have the greatest likelihood of survival and reproduction—hence, Darwin's "survival of the fittest" concept of *natural selection*.

➤ *Eugenics* is selective breeding to produce desirable characteristics in offspring.

➤ *Gene* is the unit providing heredity's chemical basis. Genes contain DNA (deoxyribonucleic acid), and DNA molecules contain the hereditary "blueprint" that controls an individual's development.

➤ Every living cell has a cell nucleus containing genes arranged in *chromosomes*. Humans have 23 chromosome pairs in each cell, a total of 46 chromosomes. The sex of an individual is determined by two chromosomes in each cell—two X chromosomes in normal females, an X and a Y chromosome in normal males. Genes at the same respective position in a pair of chromosomes control the development of a given, specific characteristic such as eye color.

➤ There is a distinction between genotype and phenotype—*genotype* being the genetic makeup of cells, and *phenotype* being the specific characteristic or trait that develops from this makeup.

➤ *Sexual recombination* describes the process that occurs in the fertilized egg. As the chromosomes from the egg and sperm combine, the zygote (newly constituted individual) has 46 chromosomes in 23 matched pairs. Because sexual mating produces an individual with a unique new gene combination, sexual recombination produces genetic diversity. By contrast, asexual reproduction (a single organism producing genetic duplicates or clones of itself) would quite severely restrict *genetic diversity.*

➤ Factors negatively impacting genetic diversity include physical *isolation*, which promotes both inbreeding and *genetic drift*, which can significantly increase or decrease a specific gene frequency in a small, isolated group across generations.

➤ *Chromosomal abnormalities* include *Down syndrome* (Mongolism) (one small chromosome 21 in triplicate rather than duplicate, the syndrome itself having distinct physical characteristics and often retardation) and *Turner's syndrome* (one X chromosome missing in females, the syndrome characterized by underdeveloped reproductive organs, and short stature); fragile X, Klinefelter's, and XYY syndromes. Behavioral genetics has developed the term *heritability*, which addresses genetic characteristics in populations. It is a current, scientific expression of the *nature-nurture issue*, which took an individual person approach and examined the extent to which a given trait was a function of nature (genetic) or nurture (environmental).

➤ *Species-typical behaviors* are characteristic behaviors generally expressed in common by all males, all females, or all members of a given species. While these behaviors can have a learned component, they have a significant component of heritability. Rigid species-typical behaviors are called *fixed-action patterns*—stimuli that trigger fixed-action patterns are called *releasing stimuli.*

➤ *Ethology*, a branch of biology, studies animal behavior in its natural habitat or environment.

➤ *Sociobiology*, the term of its pioneer (E. O. *Wilson* at Harvard), studies the evolution and biological bases of social behavior.

➤ *Personalities* include the pioneering work of *Tinbergen*, *Lorenz*, and *von Frisch* in ethology and instinctive behavior. These three shared the Nobel Prize for their ethological work in 1973. *Lorenz*, the father of ethology, has been memorialized in a classic picture of imprinted geese following him across a field. *Tinbergen* is best known for his research with aggression and courtship behaviors in stickleback, a fish species. The red underbelly of a male stickleback serves as a releasing stimulus for aggression. *Darwin*, the pioneer formulator of the theory of evolution, published his major work in 1859 (*On the Origin of Species*). Eugenics took a major step forward with the work of *Tryon* (1940), who selectively mated "maze bright" rats and discovered that through progressive mating of "maze bright" offspring he could develop a strain of rats that were very rapid maze runners. *Wilson* introduced a research field he called sociobiology, which examined social behavior evolution in several diverse species. He suggested that characteristics as diverse as aggression, sexual behavior, and altruism can evolve through natural selection.

➤ *Theories* include *Darwin's theory of evolution* and its components of natural selection and "survival of the fittest" (those that are best equipped to adapt to their environments). Within evolutionary theory it is helpful to have a general sense of the relative positions of various species in scaled comparisons of brain weight to body weight. Porpoises and humans have significantly higher ratios than other species. Chimpanzees, baboons, and wolves would be next-closest, while hummingbirds and moles would have the lowest ratios. "Bird brain" has its point. *Neotony theory* suggests that a few major gene mutations significantly slowed down the schedule of human development from that of our theorized animal ancestry.

Comparative Psychology Summary

As you can see from the difference in review coverage, much more GRE time will be given to the Physiological than to the Comparative aspect. Balance your own review time accordingly.

Several works will give you a general orientation to this area: Donald Dewsbury's *Contemporary Issues in Comparative Psychology* (New York: Simauer Assoc., 1990), James L. Gould and Carol G. Gould's *The Animal Mind* (San Francisco: W. H. Freeman, 1995), and John Maynard Smith's edited work, *Evolution Now—A Century after Darwin* (San Francisco: W. H. Freeman, 1995). Classic works in the field include Konrad Lorenz's *Studies in Animal and Human Behavior* (2 vols.) (Cambridge, Mass.: Harvard University Press, 1970), Niko Tinbergen's *The Animal in Its World* (Cambridge, Mass.: Harvard University Press, 1973), and Charles Darwin's *The Origin of Species* (New York: New American Library, 1958; 1st edition, 1859). The general orientation works will introduce you to the topics mentioned at the outset, and at this point you have become familiar with such terms as *species, species-typical behavior, fixed-action patterns, imprinting, releasers,* and the like. But before you delve too deeply into such specialized topics as adrenogenital hermaphroditism, pause to remember that your goal continues to be general, basic understanding.

Sensation and Perception

Sensation is a first cousin to the physiological and comparative areas just discussed; perception, on the other hand, adds learning to sensory phenomena. Taken together, sensation and perception constitute both an important combination of areas in their own right and a viable bridge to the discussions of learning in the next section.

SENSATION

Sensation is the process of informing the brain about some experience occurring outside the central nervous system. These experiences can be classified into seven types, or senses: visual, auditory, somatosensory (touch, temperature, pain), olfactory, gustatory, kinesthetic (movement), and vestibular (orientation). Although the message in each of these senses is quite different, the messenger, or the way of communicating with the brain, is very similar. In fact, in 1826 Johannes *Müller* published his *doctrine of specific nerve energies*, which stated that qualitative differences between the sensation of sounds and lights, for example, are not due to differences in the neural signals but to differences in the structures that the neural signals excite. In all types of sensation, a set of *receptors* is responsible for the *transduction* of the physical stimulus energy into an electrical, neural signal. Stimulus dimensions (e.g., pitch, hue) are coded, or translated, into neural signals that are relayed to the appropriate projection area in the brain. In your review of sensation, pay particular attention to the unique ways in which each sense transduces, or codes information about a stimulus, and to the route that information travels before reaching its final destination in the brain.

Because sensation is, in effect, an extension of the physiological aspects of psychology, an understanding of the basic terms and concepts in the preceding section will be essential to you now. The physiology of sensory systems provides an essential foundation for understanding thresholds and general psychophysical concepts. This foundation consists of knowledge of neural pathways and the ways in which sensory information is processed within them.

The eye, a thoroughly researched sensory system, demonstrates the area and some of its basic concepts. When light energy reaches photoreceptors (rods and cones), neural signals are sent through the visual system, producing sensations. The travel route includes the neural layers through which the light must pass before being absorbed by the photoreceptors. A photochemical reaction is triggered in the photoreceptors, producing neural signals that are transmitted first to the bipolar cells and then to the ganglion cells. Neural signals then travel along retinal ganglion cells' axons to the lateral geniculate nucleus of the thalamus. Cells in the lateral geniculate nucleus relay the signal to the occipital lobes of the brain. All of the neurons along this path have a specific *receptive field*, which is defined as the part of space that the given neuron responds to. Furthermore, the neurons are organized into systematic maps (called *retinotopic maps* in the visual system) such that neighboring neurons have neighboring receptive fields.

Of necessity, the above example has been oversimplified, but it provides a basic orientation that you will want to use for each sensory system. Although the specific terminology will vary from one sense to another, you will discover some common themes that hold across all of the sensory systems, such as sensory coding, thresholds, and receptor specificity. And with each level of understanding will come a renewed awareness and appreciation for the senses and their moment-by-moment service to us all.

Major research in the area of visual fields has been conducted by Hubel and Wiesel. Additional insights on the function of retinal ganglion cells are provided by the work of Barlow, Hill, and Levick (*Journal of Physiology*, 173 [1964], 377–407). P. Lindsay and D. Norman's *Human Information Processing*, in addition to its strength as an introductory reference source, provides excellent suggested readings lists in each topical area.

Begin your review with a general source such as S. Coren and L. Ward, *Sensation and Perception* (New York: Harcourt Brace College, 1994), H. R. Schiffman's *Sensation and Perception: An Integrated Approach* (New York: Wiley, 1990), or R. Sekular and R. Blake's *Perception* (New York: McGraw, 1993). Any of these works can provide additional references as needed.

Beyond the essential understanding of physiology and neural information processing, basic familiarity with a number of fundamental psychophysical terms and concepts will also be important.

Sensation Outline	Concepts	Names	Terms
	Dimensions of sensation		Quality (what kind)
			Intensity (how much)
			Duration (how long)

Concepts	Names	Terms
Threshold (or limen)		Absolute threshold Difference threshold Just noticeable difference (j.n.d.)
	Weber's Law (and formula) Fechner's Law (Weber's elaborated) Stevens' Law	Magnitude estimation and power
Father of psychophysics	Fechner	
Methods of measurement		Method of limits Method of constant stimuli Magnitude estimation
Signal-detection theory		Cognitive bias or expectations of sensing person
Receiver-operating- characteristics (ROC) curves		Proportion of times a signal is reported when presented and when not presented
Sensory code		Neural representation of a given sensory experience
Doctrine of specific nerve energies	Müller	Differences in experienced quality are not stimulus-based but nervous-system-based
Specificity theory vs. across-fiber theory		*Specificity:* Quality-specific neurons—given neurons signal or fire for given qualities *Across-fiber:* Quality comes from overall pattern of neural firing

Senses: What they are		Vision (Sight)
		Audition (Hearing)
		Chemical
		  Gustation (Taste)
		  Olfaction (Smell)
		Skin
		  Pressure
		  Temperature
		  Pain
		Kinesthetic
		  Limb movement feedback
		  Balance (vestibular)

**Outline Terms
Elaborated**

➤ Dimensions of sensation—*quality* (what kind of sensation), *intensity* (how much of a sensation), *duration* (how long a sensation)

➤ Threshold (or limen)—*absolute threshold* (minimum physical energy that will result in a sensory experience); *difference threshold*—j.n.d. (just noticeable difference)

➤ Laws and procedures—*Weber's Law* (and formula) for j.n.d., *Fechner's Law*, *Stevens' magnitude estimation procedure*, and his *power law*

➤ Methods of measurement—the *method of limits* (using a stimulus such as light, alternating intensity direction with each presentation), the *method of constant stimuli* (stimuli of specific intensities are presented sequentially, the measurement being whether detection occurs), *magnitude estimation* (two stimuli of different intensities are presented to a person who is then asked to compare the two and express a numerical ratio of their relative magnitudes ("First was twice as bright as the second," and so on)

➤ *Signal-detection theory* (the cognitive bias or expectations of the sensing person) and *ROC* (receiver-operating-characteristic) *curves* (the proportion of times a signal is reported when presented and the proportion of times a signal is reported erroneously when none was presented, and the variation found in these proportions as a function of "conservative reporting" versus "liberal reporting" instructions given to the subjects)

Vision and Audition

In terms of psychological emphasis, vision has been the most heavily studied modality in the sensory area, and audition has been next in prominence. Other sense modalities also receive attention, but not to the extent of these two. In keeping with this emphasis, we will begin with a review of vision and audition, then move on to other sensory modes.

In studies of visual sensation, the retina assumes primary importance—specifically the rods and cones. You will need to know the many distinctions between rods and cones (being able to compare them on such grounds as approximate numbers and distribution on the retina, shape, sensitivity to color and light, visual acuity, and neural connections). With such information, you will then be prepared to understand phenomena such as dark adaptation.

Vision

- Eye-related terms such as lens, iris, pupil, cornea, retina, photoreceptors, rods (achromatic, functioning in dim light, "party line" [sharing a bipolar cell] neural connections to the brain), cones (color sensitive, requiring brighter light, "private line" [each cone having its own bipolar cell] neural connections to the brain), cells (amacrine, bipolar, ganglion, horizontal), blind spot, fovea, optic nerve
- Visual functioning terms such as accommodation, convergence (summation, antagonism), retinal disparity, myopic, hyperopic, astigmatism, adaptation (dark, light)
- Brain-related visual terms such as columnar organization of cells (Hubel and Wiesel), ocular dominance columns, orientation columns, simple/complex/hypercomplex cells, lateral geniculate nucleus (LGN), primary visual (striate) cortex, occipital lobe
- Wave properties (frequency, amplitude, complexity), their color-vision expressions (hue, saturation, brightness), and their audition expressions (pitch, loudness/intensity [measured in decibels], timbre)

Not surprisingly, studies of sensory modalities have reached beyond the modalities themselves to the nature of the stimuli impinging upon them. In the case of vision, the most prominent "reach beyond" has encompassed color mixing and vision theory. Again, these are among the general outline terms and concepts that you will need to understand.

- Color mixing—general understanding of where, for instance, violet, blue, green, yellow, and red are located within the wavelength spectrum; distinction between subtractive and additive color mixing and knowledge of the primaries within each; ability to distinguish the terms hue, saturation, and brightness

- Color-related terms such as color solid, color circle, color mixing (additive [pigment], subtractive [light]), color primaries and complementaries
- Vision theories such as the Young-Helmholtz Trichromatic Theory (which postulates that there are three types of cones in the retina, each having primary sensitivity to a different part of the color spectrum) and Hering's proposed Opponent-Process Theory, which accepts the trichromatic thesis and further calculates differences in cone firing rates as the basis for the different colors that we see

Vision Outline

Concepts	Names	Terms
Parts of the eye		Front chamber
		Lens, iris, pupil, cornea
		Rear chamber
		Retina
		Photoreceptors
		Rods and cones
		Bipolar cells
		Ganglion cells
Vision in the brain		Magno and parvo cells
	Hubel and Weisel	Simple cells
		Complex cells
		Occipital lobe
		Primary visual cortex (V1)
	Ungerleider	"What" and "where" pathways
Visual depth		Retinal disparity
		Convergence
Near-sighted/Far-sighted		Accommodation
Dark adaptation		Rod-cone vision
Purkinje effect		
Color vision		
Additive mixing		Light: primaries = blue, green, red
Subtractive mixing		Pigment: primaries = blue, yellow, red
Properties		Frequency = hue (the color)
		Amplitude = saturation (color purity)
		Complexity = brightness (color shade)
Theories (cortical)	Hubel and Weisel	Neural firing to vertical lines
Theories (color)	Young-Helmholtz	Trichromatic
	Hurvich-Jameson	Opponent-process
Theories (contrast)	Hering	Contrasts at line junctions
	Mach	Mach bands
Negative after-image		

Audition has similar aspects, mastery of which will be essential. In addition to background familiarity with neural information processing, the following will also be important:

Hearing

- Auditory components—three parts of the ear: outer—pinna, the visible structure plus the ear canal; middle—three-part bone structure (ossicles) including hammer, anvil, and stirrup; inner—oval window (actually a kind of "front door" letting in messages); cochlea (basilar membrane, hair cells of Organ of Corti, auditory nerve, round window); understanding of the general hearing process as it relates to the above parts; familiarity with the work of Georg von Bekesy
- Auditory functioning of each basic area: outer as the initial point of entry; middle as a transformer converting large sound waves in the air into more forceful vibrations of smaller amplitude (the stirrup acting like a piston to transform the eardrum pressure into twenty-two times greater pressure on the fluid in the inner ear); inner making the conversion to neural transmission
- Auditory functioning terms such as audiometric function (lowest audible threshold energy for each frequency) and our normal audiometric hearing range and pain threshold, decibel (loudness measure, the term itself honoring Alexander Graham Bell), and a recognition familiarity with the tone oscillator and sound spectrogram ("voice print")
- Distinction between nerve deafness and ossification and their differential effects on hearing and on the prognosis for recovery of hearing function
- Audition wave properties (briefly mentioned within vision discussion): pitch/frequency (measured in hertz), loudness/amplitude/intensity (measured in decibels), and timbre (wave complexity, overtones)
- Audition theories such as Helmholtz' Place ("Piano") Theory (proposing that a given place on the basilar membrane is responsive to a specific pitch), Rutherford's Frequency ("Telephone") Theory (proposing that the entire basilar membrane vibrates, much like the diaphragm of a telephone or microphone), and Wever-Bray's Volley Theory
- Localization of sounds is based on differences between the two ears both in timing (for low frequency sounds) and loudness (for high frequency sounds). Different species have evolved to be sensitive to those frequencies that can be most easily localized (which varies with head size)
- Auditory phenomena—general hearing range sensitivity (in cycles per second); functions and threshold distinctions between "boilermaker's ear" (nerve deafness) and deafness attributable to burst eardrum or bone ossification; stimulus-related terminology: pitch, loudness, and timbre; understanding of tones, beats, and masking

Audition Outline

Concepts	Names	Terms
Parts of the ear		Outer: 　Pinna 　Ear canal Middle: 　Eardrum 　Ossicles 　　Hammer 　　Anvil 　　Stirrup

Concepts	Names	Terms
		Inner: 　Oval window 　Cochlea 　(w/ basilar membrane, hair 　cells of Organ of Corti, audi- 　tory nerve, round window)
Properties		Frequency = pitch Amplitude = loudness Complexity = timbre
Measurement units		Pitch = cycles per second (hertz) Loudness = decibels
Theories (pitch)	Helmholtz von Bekesy	Place ("piano") Wave-like motion of the basilar 　membrane (location of peaks 　varying with pitch)
	Rutherford	Frequency ("telephone or 　telegraph") (entire membrane 　vibration, frequency of vibration 　establishes pitch)
	Wever-Bray	Volley (modification of 　Rutherford—neural firing in 　volleys rather than all-at-once)
Deafness		Nerve-based (inner ear) Bone-based (middle ear)

The Chemical Senses

The chemical senses of taste and smell become our prominent concerns within this heading. The receptor cells for taste are located in clusters of cells known as the taste buds. Taste sensitivity is dependent upon a two-stage process that involves (1) the chemical stimulus penetrating the taste bud and (2) the chemical reaction that prompts the nerve impulse. Taste buds are served by branches of three cranial nerves (VII, IX, X), all of which terminate in the medulla or pons. The taste pathway subsequently reaches the posteroventral nucleus of the thalamus and terminates in the face somatic area of the cortex. Some of the most detailed work in this area has been done by Pfaffmann; his work entitled "Taste, Its Sensory and Motivating Properties" in *American Scientist* (52, 1964; pp. 187–206) is among the most basic in this area.

In smell sensitivity, the olfactory receptors are located in the roof of the nasal cavity. The olfactory epithelium contains columnar, basal, and olfactory cells; and the epithelium itself is bathed in mucus fluid—meaning that gases and mucus must be soluble in order to excite olfactory receptors. From the olfactory epithelium, axons extend to the olfactory bulb (a complex entity with its brain-destined networks of fibers and its reverberatory circuits). The final portion of the "journey" is via the olfactory tract to the cortex. What has been termed the primary olfactory cortex is actually a number of points in the ventral surface region. The region varies in size among species, depending on the relative importance of olfaction for the given species.

Compared with other species, the area is notably small in humans. As you review the chemical senses, the following should be important to you:

- Taste-related terms such as gustation (formal name for taste), the taste primaries (bitter, sour, salt, sweet) and their tongue locations, and the gustatory system (including papillae, taste buds, receptor cells)
- Smell-related terms such as olfaction (formal name for smell), elements in the olfactory system (including nasal cavity, olfactory hair cells, nerve fibers, and olfactory bulb), and the function of pheromones

Chemical Senses Outline

Concepts	Names	Terms
Gustation (taste)		Primaries
		Sweet
		Salt
		Sour
		Bitter
Adaptation		With exposure time
Contrast effect		Sweet followed by sour
Age effects		Decreasing sensitivity
Taste bud anatomy		
Taste system neuroanatomy		
Olfaction (smell)		
System parts and neuroanatomy		Olfactory bulb
		Olfactory epithelium and types of cells
		Nasal cavity
		Turbinate bones
Relationship of olfactory system to other structures in the brain		
Cues		Pheromones
		Menstrual synchrony
Interaction with gustation		The child who holds her nose while she drinks her prune juice

Attempts to formulate theories of smell have not met with notable success. However, the work of Crozier, Moncrieff, and Adey demonstrates the theoretical progression that has occurred in the field.

The Skin Senses

In the late nineteenth century, experimenters observed that the human skin is not uniformly sensitive to different types of stimuli. In further investigations, areas of skin were circumscribed and, for instance, a cold stimulus was systematically applied to determine at what points a person would report feeling coldness. Similar mapping of the identical skin area was conducted for stimuli warmer than skin temperature. It became apparent that coldness and warmth were not being felt at the same points on the skin surface. Similar mapping was conducted with touch and pain stimuli, and again the sensations were not felt at identical points on the skin surface. Woodworth and Schlosberg (*Experimental Psychology* [New York: Holt, Rinehart & Winston, 1954]) give details of experiments that were conducted in this area. These experiments led to conclusions that there were at least four primary qualities of cutaneous sensation—touch, pain, cold, and warmth. Müller's doctrine of specific nerve energies, advanced fifty years earlier, was being supported. For review purposes, we will discuss the skin senses in the general categories of pressure, temperature, and pain. Receptor categories that will be important throughout this section will be (1) free nerve endings, (2) hair follicles, and (3) encapsulated end organs; and, as was true for the previous review sections, a general knowledge of neuroanatomy will also be important.

- Touch (pressure)-related terms such as epidermis (outer layer) and dermis (hair cells, blood vessels, oil and sweat glands, receptor cells), differential touch sensitivity in different areas of the body (e.g., extremities most sensitive, back least sensitive), and cross-sensory potentials such as the capacity to "project" a visual image through tactile pressure on the back of a blind person, enabling the individual to "see" it
- Temperature-related terms such as heat receptors, cold receptors, and the sensation of paradoxical warmth or paradoxical cold, which occurs when, for example, a warm receptor is contacted with a cold stimulus or a cold receptor is contacted with a warm stimulus
- Pain-related terms such as receptors, substance effects upon pain sensation (e.g., opiates blocking pain information transfer to the brain), substance effects upon emotional response to pain sensation (e.g., tranquilizers such as Valium not affecting the sensation but dulling the emotional reaction), body-produced opiate-type hormones (endorphins and enkephalins)
- Pain-related theory such as the gate-control theory of Melzack and Wall, suggesting a "pain gate" in the spinal cord

Pressure

Geldard formally defines pressure sensation as "tissue distortion, or the mechanical deformation of skin tissue." Pressure intensity is measured in grams per millimeter. As with other senses, the level of pressure sensitivity is different in different parts of the body. In general, the closer to the extremity, the more sensitivity there will be (making the center of the back, for instance, one of the least pressure-sensitive parts of the body). To understand pressure sensitivity fully, you should also look into such terms and concepts as the types of pressure receptors (encapsulated end organs, and so on) and touch blends (cold pressure, "wetness," and so on). Your goal should be a general understanding of the area and an acquaintance with its problems.

Temperature

As mentioned previously, evidence supports the suggestion of two receptor systems—one for warmth, one for coldness. Your knowledge in this area should include an awareness that cold receptors apparently are the smaller and more numerous. In addition, you should know something about cold and heat sensitivity in different parts of the body and the "three bowl" adaptation experiment of Weber.

Pain

There are many questions relating to the nature of pain and how to stop it effectively. Initial thought that pain was a direct function of tissue damage was quickly proven to be incorrect (when, for instance, it was found that major tissue damage could go hand in hand with minor pain sensation).

The following outline provides concepts you will need to understand. In addition, you should be familiar with aspects such as the differential effects, and apparently very different pain-relieving functions, of aspirin versus a colleague anesthetic such as morphine.

Skin Senses (Cutaneous Senses) Outline

Concepts	Names	Terms
Qualities of cutaneous sensation	Müller von Frey	Specific nerve energies Four primary cutaneous senses: pressure, cold, warmth, and pain
Pressure		

Receptors: various		Among them:
		  Merkel's disk
		  Meissner's corpuscle
		  Free nerve endings
		  Digital nerve
		  Pacinian corpuscle

Sensitivity		General rule: the closer to the extremity, the more sensitive. (e.g., least sensitive is the back)
Temperature		

Receptors		Cold
		  Small and more numerous than warmth receptors
		Warmth
		  Larger than cold receptors, less numerous

Pain		
Gate Theory	Melzack and Wall	Pain messages pass through a "gate" in the spinal cord en route to the brain. In effect, pain messages may or may not be sent depending upon other sensory experiences and the moment's attention and activity.
Reducing pain		Endorphins (countering the "pain messenger" neurotransmitter "substance P") Attention distraction (e.g., Lamaze method in childbirth)

Every sensory receptor discussed to this point has had the quality of being stimulated from outside the body and providing knowledge of events external to the body. In his well-known scheme, *Sherrington* classified such senses as *exteroceptors*, in contrast to *interoceptors* and *proprioceptors*. Neither of the latter two categories receives direct stimulation from outside the body. The sensory field of the interoceptors is the gastrointestinal tract (making them the organic or visceral sensors), and the "in-betweens" (receptors in subcutaneous tissue, deep-lying blood vessels, muscles, tendons, and bone coverings) are the proprioceptors—having the common characteristic of being stimulated mainly by actions of the body itself. Among the proprioceptors Sherrington includes the labyrinthine balance function of the inner ear. This labyrinthine sense is unique in that no other sense can make good on a claim to yield no sensations of its own. If you feel dizzy, the sensations that you experience are kinesthetic, pressure, visceral—but not labyrinthine. The kinesthetic sense (which tells you where your appendages are and what they are doing) is also among the proprioceptors. Within these general areas, there are some novel and classic studies with which you should be familiar, including *Boring's "balloon" study of the gastrointestinal tract* and the *Cannon-Washburn technique* for studying *hunger sensation*.

Internal Senses Outline

Concepts	Terms
Kinesthetic	
Function	Provide feedback on limb positions and movement via muscles, joints, and tendons
Balance (Vestibular)	
Location and function	Inner ear semicircular canals contain fluid which, moving with head rotation, triggers vestibular nerve impulses. Process is critical to balance

Control center for all the sensory phenomena you've reviewed is the twelve cranial nerves. We include them simply to convey that sense of awe at this remarkable universe we carry with us daily.

Cranial Nerves Outline

Number and Name	Type	Function
I. Olfactory	Afferent	Smell
II. Optic	Afferent	Vision
III. Oculomotor	Predominantly efferent	Eye muscles
IV. Trochlear	Predominantly efferent	Eye (proprioception)
V. Trigeminal	Mixed:	
	Afferent	Face, teeth, tongue (mostly tactile, some temperature and pain)
	Efferent	Muscles of the mouth/tongue
VI. Abducens	Predominantly efferent	Eye (proprioception)
VII. Facial	Mixed:	
	Afferent	Taste, salivation, some sense of pressure and position (from facial muscles)
	Efferent	Facial nerve (motor) and intermediate nerve

Number and Name	Type	Function
VIII. Auditory/Vestibular-Cochlear	Two part: Cochlear—afferent Vestibular—mostly afferent	Transmits signals from Organ of Corti; serves inner ear for equilibrium and position orientation
IX. Glosso-pharyngeal	Mixed: Afferent	Sense of taste from posterior tongue; sensations from pharynx, eustacian tube, tonsils, soft palate
	Efferent	Muscles of pharynx, larynx, and upper esophagus (sing well!)
X. Vagus	Mixed: Afferent	Pain and temperature sensation from ear; also, pharynx, larynx, esophagus, thoracic and abdominal viscera such as heart and intestines
	Efferent	Abdominal and thoracic viscera (inhibit heart rate, stimulate gastric and pancreatic activity, gastrointestinal action)
XI. Spinal accessory	Predominantly efferent	Cardiac and laryngal nerves, et al.
XII. Hypoglossal	Efferent	Voluntary movements of neck and tongue; perhaps also teams with V in sucking, chewing, and swallowing reflexes

Sensation Summary

In studying sensation, an experimenter characteristically begins with a given stimulus (e.g., light), then varies some property of the stimulus, such as the intensity or the duration. Because human receptor cells are not infinitely sensitive, the term *threshold* becomes prominent. *Absolute threshold* deals with the minimum physical energy that will result in a sensory experience; *difference threshold* deals with the minimum *change* in physical energy that will result in a sensory-detected change. For instance, absolute threshold involves the questions "Do you see it?" and "Do you hear it?" in either/or terms. In the difference threshold study the question revolves around how much additional light or sound will be required before one can detect a change from the initial stimulus (in this case, the initial light or sound). Weber's classic work and formula ($\emptyset I/I = K$) pioneered in this area, and you will need to understand his work and be prepared for questions relating to it. The symbol $\emptyset I$ represents the detectable change in a stimulus, while I is the initial stimulus intensity, and K is a constant. *Fechner's Law* was an extension of Weber's work and suggested that the relationship between physical stimulus intensity (I) and the strength of sensation (S) is logarithmic ($S = c \log I$), c being a constant based on the unit of intensity. *Stevens' magnitude estimation procedure* would present a stimulus to the subject and assign it an intensity number. When the second stimulus was presented, the subjects would be asked to assign it a number based on their judgment of its intensity compared with the first stimulus. His general way of characterizing these relationships is known as *Stevens' power law* $(S = kI^b)$, which says, in effect, that sensation (S) is proportional to stimulus intensity (I) raised to a power (b), k being a constant based on the unit of measurement. Any of the sensation/perception works just mentioned can assist you with this understanding. A few additional books include Lindsay and Norman's work, *Human Information Processing* (New York: Harcourt Brace College, 1977), K. T. Spoehr and S. W. Lehmkuhle's *Visual Information Processing* (San Francisco: W. H. Freeman, 1982), L. Kaufman's *Perception: The World Transformed* (New York: Oxford University Press, 1979), and K. Akin's (ed.) *Perception* (New York: Oxford University Press, 1995).

You now have gone through the spectrum of sense receptors. To the extent that you understand their neuroanatomy, physiological bases, and functioning, you are now prepared for a knowledgeable review of perception.

PERCEPTION

You'll have fun reviewing this section. It's all about how we see things and how they fool us. Our senses are all primed and ready to receive input, and our past experiences and learning determine what we truly perceive. You've already had a brief dose of perception without realizing it. In the pain area, for instance, I mentioned how the perception of pain varied for different folks based on their experiences and expectations. There's the child who screams bloody murder when getting a shot at the doctor's office, while another child considers it no big deal. Expectations and past experiences make all the difference.

Sensation is physiologically based, and perception builds a bridge to our upcoming review of learning. The learning factor makes a critical difference between what comes to us through our senses and what we individually *perceive* as having been received by those senses.

In contrast to what is actually received and transmitted, perception is our *mental organization* of what is out there. It is what we *say* we saw, heard, felt, and so on—as distinct from what actually was received. Perception, therefore, contains both the sensory element (bottom-up processes) and the past experience that we bring to every situation (top-down processes). Vision again comes to the fore, and a school of thought known as Gestalt is responsible for the body of information concerning visual perception.

Whereas a thorough understanding of the term *stimulus* was relatively incidental to our previous discussions, it is essential both for perception discussions and our subsequent look at the learning area. Most definitions state that a stimulus is a physical agent that (given sufficient strength) activates one or a group of sensory receptors. Witnesses to an explosion, for instance, will find the explosion both a visual and an auditory stimulus. With such things as a traffic light, however, the stimulus will be in only one sensory modality. Having digested this all-important term, we can now take a look at the material on perception that you will need to review for the GRE.

Lindsay and Norman's chapter on "The Dimensions of Vision," and your intro book's chapter on perception will give you much of the data needed in review. For more depth, Sekular and Blake's *Perception* (New York: McGraw, 1993), or Anderson's *Cognitive Psychology and Its Implications* (San Francisco: W. H. Freeman, 1995) would be appropriate, but be careful not to get bogged down in small details.

The study of perception invariably calls for a distinction between "illusion" and "hallucination." For clarity, you can think of illusion as misperception of a stimulus and hallucination as response in the absence of any external stimulus. Inevitably, the discussion will go one step further, into extrasensory perception (ESP), and again some distinctions will be important.

- Definitional aspects of extrasensory perception—mental telepathy, clairvoyance, precognition
- Psychokinesis (or telekinesis)

Historically, J. B. Rhine's lab at Duke University served as the principal location for ESP research in the United States, and it was Rhine who developed the ESP cards used frequently in these research studies. Extrasensory perception is not a generally respected or accepted area within psychological research, but some familiarity with it is appropriate. When you've mastered the following outline you'll be a perceptual genius!

Perception Outline

Concepts	Names	Terms
Views of perceptual processes	Gibson	*Ecological*—Using information from the environment to support actions (e.g., driving)
	Rock	*Constructionist*—Constructing a representation of the environment from sensory fragments (e.g., figure closure)
	Green	*Computational*—Explaining complex computations within the nervous system that translate sensory stimulation into representations of reality (e.g., the brain's capacity to clear up retinal blood vessels, and so on, so we see clearly)

Depth perception	Gibson	Monocular cues
		  Relative size
		  Linear perspective
		  Interposition
		  Texture gradient
		  Good form
		  Height in picture plane
		  Shading
		Binocular cues
		  Retinal disparity (stereopsis)
		  Convergence
		Motion cues
		  Motion parallax
		  Optic flow

Perceptual constancies		Size Shape Brightness Color

Concepts	Names	Terms
Illusions	Muller-Lyer	Muller-Lyer
	Ponzo	Ponzo
	Zollner	Zollner
	Wundt	Wundt
	Ebbinghaus	Ebbinghaus twisted cord
	Poggendorf	Poggendorf moon
	Necker	Necker cube
	Ames	Distorted room
	Ames	Trapezoidal window
	Gestaltists	Phi phenomenon/stroboscopic movement (apparent motion)
		Autokinetic effect
		Induced movement
		Cross-cultural differences
Impossible figures	Escher	Classic drawings
Laws of perceptual organization	Gestalt: Wertheimer, Koffka, Kohler	Law of Pragnanz
		Proximity
		Similarity
		Continuity
		Common fate
		Closure/subjective contours
	Helmholtz	Maximum-Likelihood Principle
	Palmer	Common region
Perceptual expectation		Perceptual set
		Schemas
Theories	Ames	Transactional
	Brunswick	Probabilistic
ESP/Parapsychology	Rhine	Mental telepathy
		Clairvoyance
		Precognition
		Psychokinesis/Telekinesis

Outline Terms Elaborated

➤ **Depth perception:**

How do we perceive a three-dimensional world from the two-dimensional image on our retina? There are a number of cues that we use to infer the missing dimension of depth. *Monocular cues* are those that can be used by a single eye to suggest depth (linear perspective, relative size, interposition); these are cues that artists have been using for centuries to convey depth in a two-dimensional painting. Binocular cues are those that require both eyes, such as the *binocular disparity* between the slightly different images that fall on each eye. There is evidence for innate and learned aspects of depth perception; for example, the ability to use binocular disparity to perceive depth develops during a critical period early in life and can be disrupted by congenital conditions that cause a misalignment of the images on the eyes (e.g., cross-eyed).

➤ **Perceptual constancies:**

Our visual world is constantly changing. When our perception is unaltered by environmental changes that affect properties of a stimulus, this is referred to as a *perceptual constancy*. For example, if you look at the pages of this book inside under fluorescent light, then later outside under natural light, and finally at dusk as the sun is setting, you will still perceive the pages as white despite the fact that their color is actually changing. A number of constancies have been identified—lightness and color (changes in illumination do not alter the perception of brightness or color), size (perceived size does not vary with depth), shape (perceived shape does not vary with orientation).

➤ **Illusions** are fun, but they are also informative about how perception normally proceeds. For example, to see the effect that perceived distance has on size perception (the basis for size constancy), consider the Müller-Lyer, Ponzo, or moon illusions. In all of these illusions, perceived distance is misleading our perceptual system.

➤ **Laws of perceptual organization:**

In a complex visual scene, how do we determine which pieces go together? This is the problem of *perceptual organization* or segregation. A long list of factors that influence perceptual organization was first described by Max *Wertheimer*, the founder of the *Gestalt* school of psychology, and these laws of perceptual organization are on your outline.

Perception Summary

Were the terms familiar to you? If so, you are all set to move on. Realistically, catch any "loose ends" first if you need to. And, at this point, stop for a minute to reflect on the distance you have come. Taking inventory, you have been through the very difficult basic review sections on physiology/neuroscience, comparative, sensation, and perception. Now that you have these basics, you will see them come together. In the sections that follow, you will begin to get glimpses of the "whole person" and of total human development. Already you have begun to sense (maybe even perceive!) these intricate innerworkings. Take, for instance, the relationship between motivation and perception. We are all familiar with the expression "You see what you want to see!" This phrase suggests that we are motivated to see certain things and perhaps not to see others. Signal detection theory and concepts such as pain and perceptual defense have already given us clues that we clever humans are all experienced professionals in selectively attending and selectively perceiving—part of the fascination in studying us critters and our capacities to belie, mold, and shape the incoming raw data from our senses. You will see many instances of this selectivity as we review further. Reserve for yourself the right to be fascinated as you review and refresh your knowledge. Humans and their behavior are indeed a fascinating landscape.

Learning

The king had a problem. Every time it rained, all the cats in the kingdom would run across the palace's marble floor, decorating it with their very muddy feet. In his dismay, the king went to a servant with an ultimatum—either the servant solve the problem or he would lose his head. Not too pleased with the ultimatum, the servant elected to work diligently toward solving the problem. He put all the cats in a sack, took them to the woods, and initiated this sequence repeatedly—he would cough and then clobber the sack, cough and clobber the sack, cough and clobber the sack. After several repetitions of this sequence, he let the cats go. Next time it rained you can guess what he did. Right! He coughed, and the cats immediately ran for points distant.

The servant's problem-solving demonstrates a basic kind of learning or conditioning. You will come to know it as classical conditioning—the conditioning of an expectation by way of a stimulus or cue. Through their conditioning process the cats had learned that coughing was followed by clobbering. We have learned similar signals and signs in our backgrounds and environments, and may have developed a whole repertoire of positive feelings or fears related to them. As we "discover" within a given environment—finding that a given behavior leads to a positive outcome while another behavior does not—we engage in another kind of learning known as instrumental or operant. It is, in effect, the "school of trial and error learning," from which we will preserve and strengthen those behaviors that bring us positive outcomes and very likely will drop or change those behaviors that do not so reward us. The settings in which we learn are virtually limitless and endless—as a child interacting with parents, as a student interacting with classroom material and study habits, as a brother and sister interacting with each other, as a loving couple in the midst of spring. Welcome to the field of learning and to its terms which literally affect all of us daily.

The human glimpse may seem brief in this discussion of basic learning principles, but you will soon find that we have headed for practical applications of these principles that will affect all of us. Subsequent sections will cover cognition and complex human learning as well as developmental psychology and other areas of the discipline. In order not to flounder in those sections, you must master the basic learning principles. There are numerous terms and concepts you will need to know, so take a deep breath and plunge in.

Learning Outline

Concepts	Names	Terms
Forms of learning		Habituation
	Pavlov	Sensitization
	Watson	Classical conditioning (also called Respondent or Type-S)
	Skinner	Instrumental conditioning (also called Operant or Type-R)
Classical conditioning terminology		Conditioned stimulus (CS)
		Unconditioned stimulus (UCS)
		Conditioned response (CR)
		Unconditioned response (UCR)
		Temporal relations between CS and US
		Forward pairing (delayed or trace)
		Backward pairing
		Simultaneous pairing
		Second-order conditioning
		Discrimination and generalization

Concepts	Names	Terms
Instrumental conditioning terminology	Thorndike	Law of effect
		Positive reinforcement
		Negative reinforcement
		Types of reinforcers
		Appetitive stimulus
		Aversive stimulus
	Hull	Drive-reduction theory
	Premack	Premack's principle
	Skinner	Shaping
		Successive approximation
		Cumulative record
		Discriminative stimulus
Learning curve terminology		Acquisition
		Plateau/asymptote
		Extinction
		Spontaneous recovery
Schedules of reinforcement		Continuous vs. partial reinforcement
		Partial-reinforcement effect
		Fixed interval
		Variable interval
		Fixed ratio
		Variable ratio
Aversive conditioning		Escape and avoidance behavior
	Mowrer	Two-process theory
		Punishment
Neural basis for learning		Long-term potentiation
	Hebb	Hebb's law
Evolutionary perspectives on learning		Equipotentiality principle
		Biological constraints
	Garcia and Koelling	Belongingness
		One-trial learning
Clinical applications of conditioning		Behavior therapy
		Conditioned emotional response
		Phobias
		Compensatory reaction/tolerance
		Drug addiction
		Compulsive behavior
	Seligman	Depression
Cognitive learning	Rescorla/Wagner	Contiguity vs. contingency
		Blocking effect
	Seligman	Learned helplessness
	Tolman	Latent learning
		Cognitive map
	Köhler	Insight ("aha" phemoneon)

Outline Terms Elaborated

➤ **Forms of learning:**

Learning can be broadly defined as any long-lasting change in an individual's behavior that results from experience. This definition distinguishes learning from fatigue or hunger (a short-lived change in behavior), from maturation (a change that does not depend on experience), and from evolution (a change that is seen across generations). The simplest forms of learning are changes in a reflexive response caused by mere repetition of a stimulus: A decrease in responsiveness is *habituation* and an increase in responsiveness is *sensitization*. *Classical conditioning* results in a new association being formed between a previously neutral stimulus and a stimulus that elicits a reflexive response—this is the form of learning that Pavlov's salivating dogs exhibited. *Instrumental conditioning* pairs a response with a consequence in order to change the likelihood of that response; this form of learning is most associated with behaviorists *Watson* and *Skinner*.

➤ **Classical conditioning terminology:**

Classical conditioning starts with an *unconditioned stimulus (UCS)* that already elicits an *unconditioned response (UCR)*. During learning, a *conditioned stimulus (CS)* is repeatedly paired with the UCS, and eventually the CS will elicit a *conditioned response (CR)* that is similar in type to the UCR. In Pavlov's case, the UCS was the food, the CS was the bell, and the UCR and the CR were the salivation. Animals will show *generalization* of the CS to similar stimuli and *discrimination* between the CS and different stimuli. The temporal relation between the UCS and CS can vary: The UCS can precede the CS *(forward pairing)*, it can occur at the same time as the CS *(simultaneous pairing)*, or it can even follow the CS *(backward pairing)*. Forward pairing produces the best conditioning. *Second-order* conditioning occurs when a new CS is paired with a previously learned CS (instead of with a UCS) during learning.

➤ **Instrumental conditioning terminology:**

In contrast to classical conditioning, where the response or behavior of interest is automatically elicited with the appropriate stimulus, in instrumental (or operant) conditioning, the response may or may not be produced. The goal of instrumental conditioning is to change the likelihood with which the organism produces the response. The ability to change behavior with consequences in an animal was first demonstrated when Edward *Thorndike* taught a hungry cat to press a lever or pull a wire in a *puzzle box* in order to get out and obtain a food reward. His description of the cat's behavior formed the basis for his *Law of Effect*, which became the foundation for instrumental conditioning. There are a number of different categories of consequences that can be used in instrumental conditioning: Reinforcement is any consequence that increases the probability of a response. *Positive reinforcement* involves the presentation of an *appetitive stimulus* (e.g., the cat's food) as a consequence; negative reinforcement involves the termination of an *aversive stimulus* (e.g., the cat's freedom from the confining box). (Note that negative reinforcement is not the same as punishment.) Clark *Hull* described a reinforcer as anything that reduces a *drive* for a biological need (hunger, thirst) in his *drive-reduction theory*. The *Premack principle* states that any preferred response can be a positive reinforcer. In many cases, learning must begin by a period of *shaping*, in which the animal is taught what the correct response is through a series of *successive approximations*. The total number of responses that an animal has made is often plotted in a *cumulative record* of performance. In instrumental conditioning, stimulus discrimination can still occur even though the response is not elicited from a stimulus (as with classical conditioning): *discriminative stimuli* in this setting can provide a context for responding.

➤ **Learning curve terminology:**

A *learning curve* is a graph of the change in the response over time (usually magnitude of a response in classical conditioning and probability of a response in instrumental conditioning). Learning curves have the same general shape: During *acquisition* the response increases gradually and then *plateaus* at an *asymptote*. It remains here until the learning situation changes (the CS is no longer paired with the UCS or an instrumental response is not rewarded), causing the response to decline during the *extinction* period. In classical conditioning, an extinguished response may occasionally *spontaneously recover* only to be extinguished again.

➤ **Schedules of reinforcement** describe how often an animal is rewarded for an instrumental response. During instrumental conditioning, rewards can be administered on a *continuous reinforcement* schedule or on a *partial reinforcement* schedule. The *partial-reinforcement effect* describes the resistance that partial reinforcement schedules have to extinction; in other words, they are more effective at maintaining a behavior in the long run. The four types of partial reinforcement schedules are: Fixed interval (reward every *n* seconds), variable interval (on average reward every *n* seconds), fixed ratio (reward every *n* responses), variable ratio (on average reward every *n* responses). Ratio schedules give reinforcement on the basis of the number of responses made and interval schedules give reinforcement on the basis of time. Variable ratio schedules produce very high levels of responding.

➤ **Aversive conditioning** modifies responding using aversive stimuli. *Punishment* involves the administration of some aversive stimulus in order to decrease responding; the effectiveness of punishment as a consequence is debatable. Removal of an aversive stimulus can be an effective reinforcer to increase responding: Allowing an animal to *escape* from an unpleasant stimulus (typically a shock) or to *avoid* it all together is an effective way to change behavior. Punishment and escape consequences are straightforward, but *avoidance learning* is more complicated, because there is no clear reinforcer. *Mowrer* explained this phenomenon with a *two-process theory* that includes both classical conditioning (of a fear response to a neutral stimulus) and instrumental conditioning (of a response that reduces the fear).

➤ **Neural basis for learning:**

For any of the laws of learning to be effective, something in the brain must be modifiable by experience. For several decades now, scientists have believed those modifications occur at the *synapse*, the small gap between neurons. Donald *Hebb* first suggested the idea that "neurons that fire together wire together." He speculated that simultaneous activity in any pair of neurons would strengthen the synapse between those neurons; hypothetically, such a process could explain classical conditioning associations. Hebb's ideas have recently received support from neurobiologists, who have documented that experience can cause a *long-term potentiation* (or increase) in the responsiveness of a neuron. The long-lasting nature of this phenomenon makes for a tantalizing comparison to learning processes, and researchers in this area are closely examining the possibility that long-term potentiation is the cellular mechanism underlying learning.

➤ **Evolutionary perspectives on learning:**
John *Locke* used the term *tabula rasa* to describe the mind—infants are born with a "blank slate" onto which learned associations are written. It is not much of a leap to claim that any conditioned stimulus could be associated with any conditioned response, or any response with any reinforcer. This claim is called the *equipotentiality principle*, and was popular in the early days of behaviorism. However, much research now points to the *biological constraints* on what a species can learn. *Garcia* demonstrated that a rat could learn to associate a taste with an illness and a light with a shock, but could not associate a taste with a shock or a light with an illness. Garcia termed this *belongingness*—some associations are easier to learn, others are harder, and still others are impossible. Some associations are so easy to learn that *one trial* is enough to affect behavior. A classic example of this is food aversions. It is easy to see the selection pressures that favored certain one-trial learned associations (such as food with illness) in evolution!

➤ **Clinical applications of conditioning** range from phobias to drug addiction, from compulsive behavior to depression. *Behavior* therapy is used to treat a wide range of clinical disorders using learning principles; and the formation of these disorders is often well explained by simple classical and instrumental conditioning. For example, the *conditioned emotional response* between an aversive stimulus and fear may explain extreme *phobias*, and treatment of phobias often involves an attempt to extinguish the learned association. *Compensatory reactions* to drugs (creating higher *tolerance*) can be explained by classical conditioning, as can cravings associated with *drug addiction*. The *two-process* theory of avoidance learning may explain the development of *compulsive* behaviors. And contingency theory could be related to feelings of helplessness and *depression*.

➤ **Cognitive learning** focuses on the knowledge that is learned and not the behavior that is modified. Robert *Rescorla* and Allan *Wagner* described the knowledge about *contingency* (versus mere *contiguity*) that is acquired during classical conditioning. Leon *Kamin* illustrated the role that surprise plays in learning contingencies with the *blocking effect* of redundant information. Martin *Seligman* documented that the absence of contingencies (reinforcements unrelated to responses) can lead to *learned helplessness*, which may be related to *depression*. Edward *Tolman* moved away from behaviorism by distinguishing between learning and behavior; one context in which he demonstrated so-called *latent learning* was in the formation of a *cognitive map* through exploration of an environment. Wolfgang *Köhler* studied learning that was not gradual (like conditioning) but instead that was *insightful*.

Learning Summary

In our review of learning, you have been reminded of some of the powerful principles that govern much of animal and human changes in behavior. We have moved from Pavlov's dogs and Thorndike's cats, to an appreciation of some of the complex human phenemona—phobias, depression, and drug addiction—that may have their roots in these principles. However, we have also had a foreshadowing that we must move beyond the study of behavior to truly understand learning: With scientists like Wagner, Tolman, and Köhler pushing the focus onto what we *know* and not just how we *behave*, psychology moved beyond behaviorism into a fuller study of complex cognition. In our next section, we will see how much further this new approach can take us towards our understanding of the mind.

If you need to brush up on some of the items in this section, head for the learning chapter of a basic textbook. J. T. Walker's *Psychology of Learning: Principles and Processes* (New York: Prentice-Hall, 1995) or D. A. Norman's *Learning and Memory* (San Francisco: W. H. Freeman, 1995) will provide any additional depth you may need. Whatever sources you review, it will be a good idea to come back to this term-concept list afterward to see where you are in your basic understanding. When you have mastered the list, you will be set to move on.

Cognition and Complex Human Learning

During the heyday of behaviorism, words like *cognition* and *thought* were taboo. As learning theorists began to think about thought, and move away from strict behaviorism, the atmosphere was ripe for a major paradigm shift. This move was spurred by two historical events that, on the surface, have little to do with psychology. The first was World War II, which brought with it a number of applied problems, like how to train fighter pilots to read all of the information on a complex instrument panel. Psychologists like Donald *Broadbent* found that answers to these problems gave birth to the field of *information theory* or information processing, which persists today in studies of perception, attention, and memory. The second event was the advent of the computer age, which led to questions about how computers behave intelligently. Led by Allen *Newell* and Herbert *Simon*, cognitive psychologists and computer scientists began to ask similar questions about information processing, using the language of "buffers" and "storage" to describe their ideas. The focus on information—and not on behavior—became the foundation for *cognitive psychology*.

Perhaps the final nail in the behaviorist coffin was struck by linguists, led by Noam *Chomsky*, who challenged the notion that the laws of behaviorism had much to offer by way of understanding language. The field of *psycholinguistics* has taken off in its own right, which focuses on issues of language production, comprehension, structure, and development. Of all our many cognitive abilities, one of the most impressive and most unique is the human capacity for language. If you stop to contemplate some of the wonders of language—the seemingly infinite number of utterances that you are able to produce and comprehend without effort—or if you have ever spent any time with a young child who is just learning to speak, you should get a sense of the myriad of questions that psychologists who study language try to address. Work in the related fields of linguistics and computer science has also been enormously influential in the psychology of language.

The study of higher mental processes such as memory, language, and thought, form the heart of cognitive psychology today. This review may remind you of all of the wonderful and exciting capacities that make humans so special and the mind so thrilling a topic to explore.

Cognition and Complex Human Learning Outline

Concepts	Names	Terms
Memory		
Types of memory	Tulving	Semantic vs. episodic
		Intentional vs. incidental
		Verbal vs. nonverbal
	Schacter	Implicit (procedural)
	Ebbinghaus	Relearning/savings method
		Repetition priming
	Squire	Explicit (declarative)
		Recall
		Recognition
Memory processes		Encoding
		Storage
		Retrieval
Stages of memory (information-processing)	Sperling	Sensory store (iconic, echoic)
	Miller, Baddeley	Short-term store/Working memory
		Long-term store
Factors that influence memory		Serial position effect
		von Restorff effect
		Flashbulb memories
		Elaborative vs. maintenance rehearsal
	Craik & Lockhart	Levels of processing effect
	Tulving	Encoding specificity principle
		Context and state dependence
Mnemonics		Method of loci
		Visual imagery
		Chunking
		Natural language mediators
Forgetting		Decay vs. interference
		Retroactive interference
		Proactive interference
		Motivated forgetting
		Infantile amnesia
Constructive memory	Bartlett	Schemas
	Loftus	Misinformation effect/eyewitness testimony

Concepts	Names	Terms
Neurobiology of memory		Anterograde amnesia
		Retrograde amnesia
		Hippocampus (consolidation)
		Frontal lobe (working memory)
		Long-term potentiation
	Rumelhart	Neural networks
Categorization		Critical features vs. prototypes
	Rosch	Hierarchies and basic levels
		Schemas and scripts
Imagery and Visual Memory		Propositional vs. analog
	Shepard, Kosslyn	Mental rotation
	Farah	Visual imagery
	Paivio	Dual-code, picture-superiority effect
		Mental maps

Language

Concepts	Names	Terms
Linguistic analysis levels		Phonological (phonemes)
		Grammatical (morphemes and syntax)
		Semantic (word and sentence meaning)
Components of language		Phonemes
		Morphemes
		Words
		Propositions
		Subject and predicate
		Phrases and sentences
Language comprehension		Parsing
		Constituents
		Ambiguity/"garden-path" sentences
		On-line vs. off-line measurement
Language acquisition	Skinner, Mowrer	Reinforcement
	Chomsky	Inborn competence
		Stages of acquisition
		Prelinguistic
		Linguistic
		Motherese
		Comprehension vs. production
Relationship between language and thought	Whorf	Whorfian hypothesis (language determines thought)
	Brown	Thought determines language
	Fodor	Modularity position
Language in nonhuman species	Chomsky	Unique human ability
	Gardner, Rumbaugh	Animal language
Brain and language function	Broca	Language production/Broca's area
	Wernicke	Language comprehension/Wernicke's area

Concepts	Names	Terms
Thought		
Information processing	Donders, Sternberg	
Measurement		Attention and controlled operations Automatic processes Dichotic listening and shadowing task

Types of reasoning		Inductive
		  Representativeness heuristic
		  Availability heuristic
		 Deductive (e.g., syllogisms)
		 Decision making
		 Problem solving

Artificial intelligence and computer simulation		Algorithms Heuristics Expert systems
Theories and principles	Hull Spence Krechevsky Lashley Bruner	Continuity Theory Noncontinuity Theory Inductive Reasoning

Mental representations	Galton	Analogical
		  Mental images
		  Eidetic imagery
		  Spatial thinking
		 Symbolic
		  Episodic memory
		  Generic memory
		   Semantic

Models		Hierarchical network model in semantic memory Spreading activation model Parallel distributed processing (PDP) models
Problem solving	Newell and Simon Kosslyn, Holyoak	Hierarchical organization with subroutines Automatization Artificial intelligence and problem-solving strategies such as working backwards through the logic sequence Mental image manipulation of visual information
Barriers to problem solving		Stroop effect Mental set (fixation) Functional fixedness

Concepts	Names	Terms
Facilitators to problem solving		Restructuring
		Incubation
Representative research evidence		Analogical
		Mental rotation
		Image scanning
		Symbolic
		Semantic priming
Reasoning and problem solving		Deductive vs. inductive reasoning
		Algorithm, heuristic
	Newell and Simon	Search and representation
		Mental sets
		Functional fixedness
	Holyoak	Analogy
	Tversky, Kahneman	Biases in decision making

Outline Terms Elaborated

MEMORY
➤ Types of memory:

In the nineteenth century Hermann *Ebbinghaus*, a German psychologist, used the *nonsense syllable* (consonant-vowel-consonant, e.g., DAX) to study association and learning in a revolutionary way. His famous curve of retention and forgetting demonstrated that material is forgotten rapidly in the first few hours after learning—then forgetting occurs more and more slowly as time passes. There are several distinctions in the study of memory that we can draw by way of comparison to the work of Ebbinghaus. First, Ebbinghaus was studying material for memory that was *intentionally* learned. Memory can also be tested for material learned *incidentally*, that is, without making an attempt to study something for a later test. Second, Ebbinghaus used nonsense syllables to study memory for items devoid of meaning or other associations. Although this artificial situation allows for a better understanding of basic memory principles, in the past few decades psychologists have shifted their focus to more natural learning situations, for words, pictures, stories, and events. Third, Ebbinghaus assessed his memory by measuring how long it took him to relearn the same set of words day after day. This test, which Ebbinghaus called the *savings method*, or relearning, is now described by psychologists as *implicit memory*, learning that improves your performance on a task (also called *repetition priming*) without intent to recollect the information consciously. Although the study of implicit memory is currently enjoying a resurgence in the field, for most of this century psychologists have studied *explicit memory*, the conscious recollection (either *recall* or *recognition*) of prior experiences. When you try to remember a phone number or the name of your third-grade teacher, you are explicitly trying to recall a memory. The terms *procedural* and *declarative* memory are nearly synonymous with implicit and explicit memory. Fourth, Ebbinghaus studied learning of an event in his own experience. So-called *episodic memory* of events for particular occurrences (or episodes), like what you ate for breakfast this morning or what grade you got on your last history test, was distinguished by

Endel *Tulving* from generic memory of facts, called *semantic memory*, like what foods are suitable breakfast foods and the names and dates of the major battles of the Civil War.

➤ **Memory processes:**

For all types of memories, successful remembering requires three mental processes. *Encoding* is the process by which an external stimulus (e.g., a face or a word) is attended to, identified, studied, and incorporated into memory. This memory must then be retained, or *stored*, for some period of time. Finally, at *retrieval* the stored information must be recovered. Psychologists have studied each of these processes in detail.

➤ **Stages of memory:**

The process of encoding has been described with an *information-processing model* of three stages or memory systems: *sensory memory*, *short-term memory*, and *long-term memory*. Sensory memory, roughly speaking a mental afterimage, lasts for only a second, just long enough to allow attention and identification of a visual (*iconic* memory) or auditory (*echoic* memory) stimulus needed for later processing. The duration and capacity of the sensory store was first illuminated by George *Sperling*, who described the accurate storage by rapid rate of decay of letters flashed very briefly. With attention to information in the sensory store (or sensory register), information can be transferred to the *short-term store*, which can hold small amounts of information for about twenty seconds. Depending on the extent to which this information is further processed, some memories will be retained for longer periods of time in the *long-term store*. When you remember a phone number just long enough to dial it once, but then realize you have forgotten it when you encounter a busy signal on the line, that is a case of information that was in short-term memory but not transferred to long-term memory. The capacity of short-term memory is described in terms of units of information called *chunks*, which are defined in terms of meaning and not size. For example, the list of letters C-I-A-M-T-V-F-B-I would be nine bits, or chunks, of information unless the letters were grouped into three larger but meaningful chunks: CIA – MTV – FBI. George *Miller* established the capacity of short-term memory as 7 ± 2 chunks. In recent years the description of short-term memory has been modified to include any information that is in conscious awareness, whether from the sensory store or from older, long-term memories. Because this information is thought to be actively processed (i.e., thought about) while in consciousness, this form of memory has been called *working memory* by Alan *Baddeley*, who describes multiple working memory *buffers*, including one for verbal information and one for visuospatial information.

➤ **Factors that influence memory:**

Many factors influence how likely we are to remember some event. Memory for items on a list is affected by the order of those items: This *serial position effect* describes the advantage in memory of items at the beginning and end of the list. Memory may be better for unusual or novel things (the *von Restorff effect*) or for some emotionally charged events (*flashbulb memories*). The method of studying, or *rehearsal*, of information also affects how likely we are to remember something. Things we make vivid through imagery or rich associations (*elaborative rehearsal*) are processed more deeply and are better remembered than things we merely repeat by rote *(maintenance rehearsal)*: The *levels of processing effect* illustrates that there is superior memory after deep processing than after shallow processing. Additionally, the *encoding specificity principle* states that memory will improve if the context at the time of retrieval closely resembles the context during encoding. When this context describes an emotional or physical state, this effect is called *state dependence*.

➤ **Mnemonics** are learning aids or strategies that train a person to use elaboration to make information more memorable. Do you know the order of notes on the treble staff? If you thought "Every Good Boy Does Fine" to remember E-G-B-D-F, you used a mnemonic device to elaborate that information. *Chunking* is a form of *recoding* information into fewer but more meaningful units to remember. A very effective mnemonic strategy is to elaborate with *mental imagery*; one such technique is called the *method of loci*, in which to-be-remembered words are imagined in different spatial locations in a familiar place. To remember, you need only take a mental tour of that location! Another effective mnemonic device is verse: "Thirty days have September, April, June, and November . . ." This falls into the larger category of *natural language mediators* that use sounds, patterns, and meanings of words already known to assist learning new information. The principle behind all of these techniques is meaningful elaboration.

➤ **Forgetting:**
Even with all of these mnemonic devices at our disposal, our memories will still fail us. As time passes, our memories for older events can seem to fade away. But most psychologists no longer believe that memories simply *decay* with time. Rather, *interference* from other memories may be responsible for most of what we forget. *Proactive interference* is the negative effect that old information we know has on new things we are trying to learn; when you try to learn a new language or a new computer program, you may experience proactive interference. *Retroactive interference* is the effect that new learning has on information we learned before. If you can't remember your last telephone number, that's retroactive interference. Sigmund *Freud* introduced the idea of *motivated forgetting* or *repression* of particularly painful memories. One special form of forgetting, *infantile amnesia*, may be explained by changes in retrieval contexts and cues, according to the encoding specificity principle.

➤ **Constructive memory** views memory as a more active process than words like *storage* would suggest. New memories are interpreted, elaborated upon, and organized based on prior knowledge, or frameworks called *schemas*, in a constructive memory process first described by Sir Frederic *Bartlett* in the 1930s. This constructive process can lead to distortions in memory. Elizabeth *Loftus* has described the ways in which memories reported in *eyewitness testimony* can be distorted by things that happen or that are said after the event occurred; this is the *misinformation effect*.

➤ **Neurobiology of memory:**
While everyone forgets things in daily life, some people have a profound impairment in the ability to remember. There are many causes for *amnesia*, most of which affect a structure in the brain called the *hippocampus*. As a result, a person will be unable to learn new information *(anterograde amnesia)* and may have some loss of memories for a

period of time before the onset of trauma or disease *(retrograde amnesia)*. What about the movie portrayal of amnesics unable to remember their names, families, and entire childhoods? Although a convenient plot device, accidents and diseases do not result in the complete loss of long-term memories. Psychologists are beginning to understand more about different memory systems by looking at what amnesics are and are not able to learn. Memory for how to do things *(procedural memory)* is unaffected by amnesia, which devastates memory for new events *(declarative memory)*. Additionally, amnesics show *implicit memory* for events when improved performance following learning is assessed *(repetition priming)* in the absence of *explicit memory* for those events. The hippocampus is probably involved in the *consolidation* of new memories. Other regions of the brain may have different functions for memory; for example, the *frontal lobe* may play an important role in working memory. At a cellular level, the mechanism for learning in the neurons of the brain has been described as a process of *long-term potentiation* of new activity at the synapses between neurons. Some psychologists try to understand more complicated cognitive functions by constructing computational *neural networks* based on the behavior of neurons.

► Categorization:

Whereas the study of episodic memory has focused on encoding and retrieval processes, it is the storage or organization of knowledge that has dominated investigations of semantic memory. A major avenue of investigation in this area has centered on the formation and representation of *concepts*. The *critical feature* theory of concept representation defines concepts in terms of necessary and sufficient features. Eleanor *Rosch* argued, instead, for a less rigid representation of a concept, based on similarity to a representative *prototype* of a concept (e.g., a robin is a prototype bird). She also described a hierarchical organization of concepts, centered on a *basic level* at which we tend to categorize things.

► Imagery and visual memory:

Thus far, our entire discussion has focused on verbal memory. Because many of the same principles apply to memory for pictures, some psychologists have asserted that visual and spatial memories are stored as *propositions*, just as are verbal memories. However, the work of Roger *Shepard* and Steven *Kosslyn* suggests that visual thought is different from verbal thought, and that people are capable of rotating, scanning, and manipulating visual memories or *images* in ways similar to how they manipulate actual pictures. Spatial memories may be organized as *mental maps* that represent but often distort physical reality. *Paivio* suggested that we use a *dual code* of both visual and verbal memory whenever possible.

LANGUAGE

► Linguistic analysis levels:

The field of linguistics is concerned with characterizing the structure of language. A major goal of this field is to describe a set of rules, also known as a *grammar*, that is able to account for the vast number of different utterances that are possible in a language as well the regularity that these utterances possess. One of the major blows to behaviorism was its inability to account for these facts about language. A grammar consists of three major types of rules that govern language production: *Syntax* (word order and inflection), *semantics* (meaning), and *phonology* (sound structure). Because violations to all three of these types of rules occur often in normal language use, it is important to keep in mind a distinction between *linguistic competence* and *linguistic performance*. This distinction becomes particularly relevant in studies of language development. The relationship between competence and performance has been the subject of heated debates.

➤ Components of language:

The smallest element of spoken language is the *phoneme*, which corresponds to a single sound; the English language has forty phonemes. Phonemes vary from language to language, and our ability to discriminate between phonemes of other languages is very poor. Phonemes are joined together into *morphemes*, which correspond to a single meaning. A word can have one morpheme (e.g., bus) or it can have more than one morpheme (e.g., sing + ing). Morphemes like "ing" that add meaning or grammatical information to another morpheme are called *function morphemes*. Morphemes are joined into words, which are joined together to form *propositions*, which are units of meaning in a sentence. A proposition has a *subject* and a *predicate*. Propositions are incorporated into sentences that vary in structure and even meaning (e.g., shifting emphasis in the proposition by using a passive construction). *Phrase structure analysis* is an important method in understanding language processing.

➤ Language comprehension:

One of the challenges facing computer scientists is to make a computer program that can understand language—real language, as opposed to a series of simple commands. The fact that this problem has yet to be solved illustrates how difficult the task of language comprehension is, even though we do it effortlessly all the time. One of the most important steps in successful language comprehension is *parsing*, whereby words in a spoken or written message are transformed into a mental representation of the meaning of the message. There are rules that guide this transformation, and in order to apply these rules, we break sentences into smaller units, called *constituents*. For example, in the preceding sentence, a constituent would be "we break sentences into smaller units." People process the meaning of sentences one constituent at a time. How do psychologists know this? One technique psycholinguists use to study sentence processing involves interrupting people as they are reading passages and asking them to write down everything they remember. This is called an *off-line* measure of sentence processing, because it requires an interruption to measure performance. One *on-line* measure of sentence processing (one which does not require interrupting the person) uses the reader's eye movements to study parsing. Another on-line technique uses neural responses obtained from ERPs (see the review of Physiological Psychology for more information about this technique) to infer the time course of availability of different types of information during sentence processing. In order to interpret the meaning of a sentence, we use syntactic clues (e.g., word order and inflection) and semantic clues (e.g., the plausible interpretations of a word) to guide our comprehension. ERP studies have found that semantic and syntactic anomalies in sentences affect processing at different points in time and in different areas of the brain. One thing that makes language comprehension so difficult is the occurrence of ambiguities in sentences. There can be ambiguities in the meaning of single words—when you go down to the bank, are you depositing money or taking a walk by the river? There can also be ambiguities that are present in a sentence, but which are ultimately resolved. For example, if you start to read "The child painted . . ." you might begin to imagine a budding young artist in front of her canvas, until you finish the sentence: "The child painted by the artist was sleeping." Sentences that suggest one interpretation that turns out to be wrong are called *garden-path sentences*. Psychologists study how people read these sentences to understand the parsing process.

➤ **Language acquisition** is the remarkable process whereby a child achieves near mastery of a language in just a few brief years. The *behaviorists* explained language acquisition as just another example of *instrumental conditioning*; however, examination of exchanges between adults and young children revealed very few instances of correction or *reinforcement* that could lead to conditioning. An alternative hypothesis is that children are born equipped with a language capacity, not specific to any particular language of course, but rather for *language universals*. Noam *Chomsky* argued that such an innate ability to extract the rules of language is required to overcome the *"poverty of the stimulus"* that is presented to babies. Chomsky also broke from behaviorism by distinguishing between language *competence* and language *performance*. The ability to learn a language seems to peak during a *critical period*, which is most evident when comparing first and second language acquisition. Anne *Fernald* has studied a universal way in which parents speak to children, called *Motherese*, which may help the young language learner mark word and sentence boundaries. The earliest language exposure also determines which sounds an infant is capable of discriminating; by six months there are changes in phoneme discrimination (a decrease in sensitivity to foreign contrasts). The ability to understand language precedes the ability to produce language. Early language production begins with single words, followed by two-word, *telegraphic* speech. Between two and three, children begin to produce *overregularization errors* that were not present earlier, as they learn rules (such as adding –ed to the past tense, which might produce the error "eated").

➤ **Relationship between language and thought:**
Another contested issue is the relationship between language and thought. Perhaps the best known stance on this issue is the *Whorfian hypothesis*, which states that language determines the way in which a person thinks and perceives the world. For example, do Americans, who have eleven basic color words (green, yellow, etc.) perceive colors differently than the Dani (a native Indonesian culture), who have just two basic color pwords? For this question, the evidence does not support the Whorfian hypothesis; the Dani and Americans perceive

colors in a similar way. In fact, most of the research in this area suggests that language does not determine the way we think or the way in which we perceive the world. An important extension of this conclusion is called the *modularity* position, most often associated with philosopher Jerry *Fodor*, which holds that language is independent from other cognitive systems (e.g., perception). Fodor further claims that the principles that govern language acquisition and use are different than those that govern the rest of cognition. This claim has been particularly influential in the study of language acquisition: Is language acquisition governed by the same learning principles that apply to other cognitive skills? The jury is still out on this issue. As psychologists have grappled with this question, a number of important principles have been discovered. Some of these are reviewed in the pages dealing with Developmental Psychology.

➤ **Language in nonhuman species** is perhaps the most controversial issue in the field of psycholinguistics. Theories of language learning (behaviorism versus innate grammar) clearly make different predictions about the ability of nonhuman species to truly acquire language. In this debate, language must be distinguished from speaking—a parrot that speaks may not be using language, whereas an animal that cannot speak may be able to use a different form of language. This latter possibility has been investigated in chimpanzees using symbol-languages *(Rumbaugh)* and gesture *(Gardner)*. Chimps can learn words with these systems, but there is disagreement about whether they can learn syntax and whether they produce novel constructions. While the jury is still out, it is clear that even the most advanced chimp's language is less advanced that that of the typical three-year-old child.

➤ **Brain and language:**

In most people, the *left* hemisphere is dominant for language function. Paul *Broca* first described the relation between an area in the left frontal lobe, now called *Broca's area*, and language production, in his report of a patient who could only utter the sound "tan-tan" after sustaining brain damage in that area; despite this impairment the patient could understand language normally. Karl *Wernicke* described the converse pattern of language dysfunction following brain damage at the border of the temporal lobe and parietal lobe of the left hemisphere, in an area that we now call *Wernicke's area*. These patients can produce fluent utterances that are devoid of meaning, and they have grossly impaired language comprehension.

THOUGHT

➤ **Information processing** (Donders, Sternberg) (the time required to do each mental operation in a fixed sequence)
➤ **Attention and controlled operations** (each proceeding serially with conscious attention required), automatic processes (several proceeding simultaneously with no conscious attention required), dichotic listening and shadowing task (different messages sent to each ear simultaneously)
➤ **Types of reasoning,** including *inductive* (generalizing from a specific instance), *deductive* (applying a logic-based rule to new, specific situation for single-solution) (carries two error potentials: content [conclusion

undesirable] and form [conclusion invalid]), *decision making* (with its heuristics [rules of thumb, focusing on likely solution-points], in which decisions are based on recent experiences producing the most readily available information). This decision-making approach can fall prey to the conjunction or "gambler's" fallacy (e.g., that if you have just rolled "snake eyes" with dice four times in a row, you will overestimate or underestimate [far above or below random or chance probabilities] that the event will occur again). Another approach—*problem solving*—uses *productive* (new or novel approach to a problem) and *reproductive* (applying old rule to new problem) thought processes, encompasses incubation (problem-mulling while engaged in nonproblem-based activities). The reproductive can at times block creativity through the rigidity of functional fixedness (e.g., hammers are only used for hammering) and mental set (applying old problem-solving strategies).

➤ **Artificial intelligence and its computer simulation of human mental operations** through two approaches—*algorithms* (proceeding systematically, step-by-step, toward solution) and *heuristics* (proceeding more rapidly than algorithms by going to most likely solution areas and utilizing subgoal analysis [defining the problem as discrete subgoals, each addressed individually])

➤ **Personalities and their theories or principles**, including the *Continuity Theory* of *Hull and Spence* (from the learning/associationist background; it states that concepts are a product of repeated stimulus-response occurrences and generalization); *Noncontinuity Theory* of *Krechevsky and Lashley*, which states that a subject tests an hypothesis and that learning is rapid when the relevant stimulus is attended to; *Inductive Reasoning* of *Bruner*, which proceeds from a specific instance to the formation of a general rule. Global processing is an inductive-reasoning approach that tests all hypotheses simultaneously rather than sequentially. Levine's blank trials method is often utilized in global processing.

Cognition and Complex Human Learning Summary

We have come a long way since World War II, the development of computers, and a linguist named Noam Chomsky who gave birth to ideas that converged on the field of cognitive psychology. As you test your encoding and retrieval processes and fight off the effects of decay and interference on forgetting, you may find it helpful to do some elaborative rehearsal with some additional reading on the topics of memory, language, and thought.

For reading beyond your introductory psychology textbook, the following works will provide meaningful depth. (Note the use of the terms "revolution" and "new" in the titles. Cognitive psychology has indeed been an area with exciting discoveries and new frontiers over the past two decades—ones that inevitably will find common ground with the areas of brain physiology and neuroscience: B. J. Baars's *The Cognitive Revolution in Psychology* (New York: Guilford Press, 1986), H. Gardner's *The Mind's New Science: A History of the Cognitive Revolution* (New York: Basic Books, 1987), K. J. Gilhooly's *Thinking: Directed, Undirected and Creative* (San Diego, Calif.: Academic Press, 1988), S. K. Reed's *Cognition: Theory and Applications*

(Monterey, Calif.: Brooks/Cole, 1996), and John Anderson's *Cognitive Psychology and Its Implications* (New York: Worth Publishers, 2000).

Thinking has generally been characterized as a process that molds images, symbols, words, rules, and concepts into mental associations. Think of Reno or Las Vegas, for example, and a truckload of images and associations comes immediately to mind.

INTELLIGENCE

In any study of the mind, language, or thinking, you will inevitably encounter the concept of intelligence quotient (IQ). No review of the discipline of psychology could be complete without a discussion of this term and an attempt to convey a basic understanding of intelligence and its relationship to problem-solving and creativity. A definition of intelligence generally includes three elements: the ability to profit from experience, the ability to learn new information, and the ability to adjust to new situations. Theoretical work in the area has concentrated on the general nature of intelligence and whether it is a general, unitary factor or a combination of several specific factors. Scholarly work on this question began just after 1900 with *Spearman's Two Factor Theory* (a general-type factor and a specific-type factor). The next major name was *Thurstone*, who postulated seven factors in intelligence, and intelligence theory reached its peak of complexity with *Guilford's Structure of Intellect* (120 factors in three general classifications).

Two recent theoretical approaches have sought to broaden the definitional perspective of intelligence. Sternberg defines intelligence as a number of components that allow one to adapt to, select, and shape one's environment. His triarchic theory of intelligence includes more traditional notions of intelligence (componential intelligence, of linguistic and logical-mathematical skills) as well as contextual intelligence ("street smarts") and experimental intelligence (creative insight). Gardner expands on the notion of multiple intelligences to include seven domains of intelligence: linguistic, musical, logical-mathematical, spatial, bodily-kinesthetic, interpersonal, and intrapersonal. These different types of intelligence can be seen in the genius of experts from composers (musical) to dancers (bodily-kinesthetic), from teachers (interpersonal) to poets (linguistic). Both Sternberg and Gardner view intelligence not as a single or biologically determined factor, but as a number of domains that represent the interaction of the individual's biological predispositions with the environment and cultural context. From the emergence of these theories we come to know and appreciate the complexity of the term "intelligence."

In some respects, it is easier to measure intelligence than to discuss it theoretically.

Measurement began with *Binet and Simon* (French contemporaries of Spearman). Commissioned by the French minister of public instruction, they developed a test to determine which children could not profit from elementary instruction in the public schools. Their end product, later translated into English by *Terman* and named the *Stanford-Binet*, launched an era of intelligence testing in this country. In addition to creating the pioneering intelligence test, Binet and Simon gave prominence to the IQ concept and established a method for IQ computation. Other names and concepts important to the intelligence area (e.g., Wechsler) are cited here:

Intelligence Outline

Concepts	Names	Terms
Individual intelligence tests	Terman Wechsler	Stanford-Binet WAIS-III (adult) WISC-III (children) WPPSI-R (preschool)
Group intelligence tests		Otis Lorge-Thorndike California Test of Mental Maturity
Theories of intelligence	Spearman Thurstone Guilford Sternberg Gardner	Two-factor Seven-factor Structure of intellect (120 factors in 3 classifications) Triarchic theory Multiple intelligences
Intelligence quotient	Binet	$IQ = MA/CA \times 100$

Practical intelligence (tacit)	Wagner	Information-processing
		  (subtheories)
		    Componential
		    Experiential
		    Contextual

Multiple intelligences	Gardner	Linguistic Logical-mathematical Spatial Musical Bodily-kinesthetic Interpersonal and intrapersonal

Classifications	Terman	Giftedness (135 and above)
		  Longitudinal study
		Retardation
		  Mild (50–70)
		  Moderate (35–55)
		  Severe (20–35)
		  Profound (below 20)

History	Darwin Galton	Species variability Individual differences Correlation coefficient

Test-related concepts		Reliability
		  Test-retest
		  Alternative-form
		  Split-half
		Validity
		  Predictive
		  Construct
		  Concurrent
		  Face
		  Content

Concepts	Names	Terms
Nature/Nurture issues and controversies	Plomin, DeFries, McClearn	Twin studies, family studies
	Jensen	Between-group and within-group differences
Statistical concepts		Central tendency and variability Mean Standard deviation Normal curve Frequency distribution
Prenatal and postnatal influences		Environmental factors present during pregnancy and after birth (e.g., maternal drug use, smoking, alcohol use, malnutrition, AIDS, and health-related aspects of the early childhood setting)

Intelligence Summary

Although interest in intelligence measurement initiated the testing movement, applications of the technique spread quickly to the areas of aptitude, achievement, vocation, and personality. *Aptitude* is a narrower, more specific term than intelligence, and aptitude tests seek to measure much more specialized abilities (e.g., mechanical aptitude, musical aptitude, and so on) than general intelligence tests. To extend the distinction one step further, aptitude differs from achievement in that *aptitude* means *potential for successful performance* and *achievement* means *actual performance*. One could say that, on the basis of their test scores, two particular individuals are more *apt* to do well in mechanical tasks than two others. None of them has performed the tasks or become mechanically proficient as yet, but the test does predict their future performance. Your knowledge in the area should include an acquaintance with:

SAT (Scholastic Assessment Test)
Vineland Social Maturity Scale
Kuder Preference Test
Strong-Campbell Vocational Interest Test
California Achievement Tests
Sequential Tests of Educational Progress
Stanford Achievement Test

Later, as you get into personality and clinical and applied areas, you will look at some representative tests in these areas and make critical distinctions between objective and subjective approaches to testing. For now, it is sufficient to note that intelligence testing "started something" that proliferated into many other areas. In addition to the introductory textbooks, Anastasi's *Psychological Testing* (New York: Macmillan, 1989), Cronbach's *Essentials of Psychological Testing* (New York: Harper Collins, 1990), Kaplan and Saccuzzo's *Psychological Testing* (Pacific Grove, Calif.: Brooks/Cole, 1993), and the October 1981 issue of the *American Psychologist* ("Testing: Concepts, Policy, Practice, and Research") would be excellent sources. If you really are into this area, have the time, and want to do some exploring in depth, you could check into Sternberg's *Handbook of Human Intelligence* (New York: Cambridge University Press, 1982).

COGNITIVE DEVELOPMENT

Two prominent voices in opposition to the intelligence test movement were *Jean Piaget* and *Lev Vygotsky*. Piaget's keen theoretical mind, penchant for observing children, and background in Binet's laboratory equipped him for the unique contribution he made to the field of cognition. His basic disagreement with Binet centered on the notion of structuring the response possibilities for a child. Piaget preferred to let the child be "in charge" of the situation, and he merely observed and sought to systematize what he saw. In short, he attempted to get a glimpse of the child's mental world and how it functioned. His experiments and observations have yielded a wealth of insights into the cognitive capacities of the young mind and the nature of cognitive development. Piaget's world of the child was a physical world, whereas Russian psychologist Vygotsky's focus was the social world. To him, the mind was a product of its social/cultural history and the interactions that mind had with other minds. The absence of such interaction would leave the child animal-like (e.g., the Wild Boy of Aveyron). The presence of such interaction—through parents, teachers, and other key persons in the child's life and experience—socializes the child into the culture. Current research (e.g., Nelson) has taken Vygotsky's premises and studied them in the context of children's social routines. In North American culture, for example, such routines include trips to the mall, McDonald's, birthday parties, and such. In other cultures the routines would be very different—perhaps pottery-making, carrying water from a common well, and so on.

One of the major *concepts* stemming from Piaget's work has been *conservation*—a child's capacity to recognize equivalences when a specific form or arrangement changes. For example, if you took two identical glasses of lemonade and poured the contents of one of them into a thinner, taller glass, a five-year-old might tell you that there was more lemonade in the taller glass than in the original one. On the other hand, a seven-year-old who had witnessed the pouring procedure might chime in that both glasses really contained equal amounts, that the taller glass just appeared to have more lemonade in it. The seven-year-old has cognitively attained conservation in relation to such a demonstration, but the five-year-old has not yet reached such a point in cognitive development. In addition to this concept, you should further acquaint yourself with the following:

Piagetian Terms Outline

Concepts	Names	Terms
Conservation		Number
		Substance
		Length
		Area
		Weight
		Volume
General conservation sequence		Ballpark age of acquisition

Concepts	Names	Terms
Assimilation		Environment is interpreted in terms of the child's existing schema
Accommodation		Child's schema changes through interaction with the environment (i.e., "accommodates" to the environment)
Distinction between stage theory and continuity learning theory		Stage: step-like Continuity: gradual, like an inclined plane (Piaget's is a stage theory)
Stages		Sensorimotor (first 2 years) Preoperational (2–7 years) Concrete Operations (7–11 years) Formal Operations (11–15 years)

Phillips' *The Origins of Intellect: Piaget's Theory* (San Francisco: W. H. Freeman, 1975) is an authoritative source in this area.

PROBLEM SOLVING AND CREATIVITY

If you were to take the expression "thinking and _____" and ask your listeners to fill in the blank, many of them would immediately say "problem solving." Much of the time we spend in thought is directed toward problem solving; thus, the process is a logical target for psychological inquiry. Several species engage in some form of problem solving—rats, cats, pigeons, monkeys, and humans among them—and the complexity level of solution varies markedly across species. If you put a cat or a rat in a puzzle box, you would find that its method of problem solving would be strictly trial and error. Literally by accident, it would bump into the response that gained the desired result and would learn to repeat that response in a similar future situation. Much of our own learning falls into this category, but humans and monkeys also demonstrate a phenomenon that *Kohler* found comparable to *insight*. We also seem to develop a capacity for solving problems that we have never encountered in the past, and it is this capacity that *Harlow* termed *learning set*. Although set is our best friend in some problem-solving instances, it can be a barrier in others. Persistence of set, "functional fixedness" and deeply ingrained rules can sometimes prevent us from attaining the fresh, imaginative approach that some problems may require.

The next step in the problem-solving sequence is *creativity* or creative problem solving. Creativity is a phenomenon that most people can detect far more easily than they can define. "That was a creative idea!" and "She's imaginative and creative!" are much more familiar to us than "Creativity is _____." D. Krech, R. Crutchfield, and N. Livson (*Elements of Psychology*, rev. ed. [New York: Knopf, 1976], pp. 134–35) express the belief that the determinants of creative problem solving lie within (1) the stimulus pattern, (2) knowledge, and (3) the personality. They feel that the stimulus pattern, however, can cause individuals to become too rule-oriented and stimulus-bound so that their minds may tell them, as they approach a solution, that "A hammer can only be used for hammering," or "A yardstick can only be used for measuring." Creativity implies the capacity to go beyond the conventional and traditional. But if one becomes stimulus-bound, individual problem-solving methods are automatically limited to the conventional and unimaginative.

It is not surprising that knowledge can serve as both a help and a hindrance to creative problem solving. Everyone needs a certain amount of knowledge to solve a problem, but too many facts may lock us into the conventional. In the third area—personality—it appears that the creative person needs the ability to tolerate both frustration and ambiguity. Generally speaking, creativity presents an important field of investigation, which currently contains more questions than answers. Haimowitz and Haimowitz (*Human Development* [New York: Crowell, 1960], pp. 44–54) demonstrated an early awareness of the fascination held by the field—along with its unanswered questions.

Current work in the field includes several fascinating avenues of inquiry. *Amabile* cites *three cognitive/personality characteristics* she considers essential ingredients for creativity—expertise in the field; creative skills such as persistence, divergent thinking, and breaking down a problem into its component parts; and internal motivation (e.g., personal satisfaction) rather than external motivation (e.g., money or recognition). *Simonton* points to middle adulthood (46–65) as a time of peak creativity and achievement. *Csikszentmihalyi* underscores the vital importance of parental interaction with their children (e.g., reading to and talking with them, warmly supporting them, and challenging them to develop their talents). *Sternberg and Lubert* consider it essential that the creative person be firmly rooted within the society, its realities and needs, and the experience and knowledge of friends and associates. *Gardner* addresses creativity within the context of multiple intelligences outlined elsewhere in our review—linguistic, logical-mathematical, spatial, musical, body-kinesthetic, and personal. He notes that the "conventional" ways of testing only sample the first three rather than the diversity that includes musical, body-kinesthetic, and personal.

Problem Solving and Creativity Outline

Concepts	Names	Terms
Gestalt	Kohler	Insight
Learning	Harlow	Learning set (i.e., learning a creative approach to new problem settings)
Cognitive/Personality characteristics in creativity	Amabile	Essential elements: Expertise in the field Creative skills (persistence, divergent thinking, breaking down a problem into component parts) Internal motivation
Life-cycle	Simonton	Middle adulthood as peak time of creativity and achievement

Concepts	Names	Terms
Societal relationship	Sternberg and Lubert	Creative individual's firm rooting within the societal context, its realities, and the input of friends/associates
Creativity within multiple intelligences	Gardner	Moves beyond the conventionally tested realms of linguistic, logical-mathematical, spatial, into the unconventional musical, body-kinesthetic, and personal
	Maslow	Creativity within self-actualization
Tests of creativity	Guilford Mednick Barber and Wilson	Divergent thinking Remote associations Creative Imagination Scale

Problem Solving and Creativity Summary

Two of our time-tested maxims get revised in the area of creativity. Don't say them too loudly around grandma or grandpa (or perhaps even mother and dad!):

"Practice makes blindness."
(The idea here being that as you practice a given solution-attempt to a problem, you dig a rut similar to the car wheel that spins in the mud. The more you spin, the lower the likelihood that you'll see creative—and likely more efficient—problem-solving alternatives beyond that "rut.")

"If at first you don't succeed, don't try again."
(In a manner similar to the above, continual trying can create a dead-end rut. Getting away from it and coming back to it later can lend fresh perspective.)

Creativity is a fun area to talk about and an even more fun thing to possess. We wish you the best in your creative review!

As you can see, creativity and intelligence are not synonymous—a fact demonstrated vividly by M. Wallach and N. Kogan in *Modes of Thinking in Young Children: A Study of the Creativity-Intelligence Distinction* (New York: Holt, Rinehart & Winston, 1965). For additional depth in the area of creativity, look into one of these:

S. Arieti, *Creativity: The Magic Synthesis* (New York: Basic Books, 1980). K. J. Gilhooly, *Thinking: Directed, Undirected and Creative* (San Diego, Calif.: Academic Press, 1988). D. N. Perkins, *The Mind's Best Work: A New Psychology of Creative Thinking* (Cambridge, Mass.: Harvard University Press, 1983). A. Rothenberg and C. Hausman, *Creativity Question* (Durham, N.C.: Duke University Press, 1976). A. Rothenberg, *The Emerging Goddess: The Creative Process in Art, Science, and Other Fields* (New York: McGraw Reprint, 1989).

We have covered the vast areas of learning and cognition briefly, but, we trust, carefully and adequately for the purposes of this review. Next, we shall discuss developmental psychology, an even broader and more varied segment of the discipline.

Developmental Psychology

Developmental psychology, one of the most sweeping topical areas in the discipline, encompasses the psychological study of the child, that is, the child's physiological, comparative, sensory, perceptual, and learning characteristics. Thus, the study of child development actually involves everything we have been or will be talking about. For the sake of time and space, however, we will confine our discussion only to those concerns generally included in a course on the topic.

As Papalia and Olds point out in their introductory comments, child development centers upon the *quantitative and qualitative* ways in which children change over time. Not surprisingly, the quantitative changes are more easily measured because they are readily observable. The child's "quantity" changes in both weight and height, and in each instance the change can be systematically recorded. Qualitative changes pose greater problems for the would-be observer. For instance, how can one monitor a child's intellectual, emotional, social, and moral growth? And how does one determine the presence of creativity? Such questions quickly lead away from the straightforward instruments and answers that investigators rely upon in quantitative measurement.

The instruments and techniques necessary for *qualitative* measurement take various complexions. In the *naturalistic approach*, the investigator uses the method of Tinbergen and Lorenz, observing the child in his natural habitat. Large numbers of children are watched systematically at different ages, and these observations yield such data as the average age for walking, talking, parallel play, the presence of conscience, sexual interest, and so forth. *Gesell* and his associates compiled enormous amounts of observational data that enabled them to develop and publish a widely revered work and numerous articles on the average age for the emergence of specific skills and abilities in children.

Another technique, the *clinical method* of child observation, came into prominence with *Piaget*. With this method, the agenda is no longer strictly the child's in the sense that specific, open-ended questions are asked and responses are carefully studied. Whereas no intervention or structure is imposed under naturalistic observation, some intervention is evident in the clinical method—although individual freedom of response continues to be preserved. Piaget was able to use the clinical method to provide insightful glimpses into child thought processes, which previously had been totally unexplored.

A third, and most structured, measurement setting is known as the *experimental approach*. With this method, children may be grouped according to some established basis (e.g., age or socioeconomic status) and be "measured" by means of a standardized procedure, thus permitting response comparisons between groups. Statistical analysis of results enables the investigators to determine whether groups of children differ significantly on the skill or ability being measured. Everyone who has taken a school-administered IQ test has participated to some extent in a standardized, potentially experimental approach.

The development of a child begins at the point of conception, and *prenatal development* is divided into three *stages—germinal* (fertilization to two weeks), *embryonic* (two to eight weeks), and *fetal* (eight weeks to birth).

Specific events are associated with each stage. During the germinal stage, there is rapid cell division and implantation on the uterine wall. In the embryonic stage, rapid differentiation of major body systems and organ development make the embryo particularly vulnerable to influences upon the prenatal environment. Because the mother is, in effect, the prenatal environment, the available research deals with such critical questions as the effects upon the embryo of maternal diet, drug and alcohol intake, and emotional state. Equally critical are considerations relating to illness, exposure to radiation, and mother-embryo blood compatibility. In the systematic, sequential development that is characteristic of humans and animals, impaired development during the embryonic stage is major and permanent. Nature provides no opportunity for compensatory "make-up" work later in pregnancy. In the final stage, the body systems and organs of the fetus that were formed and differentiated during the preceding embryonic stage have the opportunity to grow.

At *birth*, new questions come into focus. Among them are concerns regarding the child's adjustment to the cold, bright, noisy environment beyond the womb. Physiologically, reflexes and sensory capacities are studied, and socially and emotionally, the mother-child relationship is carefully examined for possible links between the child's emotional adjustment and characteristics such as mode and schedule of feeding, maternal warmth, and the like.

During the *first two years*, the child's motor development is of primary import. Have the child's crawling, walking, and so on occurred on schedule? Invariably "the schedule" used as the reference point is the one created by Gesell.

If motor development proceeds without difficulties, language development begins to steal the spotlight. One of the most exciting days for parents is the day their child says her first word, and if that word proves to be in the "socially acceptable" category (ma-ma, da-da, and so on) the day is a joy indeed. Language development is equally exciting for child psychologists. It is obvious that a child receives and understands many words long before she can produce them, and, given the appropriate technology, the reception area may someday become an important exploration ground. For the moment, however, research emphasis centers on the accessible—language production.

Two broad categories in language production are prelinguistic (first year) and linguistic. E. and G. Kaplan ("Is There Such a Thing as a Prelinguistic Child?" in *Human Development and Cognitive Processes*, ed. J. Eliot [New York: Holt, Rinehart & Winston, 1970]) have further defined the prelinguistic category as encompassing the basic cry (first three weeks), sound variety beyond the basic cry (three weeks to four or five months), and babbling (last half of the first year). Babbling consists of vowel-like and consonant-like sounds articulated with imitations of adult intonation. One of the questions that fascinates theorists is whether the transition from babbling to recognizable words is a leap or a sequential step. A related question deals with exactly how the monkey differs from the human in the language area. At one time, *language* use was considered the standard by which humans were rated above monkeys and their relatives, but surprising and convincing studies with chimps have begun to erode that standard. Names with which you should be familiar in this area include: *Kellogg and Kellogg* (early study with "Donald" and "Gua"), *Gardner and Gardner* (work with "Washoe" and the American Sign Language for the Deaf), *Premack* ("Sarah" and "plastic sentences"), and *Rumbaugh* (the fascinating, computer-based Lana project).

Social and personality development become prominent research concerns as the child moves beyond the immediate family to the peer group, and obvious questions relate to the effects that early family influences have had upon the child's personality and social adjustment. Several personality theorists have spoken to these early years and their potential influence. Among the most prominent is Erikson, whose psychosocial theory suggests that foundations for basic trust, autonomy, and initiative are laid during the first five years of life. Freud's earlier theory took a sexual view, suggesting the possibilities of narcissism and fixations and the presence of Oedipal love characteristics. Dollard and Miller sought to combine the Freudian concept with learning principles, indicating that early experiences of hunger and crying in a child's dark bedroom could be the basis for later fear of the dark, overreaction to slight pain, apathy, and overeating. Many child psychologists who have a learning orientation concern themselves primarily with the present behavior of the child and the stimuli that prompt a given behavior. Nevertheless, few psychologists would be willing to defend a position that these early years are unimportant to the child's personality development and social adjustment.

For the *preschool* child—typically viewed as the three to five year old—mental development becomes an important concern. The effects of stimulus-enriched environments both in and beyond the home take on major importance, and most personal vocabularies now include the terms *public kindergarten*, *private kindergarten*, and *day care center*. Research has convinced several state school systems to develop kindergarten facilities for all five year olds, and the preschool years are being increasingly viewed as a time for learning as well as for social adjustment.

As the child *begins school*, she enters what child psychologists call middle childhood. Stretching from ages six to twelve, middle childhood is a critically important time for physical, mental, personality, and social development. Understandably, the development areas are complexly interwoven. A girl who grows quickly and is taller than her male peers, for instance, can expect a social experience that is quite different from that of a girl who is shorter. Erikson sees this period as a time when the child's energies are directed toward "industry" (i.e., school achievement). For many, this involvement leads to the frustration of failure and to feelings of inferiority. It also raises the question of a child's moral development strength in the wake of achievement pressure and competition. This developmental stage terminates with the onset of puberty.

Adolescence begins with the onset of puberty—a time of rapid physical and sexual development accompanied by conflicts and feelings that can make the young person's life difficult and trying. Growth spurts, concern about physical appearance, nocturnal emissions, menstruation, and masturbation are among the factors combining to form the adolescent's complex adjustment picture. Erikson sees the young person at this stage as an individual making a search for identity; he also sees successful achievement of self-identity as essential for meaningful love relationships. A search for identity is, in part, a search for values; and the young person's parental and peer group relationships become dominant factors in this search.

The preceding is a chronological approach to developmental psychology. Now let's review the outline.

Developmental Psychology Outline

Concepts	Names	Terms
Research methods		Cross-sectional (comparing children of various ages simultaneously)
		Longitudinal (studying the same children across an extended time span)
	Based on Tinbergen/ Lorenz utilized by Gesell	Naturalistic approach
	Piaget	Clinical method (partially structuring a naturalistic setting)
		Experimental (highly structured laboratory setting)
Prenatal development stages		Germinal (fertilization to two weeks)(zygote)
		Embryonic (two to eight weeks)
		Fetal (eight weeks to birth)
Teratogens		Substances producing malformations in a fetus (e.g., maternal alcohol intake, smoking, stress, drug use [tranquilizers, cocaine, marijuana], moods [depression])
Patterns of development		Cephalocaudal (head most fully developed first, i.e., a "top-down" pattern)
		Proximodistal (torso center toward extremities)
		General to specific (large motor before fine motor movement)
Relexes in the newborn		Babinski (toes outward and upward to a sole-of-the-foot touch)
		Moro (outstretched arms, legs, and crying to a sudden change in environment or loud noise)
		Rooting (head-turn toward a mild lips/cheek stimulus [e.g., breast or hand])
		Sucking (response to objects touching the lips)
		Grasping (response to objects touching hand or fingers)
		Plantar (toes curl under to a finger-press against ball of the foot)
		Eye blink (to flashed light)
Infant perceptual preferences	Fantz' "viewing box"	Complex over simple; curved over straight; human faces over random patterns or mixed features

Concepts	Names	Terms
Imprinting	Lorenz Hess Scott Harlow	Across-species pattern of following (i.e., bonding with) a moving object present during the critical period for imprinting
Bonding		Emotional attachment between newborn and primary caregiver(s) immediately after birth
Separation anxiety		Fear response when primary caregiver is absent (occurs in 8-to-15-month age range)
Heritability of temperament	Kagan Emde	Shyness Identical twins (temperament)
Stage theories	Piaget Kohlberg Freud Erikson Gesell	Cognitive Moral Psychosexual Psychosocial Physical maturation
Piagetian Stages Kohlberg Stages/Levels		See stage-listing, earlier chart Premoral Conventional morality Moral principles
	Gilligan	(Extension of Kohlberg, gender differences in caring)
Major studies	Berkeley White	Berkeley Growth Studies Harvard Early Education Project (early childhood cognitive/ intellectual development)
	Kagan	Heritability of temperament; cross-cultural study of relationship between environmental stimulation and child intelligence
Testing infant development	Fantz	"Viewing box" and early childhood sensation/perception
	Gesell Cattell Bayley	Scales
Classic studies	Gibson/Walk Sears Bandura	Visual cliff "Conscience of a child" Social learning
Determinants of development		Developmental level = heredity × environment × time (heredity × time is maturation; environment × time is learning)

Concepts	Names	Terms
Six classes of factors in behavioral development	Hebb	Genetic Chemical, prenatal Chemical, postnatal Sensory, constant Sensory, variable Traumatic
Brain development	Thompson	
Continuity vs. stage theory approach to development		
Sensory capabilities at birth		A "blooming, buzzing confusion"? Color vision? No pain in male circumcision? (Check it out!)
Genetic terminology	Tryon Mendel	Singly determined vs. multiply determined characteristics (stemming from "maze-bright/maze-dull" work); Genetics law and distinction between dominant and recessive traits Distinction in twins (monozygotic [identical] vs. dizygotic [fraternal])
Comparative-systems development patterns		Neural (earliest-developing) Reproductive Somatic (general body growth)
Abnormalities/Disorders	 Lovaas	Dwarfism Acromegaly Down syndrome Klinefelter syndrome Autism Aphasia PKU (phenylketonuria) Attention-deficit hyperactivity disorder (ADHD)

Though the preponderance of work in the developmental field has been directed toward children, a look at the entire life span has become increasingly prevalent. The "prime time" and passages of midlife, as well as the adjustment challenges and strengths of the elderly, are far more central in focus than they were ten years ago. Myths about decline in intellectual and sexual activity are being disconfirmed through research, and there is hope that one of our nation's most valuable natural resources—the experience and the insight of the retired person—can be respected and meaningfully shared. The role of the actual or surrogate grandparent in the development of young children is being acknowledged and studied.

The sex stereotypes accompanying aging have been very blatant and identifiable. In both the media and the general societal spectrum, women "age" far more quickly than men. Television drama and the print media perpetuate this inequity and its effects.

Another major focus within developmental psychology stems from the rapid increase in two-parent working households and single-parent families. The impact of both upon the child has been more and more upon the minds of researchers, reflecting, undoubtedly, a prominent uncertainty within the nation itself. Hetherington, for instance, has studied the effect of divorce upon children, an effect extending well beyond the event itself to the prospect of parents' remarrying.

As you review the areas of adolescence, adulthood, and aging, you will notice fewer terms and concepts than you found in the child development area. This distinction is partly a function of the areas themselves, and partly due to the relative recency of work in the life-span area. We have outlined a few of the basic terms and names. In your review you likely will discover others. In apportioning your study time, spend more on child development than on life-span.

Specifying age-markers for each period is somewhat arbitrary, but if they're used as guidelines rather than absolutes, they can be meaningful. Levinson outlined four eras. He based his outline on longitudinal research with forty men. Mercer, Nichols, and Doyle (1989) observed that the stages for men lacked relavance for women because motherhood, career-reentry, etc. were frequently a woman's experience. To acknowledge that difference, they carefully studied women's transitions and came up with a five-stage developmental sequence. Neither Levinson nor Mercer, Nichols, and Doyle subdivide the period beyond age 66. Gerontology researchers now speak in terms of young-old and old-old, further subdividing this age-range. A rough time-line for old-old is 80+.

Life Span Outline

Concepts	Names	Terms
Four eras (male-based)	Levinson	Adolescence (11–17) Early adulthood (18–45) Middle adulthood (46–65) Late adulthood (66+)
Five eras (female-based)	Mercer, Nichols, Doyle	Launch to adulthood (16–25) Leveling (26–30) Liberation (36–60) Regeneration/redirection (61–65) Creativity/destructiveness (66+)
Erikson's Relevant Stages	Erikson	Identity vs. role diffusion Intimacy vs. isolation Generativity vs. stagnation (or self-absorption) Integrity vs. despair
Peck's stage elaboration	Peck	*Generativity vs. Stagnation:* Valuing wisdom vs. valuing physical powers Socializing vs. sexualizing in human relationships Cathectic flexibility vs. cathectic impoverishment (ability to shift one's emotional investments from one activity and person to another)

Concepts	Names	Terms
		Ego Integrity vs. Despair: Ego-differentiation vs. work-role preoccupation Body transcendence vs. body preoccupation Ego transcendence vs. ego preoccupation
Physical, sensory, and intellectual functioning with aging		
Terminology	Bem	Secondary sex characteristics (puberty) Androgynous (incorporating equality and interchangeability in gender roles) Social clock (self-outlined developmental schedule for accomplishment) Ageism (prejudice and discrimination toward the elderly)
Gender schema theory	Bem Maccoby	That children and adolescents use gender and gender-specific roles as their way of organizing and perceiving the world
Changing lifestyles	Hetherington	Effects of divorce on children (generally speaking, less impact on younger children and an adjustment period of approximately two years)
Dementia-types		Reversible Alcoholism Malnutrition Toxic Irreversible Alzheimer's disease Multiple infarct (small-stroke-related)

Life Span Summary

Fascinating developin' critters, aren't we! For heading beyond your textbook and exploring across the life span or given parts of it, here are some reference possibilities:

Child Development

D. Papalia and S. Olds' *A Child's World: Infancy through Adolescence*. New York: McGraw, 1996.

Adolescence

David E. Balk's *Adolescent Development: Early through Late Adolescence*. Pacific Grove, Calf: Brooks/Cole, 1995 (intro-level work). Douglas C. Kimmel and Irving B. Weiner's *Adolescence: A Developmental Transition*. New York: Wiley, 1995 (more advanced work).

<u>Adulthood</u>
B. Lemme's *Development in Adulthood*. Boston: Allyn, 1994.

<u>Life-Span</u>
Barbara M. Newman and Philip R. Newman's *Development through Life: A Psychosocial Approach*. Pacific Grove, Calf.: Brooks/Cole, 1995. Jeffrey S. Turner and Donald B. Helms' *Lifespan Development*. Ft. Worth, Tex.: Harcourt Brace College, 1995

Motivation and Emotion

A quick look through any graduate school catalog will indicate that motivation and emotion—although they are perhaps not inseparable terms—are often seen together.

MOTIVATION

Motivation generally is defined as a social or psychological condition that directs an individual's behavior toward a certain goal. Drive, on the other hand, is a biological condition that performs a goal-direction function. The distinction is that a rat probably turns right in the T-maze because it has sensations of hunger or thirst, not to preserve its self-esteem. In the cases of both motivation and drive, we have to infer that they exist on the basis of what the animal or person does. We note the relationship between a stimulus and a response and then say, "Aha, the little four-legger was hungry!" or "Yep, I see a lot of love messages in the glances those two have been exchanging!" Each of these cases involves a stimulus (food pellet, lover) to which an organism responds (by turning right in the alley or sending affectionate glances). In short, on the basis of what we see, we infer.

To keep from switching terms in general discussion, the word drive is sometimes prefaced with "biological," "psychological," or "social." Our discussion of motivation will follow this pattern.

Biological Drives

Biological or primary drives have certain common elements, including: (1) the maintenance and preservation of the organism; (2) homeostasis (the tendency toward achieving and maintaining a state of balance); and (3) the quality of preempting all other drives. Entries in this group include hunger, thirst, pain, respiration, fatigue, body temperature, and bowel and bladder tension. The commonalities of biological drives can be easily illustrated. For example, if a person is hungry, his or her sonnet-writing and guitar-picking behavior stops temporarily (is preempted) until the hunger drive has been reduced. The tension of the drive itself creates a disturbing imbalance within the individual, requiring that the tension be relieved and balance be restored (homeostasis). The entire behavior sequence has survival at its root (maintenance and preservation of the organism).

Psychological Drives

These drives have the common characteristic of seeking to establish mental-emotional well-being. Psychological drives include sex, curiosity, and gregariousness. Sex seems to have many biological drive characteristics. It does not qualify as a full-fledged biological drive entity, however, because its arousal is as actively sought as its reduction (not homeostatic), and though it is essential for the survival of a species, it is not necessary for the survival of an individual organism (despite what your date may tell you!). Its power as a motivator is well known to advertisers, who utilize it as a selling aid for products ranging from magazines and entertainment to automobiles and cigarettes. Motivational research in this area has reached a point where even foods have been categorized as masculine or feminine.

The second major psychological drive—curiosity—is defined as a need to explore. Romanes, Thorndike, and Harlow have been among the researchers who have found that monkeys will perform a task or learn a response without any tangible reward except the opportunity to explore and discover. In one instance, the curiosity reward was the opportunity to see an electric train in operation. Translated to the human level, curiosity is exemplified by our desire to know what is on the moon or on Mars or Venus. Curiosity is the penchant to explore, to discover, to know.

The third psychological drive—gregariousness—is the drive for affiliation among humans and other species. One yardstick for measuring emotional trouble in a friend might be the observation that he or she stays alone a good deal and does not mix. The capacity for interaction with others is seen as an aid in maintaining mental and emotional well-being.

Social Drives

Learning is the common element among drives in this category. We must learn to associate some kind of basic need gratification with these entries, or they never gain the capacity to motivate us. The normal means by which these entries gain their motivating qualities is an association with an element (food, maybe) that satisfies a primary drive. A person learns that with this element he or she can obtain whatever is necessary to satisfy biological or psychological drives. Entries in this category include money, achievement, and freedom from anxiety. You will inevitably encounter additional entries in some of the reference books you come upon. The above-mentioned entries—particularly money and achievement—will be found universally in your sources. Surprisingly, chimps have paralleled the human social drive for money. In an apparatus called a "Chimp-O-Mat," they have been known to work diligently for tokens that they could later exchange for food.

Motivation Outline

Concepts	Names	Terms
Theories:		
Instinct	Darwin, Lorenz, Tinbergen	Adaptive function
Tension-reduction	Epicurean-based (hedonistic)	Maximize pleasure and minimize pain
	Psychoanalytic (Freud)	Tension builds and must be released
	Homeostasis (Cannon)	Primary (biological) drives preempt other activities until these drives are reduced
	(Hull)	(Hull considered this the basis of all learned behaviors.)
	Needs hierarchy (Maslow)	Physiological, safety, belongingness and love, esteem, self-actualization (Note: both a tension-reduction and enhancement entity)

Concepts	Names	Terms
Arousal-enhancement	Optimal state	
	Berlyne	Optimal-arousal
	McClelland	Optimal-incongruity
	Intrinsic motivation	
	White et al.	Competency drive
	Opponent-process	
	Solomon	Pleasurable stimuli evoke an opposing inhibitory process
	Sensation-seeking	
	Zuckerman	Sensation-seeking personality
Acquired-type	Need-Press	
	Murray	Several environment-activated needs (measured by his Thematic Apperception Test [TAT])
	Expectancy-value	
	Tolman	Repetition of behaviors bringing
	Rotter	outcomes we value
	Achievement need	
	McClelland	A basic achievement motive or
	Atkinson	need to achieve (nAch)
Terminology definitions and distinctions		
Drive		Internal state of tension prompting activities designed to reduce the tension. (Drive includes the concepts of energy, activity level, arousability, and the arousal/cue functions of stimuli.)
Incentive		External stimulus catalyst for behavior. It includes reward and response predisposition based on deprivation, learning, and heredity.
Biological aspects		Homeostasis
		Eating behavior elements such as predisposition-based weight level (role of cells and the hypothalamus)
		Precipitating factors (blood glucose, stomach, taste, and external precipitators)
Homeostasis		Organism's physiological state of equilibrium
Instinctual aspects		Ethology and fixed-action patterns
		Sign stimuli
		Action specific energy
		Imprinting (and critical periods)

Concepts	Names	Terms
Physiological regulatory mechanisms		
Blood glucose level	Mayer	Regulating hunger by the level of blood glucose. (A partial, but not total explanation.) Glucostats (glucose-sensitive neurons) appear to be liver-based, sending signals to the vagus nerve and, from there, to the hypothalamus.
Hypothalamus		Central role in regulating hunger and other physiological needs. (Stimulating the rat's lateral area prompts overeating; stimulating the rat's ventro-medial nucleus stops eating behavior.)
Insulin		Secreted by the pancreas, it enables cells to extract glucose from the blood.
Nonregulatory physiological		
Sex drive	Masters and Johnson	Phases in human sexual response cycle: excitement (vasocon-striction), plateau, orgasm, resolution
Nonphysiological motives		
Affiliation	Schachter, Maslow, Bowlby, Murray, et al.	Association and bonding need (differs for extroverts [generally high] and introverts [generally low])
		Bowlby's early work with orphans and "wasting away" suggested a physiological, survival component
Intimacy	Erikson, McAdams, et al.	Warm, close dyadic relationships
Achievement	McClelland, Atkinson	Driven by mastery of the difficult challenge
Pleasure centers	Olds and Milner	Repeated electrical self-stimula-tion to an animal's limbic system
Dopamine hypothesis		Self-stimulation most effective when stimulating nerve fibers in the medial forebrain bundle (MFB), implicated in the release of dopamine

Outline Terms Elaborated

Theories of Motivation

➤ **Instinct** (behavior patterns "wired in" and occurring automatically in the presence of certain stimuli):
Darwin, Lorenz, Tinbergen, et al. studied the adaptive significance of instinctual behaviors.

➤ **Tension-Reduction:**
Pleasure-Pain (hedonistic) (Epicurean background): Actions are selected to maximize pleasure and minimize pain.

Psychoanalytic (hydraulic model—build-up/release) (Freud): Build-up of tension, as in a pressure-cooker or boiler, which must be released (catharsis). There are life and death instincts (eros/thanatos). Drive for sexual gratification is basically motivating and is either satisfied directly or through indirect means such as fantasy and creativity.

Drive (biologically based arousal states): Principle of homeostasis (Cannon). Basis of all learned behaviors (Hull).

Needs Hierarchy: Maslow developed a five-level needs hierarchy. The first four—physiological, safety, belongingness and love, esteem—he termed "deficit needs" (as in "filling a hole"). The fifth—self-actualization—is growth-oriented and enhancing. It is here that a person realizes her potential.

➤ **Arousal-Enhancement-Type Theories:**

Optimal-State Theories: Optimal-Arousal (Berlyne): There is an optimal arousal state for maximal efficiency. Below it we are bored, and above it we are anxious. Optimal-Incongruity (McClelland): Each of us has a personal adaptation level and finds small deviations from it pleasant and stimulating. Large deviations are anxiety-producing.

Intrinsic Motivation (White et al.): There is an internal drive to develop our competencies and to accept challenges that will promote our individual growth. There is a related motivation to have personal control over events affecting our lives.

Opponent-Process (Solomon): Pleasurable affective stimuli evoke one brain-process that then triggers an opposing inhibitory process. The opposing process is gradual and lasts longer than the pleasurable stimuli, having major implications for a vicious-cycle-type phenomenon for drug users and other substance abusers. As the drug user comes down from a short-term, pleasurable high, a longer-lasting depression trough lies ahead. The reverse sequence would be true in the case of unpleasurable initial affective stimuli.

Sensation-Seeking (Zuckerman): This approach theorizes a sensation-seeking personality trait and suggests that it has four components: (1) thrill and adventure-seeking; (2) experience seeking; (3) disinhibition; (4) susceptibility to boredom. These four components are measured in Zuckerman's Sensation-Seeking Scale.

➤ **Acquired-Type:**

Need-Press (Murray): Developed by Murray and measured within his Thematic Apperception Test (TAT), the approach theorizes several needs and motives that are activated by the pressure of environmental stimuli (people and settings, for instance). Murray postulates an elaborate list of needs, including abasement, achievement, aggression, play, dominance, understanding, and so forth.

Expectancy-Value (Tolman, Rotter, et al.): Based on the purposive behavior work of Tolman, this approach suggests that we come to expect certain outcomes for given behaviors and place a value on those outcomes. We are then motivated to repeat those behaviors that bring an outcome we highly value.

Achievement (McClelland, Atkinson): This theory postulates a basic achievement motive or need to achieve (n Ach). People high in n Ach welcome new challenges and are constantly seeking to attain high standards and to excel. (Ah, just like you as you prepare for the GRE!)

Aggression is a drive that does not classify neatly into any of the above categories but has characteristics of each of them. Psychoanalytic theory views aggression as instinctual (most of us spending much of our unconscious time trying to "throttle it"); drive theorists see aggression as the result of frustration (giving it characteristics of a psychological drive perspective); and social learning theorists consider it a response that stems from observational learning and imitation (television viewing and computer/video-game playing by children is becoming an area of major concern within this perspective). With its increasing prevalence in our social milieu, it likely will remain strong as a research concern as well. Two of the classic theoretical positions influencing this field have been the Berkowitz position that frustration leads to a readiness for aggression (whether aggression itself will occur depending upon the presence or absence of aggression-eliciting stimuli in the situation) and Bandura's observational learning of aggression (children playing aggressively after viewing a television model attacking a plastic, air-filled Bobo doll). The latter has often been cited when aggression and television concerns have been expressed with regard to children. These and additional topics related to motivation will surface in our discussion of social psychology.

EMOTION

Emotion is a logical companion of motivation. When we attain (or fail to attain) a goal, words like joy, anger, delight, and depression enter the picture. We express a feeling . . . an emotion. On the physiological side, emotional expression can prompt a number of changes, including:

- Striated muscle changes controlled by the central nervous system—facial expressions, vocal expressions, muscle tension, tremors, and so on.
- Autonomic changes controlled by the autonomic nervous system and endocrine glands—heart rate, blood pressure, digestion, blood-sugar level and levels of acidity, epinephrine and norepinephrine, metabolism, breathing rate, sweating

Measurement of emotions has been prominent in the areas of:

- "Lie detector"—breathing, heart rate, galvanic skin response (GSR)
- Pupil size—increase in pupil size signifying increased interest, pleasant stimulus, heightened mental activity

A theoretical question of long standing has focused on whether the cognitive, experiential aspects of an emotion precede physiological arousal or whether, on the other hand, the emotion is experienced as a result of the physiological arousal. Theoretical positions of importance to you include:

- James-Lange Theory (emotion a result of physiological arousal)
- Cannon-Bard Theory (neurological)
- Schachter epinephrine studies

Among the cues to use in detecting someone's emotions are the following:

- Verbal (least reliable, Mehrabian)
- Facial (reliable cross-culturally for basic, simple emotions, Ekman)
- Situational context (essential to judgment of complex emotional expression, Frijda)
- Behavior

There is no doubt that prominent *learned* aspects are present in many emotional responses. For instance, a child may learn how much a cut finger hurts and how profusely to respond to such a trauma by the amount of parental fuss, alarm, and attention given similar preceding events. Where one child may cry a lot, another may hardly shed a tear—such is the parental "burden" in shaping human emotions.

Solomon's research in the *opponent-process* aspect of emotion (cited in the motivation outline) carries some far-reaching implications for the future of this field. In blatantly oversimplified form, the opponent-process theory states that our brain is oriented toward suppression of emotion—keeping our functioning at a homeostatic baseline. Consequently, an emotion being experienced prompts the brain to trigger its opposite in an effort to reinstate balance. The theory has many implications relating to abnormal psychology and the use of drugs. When a stimulant wears off, for instance, the emotional trough may be deeper than it was initially. The pattern evident with addiction—initial highs moderating over time (as the opponent process response becomes more rapid) while subsequent depression becomes more pronounced—fits this theory impressively.

Advances in brain research have provided extensive understanding of the role of brain mechanisms in emotion. We have come a long way from the days of *Phineas Gage's* railway accident in 1848, which transformed a gentle, soft-spoken man into an impulsive, irritable person with unpredictable fits of profane emotional outburst. It was then that scientists began their long road toward understanding the role of the limbic system in emotion. Subsequent understanding of brain mechanisms has revealed not only a close "working relationship" between the cerebral cortex and the limbic system, but two basic "operational loops"—one involving the cerebral cortex, the limbic sytem, and motoric (behavioral) functions, the other involving the cerebral cortex, the hypothalamus, and the autonomic nervous system (blood pressure, heart rate, skin temperature, glands, and so on). There is also convincing evidence that the right cerebral hemisphere holds primary responsibility for recognizing and mobilizing appropriate responses to emotion-eliciting stimuli and settings.

Another aspect of emotion-based research that is gaining increasing research attention and understanding is the very basic and important relationship between the emotions and physical health. With the increased pressure and complexity of American lives and lifestyles, the entire area of stress and its effects on physical health is coming under close scrutiny. *Bernard* first recognized the potential *consequences of stress*. *Cannon* was a pioneer in suggesting that we had a built-in mechanism—the *fight-or-flight reaction*—that protected us from physical danger. *Selye* further refined and extended that position, developing an understanding of the *stress-related response patterns* within the endocrine system and the autonomic nervous system. Focusing centrally on the adrenal gland, he found that a stressor prompts the organism's pituitary gland to secrete adrenocorticotropic hormone (ACTH)—this should sound familiar, based on your earlier review of the endocrine system. ACTH, in turn, signals the adrenal gland to secrete corticosterone. This hormone is key to producing the physiological changes found in the stress response. The growing area of behavioral medicine is taking a global look at the relationship between emotional and physical health. You can expect considerable spotlight in this area in the years to come.

Emotion Outline

Concepts	Names	Terms
Elements in emotion		Cognitive (subjective)
		Physiological (arousal)
		Behavioral (action)
	Plutchik	"Plutchik's Circle"—mixing emotions to produce new blends
	Lazarus	Four types: resulting from harm, loss or threat; resulting from benefits; borderline (e.g., hope and compassion); complex (e.g., grief, bewilderment, curiosity)
	Turner and Ortony	Focus on components of emotions rather than basic emotions themselves
	Lewis and Saarni	Five basic elements: Elicitors (triggering events) Receptors (brain mechanisms) States (physiological changes) Expressions (visible changes) Experience (interpretation)
Cognitive	Ekman	The smile is universally interpreted cross-culturally
Physiological Nervous system Sympathetic		Prepares body for emergency (i.e., "fight or "flight") (e.g., dilates pupils, accelerates heart rate, inhibits digestion, releases glucose)
Parasympathetic		Controls the normal operations of the body (keeps the body running smoothly) Calms everything down (e.g., heart rate) after emergency
Brain-body pathways		Two pathways: Through the autonomic nervous system releasing catecholamine hormones mobilizing the body for emergency response Through the pituitary gland and endocrine system controlling corticosteroid hormone release, increasing energy, and inhibiting tissue inflammation
Behavioral Nonverbal	Ekman and Friesen	We can correctly identify seven facial expressions: happiness, sadness, anger, fear, surprise, disgust, and contempt. (Cross-cultural agreement in facial expressions of fear, disgust, happiness, and anger interpretation.)

Concepts	Names	Terms
Theories		
Physiological	James-Lange	I run, therefore I'm afraid—the action precedes the emotion. The emotion results from the physiological arousal.
	Cannon-Bard	I'm afraid, therefore I run—challenged the James-Lange Theory.
Cognitive	Schachter-Singer	Arousal and physiological change are interpreted on the basis of context (e.g., I'll "feel" what those around me are feeling).
	Valins and Reisenzein	Arousal not a prerequisite for experiencing an emotion. Cognitive processes alone can do it. Challenged Schachter-Singer.
	Frijda	Cognitive appraisal and action tendencies occur simultanously.
Multicultural	Shaver	People universally organize their emotions with six basic categories—love, joy, anger, sadness, fear, and surprise.
Effectiveness	Yerkes-Dodson Law	Increases in motivation and arousal bring increases in emotion. A mid-range level of arousal lends to optimal performance effectiveness.
Social stimulation need	Harlow	Contact comfort (rhesus monkeys feeding on a terry cloth "mother")
	Bowlby	Early Foundling Home studies of orphans and the importance of social stimulation to survival
Measurement		Lie detector test (monitoring breathing, heart rate, and galvanic skin response [GSR])
	Holmes-Rahe	Social Readjustment Rating Scale (SRRS)
	Spielberger	State-Trait Anxiety Scale
Stress terminology		
Anxiety		Generalized fear
	Spielberger	State vs. Trait Anxiety
Stress		A nonspecific emotional response we make to real or imagined demands on us
Frustration		Resulting emotional state when a goal is thwarted or blocked
Conflict		Approach, avoidance, and approach-avoidance (the latter related to a single stimulus)

Concepts	Names	Terms
Stress and physical health	Friedman and Rosenman	Type A personality: competitive, aggressive, impatient, hostile Type B personality: relaxed, patient, easygoing, amicable Relationship to physical diseases such as rheumatoid arthritis and heart disease Relationship to a weakened immune system (Note: Both relationships are correlational and subject to controversy within the field.)
Moderating factors	Gore Kobasa Greenberg Benson Dixon Spielberger	Social support Hardiness (marked by commitment, control, and the excitement of challenge) Exercise Relaxation and mediation Humor Releasing pent-up emotions
Stress syndrome	Selye	General Adaptation Syndrome (three stages): alarm, resistance, exhaustion

Emotion Summary

Spanning several decades, Selye's work has had a profound impact upon the field. He once observed that the world is comprised of "racehorses" and "turtles." The racehorses find stress exciting and are highly motivated by it. The turtles require a calm, quiet environment for their functioning.

Having completed this much of your review, you may feel both relieved and happy; that is, you may experience both a motivation and an emotion, companions throughout human existence. Motivation and emotion lead naturally into the next two areas of psychology that we shall discuss, social and personality. You will notice that we have put social psychology before personality. Our reason is that we feel that personality builds a skillful bridge to the clinical and psychopathology areas that follow.

Social Psychology

Social psychology connects sociology and clinical psychology. Whereas the sociologist is concerned with the study of groups and the clinical psychologist works with the concerns and problems of the individual, the social psychologist studies the behavior of the individual within the group and the effects of the group upon the individual's behavior. If the area sounds sweeping to you, it is! This review spotlights some of the major areas of social psychology and discusses briefly certain aspects of each. In deference to the breadth of the field and the limitations of the review, however, a list of terms, concepts, and names concludes this section.

ATTITUDES AND ATTITUDE MEASUREMENT

If you were asked to select the most prominent area of research within social psychology, your best bet would be to select the study of attitudes. It is estimated that approximately half the research in the field deals with some aspect of attitude formation and change. Definitionally, many researchers in the field indicate that there are three components essential to the existence of an attitude: (1) cognitive; (2) emotional; and (3) behavioral. If we know something about cars (cognitive), get a "charge" out of working on them (emotional), and frequently can be spotted under the hood of some four-wheeler (behavioral), we have an attitude about cars. Knowledge alone, without emotional feeling, does not qualify; and the only way an attitude can be detected is through some form of behavior (working on cars frequently, answering an opinion poll, and so on).

Because attitudes are a prominent concern, researchers in the field have spent quite a bit of time and effort designing and standardizing attitude measurement scales. The earliest efforts in this area were those of *Thurstone*. Following very rigorous procedures for item selection, he developed a scale technique known as "equal-appearing intervals." This term encompasses both the underlying concepts and the procedures used in developing such a scale. For example, the experimenter might ask 200 people to act as judges, whose job would be to categorize a large group of statements that had been written on a specific subject (war, for instance). They would read each statement, decide to what extent it was favorable or unfavorable (i.e., for or against war), and place it in the category corresponding to their rating. There would be twelve categories into which the judges could sort these statements. Categories 1 or 2 would receive the statements that were felt to be strongly antiwar, while categories 10 or 11 would receive strongly prowar statements. As you can imagine, it would take a long time for 200 judges to sort a large group of statements into these categories.

When the judges had completed their sorting, the weeding out and selecting of statements for the final scale would begin. The best candidates for the final scale would meet two criteria: (1) low variability among the judges (meaning that a statement did not get placed into categories 1 or 2 by some judges and 10 or 11 by others); and (2) equal representation of all statement categories (meaning that the statements in the final scale would be equally distributed across the twelve-category range). The second criterion prompts the "equal-appearing intervals" description associated with Thurstone scaling procedures. After the above series of steps, the resulting scale would be a collection of approximately twenty statements. Judges would then be asked to read those statements, checking the ones that were in agreement with their respective viewpoints on the subject. By adding the category weightings of these statements (1, 2, 4, 7, 10, 11, and so on) and obtaining a mean score, the scale administrator would be able to determine where in the twelve-category range the judges' attitudes on this subject happened to be. Scale results would indicate, for instance, whether they were prowar or antiwar.

Because the judging, categorizing, and statement-selecting procedures must be repeated for each subject on which one wishes to develop a Thurstone-type scale, it is easy to understand why attempts have been made to simplify scale-development procedures. One of the earliest and best-known attempts was that of *Likert*. Likert believed that it was important to have judges express their own attitudes on a subject rather than to ask them to make general "anti" or "pro" judgments in relation to others' attitude statements. In keeping with this belief, he developed a scaling procedure known as the "*method of summated ratings.*" The response range on a Likert scale item encompassed five categories (strongly agree, agree, no opinion, disagree, strongly disagree). A strongly "pro" response on a given item was scored as a 5, and this meant that the person with the most prominent "pro" attitude on the subject received the highest overall score on a Likert scale. Correspondingly, the person with the strongest "anti" attitude on the subject received the lowest overall score on the scale. In this procedure, called "summated ratings," it is important that a person's score on each individual item in the scale correlate positively with the person's overall score.

A number of scale measurement approaches concentrating on specific measurement purposes followed these early beginnings. One was *Guttman's unidimensional approach*, in which he sought to measure a range of depth on a given attitude dimension. In a scale itself, he arranged this depth measurement sequentially. This means that, if a subject had a very slight agreement attitude on the attitude dimension, the person would agree with the first item in the scale. If a subject had a stronger agreement attitude, the person might agree with the first two scale items, and so on. In theory, it was an approach whereby Guttman claimed the ability to discern what specific items in his scale the subject has agreed with, simply by knowing that person's overall scale score. In practice, prediction has not always been that neatly accomplished, but the method proved innovative and important.

Another specific-purpose scale was *Bogardus's "social distance scale."* This scale had a seven-phrase description range that could be used in relation to a number of different identifiable ethnic groups or nationalities. For whatever groups or nationalities that were being tested in a given situation, a person had a response range from (1) "would admit to close kinship by marriage" to (7) "would exclude from my country." Several modifications of this scale technique have been made—the best-known recent one being that of Triandis.

Osgood developed the "*semantic differential scale.*" In this scale, the subject is given a concept—such as church, capital punishment, or whatever—followed by a series of bipolar adjectives (e.g., good-bad, honest-dishonest, clean-dirty, and so on). Between the two poles (good-bad, for instance) there are seven spaces, and the subject's job is to place a check in one of those spaces. A check in the spot next to "good" receives a score of 7 and, correspondingly, a check next to "bad" receives a score of 1. There are several sets of these bipolar adjectives, thus allowing for a large possible range in which scores can occur. Through factor analysis, Osgood has discovered three dimensions to be tested—evaluative, activity, potency. The first of these dimensions is tested with adjectives such as good-bad; the second with adjectives such as active-passive; and the third, with adjectives such as strong-weak. The key dimension, and the one measured most prominently within an Osgood scale, is the evaluative one.

Public opinion polling is familiar to us and constitutes another measurement approach in this area. Unlike the preceding approaches, public opinion polling seeks to obtain a response percentage figure that can serve as a base for comparison when subsequent polls are conducted on the same question or attitude dimension. The "white elephant" in this area, which served as a great lesson for subsequent pollsters, was a presidential poll conducted by the *Literary Digest* in 1936. The *Digest* used the telephone book as the source of names to be included in its samples. Conducting a poll using these names, the *Digest* predicted that Alf Landon would win the election by a landslide. When Roosevelt's strength at the ballot box smothered Landon's election hopes, it also smothered the *Literary Digest*. Because the *Digest's* managers had failed to realize that the names in the phone directory did not constitute a representative sample of the voting public, they had polled an unrepresentative sample and correspondingly had made an erroneous prediction. The *Literary Digest* went out of business, but the lesson of representative sampling was remembered well by other would-be pollsters—especially George Gallup, whose American Institute of Public Opinion has become a byword in polling. Polling techniques have become very refined, and polls are depended upon heavily by certain groups, notably politicians. Pollsters warn, however, that they are not predictors of an outcome but, instead, monitors of an opinion as it exists within a sample at a specific time.

Scaling techniques continue to develop. Among current entries on the scene is *Bem's Scale of Psychological Androgyny* (a measure of sex-role stereotypes). If your androgyny scale score were low, you would be considered high in sex-role stereotyping, and vice versa. Since current research emphases in the field provide needs for new or modified measuring instruments, the development of new scales and techniques will no doubt continue.

Attitude measurement now has ventured well into the field of physiological instruments. For a long time we have known about *galvanic skin response (GSR)* as a measure of lie detection. That time-honored device is now joined by new cousins such as the facial electromyograph (EMG), which detects subtle muscle cues of positive or negative attitudes toward a stimulus the person has just heard or seen. Cacioppo and colleagues make frequent use of the EMG and the electroencephalograph (EEG) in their attitude measurement work. We can expect more melding and blending of response scales and physiological instruments in the years ahead. Then, of course, there's that wonderful piece of impressive looking equipment that subjects are told will detect their lies and true feelings on even the most socially sensitive questions. The instrument looks convincing enough, and unwitting subjects opt toward honest responding, but in reality it doesn't measure a thing. It's called the *bogus pipeline*.

ATTITUDE CHANGE

Among the best-known names in the area of attitude change is *Festinger*. His *theory of cognitive dissonance* has been the source of a broad range of experimentation in this field. In effect, Festinger's theory says that there is a tendency for people to seek a state of consonance between their attitudes and their behavior. Someone is in a state of consonance when behavior in a given belief-area corresponds to one's attitude in that area. After formulating his theory, Festinger's next step was to create a dissonance between the person's attitude and behavior. Subjects were induced to behave in conflict with an attitude they held. He predicted that in order to regain the comfort that comes with consonance, the person's attitude would tend to change in the direction of the behavior that had been performed. For instance, a conscientious objector who had been forced to use a rifle in frontline army combat would begin to change his attitude in favor of this behavior.

Several researchers have refined Festinger's original theory. For example, Cialdini makes the point that a person's degree of cognitive dissonance will depend upon the strength of that person's need for consistency. Cooper and Fazio set out four steps they consider basic to the occurrence of cognitive dissonance. Will the attitude-discrepant behavior have *negative consequences*? Will the person feel *personal responsibility* for those consequences? Will the person be *physiologically aroused*? And will the person *attribute* that arousal to his or her behavior?

Aronson and other researchers extended this theory to the area of initiation-type settings. If we go through some pretty unpleasant behavior in order to meet the requirements for joining a group, we justify having gone through this behavior by enhancing our valuation of the group. We say, in effect, "This is a tremendous group and well worth the initiation requirements we went through in order to join." If this seems farfetched, check with some of your friends who have joined a sorority or a fraternity recently and ask them whether they are glad they joined. Better yet, ask your dad or one of his friends whether he is glad he had the experience of basic training in the military, or ask your friend whether she is glad she went through recruit-hazing at the military academy. In each of these instances, one's tendency to say that the experience was worth the trouble is an example of cognitive dissonance—a means of self-justification.

Petty and Cacioppo have developed the Elaboration Likelihood Model (ELM), which both extends and modifies some of the original work in the field. The model states that people use either a central or a peripheral route to decision making. In the central route, people are highly motivated and give careful thought and extensive deliberation to the decision they are making. In the peripheral route, people have low motivation and give very little thought or deliberation to the decision they are making. These routes are two ends of a continuum, and different influence strategies work for central and peripheral. For example, classical conditioning techniques or simple exposure work well on the peripheral route, but would have little or no impact on the highly discerning person following the central route. Correspondingly, creating a positive mood would prominently influence the low-motivation, peripheral route person but would have little or no impact on those following the central route. The central route is influenced by promoting concepts that people value and find relevant to them. Here, slight variations in expression can make the significant difference. Rather than saying, "Society will benefit from this recycling campaign," the pronoun "*You* will benefit . . ." makes the critical difference.

ATTRACTION AND AFFILIATION

Determinants of Attraction

To answer the question of why persons are attracted to one another, several possible determinants have been mentioned and investigated. *Proximity* is one of the most prominent of these determinants. Whyte found that within a new housing development the single best predictor of social attraction and friendship development was the distance between houses. Friendship and social attraction were far more likely between persons living next door to each other than, for instance, between people living down the street from each other or in different blocks. Festinger and his associates did a similar study in an apartment complex containing several two-story buildings with five apartments on each floor. Social attraction and friendship patterns again were found to be most prominent in the next-door setting and weaker as one moved additional doors away from any given apartment. This finding introduced the concept of functional distance—functional because, although two or three doors away is not all that far in terms of actual physical distance, the principle of proximity still seems to hold.

A second determinant—*similarity*—has been investigated prominently by Newcomb, Byrne, and others. Newcomb put the variables of proximity and similarity in competition with each other by setting up a dormitory room assignment procedure and carefully assigning rooms on the basis of either similar or dissimilar interests and values. Of major concern was whether sheer proximity (being roommates) would determine attraction patterns or whether similarity in interests and values would be the major determinant in attraction. The outcome revealed that proximity operated short-range but that similarity determined the long-range attraction patterns. Byrne and his associates used a questionnaire technique to establish within their subjects either perceived similarity or dissimilarity to another person's attitudes. Typically, Byrne might present his subject with the results of a questionnaire that presumably had been filled out by another person—but actually had been based on the subject's responses to an earlier questionnaire. The subject's reactions yield strong evidence of attraction on the basis of perceived similarity (i.e., agreement between the subject's responses and those of the "other person"). This evidence of attraction holds even in situations where the perceived "other person" has been represented as being a member of a different ethnic group or nationality.

Aronson and Jones are among the leading researchers who have investigated a third determinant—*rewardingness* (and its ingratiation counterpart). In effect, they have found that individuals are attracted to persons who care about them (reciprocity) and will be very wary about persons whose "care" seems to have within it the possibility of an ulterior motive. Concentrating on the rewardingness aspect of attraction, Aronson and his associates have also found that persons are more likely to be attracted to individuals who have evaluated them positively than to individuals who have negatively or neutrally evaluated them. A surprising finding was that attraction was most prominent in instances where the evaluation had moved from an initially negative one to an eventually positive one. The strength of the attraction in such instances is attributed to the combined effects of negative reinforcement (removal of an aversive stimulus) and positive reinforcement (positive evaluation); and this phenomenon provides the basis for Aronson's gain-loss model, cited later. Jones, working with ingratiation, found that persons are attracted to individuals whose positive evaluation does not carry the prospect of subsequent commitment or expectation. Counterpart to this outcome is the finding that flattery or ingratiation is most effective when directed toward an area in which the recipient has never been sure of having competence but has wished for such competence.

Anderson's work deals with *personal attributes* as a basis for social attraction. He is concerned with the general question of whether there are personal traits that people collectively find attractive. Using an adjective-rating approach, he found that the highest rating among 555 adjectives was invariably given to the traits of honesty, sincerity, and trustworthiness. Correspondingly, the lowest rating was given to words connoting liar or phony. Anderson is a pioneer in this area, and his work has been prominently utilized in the categories of attribution and person perception.

Zajonc has investigated the determinant of *familiarity* and has found it to be a prominent factor in social attraction. In one of his studies, he had persons look at Turkish words (totally meaningless to the viewing persons). He offered some words only one or two times, but showed others as often as twenty-five times. Following the viewing procedures, the persons were asked to define the words they had seen. The words seen most often were accorded the most positive definitions. This generally is referred to as the *mere exposure effect*.

Research also bears out the sad reality that we favor beauty. Not only are we attracted to physically beautiful people, but we attribute to them more positive characteristics—friendly, warm, good listeners, and so on. Snyder's classic study of men thinking they were talking with either a beautiful woman or an average-appearance woman bore out this sad reality quite dramatically. The pattern extends to lengths of sentences given by judges and people's impressions of each other in job interviews, for example. But there's a downside, too. Beautiful people can never be sure whether those who interact with them are being genuine or superficial. In the relationship context, even here, the principle of similarity seems to apply. Berscheid, Feingold, and others have found a *matching hypothesis*—that those who are dating, engaged, living together, or married are equivalent in physical attractiveness.

Attraction Models

Social psychologists have found it helpful in both their communication and their research to develop models of attraction. The following—briefly cited—are among the most prominent of these models:

Balance (A-B-X)

Developed through the work of *Heider* and the more recent theoretical concepts of *Newcomb*, this model is built upon persons A and B having attraction feelings toward each other and toward person or concept X. In the resulting A-B-X triad, the model indicates that consonance or a state of balance exists when there is an even number of negative signs. Imbalance exists where there is an odd number of negative signs. For example, suppose that Jack likes rock music, his dad does not like rock music, and Jack likes his dad. The situation within this triad is imbalance (one negative sign). Balance can be restored if Jack changes his views about either rock music or his dad (bringing a second negative sign into the triad). Obviously, all + signs in the triad also represent balance—both Jack and his dad liking rock music, and Jack liking his dad. The model is usually demonstrated as a triangularly positioned triad with signs placed between the entries. For example:

Student

\+   \+

Parent   —   Group
or Concept

The balance model is frequently used in explaining and demonstrating a phenomenon such as cognitive dissonance.

Social Exchange Theory

Gergen is one of the most prominent names associated with this theoretical view. Simply stated, the theory puts social attraction in the context of a person's rewards from interaction divided by the person's cost incurred in the interaction. When costs outrun rewards, social attraction can be expected to decline and disappear. Moreover, the most favorable fraction (rewards/costs) will be the front-runner when a choice must occur in social attraction. If, for instance, a college student is dating back home and on the campus, the back-home relationship must be proportionately more rewarding than the on-campus one to remain comparable in strength—maintaining the back-home relationship involves more cost. According to the social exchange theory, people continually scan and evaluate reward/cost in their social relationships.

Rusbult has extended these basic social exchange principles of attraction into the area of close, committed relationships. She notes that attraction principles were developed on the premise of strangers and that important additional considerations need to be added in the area of close commitment. She proposes and has researched three categories of variables: (1) the degree of positive feeling one has about her/his partner (based on the extent to which the partner gratifies this individual's important needs in areas such as intellectual, companionship, intimacy, sexuality); (2) the quality of alternatives (other options in your region and age range); (3) level of investment (resources attached to the relationship and degree of loss if it were to end). The basic attraction principles continue to apply, but, as Rusbult vividly demonstrates, they take on important additional variables as relationships move toward closeness and intimacy.

Complementarity Theory

Winch is associated with this view, the primary application of which is in the area of extensive, intimate relationships such as courtship and marriage. This theory says, in effect, that such relationships require that aspects of personality be complementary in order for the relationship to be successful. Two people who both have strong dominance needs would be seen as heading for disaster in such a relationship. Success in the relationship would be achieved only if a strong dominance need on the part of one person were met by a low dominance need on the part of the other (in effect, complementarity). Because it is relationship-specific and symbolically "messier," this theory runs no real interference with its tailor-made prospective opponent—the balance model.

Festinger's Social-Comparison

This model demonstrates how perceived similarity and social attraction tend to interact. Essentially, *Festinger* is saying that (1) people are attracted to persons they perceive as similar to themselves; and (2) they perceive the persons to whom they are attracted as more similar to themselves than is really the case. Those "perceived similar others" take on special significance in ambiguous decision-making or opinion-forming situations. When we are faced with contradictory or ambiguous information and have to make a decision, we will rely heavily on the opinion of this "perceived similar other" person. This dynamic can be potentially disastrous in close, intimate relationship decisions, because we overlook the major differences that very likely exist between us. Yes, we very well may be "attracted to perceived similar." But beware of that next step—"perceiving those to whom we're attracted as more similar than they really are." The "snowball" effect within Festinger's concept is readily apparent—social attraction feeds perceived similarity, which feeds more social attraction, and so forth.

Aronson's Gain-Loss Model

In studies such as the one performed by *Aronson and Linder*, it was found that movement from a negative to a positive evaluation of a person led to stronger social attraction toward the evaluator by the person being evaluated than did movement from a neutral position toward positive evaluation. Aronson quotes Spinoza's observation that "hatred which is completely vanquished by love passes into love and love is thereupon greater than if hatred had not preceded it." Within this kind of situation, it has been suggested that a kind of double or compound reward operates, with (1) the removal of the aversive stimulus operating as negative reinforcement and (2) the presentation of a desired stimulus operating as positive reinforcement. Unofficially, this has been termed "Aronson's law of marital infidelity." The woman who receives a compliment from a stranger finds that compliment more rewarding than an equivalent compliment received from her husband. The husband—beginning from a general position of positive reinforcement—lacks the capacity to be as rewarding as the stranger (who begins from a neutral position). Thus, the close friend or spouse constitutes a less potent source of reward but a strong and more potent source of punishment.

The distinction between attraction and affiliation is that between positively evaluating other people (attraction) and simply being with other people (affiliation). Schachter conducted a classic series of studies on the affiliation dimension and found that, in a situation of experimentally induced stress, persons were discriminating in their choice to be with other people. Given an option of simply being with other people, being with other people experiencing the same situational stress, or being alone, those persons having only the choice of simply being with other people preferred to remain alone—and those persons having the choice of being with others in the same situational stress preferred affiliation over being alone. Schachter concluded that, in the presence of fear, misery loves miserable company. Conducting similar studies in which both unrealistic fear (anxiety) and realistic fear were introduced, Sarnoff and Zimbardo found that in high-anxiety settings persons preferred to remain alone. (This was interpreted as hesitancy to share their unrealistic fear with others because of the risk of embarrassment.) Thus, the research findings indicate that people have a tendency to affiliate with "similar situation others" in cases of high fear and a tendency to prefer being alone in cases of high anxiety.

Theories of Love

Within our models of attraction, we already have touched upon many of the dynamics relating to love relationships. Ancient writers gave us six types— ludus (game-playing, uncommitted), storge (friendship), mania (demanding, possessive), pragma (pragmatic or practical), agape (giving, altruistic), erotic (passionate). In gender comparisons, men score higher than women on ludus, while women score higher than men on storge, mania, and pragma.

As you might imagine, thoughts and theories abound in this area, but we haven't the time nor space to discuss them. Two of the best known are Rubin's distinction between liking and loving and Sternberg's Triangular Theory of Love. The points of Sternberg's triangle (going top, counter-clockwise) are Intimacy, Passion, Commitment. He then makes point-linkages such as Intimacy + Passion = Romantic Love; Intimacy + Commitment = Companionate Love; Passion + Commitment = Fatuous Love.

COMMUNICATION

Two tracks operate within this heading—verbal communication and nonverbal communication. The former deals with communication via words; the latter refers to ways in which social communication occurs without words.

Verbal Communication

Specific communication patterns and leadership styles are prominent research concerns within this area. Their relevance is also strongly felt in organizational areas of applied psychology, though, and thus, to avoid duplicate review coverage, these topics will be considered in the Applied Psychology section. Janis introduced the concept of groupthink, which indicates the decision-making problems that can beset a group because of thought patterns that the sheer existence of the decision-making group can promote. He analyzed in detail the *groupthink* phenomena surrounding the Kennedy Administration's decisions that culminated in the Bay of Pigs invasion. Among the character-istics of groupthink are: (1) illusions of invulnerability; (2) evolution of a rationale (justifying the group's decision); (3) belief in the morality of the group's decisions; (4) stereotyped views of the enemy; (5) conformity pres-sures; (6) self-censorship of critical thoughts (the individual censoring self and not expressing critical thoughts to the group); (7) mindguards (persons in the group who suppress information divergent from group opinion); and (8) illusion of unanimity (an illusion of unanimity within the group despite unexpressed individual doubts).

Janis believes that groupthink is likely to occur when (1) the decision-making group is highly cohesive, (2) the group is insulated from other, more balanced information, and (3) the leader has preconceived notions of the cor-rect policy to follow. To prevent groupthink, Janis underscores the importance of arranging group conditions in such a manner that individual thought and expression are encouraged.

Among media effects, the following terms are generally familiar:

- *Two-step communication flow*—refers to the media communication pattern of first reaching the opinion makers in a given group or com-munity (step 1) so that they will then influence their respective con-stituencies (step 2). The opinion makers need not be the "pillars" of the community, but they are those persons within any given group who have the basic opinion-reference function in that group.
- *Media elite*—refers to the pattern of influence associated with specific persons in a given communications medium. For instance, in television news there are certain commentators toward whom the rest of the tele-vision commentator community turn in developing their own approaches to news events. This term, therefore, refers to an influence within the medium itself.

Nonverbal Communication

Two avenues form the basic investigation areas here—kinesics and proxemics. *Kinesics* is the study of body language—the ways in which people unwittingly communicate through their gestures, facial expressions, body positions, and so on. Pioneering work in this area was done by *Birdwhistell*. He concentrated upon the face and the development of a notation system for each aspect of facial expression. This approach was considered *micro*. A *macro* approach was undertaken by a *Birdwhistell* associate named Scheflen. Within Scheflen's approach, general patterns of interaction over a period of time were studied. *Ekman* has concentrated upon the possibility of *universal facial expressions* and has spent much time studying the smile in various cultures. He concludes that the smile is a universal expression—a general communicator across all the cultures he has studied. Other research in this area includes the work of *Kendon* and that of *Goffman*. Possessing a theoretical mind, Goffman has been the stimulus for many research studies conducted in this area.

Proxemics deals with research relating to territoriality, that is, personal space, unseen dividing lines, and the dynamics of invading another's personal space. Key work in this field was spearheaded by *Hall*, who suggested four territorial zones—intimate, personal, social, and public. The first of these zones is believed to extend to approximately eighteen inches from the body; other zones become increasingly distant. Implications for urban crowding may be a future outgrowth of work in this area.

PERSUASION

In this area, concerns relating to both noncoercive and coercive persuasion come into view. The latter includes brainwashing techniques and techniques formerly used in police interrogation; the former deals with general persuasion techniques as used in public speaking, advertising, and the like.

Techniques in General Persuasion

Several concepts have been advanced in this area. Among them is *McGuire's inoculation theory*, which states, in effect, that people can be "immunized" against a subsequent persuasive communication if they have been familiarized in advance with the persuasive arguments they are going to hear, and have heard counterarguments. *Freedman* introduced a *foot-in-the-door* technique that demonstrates that we are more likely to agree to a large, commitment-type request if we have agreed in advance to a smaller commitment request. This is the salesman's familiar approach of getting a small commitment now and returning to ask for a larger commitment later. Janis found an eating-while-reading effect that indicated that people were more likely to acquiesce to a request or agree with a viewpoint if it were presented during a pleasurable activity such as eating.

The *door-in-the-face* technique begins with a huge commitment potential, and relief comes when a more modest option is presented. Suppose we're preparing for Uncle Leroy's visit, so we head for the liquor store. The salesperson shows us a $150 bottle of wine and we find our throat sinking deep into our stomach. Just then the salesperson says, "However, we have this wine available for $20." Ah, relief! *Ask-and-You-Shall-Be-Given* relates to the high likelihood that a person will respond positively to our request on behalf of a charitable, worthy cause. *Low-balling* is our tendency to stay with a commitment we've made after the initially low stakes have been raised. The car salesperson initially told us we could have the car for $9,000. Then, by design, a discovery was made that $10,000 was the lowest they could go. We'll likely still spring for it.

The age-old notion that "actions speak louder than words" gets borne out within modeling. We remember once having heard that 75% of what children learn from parents, the parents did not intentionally teach. As we model positive behaviors, the message is a compelling one for others.

Additional concepts in this area include the sleeper effect (a comunication that has no immediate effect but proves to have long-range influence), the primacy-recency effect (whether first-communicator or last-communicator position in a presentation sequence is most effective), and two-sided/one-sided communication (whether persuasive communication will be most effective if both points of view are presented or if only one view is presented). In primacy-recency, the major question is how long after the communication will the audience members be making their decision. If the decision is soon or immediate, recency would apply (i.e., the last communicator in the sequence would be the most influential). If the decision is distant, primacy would be most effective. Out of necessity, we have oversimplified this area. Communicator characteristics and credibility are among the additional concerns central to investigations undertaken here.

Techniques in Coercive Persuasion

Schein is associated with the study of brainwashing techniques and has subdivided the general approach into a physical phase and a psychological phase. The physical phase occurs first and includes such things as exhaustive, forced marches at night (accompanied by sparse food, little or no medical attention, the leaving behind of those who cannot keep the rigorous pace, and captor explanation that all this is made necessary by the ruthless aggression of the captured soldiers' armed forces). The psychological phase begins upon arrival at the captors' camp facility. Leaders are separated from the group, original insignia of rank are no longer recognized, prisoners are rewarded for informing on fellow prisoners, incoming mail is read and only the unpleasant news is relayed, prisoners are rewarded for making confessions of their "wrongs" against the captors and for "admitting" the burden of guilt they feel at having engaged in such unfortunate aggressive behavior. The ultimate goal is to gain converts to the cause of the captors, but Schein has observed that the goal is seldom realized. Although a number of prisoners have been found to make confessions and testimonials, few convert.

GROUPS

Conformity

Sherif did the earliest work in this field with something called the *autokinetic effect*. Using a small beam of light, he would ask subjects individually to make a judgment of how much it moved (ah, but the light wasn't moving at all!). Individuals would make different judgments and he would then combine groups of three who had made divergent judgments. They had to come up with an agreed-upon judgment. Later, when again asked for their individual judgments, Sherif found that the individuals had moved toward the group judgment. *Asch* introduced the *line-judgment technique* in which seven or eight persons acted as confederates in unanimously making an obvious error in judgment. Next, the unsuspecting subject was asked to respond. Findings indicate the subject's prominent tendency to go along with the obviously wrong judgment that has preceded. If confederate unanimity is broken, such conformity is far less likely.

Crutchfield developed an indirect means of imposing conformity pressure that relieves the need to have a large number of persons serve as confederates. His technique involves five individual booths, each equipped with a light panel. Via the panel, a subject presumably sees how persons occupying the other four booths have responded to questions. In actuality, each booth occupant is being given the same light-panel-response feedback from a control room. Although this technique enables every participant to be a subject, it is one step removed from the conformity pressures imposed through direct interaction.

Additional conformity influences you will pick up within your review include *informational influence* and *normative influence*. *Informational influence* occurs when the conforming person does so because she or he believes the others are correct in their judgment. *Normative influence* occurs when a person wishes to avoid the negative consequences or, perhaps, ostracism, of differing with the group.

Hollander felt the necessity of moving beyond a conformity-nonconformity terminology. He believed that within the nonconformity category there could be both persons who were reacting against conformity and those who were behaving independently on the basis of their own preferences (regardless of the conforming trend). To characterize this distinction, he introduced the terms *anticonformity* and *independence* (replacing *nonconformity*).

Cooperation-Competition

Sherif and Sherif did a classic field study utilizing subjects from a boys' summer camp. Through prearrangements, they established two basic groups, which they soon found to be very hostile toward each other. The only technique that the investigators found effective in reducing this hostility was the introduction of a *superordinate goal*—a desirable corporate goal that neither group could accomplish alone (e.g., finding the problem with the camp's water supply, or getting the camp's disabled food truck moving again). Whereas merely bringing the groups together only served to aggravate the hostility, the superordinate goal proved effective in hostility reduction.

In a more formalized laboratory setting, *Deutsch* has studied the dynamics of *cooperation-competition*. His Acme-Bolt Trucking Game involves two players and a single main route to their respective destinations. The game has the capacity to give each player a roadblock potential, and Deutsch has found that a player who is given such threat potential is very likely to use it.

Game decision theory (gaming) has also been prominently developed for investigating the dynamics of cooperation and competition in laboratory settings. A major distinction in this area is that between the zero-sum game and the nonzero-sum game. In the *zero-sum game*, the gains of one player are made at the direct expense of the other; the *nonzero-sum game* allows each player to make intermediate gains. The nonzero-sum game has been prominently adopted in the characteristic research on cooperation-competition. A game involves a payoff matrix. Within a matrix, each player can make one of two choices. Each player knows in advance that the payoff will depend upon the choice made by the other player. In the "*Prisoner's Dilemma*," both players can make intermediate gains if they cooperatively refrain from trying to maximize individual gain. If they both try to maximize individual gains, they will both suffer great losses. The matrix concept allows several payoff possibilities to be established and investigated. Names prominent to this area include *Thibaut*, *Kelley*, and *Tedeschi*.

VIOLENCE

As a prominent social concern, violence and aggression have been natural subjects for social-psychological inquiry. Aggression can be defined as behavior intended to inflict physical or psychological injury/pain. Among boys, aggression tends to be physical—fists or weapons. Among girls, aggression tends to be verbal—the cutting remark. *Dollard and Miller* gave an early conceptual framework to the field with the *frustration-aggression hypothesis*. Their hypothesis indicates that frustration (being blocked from a goal or having the goal removed) leads to aggression. *Berkowitz* has been concerned with the effects of *aggression-eliciting stimuli* upon a potential aggressor. He has found that the presence of weapons heightens both the likelihood and the level of aggression. *Bandura* has investigated modeling effects—for instance, the effect of viewing an aggressive model on television. He finds that a child's aggression is heightened immediately following observation of a model who has been rewarded for aggressive activity. In the case of television, Siegel has suggested that a more long-range result of violence viewing is the expectation that children come to associate with specific roles in society. One of the most blatant examples of this is the role-violence differential between male and female roles as socially communicated and defined. *Wolfgang* believes that our society has, in effect, legitimized violence. Among subtle sanctions he sees in support of this position are the society's toleration of physical disciplining of children by their parents and the institutionalization of sanctioned violence through wars. *Zimbardo* investigated vandalism, violence, and his concept of deindividuation. In effect, the latter indicates that when people lose their identities or become anonymous within the larger group, they are likely to engage in aggression and violence. *Milgram* conducted perhaps one of the most frightening investigations in this area. Through a shock-administering experiment, he found that people are surprisingly obedient to commands to administer high-level shocks to other people.

Two recent models focus on the role of arousal and thought (cognition). Zillmann and Bryant link aggression to arousal and affect. To grossly oversimplify their *arousal-affect model*, if you or I have been physically aroused (perhaps just had strenuous physical activity) and someone calls us a *#@!, we're much more likely to aggress than if we had not been physically aroused prior to the insult. Berkowitz's *cognitive-neoassociation analysis* suggests that our thoughts and our feelings interact. In this context, a person interprets the situation, considers their feelings and weighs the consequences of aggressive action. In many respects, this is not far removed from the frustration-aggression hypothesis element of aggression displacement or scapegoating—not decking your boss because the consequences would be too costly, but kicking your dog when you get home.

HELPING BEHAVIOR

The investigation of helping behavior grew out of the scientific interest in thought-numbing incidents of violence. The catalyst was the Kitty Genovese murder in the Forest Hills section of Queens, New York in 1964, when thirty-eight persons were known to have watched the half-hour, gruesome ordeal. What was so shocking was the fact that no one tried to help or call the police. *Darley and Latane* spearheaded early investigations and, in their laboratory studies, found the number of other persons present to be a prominent variable—with the likelihood of anyone helping decreasing as the number of bystanders increased. *Bryan, Test, and Piliavin* have found the model variable to be important. If a model of helping has preceded the incident in which a person is called upon to help, the likelihood that that person will help is greater than the likelihood present in a no-model setting. Allen has found that directness of request is also important—that there is a greater likelihood of obtaining help when the help request has been specifically addressed to the would-be helper. Another variable that has been found to be important by Darley et al. is the clarity of the helping situation—whether the person requesting help really is in an emergency situation. Batson's research adds another critical element to the likelihood of helping. If we're in a hurry and on a tight time schedule, we're far less likely to help than if we are not time-pressured.

There are ingredients for endless debate on the question of whether we are, by nature, helpful creatures or whether we help others only to satisfy our own ego needs. Batson's research supports the view that we are by nature helpful, empathic individuals. Cialdini's research suggests a *negative state relief model*—that our empathy makes us feel sad with and for the individual and helping that individual enables us to feel good—in effect, egoistic motivation rather than altruistic. The results are inconclusive. Take your choice!

PREJUDICE

Prejudice is defined as an attitude against an identifiable group, formed without knowledge of or familiarity with specific members of the group. The word *prejudice* gives definitional meaning and clarity to this attitude. *Allport's The Nature of Prejudice* summarized early work in the area. and *Clark and Clark* provided basic early work with young children. The latter investigators found that young black children some years ago expressed a preference to be white, but recent replications such as *Hraba and Grant's* have indicated that this preference pattern no longer exists. That turnabout may be interpreted as indicative of both personal and racial pride. Rokeach et al. experimentally pitted attitude and race similarities/differences against one another to see which would prevail. Similarities in attitude proved far more favorable in attraction and liking than similarities in race. The challenge becomes that of getting to know individuals, which serves to weaken and dilute group stereotypes. Pettigrew—one of Allport's former students—is among the most prominent research authorities in the area.

Tajfel and Turner propose *social identity theory*, which allows us to enhance our individual self-esteem by our association with the groups to which we belong. This identification creates a sense of *in-group favoritism*—in effect, "us" and "them." As Cialdini has pointed out, this also enables us to engage in "BIRGing"—"Basking in Reflected Glory" of groups with whom we identify at the same time that it creates "in-groups" and "out-groups."

PERSONALITY

Adorno's The Authoritarian Personality took a post-World War II look at the question of whether attitudes (particularly anti-Semitism) were related to general personality traits and characteristics. The large, comprehensive study uncovered a relationship between the authoritarian personality and attitudes of anti-Semitism and prejudice. The authoritarianism scale developed within this study has been widely used in other contexts and is commonly referred to as the F-scale. *Rokeach* has extended this avenue of research and introduced the concept of *dogmatism*. Also related to this general area is the term *Machiavellianism* as introduced and investigated by *Christie*. Anderson's *information integration theory* proposes that our impressions of others are formed by a combination of (1) our own personal disposition (the perceiver) and (2) a weighted average of the target person's characteristics.

Related to our helping behavior discussion is the question of whether there is an altruistic personality. Batson, Eisenberg, and others have suggested that there is, and that it is based upon a combination of empathy and an internalized, high-level of moral reasoning.

STATUS AND ROLES

In this area, we will briefly concentrate upon a handful of concepts and terms. Achieved-ascribed status distinction is between status attained on the basis of one's own achievement and status accorded on the basis of given characteristics such as family line, wealth, and so on. Interrole-intrarole conflict distinction is made between conflict experienced in meeting the expectations of two different roles (e.g., daughter and fiancée, son and fiancé) and conflict experienced in meeting expectations within a single role (e.g., professor and student differences in expectations for the role of college student). The former is "inter," the latter, "intra." Distributive justice refers to comparing your reward-minus-cost to that of another worker. If, for instance, one worker is not as well educated as another but earns more money, distributive justice does not prevail and worker discontent can be anticipated. Status congruence refers to a person's tendency to make all aspects of the individual's status congruent.

Currently, the investigation of sex roles constitutes a major research emphasis within this area. *Bem* has introduced the term *androgyny* to refer to sex equality in status and role opportunities and expectations. Her Scale of Psychological Androgyny is one of the instruments used to measure the presence of sex-role stereotypes. Williams, Bennett, and Best have made a distinction between sex roles, sex-role stereotypes, and sex-trait stereotypes—a distinction that they have built into their measurement instrument in this area. Their Adjective Checklist is used to determine the presence of sex-trait stereotypes.

Eagly underscores stereotypical tendencies within her *social role theory*—a tendency to picture women as secretaries and men as CEOs, for example. Deaux and Major believe the tendency to stereotype depends on the *perceiver*, the *target*, and the *situation*. Some perceivers are *gender schematic* and will tend to have stereotypical perceptions of women and men. Other perceivers are *gender aschematic* and will have balanced, non-stereotypic perception tendencies. Targeting persons by their appearance may trigger a given gender stereotype, and given situations and settings can trigger stereotypes as well.

ATTRIBUTION THEORY

A recent and growing area of investigation, attribution theory encompasses several of the topics already reviewed. The initial model in this area was *Heider's analysis-of-behavior model*:

$$\text{Behavioral effect } (E) = f \text{ (environment + personal force)}$$

Heider's formula states that behavioral effect is a function of environment and personal force. Research is concentrated upon determining the extent to which perceivers will attribute another person's behavior to external or internal causation. Jones and Davis have found that when external forces are strong and a person goes against those forces, the person's behavior is likely to be attributed to internal causation. Similarly, there is difficulty in attributing internal causation when the person's behavior is normative or in keeping with group behavior.

A quick look at findings in the broader spectrum indicates, for example, that when men and women perform equally well on a given task, women are seen as trying harder (Taylor, Kiesler, et al.); people tend to perceive their own behavior as situationally controlled and that of other people as internally caused (Jones and Nisbett). Hastorf et al. have found that people with unusual histories (handicap, psychiatric hospitalization, and so on) will have any nonnormative actions attributed to that background. In "Lennie B" experiments concerning the severity of accidents, Walster found that there is a tendency to attribute more responsibility to the person at fault (i.e., internal causation) when the accident outcome is severe than when it is mild. Perhaps one of the most telling findings was that of Jones—discovering our tendency to attribute very high or very low performance to internal causation. Hence, the familiar comment that "the poor are poor because they're lazy and don't want to work."

To explain why people attribute internal causality to others, *Shaver* formulated a *defensive-attribution hypothesis* suggesting that the prospect of bad or unfortunate consequences occurring by chance threatens self-esteem. It therefore becomes a kind of self-defense to attribute internal causation to others. Lerner's *just-world hypothesis* indicates that people like to believe that the world is just and that individuals get what they deserve.

Theories to become familiar with include Jones' *correspondent inference theory*, which relates to our tendency to infer personality or situational causation, and Kelley's *covariation theory*. In Kelley's view, for something to be the cause of a behavior it must be present when the behavior occurs and absent when it is not. Get familiar with terms like Tversky and Kahneman's *availability heuristic* (our tendency to judge on the basis of the likelihoods that readily pop into our minds), Ross' *false consensus hypothesis* (our overestimating the extent to which others share our attitudes and opinions), and Ross' *fundamental attribution error* (our tendency to vastly overestimate the role of personal dispositional factors and vastly underestimate the role of situational factors).

Fiske and Taylor have been on the forefront of a movement called *social cognition*. It distinguishes the way people perceive things and people, and in the people context it outlines three patterns of how people are perceived. The *naïve scientist* is very methodical. The *cognitive miser* cuts corners and takes shortcuts that can head down misleading or blind alleys. The *motivated tactician* can be either very careful—perhaps even cunning—or quite careless as her or his motivations and the situation dictate.

Although it is somewhat superficial and oversimplified, we hope that this review section has given you some familiarity with the field of social psychology and its areas of research. In your further review, the concept-name-terminology sheet may provide a helpful checkpoint. As you seek mastery of concepts, names, and terminology, the following textbooks might prove valuable:

R. A. Baron and D. Byrne *Social Psychology*. Boston, MA: Allyn & Bacon, 2000 (an effective "Key Points" format throughout). S. Brehm, S. Kassin and S. Fein *Social Psychology*. Boston: Houghton Mifflin Co., 1999 (thorough with good end-of-chapter reviews). D. Myers *Social Psychology*. New York: McGraw, 1999 (good coverage breadth).

Social Psychology Outline

Concepts	Names	Terms
Attitude Formation and Change		
Cognitive dissonance theory	Festinger Aronson	Attitudes move in the direction of behavior—a drive toward consistency
	Cialdini	Strength of need for consistency
	Cooper/Fazio	Four steps basic to cognitive dissonance: negative consequences, personal responsibility, physiological arousal, and arousal attribution
Elaboration likelihood model	Petty/Cacioppo	Two routes to persuasion: central (convincing content) and peripheral (attractive or expert source)
Self-perception theory	Bem	Situational inference
Reactance theory	Brehm	Motivation to reestablish one's freedom after perceived-unjust restriction

Concepts	Names	Terms
Measurement	Thurstone	Equal-appearing intervals
	Likert	Summated ratings
	Guttman	Unidimensionality
	Osgood	Semantic differential
	Bogardus	Social distance
	Remmers	Generalized Thurstone
	Gallup	Polling and quintamensional filtration
Distinction between objective and projective techniques		
Single stimulus factor	Kelley	"Warm-cold" variable

Attraction/Affiliation		
Models	Newcomb/Heider	Balance (A-B-X)
	Festinger	Social comparison
	Winch	Complementarity
	Gergen	Behavior exchange
	Aronson	Gain-loss
Attraction determinants	Whyte/Festinger, et al.	Proximity
	Newcomb/Byrne	Similarity
	Aronson/Jones	Rewardingness/ingratiation
	Anderson	Personality attributes
	Zajonc	Familiarity
Affiliation	Schachter	Stress

Intimate Relationship Attraction		
Liking/Loving Distinction	Rubin	Friends/committed lovers
Intimate Social Exchange	Rusbult	Degree of positive feeling
		Quality of alternatives
		Level of investment
Triangular Theory of Love	Sternberg	Intimacy, passion, commitment

Communication (Verbal)		
Elements	Klapper	Source
		Channel
		Audience
Source aspects		Credibility
		Attractiveness
		Power
Patterns	Bauer	*Centralized:* Y / chain / wheel
		Decentralized: Circle, star, all-channel
	Lewin/Lippitt/White	Autocratic/democratic
Group effects	Janis	Groupthink
Media effects	Klapper	Direct and indirect effects
		Two-step communication flow
		Media elite
		Third party

Concepts	Names	Terms
Communication (Nonverbal)		
Proxemics (territoriality)	Hall Ardrey	Personal space
Kinesics (body language)	Birdwhistell Scheflen Ekman Mehrabian Kendon Goffman Wilson	Micro Macro Universal expressions Liking Dominance Responsiveness Sociological/Primal Sociobiological roots
Persuasion		
Advertising	Markin	Freudian vs. existential

Coercive techniques
  Brainwashing
  Interrogation
	
	Schein
		
		Phases:
		Physical/psychological
		Structured environment and
		  intentional distortions

Groups		

Conformity (research eras)	Sherif
	Asch
	  Crutchfield
	
	Milgram
		Autokinetic effect
		Line-judgment technique
		Booth adaptation of Asch
		  technique
		Action (as distinct from signal)
		  conformity, using a shock
		  generator and implied harm to
		  another person

Compliance-inducing techniques	McGuire
	Freedman
	Cialdini
	Doob/McLaughlin
	
	Bryan/Test
	
	Skinner
		Inoculation theory
		Foot-in-the-door
		Door-in-the-face
		"Ask-and-You-Shall-Be-Given"
		  (the tendency, if it's a worthy,
		  charitable cause)
		Low-balling (sticking to one's
		  commitment after the initially
		  low stakes have been raised)
		Modeling positive behaviors for
		  others
		Incentives for performance of
		  desired behaviors
		Primacy/recency
		Two-sided vs. one-sided
		  communication
		Sleeper effect

Cooperation-competition	Sherif and Sherif Deutsch	Superordinate goal Acme-Bolt trucking game Use of threat

Concepts	Names	Terms
Game decision theory (gaming)		"Prisoner's Dilemma"
		Payoff matrix
		Zero-sum and nonzero-sum
	Thibaut/Kelly	Fate and behavior control
	Tedeschi	Impression management
Risk-taking	Wallach/Kogan/Bem	
Theories of collective behavior	Smelser	
	Freud	
	LeBon	"The Crowd"

Violence

Concepts	Names	Terms
Frustration-aggression hypothesis	Dollard/Miller	Displacement and "scapegoating"
Aggression-eliciting stimuli	Berkowitz	
Cognitive neoassociation analysis	Berkowitz	Thought/feeling interaction
Modeling	Bandura	
Arousal/Affect Model	Zillmann/Bryant	
Socialization	Wolfgang	
	Zimbardo	Deindividuation
Obedience	Milgram	Shock generator

Helping Behavior (Altruism)

Concepts	Names	Terms
Determinants	Latane/Darley	Number of bystanders
	Bryan/Test	Model
	Piliavin	
	Allen	Directness of request
Egoistic/Altruistic Debate: Inherently Altruistic	Batson	Empathy a critical variable
Negative State Relief Model	Cialdini	Makes us feel good
Good Samaritan Model		Act is voluntary
		Act is potentially costly
		No anticipation of reward
Steps in intervention helping	Latane/Darley	Notice
		Interpret as a help-requiring situation
		Take personal responsibility
		Choose form of assistance
		Implement assistance
Concept of overload	Milgram	Adaptive responses:
		Less time to each input
		Disregard low-priority inputs
		Redraw boundaries
		Block entrance to system
		Filter
		Specialized institutions

Concepts	Names	Terms
Prejudice		
Theories	Allport	Historical Sociocultural Situational Psychodynamic Phenomenological Earned Reputation
Social Identity Theory	Tajfel/Turner	Enhance individual esteem through our group belonging
Basking in Reflected Glory	Cialdini	Basking in the successes and status of other group members "BIRGing"
Attitude/race dimensions	Rokeach	Attitude similarity prevails over race dissimilarity
Attitudes among children	Clark and Clark Hraba and Grant	Racial awareness Racial self-identification Racial preference Racial prejudice
Personality		
Authoritarian personality	Adorno	
Dogmatism	Rokeach	The open and closed mind
Machiavellianism	Christie	
Dimensions	Rotter McClelland Kuhn	Internal/external control Achievement need (nAch) Self-concept
Person perception Information Integration Theory	Schlosberg/Woodworth Anderson Anderson	Recognition of emotions Additive/averaging model Combination of perceiver disposition and weighted average of target person's characteristics
Perceptual defense	McGinnies Bruner/Postman	
Status and Roles		
Class and class measurement	Brown	Subjective Reputational Objective (based on criteria)
Role conflict		Inter-role Intra-role

Concepts	Names	Terms
	Homans	Distributive justice Status congruence
	Bem and Bem	Androgeny
Attribution		
Definitional model	Lewin/Heider	Behavioral effect $(E) = f$ (Environment + Personal force)
Principle		The degree to which we attribute other people's behaviors to external circumstances or internal motivations
Specific attribution patterns	Jones/Davis Steiner Jones/Shaver et al. Taynor/Deaux et al. Jones/Nisbett Goffman/Hastorf et al. Walster Lerner	Nonnormative Perceived freedom Ability Sex-role Self vs. other Responsibility "Lennie B" experiments Just-world hypothesis
Fundamental attribution errors Actor-observer effect		Assuming internal (motivational) causation for other people's behavior and external (situational) causation for one's own behavior
Learned helplessness	Seligman	Assuming that nothing one does can make any difference in a person's life (i.e., attributing total external causation)
Self-serving bias		"Halo"-type evaluation of one's own behavior and motives
Social cognition	Fiske/Taylor	People perceived as: naïve scientists, cognitive misers, motivated tacticians

Personality

You have all heard at one time or another the expression that someone "has personality," and you have no doubt given thought to your own personalities at times. It is easier to spot personality than to define it, but the many definitions of the term carry the common elements of: (1) relatively enduring qualities in our behavior; (2) uniqueness; and (3) comprehensiveness. "Jan swats a fly" says nothing about Jan's personality, because it is a statement about a behavior of the moment that has an automatic quality about it. In addition, everyone swats flies (even cows), so it really says nothing to distinguish Jan from anyone else. On the other hand, someone might say that "Jan reacts quickly and defensively to criticism." That person has said something about her personality—something that defines a relatively enduring characteristic distinguishing her from other people and having the comprehensive quality of being part of a total view of "Jan the person."

Review of this area logically centers on two categories: theory and measurement. *Personality theory* actually began with the work of the early Greek philosophers. With expressions such as "Know thyself" (Socrates) and "Control thyself" (Cicero), these early, brilliant minds were exploring the realm of personality. With all due respect to personality theorizing among the early philosophers (e.g., Plato, Socrates, Aristotle, and Epictetus), we will begin our review focus in the mid-nineteenth century.

Freud stunned nineteenth century Vienna when he wrote *The Interpretation of Dreams*, suggesting that our behaviors are unconsciously motivated and that dreams are the "royal road to the unconscious." His Vienna Psychoanalytic Society included many professionals who, using this as their theoretical starting points, either extended his psychoanalytic views or developed theories of their own notably different from—and in reaction to—psychoanalysis. In the following lists and narratives, you will meet these theorists and their views, and you will move beyond them to the many who never had psychoanalysis as their starting points. Here's a quick, bird's-eye view of the fascinating and lush theoretical landscape that lies just ahead.

Psychoanalysis says, "You are your instincts." In this picture, each of us is sitting on a huge dynamo of instinctual drive energy that wants immediate gratification. As we bump along the road of life with this huge dynamo whirring under us, our challenge is to stay on the civilized, narrow road. *Ego-analysis* and the *psychosocial* moved beyond Freud's view that instinct is the sole driving force. The ego-analysts believed our personalities have ego-based energy that is free from instinctual control; and the psychosocial approach of *Erikson* reinterpreted Freud's psychosexual stages in a psychosocial context—creating the well-known eight stages in the life cycle. As you will readily see in the following table, the *psychodynamic* theorists held a variety of perspectives. *Adler*, for example, believed our basic, underlying drive was not instinctual/sexual but, rather, a drive for superiority born of early inferiority feelings. Many of his therapy patients were circus performers and he noted repeatedly that the area in which they now were superior was an area in which they were inferior as children. *Jung* created the theoretical basis for what we know today as the Myers-Briggs Text—those four "magic letters" on your forehead that tell whether you're an introvert or extrovert, sensing or intuiting, thinking or feeling, and perceptual or judging. Other major names among psychodynamic theorists include *Sullivan*, with his emphasis on interpersonal relationships; *Horney*, with her perspectives on the role of culture in personality; and *Fromm*, with his distinctions in types of love. *Dollard and Miller* took psychoanalytic concepts and defined them in learning theory terms, creating a bridge to the behavioristic view that follows. It's a rich psychodynamic landscape. Note the uniqueness of each theoretical contributor and enjoy the ride.

Behaviorists say, "You are your learned behaviors." Based on the early views of John Locke, this perspective suggests that we are born "blank tablets," and the environment then writes upon our tablets. These writings begin from "Day 1," and contributors include our families, our friends, our schoolmates, our teachers, and anyone else with a "pencil or pen" who makes a mark upon us as we grow and develop. *Radical behaviorists* (e.g., *Watson, Skinner*) need to see and observe behaviors. They confine themselves to what we observably do. *Social or cognitive behaviorists* (e.g., *Bandura, Rotter*) include our expectancies and values relating to given behaviors. Where we might not play the piano for the kids on our block because they'd laugh at us, we may ride bicycles with them.

Phenomenologists say, "You are your perceptions." Jill and Jan may look out the very same window at the very same morning. The images upon their retinas may be virtually identical and yet Jill says, "What a beautiful day!" while Jan says, "What a crappy day!" The difference is not in the view. It's in how they perceive it. *Kelly* stated this difference in terms of personal constructs (i.e., the different set of glasses we wear as we look out upon our worlds). Taking a more *humanistic* view, *Rogers* spoke about the importance of our feelings and those notable moments when our rational mind has made a decision and we get that sick feeling in the pit of our stomachs. He believed our feelings are often wiser than our intellects, and we need to be in touch with those feelings. Other humanistic perspectives include *Maslow*'s view of our needs hierarchy, with the optimal attainment being self-actualization, and *Frankl*'s view of life-meaning coming through our pursuit of exciting goals.

Trait theorists say, "You are your underlying, basic characteristics." Just as we can think of different breeds of dogs and say, "That one's aggressive!" "That one's gentle and good with children!" our traits and temperaments are seen in similar terms. We are seen to have a small, select group of characteristics or traits that are basic to our personalities. *Sheldon* thought such traits were related to body types—an historical perspective to note, but a view no longer held. *Allport* believed our cardinal traits can be seen in virtually all our behavior (e.g., our quest for power, our reverence for nature). Central traits reflect in much of our behavior but are not as all-pervasive as cardinal traits. Another class, the peripheral, he terms secondary traits. Much of the significant work in trait theory has come through factor analysis—testing large groups of people, conducting multiple correlations, and finding clusters of characteristics that correlate highly together. Key work in this area has been done by Cattell and Eysenck. *Cattell*'s data come from three sources—a person's life record (L data) as gleaned from those who have known him, a person's own self-report (Q data), and objective test input (T data). Source traits are those underlying factors responsible for a highly correlating cluster. Say, for instance, that we found a highly correlating cluster of humor, gregariousness, and generosity. The source trait might be termed friendliness. The 16 PF (16 Personality Factor) Scale is the best-known instrument from Cattell's factor-analytic work. Where his 16 PF Scale encompasses normal traits, his Clinical Analysis Questionnaire (CAQ) assesses abnormal traits. *Eysenck*'s work raises the criterion threshold for identifying traits. Not only must they correlation-cluster, but they must be heritable, make sense theoretically, and have social relevance. Using these criteria, Eysenck's typology includes introversion-extroversion, stability-neuroticism, and impulse control-psychoticism. The "*Big Five*" theory of personality—first proposed by *Norman*—has now been embraced by many different personality researchers, both in and outside the trait-theory "camp." As you read the "Big Five" you'll notice the roots from which several of them have come—neuroticism (Eysenck), extroversion (Jung,

Eysenck), openness, agreeableness, conscientiousness. Not all current theorists sign on to the "Big Five" train. The interactionists take a different view.

Interactionist theorists note that traits do not predict a person's behavior in a given situation. For them, the critical "mix" blends the interaction of the person and the situation. We bring our unique traits to any given situation, and the interaction between our traits and that setting will determine our behavior. As an extrovert, you will behave very differently in a large, gala reception than will an introvert, and you likely will feel a sense of happiness and satisfaction that will elude the introvert. Early roots of this approach can be found in Rotter and Bandura's work. Studying our development from early infancy, *Thomas and Chess* have identified nine characteristics of temperament (e.g., activity level, adaptability, approach/withdrawal) and believe the key determinant of our personality is the match between our temperament and our environment. *Mischel*, *Bem*, *Allen* et al. weigh in prominently among interactionist proponents.

Now that you've had a bird's-eye view of this lush, theoretical landscape, let's look a bit more closely at those fascinating fields we just flew over. The following outline will be a helpful tool and reference point.

Personality Outline

Concepts	Names	Terms
Personality Theories		
Psychoanalytic	Freud	Personality as instinct-driven
Ego-analytic	Hartmann, Erikson	Less emphasis on id. More central role for ego.
Psychosocial	Erikson	Eight stages in life-cycle Emphasis on identity
Psychodynamic		
Individual	Adler	Basic drive is superiority-striving
Analytic	Jung	Four perceptual approaches to the environment: sensing, thinking, feeling, and intuiting
Interpersonal	Sullivan	Interpersonal relationships are the defining elements of personality
Cultural	Horney	Three ways of relating to people: moving toward, moving away from, moving against
Sociopsychoanalytic	Fromm	Five types of love: brotherly, motherly, erotic, self, and supernatural
Learning interpretation of psychoanalytic	Dollard-Miller	Translates psychosexual stages into learning-theory terms
Behaviorist		Personality as learned behaviors
Radical	Watson/Skinner	Focus on stimulus-response, observable behavior
Social	Bandura/Rotter	Focus on expectancies and values of behavioral outcomes. Stimulus-Organism-Response (as distinct from radical's S-R)
Reciprocal inhibition	Wolpe	Pair a problem behavior with an adaptive one, making it impossible to do both

Concepts	Names	Terms
Two-factor theory	Mowrer	Classically conditioned expectancy; instrumentally conditioned escape and subsequent avoidance
Phenomenological		
Personal construct	Kelly	Personality is one's perceptions. We view the world through our own set of glasses (personal constructs)
Client-centered	Rogers	"Listen to your feelings." Often they're wiser than your intellect.
Self-actualization	Maslow	Hierarchy of needs—physiological, safety, belongingness/love, esteem, self-actualization
Logotherapy	Frankl	Will to meaning (setting goals and working toward them rather than pursuing a will to power or a will to pleasure—both of which are self-defeating)
Transactional analysis	Berne/Harris	"Games People Play" (all of which are self-defeating and destructive) Parent/Adult/Child and the importance of parallel rather than crossed communication (goal of an "I'm OK, You're OK" life position)
Trait		
Physiognomy	Sheldon	Body types have distinct personality characteristics—the three basic types are endomorph (spherical), mesomorph (muscular), ectomorph (skeletal)
Functional autonomy	Allport	Traits that once had a survival function (e.g., hunting) now take on a self-perpetuating life of their own. Counters psychoanalysis with a positive view of human nature.
Factor analysis	Cattell/Eysenck	Correlational clusters enable us to identify specific personality traits.
	Cattell	Source trait identification and the Clinical Analysis Questionnaire
	Eysenck	Typology premised on introversion-extroversion, stability-neuroticism, and impulse control-psychoticism
"The Big Five"	Norman	Neuroticism (emotional stability)
	Costa	Extroversion
	McCrae	Openness
	Goldberg	Agreeableness
		Conscientiousness

Concepts	Names	Terms
Temperament	Thomas and Chess	Activity level Rhythmicity (bio-cycle regularity) Approach/withdrawal Adaptability Reactivity threshold Reaction intensity/energy Dominant mood quality Distractibility Attention span/persistence
Personology	Murray	Motivation's effect on personality. A taxonomy of needs including achievement, affiliation, dominance, play, sex, understanding, et al.
Interactionist		
	Mischel, Bem, Allen	Interaction between a given personality trait and a given situation
	Thomas and Chess	Interaction between a temperament characteristic and a situation

THEORY

A reasonable question at this point would be: Why don't personality theorists get together on a single, unified theory? The reason is that research in the field is not far enough along for the investigators to be in that enviable position. Dealing with and theorizing about the whole person is a complex task. The theorists themselves are well trained, thoroughly experienced clinical psychologists or psychiatrists who have dealt firsthand with people's adjustment problems. Their theories reflect their observations and the commonly recurring themes that they have encountered. Each theorist, in his own way, gets at important aspects of personality. All current theoretical views will at some point in the future seem as weird and archaic as early maps of the world seem now. But people's problems are occurring now, and efforts to systematize and understand in order to help must be made now, too.

In the following outline you'll visit with each of the major theorists, sharing key elements in their work.

Theory Outline

Concepts	Names	Terms
Psychoanalysis	Freud	
Divisions of psyche		Id (biological/instinctual) Ego (executive) Superego (social/perfection)
Cathexis and anticathexis		Investing emotional energy in another person (bonding) (positive feeling = cathexis, negative feeling = anticathexis)
Defense mechanisms		Repression, reaction formation, isolation, undoing, denial, projection, identification, regression and fixation, displacement, sublimation

Concepts	Names	Terms
Psychosexual stages		Oral (passive-sadistic)
		Anal (retentive-expulsive)
		Phallic (Oedipus complex and castration fear; Electra complex and penis envy)
		Latency
		Genital
Conscious, preconscious, and unconscious		Premise = our behavior is unconsciously motivated (id-driven)
Thanatos/Eros		Death/Life instinct (drive)
Parapraxes and wit		Slips of the tongue (betraying unconscious motivations)
		Wit = vehicle for getting the forbidden (sexual or aggressive) past the defense mechanisms
Dreams		"Royal road to the unconscious"
Dream interpretation		Manifest (reported) and Latent (underlying meaning)
Free association		Method of therapy
Ego Analysis	Hartmann/Erikson et al.	
Ego as conflict-free sphere	Hartmann	Not beholden to the id for borrowing its energy
Eight stages in life	Erikson	Basic trust vs. basic mistrust
		Autonomy vs. shame/doubt
		Initiative vs. guilt
		Industry vs. inferiority
		Identity vs. identity diffusion
		Intimacy vs. isolation
		Generativity vs. stagnation
		Integrity vs. despair
Psychodynamic		
Individual	Adler	Inferiority feeling/superiority striving
		Social interest as a determinant of mental health
		Family constellation (birth order and personality)
		Predisposing situations for mental illness—organ inferiority, pampering, neglect
Analytic	Jung	Archetype
		Collective unconscious
		Extroversion-introversion
		Persona
		Anima/Animus
		Shadow
		Four psychological functions: sensing, thinking, feeling, intuiting
Interpersonal	Sullivan	Modes of cognition: Prototaxic Parataxic Syntaxic
		Emphasis on schizophrenic patients
		Dynamisms
		Personifications

Concepts	Names	Terms

Cultural	Horney	Role of culture in defining normality
		Modes of relating:
		  Moving toward
		  Moving away from
		  Moving against
		Womb envy (male counterpart to Freud's penis envy concept)

Sociopsychoanalytic	Fromm	Five types of love:
		  Brotherly
		  Motherly
		  Erotic
		  Self
		  Supreme being
		Five human needs:
		  Relatedness vs. narcissism (love need)
		  Creativeness vs. destructiveness (transcendence need)
		  Brotherliness vs. incest (rootedness need)
		  Individuality vs. conformity (identity)
		  Reason vs. irrationality (frame of orientation/devotion need)

Psychoanalytic in learning-theory perspective	Dollard-Miller	Four fundamentals of learning:
		  Drive
		  Cue
		  Response
		  Reinforcement
		Four critical training situations (each with both adjustive and maladaptive potential):
		  Feeding
		  Cleanliness
		  Sex
		  Anger-anxiety
		Four types of conflict situations:
		  Approach-approach
		  Avoidance-avoidance
		  Approach-avoidance
		  Double approach-avoidance

Behaviorist/Learning Theory Radical	Watson/Skinner	Larnyx movements and muscle twitches (Watson) Operant conditioning Shaping techniques Positive reinforcement Inadequacy of punishment as a behavior controller

Concepts	Names	Terms
Social	Bandura/Rotter	Expectancies and values Perceived value of reinforcers Observational learning Situational emphasis (in contrast to early childhood emphasis within psychoanalysis)
Reciprocal inhibition	Wolpe	Reactive inhibition Reciprocal inhibition Systematic desensitization
Two-factor	Mowrer	Two factors: 　Classically conditioned fear 　Instrumentally conditioned escape/avoidance Sign-learning/solution-learning—directly related to his two factors Spread-of-effect phenomenon (whatever happens closest to a behavior occurrence determines whether the behavior will be repeated)
Phenomenological 　Client-centered	Rogers	Organized and goal-directed behavior Conscious self-structure and sensory-visceral experience Basic striving to actualize, maintain, and enhance Importance of listening to one's feelings
Hierarchy of needs	Maslow	Five levels of needs: 　Physiological 　Safety 　Belongingness/Love 　Esteem 　Self-actualization Centrality of self-actualization
Logotherapy	Frankl	Existential vacuum Existential frustration Collective neurosis Life will and meaning—will to meaning vs. will to power and will to pleasure
Personal constructs	Kelly	Constructs and contrasts Constructive alternativism C-P-C cycle (circumspection, preemption, control) Role Construct Repertory Test ("Rep" Test)
Transactional analysis	Berne/Harris	Script Parent/Adult/Child Contract Life-positions (four) Games

Concepts	Names	Terms
Trait		
Physiognomy	Sheldon	Body types: Endomorph (spherical) Mesomorph (athletic) Ectomorph (skeletal)
Dispositional	Allport	Dispositional traits: Cardinal (basic core trait[s]) Central (present throughout personality) Secondary (occasional traits, not centrally defining)
Factor analysis	Cattell	L, Q, and T-data (life record, questions regarding self, objective tests) Trait elements
	Eysenck	Personality dimensions: Introversion-extroversion Neuroticism Psychoticism
"The Big Five"	Norman Costa McCrae Goldberg	Five basic personality traits: Neuroticism (emotional stability) Extroversion Openness Agreeableness Conscientiousness
Temperament	Thomas and Chess	Nine basic characteristics of temperament: Activity level Rhythmicity (bio cycle regularity) Approach/withdrawal Adaptability Reactivity threshold Reaction intensity/energy Dominant mood quality Distractibility Attention span/persistence
Personology	Murray	Person-environment forces (needs and press) Viscerogenic (primary) needs and psychogenic (secondary) needs Specific psychogenic needs including achievement (later pursued by McClelland), social approval, et al.
Interactionist		
	Mischel, Bem, Allen	Personality's key ingredient is the interaction between one's personal trait and a given situational environment.
	Thomas and Chess	Personality's key ingredient is the interaction between one's temperament characteristic and a given situational environment.

The preceding list will provide quick reference and rapid feedback regarding the personality theory aspects of your review.

MEASUREMENT

The second portion of this personality discussion centers on measurement—the use of formal instruments to tell psychological investigators about their subjects. Instruments in this collection vary from the highly objective to the highly subjective, and it might be helpful at this point to take a look at the various devices within that broad range and some major names within the different categories.

"Dean" of the *objective measuring instruments* is the *Minnesota Multiphasic Personality Inventory (MMPI)*. Developed by *McKinley and Hathaway* in 1942, it stands as a milestone in objective personality measurement. The standardization process for the inventory was conducted with a wide range of persons judged to have specific psychological abnormalities, and as a person answers the 567 statements, his response patterns can be compared with those of the large standardization sample. Obviously, such comparison means that the inventory is oriented toward detecting abnormality. The current version—the MMPI-2—has ten clinical scales closely following the original scales. It also has seven validity scales. Both MMPI and its offspring (MMPI-2) stand as hallmarks of objective testing in the field of personality and psychopathology. Another frequently used objective scale is a real tongue-twister—the Millon Clinical Multiaxial Inventory (MCMI). Millon designed it to closely parallel the current categories of psychological disorders with the American Psychiatric Association's DSM-IV. Similar scales patterned after the MMPI (e.g., *Gough's California Psychological Inventory*) have been standardized on normal individuals and thus emphasize normality. In each of these tests, the scales are organized around the true-false statement—the test taker reads each statement and marks it either true or false. The subject's responses to the large number of statements then enable the psychologist, utilizing established procedures (or perhaps computer analysis), to develop a response profile. Objective tests of this nature have the advantage of ease of administration to large numbers of people simultaneously and ease of objective scoring. Nevertheless, the structured format of such tests does not allow unique individual expression.

Subjective measuring instruments are often described as projective techniques. In the projective technique a person is shown an ambiguous stimulus or life situation, and is asked to give his observations concerning it. The test format makes it relatively easy for a person to relate his or her own thoughts, concerns, and problems to the stimulus (generally without realizing that he is doing so). The term *projection* suggests casting upon something (or someone) "out there" that which is within. Were you depressed and lonely, for instance, you might see depression and loneliness in every life-situation picture presented to you, although the pictures did not specifically suggest such feelings. You would be, in effect, projecting onto the pictures the feelings that you have. Such techniques enable therapists to observe recurring themes and trends among subjects' responses, allowing them to get at major facets of their patients' concerns and thoughts.

The "dean" of *projective techniques* is the *Rorschach Inkblot Test*, a series of ten ambiguous-stimulus plates presented to a respondent. A life-situation instrument employing the projective-technique format is the *Thematic Apperception Test (TAT)* developed by *Murray*. Variations on each technique have been incorporated into subsequent measuring instruments (e.g., the Blacky Pictures Technique). These and additional test names are mentioned here for purposes of familiarity and quick reference.

Concepts	Names	Terms
Personality Test Outline		
Objective Tests		
Minnesota Multiphasic Personality Inventory (MMPI) now in MMPI-2 rev.	McKinley and Hathaway	Standardized on diagnosed abnormal clinical subpopulations.
Millon Clinical Multiaxial Inventory (MCMI)	Millon	Closely parallels current diagnostic categories.
California Psychological Inventory (CPI)	Gough	Standardized on a diagnosed normal sample from population.
16 Personality Factor Scale (16 PF) and the newly elaborated 12 factors in the Clinical Analysis Questionnaire (CAQ)	Cattell	16 bi-polar dimensions of personality. The new test (CAQ) contains 12 new scales (total of 28) and is based on the 16 PF. The 12 new factors measure psychopathology.
"Big Five" Personality Traits: Neuroticism Extroversion Openness Personality Inventory, Revised (NEO-PI-R)	Costa and McCrae	Has a "private" and "public" dimension—first, asks the test-taker's self-assessment; next, asks a person who knows the test-taker well to rate her/him on several dimensions.
Manifest Anxiety Scale	Taylor	Designed specifically to measure anxiety. Items are selected from the MMPI.
Eysenck Personality Questionnaire (EPQ)	Eysenck	Measures introversion-extroversion, stability-neuroticism, impulse control-psychoticism.
Q-sort	Rogers	Measures difference between the actual and the ideal self.
Internal-External Control Scale (I-E)	Rotter	Measures extent to which a person feels internal control or being controlled by external circumstances.
Social Desirability Scale	Edwards	
Allport-Vernon-Lindzey Study of Values	Allport, Vernon, Lindzey	Based on the premise that values reflect one's underlying cardinal and central traits.

Concepts	Names	Terms
Projective Tests		
Rorschach "Inkblot"	Hermann Rorschach	Ten cards with ink-blot-like pictures. Person to "tell me what you see" (and can be expected to see several things in any given ink blot). In analysis, the therapist looks for patterns across card responses.
Thematic Apperception Test (TAT)	Murray	Several cards with pictures. The person is to tell a story— "What led up to this? What's happening now? How does it turn out?"

The list is not complete, of course, but it should be sufficient for review purposes.

In addition to the objective and projective techniques, there is a set of techniques that could best be described as behavioral or situational. The OSS— World War II predecessor to the CIA—mastered this set of techniques and utilized them prominently in their screening procedures. As an OSS applicant, one might have become involved in situational testing the moment he or she walked through the front door. Such tests were designed to judge individual performance and response in actual, structured settings—providing information essential to the OSS in its selection procedures. Understandably, there are practical limitations on broad, general usage of such a procedure. To understand individuals, professionals observe carefully and theorize— developing measuring instruments to help pinpoint specific aspects of personalities. At some point in the distant future, the theories and measuring instruments now in use may seem ridiculously humorous and weird; but for now they constitute one of the major avenues for gaining increased understanding of emotional disturbances. Such understanding is the only source of hope for millions of people whose daily lives are an emotional, living nightmare, and it is these people toward whom you will now turn as you consider psychopathology.

Psychopathology

It is estimated that one out of every ten persons born in the United States will at some time be hospitalized for mental illness. Equally striking is the fact that, at any given moment, half of all hospital beds in the United States are occupied by persons suffering from emotional disturbances. Moreover, it is estimated that 30 percent of all Americans have emotional disturbances not severe enough to require hospital care, yet severe enough to interfere significantly with their life adjustment. There is much emotional pain in our midst and, consequently, much attention centered in the area of psychopathology.

What is normal? What is abnormal? And how do we know we *are* normal or abnormal? These are difficult questions—not simply for us but for professionals in the field as well. There are several approaches we could take to such questions. One would be the *subjective*, which is demonstrated by the Quaker saying, "Everyone's weird 'cept me and thee, and sometimes I wonder about thee." It says, in effect, "I'm normal, and I will now measure everyone else by the yardstick of my own normality." The *normative* approach would take perfection as normal—meaning that each of us would strive but never fully measure up. A *cultural* approach would begin from the assumption that what the majority of the people are doing is normal. The *statistical* approach would design a test and then interpret normality on the basis of scoring at or near the mean (generally scoring within one standard deviation). And the *clinical* approach to normality would be based on the assessment rendered by a trained professional in the field. That assessment might use statistical measures, but it also would use the professional's insights regarding the individual's capacity to interact, to function, and to cope in the environment. Behaviors that are bizarre and extreme (e.g., hallucinations, uncontrolled violence), behaviors that interfere with the well-being of others (e.g., spousal abuse, child molesting), emotional extremes (e.g., uncontrollable mania or depression), and behavior that interferes with daily functioning (e.g., self-destructive patterns) would be considered abnormal. The more formal expression of abnormal behavior or psychopathology is a classification system (*Diagnostic and Statistical Manual*) developed by the American Psychiatric Association. Now in its fourth revision (consequently known as DSM-IV), it uses five axes for clinical diagnosis. Axis I is called the *clinical psychiatric syndrome* and states the person's central problem (e.g., depression or paranoid disorder). Axis II outlines *personality or developmental disorders* (e.g., reading disorder or histrionic disorder). These first two axes provide the complete set of diagnostic indices. Axis III outlines *physical disorders and conditions*, giving general acknowledgment to the close relationship between physical and emotional health and balance. Axis IV addresses the *severity of psychosocial stressors*, indicating that stress can play a central role in magnifying internal conflicts and triggering abnormal behavior. Axis V is a *global assessment of functioning*, evaluating the person's highest level of adaptive functioning in the past year. Axes I and II will be primary concern as you review.

Five major models encompass current attempts to understand and address abnormality. The *biomedical model* takes the position that abnormality is an illness of the body. The *psychodynamic model* believes abnormality is a product of hidden personality conflicts. The *behavioral model* sees abnormality as learned maladaptive behaviors that can be changed through the learning of adaptive behaviors. The *cognitive model* sees abnormality as stemming from disordered thinking about oneself and the world. And the *existential-humanistic model* relates abnormality to a person's inability to successfully confront and address ultimate life questions such as the meaning of life, how you can live up to your fullest potential, and how you can face death.

The *Diagnostic and Statistical Manual (DSM-IV)* has its roots in psychiatry and the biomedical model, and as you review you will appreciate the difficulty and complexity of classifying abnormal behavior. To reduce the complexity of your *DSM* introduction, we will turn the calendar back a bit.

This classification system is a bit like B.C. and A.D. in our calendar perspective on time. B.C. in their classification system was *DSM-II* (*Diagnostic and Statistical Manual of Mental Disorders*, 2nd ed., American Psychiatric

Association). From your viewpoint it is unfortunate that it is not the current classification system—it did have the beauty of simplicity. It classified behaviors in the two general categories of psychoneurotic and psychotic disorders. The psychoneurotic disorders (sometimes called simply "neurotic") had the common characteristic of anxiety (a painful state of tension). The psychoneurotic person remained behaviorally and cognitively in contact with his environment. Psychotic disorders, on the other hand, were more severe cognitive, emotional, and behavioral disturbances characterized by hallucinations and delusions.

As diagnostics have become sharper and more focused, and as given pathologies and problems have become more prevalent and pressing, the diagnostic system itself has changed to keep pace. So let's jump right into our review of DSM-IV, using it as the framework for our preparation in psychopathology.

Place yourself, for a moment, in the role of a therapist. A client comes to see you with a problem. As you interact with the client, you will use DSM-IV to classify the individual on the five axes. You will use Axes I through III to categorize specific disorders. The disorders outlined in *Axis I* have their *onset after infancy*, and these disorders will be your most frequent experience among clients. Because of their post-infancy onset, these disorders carry the best potential for change and effective treatment. *Axis II* disorders, such as personality disorders and mental retardation, are *life-long* rather than having a specific onset-point. *Axis III* encompasses *physical disorders* such as cirrhosis of the liver and diabetes. Obviously, you will not be treating these disorders, but they may have implications relating to Axis I or II. A client's *level of stress* will be assessed within *Axis IV*. On this 1-to-6 scale, a very low level earns a 1-rating while a major traumatic event will earn a 6. On *Axis V* you will rate the client's *overall level of functioning*. If the person has attempted suicide, you will scale their functioning at 1. If the person seems quite happy and productive, the rating will be 90 (and you'll wonder why they've come to see you!). Now let's return to our major focus—Axis I.

Psychopathology Outline (Axis I)	**DSM-IV**	
	Disorder	**Axis I**
	Disorders usually first evident in infancy, childhood, or adolescence	Attention-deficit hyperactivity disorder (ADHD), attention-deficit disorder (ADD) Tourette's disorder (repetitive movements—e.g., blink, twitch, sound) Elimination disorders (e.g., bed-wetting, incontinence) Stuttering
	Delirium, dementia, and amnestic and other cognitive disorders	*Delirium*—Reduced clarity of thought, awareness, and ability to focus *Dementia*—Multiple cognitive deficits including memory impairment (may be due to Alzheimer's, HIV, head trauma, Parkinson's, Huntington's, Pick's, et al.) *Amnestic*—Memory impairment—inability to learn new information or the inability to recall previously learned information
	Mental disorders due to a general medical condition	Mental symptoms that are a direct physiological consequence of a general medical condition. These symptoms could be those of any of a number of disorders classified elsewhere within the Axes.

Disorder	Axis I
Substance-related disorders	Alcohol and drug abuse, dependence, intoxication, and withdrawal; may be alcohol, amphetamine, caffeine, cannabis, cocaine-related; inhalant-related disorders; nicotine-related disorders; opoid-related (e.g., morphine, semisynthetics such as heroin, synthetics like codeine and methadone); mind-altering (phencyclidine [PCP, Semylan]—sold illicitly under names such as PCP, Hog, Tranq, Angel Dust); sedative-, hypnotic-, or anxiolytic (antianxiety)-related (including all prescription sleeping and antianxiety medications); other substances such as anabolic steroids, nitrite inhalants, nitrous oxide ("laughing gas"), catnip, kava, antihistamines
Schizophrenia ("fractured mind") and other psychotic disorders	Major deterioration in daily, interactive functioning accompanied by thought disorders, hallucinations, delusions, or flat emotional expressiveness
Paranoid type	Delusions of grandeur (e.g., "I'm George Washington"), persecution ("Somebody's poisoning my food"), reference ("Those people in that little group are talking about me.")
Disorganized type	Disorganized speech, behavior, and flat, inappropriate affect
Catatonic type	Marked psychomotor disturbance (e.g., immobility with catalepsy or stupor, excessive motor activity, extreme negativity with rigid posture)
Undifferentiated type	Meets schizophrenia criteria but not in the specific type categories outlined above
Residual	Not "full-blown" symptoms, perhaps in transition from "full-blown" to complete remission
Other psychotic disorders	Includes at least one of the following symptoms: delusions, hallucinations, disorganized speech and/or behavior, catatonic behavior. Entries include schizophreniform, schizoaffective (bipolar or depressive), delusional (grandiose, persecutory, et al.), brief psychotic, shared psychotic ("folie a deux")
Mood disorders	Debilitating depression, mania, or bi-polar (swings between depression and mania). Includes dysthymic (chronically depressed for minimum of two years) and cyclothymic (numerous cycles of hypomanic and depressive symptom swings)
Anxiety disorders	Free-floating anxiety (present virtually constantly), anxiety (panic) attacks, acute stress or anxiety related to a specific object or thought (phobias) (often associated with obsessive-compulsive disorders)
Somatoform disorders	Physical symptoms for which there is no organic basis, paralysis in an arm that is perfectly healthy (conversion disorder), or hypochondriasis (wall-to-wall medicine chest)
Factitious disorders	Fabrication of a disorder (e.g., falsely complaining of acute abdominal pain, feigning a grand mal seizure, et al.)
Dissociative disorders	Problems of identity, memory, or consciousness that are emotion-based: dissociative amnesia, dissociative fugue (geographical distance covering by someone who has lost identity), dissociative identity (formerly multiple-personality disorder [MPD]), and depersonalization (detachment or estrangement from one's self)

Disorder	Axis I
Sexual and gender identity disorders	Problems of sexual identity (e.g., the transvestite), sexual performance (e.g., impotence, frigidity, premature ejaculation), sex object (e.g., pedophilia—the child molester; fetishism—sexual arousal to an inanimate object); exhibitionism (pleasure from public sexual exposure); frotteurism (from French "to rub," unwanted rubbing against, touching, fondling—usually in crowds)
Eating disorders	Anorexia nervosa—self-starvation Bulimia nervosa—binge eating alternating with induced vomiting or purging
Sleep disorders	*Dyssomnias* (insomnia [sleeplessness and daily fatigue], narcolepsy); *parasomnias* (sleep terror [frequent panic-awakening], nightmares, sleepwalking [walking while generally in deep stage of sleep, no later memory of it])
Impulse-control disorders	Acting on impulses that are controlled among normal people (e.g., stealing, striking someone, cursing the law enforcement officer, et al.). Includes intermittent explosive disorder, kleptomania (impulsive stealing), pyromania (impulsive fire-setting), pathological gambling, trichotillomania (impulsively pulling out one's hair)
Adjustment disorders	Behavioral/emotional symptoms in response to a stressor

Outline Terms Elaborated

We approach this discussion with all due respect. We all walk on the fringes of abnormality and, but for the grace of background, parenting, friends, and genetics, we too could easily have stepped across that fringe. We will briefly follow Axis I, commenting on each of the categories.

➤ **Disorders First Evident in Childhood or Adolescence:**
Two of the key centerpieces in this category are Attention Deficit Disorder (ADD) and Attention Deficit Hyperactivity Disorder (ADHD). The rise in prevalence and the focus on these disorders has grown rapidly in the past ten years, and the disorders carry obvious implications for learning and the school classroom. One of the familiar drug treatments is Ritalin, but it has to be administered carefully because it carries growth-stunting side effects. Other categories within this classification include disorders related to learning, pervasive developmental, motor skills, communication, feeding, tics, elimination, etc. Pervasive developmental disorders include autism. One of the tic disorders, Tourette's disorder, might manifest itself as a repetitive eye-blink, twitch, or sound. The repetitive sound often includes obscenity. Elimination disorders have natural psychological implications. Bed-wetting, for example, can be related to fears or to harsh parenting.

➤ **Delirium, Dementia, and Amnestic, etc. Cognitive Disorders:**
All disorders in the delirium category are characterized by disturbance in thinking processes and awareness. Inability to focus also is prevalent. With dementia, the cognitive deficits are multiple and include memory impairment that may be due to Alzheimer's, HIV, head trauma, Parkinson's, Huntington's, Pick's, etc.

➤ **Mental Disorders Due to a General Medical Condition:**
These symptoms might come from any of the descriptions outlined elsewhere within Axes I and II. The unifying characteristic is the general medical condition. Axis III outlines general medical conditions.

➤ **Substance-Related Disorders:**
Unfortunately and sadly, a wide range of substances are being abused by our youth—some likely in rebellion, some likely in peer conformity, others perhaps in modeling. The deadly list includes alcohol, drugs such as heroin and cocaine, mind-altering substances such as marijuana, and hallucinogens. Nicotine also has joined the list and, with alcohol, is among the fastest-growing in prevalence. The outline coverage mentions several additional abused substances and behaviors.

➤ **Schizophrenia:**
The common characteristic is the "fractured mind"—disjointed and disordered thought processes, which, within conversation, will jump unexpectedly and nonsensically from one topic to another. Rational conversation becomes difficult or impossible because of the nonsensical aspect. Another common characteristic is flat affect—an absence of the excitement or the sadness that characterize the normal range of emotions. In hallucinations, the schizophrenic may hear voices telling him a variety of things (frequently derogatory or guilt-ridden or grandiose). The delusional (paranoid) aspect is false beliefs such as a certainty that the therapist is part of a plot to kill the patient. "You're out to get me. I'm sure of it. I saw you talking in the hall about me, and somebody has been poisoning my food. I know why this is happening to me. I'm George Washington, and you're plotting to overthrow me." Each of these depicts an aspect of this disorder. The thought patterns just described are delusional and paranoid. Paranoid carries in common that someone's out to get you, and the delusions may be of persecution or grandeur. Often the persecution-grandeur delusions link in sequence as a way of explaining the persecution. And the talking about me in the hall is paranoia of reference. The outline details other types of schizophrenia and psychosis within this classification. This disorder has challenged the mental health community for several decades. There seem to be genetic roots and physiological counterparts, but characteristic interactive patterns also have been found within schizophrenic families. The prognosis operates in thirds—roughly a third will be treated and return to daily life, a third will be in and out of the hospital intermittently, and a third will remain hospitalized.

➤ **Mood Disorders:**
This has been called the common cold of our society. It's so very frequent and very prevalent among us. Depression and mania may occur separately or together. When they occur together, it's called bi-polar as the individual swings between low and high in cycles. Some people experience seasonal depression as the days grow shorter and winter sets in, but for many depressions there is no seasonal link. Two entries in this category that fall short of full-blown depression or mania are dysthymic disorders (chronic depression for at least two years) and cyclothymic (several cycle-swings between hypomanic and depressive episodes). The so-called "second-generation antidepressants" are called

serotonin reuptake blockers. Like the first-generation—the tricyclic drugs—they block the reuptake of neurotransmitters, but distinct from the tricyclics, they block serotonin specifically. This second-generation is a world of Prozac, Zoloft, Paxil, etc. They are being very heavily prescribed in the mental health community—looked upon a bit as wonder drugs. The jury is still out on long-term effects, and there is growing societal concern about their widespread use by people who are not experiencing depression.

➤ **Anxiety Disorders:**

You've been feeling anxious lately. If it's prevalent virtually all the time and seems unrelated to any triggering event in your life, it's free-floating. If it ambushes you unexpectedly, it's an anxiety attack or a panic attack. If it has an object-relationship or a setting-relationship it's a phobia. There's a wide, long list of phobias—among them, claustrophobia (closed-in places), ocholophobia (crowds), germs (mysophobia), high places (acrophobia), open spaces (agoraphobia), and…yes…the number thirteen (triskaidekophobia). We detected that little snicker on the last one, but think how many thirteenth floors there are in hotels, and so on. It's not a minor or isolated fear among us.

➤ **Somatoform Disorders:**

One of our favorite TV shows many moons ago was called "Mannix." Joe Mannix was a private detective who got into a variety of fascinating and dangerous situations. On one of the episodes a bullet slightly creased his head. It had just barely made contact with the surface of his skin, but he was blind. There was absolutely no physiological reason why he wasn't able to see. All the sensory equipment was connected and in place. It was psychological—a somatoform disorder. Other folks in this category may have a litany of minor physical complaints and a medication for each entry in the litany. You likely already have met some of these folks and may already have called them hypochondriacs.

➤ **Factitious Disorders:**

In the Army, a fellow recruit dropped out of formation complaining of a very severe, debilitating back pain. No one could prove or disprove that he had it, and—in the final analysis—he received a medical discharge. In all likelihood, it was factitious. These disorders are defined by the intentional production of physical or psychological symptoms. They may be subjective (the Army recruit acquaintance), self-inflicted (like skin-injecting saliva to produce an abscess) or elaborating on some pre-existing condition (someone with a history of seizures pretending to have a grand mal seizure).

➤ **Dissociative Disorders:**

All dissociative disorders encompass some aspect of memory loss. In amnesia it may be related to knowing who you are. In fugue, the amnesia combines with your geographically traveling or relocating. And in dissociative identity (formerly multiple-personality disorder [MPD]) two or more personalities may surface. The classic work in dissociative identity was Thigpen and Cleckley's "Three Faces of Eve"—Eve White (pure as the driven snow), Eve Black (impure as the most devilish id), and Jane (balanced and functional). The challenge was to make Jane the dominant personality so the individual could function. More recently,

"Sybil" brought us over a dozen different personalities. What was once considered a very rarely occurring disorder now has become quite frequently diagnosed. In many instances it seems related to childhood abuse and a child's attempt to escape and dissociate through a safe-haven personality or personalities. In depersonalization disorder, one is outside one's body looking in and, because there's no one "inside" to experience, feel, laugh, and cry, it's a pretty empty shell.

➤ **Sexual Disorders:**

The many aspects of sexual disorders include those related to identity, performance, object, fetishism, and exhibitionism. In identity, the transvestite may be a biological man wearing women's clothes. Performance may be related to emotional or childhood-related dynamics underlying problems with impotence, frigidity, or premature ejaculation. In object-related disorders, the individual may, for example, be a pedophile (a child molester). If you get turned on sexually by the sight of women's boots and wish to have them close by much of the time, you have a fetish. And if you let it all hang out in public, you're an exhibitionist. One of the most grotesque entries in this category is necrophilia—sexual arousal from interaction with corpses. Fortunately, it's not one of the most prevalent among these disorders.

➤ **Eating Disorders:**

These disorders are growing in prevalence—notably among intelligent, achievement-oriented women. In anorexia nervosa, the person eats only minimally—starving the body of essential nutrients. This pattern often combines with a feeling of being overweight or fat—even though the person may be quite slim or even skeletal. Bulimia nervosa blends binge eating with induced vomiting or purging. Both patterns carry devastating physiological consequences.

➤ **Sleep Disorders:**

If you awaken nonrested after a fitful night's sleep, you're likely suffering from insomnia. This experience can be natural for all of us on occasion, but when it becomes a general and ongoing experience it enters the disorder category. Sleep terror encompasses frequent panic-awakening. It may be just at the moment when the in-the-dream attacker was ready to slit your throat or it may be without any dream-related catalyst. The sleepwalker—often a child—walks within Stage 4 (deepest) sleep. There is no memory of the excursion upon waking, and contrary to common belief, the sleepwalker can suffer injury. Another injury-prone sleep disorder is narcolepsy. Here, without warning, a person may drop off to sleep in the midst of daily functioning. In yet another disorder—sleep apnea—the sleeping person is awakened by a choking or inability to breathe. One can well imagine the fitful night's sleep that brings. Insomnia and narcolepsy fall within the category of dyssomnias. The parasomnias include sleep terrors, nightmares, and sleepwalking.

➤ **Impulse Control Disorders:**

This person will do the socially unthinkable—steal an item in the store, curse the law enforcement officer to his face, strike someone in a sudden fit of rage. These disorders include going into a rage unexpectedly and without provocation (intermitten explosive disorder), the impulsive shoplifter (kleptomania), the impulsive fire-setter (pyromania), the fellow who leaves his paycheck at the race track betting window (pathological gambling), and the individual who pulls out large swaths of his own hair (trichotillomania). The absence of impulse control and predictability makes it difficult or impossible for this individual to function in daily roles such as job and family.

Psychopathology Outline (Axis II)

DSM-IV	
Disorder	**Axis II**
Mental retardation	Significantly below-average intellectual functioning

Personality disorders	
Paranoid	Consistently interpret other people's behaviors as threatening
Schizoid	Pervasive pattern of detachment from social relationships; appears indifferent, emotionally cold and detached
Schizotypal	Resembles schizophrenia but is less extreme—characterized by neglect of personal hygiene/grooming, poor interpersonal relationships, weird thought-patterns
Antisocial	Lack of affection or interpersonal bonds, highly manipulative without guilt, unlikely to keep a steady job, highly likely to get into trouble with the law
Borderline	Unstable self-image; inability to form meaningful relationships; indecision about career, values; reckless behaviors (e.g., driving, drugs, sex, et al.)
Histrionic	Hyperemotional, constant praise/attention-seeking
Narcissistic	Exaggerated self-importance and virtually total disregard for others
Avoidant	Isolationist behavior—avoiding social contact, likely having no friends
Dependent	Submissive accompanied by absence of self-initiative or self-confidence
Obsessive-compulsive	Preoccupation with orderliness, perfectionism, mental and interpersonal control; attempts to maintain control through painstaking attention to rules, trivial details, lists, schedules
Unspecified	Features of more than one personality disorder and cannot be categorized as any one single type outlined above

Outline Terms Elaborated

➤ **Mental Retardation:**
Significantly below-average intellectual functioning encompasses the categories we outlined earlier. Mildly retarded individuals score in the 50–70 range and can learn to the sixth grade level by their late teens. With proper vocational training and education they can hold a job. The moderately retarded can learn to the fourth grade level by their late teens. The can do unskilled occupations. The severely retarded (20–35 range) have only minimal speech and little or no communication skill. They can be toilet-trained but require continuous supervision. The profoundly retarded (below 20) have very minimal functioning and require nursing care.

➤ **Personality Disorders:**
Individuals with a personality disorder demonstrate rigid ways of interacting with their environment and with other people. These ways are problematic and maladaptive. The *paranoid* will find threat and suspicion

as a pattern throughout their daily functioning. A *schizotypal* borders on many of the characteristics of a schizophrenic in a less extreme form. Often characterized by poor grooming and personal hygiene, this individual has disjointed thought patterns, which translate to poor interpersonal relationships. The *antisocial* carries the proverbial chip on the shoulder. General dislike for other people often blends with a manipulative charm that can take advantage of others' well-meant and sincere intentions. Because there is no feeling of guilt or personal moral responsibility, the prognosis for such individuals in treatment is poor. Indecision and recklessness characterize the *borderline* personality disorder. These individuals have a very shaky sense of self, cannot form meaningful relationships, and are indecisive about virtually every aspect of their lives. They're likely to be reckless in many behavior areas including driving, doing drugs, safe sex, and so on. The dangers and potential consequences of this recklessness are patently obvious. A hyperemotional state treading on the borders of hysteria characterizes the *histrionic* individual. Normal-range emotional reactions get magnified many-fold, inappropriate to the context or actual event. Attention-seeking and constant-need-for-praise tendencies frequently accompany the hyperemotional. In Greek mythology a sea nymph fell deeply in love with Narcissus. When spurned by him, she prayed to the gods that he would know what it was like to love and not be loved in return. Narcissus fell in love with his own reflection and pined away in this unrequited love state. In the *narcissistic* personality disorder one's exaggerated self-importance dominates. This self-importance crowds out any care or concern for other people. An *avoidant* personality disorder is unlikely to be seen in public. Hermit-like in existence, this person avoids social contact and, for obvious reasons, will not have any friends. The *dependent* personality wishes to be cared for, much like a very young child. "You must love me because I am so weak" characterizes many of these dynamics. Self-confidence and self-initiative are notably missing from this individual's functioning. In an unhealthy relationship, this disorder can tie in with a highly domineering personality.

➤ Adjustment Disorders:

People with these disorders develop maladaptive emotional or behavioral symptoms in relation to a specific, identifiable stressor. Perhaps a major test is upcoming or a major project deadline is fast-approaching, and the person becomes severely depressed, has anxiety and panic attacks, cannot concentrate, and barely can get out of bed or function in the normal manner. The source of stress is known. The response is distinctly maladaptive and disordered.

➤ Other:

In the field of psychopathology, it's inevitable that we need an "Other" category. We humans and our problems do not fit neatly into little slots or cubicles, and the Other category covers a wide range of disorders such as: *medication-induced movement disorders* (neuroleptic Parkinson's or postural tremors), other *adverse effects or reactions to medication*, *relational problems* (parent-child, partner, sibling, and so on), problems related to *abuse or neglect* (child or adult physical/sexual abuse and child neglect). Notice the term *such as*. What has been mentioned here is not all-inclusive, and as you can see the Other category casts a very wide net.

Psychopathology Summary

In our introductory comments on psychopathology, we used the terms *medical model* and *traditional* to lead into a discussion of this classification system. If you inferred from this wording that there were other professional views in the area of psychopathology, you were right. A strong body of opinion suggests that classifications do individuals an injustice—that they fit each individual into a square containing symptoms that are not uniquely his. Critics argue that treatment is then geared to the square (the label) rather than to the individual and his special problems. More will be said about each of these views in the next section on clinical (treatment) aspects. Meanwhile, you might find it interesting to read T. Szasz' classic, "Mental Illness Is a Myth," *New York Times Magazine*, June 12, 1966. The article has been reprinted in several sources, including: Robert Guthrie, ed., *Encounter* (Menlo Park, Calif.: Cummings, 1970), pp. 278–89.

One of the major concerns of psychopathology has been the question of underlying causes of abnormal behavior. Research scientists have found answers difficult and elusive—primarily because the research itself is difficult. For example, one of the classic studies on the possibility of an hereditary basis for schizophrenia was conducted by F. J. Kallman. Among identical twins, Kallman found that in cases where one of the twins had schizophrenia, the second twin also had it in 86 percent of the cases. A corresponding figure among fraternal twins was only 14 percent, suggesting a strong hereditary contribution to the disorder. S. Arieti's *Interpretation of Schizophrenia* (New York: Aronson, 1994) provides valuable follow-up perspective.

Physiology also plays a convincing role in many instances—notably with regard to blood protein content found to accompany functional psychoses. It is a case of being able to say, "We've found something physiologically different among these people, but why is the difference there and what is its significance?" Such findings raise further questions, as yet unanswered. To complicate the picture even more, life-history comparisons of normal and mentally disturbed persons have revealed marked differences in the areas of parental relationships, home and social environments, and traumatic emotional events. As you sort through what we have just said, you will grasp the complex interrelationship between heredity and environment. There can be little wonder why research in this area is so difficult—and equally little wonder why it must continue. As it does continue, we can expect increasingly closer cooperation between psychologists and physiologists; indeed, the finding of essential answers will depend heavily upon such cooperation. In the meantime, emotional disturbances exist and must be treated—which brings us to the clinical aspect of psychology, next in our review.

Clinical Psychology

Clinical psychology, is, in effect, treatment psychology. Not surprisingly, treatment approaches reflect the viewpoints held by professionals in the areas of theory, measuring instruments, and psychopathology. To get acquainted with this whole area, a logical starting point is to examine the ways in which each theoretical viewpoint approaches the clinical aspect. For purposes of clarity, you should take your initial glimpse via the outline used in the personality discussions.

PSYCHOANALYSIS

The assumption is made in psychoanalysis that the *personality's core elements* are established in the first few years of life. Treatment, therefore, is oriented toward reaching back into those early years and "laying bare" the guilt and conflict in the situations where they occurred initially. In the classical approach to treatment, the method used for this uncovering process is *free association* (subject lies on his back on a couch with instructions to say everything that comes to mind). It is assumed that the relaxed setting and these instructions will enable the person both to become aware of and reveal thoughts that have been kept from awareness by the usual *psychological defense system* prominent within daily life. *Dream interpretation* is central to this process—dreams being considered, in Freud's words, "the royal road to the unconscious." In addition to dream interpretation, the Rorschach Test is frequently used as another means of probing the unconscious. Complete psychoanalysis can require several years (and, obviously, a sizable sum of money). It also requires a patient with a reasonable degree of intelligence and some capacity for thought and insight. The assumptions underlying such treatment are that a change in personality can occur only through return to "the scene of the crime" (that is, the source of guilt and conflict) and that the "laying bare" process will enable the person to initiate a desirable change.

EGO ANALYSIS

Followers of this method believe that they have modified the classical psychoanalytic approach in the way Freud himself might have done if he were alive today. As the title suggests, this approach frees the individual from a "slavery" to id urges and promotes the importance of ego. Although free association and dream interpretation are still important parts of this view, the play-by-play "laying bare" process within early childhood is relieved somewhat by the ego emphasis. A primary goal of this treatment is an understanding of child-based conflicts, coupled with a wholesome strengthening of the person's ego.

PSYCHODYNAMIC ANALYSIS

In this and the above two approaches, the therapist talks with the subject in a one-to-one setting. However, psychodynamic treatment is less formal than psychoanalysis, and treatment does not include free association and the necessity for several years of treatment. Again, the goal is insight and self-understanding as the means of initiating behavior change. Specific methods used to reach this goal reflect the unique aspects of a given theoretical position. For instance, *Adler's* approach to insight might include replacing inferiority feelings with self-respect and social interest, but *Jung's* approach might feature a balance among the psychological functions of sensing, thinking, feeling, and intuiting. We could expect *Sullivan* to use spadework directed toward removal of lingering parataxic cognitions still present and problematic in our adult thinking. *Horney* would emphasize adjustment to one's culture and the development of effective modes of relating within it. *Fromm's* method stresses relationships that carry within them a love between equals and emphasizes a personality strong in relatedness, creativeness, brotherliness, individuality, and reason. As they begin to build the learning-theory bridge, *Dollard* and *Miller* seek to grant a person learning-based understanding of early childhood conflicts. Because of its learning base, the heart of this treatment approach rightfully belongs in the next section.

BEHAVIORIST AND LEARNING THEORY

The general emphasis of this approach is to remove faulty learning and replace it with learning that enables the subject to function and cope effectively. Virtually all the terms that you encountered in classical and operant conditioning come into play here because of the learning principles that are utilized. *Dollard* and *Miller* speak of the process as *counterconditioning* (i.e., running an effective response in direct and strong competition with the person's current ineffective one). Because this theory is a bridge between psychotherapy and learning theory, emphasis is given to insight—the ability to realize how faulty learning occurred in the early years and the learning capacity to change current problem behavior on the basis of this knowledge.

Behavior theorists place little importance on insight. They view psychopathology as one or a combination of several noncoping behaviors, and their goal is to change those behaviors. The method for doing so is to establish a learning situation or, in some instances, a complete environment, within which predetermined behaviors can be systematically encouraged through reinforcement and other behaviors (considered problem behaviors) can be either ignored or punished (depending on the approach). This spectrum of approaches follows, generally, one of the subsequent classifications.

The *behaviorist-learning theory* techniques provide the most readily demonstrable results in behavior change. Such techniques operate on the premise that the primary goal must be to change the current, maladaptive behavior and that a time-consuming, expensive return to one's childhood for purposes of unraveling and new insight is not important. Behaviorists believe that a person does not need insight into childhood conflicts in order to effectively change current behaviors. It is a "now" orientation based on systematic structuring of stimuli and responses. The technique initially identifies the problem behaviors and develops a conditioning program to change the responses customarily given to problem stimuli. It lives up to its name— placing emphasis on observable behavior without concerning itself with intrapsychic constructs such as id.

Desensitization   *Watson* pioneered in this method when he created within a child intense fear of white rats and then proceeded to remove the fear by a systematic procedure containing gradual steps (white objects at a distance, then moved closer to the child and approximating the feared object more and more in each successive treatment session). What Watson instituted was a *desensitization process*. This approach is widely used in cases of intense fear and phobia. Suppose, for instance, that you had an intense fear of butterflies and you were a summer lifeguard at an outdoor pool. Butterflies would no doubt appear and might well cause you both problems and embarrassment. To desensitize you, a professional might first have you read about butterflies in general, then later about the species that bother you the most. Next, you might be asked to collect pictures of them. And, to pass your "final exam," you might be given a butterfly net with instructions to catch a butterfly and return it to the therapist. The entire procedure would constitute desensitization. A prominent, controversial name in the field is that of Wolpe. Wolpe's treatment approach begins with development of an anxiety stimulus hierarchy (careful listing of most-to-least anxiety-producing situations). He then teaches the subject to relax all the muscles in his body. Desensitization begins as Wolpe introduces one or two of the least anxiety-producing situations and asks the person to relax (a response in direct conflict with the individual's normal behavior in these situations). Subsequent sessions move systematically toward the more severe anxiety-producing situations, again with instructions to the subject to relax.

Implosion Therapy (Flooding)

Stampfl's flooding or implosion therapy forms a direct contrast to the systematic desensitization approach. Rather than gradually exposing the person to the feared object or situation, this approach "floods" the person with feared-object or idea exposure suddenly and all-at-once. Because our sympathetic nervous systems cannot maintain this high level of arousal for an extended period of time, the person inevitably will "come back down" and feel more relaxed somewhere along this sequence. It's as though "I went through the worst possible. I made it through, and I'm OK." What once threatened to overwhelm has now been gone through at its worst, and the "worst" didn't prove as bad as the expectation.

Observational Learning

This approach relies on observation as a means of relieving intense fear and anxiety. Suppose you were intensely afraid of dogs. If this approach were used in treating you, you would be asked to observe someone with whom you could identify closely as this person moved gradually closer and closer to the feared object (a dog). Because you would be observing from a safe place, the initial threat of direct contact would be greatly reduced. Eventually (in the final stage of observation), however, you would be called upon to join your model in petting a dog. *Bandura* developed this approach and continues to be the most prominent name in the area.

Conditioned Aversion

Anyone who has seen the movie *A Clockwork Orange* is familiar with facets of this approach, which is used in cases where the subject finds great pleasure and positive reinforcement in some problem behavior. Sexual problems such as fetishism and transvestism are among the behaviors treated by this method. Generally speaking, it is a method utilized when other methods have failed; and the subject must have advance knowledge of and give consent for any treatment. For example, suppose a man achieved great sexual satisfaction and orgasm while wearing women's undergarments. The treatment would involve his wearing the undergarments at the same time that a drug-induced nausea was making him feel quite ill. The pairing of his former source of great pleasure with the drug-induced nausea would continue. Over a period of time, the drug level could be reduced, but the thoughts and feelings of nausea would continue to accompany the former pleasure objects. In other cases, the stimulus object might be nude child photos (pedophilia), a drink of Scotch whiskey (alcoholism), and so on. The major objective is to develop the nausea response as dominant over the former pleasure response, thus discouraging the problem behavior.

Changing Behavior Consequences

This technique emphasizes the manipulation of positive reinforcement. In general, it involves the withdrawal of positive reinforcement from maladaptive behaviors and the association of reinforcement with appropriate, adaptive behaviors. Suppose that problem child George frequently screams and kicks, uses derogatory language, and takes off his clothes. Normally, each of these situations gets his mother's attention (in effect, a positive reinforcement). Under this technique, however, the consequence of George's problem behavior would change because George's mother would be instructed to signal George when his behavior was disruptive. If the behavior continued he would be put in a dull, drab isolation room and brought out only when the behavior ceased. He would, of course, be praised whenever a behavior occurred that was appropriate and desirable. The technique involves all the specifics of the shaping process familiar to you from the learning section review. It is this type of procedure that is generally being referred to when you hear the term behavior modification.

Therapeutic Communities

In certain instances, a person's entire environment can be set up with systematic reinforcement contingencies. The mental hospital and the prison setting are two environments having such contingencies, and behavior modification techniques in these instances would seek to change reinforcements and consequences in such a manner that desired behaviors would be encouraged and motivation toward such behaviors would be prompted. In effect, a therapeutic community involves a total-environment usage of behavior modification techniques and the changing of behavior consequences. Ethics controversies enshroud some of these usages. Currently, questions such as whether prisoners can be forced to rehabilitate within such a modification program are being raised. Such controversies can be expected to continue, as there are no simple solutions to them.

PHENOMENOLOGICAL

Perhaps the least systematic collection of views are those found under this heading. The main idea holding this collection together is an emphasis on individual perception. In the perception discussions earlier in this book, it was indicated that perception combined the sensory experience (what is received physiologically) with past learning (what one expects to receive). Two people can wake up at the same hour on the same morning with very different outlooks on the day. These two people may encounter virtually the same events during the day, and yet one may have a positive outlook and exhibit optimism toward these events, and the other may demonstrate a negative outlook and pessimism. Phenomenologists believe that the essential goal of a clinical technique is to change the subject's perception of himself and his environment. Where such perception is hampering a person, the technique seeks to free the individual to be what he can be. As *Maslow* once stated, "What a person can be, he must be." Translated into actual settings, the approach uses therapist-person discussions on a one-to-one basis. For persons such as Rogers, Berne, and Harris, various approaches to group therapy are also important techniques. Group techniques are less expensive for the individual, and they provide clients with an opportunity to see how other people will respond to them and to what they are saying in a safe, controlled setting.

The basic premise throughout this approach is that if you can change perception, behavior will change as a consequence.

Fixed Role Therapy

Kelly believes the critical role of the therapist is to act as a validator for the client's experience. Within this process—through the Role Construct Repertory Test (REP Test)—the therapist becomes familiar with the client's faulty constructs and helps the client to break down the faulty and reconstruct adaptively. The therapist's role is to serve as validator of the client's new constructs.

Client-Centered Therapy

Carl *Rogers* founded this approach and the term *client*, which we have used frequently within other therapeutic descriptions. In Rogers' view, the person who comes for therapy is a client (an equal) who has engaged the services of the therapist as a consultant. This perspective is vastly different from the patient-therapist scenario in which roles are distinctly unequal and the therapist is the expert provider of mental health knowledge and procedures. Rogers' therapy is premised on giving the client unconditional positive regard and acceptance, clarifying what the client says by reflecting it back, and helping the client to get in touch with feelings. Where conscious self-structure from one's past is notably different from sensory visceral experience in one's present, the process will seek to bring the conscious self-structure more closely aligned with present experience.

Logotherapy

Founded by Viktor *Frankl*, this approach is premised on paradoxical intent. The client may say, "I think I am going to faint." The therapist may respond, "Go ahead, faint." And when the eventuality doesn't happen, the therapist and client share the humor of this nonhappening and build on the distinction between thought and reality.

Gestalt Therapy

Fritz *Perls* formulated this approach to therapy. It stems from the premise that our words frequently say very different things than our bodies are expressing, and the therapist seeks to bring out the bodily expressed message—pointing out the duality and contrast. Perls believed frustration to be an essential ingredient of growth, and within the therapy session he sought to frustrate the client (e.g., "What is your hand doing now?" "What is your foot doing now?" and so on). Perls believed we disown major parts of our personality (frequently aspects relating to sex), and it is the therapist's role to help us reown those disowned parts, becoming whole once again.

Rational-Emotive Therapy

Founded by Albert *Ellis*, this approach targets the irrationality in many of our thoughts and beliefs that carry negative psychological consequences. Ellis points to the eleven universally inculcated irrational thoughts or values he perceives as prevalent in Western societies. Among these eleven are the beliefs that we must be liked by everyone, we must be perfectly competent, we should be dependent and must have someone stronger on whom to rely, there's always a right or perfect solution to every problem, and it's easier to avoid certain difficulties and responsibilities than to face them. In therapy Ellis seeks to target and point out the irrational, replacing it with rational, adaptive thoughts and beliefs.

Cognitive Therapy

Aaron *Beck*'s cognitive therapy focuses on faulty cognitions—especially among those who are depressed. He believes depressed people have a "negative cognitive triad of depression" containing automatic thoughts that feed on themselves in a destructive cycle. The self messages within the triad are "I am deprived or defeated. The world is full of obstacles. The future is devoid of hope." With this triad cycling, the depressed person has little option but to sink deeper into the trough. Beck seeks to substitute more favorable beliefs for those in the destructive triad.

Cognitive-Behavior Therapy

Cognitive-behavior therapy blends aspects of behavior therapy and cognitive therapy. Like the behavior therapist, cognitive-behavior therapists such as *Meichenbaum* (founder and principal spokesperson) set behavior-change-based goals for their clients, but in contrast to behaviorists, the cognitive-behavior therapist puts more emphasis on a person's interpretation of his situation. Within past as well as present events, the therapist illumines the person's interpretive distortions and helps the client to reinterpret more accurately and adaptively.

Multi-modal Therapy

Richard *Lazarus* points out that how much a given event stresses a given individual depends on how the individual interprets the event and what action options they see for themselves within it. The pregnant, unmarried 14-year-old is likely to experience far greater stress than the pregnant, married 30-year-old. Situations and perceptions of options are vastly different. The element of familiarity with a potentially stressful situation is central to Lazarus, and part of his approach is to help the client anticipate potentially stressful situations and formulate response-options within them.

Trait (and State)

It seems fair to say that trait theorists are more concerned with theoretical approach than with clinical technique in behavior change. They believe that it is possible to predict behaviors and personality characteristics on the basis of specific, measurable traits. Professionals steeped in this approach make much use of objective measuring instruments such as the MMPI. Beyond their use of such instruments, their techniques for behavior change tend to be eclectic—combining the elements of several of the preceding approaches.

It is important to distinguish trait from state. In anxiety, for example, an anxiety trait is a motive or acquired behavioral disposition that predisposes a person to perceive a wide range of objectively harmless circumstances as threatening. Anxiety state is a subjective, consciously perceived feeling of apprehension and fear-arousal with activation of the autonomic nervous system (ANS). If you have an anxiety trait, you are highly likely to be in an anxiety state in any given set of circumstances (*Spielberger*).

Drug Therapy

One of the most exciting breakthrough areas in treatment has been the area of drug therapy. The "straight-jackets," chains, and shackles of yesteryear have been replaced by a battery of drug therapies that promote behavioral balance and functionality while enabling the individual to work on underlying problems. These drugs exist across virtually the entire spectrum of disorders, and new pharmacology discoveries are entering the line-up constantly. Among the most exciting new entries have been the second-generation anti-depressant drugs. The suspects in depression have been norepinephrine and serotonin neurotransmitters, and the goal has been to help neurotransmitter activity. Until recently, two classes of drugs—monoamine oxidase (MAO) inhibitors and tricyclic antidepressants—had been called upon for this mission. Now serotonin reuptake inhibitors, among them Prozac, Zoloft, and Paxil, largely have replaced their tricyclic predecessors. There's a prediction that somewhere in the not-distant future these drugs will be available over-the-counter. They are among the most prevalently prescribed and used among our population today. Antimanic medications include lithium carbonate (Eskalith), and Valium and Librium rank among the frontrunners in treating anxiety. Antipsychotic drugs include haloperidol (Haldol), chlorpromazine (Thorazine), clozapine (Clozaril), and resperidone (Resperdol). Attention Deficit Disorder (ADD) and Attention Deficit Hyperactivity Disorder (ADHD) have been effectively treated with Ritalin and Cylert.

As mentioned earlier, drug therapy may be a mixed blessing. On the one hand, behavior is controlled, paving the way for other therapeutic interventions. The infamous straight-jacket has long ago been discarded and extreme behaviors are being drug-controlled. Many who could not function outside the institutional setting can now function effectively and hold jobs. These are no minor or insignificant strides. On the other hand, drugs are overprescribed—often for individuals who do not need them and do not have a disorder—and the jury is still out on long-term effects of drug usage. As for the automobile industry, the general public tests the long-term effects, and many years down the road we could make discoveries of long-term effects that are irreversible. For example, the long-term use of antipsychotic drugs has been linked with symptoms similar to those found in Parkinson's disease ("pseudo-parkinsoniansim"). Current users, for the most part, see present benefits as overriding long-term potential risks. It is difficult at this juncture to predict what chemotherapy's future will be—whether it will become the clinical mainstream or simply one of many techniques in prominent usage. For now and the foreseeable future, it is very much with us.

Electroconvulsive Shock Therapy

Another technique used within the institutional setting for specific types of depression and manic disorders is electroconvulsive shock therapy (ECT), often shortened to the term electroconvulsive therapy. After anesthesia and a muscle relaxant, a light electric current is sent across the patient's temples for a split-second, producing a convulsion. Treatment for a severely depressed patient typically requires 6 to 12 treatments within a one-month time period. Anesthesia wears off within an hour or so of treatment, as does the immediate amnesia. Recovery from memory loss generally occurs within six months or a year, and the treatment itself has been found effective with severely depressed patients.

Because our image of this treatment resembles "Big Brother," brainwashing, or mind-programming, it is understandably controversial. The state of California at one point outlawed it, and for some time it was the unwanted stepchild within the public psyche. Responding to concerns, the National Institute of Mental Health (NIMH) named a panel to evaluate ECT. They confirmed its effectiveness in treating severe depression and found side effects minimal and complications exceedingly rare. Risks were no greater than those for anesthesia itself. After having been the little-utilized stepchild for many years, there has been a recent resurgence in ECT use.

Pragmatic Therapy

Steeped in the psychoanalytic tradition, Otto *Rank* advanced the therapeutic premise that "if it works, use it." His approach had a major impact upon one of his younger child-guidance-clinic colleagues, Carl Rogers. Rogers integrated this conceptual approach into the development of his own theoretical views and approach to therapy.

Primal Therapy

Primal therapy of *Janov* takes us back to the very beginnings of our life-journey. One must make and experience the primal scream. In some groups, they lay out a carpet-runner across the floor and an individual lies on it at one end, pushing across while other members of the group support, encourage, and spur the individual on. The point is to recreate the birth process and to experience the primal scream and joy upon entry to the outer world. Controversial? Perhaps a bit.

Transactional Analysis

Founded by *Berne*, it is based on the premise that people play destructive games with one another. All of us have the entities of Parent, Adult, and Child within us, and a challenge for us as adults is to "turn off the shoulds" of the Parent and get in touch with our feelings and spontaneity within the Child. *Harris* frames this latter challenge within the context of finding and maintaining an "I'm OK–You're OK" life position as distinct from the "I'm Not OK–You're OK" position we naturally inherited from childhood life among those adult, seemingly giant figures.

Reality Therapy

Founded by *Glaser*, a key aspect of reality therapy is the formation of a contract agreement between the client and the therapist. By signing the contract, we have signed and sealed our commitment to the therapeutic process and to the change-goals set within it. Ignoring the typical DSM categories, this approach seeks to make the client more proactive in his life and environment, actively pursuing adaptive and fulfilling goals.

Psychodrama

It has often been said, "if we could only see ourselves as others see us." *Moreno's* approach provides this self-enlightenment opportunity within the framework of role-play and role-reversal. As we see how we're perceived by others, the message can be a startling one, which spotlights aspects of ourselves we may have ignored or denied. Within this supportive setting, we have the opportunity to work toward change. In the broader context, this approach takes the view that the more roles we become familiar with, the better prepared we are for any future eventualities and role-expectations that may come our way.

Family Therapy

The overriding premise within all of family therapy is that an individual does not have a problem. Rather, the individual reflects symptoms of an interactive system problem. Therefore, the system needs to be treated and restructured. Taking this as our definitional baseline, there are *four major schools* within family therapy. *Object relations theory*, traced to *Melanie Klein*, sees the purpose of interpersonal interaction being self-development, as distinct from instinctual need fulfillment. *Bowen theory*, from *Murray Bowen*, posits the triangle as the basic construction within a flawed family-interaction system. The goal of this approach is to differentiate oneself from the family, attaining a stand-alone, solid, individual identity. *Structural family theory*, associated with *Salvador Minuchin*, focuses on the present family interactive patterns rather than their past roots. The goal is to realign the family members within their structural system, thereby changing their experience of one another. *Communication theory* stems directly from the work of *Bateson* and the concept of the double-bind. It views family pathology as a communication problem. Like Minuchin, the present is emphasized and the goal is to change the communication rules within the system.

Clinical Psychology (Treatment) Outline

Concepts	Names	Terms
Psychoanalysis	Freud	Free association (revisiting and working through early childhood conflicts)
Ego analysis	Hartmann, White	Free association (with emphasis on ego rather than early childhood)
Psychodynamic	Adler, Sullivan, Horney, Jung	One-on-one interaction with the person—goal being self-insight and understanding
	Jung	Discovering an individual's complexes and working through them.
Behaviorist Changing behavior consequences (shaping)	Skinner	Behavior modification by reinforcing desired responses and ignoring maladaptive ones
Observational learning	Bandura	Reduction of fear through observation of another person with whom one identifies approaching the feared object
Desensitization	Watson, Wolpe	Within a familiar, positively reinforcing environment, gradually move the person step-by-step toward the feared object or stimulus (countering fear with relaxation en route)
Implosion (flooding)	Stampfl	Suddenly and intensely expose the person to the feared stimulus, knowing the panic response can only last briefly
Conditioned aversion	Wolpe et al.	Change the outcome of a previously pleasurable problem behavior (e.g., pedophilia) to one of drug-induced nausea
Therapeutic communities	Skinner	Outline behavior contingencies and reinforce desired behaviors within a controlled setting (e.g., hospital or prison)
Phenomenological Fixed role	Kelly	Validate the client's experience in trying out new, adaptive constructs

Concepts	Names	Terms
Client-centered	Rogers	Provide unconditional positive regard for the client, reflect back to the client, and help him get in touch with feelings
Logotherapy	Frankl	Utilize paradoxical intent to demonstrate and change unrealistic thoughts
Gestalt	Perls	Focus on bodily movements and expressions, enabling clients to gain synchronicity between their feelings (nonverbal) and their words (verbal)
Rational-emotive	Ellis	Illuminating a client's irrational thoughts (e.g., everyone must like me) and moving him toward effective, rational thought
Cognitive	Beck	Focus on faulty cognitions—especially the "negative triad" within depressed persons—and substitute favorable cognitions
Cognitive-behavior	Meichenbaum	Set behavior-change goals for the client, emphasizing a person's interpretation of his life situation
Multi-modal	Lazarus	Help the client anticipate potentially stressful situations and formulate response-options within them
Medical		Medical interventions (drug therapy or ECT)
Drug therapy		Use of drugs to moderate and control behaviors. Among the applications: For antidepression: MAO inhibitors, tricyclics, and serotonin reuptake inhibitors (Prozac, Zoloft, et al.) For antimanic: Lithium carbonate (Eskalith) For antianxiety: Valium and Librium For antipsychotic: Halperidol (Haldol), Chlorpromazine (Thorazine), Clozapine (Clozaril), and Resperidone (Resperdol) For ADD/ADHD: Ritalin and Cylert
Electroconvulsive		Split-second shock to the temples with resulting convulsion. Used for severe depression and mania.

Concepts	Names	Terms
Eclectic		A blend of theoretical approaches
Pragmatic	Rank	"If it works, use it"—drawing from a variety of theoretical backgrounds
Primal	Janov	Revert to the primal scream and, in effect, the first moment of daylight (simulating emergence from the birth canal) as an emotionally cleansing and liberating exercise
Transactional analysis	Berne/Harris	Point out crossed lines of communication among the Parent/Adult/Child entities in our interactions with others. Work toward an "I'm OK–You're OK" life position.
Reality	Glasser	Eschews the diagnostic categories—placing people in the generally happy/generally miserable categories. Helps the miserable to be more proactive in their lives, selecting behaviors that will fulfill their innate needs and goals. Client makes a signed "contract" with the therapist.
Psychodrama	Moreno	Focuses on role-play and role-reversal. Takes the premise that the more roles an individual becomes familiar with and can assume, the better prepared the individual is for the requirements of any future situation.
Family	Klein, Bowen, Minuchin, Bateson et al.	Treats the family as an interactive system rather than treating an individual. Seeks to restructure the interactive patterns within the system.

Having viewed the range of clinical techniques, from the couch and free association to chemotherapy and electroconvulsive shock, you now have an idea of the variety of methods that are directed toward the common objective of changing maladaptive behavior. We are a long distance from rebuilt-brain transplants, and, in the meantime, people need emotional help. Clinical techniques seek to provide such help and relieve the accompanying emotional pain.

Methodology

Because psychology is a social science, investigators in all aspects of the discipline adopt the scientific approach to new information. The scientific method is, in effect, an objective way of observing, describing, and classifying. It is quantitative, and quantitative classification must work with objectively measurable characteristics involving "more than" and "less than" relationships.

Qualitative classification, on the other hand, involves simply categorizing on the basis of a specific characteristic, e.g., hair color. To gain some understanding of the distinctions, a brief look at the words *nominal*, *ordinal*, *interval*, and *ratio* can prove helpful.

Numbers used in *nominal* ways are, in effect, labels. The number on your house or apartment falls into this category. The fact that your house number is 1054 and someone else's is 1020 does not mean that your house is bigger than the other person's. The numbers simply serve a labeling, categorizing function. *Ordinal* use of numbers involves rank ordering. Judges at the county fair use numbers in this manner. A given ordinal number can indicate more of a quality than another number, but it does not indicate that the distance between first and second, for instance, is equivalent to the distance between second and third. Ordinal is rank ordering of some characteristic and does not go beyond that ordering to any suggestion of equal intervals between. The latter suggestion is reserved for the *interval* aspect of quantitative number usage. Such intervals are judged to be equal. An applied example of this type of usage involves temperature. The difference between 90 and 100 degrees Fahrenheit is considered equivalent to the difference between 70 and 80 degrees Fahrenheit. Though these differences may not seem equivalent when you are trying to find relief from the hot sun, in thermometer and interval terms they are. A psychological example that approximates interval measurement is the intelligence test. Though currently embroiled in controversy, these tests were developed on the premise that intervals were equivalent—that 15 IQ points at one point on the scale were equivalent to 15 IQ points at another point on the scale. This kind of testing provides one of psychology's strongest bids for interval use of numbers. The final type of numerical quantity, *ratio*, presumes an absolute zero point. When you have been able to establish an absolute zero, you have reached a point where you can make statements such as "twice as much as" or "three times as much as." Psychologists are certainly not yet prepared to suggest that a person having a 150 IQ is twice as intelligent as a person having a 75 IQ. This type of number usage is possible in natural science, but social scientists have not yet discovered an absolute zero and must concentrate their number usage in the ordinal and interval areas.

To maintain objectivity, the scientific method adopts an established set of procedures to be followed in the testing of hypotheses. Suppose, for instance, that you had made general observations that seemed to link the eating of carrots with reading speed. To determine whether these observations had any scientific validity, you would need to develop an hypothesis to be tested. You would be hypothesizing that carrot eating affects reading speed. As you translate this hypothesis into formally established testing procedures, this is what you would have:

STEP 1: SET UP THE NULL HYPOTHESIS

Null hypothesis means "no difference." Your null hypothesis would be that reading speed is not affected one way or the other by carrot eating. Actually, you believe that carrot eating has an effect on reading speed, so this hypothesis is one that you hope to disprove later in the procedure. You are hoping that the difference you find will be sufficiently great that you can disprove (reject) the null hypothesis expressed here. Note, however, that rejecting the null hypothesis does not mean you prove that carrot eating affects reading speed. A research hypothesis is never proven, per se.

STEP 2: COLLECT THE DATA SAMPLE

(A) Set up the experimental and control groups.

Through careful thought and planning, you will need to develop your experimental design. At this point, you must familiarize yourself with such terms as *independent variable* and *dependent variable*, and learn their specific translation within your experimental situation. In this instance, the independent variable will be carrots—the stimulus element that is placed in the experimental situation to see whether it makes a difference in reading speed. The dependent variable will be reading speed—the response obtained in relation to the stimulus element introduced. To compare the responses of your experimental and control groups, you should administer carrots to the experimental group, no carrots to the control group. Because the control group will not be receiving the independent variable, this group will enable you to determine later to what extent an observed response change was a function of the carrot eating (independent variable) within the experimental group. Obviously, it is important to keep all other potential variables between the two groups the same. For example, you may want to use only girls (or boys) to remove the possibility of performance differences resulting from sex differences. The reading material that you select must be equivalent for the two groups, and you must be certain that there has been no previous familiarity with this material. It will be essential to measure the reading speeds of all subjects *before* you institute the independent variable in order to get an accurate measure of any changes in reading speed after the experimental group has gobbled its carrots. And it will be important to be sure that each person consumes the same amount of carrots. In addition, situational variables must be controlled—lighting must be equivalent for all subjects, and so on. Having proceeded with care in subject selection and control of potential variables, you can move into the second aspect of data collection.

(B) Decide on a statistical procedure and collect data in a form compatible with that procedure.

One of the most deplorable and traumatic scenes that any statistician can relate involves the sight of someone on the doorstep who has collected a batch of data and now wants to know what he can do with it statistically. Such decisions must be made *before* the data is collected. The GRE will assume that you are very familiar with the range of statistical procedures and the experimental situations in which each should be utilized. But before you can get acquainted with the specific statistical procedures, you need a thorough understanding of the foundations upon which they are built. Therefore, take a brief look at some of the basic terms and concepts as presented below; we will also suggest books to which you can refer for additional review.

Distinction Between Descriptive and Sampling Statistics

The *descriptive-statistics* approach requires a person to specify a given population of interest and then collect measurements from *all* the members of that population. You can begin to imagine the difficulty of accomplishing this kind of measurement collection when you think of a population such as Democrats, Republicans, or Independents! The more typical situation would involve having measurement access to a smaller group selected from the larger population of interest. This smaller group is known as a sample, and the statistics used in analyzing data collected from the smaller group are known as *sampling statistics*. Analyzing the data from the sample—assuming that a sample that is representative of the population has been obtained—you can then make generalizations from the sample to the population.

Statistical Inference and the Concept of Random Sample

Statistical inference refers to sampling statistics and the process through which inference is made to whole populations through sampling procedures. Such inference requires careful attention to the concept of randomness in sampling. *Randomness* means that in selecting a sample each member of the specific population has an equal chance of being selected—that no weight or preference will enhance selection chances for some members and weaken those chances for others. As mentioned in the section on social psychology, public opinion polling relies heavily on the concept of random sampling.

Parameter-Statistic Distinction

Values obtained from populations are called *parameter*s, and values obtained from samples are called *statistics*. Parametric tests (statistical procedures) are based on the assumption that the population from which a sample has been drawn is a normal distribution. Correspondingly, nonparametric tests are not dependent upon this normal distribution assumption. Most of the statistical procedures with which you will become familiar are parametric. Among the few nonparametric procedures you will need to know is the chi-square test.

Central Tendency

In any distribution, it becomes necessary to measure central tendency. Three methods of measuring are available—mean, median, and mode. Most statistical procedures rely upon the *mean* (an average of the scores in the sample). The *median* constitutes a midpoint of the sample scores, and the *mode* is the most frequently occurring score. Use of mean can lead to problems in distributions where there are a few extremely divergent scores. Because it is an average, it tends to be prominently influenced by these extreme scores. In such instances, the median as the midpoint score (half the scores greater than, half smaller than) makes a more appropriate measure of central tendency.

You might ask what happens to the mean of a distribution when a fixed number is added to each score in that distribution. The answer is that the mean value is increased by this fixed number. In similar fashion, if each score in a distribution were to be multiplied by a fixed number, the resulting mean would be the original mean multiplied by this fixed number. Division would have a similar effect. In summary, the same effect that has occurred with the individual scores in the distribution also occurs with the mean.

Variability

Variability refers to the relationship among all the scores in a distribution. Are they clustered closely around the mean, or are they widely scattered? The terms *variance* and *standard deviation* are measures of this variability. The *standard deviation* is, in effect, the positive square root of the variance. Interpretively, if you were comparing two standard deviations (one being 3.7 and the second being 1.2), you would know that the scores in the second distribution are generally closer to the mean and less scattered than the scores in the first distribution.

If you increase or decrease each term in a distribution by a fixed amount, the variance and standard deviation remain unchanged. In effect, you have not changed the "scatter" of the distribution around the mean. If each term in a distribution is multiplied by a constant, the original standard deviation would be affected in the same manner as every other score in the distribution (the resulting standard deviation being the original standard deviation times the constant).

Because a standard deviation squared would be its corresponding variance, the effect upon variance of multiplying each score in a distribution by a constant would be that of multiplying the original variance by the square of that constant. For example, if each score in a distribution were multiplied by 2 and the original variance had been 6, the resulting variance would be 24. Squaring the constant makes it 4, and 4 times 6 equals 24. In cases of division by a constant, division by the square of the constant would yield the resulting variance.

Z-Scores

Imagine that Distribution 1 has a mean of 40 and a standard deviation of 2.5, while Distribution 2 has a mean of 40 and a standard deviation of 2.0. Now, if someone were to ask how a score of 45 in Distribution 1 would compare with a score of 46 in Distribution 2, a quick score comparison would be difficult to make, to say the least. The computation of z-scores is a way of translating these different standard deviations and different means into a common language that facilitates comparison. Computed as score minus the mean divided by the standard deviation, the z-score makes score comparisons quite simple. In the above example, for Distribution 1 a score of 45 minus 40 = 5. This 5 divided by the standard deviation of 2.5 produces a z-score of +2. In Distribution 2, 46 minus 40 = 6. This 6 divided by 2 produces a z-score of +3.0. Therefore, through the use of the z-score translation, it becomes easy to see that the score of 46 in Distribution 2 is significantly better than a score of 45 in Distribution 1. Note that the z-score in these instances was preceded by a plus sign. If the score had been below the mean, it would have been preceded by a minus sign.

Central tendency, variability, and z-scores are intricately related to the concept of a normal distribution. Because the z-score is based on the assumption of a normal distribution, it is possible to speak in terms of probabilities. In a normal distribution (which you can find outlined in table form in any basic statistics text), approximately 34 percent of the scores occur between the mean and a z-score of +1 (one standard deviation above the mean). Approximately 14 percent more occur between z-scores of +1 and +2 (between one and two standard deviations above the mean), and approximately 2 percent of the scores in the distribution occur beyond a z-score of +2. So, if we refer to Distribution 1 momentarily and ask what the probability is of a score of between 42.5 and 45, we can immediately state that probability as 14 percent. Because a normal distribution is symmetrical, exact percentages hold for scores occurring below the mean. For example, the probability of a score between 35 and 37.5 in Distribution 1 would be 14 percent. Part of the data you will receive regarding your GRE performance will involve your percentile rank. That rank will indicate the percentage of test takers scoring either the same as or below you—a computation strikingly similar to the ones made above.

Probability Type I and Type II Error

You have ten balls in your backpack. Five are red, three are green, two are yellow. Your backpack is specially designed with a ball dispenser (sure it is!), and when you shake the backpack, only one ball can come through the dispenser at a time. Since half of the entire group is red, the probability of a red ball coming through is .5; of a green ball, .3; and of a yellow ball, .2. Assuming you return all the balls to the backpack each time before dispensing, these probabilities will continue unchanged. The normal distribution discussed earlier is a bit like the colored balls. They're just stacked up in a very normal, symmetrical way. The probability of a ball being within one standard deviation of the mean is .68 (.34 on each side of the mean); between one and two standard deviations of the mean, .28 (.14 on each side of the mean); beyond two standard deviations from the mean, .04 (.02 on each side of the mean). When scientists set a significance level (as you will in Step 4 upcoming), they ask themselves, "What is the chance probability of mistakenly rejecting a null hypothesis? (Type I error) or mistakenly accepting a null hypothesis? (Type II error)." The scientists set their significance level based on the risk they're willing to take of making an erroneous rejection (Type I error) or acceptance (Type II error). We did a bit of repetition on these because they're all-too-easy to get reversed or mixed up. Do you have "RA's" (Residence [Hall] Advisers) at your institution? Just think of this as RA's—first comes the R (Type I and erroneously rejecting a null), second comes A (Type II and erroneously accepting a null). Yeah, we've repeated ourselves enough. You're ready to head on.

PERCENTILE RANK

Got a spare piece of paper? Put it over one of those beautiful bell-shaped curves we just talked about. Now slowly move the paper to the right, little-by-little exposing the left side of the curve. What you're doing relates directly to percentile ranks. Percentiles begin at the far left side of the distribution— a zero assumed at the far left. As your paper moves further and further to the right, the percentile rank steadily increases. When you get to the midpoint (mean, median, and mode of this normal distribution) you have reached the 50th percentile. If your score came at the 50th percentile it would mean 50 percent of all those who took the test scored equal to or below you. As you continue to move your paper further to the right you'll reach 60th, 70th, 80th, and 90th percentiles. Just for fun, let's move the paper just a tad further—to the 95th percentile. This means 95 percent of all those who took the test scored equal to you or below you. And you can be very, very sure there weren't many equal to you. Has a nice ring to it, doesn't it!

At this point, you can see the intricate relationships among the concepts of central tendency, variability, *z*-score, normal distribution, probability, and percentiles. As you seek for more depth within one of the introductory statistics books, we suggest that you attempt to gain a basic understanding of the following concepts and terms:

Methodology Outline

Concepts	Terms
Uses of numbers	Nominal—to label
	Ordinal—to rank
	Interval—to express consistent interval values at different points in a distribution (e.g., the difference between 15 and 20 degrees Fahrenheit equivalent to the difference between 85 and 90 degrees Fahrenheit)
	Ratio—premised on an absolute zero, it can express "twice as much," "three times as much," (e.g., weight, height)

Concepts	Terms
Central tendency measures (in both grouped and nongrouped data)	Mean—the average score Median—the midpoint score (half the distribution scores are higher than, half are lower than) Mode—the most frequently occurring score in a distribution
Parameter and statistic	Parameter—a descriptive measure of the population Statistic—a descriptive measure of a sample
Binomial distribution	Values in this distribution are either 0 or 1.
Independent and dependent variable	Independent—Experimenter puts this variable into the design within the "experimental group" (as distinct from the control group) Dependent—Subject response (and a comparison of differences in response between subjects in the experimental and control groups) For example: The Effect of Carrot-Eating on Reading Speed—Carrot-Eating = the independent variable, Reading Speed = the dependent variable. Only the experimental group will eat carrots.
Inferential statistics	Inferring characteristics of a population from a sample of data
Variability	Standard deviation—a measure of difference from the mean of a distribution (if high, it's a widely scattered distribution; if low, it's bunched closely around the mean); Variance—another statistical expression of difference from the mean (it's the standard deviation squared)
Frequency distribution	The "scatter-pattern" of scores
Frequency polygon and histogram	Distinction: Polygon = Lines connecting points on the graph Histogram = Bar graph representing score intervals
Methods of data grouping	Frequency (characteristic of the polygon) Interval (characteristic of the histogram)
Concept of a normal distribution	Proportions of distribution scores occurring within 1, 2, and 3 standard deviations of the mean: Within 1 = 68 Within 2 = 96 (28 between 1 and 2 s.d.'s) Within 3 = virtually all scores (4 between 2 and 3 s.d.'s)

Concept of positive and negative skew and its effect upon location of mean, median, and mode	Negative skew = scores bunched at the right and tail off (or skew) to the left
	Positive skew = scores bunched at the left and tail off (or skew) to the right
	"Cardinal Rule"—The mean moves in the direction of the skew
	   Central tendency sequential occurrence in a negatively skewed distribution is mean, median, mode
	   Central tendency sequential occurrence in a positively skewed distribution is mode, median, mean

Percentile rank	Zero at the left side of a normal distribution, gradually increasing as one moves to the right.

Concepts	Terms
Probability in relation to the normal distribution	The likelihood of a given score occurring.

Concept of risk in decision making and the distinction between Type I and Type II error	*Type I Error:*
	    Mistakenly rejecting a null hypothesis
	Type II Error:
	    Mistakenly accepting a null hypothesis

Concept of significance level as it relates to probability and types of errors	Typically set at .05 (in effect, risking that five times in 100, I'll make a Type I or Type II error) More stringent = .01 level (risking only one time in 100)
Difference between one-tailed and two-tailed tests	One-tailed puts the entire significance level on a designated side of the distribution Two-tailed evenly divides it on both sides of the distribution (e.g., if .05 level, .025 of it will be on the left, .025 will be on the right)
Degrees of freedom	The number of frequencies free to vary for any given n (e.g., if there are three brands of soda being tested with a chi square design, the $df = 2$ [$n-1$]).
Confidence interval and confidence limits	Estimating a population mean on the basis of our sample mean, for example, and stating our level of confidence that the population mean falls within our estimate
Correlation	A co-relation between two sets of variables. If they vary in direct relation to each other, (e.g., a high score in one set is a high score in the other, a low score in one set is a low score in the other) it is a positive correlation. If they vary inversely (e.g., a low score in one set is a high score in the other, a high score in one set is a low score in the other), it is a negative correlation. Correlation range is -1.0 to $+1.0$ (Note: When you get a correlation of $+1.5$, check your calculations!)
Regression	Line drawn among a group of correlation-distribution points to represent a trend (e.g., how much Y varies when X varies by one unit).

Don't get too bogged down in concepts like degrees of freedom. You'll be in the field for several years and will still be fascinated by that concept!

With this basic statistical background, you are now ready to consider different statistical procedures and the situations in which they are utilized. Among the most prominent testing procedures are the *t*-tests for (1) the difference between sample and population means, (2) two independent means, and (3) related measures.

A typical example of the *first* instance (difference between sample and population means) would be a situation in which the researcher knows a national average for the dimensions being measured (e.g., average weight of twelve year olds) and now must determine whether the weight of twelve year olds in the sample is significantly different from the population mean (the national average).

To demonstrate the *second* instance (two independent means), suppose that a researcher wants to determine whether there is a significant difference between the IQ scores of twelve-year-old boys and those of twelve-year-old girls in a given school. The scores of the boys and those of the girls have been obtained independently and, in effect, the comparison is between two sample means. This kind of setting—a comparison of two independent means—is perhaps the most common and most often used *t*-test procedure.

In the *third* procedure (related measures) there is a relationship between the measures being obtained. For example, one might take the above group of twelve-year-old boys and give them an IQ test just before instituting an intensive educational program and then administer the IQ test again at the conclusion of the program. The *t*-test would be comparing two sets of measures obtained on the same people (before and after an experimental procedure was introduced) to determine whether significant change had occurred in their IQ scores. In addition to using this procedure to test the same people twice, it is possible to use it to compare the performances of matched groups. In such groups each member of Group 1 has been matched with a specific member of Group 2 in the critical dimensions (age, sex, background, and so on). On the rare occasions when developmental psychologists have been able to assemble a large group of identical twins, it has been the norm to assign identical twin A to Group 1, identical twin B to Group 2. By following a similar procedure for each set of identical twins, the researchers could be sure of matched groups since, for each person in Group 1, there was a person in Group 2 with identical hereditary background. The researchers could now institute an experimental procedure with one of the groups and test each group at the conclusion of the procedure to determine how much performance change was a function of the experimental procedure. Such comparisons could utilize the *t*-test for related measures.

Correlation

By its name, correlation suggests a co-relation. It is used to determine whether there is any systematic relationship between two sets of measurements or observations. The correlation coefficient used to describe such a relationship is expressed in a range from +1 to −1. A zero would indicate no relationship, a +1.0 would indicate a perfect positive relationship, a −1.0 would indicate a perfect negative relationship, and a + or −1.1 or above would indicate that a computational error had been made! Correlation coefficients never exceed 1.0. It is important to realize that the degree of correlation is expressed by the number itself and not by its sign. For example, between the numbers +0.5 and −0.7 the greatest degree of correlation is expressed by −0.7. The sign merely indicates in what direction the relationship exists, and direction will become better understood as we consider the following situation.

Spearman Rank-Order Correlation

Suppose that two judges were ranking the entries in a dog show. To simplify the outcome, imagine that the rankings looked like this:

	Rankings	
Dog	Judge 1	Judge 2
A	1	5
B	2	4
C	3	3
D	4	2
E	5	1

By comparatively scanning the above rankings, one can see that the dog ranked highest by Judge 1 was ranked lowest by Judge 2, that the dog ranked next highest by Judge 1 was ranked next lowest by Judge 2, and so forth. There is definitely a systematic relationship in a negative direction. Spearman's rho formula yields a correlation coefficient of –1.0. If the rankings in Judge 2's column had been reversed (1 for dog A, 2 for dog B, and so on), there would have been a perfect positive relationship between the judges' rankings, and the resulting Spearman rho coefficient would have been +1.0. Obviously, most judges are not likely either to agree or disagree this perfectly, so correlation coefficients generally are less than 1.0.

Pearson Product-Moment Correlation

This correlation procedure applies in situations where the researcher wants to determine whether there is a relationship between two groups of paired numbers. Pairing generally means that two scores exist for the same person; thus, in a typical situation utilizing this procedure, you would expect to have two sets of scores for each of several individuals and would now want to determine whether the scores were in any way related. To illustrate, imagine that you have just obtained IQ scores and foreign-language proficiency scores for a group of college sophomores. The question now arises of whether there is any relationship between intelligence and foreign-language proficiency. To answer the question, you conduct a Pearson Product-Moment Correlation on the two sets of scores. If the resulting correlation is in the +0.6 range or above, there would appear to be a high degree of relationship between these two factors. You can begin to see how many factors and aspects of personal and social life can be examined with this method. For instance, correlations have been made between high school and college performance levels, and obviously correlations have been made between performance on the GRE and success in the graduate program.

Correlation does not mean causation. It means that a systematic relationship has been found between two factors. When government and foundation sources discovered a correlation between cigarette smoking and incidence of lung cancer, cigarette industry spokesmen were quick to remind the researchers that they had only found a relationship and could not suggest causation.

If you think for a moment, you probably will realize that this correlation involves the same basic setting described for the use of the *t*-test for related measures. The difference is that in the case of the *t*-test you are comparing the same measure (taken at two different times or in matched groups) and are looking for a significant difference instead of for a systematic relationship.

Point-Biserial Correlation

If, in the above-described correlation setting, one of the scores you obtained was dichotomous, you would need a Point-Biserial Correlation to conduct the correlation. *Dichotomous suggests "either-or"* in contrast to a score continuum. If you compare IQ scores with whether a person obtains an above-B or below-B grade-point average in college, the latter situation is dichotomous. In tabling that dichotomous situation for purposes of the correlation, you might want to represent the above-B performances by the number 1 and the below-B by 0. The IQ scores can occur in a large, continuous range, and therefore your comparison would contain one continuous and one dichotomous measure for each person. Otherwise, the basic format would resemble the one that you would establish for the Pearson Product-Moment Correlation.

Chi-square

In discussing the nonparametric area of statistics, we mentioned that chi-square was one of the most prominent methods. Chi-square seeks to determine whether two variables are independent in a population from which a sample has been obtained. Chi-square deals with variables that are discrete categories rather than continuous measurements. For example, this statistic might be used to determine whether the variables of political party registration and sex are related. In the simplest chi-square settings, you would be working with two categories for each of the dimensions (in this instance, female-male and Democrat-Republican). The question is whether sex and political party affiliation are related in the population from which the sample was drawn. Because there are two discrete categories on each of the two variables, the resulting table resembles a square, four-paned window. In the procedure itself, you will obtain a value known as a phi coefficient (similar to a correlation coefficient) which can then be used to obtain a final chi-square value. Terms you can expect to find within chi-square procedures include *expected frequency*, *obtained frequency*, and *degrees of freedom*. Understanding of this statistic should come after you have worked your way through several examples. One of the basic introductory books in statistics can be a valuable reference source for this purpose. From a clear, simplified, conceptual presentation standpoint, we would recommend Weinberg and Schumaker's *Statistics: An Intuitive Approach* (Belmont, Calif.: Brooks/Cole, 1980). The following is a list of other statistics:

- *F*-test and *F*-maximum test
- Analysis of variance
  Completely randomized design
  Factorial design—two factors, three factors
  Treatments-by-levels design
  Treatments-by-subjects design (repeated measures design)
  Treatments-by-treatments-by-subjects design
  Two-factor mixed design (repeated measures on one factor)
  Three-factor mixed design (repeated measures on one factor)
  Three-factor mixed design (repeated measures on two factors)
- Latin square design

With the statistics listed above, work for *general* familiarity with situations in which they would be used rather than for mastery of their fundamentals. To calm any fears that you may be having, let's say that, where the *t*-test can only handle two groups of measures simultaneously, these measures have been devised to work with more than two sets of measures simultaneously. Bruning and Kintz's section introducing the different analysis-of-variance procedures can provide further clarity (and fear reduction). With regard to statistical procedures, your main objective is knowing the settings in which they would be used. For instance, suppose that a question on the GRE outlined five experimental formats and asked which one measured learning transfer—could you identify it? Basic familiarity both here and within the area of learning transfer will prepare you to answer such questions.

Books that can assist you in this review include the following:

James Bruning and B. L. Kintz, *Computational Handbook of Statistics* (Glenview, Ill.: Scott, Foresman, 1987). (Brief, narrative sections helpful in understanding design usages). Richard S. Lehman, *Statistics in the*

Behavioral Sciences: A Conceptual Introduction. (Pacific Grove, Calif.: Brooks/Cole, 1995). ("User friendly" conceptual introduction). R. Mark Sirkin, *Statistics for the Social Sciences* (Newbury Park, Calif.: Sage, 1994). (In-depth coverage). Rand P. Wilcox, ed., *Statistics for the Social Sciences* (New York: Academic, 1995), (Authoritative)

That may have seemed like a mammoth second step, and it was—encompassing all basic understanding in statistics. Because you have now mastered these essential concepts, however, the subsequent steps in hypothesis testing can go quickly; and as you review them you will understand their underlying rationale.

STEP 3: SET A SIGNIFICANCE LEVEL

In psychological research, the significance level is generally either .05 or .01. The .05 level indicates that you are willing to consider significant a difference that could occur by chance only five times in each hundred cases. The .01 level is more stringent, accepting as significant a difference that could occur by chance only one time in each hundred cases. Notice that the significance level is set before statistics are computed. This sequence is essential. Otherwise, an experimenter might decide after the fact which significance level to choose—the decision then being based on the size of the difference actually found. Throughout your perusal of psychological literature, you will find expressions like "significant at the .01 level" or "significant at the .05 level." Be sure you understand both their meaning and how they relate to proportions under the normal curve and probability.

STEP 4: COMPUTE STATISTICS

Having selected the experimental design in Step 2 and the significance level in Step 3, you should find this fourth step self-explanatory. Depending on the design that you have selected, you may have a t-value, z-value, F-value, and so on. In each instance, for the n or df in your experiment (based on the number of subjects you have in each group), you will refer to the appropriate table (z, t, F) to determine whether the value you have obtained is larger than the value required for significance at the level selected.

STEP 5: MAKE DECISION

If the number obtained in your computation is larger than the number found in the table for your significance level (at your appropriate n or df), you can reject the null (no difference) hypothesis. As mentioned earlier, every experimenter hopes that the difference found will be large enough for such rejection of the null. On the other hand, if the number you find in computation is smaller than the table value for your established significance level, you have failed to reject the null (meaning in this case that carrot eating did not have a significant effect on reading speed). Obviously, significant results are the prime candidates for publication in experimental-professional journals; and the findings most impressive to journal editors are those involving experiments in which a large number of subjects have been used. Relating all this to your specific situation, suppose that you selected the .05 significance level and obtained a z-score of 2.05 in your statistical computation. As you move to the appropriate column in the z-table (normal distribution table), you find that the score required for significance at the .05 level is 1.96. Since your score is larger, you can reject the null hypothesis and conclude that carrot eating has had a significant effect upon reading speed. The table reference will change as a function of the statistical procedure that you have selected, but the basic reference and decision-making procedure will remain the same.

You have now been duly initiated into the scientific method. This method is utilized by researchers in all areas of psychology in their quest for information and further understanding of behavior. Because of this prominence and virtual omnipresence throughout psychology, your understanding of its various aspects should be thorough.

Applied Psychology

Psychological concepts from all aspects of the field have their counterparts in practical settings, and throughout your daily experience you constantly encounter these applications. Signboards and cereal boxes utilize colors that will attract and hold attention in given intensities of light, speakers convey warmth and seek to influence opinions, newspaper ads strive to achieve the von Restorff (novel stimulus) effect, and movies appeal to motivations and emotions. Each of these methods is applied, and each is psychological. The specific intent of this applied psychology section, however, is to study industrial, human engineering, and organizational applications.

To gain a general perspective of this area, it may be helpful to concentrate briefly on each of these headings—*industrial psychology*, *human engineering*, and *organizational psychology*. They enable us to think of distinct concerns within the general framework of applied psychology, concerns that relate to one another like the threads of an intricate design in a woven fabric.

The term *industrial* implies production, and several aspects of this heading are product-related. Major considerations in this area include such questions as how to achieve both worker satisfaction and efficient production, how to match persons to the jobs for which they are best suited, and how to achieve high worker morale and motivation.

Human engineering relates more specifically to the work space of the individual worker. Here, some of the primary aspects can be expressed in such questions as whether the lighting, temperature, and noise levels are such that the worker can be effective. Additional concerns relate to promoting smooth work flow and eliminating bottlenecks in the production process. Within the work space of the individual employee, attention should be given to the location of equipment controls and to whether they are designed to promote both worker efficiency and safety. For obvious reasons, one work space that has been of prominent human engineering concern is the airplane cockpit. Here again, the problem is how to promote both maximal efficiency and safety.

Organizational psychology introduces concerns relating to the nature and effects of an organization's structure, communication patterns, processes in organizational decision making, and styles of leadership and leadership development. Whereas human engineering has a very specific focus upon work space, organizational psychology takes a broad-range perspective. As you proceed with this review, you will find elements from each of these headings interwoven within the context of applied psychology.

As we think of the organization and the worker, a natural emphasis at the outset is on analyzing jobs and their performance requirements and correspondingly selecting personnel whose aptitudes best match individual job descriptions. It is more than just a question of whether a person has, for instance, the finger dexterity needed to install screws quickly in automobile door handles; it is equally a question of whether the individual's personality and interests are compatible with the job and the work environment. The gardening or camping enthusiast may be discontent in a tiny office cubicle, and a basically shy radio performer may be personally unsuited for work in the television medium. In each instance, the emphasis is upon making the proper person-to-job match.

Such matching requires the use of personnel selection techniques that can produce the aptitude, personality, interest, and achievement information necessary for appropriate assessment and decision making. The required test "arsenals" are large and, in many cases, specific to the requirements of a given work setting, but among them are familiar names from your review of cognition and complex human learning. Several of the aptitude tests are prefaced with the words Purdue or Minnesota, prominent test contributors in this area. Personality tests include the Bernreuter and MMPI, and interest tests include the Strong-Campbell and the Kuder. Achievement tests range from a written test for factual knowledge to a performance test on a job-related task. Each instrument carries its unique function within the personnel selection process.

Once hired, the worker will continue to be evaluated, and the hiring organization must devise equitable, effective methods for appraising job performance. Such appraisals take on critical importance in areas such as wages and salaries, promotions, on-the-job training, and so forth. Likert-type checklist rating techniques and interview methods are among the procedures frequently employed in such appraisals. It is critical that appraisal procedures be sufficiently controlled to prevent a final evaluation based largely on the opinions of a single individual. It is equally critical to control for such elements as "halo" effect (the rater's tendency to give a totally positive evaluation to a person whom he or she likes) and constant error (the rater's general tendency toward leniency or harshness in evaluation procedures). It becomes obvious that, in order to be both effective and equitable, the components of an overall appraisal procedure must be skillfully designed and carefully implemented.

Beyond the person-centered aspects of selecting the appropriate individual and evaluating him equitably, there are major concerns relating to worker environment. In the specific work setting, these can be the human engineering questions of how to arrange equipment, knobs, lights, and traffic patterns to promote the least amount of lost motion and the most efficient worker performance. At the broader, organizational level, the question expands to that of the industry's general view of its workers.

The *industrial view toward workers* has never been a singular one that could be isolated in time and labeled unanimously scientific or consistently humanistic. Nevertheless, general climates have been evident during specific time periods in our nation's industrial history. The earliest climate, characteristic of the first quarter of the twentieth century, was one of scientific management. Within it, the emphasis was placed on production. Its principal advocates believed that work in general, and specific jobs in particular, should be defined clearly to the worker and that, given a knowledge of expectations and a product-designed work setting, reinforcements and punishments should be arranged in a manner designed to obtain highest output per worker input. This method sounds impersonal, and it is. Production emphasis, giving its attention to time-and-motion studies and piecework incentives, makes no provision for viewing the worker as a unique individual. In the purest sense, scientific management involves viewing the worker as part of the production machine.

The *human relations approach* emerged from the now classic "*Hawthorne effect.*" While studying ways to improve lighting and production-oriented features of a specific work setting, management at the Hawthorne Plant of the Western Electric Company discovered that productivity was increasing in the absence of any changes in work setting. The only viable explanation for this phenomenon was the attention being given to the workers themselves, and the results provided convincing support for the view that one can increase productivity by increasing worker satisfaction. Workers were being viewed on an individual basis, and the philosophy that a satisfied worker is a productive worker gained a foothold. In some industries, counseling psychologists were hired with responsibilities for helping workers solve personal problems. Techniques were devised for making workers feel that they were participants in decision-making processes. Plant newspapers, suggestion boxes, and corporate sharing were among the changes that emerged. Industry was acknowledging the worker as a human being with feelings and needs.

Both the human relations and the scientific management approaches are currently found on the industrial scene. Also frequently used in evaluating specific organizations is the *Blake-Mouton Grid*, based on the premise that an efficient organization demonstrates strong and equal levels of concern for people and for production. This measure and several other current approaches within industry reflect an attitude to the worker environment that is both human- and production-oriented.

The human relations approach has prompted numerous psychological studies of worker satisfaction. *Katz and Kahn* have applied the level-of-involvement model and suggest that certain jobs are inherently more satisfying than others because of the degree of worker involvement characterizing them. Utilizing *Kelman*'s categories, they point to the job of guard as an example of minimal involvement in one's work. They see it as a compliance-type position that calls upon the person simply to "be there." Individuality, sense of personal worth, and involvement are lacking in the job itself. At the other end of the involvement spectrum, the manager and the creative worker have built-in opportunities to internalize their work. This means that their values and goals can be very much in keeping with the goals and objectives characterizing their work positions. Within their work responsibilities, they have a sense of personal input. One of the major challenges for management has been to take jobs such as that of guard and bring a sense of personal involvement to them. To define the situation from a slightly different perspective, *Maslow* suggested that the more a work position engages a person's potentials, the deeper the satisfaction it provides. A kind of team approach has been used successfully in several industries to enhance the worker's sense of involvement. In coal mining, the perfection of conveyor systems destroyed team feeling and interaction among workers. It was a case where implementation of an obviously more efficient scientific method led to increased absenteeism and lower production. By contrast, miners working in teams felt a sense of responsibility to those teams, could identify with team goals, and received team support for their individual contributions.

A similar kind of distinction within industry has been made between the process and product models for workers. In the *process model*, the emphasis is "plugging in" the worker to an ongoing industrial process. The *product model* seeks to identify the worker with the final product. To accomplish such identification, an organization may take assembly-line workers and rotate them among different points in the assembly process. This rotation allows the individual worker to be involved with the product at different stages of completion, enhancing the possibility of his identification with the end product toward which work is being directed.

Communication patterns and leadership styles profoundly affect the working climate and consequent satisfaction that a worker experiences. A communication pattern can promote either autocratic or democratic feeling throughout the work force and can do much to establish positions of power within the communication process. Consider briefly the following patterns of communication.

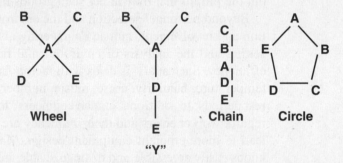

The wheel, "Y," and chain are centralized communication networks. They share the advantages of facilitating efficient performance of routine tasks, strengthening positions of leadership, and allowing for quick formation of stable patterns of interaction among group members. The most central position within each of these patterns is A, and the person occupying this position has built-in power, potential leadership, and the greatest likelihood of experiencing satisfaction. Peripheral positions such as C and E can be expected to experience the least satisfaction.

The circle is an example of a decentralized communication network. All positions have equal communication access. Although the decentralized network is less efficient than the centralized patterns, participants in such a circle-type pattern register much stronger feelings of satisfaction and seem better prepared to handle nonroutine, unpredictable situations than participants in the other patterns. Once can readily see the variables in worker climate that can develop through communication network patterns.

In a specific communication setting—the interaction process of groups involved in decision making—*Bales* established analytical categories that have attained wide use and acceptance. His twelve categories are grouped in the following four areas:

(A) Positive reactions—Shows solidarity, shows tension release, shows agreement

(B) Problem-solving attempts—Gives suggestions, gives opinions, gives orientation

(C) Questions—Asks orientation, asks opinions, asks suggestions
(D) Negative reactions—Shows disagreement, shows tension increase, shows antagonism

Areas B and C are used to determine a group member's task orientation, and areas A and D are indicative of the member's sociability. Analysis centers upon the frequency of a person's interaction within each of the categories.

To point out another facet of the communication process operating within decision-making groups, *Janis* advanced the concept of *groupthink*. He believes that the highly cohesive group can foster a number of illusions among its membership. In discussing his illusion of invulnerability, Janis expresses the view that the group may decide to take risks that its members individually would not be willing to take. The illusion of morality involves the group's tendency to consider any actions that it may take as being moral. An illusion of unanimity indicates that although the group may appear to have made a unanimous decision, individual members may have censored themselves and silenced their dissent. Other factors in groupthink include shared stereotypes, rationalization, self-censorship, direct pressure, and mindguards. The cohesive group shares the benefits of high morale, but Janis points out the pitfalls that may affect such groups in their decision making.

Beyond personnel selection and the environmental factors of job satisfaction and involvement, human engineering also deals with the specific work setting and the analysis of environmental factors as they relate to worker efficiency. Such analysis deals with factors involving illumination, air flow, temperature, humidity, noise, music, number of hours in the work day, and rest periods. In addition, "human engineers" look at equipment design. In this regard, worker errors and their frequency are studied for insights that might lead to more efficient equipment design. Making dials easily readable and knobs easily accessible and distinguishable are part of the human engineering goal. As you board an airplane for some distant destination, you begin to take a strong personal interest in how well the human engineer has done his job. Efficiency in cockpit control-panel design is among the major concerns of human engineering.

Because industry cannot function without the consumers, marketing is of special corporate interest. Though some industries are meeting an already existing consumer need, other corporations must create a need among potential consumers. In either case, the marketing process must involve careful attention to consumers' attitudes, motivations, and perceptions. Instruments such as attitude surveys, questionnaires, and interviews assist the corporation in tapping consumer opinion. The relationship between sales and specific marketing techniques is carefully studied, and distinct changes in approach are made in response to generally negative attitudes from consumers and/or disappointing sales for a given product. Although marketing may seek to shape consumer behavior, it is also obvious that consumer response can shape an industry's product directions.

From the moment that you begin looking for a job, applied psychology is all around you. Personnel selection, general worker climate, specific work setting, and product sales combine to form a complex picture of which the following are among the central names and concepts:

Applied Psychology Outline

Concepts	Names	Terms
Industrial		
Production emphasis	Taylor	Scientific management
Time-and-motion		Minimize both time and motion to maximize efficiency
Piecework		Pay on the basis of number of pieces completed, setting target thresholds to be met
Process model		Focus on the process (e.g., the assembly line) rather than worker identity with product
Personnel selection		
Job analysis		Identifying job requirements
Recruitment		Methods for obtaining people to fill job requirements
Interviews		Poor predictor of individual's job performance
Structured		Prescribed set of questions
Situational		Hypothetical work situations
Testing		Knowledge and skills required for a particular job
Assessment centers	AT&T-initiated in 1950s (Generally independent, noncompany-related facilities)	Evaluate a small number of candidates over a series of days, placing them in stressful situations, giving them a challenging "in-basket," and so on
Organizational		
Human relations approach		
Hawthorne Effect	Western Electric, 1929–32 (Mayo's research interpretation that fostered the human relations movement)	Importance of treating workers as unique and important individuals
Blake-Mouton Grid	Blake-Mouton	On a nine-point grid (vertical and horizontal axis), it evaluates the degree to which a company emphasizes process (production orientation) and human relations (worker concern)
Theories		
Need-achievement	McClelland/Atkinson	High need to achieve (n Ach) associated with executive success
Needs-hierarchy	Maslow	The importance of attending to workers' physiological, safety, belongingness and love, esteem, and self-actualization needs
ERG	Alderfer	Relates three of Maslow's needs (existence, relatedness, and growth) to the workplace
Motivator-hygiene	Herzberg	Suggests that only meeting higher-order needs (Maslow's self-actualization) can attain worker satisfaction

Concepts	Names	Terms
Job-characteristics	Hackman/Oldham	Relates job characteristics and the individual worker's need for growth with resulting job satisfaction
Expectancy	Vroom	Reward-expectancy governs the choices and behaviors of workers in the workplace.
	Lawler-Porter Modification	Motivation, ability, and *role perceptions* govern worker performance
Goal-setting	Locke	Clarity and participation in goal-setting is basic to worker success and satisfaction in the workplace
Equity	Adams	Worker comparison of inputs and outcomes with those of other workers for judgment of fairness

Concepts	Names	Terms
Work-group Distinctions		
Formal		Hierarchy chart of company
Informal		Friendship and common interest groups
Work norms		Generally established within the informal work groups

Concepts	Names	Terms
Leadership		
Research eras		
Trait	Aristotle	Leaders are born with leadership traits
Leader-behavior	Hemphill (later Komaki, Lord & Maher)	Importance of studying leader-behaviors for clues to effective leadership—two basic dimensions: Initiating structure Consideration
Interaction	Fiedler (Fiedler and Garcia elaboration is termed *cognitive-resource utilization theory*)	Contingency Model—matching *task-centered* and *person-centered* leaders to the appropriate leadership settings (believes the match, not birth-given traits is the key to leadership success)
Types		
Authoritarian		Leader-dominated
Democratic		Participatory
Transactional		Provide worker support to help achieve job satisfaction
Transformational		Motivate through charisma and vision to goals beyond worker expectation

Concepts	Names	Terms
Assessment	Bass & Avolio	Multifactor leadership questionnaire (MLQ)
Modes of attainment		
Appointed		From outside the group
Emergent		From within the group

Concepts	Names	Terms
Communication patterns		
Centralized		Wheel, Y, chain
Decentralized		Circle, all-channel
Group interaction process		
Categories	Bales	Positive reactions, problem-solving, questions, negative-reactions
Groupthink	Janis	Self-defeating process characteristic of cohesive groups; characterized by: Illusion of invulnerability Illusion of morality Illusion of unanimity Self-censorship Mindguards Shared stereotypes Rationalization Direct pressure
Human Factors		
Efficiency		
Ergonomics	From Greek "ergon" (work) and "nomos" (natural laws)	Matching displays and controls to natural human physiology
Applications		
Traffic safety		
Environmental	McGinnis	Brake-light position (centered and high-mounted)
Personal	Laux & Brelsford	The driving needs of an increasingly aging population
Behavioral	Ludwig & Geller	Seat belt use
Information displays		Lights vs. meters and multi-sensory (e.g., visual + audio)
Controls		Shape-coded knobs for use in aircraft cockpits; for example, standardizing the functional outcomes of a given knob, pedal, or wheel movement
Human-computer		Facilitating operator learning and minimizing stress and strain related with video display terminals (VDT's)
Space exploration		Extra-vehicular activity (EVA), its unique problems and challenges
Environmental		
Definition		Studying the impact of specific environments on behavior
Applications		
Urban density		The effects of crowding on mental health, crime, families, etc.

Concepts	Names	Terms
Noise		Effects on health and functioning, and distinctions between the effects of short-term and long-term noise exposure

School		
Roles		
Assessment		Both academic and personality
Intervention		To improve the learning environment and the experience of individual students within it
Program evaluation		Through teamwork and consultation with parents and community professionals

The preceding list is but a sampling. Beyond it, the *Journal of Applied Psychology* can give you the topically diverse flavor of the field. To review in a more systematic fashion, one of the following books would be helpful:

Jerald Greenberg's *Behavior in Organizations.* New York: Prentice-Hall, 1996. Dubrin's *Organizational Behavior: An Applied Perspective*. Ohio: South Western Educational Publishers, 1997. Paul Spector's *Industrial and Organizational Psychology: Research and Practice.* New York: Wiley, 1995.

As in the other areas of your review, you cannot expect to gain Ph.D.-level mastery of applied psychology, but acquaintance and familiarity with its primary aspects will be important to you. The field is a rapidly growing one.

Beyond "The Topics"

In any administration of the GRE you will find a sprinkling of questions that do not fit any given topic area but cut across areas or "fall in the cracks" between them. They relate to general knowledge and familiarity with the field. Some of these questions might be classified as "History and Systems"—knowledge of the historical schools of thought within the field and its background. Still others of these questions might be characterized as day-to-day familiarity with psychology—knowing, for instance, that the American Psychological Association (APA) is the official professional organization for the field, that it is based in Washington, D.C., and that it publishes several journals in the field, and so forth. Another organization, the American Psychological Society (APS) has more recently formed and places its primary focus on academic settings and research. The APS also is based in Washington, D.C. Obviously, you do not want to concentrate your major review time on these "beyonds," but a quick-glance familiarity might prove helpful, especially in the History and Systems area. To help with that final brief look, here are some aspects to include in your quick glimpse "beyond."

History and Systems

Schools:

Structuralism: *Wundt* founded the *first psychological laboratory* at Leipzig, Germany, in 1879 (a date as basic to psychology as Columbus and 1492 is to the United States). The structuralists studied the mind through *introspection* (in effect, being trained to observe your own conscious experience). *Titchener* was the major spokesperson for this school of psychology within the United States. The approach never really got a strong foothold in the United States because it *lacked objectivity*.

Functionalism: Emphasized adaptation to one's environment (and the mind as an adaptive tool). Strongly influenced by the work of Darwin, its chief advocates were *Dewey* and *William James*. Critical of structuralism, it emphasized behavior and adjustment rather than isolated mental states.

Behaviorism: A kind of "objective functionalism." Strongly influenced by the functionalist approach and the work of Pavlov, it insisted on objective observation—excluding conscious experience (the structuralism mainstay) as beyond the realm of appropriate study for scientific research. Its early advocate was *Watson*, and more recently, *Skinner* (each covered in more detail within the Personality review section).

Gestalt: A reaction to behaviorism (and its reduction of behavior to muscle-twitch elements), it emphasized studying the whole person. Its primary definitional "byline" is "The whole is greater than the sum of its parts." Its founder was *Wertheimer*. Kohler and Koffka also were key figures within this school.

Psychoanalysis: Begun with the clinical work of *Freud*, it was prevalent in Europe at the time functionalism was prevalent in the United States. It held the position that behavior was determined by unconscious motivations—many of them rooted in a child's early psychosexual development. (Further discussion of this school of thought is found within the earlier Personality review section.)

These works can provide meaningful reference in the history/systems area without heading you for five-volume detail: M. Marx and William A. Cronan-Hillix, *Systems and Theories in Psychology* (New York: McGraw, 1987), (Has an excellent "schools time chart" just after its Preface; the standard history/systems work in the field.) M. Wertheimer, *A Brief History of Psychology* (New York: Holt, Rinehart & Winston, 1987), (Not the founder of the Gestalt school! It's very readable and traces the emergence of psychology from its Greek/philosophical beginnings.) More current works include:

James F. Brennan's *History and Systems of Psychology*. New York: Prentice-Hall, 1993. Malone's *History and Systems of Psychology*. Pacific Grove, Calif.: Wadsworth, 1997.

Professional Information

Journals published by the American Psychological Association include:

Contemporary Psychology
Journal of Abnormal Psychology
Journal of Applied Psychology
Behavioral Neuroscience

Journal of Comparative Psychology
Journal of Consulting and Clinical Psychology
Journal of Educational Psychology
Psychological Bulletin
Journal of Personality & Social Psychology
Developmental Psychology
Professional Psychology
Journals of Experimental Psychology
  There are four of them, each with the *JEP* heading:
  General
  Learning, Memory, & Cognition
  Human Perception & Cognition
  Animal Behavior Processes
Psychology and Aging
Psychological Abstracts

The official journal received by all APA members is the *American Psychologist*, and the official monthly newspaper is the *APA Monitor*. The official journal of the APS received by all members is *Psychological Science*, and the official bimonthly newspaper is the *APS Observer*.

Feel official now? Great. Be familiar here, but don't "invest your life savings." A few questions on the GRE may tap this day-to-day, working knowledge.

Remember, a strong introductory textbook is your best primary review source. See Chapter 1 book recommendations and keep your book close at hand throughout your review.

4 Diagnostic Test 2 for Review Analysis

Now that you've intensively reviewed each of the areas, let's see how you're doing. Find a good test-taking place equipped with a couple of sharp pencils and good erasers. Set your timer for 170 minutes, note how many questions are on the test (GRE tests vary between the 190s and 220s), and give it your best. Good luck!

Diagnostic Test 2

Time: 170 minutes

Directions: Each of the following questions contains five possible responses. Read the question carefully and select the response that you feel is most appropriate. Then completely darken the oval on your answer grid that corresponds with your choice.

1. A physical stimulus is converted into a neural impulse by a process known as

   (A) transposition   (B) transaction   (C) transduction
   (D) transition   (E) transference

2. The glands of the body serve as

   (A) receptors   (B) effectors   (C) nodes
   (D) afferent nerves   (E) efferent nerves

3. As one moves from external stimulus to motor response, which of the following constitutes an accurate sequential pattern?

   (A) afferent nerve, interneuron, efferent nerve
   (B) efferent nerve, interneuron, afferent nerve
   (C) afferent nerve, efferent nerve, neural modulator
   (D) efferent nerve, afferent nerve, neural modulator
   (E) neural modulator, efferent nerve, afferent nerve

4. Synaptic transmission and the function of the synapse were first discovered and outlined by

   (A) Descartes   (B) Delgado   (C) Penfield
   (D) Sherrington   (E) Olds

5. The antagonistic actions of skeletal muscles are termed

   (A) associative inhibition
   (B) synaptic transmission
   (C) reciprocal extension
   (D) counterconditioning
   (E) reciprocal inhibition

6. Which of the following is *not* a neurotransmitter?

   (A) acetylcholine   (B) serotonin   (C) dopamine
   (D) epinephrine   (E) opioid peptides

7. A neuron does *not* contain

   (A) a cell body   (B) septum   (C) axon
   (D) myelin sheath   (E) dendrites

8. The divisions of the peripheral nervous system are the

(A) CNS and somatic
(B) CNS and PNS
(C) somatic and visceral
(D) somatic and autonomic
(E) visceral and central

9. The head-injured patient lost the ability to breathe. Autopsy revealed neural damage in the

(A) medulla   (B) midbrain   (C) cerebellum
(D) hypothalamus   (E) pons

10. _____ demonstrated that stimulation to the motor cortex can elicit body movements.

(A) Cajal   (B) Sherrington   (C) Penfield
(D) Descartes   (E) Olds

11. *Not* among the major brain divisions is

(A) frontal   (B) cerebellum   (C) brain stem
(D) forebrain   (E) reticular activating system

12. The alcoholic staggered even when not drunk. Damage had occurred to the

(A) cerebellum   (B) reticular activating system   (C) medulla
(D) pons   (E) thyroid gland

13. Left hemisphere is to right hemisphere as

(A) hearing is to speaking
(B) spatial ability is to language function
(C) balance is to movement
(D) language function is to spatial ability
(E) Broca's area is to Wernicke's area

14. You are a right-handed, split-brain patient. You have just been very briefly shown a telephone picture to the left of your center-vision point. You will

(A) immediately say telephone
(B) indicate that you saw nothing
(C) speak at length about telecommunications
(D) find yourself becoming dizzy
(E) immediately think of your last phone conversation

15. The two major divisions of the autonomic nervous system are

(A) somatic and peripheral
(B) brain and spinal cord
(C) sympathetic and parasympathetic
(D) parietal and occipital
(E) septum and hippocampus

16. _____ measures brain-wave activity, more specifically, emitted potentials.

(A) MRI   (B) CAT scan   (C) EKG   (D) ESB   (E) EEG

17. _____ is a neurotransmitter-related brain disorder associated with acetylcholine deficiency.

(A) Alzheimer's   (B) Parkinson's   (C) Wernicke's
(D) schizophrenia   (E) Down syndrome

18. _____ is the cerebral "alarm clock," which selectively filters incoming stimuli.

(A) medulla   (B) pons   (C) reticular formation
(D) cerebellum   (E) limbic system

19. For the diabetic, the basic problem is that the_____ is not producing _____.

(A) adrenal medulla, epinephrine
(B) adrenal cortex, carbohydrate
(C) thyroid, acetylcholine
(D) pituitary, somatotropin
(E) pancreas, insulin

20. A patient who is taking Eskalith (lithium carbonate) is most likely experiencing the problem of _____.

(A) anxiety   (B) depression   (C) psychosis
(D) mania   (E) memory loss

21. The narcotics/opiates do *not* include

(A) cocaine   (B) codeine   (C) heroin
(D) morphine   (E) opium

22. Jo Nell is suffering from depression. She most likely is taking which of the following:

(A) Haldol   (B) Zoloft   (C) Resperdol
(D) Clozaril   (E) Thorazine

23. Genotype is to phenotype as _____ is to _____.

(A) trait characteristics, cell genetic make-up
(B) living cell, sex determinant
(C) cell genetic make-up, trait characteristics
(D) eugenics, genetic drift
(E) genetic drift, inbreeding

24. _____ has been a central figure in the field of sociobiology.

(A) Darwin   (B) Wilson   (C) Lorenz
(D) Tinbergen   (E) Mendel

25. _____ paired maze-bright and maze-dull rats in a field called _____.

    (A) Lorenz, imprinting
    (B) Tinbergen, fixed-action patterns
    (C) Darwin, natural selection
    (D) Tryon, eugenics
    (E) Mendel, dominance and recessiveness

26. Fechner's Law ($S = k \log I$) states that

    (A) a constant stimulus intensity causes a logarithmic decrease in sensation
    (B) an increase in the stimulus causes a logarithmic decrease in sensation
    (C) an increase in the stimulus causes a logarithmic increase in sensation
    (D) an increase in sensation means a logarithmic increase in stimulus intensity
    (E) an increase in sensation means a logarithmic decrease in stimulus intensity

27. You are holding a weight of 10 lb, and 2 lb are added before you can report a difference. According to Weber's Law, if you were holding a 20-lb weight, _____ lb would need to be added before you could report a difference.

    (A) 3   (B) 8   (C) 4   (D) 6   (E) 2

28. You have just been presented with a 1,000-cycle-per-second tone. As the frequency is slowly increased, you are instructed to tell the experimenter when you notice a difference in pitch. At 1,050 cps you report noticing a difference. The 50 cps change is your

    (A) absolute threshold
    (B) difference threshold
    (C) criterion threshold
    (D) minimum threshold
    (E) maximum threshold

29. The person is seeing a tree. Proximal is to distal as _____ is to _____.

    (A) retinal image, tree
    (B) tree, retinal image
    (C) perception, sensation
    (D) tree, perception
    (E) tree, sensation

30. Transduction is

    (A) the light source from the distal stimulus
    (B) the transfer of energy from proximal stimulus to distal stimulus
    (C) the psychological experience of a stimulus
    (D) the transformational activity in the medulla, converting the light waves
    (E) the conversion process whereby proximal stimulus becomes neural impulse

31. In signal-detection research, when no stimulus is presented and the subject reports seeing one, it is called

    (A) a hit   (B) a miss   (C) a false alarm
    (D) a false positive   (E) an hallucination

32. Two persons are equal in sensitivity but quite different in response biases. Their ROC curves will be

    (A) markedly different   (B) slightly different
    (C) biased and invalid   (D) identical   (E) uninterpretable

33. Specificity theory—as distinct from across-fiber theory—advances the position that

    (A) there are quality-specific neurons
    (B) quality is derived from the overall pattern of neural firing
    (C) specific brain cells store specific visual and facial memories
    (D) a broad range of brain cells randomly store visual and facial memories
    (E) specific cognitive bias affects the storage of given visual memories

34. The doctrine of specific nerve energies was advanced by

    (A) Weber   (B) Fechner   (C) Stevens
    (D) Gallaudette   (E) Muller

35. Jill can sense the position of her leg and foot as she walks. This feedback comes courtesy of her _____ sense.

    (A) vestibular   (B) cerebellar   (C) olfactory
    (D) kinesthetic   (E) chemical

36. A specific sound frequency is sent to the subject, followed by another specific frequency, and another. The subject is to signal whenever she or he detects a sound. This method is called the method of _____.

    (A) difference threshold   (B) constant stimuli
    (C) magnitude estimation   (D) limits   (E) signal detection

37. The trichromatic theory is associated with the work of _____.

    (A) Young   (B) Hering   (C) Hubel
    (D) Helmholtz   (E) Wiesel

38. Visual depth is due, in part, to

    (A) rod vision   (B) cone vision   (C) accommodation
    (D) opponent-process   (E) retinal disparity

39. Pinna is part of the

    (A) oval window   (B) outer ear   (C) ossicles
    (D) cochlea   (E) anvil

40. After two college roommates have been living together for a year, they find that their menstrual cycles have synchronized. Researchers would attribute this synchrony, in part, to

    (A) observational learning   (B) olfactory cues
    (C) auditory cues   (D) spatial cues   (E) transmodulation

41. Gate-control theory is associated with _____ and the sensation of _____.

    (A) Melzack, pain   (B) Olds, pleasure   (C) Weber, touch
    (D) Helmholtz, vision   (E) Baker, audition

42. *Not* a monocular cue for depth is

    (A) relative size   (B) interposition   (C) convergence
    (D) linear perspective   (E) shading

43. In closure we tend to

    (A) complete figures that have a gap in them
    (B) prefer differential contours
    (C) associate the distal and proximal stimuli
    (D) view on the basis of texture gradient
    (E) rely on component process

44. In dichotic listening, _____ is presented to _____.

    (A) the same stimulus, each ear simultaneously
    (B) a different stimulus, each ear simultaneously
    (C) a single stimulus, one ear only
    (D) a single stimulus, randomly to both ears
    (E) a different stimulus, sequentially to both ears

45. Stationary lights on a neon sign blink sequentially and appear to move. This appearance is called the _____.

    (A) Ponzo illusion   (B) von Restorff effect   (C) Necker illusion
    (D) phi phenomenon   (E) induced movement effect

46. Half of a line has arrows or fins pointing outward. The remaining half has arrows or fins pointing inward. The first half looks longer than the second half. This is the _____ illusion.

    (A) Zollner   (B) Wundt   (C) Poggendorf
    (D) Escher   (E) Muller-Lyer

47. We come from a straw-thatch village where there are no carpentered right-angles or high-rise buildings. Compared to someone in urban, Western society, we would be _____ to see the _____.

    (A) more likely, trapezoidal room illusion
    (B) more likely, Escher illusion
    (C) less likely, moon illusion
    (D) less likely, Taylor illusion
    (E) less likely, Ames window illusion

48. The rectangular table appears rectangular regardless of the distance or angle at which it is viewed. This is an example of

    (A) brightness constancy
    (B) size constancy
    (C) shape constancy
    (D) height constancy
    (E) monocular constancy

49. The major laws of perceptual organization were developed by the

    (A) Gestaltists   (B) Phenomenologists   (C) Cognitivists
    (D) Probabilists   (E) Transactionalists

50. Top-down processing refers to

    (A) activating higher-order units of perception, which influence items of lower order
    (B) activating lower-order units of perception, which influence items of higher order
    (C) activating both higher-order and lower-order units simultaneously
    (D) the flow process within a cognitive hierarchy
    (E) moving from phonemes to morphemes rather than vice versa

51. The conditioned stimulus gets its reinforcing power from association with the _____.

    (A) unconditioned response
    (B) unconditioned stimulus
    (C) discriminative stimulus
    (D) generalized stimulus
    (E) stimulus transfer

52. When a light paired with a bell takes on reinforcing characteristics, the phenomenon is called _____.

    (A) third-order conditioning
    (B) anomalous conditioning
    (C) distinctive conditioning
    (D) higher-order conditioning
    (E) counterconditioning

53. The Law of Effect was developed by _____.

    (A) Skinner   (B) Watson   (C) Thorndike
    (D) Pavlov   (E) Sullivan

54. Tom receives a salary at the end of each month. His reinforcement schedule is

    (A) variable interval   (B) fixed interval   (C) variable ratio
    (D) fixed ratio   (E) none of the above

55. The gambler's disease is a striking and devastating result of

    (A) variable interval   (B) fixed interval   (C) variable ratio
    (D) fixed ratio   (E) phylogenetic characteristics

56. Classical conditioning is to instrumental conditioning as _____
    is to _____.

    (A) Type R, Type S
    (B) Type S, respondent
    (C) Type R, operant
    (D) respondent, operant
    (E) solution, sign

57. "Give me a child till that child is five years old, and I will make of him anything you want—doctor, lawyer, thief." A likely quote from _____.

    (A) Thorndike   (B) Hull   (C) Spence
    (D) Pavlov   (E) Watson

58. In learning transfer, you perform more poorly on a later task because you had learned an earlier task that interfered. This is called _____.

    (A) proactive facilitation
    (B) retroactive facilitation
    (C) constructive inhibition
    (D) retroactive inhibition
    (E) proactive inhibition

59. The plateau point in a learning curve is the point at which

    (A) physiological limit of capability has been reached
    (B) incubation is occurring and performance will increase later
    (C) response has been extinguished
    (D) spontaneous recovery occurs
    (E) learning set demonstrates its effectiveness

60. Which of the following is an accurate learning-acquisition sequence?

    (A) drive, cue, response, reinforcement
    (B) cue, drive, response, reinforcement
    (C) cue, response, drive, reinforcement
    (D) drive, response, cue, reinforcement
    (E) response, cue, drive, reinforcement

61. The most effective technique in classical conditioning is

    (A) forward pairing—delayed
    (B) forward pairing—trace
    (C) backward pairing—delayed
    (D) backward pairing—trace
    (E) simultaneous pairing

62. The cognitive field theory was developed by

    (A) Harlow (B) Premack (C) Hull
    (D) Rescorla (E) Tolman

63. Until they are reduced to a given level of satiation, primary (biological) drives preempt all other drives. This statement reflects the concept of

    (A) arousal-enhancement (B) expectancy-value
    (C) homeostasis (D) need-press (E) opponent-process

64. Which of the following is an *incorrect* pairing?

    (A) competency drive—White
    (B) achievement need—Solomon
    (C) expectancy/value—Rotter
    (D) sensation-seeking—Zuckerman
    (E) needs hierarchy—Maslow

65. The researcher stimulates the lateral area of the rat's hypothalamus. The resulting behavioral outcome is

    (A) cessation of eating (B) overeating (C) sexual arousal
    (D) onset of sleep (E) hyperactivity

66. When Olds and Milner stimulated an animal's limbic system, the net outcome effect was

    (A) aggression (B) hyperactivity (C) pleasure
    (D) maternal behavior (E) sexual mounting behavior

67. The parachutist landed safely, and initial exhilaration was immediately followed by tears and crying. This sequence could best be explained by _____.

    (A) Solomon (B) Cannon (C) Selye
    (D) Bernard (E) James

68. We see something frightening. _____ would say we run and then we're scared. _____ would say we're scared and then we run.

    (A) Solomon, Bernard (B) Selye, Lazarus (C) Lewis, Saarni
    (D) James, Cannon (E) Turner, Ortony

69. "Stay calm!" this physiological system says. No "fight-or-flight" preparation here.

    (A) sympathetic (B) parasympathetic (C) medulla
    (D) pons (E) limbic

70. Increases in motivation and arousal bring increases in emotion.

    (A) Bowlby (B) Harlow (C) Frijda
    (D) Schachter-Singer (E) Yerkes-Dodson

71. Rhesus monkeys that feed on a terry cloth mother are notably better adjusted than those who feed on a wire mother. And, given the option, a monkey will go to the terry cloth mother. The researcher and the principle are _____ and _____.

    (A) Harlow, contact comfort
    (B) Schachter-Singer, emotional arousal based on context
    (C) Bowlby, social stimulation
    (D) Spielberger, state vs. trait
    (E) Gore, social support

72. You are in a state of physiological arousal. You look to those around you for cues regarding what you should be feeling. If they're panicky, you panic. If they're depressed, you get depressed. If they're hyper, you feel hyper. Which of the following would say, "I told you so!"

    (A) Shaver   (B) Cannon-Bard   (C) James-Lange
    (D) Schachter-Singer   (E) Gore

73. Competitive, aggressive, hostile, impatient . . . finds waiting in lines the absolute pits. This person would be considered _____.

    (A) Type B personality   (B) cyclothymic   (C) state-anxious
    (D) Type A personality   (E) Avoidant personality

74. Selye's General Adaptation Syndrome has three stages. Which of the following constitutes an accurate sequential order?

    (A) exhaustion, resistance, alarm
    (B) resistance, alarm, exhaustion
    (C) denial, anger, bargaining
    (D) anger, bargaining, denial
    (E) alarm, resistance, exhaustion

75. Your mother has just died, your spouse just left you, and you've started a new job. According to _____ you're in very stressful, dangerous emotional territory.

    (A) Holmes-Rahe   (B) Schachter-Singer   (C) James-Lange
    (D) Anderson-Gore   (E) Cannon-Bard

76. A major distinction between episodic and semantic memory was central to the work of

    (A) Miller   (B) Skinner   (C) Tulving
    (D) Ebbinghaus   (E) Bates

77. When Ebbinghaus set out to study human memory, he had a basic problem to resolve. He needed to

    (A) move beyond the introspection practices of the structuralists
    (B) find a novel-type stimulus his subjects wouldn't already know
    (C) mask familiar words in the paired-associates method of presentation
    (D) find a way to tap long-term rather than short-term memory
    (E) tap primitive beliefs as well as central traits

78. In the depth-of-processing theory of memory, which of the following represents an accurate increasing-depth-sequence?

    (A) semantic, physical, acoustic
    (B) acoustic, semantic, physical
    (C) encoding, storage, retrieval
    (D) storage, retrieval, encoding
    (E) physical, acoustic, semantic

79. "One is a bun. Two is a shoe. Three is a tree. Four is a door." This is part of the _____ method of improving memory.

    (A) pegword   (B) loci   (C) visual imagery
    (D) flashbulb   (E) permastore

80. *Not* among the basic theories of memory is _____.

    (A) dual-memory   (B) network   (C) elaborative
    (D) depth-of-processing   (E) set

81. Jill has learned something and now has been away from it for several months. A researcher measured how long it took her to learn it initially and now will measure how long it takes her to relearn it. By comparing the difference in the two times required for learning, the researcher has instituted the _____ method of measuring memory.

    (A) PQ4R   (B) savings   (C) meaningfulness
    (D) sensory   (E) maintenance

82. Which of the following will be *least* effectively retained? Learning to _____.

    (A) swim
    (B) ride a bicycle
    (C) drive a car
    (D) recite a poem
    (E) find your way through the streets of your hometown

83. The "magical number 7 plus or minus 2" refers to _____ and _____.

    (A) Brown, flashbulb memories
    (B) Tulving, semantic memory
    (C) Bahrick, permastore
    (D) Miller, short-term memory
    (E) Forester, sensory register memory

84. According to _____ and the _____ we have a tendency to remember the unfinished task.

    (A) Ziegarnik, Ziegarnik effect
    (B) von Restorff, von Restorff effect
    (C) Brown, tip-of-the-tongue
    (D) Coates, serial position effect
    (E) Tulving, episodic memory effect

85. Laboratory techniques for measuring retention have *not* included

    (A) serial-recall   (B) recognition   (C) free recall
    (D) paired-associates   (E) memory trace

86. According to _____, there is an inborn competence for language acquisition and a set acquisition pattern that will be followed regardless of the culture in which one is born.

    (A) Skinner   (B) Mowrer   (C) Chomsky
    (D) Gardner   (E) Rumbaugh

87. "I am the smallest unit of sound—'p,' 'd,' 'k.' I am _____."

    (A) a morpheme   (B) a subject   (C) a proposition
    (D) a typicality   (E) a phoneme

88. Language comprehension is associated with _____ area of the brain.

    (A) Wernicke's   (B) Broca's   (C) Rescorla's
    (D) Gage's   (E) Forester's

89. Which of the following is an *incorrect* pairing?

    (A) Hull—continuity theory
    (B) Krechevsky—noncontinuity theory
    (C) Bruner—inductive reasoning
    (D) Sternberg—parallel distribution theory
    (E) Tolman—cognitive maps

90. Jack and Jill went up the hill to fetch a pail of water. Jack fell down and broke his crown and just afterwards couldn't remember walking up the hill with Jill. This is a case of

    (A) anterograde amnesia   (B) retrograde amnesia
    (C) proactive amnesia   (D) early senility   (E) Alzheimer's

91. In the Stroop effect, we may be asked to remember the word "blue" when the color of the word itself actually was yellow. Our response tendencies demonstrate

    (A) transduction   (B) chaining   (C) loci
    (D) automatization   (E) PQ4R

92. Joan has a so-called "rule of thumb" she uses in working toward puzzle solutions. She is using a(n) _____.

    (A) mental representation   (B) cryptogram   (C) algorithm
    (D) heuristic   (E) mental set

93. MYCIN is one type of _____.

    (A) chaining   (B) expert system   (C) logarithm
    (D) algorithm   (E) schema

94. All cows are animals. All animals are living. Therefore, all cows are living.

    (A) heuristic (B) logarithm (C) expert system
    (D) transformation (E) syllogism

95. A young child learns that daddy has two legs, spectacles, and is a bit balding. One day on the street, while passing a balding man, the child says, "Daddy." This is a case of

    (A) using an algorithm
    (B) using a semantic logarithm
    (C) extending a morpheme
    (D) overgeneralizing
    (E) conceptual anomie

96. Thought models do *not* include

    (A) hierarchical network
    (B) parallel distributed processing
    (C) automatization
    (D) spreading activation
    (E) all of the preceding are thought models

97. Which of the following includes the *most* symbolic mental representation entries?

    (A) mental images, spatial thinking
    (B) episodic memory, spatial thinking
    (C) mental images, generic memory
    (D) eidetic imagery, spatial thinking
    (E) episodic memory, generic memory

98. Which is the last of the prelinguistic stages in a child's development of speech?

    (A) phonemes (B) basic cry (C) hierarchical
    (D) babbling (E) anagrammatic

99. The combination of a subject and a predicate is called a(n) _____.

    (A) morpheme (B) phoneme (C) proposition
    (D) sequence (E) analog

100. According to prototype theory, a prototype for a concept

    (A) must contain all features necessary to the definition within that class
    (B) must contain most, but not all, of the features necessary for definition within that class
    (C) is an eidetic image of a concept
    (D) must follow the principle advanced by Kohler
    (E) must follow the principle advanced by Rescorla

101. A correct sequential rendering of the prenatal development stages is
_____.

    (A) germinal, embryonic, fetal
    (B) fetal, germinal, embryonic
    (C) germinal, fetal, embryonic
    (D) embryonic, germinal, fetal
    (E) embryonic, fetal, germinal

102. This method of study compares children at various ages simultaneously.
It is the _____ method.

    (A) longitudinal   (B) clinical   (C) experimental
    (D) cross-sectional   (E) naturalistic

103. If a fetus has received a teratogen, you can expect

    (A) a brilliant newborn
    (B) a newborn with mostly recessive genetic features
    (C) a newborn with mostly dominant genetic features
    (D) a fetal self-abortion
    (E) a fetal malformation

104. The patterns of development are from the head down and from the center
of the torso toward the extremities. These two patterns are termed
_____ and _____, respectively.

    (A) cephalomodal, proximocaudal
    (B) anatodistal, ecolomodal
    (C) oxylocaudal, cephalodistal
    (D) oxylodistal, cephalocaudal
    (E) cephalocaudal, proximodistal

105. This newborn demonstrates the Babinski reflex. You would expect

    (A) outstretched arms, legs, and crying to a sudden change in environ-
    ment
    (B) head-turn toward a mild lips or cheeks stimulus
    (C) grasping in response to an object touching the hands or fingers
    (D) eye-blink to a flashed light
    (E) toes stretched outward and upward to a sole-of-the-foot touch

106. He walked across a field and a string of tiny goslings followed him.
The researcher was _____ and the demonstrated phenomenon
was _____.

    (A) Lorenz, imprinting
    (B) Harlow, contact comfort
    (C) Fantz, human face bonding
    (D) Gesell, physical bonding
    (E) Skinner, behavior modification

107. Separation anxiety occurs when the newborn is

   (A) 1 to 2 months old
   (B) 3 to 4 months old
   (C) 8 to 15 months old
   (D) 24 to 30 months old
   (E) 3 years old

108. Which of the following is an *incorrect* stage theory pairing?

   (A) Piaget—cognitive
   (B) Kohlberg—physiological
   (C) Freud—psychosexual
   (D) Erikson—psychosocial
   (E) Gesell—physical maturation

109. You know that even though the toy boat has been placed in the filled aquarium tank, the tank itself still contains the same amount of water. In Piagetian terms this is _____ conservation.

   (A) number
   (B) substance
   (C) length
   (D) area
   (E) volume

110. Which of the following *correctly* states the sequence of Piagetian stages?

   (A) sensorimotor, preoperational, formal operations, concrete operations
   (B) preoperational, sensorimotor, formal operations, concrete operations
   (C) sensorimotor, preoperational, concrete operations, formal operations
   (D) preoperational, sensorimotor, concrete operations, formal operations
   (E) preoperational, formal operations, concrete operations, sensorimotor

111. The child cognitively believes that the ocean's waves only roll in when s/he is there watching them. This child is expressing _____ and has not yet attained _____.

   (A) accommodation, assimilation
   (B) conservation, acquisition
   (C) assimilation, acquisition
   (D) acquisition, extinction
   (E) assimilation, accommodation

112. Hebb's six classes of factors in behavioral development do *not* include:

   (A) chemical, prenatal
   (B) chemical, postnatal
   (C) sensory, constant
   (D) sensory, variable
   (E) sensory, prenatal

113. Five blue buttons are laid out on a table. Five red buttons are laid out with more space between buttons. A four-year-old looks at the two sets of buttons and is asked if there are more blue or red buttons. The child answers _____ demonstrating the concept of _____ .

    (A) red buttons, number conservation has not been attained
    (B) blue buttons, number conservation has not been attained
    (C) blue buttons, number conservation has definitely been attained
    (D) red buttons, number conservation has definitely been attained
    (E) neither has more, number conservation has definitely been attained

114. Socially the young child can only attend to one dimension at a time. In cognitive terms this is called _____.

    (A) accommodation   (B) egocentrism   (C) assimilation
    (D) reversibility   (E) empiricism

115. At birth a newborn's head is approximately _____ percent of its total body length.

    (A) 15   (B) 25   (C) 40   (D) 50   (E) 60

116. When a harmful substance is taken by the mother, the aspect of fetal development most seriously affected is _____.

    (A) invariably the heart
    (B) the lungs
    (C) the cortex
    (D) the limbs
    (E) that which is most rapidly developing at the time the substance is consumed

117. _____ is the continuing function of heredity after birth.

    (A) maturation   (B) learning   (C) habituation
    (D) transduction   (E) nativism

118. Which of the following is true for individuals in middle-adulthood?

    (A) lower work satisfaction than in earlier years
    (B) no decline in strength or tissue elasticity
    (C) loss of skill on informational tasks but not on timed tasks
    (D) decrease in estrogen production for women
    (E) increase in testosterone production for men

119. Middle-adulthood is a time when

    (A) a person feels caught between generations—"children at both ends"
    (B) marriage gets reevaluated
    (C) career gets reevaluated
    (D) time orientation changes from years lived to years left to live
    (E) all of the above

120. The notion that children develop more in the pattern of an inclined plane than in the pattern of steps is characteristic of

(A) stage theory   (B) status theory   (C) continuity theory
(D) contiguity theory   (E) developmental theory

121. A major criticism of stage theories relates to the point that

(A) they ignore developmental norms
(B) they fail to account for sudden changes in behavior
(C) they are overly predictable
(D) they oversimplify and ignore individual variations
(E) they stem almost exclusively from psychoanalysis

122. Kohlberg's moral development stages are closely related to

(A) Freud's psychosexual stages
(B) Piaget's cognitive development stages
(C) Erikson's psychosocial stages
(D) Sullivan's interpersonal stages
(E) Dollard and Miller's learning stages

123. Between the ages of 2 and 3 years, a child's language development increases from approximately _____ words to _____ words.

(A) 50, 1000   (B) 2, 10   (C) 20, 50
(D) 50, 100   (E) 100, 200

124. The toy train disappears into a tunnel. From the child's cognitive perspective, the train is gone (in effect, no longer exists). This cognitive experience expresses an absence of _____ and is characteristic of _____.

(A) reversibility, the conservation stage
(B) assimilation, the conservation stage
(C) accommodation, the concrete operations stage
(D) object permanence, the sensorimotor stage
(E) object permanence, the concrete operations stage

125. In early junior high school, you would expect

(A) boys to be taller than girls
(B) girls to be taller than boys
(C) boys and girls to be the same height
(D) boys to excel in finger dexterity tasks
(E) boys to be notably better than girls in musical ability

126. That one's attitudes move in the direction of one's behaviors is a basic premise of

(A) Festinger   (B) Schachter   (C) Kelman
(D) Milgram   (E) Hathaway

127. "Checkmark the statements you agree with" would be an instruction found in a(n) _____ scale.

    (A) Likert (B) Osgood (C) Guttman
    (D) Thurstone (E) Kuder

128. This scale is developed on the premise that if an individual statement does not correlate positively with the overall score on the scale, it needs to be deleted.

    (A) Likert (B) Osgood (C) Guttman
    (D) Thurstone (E) Bogardus

129. You like your mother. Your mother does not like heavy metal. You like heavy metal. The triad is

    (A) balanced
    (B) imbalanced
    (C) balanced for your mother but imbalanced for you
    (D) carrying a valence of –2
    (E) carrying a valence of –3

130. Interactions are comparisons of rewards and costs. When costs outrun rewards, a given dyadic relationship will likely end. This is indicative of the _____ Model.

    (A) Balance (B) Social Comparison (C) Behavior Exchange
    (D) Complementarity (E) Gain-Loss

131. When Newcomb set up an experimental dorm, he found which of the following to be the most salient element in attraction?

    (A) proximity
    (B) rewardingness
    (C) proximity at first, similarity long-range
    (D) similarity at first, proximity long-range
    (E) similarity at first, rewardingness long-range

132. We like those people who agree with us. _____ found this dramatically to be true within his research.

    (A) Milgram (B) Aronson (C) Sherif
    (D) Schachter (E) Festinger

133. Under stressful conditions, there is a strong desire to affiliate with _____.

    (A) authority figures
    (B) anyone
    (C) experts
    (D) ingratiators
    (E) others in the same stressful circumstances

134. John kept the critical researcher's input from reaching the board meeting in which a decision would be made about marketing the weight-reducing pill. John was functioning as a(n) _____.

(A) mindguard
(B) creator of an illusion of invulnerability
(C) direct pressure agent
(D) facilitator
(E) unanimity advocate

135. Each of us has a bubble around us that extends roughly 18 inches. This relates to _____ work in the area of _____.

(A) Hall's, proxemics
(B) Birdwhistell's, kinesics
(C) Goffman's, anthropology
(D) Scheflen's, macro
(E) Kelman's, levels of influence

136. John was shown some Turkish words five times within a presentation series. Others he saw perhaps ten times, and still others only once. When asked to define the words, he _____.

(A) defined most positively the words he had seen least often
(B) defined most positively the words he had seen most often
(C) defined moderately positively all the words he had seen
(D) defined moderately negatively all the words he had seen
(E) defined most negatively the words he had seen most often

137. A political candidate has just told our group that the opposing candidate will be coming through next week. She has gone on to say some of what we will hear from the opposing candidate and has given us counterarguments to those points. This demonstrates _____.

(A) Newcomb's Balance Theory
(B) Ekman's Universality Theory
(C) McGuire's Inoculation Theory
(D) Bryan's Modeling Theory
(E) Sherif's Superordinate Theory

138. Research into television violence effects upon children makes frequent reference to the classic work of _____.

(A) Milgram   (B) Cialdini   (C) Sherif
(D) Bandura   (E) Asch

139. Which of the following is an *incorrect* pairing?

(A) Freedman—foot-in-the-door
(B) Cialdini—door-in-the-face
(C) Sherif—superordinate goal
(D) Zimbardo—deindividuation
(E) Deutsch—ingratiation

140. According to _____ research, _____ is a critical element in helping behavior.

    (A) Latane and Darley's, number of bystanders
    (B) Asch's, status of prospective helper
    (C) Milgram's, obedience-seeking tendency
    (D) Kelman's, compliance level
    (E) Allen's, overload

141. The Pope's highest-ranking cardinal speaks out in favor of abortion. There is a tendency to find his position exceedingly credible because it is _____.

    (A) based on the just-world hypothesis
    (B) premised on self vs. other attribution
    (C) nonnormative
    (D) extreme
    (E) responsibility-based

142. According to _____ we are _____.

    (A) phenomenologists, instinct-driven
    (B) behaviorists, perception-driven
    (C) trait theorists, stimulus-driven
    (D) psychoanalysts, learning-driven
    (E) none of the above

143. Brotherly love is among the most powerful because it is love between equals. _____ would agree.

    (A) Watson   (B) Horney   (C) Fromm
    (D) Adler   (E) Jung

144. Stage theories of personality include

    (A) Allport   (B) Adler   (C) Horney
    (D) Erikson   (E) all of the preceding

145. *Correctly* paired is

    (A) Freud—psychodynamic
    (B) Sullivan—interpersonal
    (C) Kelly—traits
    (D) Mowrer—reciprocal inhibition
    (E) Maslow—logotherapy

146. Rogers' concept of conscious-self-structure relates to

    (A) our current setting and discovery of our abilities within it
    (B) all the untested ability messages given to us in the past
    (C) sensory-visceral experience
    (D) unconditional positive regard
    (E) the Jonah Complex

147. We have a will to power and a will to pleasure, and both of them are self-defeating. This is the theoretical view of

    (A) Sullivan   (B) Allport   (C) Adler
    (D) Maslow   (E) Frankl

148. The 16 PF Scale is based on the work of _____ .

    (A) Eysenck   (B) Allport   (C) Sheldon
    (D) Cattell   (E) Murray

149. The basic theoretical background for the Myers-Briggs test is found in the work of

    (A) Erikson   (B) Hartmann   (C) Horney
    (D) Fromm   (E) Jung

150. A child who has almost drowned is now being beckoned into the water by her very closest friends. She is experiencing _____ conflict.

    (A) approach-approach
    (B) avoidance-avoidance
    (C) approach-avoidance
    (D) double approach-avoidance
    (E) none of the preceding

151. When a maladaptive response has just occurred, it is in a temporary state of exhaustion during which an adaptive response can be introduced with strong success potential. This approach is characteristic of

    (A) reciprocal inhibition
    (B) systematic desensitization
    (C) assertiveness
    (D) radical behaviorism
    (E) implosion

152. *Incorrectly* matched is

    (A) Mowrer—classical and instrumental conditioning in escape and avoidance
    (B) Kelly—Role Construct Repertory Test
    (C) Cattell—L, Q, and T data
    (D) Eysenck—inferiority feeling, superiority striving
    (E) Sheldon—endomorph, mesomorph, ectomorph

153. "This is a story-telling test. . . Tell what has happened before and what is happening now. Say what the people are feeling and thinking and how it will come out." These are instructions associated with the _____ in personality.

    (A) Rorschach Test
    (B) Thematic Apperception Test
    (C) Myers-Briggs Test
    (D) 16 PF Test
    (E) Minnesota Multiphasic Personality Test

154. He is a social behaviorist who devised an Internal-External Control Scale.

    (A) Allport   (B) Maslow   (C) Rotter
    (D) Frankl   (E) Harris

155. Tourette's disorder carries the symptoms of

    (A) bed-wetting   (B) stuttering   (C) repetitive movements
    (D) ADHD   (E) ADD

156. The soldier went into combat and suddenly his right arm was paralyzed. There was no injury causing the paralysis.

    (A) schizophrenia   (B) somatoform disorder
    (C) anxiety disorder   (D) mood disorder   (E) paranoia

157. The man went off on a fishing trip and lost all memory of who he was. Years later his original family, who had presumed him dead, read a newspaper article about a citizen award he had received in another community.

    (A) fugue   (B) multiple personality   (C) amnesia
    (D) mood disorder   (E) associative disorder

158. Bi-polar disorders are

    (A) mood related   (B) anxiety related   (C) delusional
    (D) substance-related   (E) schizophrenic

159. DSM-IV is organized along _____ axes.

    (A) 2   (B) 3   (C) 4   (D) 5   (E) 6

160. As you were walking down the hall, three people standing there were talking about you. You're sure of it.

    (A) delusional   (B) schizophrenic   (C) dissociative
    (D) somatoform   (E) anxiety

161. *Sybil* was a notable example of _____.

    (A) schizophrenia
    (B) substance-related disorder
    (C) paranoia
    (D) somatoform disorder
    (E) dissociative disorder

162. They are serotonin reuptake blockers—a "second generation" of drugs to treat

    (A) anxiety disorders
    (B) somatoform disorders
    (C) sexual disorders
    (D) sleep disorders
    (E) mood disorders

163. Jill is dreadfully fearful of heights. Her fear is formally described as

    (A) acrophobia   (B) ochlophobia   (C) agoraphobia
    (D) claustrophobia   (E) mysophobia

164. Which of the following is *not* true of sleep disorders?

    (A) The sleepwalker generally walks within Stage 4, deep sleep.
    (B) Sleep terror involves frequent panic-awakenings.
    (C) Narcolepsy occurs when an individual has taken a drug overdose.
    (D) Sleep apnea awakens a person because of inability to get a breath.
    (E) A fitful night's sleep is characteristic of insomnia.

165. You strike someone without provocation. You curse the law enforcement officer to her face. You steal an item from the store. All of these are symptomatic of

    (A) somatoform disorders
    (B) sexual disorders
    (C) eating disorders
    (D) mood disorders
    (E) impulse control disorders

166. DSM's Axis II encompasses _____ personality disorders.

    (A) borderline   (B) narcissistic   (C) avoidant
    (D) histrionic   (E) all of the preceding

167. Jan lacks any affection or interpersonal bonds. She's highly manipulative without guilt. Her symptoms are consistent with those of _____ personality disorder.

    (A) dependent   (B) antisocial   (C) paranoid
    (D) histrionic   (E) borderline

168. In this therapeutic approach, your worst fears are relived vividly and in living color. Conceptually, there's the premise that once you have been through your perceived worst, your fears will dissipate and your self-confidence will build. The therapeutic approach described is _____.

    (A) implosion
    (B) explosion
    (C) systematic desensitization
    (D) assertiveness
    (E) paradoxical intent

169. Which of the following is *not* a major school of family therapy?

    (A) Object Relations (Klein)
    (B) Contextual Family (Meichenbaum)
    (C) Bowen Theory (Bowen)
    (D) Communication Theory (Bateson)
    (E) Structural Family (Minuchin)

170. Therapeutic communities institute _____ approaches throughout a given institution such as a hospital or a prison.

    (A) analytic   (B) client-centered   (C) behavioristic
    (D) rational-emotive   (E) cognitive

171. "What is your finger doing now? What is your hand doing now?" With this focus on bodily movements as expressions of one's feelings, you would expect to be seated in the presence of a _____ therapist.

    (A) behavior   (B) cognitive   (C) Gestalt
    (D) Logo   (E) psychodynamic

172. This therapist focuses primarily on faulty cognitions experienced by depressed people. He cites a "negative triad" to be replaced with favorable cognitions.

    (A) Beck   (B) Meichenbaum   (C) Lazarus
    (D) Rank   (E) Perls

173. George is taking a prescribed drug, Thorazine (chlorpromazine). From your knowledge of medical treatments you conclude that he needed an _____ medication.

    (A) antidepressant   (B) antimanic   (C) antianxiety
    (D) antipsychotic   (E) ECT

174. Electroconvulsive shock therapy (ECT) entails_____.

    (A) placing electrodes near the heart to deliver a rhythmic shock
    (B) an electrode-induced convulsion that produces anterograde amnesia
    (C) placing electrodes on the arms and legs
    (D) a split-second shock across the temples producing convulsion
    (E) none of the above

175. In this therapeutic approach, the individual makes a signed contract with the therapist.

    (A) psychodrama   (B) reality   (C) primal
    (D) transactional analysis   (E) Gestalt

176. In the history of the mental health movement, which of the following had a major impact in changing the way emotionally disturbed people were treated?

    (A) Hippocrates   (B) Pinel   (C) Beers
    (D) Nightingale   (E) three of the preceding

177. Because mentally disturbed individuals were believed to be possessed by evil spirits, early treatments included _____.

    (A) flogging   (B) starving   (C) burning
    (D) magic   (E) all of the preceding

178. Within the current diagnostic system (DSM-IV), Posttraumatic Stress Disorder (PTSD) is classified as a(n) _____ disorder.

    (A) mood   (B) anxiety   (C) delusional
    (D) dissociative   (E) schizophrenic

179. Early fears are to enzyme deficiency as _____ is to _____.

    (A) psychogenic, somatogenic
    (B) sociogenic, androgenic
    (C) psychoanalytic, phenomenological
    (D) behavioristic, perceptual
    (E) id-based, ego-based

180. When we speak of "Down syndrome" or some other syndrome, the term refers to

    (A) a substance-related disorder
    (B) a teratogenic disorder
    (C) a state of mental confusion
    (D) a set of symptoms generally occurring together
    (E) none of the preceding

181. Dr. Arnett is treating Fred for depression. She notes Fred's depression-related behaviors and sets up a series of reinforcement schedules for change. The therapy Dr. Arnett is utilizing is within the _____ model.

    (A) cognitive
    (B) psychodynamic
    (C) learning
    (D) medical
    (E) pathology

182. According to cross-cultural studies, the incidence of schizophrenia is most prevalent within the _____ classes.

    (A) upper
    (B) upper-middle
    (C) lower-middle
    (D) lower
    (E) no class differences found

183. Jonathan plans to talk with his dad about his weekly allowance. It's currently $1, and he wants it to be increased. He gathers data from several of his friends—$2, $3, $3, $5, $7, $20. To make his best possible case to his dad, Jonathan would be well-advised to use which measure of the following?

    (A) median
    (B) mode
    (C) mean
    (D) standard deviation
    (E) variance

184. Emily scores at the 85th percentile. This means

    (A) 85 percent of those taking the test were above her
    (B) 15 percent of those taking the test were equal to her
    (C) 15 percent of those taking the test were below her
    (D) 85 percent of those taking the test were equal to or below her
    (E) none of the above

185. You plan to study the effect of sunshine on mood. Sunshine is your _____.

    (A) parameter
    (B) inference
    (C) independent variable
    (D) dependent variable
    (E) nominal variable

186. My number is 1745 Periwinkle Lane. My friend lives at 1784 Periwinkle Lane. These number usages are _____.

    (A) nominal
    (B) ordinal
    (C) interval
    (D) ratio
    (E) integer

187. Parameter is to statistic as _____ is to _____.

    (A) mean, mode
    (B) population, sample
    (C) value, dichotomous
    (D) deduction, inference
    (E) none of the preceding

188. In a negatively skewed distribution, moving from left to right we will encounter which of the following sequences?

    (A) mode, median, mean
    (B) mode, mean, median
    (C) mean, median, mode
    (D) median, mode, mean
    (E) median, mean, mode

189. The 64th percentile of a normal distribution is equivalent to a *z*-score of _____.

    (A) 5   (B) 4   (C) 3   (D) 2   (E) 1

190. Which of the following is *not* true?

    (A) Histograms are bar graphs representing score intervals.
    (B) Polygons are comprised of points connected by lines.
    (C) Standard deviation is the average difference between *z* scores.
    (D) Standard deviation is the square root of the variance.
    (E) All the above are true.

191. Ashley wants to minimize her chances of mistakenly rejecting a null hypothesis. She is seeking to avoid committing a Type _____ error.

    (A) I   (B) II   (C) III   (D) IV   (E) V

192. Egbert is estimating a population mean on the basis of his sample mean and is stating his level of certainty that the population mean falls within his estimate. He has just set up a(n) _____.

    (A) point biserial interval
    (B) confidence interval
    (C) estimation interval
    (D) judgment interval
    (E) correlational interval

193. We've compared two sets of data and have come up with a correlation of +.8. We can legitimately conclude that there's a _____ between our measures.

    (A) strong inverse relationship
    (B) weak inverse relationship
    (C) weak positive relationship
    (D) no relationship
    (E) strong positive relationship

194. If Ignatius plans to conduct a one-tailed test, we know that he's

    (A) only willing to consider significant differences above the mean
    (B) only willing to consider significant differences below the mean
    (C) only willing to consider significant differences in a single direction
    (D) considering only correlations in the 0 to .5 range
    (E) considering only correlations in the .5 to 1.0 range

195. Ellen is going to give a set of subjects a performance test, teach them a new skill, and give them the performance test again. She is using a _____ design.

    (A) three-factor mixed
    (B) repeated measures
    (C) chi-square
    (D) completely randomized
    (E) none of the preceding

196. You have randomly assigned individuals to each of two groups. One group will receive an experimental manipulation, after which you will measure the performance of both groups. The analysis you have elected to use is the *t*-test for _____.

    (A) sample and population means
    (B) independent measures
    (C) related measures
    (D) correlated measures
    (E) random measures

197. A perfectly horizontal regression lines indicates
   I.   zero correlation between two variables
   II. +1 correlation between two variables
   III. −1 correlation between two variables

   (A) both I and II   (B) I, II, and III   (C) only II and III
   (D) only I   (E) only II

198. Tara wants to determine whether there are proportionately more girls than boys born in August. She will be best advised to use a(n)

   (A) analysis of variance   (B) chi-square test
   (C) correlation   (D) z-test   (E) f-test

199. Which of the following is true?
   I.   Correlation does not mean causation.
   II. The mean always moves in the direction of a distribution's skew.
   III. Dichotomous measures are "either-or" measures, typically 0 and 1.

   (A) I, II, and III are true
   (B) only I and II are true
   (C) only II and III are true
   (D) only I is true
   (E) only II is true

200. A critical ratio is
   I.   the difference between sample means
   II. a variance
   III. a z-score

   (A) III only   (B) both I and II   (C) both II and III
   (D) II only   (E) I only

201. Standard error is the

   (A) standard deviation of a distribution of population means
   (B) standard deviation of a distribution of sample means
   (C) variance of a distribution of population means
   (D) variance of a distribution of sample means
   (E) none of the above

202. A research design has more than two groups. A(n) _____ will be an appropriate test of statistical significance.

   (A) analysis of variance   (B) t-test   (C) z-test
   (D) point biserial correlation   (E) none of the preceding

203. Scientific management puts an emphasis on
   I.   time-and-motion studies
   II. piecework
   III. process

   (A) I and III only   (B) II and III only   (C) I only
   (D) II only   (E) I, II, and III

204. To find all available psychological research data on the topic of substance-related depression, one would consult

(A) *Psychological Bulletin*
(B) *Journal of Personality and Social Psychology*
(C) *Psychological Abstracts*
(D) *Psychological Review*
(E) *Annual Review of Psychology*

205. Which of the following is primarily an organizational psychology focus rather than an industrial psychology focus?

(A) job analysis
(B) team-building
(C) recruitment
(D) interviewing
(E) testing

206. An assessment center
   I.   is generally an independent, noncompany entity
   II. evaluates a small number of executive-candidates intensively
   III. places candidates in challenging problem-solving situations

(A) I, II, and III   (B) I and II only   (C) II and III only
(D) II only   (E) III only

207. Reward expectancy governs the choices and behaviors of workers in the workplace.

(A) Locke   (B) Adams   (C) Maslow
(D) Vroom   (E) Herzberg

208. The ERG organizational theory relates to _____ and was developed by _____.

(A) evaluation, reorganization, growth / Hackman
(B) estimation, restructuring, goal-setting / Herzberg
(C) estimation, reorganization, growth / Lawler
(D) existence, relatedness, growth / Alderfer
(E) executive, relatedness, governing / Adams

209. Cognitive resource utilization theory in leadership research was developed by

(A) Aristotle   (B) Fiedler and Garcia   (C) Hemphill
(D) Lord and Maher   (E) Komaki

210. This leadership type motivates through charisma and vision to set and attain goals beyond worker expectation.

(A) transformational
(B) transactional
(C) democratic
(D) authoritarian
(E) egalitarian

211. Compared with decentralized patterns, the centralized patterns of organizational communication
    I.   generate lower worker morale
    II. require more time to solve complex problems
    III. make fewer errors in solving complex problems

    (A) I only   (B) II only   (C) III only
    (D) I and II only   (E) II and III only

212. "Those FDA guys are trouble-makers." This comment in a drug manufacturer's high-level decisionmaking meeting is indicative of Janis'

    (A) illusion of unanimity
    (B) illusion of morality
    (C) shared stereotypes
    (D) direct pressure
    (E) rationalization

213. The research area that matches displays and controls to natural human physiology is

    (A) ecology   (B) ergonomics   (C) micronics
    (D) kinesics   (E) proxemics

214. In the human factors area, the term EVA refers to

    (A) ecological valuation assessment
    (B) ergonomic vulnerability assay
    (C) environmental valuation assessment
    (D) extra-vehicular activity
    (E) none of the preceding

215. Structuralism is to functionalism as _____ is to _____.

    (A) introspection, adaptation
    (B) objective measurement, holism
    (C) nomothetism, idiographism
    (D) counterconditioning, reflex
    (E) observation, assessment

216. The whole is greater than the sum of its parts is a central tenet of _____.

    (A) functionalism   (B) behaviorism   (C) Gestalt
    (D) psychoanalysis   (E) structuralism

217. The recently formed national membership organization representing psychology is the

    (A) American Psychological Institute (API)
    (B) American Psychological Society (APS)
    (C) American Psychological Association (APA)
    (D) American Psychological Union (APU)
    (E) National Psychological Society (NPS)

218. The *Observer* is the bi-monthly membership publication of the

(A) American Psychological Institute (API)
(B) American Psychological Society (APS)
(C) American Psychological Association (APA)
(D) American Psychological Union (APU)
(E) National Psychological Society (NPS)

219. Historically, the European schools of psychology were oriented toward
_____ while the American schools were oriented toward
_____.

(A) conscious thought, unconscious thought
(B) cathexis, anticathexis
(C) introspection, observable behavior
(D) kinesics, proxemics
(E) body, soul

220. The major spokesperson for structuralism in the United States was

(A) Watson   (B) Bandura   (C) Cattell
(D) O'Leary   (E) Titchener

Diagnostic Test 2: Answer Comments

1. (C) Neurons attached to receptor cells respond to various external stimuli such as touch, light, and so on. These receptor cells transduce the physical stimuli into electrical impulses, which, in turn, trigger an impulse in other neurons.

2. (B) The muscles and glands are the organs of action—the effectors. They respond to efferent nerve fibers. The term *efferent* comes from the Latin, *effere*, "to bring forth."

3. (A) An accurate sequential pattern is afferent nerve, interneuron, efferent nerve. A stimulus occurs and afferent nerves (bundles of nerve fibers) send the message to intermediate nerve cells (interneurons) in the brain or spinal cord. The interneurons send action commands to muscles and glands via the efferent nerve fibers.

4. (D) The concept of the synapse—a gap between neurons across which they must communicate—was envisioned by an English physiologist, Sir Charles Sherrington. His nineteenth and early twentieth century work was conducted with dogs.

5. (E) The antagonistic actions of skeletal muscles are termed *reciprocal inhibition*. Sherrington found that what excited the flexor, relaxed the extensor—that flexors and extensors seemed to function cooperatively in pairs (assuring that both were not excited simultaneously).

6. (E) Acetylcholine, serotonin, the catecholamines (dopamine, norepinephrine, epinephrine), and GABA are neurotransmitters. Opioid peptides and substance P are neuromodulators.

7. (B) Neurons contain a cell body, axon, dendrites, and other accessories such as soma, myelin sheath, Nodes of Ranvier, and synapse. The septum is part of the limbic system in the forebrain.

8. (D) The divisions of the peripheral nervous system are the somatic (concerned with skeletal muscles and sense organs) and autonomic, or ANS, concerned with keeping our life-machine functioning smoothly, including the heart, blood vessels, digestive systems, genital organs, and so on.

9. (A) The hindbrain contains the medulla and the cerebellum. The medulla controls vital life-sustaining functions including heartbeat, circulation, and respiration.

10. (C) Penfield conducted brain surgery with patients under local anesthesia. By stimulating the brain, he was able to conduct function-mapping. He found the cortical motor area to be located in a region of the frontal lobe.

11. (E) The reticular activating system (RAS) is part of the brain stem.

12. (A) The alcoholic who's staggering when not drunk has a damaged cerebellum. Balance is a critical function of the cerebellum.

13. (D) Language function is predominantly centered in the left hemisphere and spatial ability in the right hemisphere.

14. (B) Because the picture was flashed to your right hemisphere, you will respond as though you saw nothing. The right hemisphere, being spatial, lacks the language to describe.

15. (C) The autonomic nervous system (ANS) contains the sympathetic and parasympathetic. The sympathetic prepares us "for fight or flight," while the parasympathetic calms our system down.

16. (E) The EEG measures brain-wave activity. The emitted potentials are received by electrodes placed on the head. Wave activity is recorded on a continuously moving paper roll or stored within a computer.

17. (A) Alzheimer's is a neurotransmitter-related brain disorder associated with acetylcholine deficiency.

18. (C) The reticular formation or reticular activating system (RAS) is the brain's "alarm clock." By selectively filtering stimuli, it identifies those critical to the given individual's roles (e.g., the cry of the parent's baby, the doctor's telephone ring, and so on).

19. (E) The diabetic's basic problem is that the pancreas is not producing insulin. This insulin is a critical ingredient in the body's ability to extract glucose from the blood stream.

20. (D) Patients taking Eskalith (lithium carbonate) are likely experiencing mania. Eskalith is a major antimanic medication.

21. (A) The narcotics/opiates include codeine, heroin, morphine, and opium. Cocaine is an amphetamine (functioning as a stimulant).

22. (B) Jo Nell likely will be taking Zoloft or one of the other serotonin reuptake inhibitors such as Prozac or Paxil for her depression. Zoloft's generic name is sertaline; Prozac's, fluoxetine.

23. (C) Genotype refers to the genetic make-up of cells and phenotype refers to the trait characteristics developing from the cell genetic make-up.

24. (B) Sociobiology is a relatively new entry in the area of built-in social behaviors. Wilson has pioneered this field, which focuses on the evolutionary history underlying many of our human social behaviors.

25. (D) Tryon paired maze-bright and maze-dull rats across several generations, finding a widening gap between the two groups' abilities to run mazes. Eugenics refers to such mating to bring out specified characteristics in offspring.

26. (D) Fechner's Law ($S = k \log I$) states that an increase in sensation means a logarithmic increase in stimulus intensity.

27. (C) Weber's Law suggests a constant ratio. If 2 lb added are noticeable with a weight of 10 lb, a 4-lb addition would be needed when holding 20 lb.

28. (B) Difference threshold is the minimum change at which you detect a difference.

29. (A) The retinal image is the proximal, and the distal is the external stimulus.

30. (E) Transduction is the conversion process whereby proximal stimulus becomes neural impulse.

31. (C) False alarm is reporting a stimulus when none is present. A miss is not reporting a stimulus when one is present.

32. (D) The ROC (receiver-operating-characteristic) curve will be identical for two people of equal sensitivity but different response biases. Where one subject may have several more false alarms than another, they also will have proportionately more misses.

33. (A) Specificity theory expresses the view that there are quality-specific neurons that signal or fire for given qualities.

34. (E) Muller advanced the doctrine of specific nerve energies. It holds that differences in experienced quality are not stimulus based but are nervous system based.

35. (D) The kinesthetic sense tells us the position of our limbs—vividly portrayed when your leg and foot "go to sleep" and you momentarily do not have that sense.

36. (B) The method of constant stimuli is a stimulus presented at a given and constant frequency. In the method of limits, frequencies are varied across trials in alternating ascending/descending order.

37. (D) Helmholtz advanced the trichromatic theory of three sets of fibers in the retina, each sensitive to one of the primary colors.

38. (E) Retinal disparity (the stimulus falling on a different part of each retina) is central to visual depth. Convergence (the two eyes focusing on a given object) also is central.

39. (B) Pinna is part of the outer ear. It's the visible part we have and see. Another part of the outer ear is the ear (or auditory) canal.

40. (B) The olfactory sense is credited with a central role in menstrual synchrony.

41. (A) Gate-control theory is associated with Melzack and the sensation of pain. Melzack suggests a "pain gate" in the spinal cord.

42. (C) Convergence is a binocular depth cue. Relative size, interposition, linear perspective, and shading are monocular.

43. (A) In closure we tend to complete familiar figures that have a gap in them (almost-complete squares and circles, for example).

44. (B) In dichotic listening, a different stimulus is presented to each ear simultaneously. If the subject is asked to attend to the stimulus coming through one earphone, she or he will virtually ignore and "shut out" the message incoming on the other earphone.

45. (D) When lights blink sequentially on a neon sign, creating the appearance of movement, it is what the Gestaltists termed the phi phenomenon or the stroboscopic effect. Another dramatic example is movies, which are stationary frames moving in sequence.

46. (E) The line with half-outer and half-inner-pointing fins is a classic Muller-Lyer illusion.

47. (E) Coming from a thatched-hut village without carpentered right angles, you would be less likely to see the Ames window illusion than someone coming from carpentered and "angled" Western culture.

48. (C) The fact that we see a rectangular table regardless of the angle at which we're viewing it is a dramatic example of shape constancy.

49. (A) The major laws of perceptual organization were developed by the Gestaltists. These laws include proximity, similarity, continuity, common fate, and closure.

50. (A) Top-down processing refers to activating higher-order units of perception, which then influence items of lower order. Pattern recognition is often top-down processing. Bottom-up begins with a specific feature and gradually builds up to a larger unit.

51. (B) The conditioned stimulus gets its reinforcing power from association with the unconditioned stimulus.

52. (D) When one conditioned stimulus can be paired with another conditioned stimulus and the second CS gets a response, higher-order conditioning has occurred.

53. (C) The Law of Effect was developed by Thorndike. The consequences of a response determine whether it will be strengthened or weakened. Responses associated with positive consequences (e.g., reinforcements) will be strengthened.

54. (B) Tom's salary is time-based. Occurring at the end of each month, it is a fixed interval.

55. (C) The gambler's disease is a devastating result of variable ratio. Because it happens after an unpredictably variable number of responses, it is highly resistant to change.

56. (D) Respondent is another term for classical conditioning; and operant, a synonym for instrumental.

57. (E) John Watson made the bold statement about making of the young child anything you wanted to make him. The premise is that the child is a blank slate (a Lockean, "tabula rasa") on which the environment writes.

58. (E) The first term indicates direction (whether earlier-to-later [proactive] or later-to-earlier [retroactive]). The second term indicates whether helpful (facilitation) or detrimental (inhibition). Because an earlier learning interfered with a later one in this instance, it was proactive inhibition.

59. (B) At the plateau point in a learning curve, incubation is occurring. Though performance seems to have leveled off, it will notably improve later.

60. (A) The basic learning sequence is drive, cue, response, reinforcement. The sequence will never begin without the organism having a drive (i.e., a need). The drive will need distinct signals or cues, and once a response is made to these signals or cues, reinforcement will be critical to response repetition in the future.

61. (A) The most effective technique in classical conditioning is forward pairing - delayed. In this technique, the CS comes on and stays on through the presentation of the UCS. In the forward pairing - trace technique, the CS goes off before the UCS is presented, forcing greater reliance on the animal's memory capacity.

62. (E) The cognitive field theory was developed by Tolman. In contrast to the reinforcement view of Thorndike and Skinner, Tolman believed the animal forms an internal representation of the response-reinforcer relationship sequence. Whether or not this representation will lead to response repetition in the future will depend upon the animal's drives and needs.

63. (C) Cannon's motivation theory of homeostasis expresses the view that biological drives preempt other activities until these drives are reduced. In homeostasis there is a drive toward establishing and maintaining balance.

64. (B) McClelland and Atkinson are associated with achievement need (n Ach). Solomon is associated with opponent process.

65. (B) Stimulating the lateral area of the hypothalamus promotes overeating. Stimulating the ventromedial nucleus stops eating.

66. (C) When Olds and Milner stimulated the rat's limbic system, the rats found it highly pleasurable . . . so much so that they would quickly learn mazes to get the stimulation.

67. (A) Solomon advanced the opponent-process theory that our bodies, in an attempt to maintain homeostasis, will invoke an inhibitory response to offset a highly pleasurable one.

68. (D) James would say we run and then we're scared. Cannon would say we're scared and then we run.

69. (B) The parasympathetic system controls normal operations of the body and calms everything down after an emergency response.

70. (E) The Yerkes-Dodson Law states that increases in motivation and arousal bring increases in emotion. A mid-range level of arousal contributes to optimal performance effectiveness.

71. (A) Observing that rhesus monkeys spent considerable time on the terry cloth mother—even when this mother was not the food source—Harlow advanced the concept of contact comfort.

72. (D) Shachter and Singer's research has demonstrated that subjects in a high state of arousal look to those around them for cues regarding what they should be feeling.

73. (D) Being competitive, aggressive, hostile, impatient, and hating lines and waiting are descriptive elements in Type A personality.

74. (E) Selye's General Adaptation Syndrome carries the stages of alarm, resistance, and exhaustion.

75. (A) With your mother's death, your spouse's departure, and starting a new job, the Social Readjustment Rating Scale (SRRS) of Holmes and Rahe would rate you as highly overstressed and vulnerable.

76. (C) Tulving distinguished episodic from semantic memory. *Episodic* is memory for specific events, and *semantic* is memory for ideas, rules, and concepts.

77. (B) Ebbinghaus needed to find a novel-type stimulus his subjects did not already know. Otherwise, he knew that the meaningfulness of content would skew any research results.

78. (E) In the depth-of-processing theory of memory, the sequential path to increasing depth is physical, acoustic, semantic. Physical relates to the physical characteristics of a stimulus. Acoustic "sounds it out," and semantic looks for meaning.

79. (A) The pegword method features a ten-line rhyme beginning with "One is a bun. Two is a shoe. Three is a tree. Four is a door." Once a person has memorized the rhyme, he or she can then relate an item (e.g., a word) with each line of the rhyme, finding a novel way of picturing it within that line. One then has the potential to remember ten items.

80. (C) Elaborative is not a basic theory of memory. Dual-memory, network, depth-of-processing, and set are among the basic theories.

81. (B) The savings method of measuring memory subtracts the relearning time from the initial learning time. The difference is the savings (i.e., the time saved by having learned the material originally).

82. (D) Swimming, bike-riding, car-driving, and your hometown streets—being motor and spatial tasks—are quite well retained. A poem recitation is verbal—more prone to forgetting.

83. (D) Miller credited short-term memory with the capacity to learn the "magical number" of 7 items plus or minus 2. It's interesting that most phone numbers (7 digits) clearly agree with him.

84. (A) Ziegarnik advanced the premise that we are far less likely to remember finished tasks than unfinished ones.

85. (E) Laboratory techniques of measuring retention have included serial-recall, recognition, free recall, and paired-associates. Memory trace is not a retention-measuring technique. It is part of a theory of forgetting.

86. (C) Chomsky and Lenneberg hold the position that there is an inborn competence for language acquisition and that a consistent acquisition pattern is followed regardless of the culture in which one is born.

87. (E) Phonemes are the smallest units of sound—"p," "d," "k,"and so on.

88. (A) Language comprehension is associated with Wernicke's area of the brain. Language production is associated with Broca's.

89. (D) Sternberg is associated with information processing.

90. (B) By not remembering having walked up the hill with Jill, Jack was experiencing retrograde amnesia. Anterograde amnesia would relate to memories Jack had established *after* he had fallen down and broken his crown.

91. (D) The Stroop effect pits a color word (for example, blue) against the color in which it actually is written (for example, yellow). Within the automatization response tendency, a subject is highly likely to come out with the response "yellow"—the color in which the word is written.

92. (D) Joan's "rule of thumb" is an heuristic she uses in working toward puzzle solutions.

93. (B) MYCIN is an expert system, problem-solving computer program. Such problem-solving computer programs are exceedingly narrow in knowledge focus and scope.

94. (E) This three-part approach—All cows are animals. All animals are living. Therefore, all cows are living.—is an example of a syllogism. Syllogisms contain two premises and a conclusion.

95. (D) Calling the man on the street "daddy" because he has some characteristics of his own daddy is an instance of overgeneralizing. Such overgeneralizing is common in the early stages of a child's concept formation.

96. (C) Thought models do not include automatization. The hierarchical network, parallel distributed processing, and spreading activation are all thought models.

97. (E) Episodic memory and generic memory are symbolic mental representations. Analogical mental representations include mental images, eidetic imagery, and spatial thinking.

98. (D) Babbling is the final and most critical prelinguistic stage of a child's development of speech. It is here that a child experiments with consonant-vowel-consonant combinations that will serve as the practice-prelude to meaningful words.

99. (C) The combination of a subject and a predicate is called a proposition. Any given sentence can have more than one proposition.

100. (B) Prototypes represent a person's internal mental average of all the examples that person has seen of a given concept. Any new stimulus must contain most, but not all, the features. A goldfinch likely will register as a good representation of the concept "bird." On the other hand, a penguin—with few of the concept features—will register as a poor representation.

101. (A) The germinal stage extends from fertilization to the first two weeks. The embryonic stage extends from two weeks to eight weeks. The fetal period extends from eight weeks to birth.

102. (D) The cross-sectional method compares children of different ages simultaneously.

103. (E) Teratogens are substances producing malformations in a fetus. Such teratogens may include maternal alcohol intake, smoking, stress, drug use, and major mood swings.

104. (E) The newborn's development is characterized by the patterns from the head down (cephalocaudal) and from the torso center toward the extremities (proximodistal).

105. (E) In the Babinski reflex, the newborn's toes stretch outward and upward when the sole of the foot is touched.

106. (A) One of the most classic pictures in all of psychology is that of Konrad Lorenz walking across a field with a string of tiny goslings following him. He was their central, moving stimulus during the critical period for imprinting.

107. (C) Separation anxiety in the newborn occurs within the 8 to 15 month old range.

108. (B) Kohlberg's stage theory outlines the stages in the development of moral reasoning. It is closely related to Piaget's stage theory of cognitive development.

109. (E) This sophisticated form of conservation is volume conservation. It relates to the principle of volume displacement.

110. (C) Piaget's cognitive stages begin with the sensorimotor, followed by the preoperational, concrete operations, and formal operations.

111. (E) The child who thinks the waves only roll in when she's there is expressing assimilation.

112. (E) Sensory, prenatal is not one of Hebb's six classes of factors in behavioral development. The factors are genetic, chemical prenatal/postnatal, sensory constant/variable, and traumatic.

113. (A) A child who had achieved number conservation would have said that there were the same number of blue and red buttons, even though the red ones were more spread out.

114. (B) In Piagetian terms, a child's inability to attend to more than one dimension at a time is called egocentrism.

115. (B) At birth a newborn's head is approximately 25% of its body length. By adulthood it will change proportionately from one-fourth to one-eighth.

116. (E) The aspect of fetal development most prominently affected by a harmful substance taken by the expectant mother is the aspect most rapidly developing at the time the substance is consumed.

117. (A) Maturation is the continuing function of heredity after birth.

118. (D) For individuals in midlife there is a decrease in estrogen production for women. There is also a decrease in testosterone production for men. People in this age-range generally have higher work satisfaction than they did in their earlier years, experience some decline in strength and tissue elasticity, and lose skill on timed memory tasks more so than on informational ones.

119. (E) All of the aspects mentioned—caught between generations, marriage/career reevaluation, and change in time orientation to years left to live—characterize middle-adulthood.

120. (C) Suggesting an inclined-plane-type pattern of child development rather than a series of steps is characteristic of continuity theory.

121. (D) Critics point out that stage theories oversimplify and ignore individual variation in development.

122. (B) Kohlberg's moral development stages are closely related to Piaget's cognitive development stages.

123. (A) This is one of the most astounding changes within a child's development. From a 50-word vocabulary at age 2, a child moves to an awesome 1000-word vocabulary by age 3.

124. (D) A child's absence of object permanence is characteristic of the sensorimotor stage.

125. (B) Girls mature at an earlier age than boys. Where a girl may reach somatic maturity by age 11 or 12, a boy will likely not reach somatic maturity till age 15 or 16. It makes for some fascinating dance-partner match-ups.

126. (A) Festinger's cognitive dissonance theory states that our attitudes move in the direction of our behaviors. "When you say something you don't believe, you begin to believe what you're saying."

127. (D) Thurstone's equal-appearing-intervals scale typically carries the instruction to "Checkmark the statements you agree with." The final scale results from a very rigorous statement-selection procedure designed to represent all levels of an attitude and its expression.

128. (A) Likert's summated ratings scale is based on the premise of high correlation between responses on individual scale items and the overall scale score. Where an individual-item correlation is low, that item does not contribute to the overall scale score and needs to be deleted.

129. (B) If you like your mother, your mother doesn't like heavy metal, and you do like heavy metal, the triad is imbalanced. You wish to have people you like see things the same way you do. In the Balance Theory Model of Heider and Newcomb, an odd number of negatives represents imbalance. An odd number of positives represents balance.

130. (C) Gergen's Behavior Exchange Model sees interactions in the context of reward/cost. When cost outruns reward a given dyadic relationship will likely weaken or end.

131. (C) Newcomb found proximity most salient at first (roommate attraction to roommate), but then individuals discovered those of similar interests, and similarity became the most salient element in attraction long-range.

132. (D) Schachter's research into affiliation found that people are strongly attracted to those who agree with them. The dissenters were distinctly excluded from subsequent group membership.

133. (E) Under stressful conditions, there is a strong desire to affiliate with others in the same stressful circumstances (the research of Schachter).

134. (A) By keeping the critical researcher's input from reaching the board meeting in which a decision would be made about marketing the weight-reducing pill, John was functioning as a mindguard. Within Janis' groupthink concept, this is precisely the function of the mindguard.

135. (A) Hall's research in proxemics (personal space) theorized that Western society has four distance zones: intimate, personal, social, and public. The outer limits of the close intimate distance zone form an 18-inch-radius bubble around the individual.

136. (B) Zajonc found that subjects defined most positively the words they had seen most often. In summary, familiarity breeds liking.

137. (C) In McGuire's Inoculation Theory one gives a group a small dose of what they will be hearing more of later. The dose is designed to build immunity to what they will subsequently be hearing.

138. (D) Bandura's classic work on modeling is frequently cited as a background for discussing the aggression-eliciting effects television-violence viewing has upon children.

139. (E) Deutsch conducted research into cooperation and competition utilizing the classic Acme-Bolt Trucking Game.

140. (A) Latane and Darley conducted the central research series in the area of helping behavior and found number of bystanders to be a critical element in whether a person receives help. An individual is most likely to receive help when there's only one person around. The likelihood of receiving help steadily decreases as the number of bystanders grows.

141. (C) The cardinal's outspoken position in favor of abortion is highly credible because it stands in sharp contrast to what one would expect the cardinal's position to be.

142. (E) None of these choices is accurate. Phenomenologists see us as perception-driven; behaviorists, as learning-driven; trait theorists, as trait-driven; psychoanalysts, as instinct-driven.

143. (C) Fromm considers brotherly love the most powerful because it is love between equals. His five types of love are brotherly, motherly, erotic, self, and supernatural.

144. (D) Erikson's stage theory outlines eight psychosocial stages within the life span.

145. (B) The correct pairing is Sullivan—interpersonal. In his view, personality is interpersonal relationships.

146. (B) Rogers' concept of conscious-self-structure is all the untested ability messages given to us in the past. It's all those people who gave us the untested message that we'd make a wonderful doctor, but we had yet to face the sensory-visceral experience of organic chemistry.

147. (E) Frankl indicated that we have a will to power and a will to pleasure, both of which will be self-defeating. Only a will to meaning (setting individual goals that tap into our "deepest running currents") will truly bring us happiness.

148. (D) The 16 PF (Personality Factor) Scale is based on the factor analytic work of Cattell.

149. (E) The basic theoretical background for the Myers-Briggs test is found in the work of Jung (his concepts of introversion-extraversion, sensing, thinking, feeling, and intuiting).

150. (C) The child who had almost drowned, now being beckoned into the water by her very closest friends, is experiencing approach-avoidance conflict. She wants to be with her friends, and she wants to avoid the water. If the attraction of her friends is strong enough, she will go into the water, gradually overcoming the fear that has prompted her to avoid it.

151. (A) Wolpe's reciprocal inhibition states that when a given maladaptive response has just occurred, it is in a temporary state of exhaustion during which an adaptive response can be introduced with strong success potential.

152. (D) Eysenck is incorrectly paired. His work in the factor analysis area formed a typology premised on introversion-extraversion, stability-neuroticism, and impulse control-psychoticism.

153. (B) These story-telling instructions are characteristic of Murray's Thematic Apperception Test (TAT).

154. (C) Rotter is a social behaviorist who devised an Internal-External Control Scale.

155. (C) Tourette's disorder carries the symptoms of repetitive movements (e.g., eye-blink, twitch, repetitive sound, and so on.)

156. (B) Somatoform disorders are bodily symptoms such as paralysis that have no underlying physiological cause.

157. (A) Fugue is a form of amnesia that includes a change of geographical location.

158. (A) Bi-polar disorders are mood related. As the "bi" prefix suggests, they include swings between mania and depression.

159. (D) DSM-IV is organized along five axes. Specific disorders are categorized in Axes I through III; level of stress, in Axis IV; and level of functioning, in Axis V. Axis I and Axis II are most central to your review.

160. (A) The thought that people are talking about you as you walk down the hall is delusional. It is called paranoia of reference.

161. (E) *Sybil* was a notable example of multiple personality disorder—a dissociative disorder. She had more than a dozen separate personalities.

162. (E) The serotonin reuptake blockers are a "second generation" of drugs to treat mood disorders. Among them are Prozac, Zoloft, and Paxil. The "first generation" were the tricyclic drugs.

163. (A) Jill's fear of heights is formally called acrophobia. The other terms given as options were ochlophobia (crowds), agoraphobia (open spaces), claustrophobia (closed-in places), and mysophobia (germs).

164. (C) Narcolepsy occurs without warning. The person simply falls asleep within virtually any aspect of daily activity.

165. (E) Striking someone without provocation, cursing the law enforcement officer to her face, and stealing from the store are all symptomatic of an impulse control disorder.

166. (E) DSM's Axis II encompasses mental retardation and all personality disorders including borderline, narcissistic, avoidant, histrionic, paranoid, schizotypal, antisocial, and dependent.

167. (B) Lacking any affection or interpersonal bonds is characteristic of the antisocial personality disorder.

168. (A) Therapeutically reliving your worst fears vividly and suddenly is characteristic of Stampfl's implosion technique.

169. (B) Contextual Family (Meichenbaum) is not a school of family therapy. The term is made up (were you impressed?), and Meichenbaum is a founder of cognitive behavior therapy. The major schools of family therapy are Object Relations (Melanie Klein), Bowen Theory (Murray Bowen), Structural Family Theory (Salvador Minuchin), and Communication Theory (Bateson).

170. (C) Therapeutic communities such as hospitals and prisons set up clearly outlined goals and reinforcements and use behavior modification techniques on an institution-wide basis.

171. (C) Gestalt therapy draws frustratingly close attention to what the client is expressing within bodily movements. The goal is to sensitize the client and enable her/him to "speak with one voice" both verbally and bodily.

172. (A) Aaron Beck focuses on the "negative triad" of faulty cognitions experienced by individuals who are depressed. The triad says, "I am deprived or defeated. The world is full of obstacles. The future is devoid of hope."

173. (D) Thorazine (chlorpromazine) is an antipsychotic medication. Others in this drug family include Haldol (halperidol), Clozaril (clozapine), and Resperdol (resperidone).

174. (D) Electroconvulsive shock therapy (ECT) entails a split-second shock to the temples producing a convulsion and temporary retrograde amnesia.

175. (B) In Glasser's Reality Therapy, the individual makes a signed contract with the therapist.

176. (E) Hippocrates, Pinel, and Beers had major impacts on the mental health movement. Hippocrates initiated treatment with care and kindness. Pinel reformed asylums in France. And Beers, himself a hospital patient, had a major impact on reforming institutional approaches to mental health in the United States.

177. (E) Because mentally disturbed individuals were believed to be possessed by evil spirits, early treatments included flogging, starving, burning, herbs, and magic. The intent was to make the body an unpleasant and uninviting place for evil spirits to be.

178. (B) In DSM-IV, Posttraumatic Stress Disorder (PSTD) is classified as an anxiety disorder. It involves direct personal experience of an event involving actual or threatened death or serious injury; threat to the physical integrity of another; or learning about violent family/friend death. Symptoms include intense fear, helplessness, horror, persistent reexperiencing of the traumatic event, persistent avoidance of stimuli associated with the trauma, and a numbing of general responsiveness.

179. (A) Early fears are to enzyme deficiency as psychogenic is to somatogenic. Psyche suggests mind, whereas soma suggests body.

180. (D) A syndrome is a set of symptoms generally occurring together.

181. (C) The learning model looks upon problem behaviors as faulty learning. The approach seeks to replace the faulty learning with adaptive responses by setting up reinforcement schedules for the desired behaviors.

182. (D) Incidence of schizophrenia is most prevalent within the lower socioeconomic classes. The reasons for this class-specific prevalence are not known.

183. (C) Jonathan will make his best-possible allowance case to his dad by quoting the mean of the data he gathered. The mean is prominently affected by extreme scores, and one of his friends is receiving a weekly allowance of $20.

184. (D) Emily's score at the 85th percentile indicates that 85 percent of those taking the test were equal to or below her. To be sure, most of that group were below her.

185. (C) Whenever you see a title that reads "The effect of . . ." the next word is your independent variable. Whatever follows the preposition "on" is your dependent variable. In this instance it's "the effect of sunshine on mood"—sunshine being the independent variable, mood being the dependent variable.

186. (A) When numbers are used as labels, the usage is called nominal. Numbers used to express rank are ordinal. Consistent intervals (e.g., 15 points on an IQ scale) is the interval use of numbers. Ratio number usage has an absolute zero and can state "twice as much as," "three times as much as," and so on.

187. (B) Population measures are expressed as parameters. Sample measures are expressed as statistics.

188. (C) The mean of a distribution always moves in the direction of the skew. It is the central tendency measure most prominently affected by extreme scores.

189. (E) The 64th percentile of a normal distribution is one standard deviation above the mean. This point is expressed by a z of +1.

190. (C) A standard deviation within a frequency distribution is the square root of the variation.

191. (A) Mistakenly rejecting a null hypothesis is a Type I error. Mistakenly accepting a null hypothesis is a Type II error. Remember your "RA" in college? "R" comes first. R is for reject and A is for accept.

192. (B) When Egbert estimates a population mean on the basis of a sample mean and states a level of certainty that the population mean falls within this estimate, he has just set up a confidence interval.

193. (E) A correlation of +.8 expresses a strong positive relationship between the two sets of measures.

194. (C) A one-tailed test only considers significant differences in a single direction.

195. (B) Giving the same set of subjects a pretest, experimental procedure, and posttest is the repeated measures design. It also is called a treatments-by-subjects design.

196. (B) In a *t*-test for a difference between two independent means, subjects generally are randomly assigned to the two groups. One group receives an experimental procedure, and both groups are then measured again. This is the most commonly used *t*-test design.

197. (D) A perfectly horizontal regression line indicates a zero correlation between two variables. (Note: The Educational Testing Service likes to use this "I, II, III" format. Don't let it throw you. Stick with what you know, go with your first response, and don't second-guess yourself.)

198. (B) When one seeks to test a proportion, we have entered the realm of nonparametric tests and, key among them, chi-square.

199. (A) All the choices are true. Correlation does not mean causation. It merely expresses a relationship between two sets of variables. The mean always moves in the direction of a distribution's skew. And dichotomous measures (binomials) are "either-or" measures, typically 0 and 1.

200. (A) In formula terms a critical ratio = (obtained sample mean – population mean) divided by the standard error of the mean.

201. (B) Standard error is the standard deviation of a distribution of sample means. Standard error decreases as the number of measures in a distribution increases.

202. (A) Where a research design has more than two groups, an analysis of variance is an appropriate test of statistical significance.

203. (E) Scientific management puts an emphasis on time-and-motion studies, piecework, and process. Features of the workplace are emphasized. Concern for workers as individuals is notably absent.

204. (C) *Psychological Abstracts* is the basic resource for locating available research data on a given topic.

205. (B) Team-building is a central focus within organizational psychology. Industrial psychology is primarily concerned with functions such as job analysis, recruitment, interviewing, and testing.

206. (A) Assessment centers are generally independent, noncompany entities to which corporations send a small number of executive-candidates for intensive evaluation and challenging problem-solving exercises.

207. (D) Vroom's Expectancy Theory states that reward expectancy governs the choices and behaviors of workers in the workplace.

208. (D) The ERG organizational theory was developed by Alderfer. He relates three of Maslow's needs—existence, relatedness, and growth—to the workplace.

209. (B) Fiedler and Garcia developed the cognitive resource utilization theory in leadership. It elaborates upon Fiedler's earlier contingency model, which identified task-centered and person-centered leaders and underscored the importance of matching leaders to the leadership contexts that fit them.

210. (A) Transformational leadership motivates through charisma and vision to set and attain goals beyond worker expectation.

211. (D) Compared with decentralized patterns, the centralized patterns of organizational communication generate lower worker morale, require more time to solve complex problems, and make more errors in solving complex problems.

212. (C) As a group member says, "Those FDA guys are trouble-makers," she or he has stereotyped the FDA for this decisionmaking group. In Janis' groupthink terms, this is shared stereotypes.

213. (B) Ergonomics matches displays and controls to natural human physiology.

214. (D) In the human factors area, EVA refers to extra-vehicular activity and its unique problems and challenges within space exploration.

215. (A) The key word within structuralism is introspection—the research method used by structuralism to study the mind. The key word within functionalism is adaptation—the role of the mind as an adaptive tool.

216. (C) The Gestalt school espouses the view that "the whole is greater than the sum of its parts." This view has been a major element within the phenomenological view of personality—a view that treats individuals holistically rather than as elements such as ids, egos, and superegos.

217. (B) The American Psychological Society (APS) is the most recently formed national membership organization representing psychology. It focuses on academic psychology to the virtual exclusion of practicing psychology.

218. (B) The *Observer* is the bi-monthly membership publication of the American Psychological Society (APS). The American Psychological Association's monthly membership publication is the *Monitor*.

219. (C) Historically, the European schools of psychology were oriented toward introspection while the American schools were oriented toward observable behavior. While structuralism reigned in Europe, functionalism and behaviorism were predominant in the United States.

220. (E) Edward Titchener brought structuralism to the United States and served as its major spokesperson. Even with all his brilliance and eloquence, it never "caught on" in the United States as a major school.

Diagnostic Test 2: Evaluating Your Score

Abbreviation Guide for Quick Reference (Translation)

PC:	Physiological/Comparative
SnP:	Sensation/Perception
LM:	Learning/Motivation/Emotion
CHL:	Cognition/Complex Human Learning
D:	Developmental
PrS:	Personality/Social
PyCl:	Psychopathology/Clinical
M:	Methodology
Ap:	Applied

TALLY CHART																			
Checkmark to the left of the items you missed.																			
	1		23		45		67		89		111		133		155		177		199
	2		24		46		68		90		112		134		156		178		200
	3		25		47		69		91		113		135		157		179		201
	4		26		48		70		92		114		136		158		180		202
	5		27		49		71		93		115		137		159		181		203
	6		28		50		72		94		116		138		160		182		204
	7		29		51		73		95		117		139		161		183		205
	8		30		52		74		96		118		140		162		184		206
	9		31		53		75		97		119		141		163		185		207
	10		32		54		76		98		120		142		164		186		208
	11		33		55		77		99		121		143		165		187		209
	12		34		56		78		100		122		144		166		188		210
	13		35		57		79		101		123		145		167		189		211
	14		36		58		80		102		124		146		168		190		212
	15		37		59		81		103		125		147		169		191		213
	16		38		60		82		104		126		148		170		192		214
	17		39		61		83		105		127		149		171		193		215
	18		40		62		84		106		128		150		172		194		216
	19		41		63		85		107		129		151		173		195		217
	20		42		64		86		108		130		152		174		196		218
	21		43		65		87		109		131		153		175		197		219
	22		44		66		88		110		132		154		176		198		220

Record the number of questions you missed (checkmarked) in each area.

PC (1–25) _____ SnP (26–50) _____ LM (51–75) _____
CHL (76–100) _____ D (101–125) _____ PrS (126–154) _____
PyCl (155–182) _____ M (183–202) _____ Ap (203–220) _____

Test Score Scaling

You are a real "pro" at this scaling by now. As you did in the initial diagnostic test, subtract the number of questions you missed in a given subject area from the total number of questions in that area. Compare the result with the 75th percentile number. If the number is equal to or larger than the 75th percentile number, you know that area pretty well. If your number is smaller than the 75th percentile number, review that area a bit more.

PC Area: 25 – _____ (your number missed) = _____ // 20 = 75th percentile
SnP Area: 25 – _____ (your number missed) = _____ // 20 = 75th percentile
LM Area: 25 – _____ (your number missed) = _____ // 20 = 75th percentile
CHL Area: 25 – _____ (your number missed) = _____ // 20 = 75th percentile
D Area: 25 – _____ (your number missed) = _____ // 20 = 75th percentile
PrS Area: 29 – _____ (your number missed) = _____ // 22 = 75th percentile
PyCl Area: 28 – _____ (your number missed) = _____ // 21 = 75th percentile
M Area: 20 – _____ (your number missed) = _____ // 14 = 75th percentile
Ap Area: 18 – _____ (your number missed) = _____ // 13 = 75th percentile

How was "Diagnostic Round Two?" We bet your hard work is paying off. Touch up any of the areas where your score dipped below the 75th percentile. Then you'll be all set to try out more of the practice tests.

Just a Thought or Two

Here are a few more observations and thoughts to blend with those we shared after the first diagnostic test. Just tuck 'em in that clever strategy-arsenal you've been building.

- You can expect about a half-dozen or so of those cute little "I only," "II only," and so on question formats. Don't let them throw you. Jennifer Palmer graciously passed along a successful test-taking strategy she used on these GRE items, so gather 'round and let's listen in. The format you'll see will be some variation of this: "I only," "II only," "III only," "I and II only," "II and III only." Sometimes you'll see a "I, II, and III." Whatever format you encounter, the key approach is this— *Look at the individual answer choices rather than the combinations!* Take one statement at a time! Here, we'll show you what we mean:

  (A) I only
  (B) II only
  (C) III only
  (D) I and II only
  (E) II and III only

  Start with (A). If it's true then you can eliminate (B), (C), and (E). If it's false you can still eliminate (A) and (D). As Jennifer observed, it's generally more advantageous to decide definitively that a statement is true because that decision allows you to eliminate more answer choices. But since we don't always have that luxury, the strategy is to definitively decide something about one statement and work from there. Let's hear that round of applause for Jennifer! Thanks, Jennifer, for that special sharin'!
- Be familiar enough with your content to be able to apply it in different contexts. There's a major difference between barely hanging onto facts and having the flexibility to apply them in whatever setting a test question gives you. When you can do the latter, it's more fun and you'll feel more confident with any setting a test item presents to you.
- Test yourself on the quick-reference table concepts, names, and terms we've provided. They will help you mentally to organize information, make logical relationships, and check up on any spots that may need a bit more review.
- When reviewing within your selected text, remember the PQRST method. Preview a given section of material originally (like flying

quickly and low over a landscape). Then, before you read, phrase in your mind a question you're seeking to answer, much like a detective would. As you read you'll be actively seeking to answer the question you've phrased. Next, self-recite key material. It puts your learning in a different modality—you're hearing as well as seeing. Finally, test yourself by going back to given headings or section titles and seeing what you remember within them. Yeah, it's Preview, Question, Read, Self-Recite, Test, and you'll do just fine.

- Don't forget the importance of moving rapidly through the test items and guessing if you can eliminate even one answer choice.

5 Sample Tests

This section contains four sample GRE Psychology Tests, each based on the actual exam. Their length, the type of question used (multiple choice), and their content approach the official test as closely as possible. By simulating actual testing conditions as you take these tests, you should be able to get a good idea of how well you are progressing in your review, which subject areas need more work, and what your prospects for success on the actual test should be.

How to Use the Sample Tests

Each test has an answer grid, answers with explanations, and a scale for evaluating your score in each subject area. Best results can be obtained by following a few simple procedures.

When taking a sample test, it is a good idea to simulate actual testing conditions. To do this, find a quiet area away from distractions. Have several sharpened pencils and a watch or suitable timer handy. Since the time allotted for the official test is 170 minutes, plan to limit yourself to this time span. Don't consult notes or the review section of this book while taking the sample test. Use the answer grid to record your answers.

After you have completed a test, check your responses with the correct answers for that test. (The answer explanations will help you understand any questions you might have missed.) Next, turn to the section at the end of the test entitled "Evaluating Your Score." The different subject areas on the test are listed with abbreviations. To find out which areas you may need more work in, find the numbers in the Tally Chart that correspond with the numbers of the test questions you missed. The abbreviation next to each number will indicate which area that particular question deals with. In the space provided below the chart, record the total number of questions you missed in each of the subject areas. You can then check the Test Score Scale to see how your scores compare with the norm. To do this, subtract the number you had wrong from the total number of test questions in a certain area as shown on the Scale and compare the result with the 75th percentile number also given. Any score below this percentile indicates an area for more review. After you have determined which areas need more work, return to those sections in Chapter 3.

By taking one test at a time and evaluating your score after each one, you can chart your progress and make the most of your review time.

Test 1: Answer Grid

1. Ⓐ Ⓑ Ⓒ Ⓓ Ⓔ	51. Ⓐ Ⓑ Ⓒ Ⓓ Ⓔ	101. Ⓐ Ⓑ Ⓒ Ⓓ Ⓔ	151. Ⓐ Ⓑ Ⓒ Ⓓ Ⓔ
2. Ⓐ Ⓑ Ⓒ Ⓓ Ⓔ	52. Ⓐ Ⓑ Ⓒ Ⓓ Ⓔ	102. Ⓐ Ⓑ Ⓒ Ⓓ Ⓔ	152. Ⓐ Ⓑ Ⓒ Ⓓ Ⓔ
3. Ⓐ Ⓑ Ⓒ Ⓓ Ⓔ	53. Ⓐ Ⓑ Ⓒ Ⓓ Ⓔ	103. Ⓐ Ⓑ Ⓒ Ⓓ Ⓔ	153. Ⓐ Ⓑ Ⓒ Ⓓ Ⓔ
4. Ⓐ Ⓑ Ⓒ Ⓓ Ⓔ	54. Ⓐ Ⓑ Ⓒ Ⓓ Ⓔ	104. Ⓐ Ⓑ Ⓒ Ⓓ Ⓔ	154. Ⓐ Ⓑ Ⓒ Ⓓ Ⓔ
5. Ⓐ Ⓑ Ⓒ Ⓓ Ⓔ	55. Ⓐ Ⓑ Ⓒ Ⓓ Ⓔ	105. Ⓐ Ⓑ Ⓒ Ⓓ Ⓔ	155. Ⓐ Ⓑ Ⓒ Ⓓ Ⓔ
6. Ⓐ Ⓑ Ⓒ Ⓓ Ⓔ	56. Ⓐ Ⓑ Ⓒ Ⓓ Ⓔ	106. Ⓐ Ⓑ Ⓒ Ⓓ Ⓔ	156. Ⓐ Ⓑ Ⓒ Ⓓ Ⓔ
7. Ⓐ Ⓑ Ⓒ Ⓓ Ⓔ	57. Ⓐ Ⓑ Ⓒ Ⓓ Ⓔ	107. Ⓐ Ⓑ Ⓒ Ⓓ Ⓔ	157. Ⓐ Ⓑ Ⓒ Ⓓ Ⓔ
8. Ⓐ Ⓑ Ⓒ Ⓓ Ⓔ	58. Ⓐ Ⓑ Ⓒ Ⓓ Ⓔ	108. Ⓐ Ⓑ Ⓒ Ⓓ Ⓔ	158. Ⓐ Ⓑ Ⓒ Ⓓ Ⓔ
9. Ⓐ Ⓑ Ⓒ Ⓓ Ⓔ	59. Ⓐ Ⓑ Ⓒ Ⓓ Ⓔ	109. Ⓐ Ⓑ Ⓒ Ⓓ Ⓔ	159. Ⓐ Ⓑ Ⓒ Ⓓ Ⓔ
10. Ⓐ Ⓑ Ⓒ Ⓓ Ⓔ	60. Ⓐ Ⓑ Ⓒ Ⓓ Ⓔ	110. Ⓐ Ⓑ Ⓒ Ⓓ Ⓔ	160. Ⓐ Ⓑ Ⓒ Ⓓ Ⓔ
11. Ⓐ Ⓑ Ⓒ Ⓓ Ⓔ	61. Ⓐ Ⓑ Ⓒ Ⓓ Ⓔ	111. Ⓐ Ⓑ Ⓒ Ⓓ Ⓔ	161. Ⓐ Ⓑ Ⓒ Ⓓ Ⓔ
12. Ⓐ Ⓑ Ⓒ Ⓓ Ⓔ	62. Ⓐ Ⓑ Ⓒ Ⓓ Ⓔ	112. Ⓐ Ⓑ Ⓒ Ⓓ Ⓔ	162. Ⓐ Ⓑ Ⓒ Ⓓ Ⓔ
13. Ⓐ Ⓑ Ⓒ Ⓓ Ⓔ	63. Ⓐ Ⓑ Ⓒ Ⓓ Ⓔ	113. Ⓐ Ⓑ Ⓒ Ⓓ Ⓔ	163. Ⓐ Ⓑ Ⓒ Ⓓ Ⓔ
14. Ⓐ Ⓑ Ⓒ Ⓓ Ⓔ	64. Ⓐ Ⓑ Ⓒ Ⓓ Ⓔ	114. Ⓐ Ⓑ Ⓒ Ⓓ Ⓔ	164. Ⓐ Ⓑ Ⓒ Ⓓ Ⓔ
15. Ⓐ Ⓑ Ⓒ Ⓓ Ⓔ	65. Ⓐ Ⓑ Ⓒ Ⓓ Ⓔ	115. Ⓐ Ⓑ Ⓒ Ⓓ Ⓔ	165. Ⓐ Ⓑ Ⓒ Ⓓ Ⓔ
16. Ⓐ Ⓑ Ⓒ Ⓓ Ⓔ	66. Ⓐ Ⓑ Ⓒ Ⓓ Ⓔ	116. Ⓐ Ⓑ Ⓒ Ⓓ Ⓔ	166. Ⓐ Ⓑ Ⓒ Ⓓ Ⓔ
17. Ⓐ Ⓑ Ⓒ Ⓓ Ⓔ	67. Ⓐ Ⓑ Ⓒ Ⓓ Ⓔ	117. Ⓐ Ⓑ Ⓒ Ⓓ Ⓔ	167. Ⓐ Ⓑ Ⓒ Ⓓ Ⓔ
18. Ⓐ Ⓑ Ⓒ Ⓓ Ⓔ	68. Ⓐ Ⓑ Ⓒ Ⓓ Ⓔ	118. Ⓐ Ⓑ Ⓒ Ⓓ Ⓔ	168. Ⓐ Ⓑ Ⓒ Ⓓ Ⓔ
19. Ⓐ Ⓑ Ⓒ Ⓓ Ⓔ	69. Ⓐ Ⓑ Ⓒ Ⓓ Ⓔ	119. Ⓐ Ⓑ Ⓒ Ⓓ Ⓔ	169. Ⓐ Ⓑ Ⓒ Ⓓ Ⓔ
20. Ⓐ Ⓑ Ⓒ Ⓓ Ⓔ	70. Ⓐ Ⓑ Ⓒ Ⓓ Ⓔ	120. Ⓐ Ⓑ Ⓒ Ⓓ Ⓔ	170. Ⓐ Ⓑ Ⓒ Ⓓ Ⓔ
21. Ⓐ Ⓑ Ⓒ Ⓓ Ⓔ	71. Ⓐ Ⓑ Ⓒ Ⓓ Ⓔ	121. Ⓐ Ⓑ Ⓒ Ⓓ Ⓔ	171. Ⓐ Ⓑ Ⓒ Ⓓ Ⓔ
22. Ⓐ Ⓑ Ⓒ Ⓓ Ⓔ	72. Ⓐ Ⓑ Ⓒ Ⓓ Ⓔ	122. Ⓐ Ⓑ Ⓒ Ⓓ Ⓔ	172. Ⓐ Ⓑ Ⓒ Ⓓ Ⓔ
23. Ⓐ Ⓑ Ⓒ Ⓓ Ⓔ	73. Ⓐ Ⓑ Ⓒ Ⓓ Ⓔ	123. Ⓐ Ⓑ Ⓒ Ⓓ Ⓔ	173. Ⓐ Ⓑ Ⓒ Ⓓ Ⓔ
24. Ⓐ Ⓑ Ⓒ Ⓓ Ⓔ	74. Ⓐ Ⓑ Ⓒ Ⓓ Ⓔ	124. Ⓐ Ⓑ Ⓒ Ⓓ Ⓔ	174. Ⓐ Ⓑ Ⓒ Ⓓ Ⓔ
25. Ⓐ Ⓑ Ⓒ Ⓓ Ⓔ	75. Ⓐ Ⓑ Ⓒ Ⓓ Ⓔ	125. Ⓐ Ⓑ Ⓒ Ⓓ Ⓔ	175. Ⓐ Ⓑ Ⓒ Ⓓ Ⓔ
26. Ⓐ Ⓑ Ⓒ Ⓓ Ⓔ	76. Ⓐ Ⓑ Ⓒ Ⓓ Ⓔ	126. Ⓐ Ⓑ Ⓒ Ⓓ Ⓔ	176. Ⓐ Ⓑ Ⓒ Ⓓ Ⓔ
27. Ⓐ Ⓑ Ⓒ Ⓓ Ⓔ	77. Ⓐ Ⓑ Ⓒ Ⓓ Ⓔ	127. Ⓐ Ⓑ Ⓒ Ⓓ Ⓔ	177. Ⓐ Ⓑ Ⓒ Ⓓ Ⓔ
28. Ⓐ Ⓑ Ⓒ Ⓓ Ⓔ	78. Ⓐ Ⓑ Ⓒ Ⓓ Ⓔ	128. Ⓐ Ⓑ Ⓒ Ⓓ Ⓔ	178. Ⓐ Ⓑ Ⓒ Ⓓ Ⓔ
29. Ⓐ Ⓑ Ⓒ Ⓓ Ⓔ	79. Ⓐ Ⓑ Ⓒ Ⓓ Ⓔ	129. Ⓐ Ⓑ Ⓒ Ⓓ Ⓔ	179. Ⓐ Ⓑ Ⓒ Ⓓ Ⓔ
30. Ⓐ Ⓑ Ⓒ Ⓓ Ⓔ	80. Ⓐ Ⓑ Ⓒ Ⓓ Ⓔ	130. Ⓐ Ⓑ Ⓒ Ⓓ Ⓔ	180. Ⓐ Ⓑ Ⓒ Ⓓ Ⓔ
31. Ⓐ Ⓑ Ⓒ Ⓓ Ⓔ	81. Ⓐ Ⓑ Ⓒ Ⓓ Ⓔ	131. Ⓐ Ⓑ Ⓒ Ⓓ Ⓔ	181. Ⓐ Ⓑ Ⓒ Ⓓ Ⓔ
32. Ⓐ Ⓑ Ⓒ Ⓓ Ⓔ	82. Ⓐ Ⓑ Ⓒ Ⓓ Ⓔ	132. Ⓐ Ⓑ Ⓒ Ⓓ Ⓔ	182. Ⓐ Ⓑ Ⓒ Ⓓ Ⓔ
33. Ⓐ Ⓑ Ⓒ Ⓓ Ⓔ	83. Ⓐ Ⓑ Ⓒ Ⓓ Ⓔ	133. Ⓐ Ⓑ Ⓒ Ⓓ Ⓔ	183. Ⓐ Ⓑ Ⓒ Ⓓ Ⓔ
34. Ⓐ Ⓑ Ⓒ Ⓓ Ⓔ	84. Ⓐ Ⓑ Ⓒ Ⓓ Ⓔ	134. Ⓐ Ⓑ Ⓒ Ⓓ Ⓔ	184. Ⓐ Ⓑ Ⓒ Ⓓ Ⓔ
35. Ⓐ Ⓑ Ⓒ Ⓓ Ⓔ	85. Ⓐ Ⓑ Ⓒ Ⓓ Ⓔ	135. Ⓐ Ⓑ Ⓒ Ⓓ Ⓔ	185. Ⓐ Ⓑ Ⓒ Ⓓ Ⓔ
36. Ⓐ Ⓑ Ⓒ Ⓓ Ⓔ	86. Ⓐ Ⓑ Ⓒ Ⓓ Ⓔ	136. Ⓐ Ⓑ Ⓒ Ⓓ Ⓔ	186. Ⓐ Ⓑ Ⓒ Ⓓ Ⓔ
37. Ⓐ Ⓑ Ⓒ Ⓓ Ⓔ	87. Ⓐ Ⓑ Ⓒ Ⓓ Ⓔ	137. Ⓐ Ⓑ Ⓒ Ⓓ Ⓔ	187. Ⓐ Ⓑ Ⓒ Ⓓ Ⓔ
38. Ⓐ Ⓑ Ⓒ Ⓓ Ⓔ	88. Ⓐ Ⓑ Ⓒ Ⓓ Ⓔ	138. Ⓐ Ⓑ Ⓒ Ⓓ Ⓔ	188. Ⓐ Ⓑ Ⓒ Ⓓ Ⓔ
39. Ⓐ Ⓑ Ⓒ Ⓓ Ⓔ	89. Ⓐ Ⓑ Ⓒ Ⓓ Ⓔ	139. Ⓐ Ⓑ Ⓒ Ⓓ Ⓔ	189. Ⓐ Ⓑ Ⓒ Ⓓ Ⓔ
40. Ⓐ Ⓑ Ⓒ Ⓓ Ⓔ	90. Ⓐ Ⓑ Ⓒ Ⓓ Ⓔ	140. Ⓐ Ⓑ Ⓒ Ⓓ Ⓔ	190. Ⓐ Ⓑ Ⓒ Ⓓ Ⓔ
41. Ⓐ Ⓑ Ⓒ Ⓓ Ⓔ	91. Ⓐ Ⓑ Ⓒ Ⓓ Ⓔ	141. Ⓐ Ⓑ Ⓒ Ⓓ Ⓔ	191. Ⓐ Ⓑ Ⓒ Ⓓ Ⓔ
42. Ⓐ Ⓑ Ⓒ Ⓓ Ⓔ	92. Ⓐ Ⓑ Ⓒ Ⓓ Ⓔ	142. Ⓐ Ⓑ Ⓒ Ⓓ Ⓔ	192. Ⓐ Ⓑ Ⓒ Ⓓ Ⓔ
43. Ⓐ Ⓑ Ⓒ Ⓓ Ⓔ	93. Ⓐ Ⓑ Ⓒ Ⓓ Ⓔ	143. Ⓐ Ⓑ Ⓒ Ⓓ Ⓔ	193. Ⓐ Ⓑ Ⓒ Ⓓ Ⓔ
44. Ⓐ Ⓑ Ⓒ Ⓓ Ⓔ	94. Ⓐ Ⓑ Ⓒ Ⓓ Ⓔ	144. Ⓐ Ⓑ Ⓒ Ⓓ Ⓔ	194. Ⓐ Ⓑ Ⓒ Ⓓ Ⓔ
45. Ⓐ Ⓑ Ⓒ Ⓓ Ⓔ	95. Ⓐ Ⓑ Ⓒ Ⓓ Ⓔ	145. Ⓐ Ⓑ Ⓒ Ⓓ Ⓔ	195. Ⓐ Ⓑ Ⓒ Ⓓ Ⓔ
46. Ⓐ Ⓑ Ⓒ Ⓓ Ⓔ	96. Ⓐ Ⓑ Ⓒ Ⓓ Ⓔ	146. Ⓐ Ⓑ Ⓒ Ⓓ Ⓔ	196. Ⓐ Ⓑ Ⓒ Ⓓ Ⓔ
47. Ⓐ Ⓑ Ⓒ Ⓓ Ⓔ	97. Ⓐ Ⓑ Ⓒ Ⓓ Ⓔ	147. Ⓐ Ⓑ Ⓒ Ⓓ Ⓔ	197. Ⓐ Ⓑ Ⓒ Ⓓ Ⓔ
48. Ⓐ Ⓑ Ⓒ Ⓓ Ⓔ	98. Ⓐ Ⓑ Ⓒ Ⓓ Ⓔ	148. Ⓐ Ⓑ Ⓒ Ⓓ Ⓔ	198. Ⓐ Ⓑ Ⓒ Ⓓ Ⓔ
49. Ⓐ Ⓑ Ⓒ Ⓓ Ⓔ	99. Ⓐ Ⓑ Ⓒ Ⓓ Ⓔ	149. Ⓐ Ⓑ Ⓒ Ⓓ Ⓔ	199. Ⓐ Ⓑ Ⓒ Ⓓ Ⓔ
50. Ⓐ Ⓑ Ⓒ Ⓓ Ⓔ	100. Ⓐ Ⓑ Ⓒ Ⓓ Ⓔ	150. Ⓐ Ⓑ Ⓒ Ⓓ Ⓔ	200. Ⓐ Ⓑ Ⓒ Ⓓ Ⓔ

Test 1

Time: 170 minutes

Directions: Each of the following questions contains five possible responses. Read the question carefully and select the response that you feel is most appropriate. Then completely darken the oval on your answer grid that corresponds with your choice.

1. The law of specific nerve energy refers to

   (A) their electrical potential
   (B) a receptor's capability to give only one quality of experience (e.g., auditory), regardless of how it was stimulated
   (C) a receptor's capability to give several different qualities of experience (e.g., temperature, pain, and so on), which vary with the quality of stimulus received
   (D) postsynaptic potential
   (E) presynaptic potential

2. Alpha wave would be most prevalent in which of the following instances?

   (A) deep sleep
   (B) REM sleep
   (C) eyes closed in relaxed, wakeful state
   (D) solving a multiplication problem "in your head"
   (E) eyes open in relaxed, wakeful state

3. "In no case may we interpret an action as the outcome of the exercise of a higher psychical faculty if it can be interpreted as the outcome of the exercise of one which stands lower in the psychological scale." The quotation expresses

   (A) natural selection (Darwin)
   (B) law of imprinting (Lorenz)
   (C) law of phylogeny (Tinbergen)
   (D) theory of tropisms (Loeb)
   (E) law of parsimony (Morgan)

4. Which of the following would *not* be characterized as a stimulant?

   (A) caffeine   (B) barbiturates   (C) nicotine
   (D) cocaine   (E) benzedrine

5. The animal laboratory would be the most likely work setting for which of the following comparative psychologists?

   (A) Lorenz
   (B) Tinbergen
   (C) Lashley
   (D) Romanes
   (E) Morgan

6. An individual who receives normal sight following blindness in the early years of life

   (A) cannot achieve the skills of shape discrimination
   (B) will not develop the size-constancy aspect of perception
   (C) will adjust to the visual world almost instantly
   (D) will experience long-term muscle coordination problems because of changes in reference points
   (E) will have to relearn auditory and tactile associations necessary to accommodate the visual frame of reference

7. Inability to monitor the movements of one's feet and the absence of feedback regarding their position and relationship to the ground would suggest problems with the

   (A) labyrinthine sensory system
   (B) kinesthetic sensory system
   (C) thermal sensory system
   (D) visceral sensory system
   (E) peripheral sensory system

8. The perceptual theory known as "Sensory-Tonic" was developed by

   (A) Dember   (B) Wertheimer   (C) Werner-Wapner
   (D) Allport   (E) Ricco

9. Which of the following is *not* part of the brainstem?

   (A) medulla   (B) pons   (C) midbrain
   (D) reticular formation   (E) corpus callosum

10. Kohler has found that with "squint glasses"

    (A) greater adaptation occurs than with inversion glasses
    (B) no adaptation occurs to the phi phenomenon experience
    (C) no adaptation occurs to the color-stereo effect
    (D) strong adaptation occurs to color-stereo but not to phi
    (E) surprising adaptation occurs to both color-stereo and phi

11. Reflexes occur primarily in the

    (A) cerebellum   (B) spinal cord   (C) frontal lobe
    (D) limbic system   (E) medulla oblongata

12. Which of the following is *not* closely related to attribution theory?

    (A) Nisbett's person perception
    (B) Kelley's covariation
    (C) Heider's dispositional properties
    (D) Festinger's cognitive dissonance
    (E) Gergen's role behavior

13. Which of the following is central to the stress response?

    (A) DNA   (B) TOTE   (C) GABA
    (D) ACTH   (E) NMR

14. The process of maintaining constancy in the normal internal environment of an organism is called

(A) homeostasis   (B) adaptation   (C) consistency
(D) physiological equivalence   (E) psychological motivation

15. As stimulus patterns become increasingly similar, reaction times based on stimulus discrimination

(A) become shorter
(B) become longer
(C) remain unchanged
(D) become shorter for auditory stimuli, longer for visual ones
(E) become shorter for visual stimuli, longer for auditory ones

Questions 16 and 17 are based on the following passage.

One can think of collective behavior from a number of different, and unique, perspectives. On the one hand, the Marxian model suggests that workers will combine in revolt when their life situations become intolerable. A second perspective, expressed by LeBon, suggests that a crowd takes on characteristics such as impulsiveness and irrationality that are not necessarily characteristic of individual persons within the crowd. A third perspective, held by Freud, sees Oedipal implications in crowd behavior as individuals identify with the crowd leader, expressing a kind of familial love within this identification. Still a fourth perspective is seen in Turner's emphasis on the emergent-norm model—the theory that the ambiguity of a crowd situation prompts the crowd members to adopt as their norm the behavior of a handful of the group's most visible members. Hall adds an additional perspective with the suggestion that crowd behavior tends to violate personal space.

16. Which of the above perspectives would be *least* likely to associate crowd behavior with the immediate, environmental factors?

(A) Marxian   (B) LeBon   (C) Freud
(D) Turner   (E) Hall

17. The view that speaks most directly to the concept of territoriality is that of

(A) Marx   (B) LeBon   (C) Freud
(D) Turner   (E) Hall

18. Primaries in additive color mixing

(A) are synonymous with subtractive color mixing
(B) are blue, green, and red
(C) are utilized in the mixing of paints
(D) have become obsolete and no longer are used as a theoretical reference
(E) are blue, yellow, and red

19. In perceiving the distance of a sound, a person must depend heavily upon

(A) complexity and resonance   (B) brightness and saturation
(C) dystonia   (D) loudness and timbre   (E) beats

20. The body's own self-produced "pain killers" are

(A) epinephrine and norepinephrine
(B) opium and heroin
(C) endorphins and enkephalins
(D) serotonin and acetylcholine
(E) GABA and ACTH

21. Which of the following was an unexpected finding among subjects in early sensory deprivation experiments?

(A) delusions
(B) hallucinations
(C) "phantom limb" phenomenon
(D) experience of motion parallax
(E) convergence

22. A term unrelated to ESP is

(A) clairvoyance   (B) psychokinesis   (C) psychosynesis
(D) telepathy   (E) telekinesis

23. In a Sarason-type experiment, Group 1 is told that it is not expected to finish its task, while Group 2 is told that it is expected to finish. Which of the following would be the anticipated result?

(A) Group 1 finishes; Group 2 does not.
(B) Both Group 1 and Group 2 finish with equal speed.
(C) Group 2 completes more of the task than Group 1.
(D) Both groups experience a type of situational neurosis preventing performance on the task.
(E) The experimenter-monitored group—regardless of the instructions —finishes last.

24. Among the following, the conceptual term *least* important to Hull would be

(A) habit strength   (B) reaction potential   (C) drive
(D) stimulus   (E) interaction potential

25. Auditory receptor cells are located in the

(A) anvil   (B) stirrup   (C) cochlea
(D) eustachian tube   (E) pinna

26. In his own words, Tolman called his theoretical views

(A) S-O-R psychology
(B) radical behaviorism
(C) purposive behaviorism
(D) dynamic behaviorism
(E) motivational behaviorism

27. In the early, classic experiments of Cannon and Washburn, their subjects were required to swallow balloons. This procedure enabled the experimenters to study

(A) the amount of food intake
(B) hormonal secretions
(C) the physiological mechanism known as the "start" factor
(D) dietary self-selection
(E) gastric contractions of the stomach

28. Which of the following name combinations constitutes a chronological time sequence in motivation research?

(A) James, McKinsey, Atkinson
(B) Freud, Adler, Rank
(C) James, McDougall, Atkinson
(D) Freud, Skinner, Berne
(E) James, McClelland, Freud

29. "There is an optimal arousal state for maximal efficiency. Below it we are bored, and above it we are anxious." These statements and their corresponding theory are

(A) Zuckerman's (B) Solomon's (C) Berlyne's
(D) Murray's (E) White's

30. Sleepwalking and talking
(A) occur primarily during the dreaming period
(B) occur mostly in nondreaming stages, since the dreaming person is almost totally immobile
(C) signify hypnagogic activity
(D) correlate strongly with the incidence of alexia
(E) occur far more frequently among women than among men

31. Research indicates that Alzheimer's disease may be related to a deficiency in

(A) dopamine (B) serotonin (C) epinephrine
(D) acetylcholine (E) GABA

32. Which of the following is the control responsibility of the parasympathetic nervous system?

(A) respiration increase
(B) pupil dilation
(C) heart-rate inhibition
(D) salivation inhibition
(E) piloerection

33. Muscles are prominent and familiar examples of

(A) receptors (B) affectors (C) end plates
(D) effectors (E) ganglia

34. Lindsley's activation theory of emotion centers upon the role of

   (A) the limbic system
   (B) classical conditioning
   (C) the reticular formation
   (D) instrumental conditioning
   (E) the galvanic skin response

35. According to Atkinson, which of the following would be true?

   (A) Motivation deals with immediate influences on direction, vigor, and persistence of action.
   (B) Motivation is synonymous with perception.
   (C) Motivation is synonymous with emotion.
   (D) Motivation is synonymous with the study of behavior change.
   (E) Motivation deals primarily with intelligence.

36. When sleep is regularly and experimentally interrupted at the onset of dream activity, it is found that, on subsequent nights,

   (A) normal dream frequency is evident
   (B) normal dream length is evident
   (C) lower dream frequency is evident
   (D) much longer than normal dream length is evident
   (E) there is a surprising absence of any dream activity

37. *Incorrectly* paired are

   (A) spinal cord—a center for reflex behavior
   (B) medulla—centers for respiration and cardiac activity
   (C) ventricular system—glandular hormonal secretions into the blood
   (D) midbrain—conduction of impulses between higher and lower centers of the nervous system
   (E) cerebellum—coordination of sensory and motor impulses

38. Studies by Denenberg indicate that early handling tended to make animals

   (A) more fearful as adults
   (B) less active as adults
   (C) less emotional as adults
   (D) more active as adults
   (E) equivalent in all respects to nonhandled control animals

39. In the exhaustion stage of Selye's general adaptation syndrome, a person demonstrates

   (A) hyperventilation
   (B) apparent calm
   (C) GSR
   (D) more visceral activity
   (E) the alarm-type reaction

40. Hyperactivity through glandular secretion is most directly related to

(A) the cerebellum   (B) the gonads   (C) the thyroid gland
(D) the adrenal medulla   (E) the Sylvian fissure

41. A person who is in the circus because he is nine feet tall and has very large hands and feet and a protruding jaw can attribute his physiological abnormality to an overactive

(A) thyroid gland   (B) parathyroid gland   (C) adrenal gland
(D) pancreas   (E) pituitary gland

42. The brain and spinal cord comprise the

(A) sympathetic nervous system
(B) parasympathetic nervous system
(C) central nervous system
(D) peripheral nervous system
(E) somatic nervous system

43. A peculiar, intoxication-type behavior in which a person loses normal control of his emotions is characteristic of

(A) fatigue   (B) oxygen starvation   (C) thirst
(D) hunger   (E) sexual deprivation

Questions 44–46 are based on the following information.

Among theoretical approaches to personality the terms *nomothetic* and *idiographic* serve to identify two basically different avenues. The idiographic approach places emphasis upon the individual person as a unique entity; the nomothetic approach experimentally looks for personality factors and characteristics that are common to people in general.

44. Which of the following points might be made in defense of the idiographic approach?

(A) The person's unique qualities constitute the essence of his or her personality.
(B) Correlations designed to find common personality characteristics are essential for progress in the field.
(C) The function of an organism in response to a specific stimulus is the key to personality study.
(D) Personality is essentially a matter of physiochemistry and hormonal secretions.
(E) Id, ego, and superego are the principal factors in personality.

45. Which of the following correctly pairs an advocate of the nomothetic approach with an advocate of the idiographic approach?

(A) Rogers—Kelly   (B) Frankl—Perls   (C) Watson—Skinner
(D) Maslow—Tolman   (E) Freud—Adler

46. Which of the following terms and concepts is *not* associated with the idiographic approach?

    (A) individual psychology
    (B) client-centered therapy
    (C) personal construct
    (D) systematic desensitization
    (E) Gestalt therapy

47. The Bunson-Roscoe Law

    (A) holds for photochemical processes
    (B) holds exclusively for audition
    (C) relates exclusively to pain sensitivity
    (D) holds for synesthesia
    (E) relates exclusively to kinesthesis

48. REM sleep signals

    (A) high GSR   (B) dreaming   (C) reciprocal innervation
    (D) stage IV sleep   (E) stage II sleep

49. The method of summated ratings refers to which of the following scales?

    (A) Thurstone   (B) Likert   (C) Semantic Differential
    (D) Guttman   (E) Bogardus

50. In the McClelland-type ring toss game, which of the following groups of men would be expected to take the most shots from an intermediate distance?

    (A) those high in test anxiety
    (B) those high in both test anxiety and achievement need
    (C) those low in achievement need
    (D) those low in both achievement need and test anxiety
    (E) those high in achievement need and low in test anxiety

Questions 51–53 are based upon the following diagram.

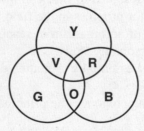

Key
V – Violet
G – Green
O – Orange
B – Blue
R – Red
Y – Yellow

51. Momentarily assuming the above diagram to be an accurate color wheel, what would be the after-image of exposure to red?

    (A) yellow   (B) violet   (C) green
    (D) orange   (E) blue

52. What combination of colors would produce green?

(A) violet and orange   (B) violet and red   (C) blue and yellow
(D) orange and red   (E) blue and red

53. What color would be the complementary of green?

(A) violet   (B) blue   (C) orange
(D) red   (E) violet-orange

Questions 54–56 are based upon the following diagram.

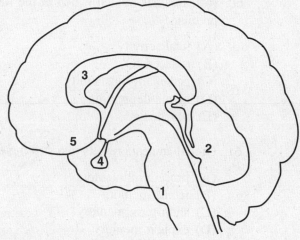

Assume that the human brain has been "halved" and that in the above drawing you are viewing from midbrain the central, interior portion of the right hemisphere.

54. Identify the rhinencephalon.

(A) 1   (B) 2   (C) 3   (D) 4   (E) 5

55. Locate the cerebellum.

(A) 1   (B) 2   (C) 3   (D) 4   (E) 5

56. Find the corpus callosum.

(A) 1   (B) 2   (C) 3   (D) 4   (E) 5

57. Dogs have been trained to make a response when the stimulus is an oval but not when the stimulus is a circle. The animals have been food-deprived and receive food reinforcement for each correct response. On subsequent trials the oval shape that is presented looks more and more circular. At the point where the dogs' previously high level of correct responding becomes random in accuracy, the likely cause of the change is

(A) satiation
(B) anxiety
(C) nondiscriminative stimulus
(D) figure-ground reversal
(E) response generalization

58. The third stage of labor in childbirth is called

    (A) cervix dilation   (B) actual newborn emergence
    (C) the afterbirth   (D) breech   (E) vertex

59. Betsy is brown-eyed (heterozygous) and Bob is brown-eyed (heterozygous). The statistical likelihood of their producing a brown-eyed child is

    (A) 1 in 4   (B) 3 in 4   (C) 2 in 4
    (D) 4 in 4   (E) 0 in 4

60. Research has related which of the following to maternal stress during pregnancy?

    (A) fetal activity
    (B) reduced IQ
    (C) personality instability
    (D) manic-depression
    (E) psychosis

61. Global amnesia results in a striking disruption of

    (A) procedural memory
    (B) iconic memory
    (C) short-term memory
    (D) explicit memory
    (E) implicit memory

62. Which of the following is produced by tactile stimulation of a newborn's cheek?

    (A) Babkin response
    (B) Babinski response
    (C) rooting response
    (D) Moro response
    (E) grasping reflex

63. The fact that Siamese twins, connected at their backs, have been observed in alternate periods of sleep and wakefulness (e.g., one has been sleeping while the other is awake) suggests the importance of which of the following as a mechanism in sleep?

    (A) brain rhythms   (B) prolactin   (C) blood-sugar level
    (D) chemical stimulation   (E) epinephrine

64. In the Dollard and Miller schema, the avoidance gradient is

    (A) steeper than the approach gradient
    (B) equivalent to the approach gradient at all distances from the goal
    (C) weaker than the approach gradient near the goal
    (D) equivalent to the approach gradient when the goal is reached
    (E) stronger than the approach gradient when the goal is distant

65. The fact that a task interrupted prior to completion is remembered better than a completed task is called

(A) proactive facilitation
(B) proactive inhibition
(C) Zeigarnik effect
(D) von Restorff effect
(E) serial position effect

66. Guthrie is most closely associated with which of the following in learning theory?

(A) reinforcement
(B) habit strength
(C) contiguity of S and R
(D) S-R connection
(E) cognitions

67. A person has just learned a new response to be substituted for an old one. Introduction of stress to the response situation will most likely

(A) enhance responding
(B) have no effect upon responding
(C) interfere with responding
(D) crystallize and "cement" the newly learned response
(E) promote reminiscence

68. In toilet training, parents can expect

(A) defecation control to precede urination control
(B) urination control to precede defecation control
(C) simultaneous defecation and urination control
(D) defecation control by the end of the first year
(E) the control pattern that was true in the parents' own childhoods

69. An inability to learn new information and form new long-term memories is called

(A) retroactive amnesia
(B) proactive amnesia
(C) anterograde amnesia
(D) infantile amnesia
(E) implicit amnesia

70. "With the possible exception of old age, no other phase of individual development is so clearly marked by negative connotations and lack of positive sanctions." This is a reference by Goldblatt to

(A) age 1
(B) Erikson's age of autonomy versus shame and doubt
(C) the general preschool period
(D) early adolescence
(E) early adulthood

71. The set-point theory has been advanced in the area of

    (A) visual illusions   (B) learned helplessness   (C) obesity
    (D) schizophrenia   (E) depression

72. In research with newborns, the cautious experimental hunch now being advanced is that

    (A) fast habituators may be brighter than slow habituators
    (B) slow habituators may be brighter than fast habituators
    (C) intelligence may be related to the presence and strength of initial reflexes
    (D) early onset of pleasant emotions in the newborn means healthy personality later
    (E) block design may be an accurate measure of intelligence as early as one month of age

73. The term *general-to-specific* in child development refers to

    (A) visual acuity   (B) auditory sensitivity   (C) motor movements
    (D) cortex development   (E) pain sensitivity

74. The neonate has well-developed

    (A) temperature-regulating mechanisms
    (B) pain sensitivity
    (C) immunity to various infections
    (D) lower torso
    (E) auditory acuteness

75. Gibson's theory of motion perception centers primarily on the

    (A) stroboscopic effect
    (B) relation of moving object to immobile background
    (C) relation to phi phenomenon to immobile background
    (D) binocular disparity
    (E) shape constancy

76. The motor primacy principle in development means that

    (A) muscle development precedes neural development
    (B) striated muscle development precedes smooth muscle development
    (C) virtually any motor skill can be learned shortly after birth, if the infant is given sufficient training
    (D) maturation of neuromuscular structures to a given stage precedes ability to respond
    (E) motor development precedes glandular development

77. Scientific inquiry utilizing rules of logical inference from established premises and laws is known as

    (A) inductive   (B) reductive   (C) deductive
    (D) teleological   (E) probabilistic

78. Innate behavior patterns develop primarily as a function of

   (A) instrumental conditioning
   (B) maturation
   (C) learning
   (D) infant stimulation
   (E) successive approximation

79. The newborn

   (A) vocalizes socially
   (B) smiles socially
   (C) tracks moving objects behind stationary objects
   (D) has the capability for basic learning
   (E) engages in babbling

80. In comparative physical growth curves, females

   (A) develop more slowly than males
   (B) develop more rapidly than males
   (C) develop at the same rate as males
   (D) develop more rapidly than males during the first six years and
       more slowly thereafter
   (E) develop more slowly than males during the first six years and
       more rapidly thereafter

81. If a female human fetus in the early stages of its development received
    large injections of androgen, which of the following could be expected
    in the newborn?

   (A) stillbirth
   (B) anoxia
   (C) brain damage
   (D) abnormal, exaggerated female sex characteristics
   (E) abnormal, exaggerated male sex characteristics

82. Which of the following constitutes a disadvantage of the rooming-in
    procedure with newborns?

   (A) Needs are met with minimal crying.
   (B) Trained nurses are easily accessible.
   (C) No adjustment required to handling by several people
   (D) Constant demands are made upon the new mother.
   (E) Rigid feeding schedule is adhered to.

83. Continued improvement in the absence of further practice is known as

   (A) spontaneous recovery   (B) platikurtic   (C) savings
   (D) reminiscence   (E) recall

84. George Sperling demonstrated that iconic memories decay in under
    two seconds from the

   (A) short-term store   (B) sensory register   (C) hippocampus
   (D) long-term store   (E) working memory

85. In developmental terminology, PKU refers to

    (A) the effects of thalidomide
    (B) Down syndrome
    (C) sickle cell
    (D) a hereditary enzyme deficiency
    (E) syphilis in the newborn

86. Jill remembers a phone number by rehearsing the digits aloud. She is using

    (A) an acoustical code
    (B) a computer code
    (C) a semantic code
    (D) a visual code
    (E) an acuity code

87. Any activity in a reinforcement hierarchy is reinforced by an activity above it in the hierarchy and may reinforce any activity below it. This principle was developed by

    (A) Watson   (B) Premack   (C) Rotter
    (D) Skinner   (E) Rogers

88. The process through which environmental information is received and labeled by the human is called

    (A) decoding   (B) generativity   (C) mediation
    (D) encoding   (E) programming

89. According to Piaget, the process through which a young child relates something he sees to something he already knows is called

    (A) accommodation   (B) assimilation   (C) convergence
    (D) concrete operation   (E) formal operation

90. Temporal conditioning

    (A) is synonymous with trace conditioning
    (B) is synonymous with delayed conditioning
    (C) is synonymous with simultaneous conditioning
    (D) presents an UCS on a fixed time schedule
    (E) utilizes a CS that is in itself inherently rewarding

91. Existing research suggests that an active, outgoing, socially assertive child is most likely to have come from a family background that has been

    (A) warm and restrictive
    (B) distant and demanding
    (C) distant and democratic
    (D) warm and permissive
    (E) distant and permissive

92. Lorenz has suggested that

   (A) aggression is innate and biologically based
   (B) phonemes are the key factors in child language development
   (C) language determines thought processes
   (D) duck imprinting cannot be replicated in humans
   (E) the general notion of imprinting is not supported by experimental evidence

93. Punishment is most effective as an aid to learning when used

   (A) at the beginning of a series of trials
   (B) at the end of a series of trials
   (C) to extinguish previously rewarded responses
   (D) in combination with reward
   (E) in the middle of a series of trials

94. Theoretical separation between imagery and verbal processes has

   (A) not been supported by neurological investigations
   (B) been strongly supported by neurological investigations
   (C) been supported by investigations of the left temporal lobe only
   (D) been supported by investigations of the right temporal lobe only
   (E) been supported by the work of Kimura but not by that of Milner

95. Developmentally speaking, the earliest group in which a person participates is

   (A) dyadic
   (B) monadic
   (C) triadic
   (D) quadratic
   (E) parallel play group

96. Among the features by which we distinguish letters, a three-year-old child is proficient only in

   (A) curvature (U vs. V)
   (B) closedness (O vs. C)
   (C) direction (P vs. d)
   (D) size (a vs. A)
   (E) shape

97. Which of the following is stated by a null hypothesis?

   (A) significant difference
   (B) no significant difference
   (C) normal frequency distribution
   (D) minimized Type II error
   (E) 0.05 significance level

98. Which of the following has *not* been a finding within developmental psychology research?

    (A) The degree of mother responsiveness to a baby's needs affects the quality of the child's attachment to the mother.
    (B) Frequent mother-child separations during the first two or three years can produce anxious attachment.
    (C) The discipline technique of expressing disapproval through love withdrawal has been found to be one of the most effective.
    (D) Failure to form attachments to significant, caretaking persons during childhood relates to the inability to form close personal relationships in adulthood.
    (E) The young child is much more willing to explore strange surroundings when mother is present than when she is not.

99. The standard deviation obtained from a sample distribution of scores is

    (A) an inferential statistic
    (B) a descriptive statistic
    (C) a measure of correlation
    (D) a squared variance
    (E) a measure of central tendency

100. Eleanor Rosch suggested that category membership is determined by similarity of an exemplar to the concept's

    (A) chunk   (B) schema   (C) critical features
    (D) prototype   (E) icon

101. Which of the following should be the source of greatest parental concern about a child's emotional health?

    (A) frequent laughing
    (B) frequent noisiness
    (C) long periods of sleep
    (D) frequent temper tantrums
    (E) frequent crying

102. Current trends indicate that breast feeding is most prevalent among which of the following groups?

    (A) lower-class white mothers
    (B) lower-class black mothers
    (C) middle-class, well-educated mothers
    (D) middle-class, poorly educated mothers
    (E) all social strata

103. Not among the elements that Thurstone found comprising intelligence is

    (A) verbal comprehension
    (B) memory
    (C) reasoning
    (D) space visualization
    (E) creative problem solving

104. In the present intelligence classification system, the former category of moron would now be included within

(A) profoundly retarded
(B) educable
(C) severely retarded
(D) trainable
(E) mildly retarded

105. In studying the relationship between test frequency and content mastery, a researcher finds a correlation of +1.20. On the basis of this finding, he can conclude that there is

(A) strong positive correlation
(B) strong negative correlation
(C) low positive correlation
(D) low negative correlation
(E) a computational error

106. When asked what time it is, four-year-old Johnny correctly responds that it is 4:30. Johnny's time concept has developed
(A) more rapidly than one normally would expect
(B) more slowly than one normally could expect
(C) through parental instructions and careful guidance
(D) as a function of training received through a sibling
(E) as a function of his work in spatial relations

107. Determining a rule of structure from incomplete evidence and then identifying items that fulfill the rule would be a demonstration of

(A) interpolation   (B) extrapolation   (C) interposition
(D) structuring   (E) modeling

108. Dual process refers to a theory of

(A) short- and long-term memory
(B) axon and dendrite
(C) rod and cone vision
(D) sympathetic and parasympathetic nervous system
(E) neurosis and psychosis

109. During a political campaign, it is common for one to remember falsely a candidate's opinions as more consistent with that candidate's party's platform than they really are. The tendency to remember an expected statement instead of an actual statement is an example of a(n)

(A) iconic memory
(B) implicit memory
(C) schema-consistent distortion
(D) algorithm
(E) concept prototype

110. Hebb found that "super span" tests involving long strings of digits repeated periodically after many intervening spans

(A) left no memory trace
(B) left a demonstrable memory trace
(C) created unique number-span retention capacities
(D) suggested strictly transient neural activity
(E) suggested the "isometric digit" problem

111. A student has several weeks in which to plan study for an upcoming test. Which of the following time-allotment strategies would the student be best advised to use?

(A) massing study time in the third week before the test
(B) massing study time just before the test
(C) distributing study time throughout the several-week period
(D) studying on every fifth day
(E) studying "round-the-clock" in the 24 hours before the test

112. Kohlberg indicates that at the most primitive level of moral development, morality is decided by
(A) individual rights and social contracts
(B) reward and punishment
(C) individual conscience
(D) social approval or disapproval
(E) religious values

113. Telegraphic speech refers to

(A) a child's first word
(B) verbal expression that emphasizes only vowel sounds
(C) the consistent use of three-syllable words
(D) a child's early grammatical constructions
(E) the basic consonant elements present in every language

114. In experiments such as Pavlov's surgical isolation of a portion of a dog's stomach, it has been found that the effect of food upon digestive processes depends upon

(A) solely the tasting behavior
(B) solely the swallowing behavior
(C) solely the entry of food into the stomach
(D) a combination of both the stomach and the mouth activities
(E) neither the stomach nor the mouth activity

115. Which of the following is *least* characteristic of the kibbutzim?

(A) professional caretakers for children in houses separate from those of the parents
(B) marked retardation in the social and intellectual development of the children
(C) parental visits primarily in the evenings and on weekends
(D) a warm, permissive approach to toilet training
(E) operation by the state

Questions 116 and 117 are based on the following diagram.

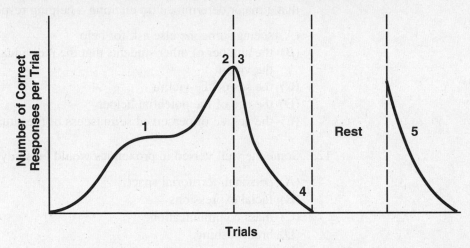

116. In the above diagram, the process of extinction began at which point?

(A) 1   (B) 2   (C) 3   (D) 4   (E) 5

117. The phenomenon occurring at point 1 would be indicative of

(A) asymptote   (B) extinction   (C) plateau
(D) reminiscence   (E) spontaneous recovery

118. According to psychoanalytic theory, defense mechanisms develop as a function of

(A) repression   (B) depression   (C) superego
(D) anxiety   (E) reaction formation

119. Kelley's "warm-cold" experimentation demonstrated the effect of which of the following on a person's attitude toward a group speaker?

(A) room temperature
(B) the warmth or coldness of the speaker himself
(C) the variation in a single descriptive adjective
(D) the warmth or coldness of the experimenter
(E) the warmth or coldness of the audience

120. Interpersonal attraction based on rewards and costs is a prominent aspect of the

(A) theory of similarity
(B) theory of complementarity
(C) social exchange theory
(D) theory of cognitive dissonance
(E) distributive justice theory

121. Which of the following experimenters developed a test in which black and white dolls are presented to black and white children with the question, "Which one looks like you?"

(A) Ammons   (B) Pettigrew   (C) Clark
(D) McCandless   (E) Kelly

122. In Darley and Latane's "epileptic attack" study, the investigators found that a major determinant in eliciting a helping response was

    (A) seeing someone else ask for help
    (B) the number of other students that the individual thought had heard the victim
    (C) the sex of the victim
    (D) the age of the potential helper
    (E) the degree of perceived seriousness of the situation

123. Someone well versed in proxemics would be studying

    (A) personal, territorial space
    (B) facial expressions
    (C) mass communication
    (D) brainwashing
    (E) nonzero sum games

124. Which one of the following has said in regard to personality that every child is a scientist, developing and testing his own hypotheses?

    (A) Freud   (B) Jung   (C) Rogers
    (D) Allport   (E) Kelly

125. The personality approaches of Cattell and Eysenck rely heavily upon

    (A) inner forces (cathexes-anticathexes)
    (B) percept and concept
    (C) observable action
    (D) factor analysis
    (E) script and contract

126. The therapy technique known as free association had its early beginnings in the work of

    (A) James   (B) Freud   (C) Watson
    (D) Jung   (E) Brucke

127. The terms *script* and *contract* are prominent within which of the following approaches?

    (A) psychoanalysis
    (B) systematic desensitization
    (C) reciprocal inhibition
    (D) implosive therapy
    (E) transactional analysis

128. Definitionally central to personality as viewed within behaviorism is

    (A) inner motivation
    (B) percept and concept
    (C) observable action
    (D) reenactment of birth trauma
    (E) factor analysis

129. Within Newcomb's A-B-X model, if person A likes X, person B likes X, and person A dislikes person B, the triad is said to be

(A) cooriented   (B) asymmetric   (C) congruent
(D) bipolar   (E) inoculated

130. In Adler's approach to personality, the presence of an inferiority complex within a person will be followed by

(A) heightened sexual activity   (B) need for maternal love
(C) desire for peace   (D) superiority striving   (E) thanatos

131. A researcher has designed a Likert-type scale on which all the "Strongly Agree" items are strongly favorable responses toward the topic being measured. When the test is administered, which of the following misgivings would be quite legitimate?

(A) that the "Strongly Agree" portion of the scale has been underrepresented
(B) that the "Strongly Disagree" portion of the scale has been underrepresented
(C) that equal-appearing intervals were not developed
(D) that a random responder may be falsely interpreted
(E) that social distance has not been maintained

132. When Berkowitz refers to the F-A hypothesis, he means

(A) frustration-affection
(B) frustration-aggression
(C) feeling-affect
(D) feeling-aggression
(E) fixation-accommodation

133. In the Allport-Vernon-Lindzey scale, which type of person will most highly value the search for truth and order?

(A) economic   (B) philosophical   (C) theoretical
(D) aesthetic   (E) religious

134. According to the Life Change Scale, which of the following events would be most stressful?

(A) marital separation   (B) retirement   (C) marriage
(D) son or daughter leaving home   (E) foreclosure of mortgage

135. Studies of MAO levels suggest that
(A) people may differ in an enzyme level that affects emotion
(B) multiple action orientation is prevalent among schizophrenics
(C) management accounting options have been effective in organizational psychology
(D) people may differ in intelligence as a direct function of head size
(E) visual connection in the brain is not through the optic chiasm as originally thought

136. Kagan's work reopens debate and challenges the basic assumption regarding

    (A) a critical early-childhood period in social development
    (B) a critical early-childhood period in cognitive-intellectual development
    (C) a critical early-childhood period in emotional development
    (D) the Erikson psychosocial stages
    (E) the Freudian views regarding thanatos

137. A decision to establish status on the basis of individual income, education, and occupation utilizes the

    (A) objective method
    (B) reputational method
    (C) subjective method
    (D) situational method
    (E) projection method

138. According to the expectancy-value theory

    (A) unattractive women are likely to find attractive male partners
    (B) males and females of equal attractiveness are likely to be matched
    (C) extrovert personality types are likely to pair with introverts
    (D) attitudes will change in the direction of one's behavior
    (E) attractive women are likely to find unattractive male partners

139. Which of the following makes the most prominent use of statistics in its scoring procedures?

    (A) Rorschach Test
    (B) TAT
    (C) Blacky Test
    (D) MMPI
    (E) Sentence Completion Test

140. The general message about early childhood that can be gleaned from personality theorists is that that period is

    (A) not very critical to long-term development
    (B) critically important to later personality development
    (C) critical in the physiological sense but not in the social
    (D) critical in the social sense but not in the physiological
    (E) important only in terms of language development

141. Aronson and Mills's study involving "frank discussion of sexual matters" revealed that strength of initiation

    (A) does not correlate with group attraction
    (B) has strong positive correlation with group attraction
    (C) has weak positive correlation with group attraction
    (D) has strong negative correlation with group attraction
    (E) has weak negative correlation with group attraction

142. The Oedipal conflict is successfully resolved when the child

    (A) identifies with the opposite-sex parent
    (B) identifies with the same-sex parent
    (C) achieves satisfactory toilet training
    (D) has been satisfactorily weaned
    (E) adjusts to the anger-anxiety conflict

143. Existing research would suggest which of the following as an approach to problems of prejudice?

    (A) simply bringing the groups together
    (B) engaging the groups in competitive activities
    (C) developing a superordinate goal
    (D) initiating a letter-writing program between groups
    (E) individual psychotherapy

144. Selecting colors for a sign that must show up prominently at dusk, one might be best advised to choose

    (A) red   (B) yellow   (C) orange
    (D) violet   (E) pink

145. One of the major reasons that circadian rhythm has become a focus of attention in studying pilots is its relationship to

    (A) sleeplessness   (B) anemia   (C) apraxia
    (D) fatigue   (E) strokes

146. A desire to guide and contribute to the development of a generation younger than oneself would *not* be characteristic of

    (A) generativity   (B) genital stage   (C) self-actualization
    (D) narcissism   (E) social interest

147. The socially "good" or "proper" within Freudian theory is conceptually defined as the

    (A) id   (B) ego   (C) superego
    (D) archetype   (E) preconscious

148. A primary problem encountered in treating drug addicts, alcoholics, and sociopaths is

    (A) their contentedness with their present life-style
    (B) their lack of effective verbal communication skills
    (C) their related sexual problems
    (D) their consistently low IQ levels
    (E) resistance from families and close relatives

149. Within DSM-IV, Huntington's disease would be categorized as which type of disorder?

    (A) schizophrenic   (B) dissociative   (C) affective
    (D) delirium/dementia   (E) factitious

150. The learned helplessness theory of depression has been the work of

    (A) Rotter   (B) Seligman   (C) Maslow
    (D) Bandura   (E) Watson

151. Freud first became familiar with the concept of "talking cure" through an association with

    (A) Charcot   (B) Breuer   (C) Bennett
    (D) Selye   (E) Rank

152. The person smokes a cigarette and, because of earlier drug administration, becomes nauseous in a technique known as

    (A) chaining   (B) therapeutic community   (C) extinction
    (D) aversive conditioning   (E) reciprocal inhibition

153. Which of the following would most accurately describe the delusional situation in which a person believes others are talking about her?

    (A) delusions of sin and guilt
    (B) hypochondriacal delusions
    (C) delusions of grandeur
    (D) nihilistic delusions
    (E) delusions of reference

154. Eysenck's personality framework contains which of the following among its main dimensions?

    (A) parapraxic-syntaxic
    (B) depressive-obsessional
    (C) introversion-extraversion
    (D) hysteric-psychopathic
    (E) adaptive-maladaptive

155. The soldier who in the heat of battle curls up in a fetal position and cries is demonstrating
    (A) phobia   (B) regression   (C) projection
    (D) psychosomatic disorder   (E) hypochondriasis

156. Elevators seem to "close in" and small rooms create feelings of fear that seem unbearable in

    (A) anxiety reaction   (B) claustrophobia   (C) acrophobia
    (D) ochlophobia   (E) obsessive-compulsion

157. Fundamental to all sensitivity and encounter groups is

    (A) open interactions
    (B) nudity
    (C) the breakdown of defenses through the use of fatigue
    (D) an attempt by each member to "shock" the group
    (E) the arrangement of chairs in a semicircle and the presence of two trained therapists

158. Which of the following statements is incorrect?

(A) Wolpe's method has been used with homosexual patients.
(B) Behavior and reinforcement therapists include Skinner and Lindsley.
(C) Behavior therapy has been attacked on grounds that it threatens man's freedom.
(D) ESB is in common usage as a therapeutic technique.
(E) Frankl's logotherapy seeks to remove the existential vacuum experienced by the patient.

159. A man went on a fishing trip and did not return home. Much later, he was discovered in another part of the country with a new marriage, family, and job and no recollection of his previous family or identity. His emotional disturbance would be classified as

(A) dissociative amnesia
(B) dissociative fugue
(C) dissociative identity
(D) conversion reaction
(E) affective reaction

160. A respectable president of a corporation greets people who come by his office by shaking hands with only his little finger; then he excuses himself long enough to wash the finger thoroughly in his adjacent lavatory. His behavioral symptoms indicate

(A) schizophrenia   (B) psychosis   (C) mysophobia
(D) pyromania   (E) mood disorder

161. A person thinks that she sees a snake moving stealthily through the weeds on a distant hillside. As she gets closer, she discovers that it was only a dark piece of rope. This is a perceptual phenomenon known as

(A) telekinesis   (B) illusion   (C) delusion
(D) hallucination   (E) motion parallax

162. Statistics on psychopathology indicate that since 1900

(A) childhood schizophrenia incidence has increased
(B) autism has increased
(C) mental disorders stemming from alcoholism have decreased
(D) psychosis incidence in people under forty has not increased
(E) mental disorders as a function of age have decreased

163. A person is completely unresponsive, stares blankly into space, and never moves. She shows symptoms related to

(A) paranoia
(B) schizoaffective
(C) catatonic schizophrenia
(D) residual-type schizophrenia
(E) narcissistic personality disorder

164. In Bandura's behavioral psychotherapy, a withdrawn child in a kindergarten room would be reinforced for

(A) remaining alone
(B) joining the group
(C) drawing a picture
(D) writing his name
(E) playing with blocks

165. A team approach to therapy in which the entire life situation and the activities of the patient are brought into the therapeutic plan is known as

(A) milieu therapy
(B) sociotherapy
(C) nondirective therapy
(D) nonanalytical therapy
(E) Gestalt therapy

166. "Sour grapes" is an example of the defense mechanism called

(A) reaction formation
(B) compensation
(C) compartmentalization
(D) rationalization
(E) projection

167. A child had a very traumatic water-related experience of almost drowning. Now the child's best friends are standing in the water and are calling to the child to join them. This approach to the child's fear problem would be an example of

(A) learning reversal
(B) counterconditioning
(C) implosion
(D) incidental learning
(E) conditioned aversion

168. In which of the following would spontaneous recovery be most likely?

(A) paranoid state
(B) narcissistic personality disorder
(C) sexual deviation
(D) stuttering
(E) antisocial personality disorder

169. Abreaction would be most common as a result of

(A) psychosurgery
(B) Metrazole shock therapy
(C) electroconvulsive shock therapy
(D) LSD therapy
(E) psychotherapy

170. Each of the scores in a distribution has been multiplied by 7. The standard deviation is

   (A) increased by 7
   (B) increased to 7 times its original value
   (C) increased by its original value divided by 7
   (D) increased by 14
   (E) unchanged from its original value

171. An inanimate object would be central to which of the following sexual deviations?

   (A) voyeurism   (B) masochism   (C) fetishism
   (D) pedophilia   (E) sadism

172. *Not* part of a symptom nucleus for anxiety disorders is

   (A) inadequacy   (B) fearfulness   (C) tension
   (D) egocentricity   (E) high stress tolerance

173. Which of the following would seem unrelated to the "anniversary reaction"?

   (A) specific age attainment by the patient
   (B) awareness of the age of a family member when tragedy befell him
   (C) specific day of the week
   (D) wholesome potential to act as "releaser"
   (E) divorce and remarriage

174. For best research control of genetic factors, which of the following should be used in experimentation?

   (A) newborns   (B) siblings   (C) identical twins
   (D) factor analysis   (E) longitudinal approach

175. One type of test reliability is

   (A) the degree to which the test measures what it is intended to measure
   (B) the degree to which repeated measurements give the same score result
   (C) the degree to which the test measures content
   (D) the degree to which it is predictive
   (E) the degree of thoroughness

176. For simple testing of differences between the means of an experimental and a control group, a researcher would be likely to use

   (A) chi-square   (B) *t*-test   (C) correlation
   (D) regression   (E) *F*-test

177. That its findings cannot be checked by other researchers is a criticism frequently leveled at proponents of

   (A) behaviorism   (B) eclecticism   (C) functionalism
   (D) introspectionism   (E) neobehaviorism

178. A political gathering precedes election night by two months. Given a choice of speaking positions on the program, a political candidate would be wise to choose to be

(A) the first speaker
(B) the middle speaker
(C) the last speaker
(D) either the first or the last speaker
(E) in any of the three speaking positions

179. Given a grouping of data that is heterogeneous, you can expect a standard deviation to be

(A) small   (B) large   (C) small if sample size is small
(D) large only if sample size is large   (E) below .9

180. A disreputable jeweler would have the best chance of selling an inferior diamond in which of the following display settings?

(A) positioned on red velvet under red light
(B) positioned on blue velvet under blue light
(C) positioned on blue velvet under red light
(D) positioned on red velvet under blue light
(E) positioned on yellow velvet under blue light

181. Persons on stage will be noticed if the light beamed upon their blue outfits is

(A) red   (B) orange   (C) yellow
(D) violet   (E) pink

182. In a "stop smoking" campaign, which of the following persons would be most likely to quit successfully?

(A) a person who has read statistics on cancer research
(B) a person who knows the mg tar content of her cigarette
(C) a person who hears an expert deliver a talk on the subject
(D) a person who hears one of her friends deliver a talk on the subject
(E) a person who personally delivers a talk on the subject

183. Psychodrama is a form of which of the following managerial training techniques?

(A) incident   (B) case   (C) sensitivity
(D) role playing   (E) free association

184. Which of the following is *not* a characteristic of teaching-machine instruction?

(A) small, graduated steps
(B) knowledge of results
(C) multiple-choice format
(D) essay, reconstruction-type format
(E) immediate feedback

185. In screening applicants whose employment would involve winding small electronic coils, which of the following would be most useful?

    (A) intelligence tests
    (B) pursuit rotor
    (C) personality tests
    (D) finger dexterity tests
    (E) electrical knowledge tests

186. In which of the following settings would a victim be most likely to receive help?

    (A) several men watching the mishap
    (B) several women watching the mishap
    (C) several members of a mixed group watching the mishap
    (D) three people watching the mishap
    (E) one person watching the mishap

Questions 187–189 are based on the following choices.

Given a normal distribution with a mean of 68 and a standard deviation of 10, use the following set of choices to answer questions 187–189.
    (1) .68
    (2) .84
    (3) .16
    (4) .32
    (5) none of the above

187. What is the probability of a score above 78?

    (A) 1   (B) 2   (C) 3   (D) 4   (E) 5

188. What is the probability of a score below 48?

    (A) 1   (B) 2   (C) 3   (D) 4   (E) 5

189. What is the probability of a score either below 58 or above 78?

    (A) 1   (B) 2   (C) 3   (D) 4   (E) 5

190. A personnel selection test that requires previous knowledge and mastery of a given body of material is, in effect,

    (A) an aptitude test
    (B) an achievement test
    (C) an intelligence test
    (D) a test for creativity
    (E) a test for sociability

191. The fact that repeated administrations of a particular test result in consistent scores is evidence of

    (A) validity   (B) reliability   (C) split-half correlation
    (D) objectivity   (E) reliability and consistency

192. An experimenter investigates test anxiety in military academy cadets by utilizing galvanic skin response measurement. The GSR represents

    (A) dependent variable and operational definition of anxiety
    (B) independent variable and operational definition of anxiety
    (C) intervening variable and operational definition of anxiety
    (D) only operational definition of anxiety
    (E) only dependent variable

193. Terman's study of gifted children would be considered

    (A) latitudinal
    (B) longitudinal
    (C) laboratory method
    (D) representational method
    (E) nomothetic

194. Which of the following scales could be developed and implemented with the least amount of standardization?

    (A) Thurstone type
    (B) Remmers type
    (C) Likert type
    (D) Stanford-Binet type
    (E) Osgood type

195. In a specific hearing test for children, *separate* tones are presented in a range of frequencies and intensities. The child is given general instructions to press a button whenever she hears a tone. This test is an application of the

    (A) method of limits
    (B) difference limen
    (C) paired-comparisons method
    (D) differential-threshold method
    (E) Fechner method

196. Among human engineering principles relating to human-machine systems, a familiar control principle states that the best system provides

    (A) only one action pathway to achieve a given effect
    (B) at least six action pathways to achieve a given effect
    (C) at least two action pathways to achieve a given effect
    (D) a maximum of three action pathways to achieve a given effect
    (E) a maximum of four action pathways to achieve a given effect

197. The function of "white noise" is to

    (A) intensify the decibel level of existing noise
    (B) reduce the decibel level of existing noise
    (C) blot out or "overshadow" existing noise
    (D) accomplish synesthesia
    (E) rehabilitate in cases of temporary hearing loss

198. In comparison with centralized networks, which of the following constitutes a distinct advantage of the decentralized communication network?

(A) increased worker productivity
(B) quickly formed interaction stability
(C) more rigid structure
(D) increased worker satisfaction
(E) fewer messages required for making a given decision

199. To convert a standard deviation into a variance, one must

(A) take the square root of the standard deviation
(B) divide the standard deviation by N
(C) multiply the standard deviation by $1/z$
(D) multiply the standard deviation by N
(E) square the standard deviation

200. Researchers in kinesics believe that

(A) the territorial space concept is a myth
(B) findings will have relevance to parent-child communication and understanding
(C) the future of the field will be primarily within proxemics
(D) Hall's work is the field's pinnacle achievement
(E) interpersonal communication is primarily verbal

Test 1: Answer Comments

1. (B) Specific energy of nerves refers to a receptor's capability to give only one quality of experience (e.g., visual or auditory), regardless of how it was stimulated.

2. (C) Alpha waves are most prevalent when a person is in a relaxed, wakeful state with his or her eyes closed.

3. (E) Referred to as Occam's razor or "Morgan's canon," the quotation states a basic interpretive principle in comparative psychology.

4. (B) Barbiturates are depressants, not stimulants. Remember that many of the stimulants carry "ine" word-endings (e.g., caffeine, cocaine, nicotine, amphetamine, and so on).

5. (C) The question deals with a basic difference in study methods among comparative psychologists. Lorenz, Tinbergen, and Romanes are part of a European naturalistic observation tradition; Morgan used the problematic anecdotal method; Lashley has been a major contributor within the American experimental laboratory approach.

6. (E) The individual receiving normal sight after several years of blindness must relearn the auditory and tactile associations necessary to accommodate the visual frame of reference.

7. (B) The kinesthetic sensory system enables us to monitor the movements of our feet and know their position in relation to the ground.

8. (C) Werner-Wapner developed the perceptual theory known as "Sensory-Tonic." It states, in effect, that any percept is determined by the interaction between sensory (afferent) and proprioceptive (tonic) activity.

9. (E) The corpus callosum is not part of the brainstem. It is the thick band of fibers connecting the two cerebral hemispheres, enabling them to "communicate" with each other and with other parts of the nervous system.

10. (C) Kohler found no adaptation to the color-stereo effect when wearing "squint glasses." Squint glasses are prism-type filters worn over the eyes.

11. (B) Reflexes occur primarily in the spinal cord. The fact that the cerebral cortex is not involved accounts for the instantaneous nature of the reflexive response.

12. (D) Currently an area of prominent attention in social psychology, attribution theory involves the processes through which a person interprets the motivations underlying another person's behavior and, in effect, attributes causality. The work of Nisbett, Kelley, Heider, and Gergen is central to this area; that of Festinger is not.

13. (D) ACTH—adrenocorticotropic hormone, secreted by the pituitary —signals the adrenal gland to secrete corticosterone. This hormonal sequence produces the physiological changes found in the stress response.

14. (A) The process of maintaining constancy of the normal internal environment of an organism is called homeostasis.

15. (B) As stimulus patterns become increasingly similar, reaction times become longer because stimulus discrimination is more difficult.

16. (C) Freud's perspective places primary emphasis upon the presence of unresolved personal conflicts brought by the individual to the crowd situation.

17. (E) Hall's concept of personal space is, in effect, a concept of territoriality (i.e., of protecting one's personal "turf").

18. (B) The primaries in additive (light) color mixing are blue, green, and red. Primaries in subtractive (pigment) color mixing are blue, yellow, and red.

19. (D) To perceive the distance of a sound, a person must rely heavily upon loudness and timbre (sound wave complexity).

20. (C) Endorphins and enkephalins are the body's own "pain killers." It is the rush of endorphins that seems central to the pain-relieving effects of acupuncture and the "runner's high" of the marathon runner.

21. (B) Sensory deprivation researchers found the unexpected occurrence of hallucinations, as though the subjects were compensating visually for their lack of stimulation.

22. (C) Although it sounds similar to ESP terms, psychosynesis is a "clunker" (meaningless distractor).

23. (C) In the Sarason-type study, experimenter-conveyed expectation of task completion prompts better subject performance.

24. (E) Although the terms *habit strength*, *reaction potential*, *drive*, and *stimulus* are integral to Hull, the term *interaction potential* is not.

25. (C) Auditory receptor cells are located in the cochlea, the point at which transformation to neural impulse occurs.

26. (C) Tolman called his learning theory views *purposive behaviorism*.

27. (E) Cannon and Washburn's procedure was designed to study gastric contractions as the potentially critical factor in the experience of hunger.

28. (C) James was one of the prime movers in motivation research, followed by McDougall and, more recently, Atkinson.

29. (C) Berlyne developed the theory of optimal-arousal. The other choices within this question are paired with theories as follows: Zuckerman (sensation-seeking), Solomon (opponent-process), Murray (need-press), White (intrinsic motivation).

30. (B) Sleepwalking and talking occur in stage IV sleep, but dreaming occurs during REM stage I.

31. (D) Research suggests a relationship between acetylcholine deficiency and Alzheimer's disease. Abundantly present in the brain, it has a major role in learning and memory.

32. (C) Heart-rate inhibition lies within the responsibilities of the parasympathetic nervous system.

33. (D) Some of the best, most common examples of effectors are skeletal muscles.

34. (C) Lindsley's activation theory of emotion is based upon the function of the reticular formation in organismic arousal.

35. (A) In Atkinson's view, motivation deals with immediate influences on direction, vigor, and persistence of action.

36. (D) Dreaming appears essential to the human organism, and dream overcompensation will occur in sleep that follows that in which dreaming has been interrupted and virtually prohibited.

37. (C) The ventricular system supplies the brain and spinal cord with cerebrospinal fluid.

38. (D) Denenberg found that early handling had the long-range effect of making animals less fearful and more active in adulthood.

39. (E) The alarm-type reaction is demonstrated in the exhaustion stage of Selye's general adaptation syndrome.

40. (C) High levels of thyroxine output from the thyroid gland would be associated with hyperactivity.

41. (E) The pituitary gland secretes hormones related to body growth and maintenance. The fact that a person is nine feet tall (and thus in the circus) can be attributable to pituitary gland malfunction.

42. (C) The central nervous system contains the brain and the spinal cord.

43. (B) An intoxication-type behavior in which a person loses control of his emotions is characteristic of oxygen starvation. This result has been produced in experimental settings in which a person inhaled carbon dioxide.

44. (A) That a person's unique qualities constitute the essence of his personality is a point frequently made in defense of the idiographic approach.

45. (E) Freud's psychoanalytic approach is nomothetic and Adler's individual psychology approach is distinctly idiographic.

46. (D) Whereas individual psychology, client-centered therapy, personal construct, and Gestalt therapy focus upon individual uniqueness (idiographic), systematic desensitization is a general approach often used in cases of phobia.

47. (A) The Bunson-Roscoe Law holds for photochemical receptors. It is sometimes called the reciprocity or photographic law, and expresses a reciprocal relationship within vision between intensity and time.

48. (B) REM (rapid eye movement) stage I sleep signals dreaming.

49. (B) The Likert scaling technique is known as the method of summated ratings, expressing a relationship between a person's high score on individual response items and an overall high score on the scale.

50. (E) In a ring-toss game, McClelland found persons high in achievement need and low in test anxiety were taking intermediate-level risks.

51. (C) Utilizing the diagram, the afterimage of red would be the color directly across from it in the color wheel—green.

52. (A) According to this diagram, violet and orange combined would produce green—the color that occurs between them in the sketch.

53. (D) In this case, the complementary of green would be red—the color directly across from it.

54. (E) The rhinencephalon is an area in the brain stem that contains primitive cortex and subcortical structures relating to olfaction and emotion. It is the oldest portion of the cerebral hemispheres.

55. (B) Located adjacent to the occipital lobe and the brain stem, the cerebellum coordinates movements necessary for maintenance of balance and posture.

56. (C) This heavy bundle of fibers—*the corpus callosum*—connects the two hemispheres of the brain.

57. (C) At a certain point the oval is so close to the circle in shape that it no longer has a distinctive cue quality as a stimulus. It then has become a nondiscriminative stimulus—lacking the distinctiveness that formerly had given it response strength.

58. (C) The three stages, sequentially, are cervix dilation, actual newborn emergence, and afterbirth. The third stage involves delivery of the placenta with its accompanying amniotic and chorionic membranes.

59. (B) Heterozygous indicates the presence of genetic potential for either brown-eyed or blue-eyed children. Because brown eyes are a dominant characteristic, only one among the four possible combinations would result in blue eyes.

60. (A) Positive correlations have been found between the amount of maternal stress during pregnancy and the extent of fetal activity.

61. (D) Global amnesia results in an impairment on explicit memory tests of recent events in long-term memory.

62. (C) Rooting response, in effect a search for the nipple, is prompted by tactile stimulation of a newborn's cheek.

63. (A) The observations of Siamese twins yielded early indicators that brain rhythms had a central function in sleep. Subsequent research began moving away from the chemical theory of sleep toward a search for brain mechanisms.

64. (A) Avoidance is steeper, meaning that it will take on prominence and power as a person approaches the goal.

65. (C) The Zeigarnik effect suggests better retention of uncompleted tasks than of completed ones.

66. (C) One of the theory aspects most prominently identified with Guthrie has been the word *contiguity* (closeness) in reference to stimulus response.

67. (C) Newly learned responses are much more vulnerable to stress than their well-established predecessors.

68. (A) Physiological readiness for defecation control occurs in the young child before similar readiness for urination control. The latter must await sphincter-muscle development.

69. (C) In anterograde amnesia, a patient is unable to learn new information or remember events occurring after the onset of the disorder.

70. (D) Goldblatt is describing the combination of capability and prohibition that besets the early adolescent period of development.

71. (C) Set-point theory would suggest that sensitivity to food stimuli is a result of obesity rather than a cause of it. In effect, the body's food-sensitivity set point has been established at the current level of intake. Recent research suggests that sensitivity to food stimuli remains essentially constant with weight gain or weight loss—thereby challenging the basic premise of the set-point theory.

72. (A) The potential relationship between speed of habituation in the infant and intelligence is currently prominent in child psychology research. Initial findings have been encouraging.

73. (C) Massive motor movements (e.g., movements of whole arms or large portions of the body) precede more specific motor movements (e.g., those of wrists or fingers).

74. (C) The newborn has a natural immunity that wears off during its first six months.

75. (B) Gibson's theory of motion is based on the moving object's constantly covering and uncovering different aspects of the stationary background. The theory explains well the perception of motion in well-lighted settings but not motion perceived in darkness.

76. (D) The motor primacy principle refers to maturation as preceding response capability.

77. (C) Deductive reasoning combines separate elements of existing knowledge to reach a conclusion. Such reasoning is in contrast to the inductive approach, which takes the "known" as starting point and makes an intuitive leap toward the unknown via hypotheses.

78. (B) The terms *innate* and *maturation* both refer to hereditary elements in behavior.

79. (D) Such basic learning capability is evident in both the newborn and the late fetal stages of development.

80. (B) This male-female growth differential is especially evident during early adolescence—when many girls are embarrassed because they are taller than their male counterparts.

81. (E) Large injections of androgen (a male sex hormone) have been known to produce abnormal, exaggerated male sex characteristics in the female newborn.

82. (D) Although the rooming-in procedure gives the mother closeness to the newborn and prompt responsiveness to infant needs, the potential price is that of constant demands upon the new mother.

83. (D) Reminiscence constitutes performance improvement without intervening practice on the task.

84. (B) George Sperling used the "partial-report procedure" to demonstrate that a large amount of visual information can be stored for only a fraction of a second in a sensory register.

85. (D) The letters refer to phenylketonuria, a defect in the enzyme that metabolizes phenylalanine. Uncorrected by dietetic measures, the disorder can cause brain damage and mental deficiency.

86. (A) Information can be encoded in short-term memory in several ways. Rehearsing it aloud is an acoustical code. Trying to form a mental picture is a visual code. Giving the information meaning by relating it to something else would be a semantic code.

87. (B) Doing your homework before heading out for snack or play is a familiar example of the Premack principle. The snack or play—being higher in the reinforcement hierarchy— reinforces the activity of homework (which is lower in the reinforcement hierarchy).

88. (D) The encoding (labeling) process is essential to human language and thought.

89. (B) Assimilation is a Piagetian term describing the cognitive process of relating a perceived stimulus to the conceptual information that a child already has.

90. (D) A regular, fixed time schedule is the critical factor in temporal conditioning.

91. (D) Warmth and permissiveness are positively correlated with outgoing, socially assertive characteristics in children, whereas similar correlation is not found for distant, restrictive, demanding, authoritarian family settings.

92. (A) Lorenz's work centers on the biological bases for behavior and spans a range from imprinting to the innate aspects of aggression.

93. (D) Punishment, in combination with a presented behavioral alternative and an associated reward, enhances effectiveness.

94. (B) Brain mapping and localization of functioning has been one research area supporting this separation of processes.

95. (A) The earliest group is the mother-child dyad.

96. (B) The capacity for distinguishing letters on the basis of closedness is characteristic of the three-year-old. More sophisticated distinctions such as curvature will occur later.

97. (B) The null hypothesis is, in effect, the "no difference" hypothesis that a researcher hopes to be unable to accept on the basis of his research findings.

98. (C) The work of Hoffman and others indicates that love withdrawal as a discipline technique can produce overdependence upon adult approval. Explaining how the behavior is harmful and undesirable (a reasoning method) has been found to be more effective.

99. (B) The number of scores in a distribution, the measure of central tendency, and the measure of variability are three measures generally called descriptive statistics. On the basis of one's description of the sample, the investigator can make inferences about the probable characteristics of the specific population that could not be measured in its entirety (inferential statistics).

100. (D) Rosch used category classification reaction times to demonstrate that an object will be classified as a member of a category on the basis of similarity to the prototype (i.e., most representative example) of the category.

101. (D) Frequent temper tantrums among children constitute an emotional health signal to be heeded.

102. (C) Middle-class, well-educated mothers are the group most prominently utilizing the breast-feeding method in child rearing. This practice reflects their prominent concern for cognitive-emotional-social development in young children.

103. (E) Thurstone's elements included verbal comprehension, numerical ability, perceptual speed, space visualization, reasoning, word fluency, and memory.

104. (E) Moron referred to the IQ range between 50 and 70, now covered by the "mildly retarded" classification.

105. (E) A score indicating highest possible, i.e., perfect, correlation would be 1.00. Any figure higher than 1 is erroneous.

106. (A) Such time-concept mastery would be characteristic of the six-year-old.

107. (B) Extrapolation, by definition, involves making inferences on the basis of existing data or facts.

108. (A) Dual-process theory refers to the relationship between short-term and long-term memory. It assumes that information initially enters short-term memory, which has limited capacity. To be encoded in long-term memory would require transfer from short-term memory. This transfer would entail the information learning and retention techniques (e.g., chunking, rehearsal, associating, and PQ4R).

109. (C) Sir Frederic Bartlett demonstrated that we distort memories to make them more consistent with our schemas, or expectations.

110. (B) Hebb found such a digit-span memory trace to be demonstrably evident.

111. (C) This student has ample time to plan study patterns for the test, and given this ample time the best approach would be to distribute study time throughout the several-week period. If the student planned to allot only a few hours to study, the only choice would be to mass it just before the test ("cramming") and to expect the inevitable worst.

112. (B) Kohlberg is a prominent researcher in the area of moral development within children and has been very strongly impressed by the importance of reward and punishment in moral determinations.

113. (D) Telegraphic speech refers to the child's early grammatical constructions. These spontaneous speech patterns are observed when the child is about two years of age and frequently are attempts to imitate parental speech. Such attempts are characterized by the omission of prepositions, articles, suffixes, and so on. Representative of telegraphic speech would be a sentence such as "Go mommy store."

114. (D) Both stomach and mouth activities appear to have important roles in the digestive processes relating to food.

115. (B) The kibbutzim—collective farm—concept in childrearing is an Israel-based, state-supported approach that involves professional caretakers providing twenty-four-hour-per-day child care in a communal setting outside the home of the natural parents. Parental visits occur primarily in the evenings and on weekends. The child development atmosphere is characterized as warm and permissive. Recent studies indicate that these children are equal in physical, social, and intellectual development to their Israeli counterparts who have been raised in private homes.

116. (C) At point 3 there began a steady decline in number of correct responses per trial, indicating that reinforcement had been withdrawn and that the extinction process was underway.

117. (C) A temporary leveling in the response acquisition curve is known as a plateau. Such leveling is followed by an increase in the number of correct responses per trial.

118. (D) Initiated theoretically within psychoanalysis, defense mechanisms have the function of reducing the anxiety caused by fear that an id impulse may emerge.

119. (C) The Kelley experiment demonstrated the tremendous change in attitude that can be produced by the variation of a single word in a description. A subsequent speaker gave to various individuals descriptions that contained within them either the word warm or the word cold. Evaluation of the speaker varied accordingly.

120. (C) The social exchange theory of interpersonal attraction speaks of continually changing balances between reward and cost in any given interaction.

121. (C) The well-known Clark procedure utilized comparative presentation of black dolls and white ones to study prejudice in children.

122. (B) Darley and Latane found that the major determinant in eliciting help was the number of other students that the individual thought had heard the victim.

123. (A) Proxemics is the study of personal, territorial space. In the American culture, it is believed that each person has a kind of "invisible shield" approximately eighteen inches from his or her body. Anyone who comes closer than this and who is not an intimate friend is violating the person's territorial, personal space.

124. (E) Kelly views every child as a scientist forming constructs and testing hypotheses.

125. (D) Cattell and Eysenck are prominently concerned with factor analysis—e.g., correlation and grouping of traits.

126. (B) The therapeutic technique known as free association was initiated by Freud and remained central to his work throughout his career.

127. (E) The transactional analysis of Berne makes prominent use of the terms *script* and *contract*.

128. (C) Behaviorism focuses upon observable behavior and the means through which a person's environment can be restructured to effect a change in problem behavior.

129. (B) The triad is in a state of asymmetry or imbalance. Symmetry would be achieved if the triad contained an even number of negative (dislike) components. Such would be the case if person A liked person B, person A disliked X, and person B disliked X. Obviously, symmetry would also be attained if the triad contained no negative components—person A liking person B, person A liking X, and person B liking X.

130. (D) Adler believed that the major personality energizer was not a sexual drive (psychoanalytic view) but a superiority striving.

131. (D) By designing a Likert-type scale in which all the "Strongly Agree" items are strongly favorable responses toward the topic, the researcher has made the fatal error of being unable to detect the respondent who, for instance, check-marked all the "Strongly Agree" items without even bothering to read the statements. In design of the scale, half the "Strongly Agree" items should have been strongly negative responses on the topic—giving the scale "left-right" balance.

132. (B) The F-A hypothesis in Berkowitz's usage refers to the frustration-aggression hypothesis: that frustration will be followed by aggressive behavior.

133. (C) In Allport-Vernon-Lindzey scaling, a person rating high in theoretical value would espouse a search for truth and order.

134. (A) The top three stress indicators on the Life Change Scale are death of spouse, divorce, and marital separation. The scale is also known as the Holmes and Rahe Social Readjustment Rating Scale.

135. (A) The enzyme affects neural transmission and is believed to have a prominent role in emotional behavior. Zuckerman has found low levels of MAO (monoamine oxidase) in persons scoring high in sensation-seeking scale (as compared with high levels of MAO among persons scoring low). This research link is tentative but suggests the complex physiological/biochemical processes that may function in personality determination.

136. (B) Kagan's research challenges the long-held premise of a critical period in cognitive-intellectual development. His study is cross-cultural, dealing with children who would be deprived of their usual habitat at the critical age for cognitive-intellectual development.

137. (A) Status determination on the basis of individual income, education, and occupation would be characteristic of the objective method—determining fixed criteria and placing people within them.

138. (B) Expectancy-value theory is intrinsic to the social psychology principle of behavior exchange—in effect, a marketplace model. In this formula a person takes the value of a physically attractive partner and multiplies it by their expectancy of obtaining such a partner. This means we tend not to "overshoot" and risk rejection but end up with a partner similar to ourselves in attractiveness.

139. (D) The Minnesota Multiphasic Personality Inventory utilizes a very rigorous statistical procedure for analysis.

140. (B) Although some of their explanatory views vary, most personality theorists see early childhood as critically important to later personality development.

141. (B) Aronson, Mills, and others in the field of cognitive dissonance have found the amount of initiation to be positively correlated with an individual's degree of attraction to a group. Because your fraternity or sorority initiation was rigorous, for example, the group may be more attractive to you than a fraternity or sorority would be to someone who did not have such a rigorous initiation.

142. (B) The Oedipus complex—sexual attraction to the opposite-sex parent—is resolved when the child identifies with the same-sex parent.

143. (C) Notably, the "Robber's Cave" research of Sherif would underscore the development of superordinate goals as a positive approach to prejudice-related problems.

144. (D) The color corresponding to shortest wavelength would show up most prominently. In this grouping, violet holds that comparative position.

145. (D) Circadian rhythm—a cyclic body rhythm—has been studied in commercial pilots because of its relationship to "jet lag" (crossing time zones) and fatigue.

146. (D) Narcissism is complete devotion to self-pleasure. One of the behaviors exemplifying narcissism would be masturbation.

147. (C) Within Freud's psychoanalytic theory, moral regulations and restrictions are the province of the superego, which functions in the context of (1) ego ideal or a perfection striving, and (2) conscience or psychological punishment and guilt.

148. (A) Contentedness with present life style and insufficient desire to change are major problems in the treatment of drug addicts, alcoholics, and sociopaths.

149. (D) Within DSM-IV, Huntington's disease is categorized as delirium/dementia. It is a degenerative disease of the nervous system.

150. (B) Seligman developed learned helplessness theory, which states that an interpretation of events as being beyond one's control can lead to depression.

151. (B) Breuer introduced Freud to the concept of "talking cure"—a method that Breuer had tried successfully in hysteria cases. Freud later utilized the concept in his free-association method.

152.   (D)   This method is aversive conditioning, one of the last resorts therapeutically when other methods have proved ineffective and the problem behavior is a source of pleasure.

153.   (E)   One's delusional belief that other persons are talking about her is known as delusions of reference.

154.   (C)   Two of Eysenck's major classification categories for maladaptive behavior are introversion and extraversion. Among his other major dimensions are neuroticism-nonneuroticism and psychoticism-nonpsychoticism.

155.   (B)   The soldier curled up in a fetal position and crying is manifesting maladaptive regression behavior.

156.   (B)   The person who experiences fear and anxiety in small rooms or elevators would be expressing claustrophobia.

157.   (A)   Although nudity, fatigue, and so on, have specific encounter-group prominence, open interaction characterizes all sensitivity and encounter groups.

158.   (D)   ESB means electrical stimulation of the brain and has no relationship to electroconvulsive shock techniques occasionally used within clinical psychology.

159.   (B)   The combined elements of amnesia and geographical flight are indicative of the dissociative reaction known as fugue.

160.   (C)   This man has an obsessive fear of germs (mysophobia). Because of it he engages in compulsive—often embarrassing—hand-washing behavior.

161.   (B)   Misperception of an actual stimulus is a basic characteristic of illusions.

162.   (D)   Statistics indicate that the incidence of psychosis in people under forty has not increased since 1900.

163.   (C)   Lack of movement is indicative of catatonic schizophrenia. Muscular rigidity and motionlessness are characteristic of this disorder.

164.   (B)   In his behavioral psychotherapy settings, Bandura would reinforce a withdrawn child for joining the group.

165.   (A)   In milieu therapy, the family, close associates, and natural setting become parts of the therapeutic process.

166.   (D)   One of the classic rationalizations is the "sour grapes" phenomenon. As the story goes, the fox could not reach the grapes he wanted and rationalized that it was just as well because they were sour anyway.

167.   (B)   In counterconditioning the problem response (in this instance, avoidance of the water) is placed in direct competition with an adaptive response (e.g., close friends in the water beckoning to the person to join them). The problem will have been resolved when the adaptive response becomes the dominant one. Desensitization techniques use counterconditioning—relaxation (the adaptive response) placed in direct competition with tenseness and anxiety (the problem response).

168. (A) Of the disorders listed, spontaneous recovery would be most likely within the paranoid state. In each of the other instances, some form of therapy is virtually essential.

169. (E) Abreaction refers to the expressing of pent-up emotions. It is most likely to occur within psychotherapy.

170. (B) The standard deviation increases by the same multiple as each of the scores in the distribution—in this case, 7.

171. (C) Sexual stimulation attained from the sight or closeness of a given object or type of object is characteristic of fetishism.

172. (E) One of the characteristics of anxiety disorders is low stress tolerance.

173. (E) Although Pollock's "anniversary reaction" involves such elements as specific age attainment, specific day of the week, and awareness of the age at which tragedy befell a family member, it has no direct relationship to divorce or remarriage. The reaction holds that wholesome potential acts as a "releaser" and involves emotionally reliving a highly stressful event on its calendar anniversary date.

174. (C) Research control of genetic factors is most effectively achieved through the use of identical twins.

175. (B) Statistical reliability of a test refers to the extent to which repeated administrations will give the same score result. In addition, a test must also have validity—that is, it must measure that which it was constructed to measure (e.g., intelligence or mechanical aptitude).

176. (B) The t-test would be used for simple testing of differences between the means of experimental and control groups.

177. (D) One of the basic problems with the structuralist school of Wundt and Titchener was the fact that their method of introspection did not permit confirmation of results by other researchers—a basic criticism leveled by functionalists and, later, behaviorists.

178. (A) Two months before election night (a comparatively long time), a political candidate stands the best chance of being remembered if she is the first speaker on the program. If, on the other hand, it is the day before the election, being the last speaker is the wisest choice.

179. (B) With a heterogeneous data grouping, standard deviation would be large. Homogeneous data would suggest a small standard deviation.

180. (B) The blue light would bring out the blue pigment in the velvet, making the diamond look beautiful and irresistible. The other combinations of light-pigment mentioned would not have comparable effectiveness.

181. (D) Blue is "next door" to violet on the subtractive color wheel; thus, because hues rarely are pure, the violet light would accentuate the blue pigment.

182. (E) A person who delivers a talk on stopping smoking would be most likely to quit successfully. They are—through their personal involvement—more likely to believe the arguments and experience a consequent behavior change than a person who merely has heard the information passively.

183. (D) Psychodrama was popularized as a therapeutic technique by Moreno. It involves patients taking the roles of persons related to their conflict situation.

184. (D) Graduated steps, knowledge of results, immediate feedback, and multiple-choice format characterize teaching machine instruction, but sentence completion is not an aspect of such methodology.

185. (D) In this situation, a finger dexterity test would most closely approximate the actual task for which the individuals are being screened.

186. (E) Research indicates that the greater the number of persons watching a mishap, the lower the likelihood that any one of them will render help to a victim.

187. (C) Since it is one standard deviation above the mean, the probability of a score above 78 is approximately 16 percent.

188. (E) Below 48 would be a score lower than two standard deviations below the mean, an approximately 2 percent probability.

189. (D) This item refers to the area beyond one standard deviation to each side of the mean—approximately 32 percent.

190. (B) Previous knowledge and mastery of a body of material would characterize an achievement test.

191. (B) Consistent scores on repeated administrations would be evidence of test-retest reliability.

192. (A) GSR measure here is both the dependent variable (subject response) and the operational definition on which the presence and extent of anxiety will be determined.

193. (B) Terman's follow-up study of several gifted children at different points in their lives was one of the best-known longitudinal studies.

194. (E) The Osgood-type semantic differential scale could be implemented with the least amount of standardization. Its administration ease and flexibility are its primary assets.

195. (A) Many hearing tests involve a practical application of the psychophysical method of limits—presentation of fixed stimuli at frequencies both above and below threshold.

196. (A) In human engineering control principles, the best system provides for only one action pathway to achieve a given effect. With more than one pathway, the result could be inefficiency and confusion.

197. (C) "White noise" serves to blot out or "overshadow" existing noise.

198. (D) Increased worker satisfaction has been found within decentralized communication networks.

199. (E) Standard deviation can be expressed as the square root of the variance. Therefore, one can obtain a variance by squaring a standard deviation.

200. (B) Kinesics researchers believe that their study of nonverbal communication and body language will have critical importance in understanding and relating to children.

Test 1: Evaluating Your Score

Abbreviation Guide for Quick Reference (Translation)

PC:	Physiological/Comparative
SnP:	Sensation/Perception
LM:	Learning/Motivation/Emotion
CHL:	Cognition/Complex Human Learning
D:	Developmental
PrS:	Personality/Social
PyCl:	Psychopathology/Clinical
M:	Methodology
Ap:	Applied

TALLY CHART

- Checkmark to the left of each number you missed.
- In the column to the right of the number note the area your check-marked question is in.
- Move your check mark to the appropriate area column.
- Sum your check marks in each area column.
- Carry these sums to the blanks on the next scaling page.

Q#		PC	SnP	LM	CHL	D	PrS	PyCl	M	Ap
1	PC									
2	PC									
3	PC									
4	PC									
5	PC									
6	SnP									
7	SnP									
8	SnP									
9	PC									
10	SnP									
11	PC									
12	PrS									
13	LM									
14	PC									
15	SnP									
16	AP									
17	AP									
18	SnP									
19	SnP									
20	PC									
21	SnP									
22	SnP									
23	LM									
24	LM									
25	SnP									
26	LM									
27	PC									

Q#		PC	SnP	LM	CHL	D	PrS	PyCl	M	Ap
28	LM									
29	LM									
30	PC									
31	PC									
32	PC									
33	PC									
34	PC									
35	LM									
36	PC									
37	LM									
38	LM									
39	LM									
40	PC									
41	PC									
42	PC									
43	LM									
44	PrS									
45	PrS									
46	PrS									
47	SnP									
48	PC									
49	PrS									
50	LM									
51	SnP									
52	SnP									
53	SnP									
54	PC									
55	PC									
56	PC									
57	LM									
58	D									
59	D									
60	D									
61	CHL									
62	D									
63	D									
64	LM									
65	CHL									
66	LM									
67	CHL									
68	D									
69	CHL									
70	D									
71	LM									

Q#		PC	SnP	LM	CHL	D	PrS	PyCl	M	Ap
72	D									
73	D									
74	D									
75	SnP									
76	D									
77	M									
78	D									
79	D									
80	D									
81	D									
82	D									
83	CHL									
84	CHL									
85	D									
86	CHL									
87	LM									
88	CHL									
89	D									
90	LM									
91	D									
92	D									
93	LM									
94	CHL									
95	D									
96	D									
97	M									
98	D									
99	M									
100	CHL									
101	D									
102	D									
013	CHL									
104	CHL									
105	M									
106	D									
107	CHL									
108	CHL									
109	CHL									
110	CHL									
111	CHL									
112	D									
113	CHL									
114	LM									
115	D									

Q#		PC	SnP	LM	CHL	D	PrS	PyCl	M	Ap
116	LM									
117	LM									
118	PrS									
119	PrS									
120	PrS									
121	PrS									
122	PrS									
123	PrS									
124	PrS									
125	PrS									
126	PrS									
127	PrS									
128	PrS									
129	PrS									
130	PrS									
131	PrS									
132	PrS									
133	PrS									
134	PrS									
135	PrS									
136	Ap									
137	PrS									
138	PrS									
139	PrS									
140	Ap									
141	PrS									
142	PrS									
143	Ap									
144	Ap									
145	Ap									
146	PrS									
147	PrS									
148	PyCl									
149	PyCl									
150	PyCl									
151	PyCl									
152	PyCl									
153	PyCl									
154	PyCl									
155	PyCl									
156	PyCl									
157	PyCl									
158	PyCl									
159	PyCl									

Q#		PC	SnP	LM	CHL	D	PrS	PyCl	M	Ap
160	PyCl									
161	PyCl									
162	PyCl									
163	PyCl									
164	PyCl									
165	PyCl									
166	PyCl									
167	PyCl									
168	PyCl									
169	PyCl									
170	M									
171	PyCl									
172	PyCl									
173	PyCl									
174	M									
175	M									
176	M									
177	M									
178	Ap									
179	M									
180	Ap									
181	Ap									
182	Ap									
183	Ap									
184	Ap									
185	Ap									
186	Ap									
187	M									
188	M									
189	M									
190	Ap									
191	M									
192	M									
193	M									
194	Ap									
195	Ap									
196	Ap									
197	Ap									
198	Ap									
199	M									
200	Ap									
Sum										

Test Score Scaling

As you bring your tally sums forward from the previous page and tuck them into the blanks below, you'll spot any areas still needing attention. Are you improving? We're willing to bet on it!

PC Area: 23 – _____ (your number missed) = _____ // 18 = 75th percentile

SnP Area: 15 – _____ (your number missed) = _____ // 11 = 75th percentile

LM Area: 22 – _____ (your number missed) = _____ // 17 = 75th percentile

CHL Area: 18 – _____ (your number missed) = _____ // 14 = 75th percentile

D Area: 28 – _____ (your number missed) = _____ // 21 = 75th percentile

PrS Area: 30 – _____ (your number missed) = _____ // 23 = 75th percentile

PyCl Area: 25 – _____ (your number missed) = _____ // 19 = 75th percentile

M Area: 17 – _____ (your number missed) = _____ // 13 = 75th percentile

Ap Area: 22 – _____ (your number missed) = _____ // 17 = 75th percentile

Test 2: Answer Grid

1. Ⓐ Ⓑ Ⓒ Ⓓ Ⓔ	51. Ⓐ Ⓑ Ⓒ Ⓓ Ⓔ	101. Ⓐ Ⓑ Ⓒ Ⓓ Ⓔ	151. Ⓐ Ⓑ Ⓒ Ⓓ Ⓔ
2. Ⓐ Ⓑ Ⓒ Ⓓ Ⓔ	52. Ⓐ Ⓑ Ⓒ Ⓓ Ⓔ	102. Ⓐ Ⓑ Ⓒ Ⓓ Ⓔ	152. Ⓐ Ⓑ Ⓒ Ⓓ Ⓔ
3. Ⓐ Ⓑ Ⓒ Ⓓ Ⓔ	53. Ⓐ Ⓑ Ⓒ Ⓓ Ⓔ	103. Ⓐ Ⓑ Ⓒ Ⓓ Ⓔ	153. Ⓐ Ⓑ Ⓒ Ⓓ Ⓔ
4. Ⓐ Ⓑ Ⓒ Ⓓ Ⓔ	54. Ⓐ Ⓑ Ⓒ Ⓓ Ⓔ	104. Ⓐ Ⓑ Ⓒ Ⓓ Ⓔ	154. Ⓐ Ⓑ Ⓒ Ⓓ Ⓔ
5. Ⓐ Ⓑ Ⓒ Ⓓ Ⓔ	55. Ⓐ Ⓑ Ⓒ Ⓓ Ⓔ	105. Ⓐ Ⓑ Ⓒ Ⓓ Ⓔ	155. Ⓐ Ⓑ Ⓒ Ⓓ Ⓔ
6. Ⓐ Ⓑ Ⓒ Ⓓ Ⓔ	56. Ⓐ Ⓑ Ⓒ Ⓓ Ⓔ	106. Ⓐ Ⓑ Ⓒ Ⓓ Ⓔ	156. Ⓐ Ⓑ Ⓒ Ⓓ Ⓔ
7. Ⓐ Ⓑ Ⓒ Ⓓ Ⓔ	57. Ⓐ Ⓑ Ⓒ Ⓓ Ⓔ	107. Ⓐ Ⓑ Ⓒ Ⓓ Ⓔ	157. Ⓐ Ⓑ Ⓒ Ⓓ Ⓔ
8. Ⓐ Ⓑ Ⓒ Ⓓ Ⓔ	58. Ⓐ Ⓑ Ⓒ Ⓓ Ⓔ	108. Ⓐ Ⓑ Ⓒ Ⓓ Ⓔ	158. Ⓐ Ⓑ Ⓒ Ⓓ Ⓔ
9. Ⓐ Ⓑ Ⓒ Ⓓ Ⓔ	59. Ⓐ Ⓑ Ⓒ Ⓓ Ⓔ	109. Ⓐ Ⓑ Ⓒ Ⓓ Ⓔ	159. Ⓐ Ⓑ Ⓒ Ⓓ Ⓔ
10. Ⓐ Ⓑ Ⓒ Ⓓ Ⓔ	60. Ⓐ Ⓑ Ⓒ Ⓓ Ⓔ	110. Ⓐ Ⓑ Ⓒ Ⓓ Ⓔ	160. Ⓐ Ⓑ Ⓒ Ⓓ Ⓔ
11. Ⓐ Ⓑ Ⓒ Ⓓ Ⓔ	61. Ⓐ Ⓑ Ⓒ Ⓓ Ⓔ	111. Ⓐ Ⓑ Ⓒ Ⓓ Ⓔ	161. Ⓐ Ⓑ Ⓒ Ⓓ Ⓔ
12. Ⓐ Ⓑ Ⓒ Ⓓ Ⓔ	62. Ⓐ Ⓑ Ⓒ Ⓓ Ⓔ	112. Ⓐ Ⓑ Ⓒ Ⓓ Ⓔ	162. Ⓐ Ⓑ Ⓒ Ⓓ Ⓔ
13. Ⓐ Ⓑ Ⓒ Ⓓ Ⓔ	63. Ⓐ Ⓑ Ⓒ Ⓓ Ⓔ	113. Ⓐ Ⓑ Ⓒ Ⓓ Ⓔ	163. Ⓐ Ⓑ Ⓒ Ⓓ Ⓔ
14. Ⓐ Ⓑ Ⓒ Ⓓ Ⓔ	64. Ⓐ Ⓑ Ⓒ Ⓓ Ⓔ	114. Ⓐ Ⓑ Ⓒ Ⓓ Ⓔ	164. Ⓐ Ⓑ Ⓒ Ⓓ Ⓔ
15. Ⓐ Ⓑ Ⓒ Ⓓ Ⓔ	65. Ⓐ Ⓑ Ⓒ Ⓓ Ⓔ	115. Ⓐ Ⓑ Ⓒ Ⓓ Ⓔ	165. Ⓐ Ⓑ Ⓒ Ⓓ Ⓔ
16. Ⓐ Ⓑ Ⓒ Ⓓ Ⓔ	66. Ⓐ Ⓑ Ⓒ Ⓓ Ⓔ	116. Ⓐ Ⓑ Ⓒ Ⓓ Ⓔ	166. Ⓐ Ⓑ Ⓒ Ⓓ Ⓔ
17. Ⓐ Ⓑ Ⓒ Ⓓ Ⓔ	67. Ⓐ Ⓑ Ⓒ Ⓓ Ⓔ	117. Ⓐ Ⓑ Ⓒ Ⓓ Ⓔ	167. Ⓐ Ⓑ Ⓒ Ⓓ Ⓔ
18. Ⓐ Ⓑ Ⓒ Ⓓ Ⓔ	68. Ⓐ Ⓑ Ⓒ Ⓓ Ⓔ	118. Ⓐ Ⓑ Ⓒ Ⓓ Ⓔ	168. Ⓐ Ⓑ Ⓒ Ⓓ Ⓔ
19. Ⓐ Ⓑ Ⓒ Ⓓ Ⓔ	69. Ⓐ Ⓑ Ⓒ Ⓓ Ⓔ	119. Ⓐ Ⓑ Ⓒ Ⓓ Ⓔ	169. Ⓐ Ⓑ Ⓒ Ⓓ Ⓔ
20. Ⓐ Ⓑ Ⓒ Ⓓ Ⓔ	70. Ⓐ Ⓑ Ⓒ Ⓓ Ⓔ	120. Ⓐ Ⓑ Ⓒ Ⓓ Ⓔ	170. Ⓐ Ⓑ Ⓒ Ⓓ Ⓔ
21. Ⓐ Ⓑ Ⓒ Ⓓ Ⓔ	71. Ⓐ Ⓑ Ⓒ Ⓓ Ⓔ	121. Ⓐ Ⓑ Ⓒ Ⓓ Ⓔ	171. Ⓐ Ⓑ Ⓒ Ⓓ Ⓔ
22. Ⓐ Ⓑ Ⓒ Ⓓ Ⓔ	72. Ⓐ Ⓑ Ⓒ Ⓓ Ⓔ	122. Ⓐ Ⓑ Ⓒ Ⓓ Ⓔ	172. Ⓐ Ⓑ Ⓒ Ⓓ Ⓔ
23. Ⓐ Ⓑ Ⓒ Ⓓ Ⓔ	73. Ⓐ Ⓑ Ⓒ Ⓓ Ⓔ	123. Ⓐ Ⓑ Ⓒ Ⓓ Ⓔ	173. Ⓐ Ⓑ Ⓒ Ⓓ Ⓔ
24. Ⓐ Ⓑ Ⓒ Ⓓ Ⓔ	74. Ⓐ Ⓑ Ⓒ Ⓓ Ⓔ	124. Ⓐ Ⓑ Ⓒ Ⓓ Ⓔ	174. Ⓐ Ⓑ Ⓒ Ⓓ Ⓔ
25. Ⓐ Ⓑ Ⓒ Ⓓ Ⓔ	75. Ⓐ Ⓑ Ⓒ Ⓓ Ⓔ	125. Ⓐ Ⓑ Ⓒ Ⓓ Ⓔ	175. Ⓐ Ⓑ Ⓒ Ⓓ Ⓔ
26. Ⓐ Ⓑ Ⓒ Ⓓ Ⓔ	76. Ⓐ Ⓑ Ⓒ Ⓓ Ⓔ	126. Ⓐ Ⓑ Ⓒ Ⓓ Ⓔ	176. Ⓐ Ⓑ Ⓒ Ⓓ Ⓔ
27. Ⓐ Ⓑ Ⓒ Ⓓ Ⓔ	77. Ⓐ Ⓑ Ⓒ Ⓓ Ⓔ	127. Ⓐ Ⓑ Ⓒ Ⓓ Ⓔ	177. Ⓐ Ⓑ Ⓒ Ⓓ Ⓔ
28. Ⓐ Ⓑ Ⓒ Ⓓ Ⓔ	78. Ⓐ Ⓑ Ⓒ Ⓓ Ⓔ	128. Ⓐ Ⓑ Ⓒ Ⓓ Ⓔ	178. Ⓐ Ⓑ Ⓒ Ⓓ Ⓔ
29. Ⓐ Ⓑ Ⓒ Ⓓ Ⓔ	79. Ⓐ Ⓑ Ⓒ Ⓓ Ⓔ	129. Ⓐ Ⓑ Ⓒ Ⓓ Ⓔ	179. Ⓐ Ⓑ Ⓒ Ⓓ Ⓔ
30. Ⓐ Ⓑ Ⓒ Ⓓ Ⓔ	80. Ⓐ Ⓑ Ⓒ Ⓓ Ⓔ	130. Ⓐ Ⓑ Ⓒ Ⓓ Ⓔ	180. Ⓐ Ⓑ Ⓒ Ⓓ Ⓔ
31. Ⓐ Ⓑ Ⓒ Ⓓ Ⓔ	81. Ⓐ Ⓑ Ⓒ Ⓓ Ⓔ	131. Ⓐ Ⓑ Ⓒ Ⓓ Ⓔ	181. Ⓐ Ⓑ Ⓒ Ⓓ Ⓔ
32. Ⓐ Ⓑ Ⓒ Ⓓ Ⓔ	82. Ⓐ Ⓑ Ⓒ Ⓓ Ⓔ	132. Ⓐ Ⓑ Ⓒ Ⓓ Ⓔ	182. Ⓐ Ⓑ Ⓒ Ⓓ Ⓔ
33. Ⓐ Ⓑ Ⓒ Ⓓ Ⓔ	83. Ⓐ Ⓑ Ⓒ Ⓓ Ⓔ	133. Ⓐ Ⓑ Ⓒ Ⓓ Ⓔ	183. Ⓐ Ⓑ Ⓒ Ⓓ Ⓔ
34. Ⓐ Ⓑ Ⓒ Ⓓ Ⓔ	84. Ⓐ Ⓑ Ⓒ Ⓓ Ⓔ	134. Ⓐ Ⓑ Ⓒ Ⓓ Ⓔ	184. Ⓐ Ⓑ Ⓒ Ⓓ Ⓔ
35. Ⓐ Ⓑ Ⓒ Ⓓ Ⓔ	85. Ⓐ Ⓑ Ⓒ Ⓓ Ⓔ	135. Ⓐ Ⓑ Ⓒ Ⓓ Ⓔ	185. Ⓐ Ⓑ Ⓒ Ⓓ Ⓔ
36. Ⓐ Ⓑ Ⓒ Ⓓ Ⓔ	86. Ⓐ Ⓑ Ⓒ Ⓓ Ⓔ	136. Ⓐ Ⓑ Ⓒ Ⓓ Ⓔ	186. Ⓐ Ⓑ Ⓒ Ⓓ Ⓔ
37. Ⓐ Ⓑ Ⓒ Ⓓ Ⓔ	87. Ⓐ Ⓑ Ⓒ Ⓓ Ⓔ	137. Ⓐ Ⓑ Ⓒ Ⓓ Ⓔ	187. Ⓐ Ⓑ Ⓒ Ⓓ Ⓔ
38. Ⓐ Ⓑ Ⓒ Ⓓ Ⓔ	88. Ⓐ Ⓑ Ⓒ Ⓓ Ⓔ	138. Ⓐ Ⓑ Ⓒ Ⓓ Ⓔ	188. Ⓐ Ⓑ Ⓒ Ⓓ Ⓔ
39. Ⓐ Ⓑ Ⓒ Ⓓ Ⓔ	89. Ⓐ Ⓑ Ⓒ Ⓓ Ⓔ	139. Ⓐ Ⓑ Ⓒ Ⓓ Ⓔ	189. Ⓐ Ⓑ Ⓒ Ⓓ Ⓔ
40. Ⓐ Ⓑ Ⓒ Ⓓ Ⓔ	90. Ⓐ Ⓑ Ⓒ Ⓓ Ⓔ	140. Ⓐ Ⓑ Ⓒ Ⓓ Ⓔ	190. Ⓐ Ⓑ Ⓒ Ⓓ Ⓔ
41. Ⓐ Ⓑ Ⓒ Ⓓ Ⓔ	91. Ⓐ Ⓑ Ⓒ Ⓓ Ⓔ	141. Ⓐ Ⓑ Ⓒ Ⓓ Ⓔ	191. Ⓐ Ⓑ Ⓒ Ⓓ Ⓔ
42. Ⓐ Ⓑ Ⓒ Ⓓ Ⓔ	92. Ⓐ Ⓑ Ⓒ Ⓓ Ⓔ	142. Ⓐ Ⓑ Ⓒ Ⓓ Ⓔ	192. Ⓐ Ⓑ Ⓒ Ⓓ Ⓔ
43. Ⓐ Ⓑ Ⓒ Ⓓ Ⓔ	93. Ⓐ Ⓑ Ⓒ Ⓓ Ⓔ	143. Ⓐ Ⓑ Ⓒ Ⓓ Ⓔ	193. Ⓐ Ⓑ Ⓒ Ⓓ Ⓔ
44. Ⓐ Ⓑ Ⓒ Ⓓ Ⓔ	94. Ⓐ Ⓑ Ⓒ Ⓓ Ⓔ	144. Ⓐ Ⓑ Ⓒ Ⓓ Ⓔ	194. Ⓐ Ⓑ Ⓒ Ⓓ Ⓔ
45. Ⓐ Ⓑ Ⓒ Ⓓ Ⓔ	95. Ⓐ Ⓑ Ⓒ Ⓓ Ⓔ	145. Ⓐ Ⓑ Ⓒ Ⓓ Ⓔ	195. Ⓐ Ⓑ Ⓒ Ⓓ Ⓔ
46. Ⓐ Ⓑ Ⓒ Ⓓ Ⓔ	96. Ⓐ Ⓑ Ⓒ Ⓓ Ⓔ	146. Ⓐ Ⓑ Ⓒ Ⓓ Ⓔ	196. Ⓐ Ⓑ Ⓒ Ⓓ Ⓔ
47. Ⓐ Ⓑ Ⓒ Ⓓ Ⓔ	97. Ⓐ Ⓑ Ⓒ Ⓓ Ⓔ	147. Ⓐ Ⓑ Ⓒ Ⓓ Ⓔ	197. Ⓐ Ⓑ Ⓒ Ⓓ Ⓔ
48. Ⓐ Ⓑ Ⓒ Ⓓ Ⓔ	98. Ⓐ Ⓑ Ⓒ Ⓓ Ⓔ	148. Ⓐ Ⓑ Ⓒ Ⓓ Ⓔ	198. Ⓐ Ⓑ Ⓒ Ⓓ Ⓔ
49. Ⓐ Ⓑ Ⓒ Ⓓ Ⓔ	99. Ⓐ Ⓑ Ⓒ Ⓓ Ⓔ	149. Ⓐ Ⓑ Ⓒ Ⓓ Ⓔ	199. Ⓐ Ⓑ Ⓒ Ⓓ Ⓔ
50. Ⓐ Ⓑ Ⓒ Ⓓ Ⓔ	100. Ⓐ Ⓑ Ⓒ Ⓓ Ⓔ	150. Ⓐ Ⓑ Ⓒ Ⓓ Ⓔ	200. Ⓐ Ⓑ Ⓒ Ⓓ Ⓔ

Test 2

Time: 170 minutes

Directions: Each of the following questions contains five possible responses. Read the question carefully and select the response that you feel is most appropriate. Then completely darken the oval on your answer grid that corresponds with your choice.

1. Mallard duckling imprinting on a moving dummy is studied at varying time periods after birth in the experiments of

   (A) Hebb   (B) Hess   (C) Scott
   (D) Harlow   (E) Webb

2. The perceptual phenomenon of apparent tilt is

   (A) heavily dependent upon brightness and hue
   (B) a function of saturation
   (C) least prominent among persons relying on bodily clues
   (D) related to intelligence
   (E) strongly dependent upon retinal disparity

3. The cerebellum functions prominently in which of the following areas?

   (A) heart activity
   (B) blood pressure
   (C) muscle-movement coordination
   (D) verbal association
   (E) respiration

4. Historically, the European and American approaches to comparative psychology distinctly differed in the prominence given to

   (A) intelligence   (B) behavior   (C) learning
   (D) memory   (E) naturalistic observation

Questions 5–7 are based on the following information.

For 200 ninth-grade students whose IQ scores were available, Guilford and his associates were able to obtain divergent production scores. The findings are presented in the table.

LP Score	INTELLIGENCE QUOTIENT								
	60–69	70–79	80–89	90–99	100–109	110–119	120–129	130–139	140–149
50–59						1	3		1
40–49						2	4	1	
30–39			2	3	4	11	17	6	2
20–29			1	3	10	23	13	7	
10–19	1	5	3	9	11	19	7	3	1
0–9	1	3	1	4	10	11	2		

5. On the basis of this table, it would be appropriate to make the interpretation that there is

   (A) a direct, one-to-one relationship between IQ and divergent production
   (B) an almost perfect negative relationship between IQ and divergent production (the lower the IQ, the higher the likelihood of divergent production)
   (C) apparently a complete absence of relationship between IQ and divergent production
   (D) greater likelihood of divergent production in the 120–129 IQ range than in the 110–119 range
   (E) greater likelihood of divergent production in the 100–109 IQ range than in the 130–139 range

6. Interpretations of data such as those presented in this table would rely heavily upon the assumption that the children

   (A) were in the same school
   (B) participated in standardized testing and scoring procedures
   (C) were of the same sex
   (D) received their testing on the same day within the same test setting
   (E) represented all parts of the country

7. The table data suggest the greatest statistical likelihood of divergent production by persons in which of the following IQ groups?

   (A) 60–69   (B) 70–79   (C) 120–129
   (D) 130–139   (E) 140–149

8. In Brady's work with "executive monkeys," those that developed ulcers had

   (A) mother-deprived backgrounds
   (B) father-deprived backgrounds
   (C) sibling-deprived backgrounds
   (D) capacity to control shock onset
   (E) no capacity to control shock onset

9. Phineas Gage experienced a major personality change after a railroad tamping rod went through his skull. This tragic accident alerted scientists to the role in emotions of the

   (A) limbic system   (B) parietal lobe   (C) temporal lobe
   (D) occipital lobe   (E) cerebellum

10. Sound vibrations in the ear create neural impulses received in which of the following cortex locations?

   (A) temporal lobe   (B) central fissure   (C) occipital lobe
   (D) parietal lobe   (E) auditory lobe

11. Pitch is determined by

   (A) amplitude   (B) complexity   (C) frequency
   (D) decibels   (E) amplification

12. The autokinetic effect is most commonly demonstrated with which of the following stimuli?

   (A) a spot of light in a darkened room
   (B) lights flashing on and off in a patterned sequence
   (C) lights rotating around a single, central spot of light
   (D) a color wheel containing a black-white color disc
   (E) a steady blue light consistently viewed near dusk

13. Alcohol consumption

   (A) shortens reaction time
   (B) lengthens reaction time
   (C) shortens auditory reaction time while lengthening visual
   (D) shortens visual reaction time while lengthening auditory
   (E) shortens all except pain reaction time

14. Which of the following is an *incorrect* pairing?

   (A) spike potential—the nerve impulse, characterized by a very rapid change of neuronal potential
   (B) threshold—a transition from graded potential to spike potential
   (C) absolute refractory period—complete depression following a spike
   (D) all-or-none law—refers to and focuses upon graded potential
   (E) autonomic system chemical transmitters—acetylcholine, norepinephrine

15. A brain wave not evident in the newborn is the

   (A) beta   (B) alpha   (C) delta
   (D) theta   (E) gamma

16. The concept of equipotentiality was formulated on the basis of a systematic experimental program conducted by

   (A) Lindsley   (B) Tolman   (C) Lashley
   (D) Skinner   (E) Terman

17. Which of the following is an *incorrect* statement?

   (A) Receptive disorders such as agnosias and sensory aphasias are primarily localized in the posterior cerebral cortex.
   (B) Expressive disorders such as apraxias and motor aphasias are primarily localized in the frontal lobes.
   (C) Alexia is a type of visual aphasia associated with word blindness.
   (D) Apraxia refers to disturbances in audition, commonly called word deafness.
   (E) Inability to write or say a word that has been perceived is a type of aphasia.

18. Perceptual phenomena have been most prominently explored within

(A) structuralism   (B) Gestalt   (C) behaviorism
(D) functionalism   (E) eclecticism

19. ROC curves are

(A) retrograde-obsessive-compulsive
(B) remote-optical-chromatic
(C) respondent-operant-capacity
(D) receiver-operating-characteristic
(E) ratings-of-capability

20. Which of the following is *not* a taste primary?

(A) bitter   (B) sour   (C) sweet
(D) salty   (E) bland

21. The inability to recognize printed words because of brain damage is called

(A) kinesthesia   (B) somatic aphasia
(C) labyrinthine aphasia   (D) alexia   (E) acromegaly

22. The fact that a cold-blooded animal can remain alive and make coordinated muscle movements for some time after decapitation is possible because of

(A) spinal cord sufficiency for complicated patterns of reflexive behavior
(B) pons activity and increased compensatory functioning
(C) the role of the cerebellum in reflexive behavior
(D) inhibitory postsynaptic potential
(E) facilitating (excitatory) postsynaptic potential

23. A physiological psychologist would be most likely to find the term *reciprocal innervation* in discussions related to

(A) EEG
(B) digestion
(C) heartbeat
(D) muscle movements in walking
(E) subsequent learning interfering with previously learned responses

24. When a subject's sleep is interrupted during nondreaming periods rather than during dreaming periods

(A) subsequent sleep patterns equivalent to dream-period interruption are noted
(B) significantly higher subsequent dream attempts are noted
(C) subsequent dreams are much longer than usual
(D) significantly lower than normal subsequent dream attempts are noted
(E) subsequent dream attempts normal in both frequency and length are noted

25. The capacity for detecting the direction of incoming sound is

    (A) prominent among persons with hearing in only one ear
    (B) possible only when hearing exists in both ears
    (C) frequently termed monaural hearing
    (D) explained within the Young-Helmholtz theory of audition
    (E) heavily depending on the Meissner receptor

26. The SOC one passes through going from sleeping to waking is called the

    (A) twilight zone   (B) hypnagogic state   (C) hypnotic trance
    (D) hypnopompic state   (E) syntonic state

27. The lowest frequency in brain waves occurs within the

    (A) alpha rhythm   (B) beta rhythm   (C) gamma rhythm
    (D) delta rhythm   (E) theta rhythm

28. The brain area central to language production is
    (A) Broca's area   (B) Sylvian fissure   (C) Wernicke's area
    (D) Gage's area   (E) fissure of Rolando

29. The earliest emotion evident in the newborn is

    (A) delight   (B) shame   (C) shyness
    (D) excitement   (E) affection

30. *Not* among stimulus cues that can aid perception of depth is

    (A) texture   (B) light and shadow   (C) relative position
    (D) linear perspective   (E) convergence

31. Tinbergen's fixed action patterns

    (A) are elicited by a complex arrangement of external stimuli
    (B) are hormonally induced without reference to external stimuli
    (C) are elicited by simple, specific external stimuli
    (D) are synonymous with Watson's concept of nest habits
    (E) are instrumentally conditioned

32. Which of the following mobilizes the body by secreting epinephrine in stressful situations?

    (A) adrenal cortex   (B) pituitary   (C) gonads
    (D) pancreas   (E) adrenal medulla

33. Receptors generally referred to as chemical are

    (A) temperature and pain
    (B) visual and auditory
    (C) auditory and temperature
    (D) temperature and pressure
    (E) gustation and olfaction

34. The Frequency Theory of Audition is best suited to explain hearing in

    (A) the low frequency range
    (B) the high frequency range
    (C) the intermediate frequency range
    (D) all frequency ranges
    (E) the specific range between 3,000 and 10,000 cycles per second

35. Which of the following is an endocrine gland controlling growth and stimulating other endocrine glands?

    (A) pituitary   (B) adrenal   (C) thyroid
    (D) parathyroid   (E) pineal

36. Rat experimentation investigating the role of the cerebral cortex in sexual behavior indicates that

    (A) sexual behavior survives fairly extensive cortical destruction in male animals
    (B) the cerebral cortex is essential for copulation to occur in females
    (C) the cerebral cortex has no effect upon the ordering of responses that make up the pattern of sexual behavior in females
    (D) complete cortical destruction has no effect on arousal in male animals
    (E) cortical destruction affects motor but not sensory and perceptual functions

37. The study of motivation had its primitive, early beginnings with

    (A) Wundt and Weber
    (B) Fechner and Hull
    (C) Freud and James
    (D) Breuer and Charcot
    (E) Jung and Adler

38. Which of the following was *not* a facet of Freud's work having importance within the field of motivation?

    (A) underlying motives expressed consciously in disguised form
    (B) the function of unconscious processes in motivation
    (C) unconscious determinants of thought and action
    (D) relation of everyday slips and errors to underlying motivations
    (E) the manner in which habit combines with drive to express the content of emotion

39. Putting animals in puzzle boxes to study their intelligence was initially undertaken by

    (A) Darwin
    (B) James
    (C) Thorndike
    (D) Atkinson
    (E) Lewin

40. Hebb's consolidation theory of memory trace expresses the position that

(A) a type of learning consolidation activity occurs simultaneously with the learning event, "locking in" the memory trace instantly
(B) a type of learning consolidation activity occurs for minutes and even hours after the learning event
(C) electroconvulsive shock impairment of long-term, but not recent, memory provides basic support for his theoretical position
(D) children fit his theoretical model but adults do not
(E) adults fit his theoretical model but children do not

41. "A group of individuals capable of interbreeding under natural conditions and reproductively isolated from other such groups," most directly constitutes a definition of

(A) phylum   (B) class   (C) order
(D) family   (E) species

42. At which of the following ages would you expect clock-time concepts to be mastered initially by a child?

(A) two years
(B) three years
(C) four years
(D) between five and six years
(E) between seven and eight years

43. Reaction time

(A) decreases with age up to approximately forty years
(B) increases with age up to approximately forty years
(C) decreases with age up to approximately thirty years
(D) increases with age up to approximately thirty years
(E) decreases with age throughout the life span

44. Auditory sensations are transformed from "air waves" to nerve impulses by the

(A) vestibular system   (B) pinna   (C) ossicles
(D) cochlea   (E) round window

45. Studies of emotion involving transections at various levels of the brain stem in animals reveal that

(A) the integrated "attack reaction" found in normal animals remains intact
(B) organization of intense emotional responses apparently occurs at a level above the midbrain
(C) auditory stimuli retain their normal effectiveness in evoking emotional responses
(D) visual stimuli retain their normal effectiveness in evoking emotional responses
(E) there are no emotional response differences distinguishable from those found in normal animals

46. The terminal point for efferent fibers is

(A) the spinal cord
(B) the central nervous system
(C) the cerebral cortex
(D) muscles or glands
(E) the myelin sheath

47. When Tolman summarized Watson's definition of emotions, he did so in terms of

(A) field theory
(B) law of effect
(C) law of exercise
(D) stimuli and responses
(E) sensations and perceptions

48. A term collectively describing muscles and glands is

(A) receptors   (B) effectors   (C) innervators
(D) affectors   (E) constrictors

49. The Ames room was specifically designed to test

(A) shape constancy
(B) size constancy
(C) motion parallax
(D) interposition
(E) continuity

50. Experiments that have been able to restrict a specific visual input to a specific location on the retina have found

(A) increased stimulus clarity
(B) slight, but not total, fading
(C) gradual and complete fading
(D) partial Ganzfeld
(E) increased visual concentration capacities

51. Which of the following has been experimentally associated with LSD use?

(A) permanent insanity
(B) increased creativity
(C) therapeutic growth and insight
(D) cognitive experience similar to psychosis
(E) telekinesis

52. Which of the following is most deficient in color vision?

(A) turtles   (B) fish   (C) rats
(D) monkeys   (E) humans

Questions 53–56 are based on the following hearing diagram.

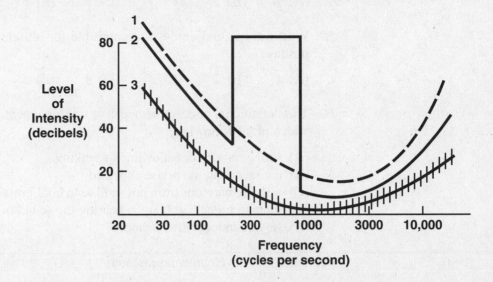

53. Which of the above lines would indicate nerve damage?

(A) 1   (B) 2   (C) 3   (D) 1 and 3   (E) all of the above

54. Which of the above lines would suggest ossification?

(A) 1   (B) 2   (C) 3   (D) 1 and 3   (E) all of the above

55. Which of the above lines would be unusually acute for human hearing?

(A) 1   (B) 2   (C) 3   (D) 1 and 3   (E) all of the above

56. Which of the above lines would represent the effects of aging?

(A) 1   (B) 2   (C) 3   (D) 1 and 3   (E) all of the above

Questions 57–59 are based on the following drawing.

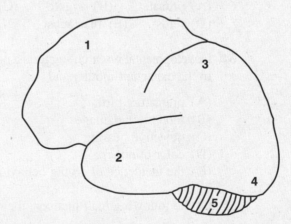

57. Audition functions would be located in which of the above cerebral areas?

(A) 1   (B) 2   (C) 3   (D) 4   (E) 5

58. Which of the areas has cerebral responsibility for vision?

    (A) 1   (B) 2   (C) 3   (D) 4   (E) 5

59. Which of the brain areas is responsible for muscle coordination and posture?

    (A) 1   (B) 2   (C) 3   (D) 4   (E) 5

60. The definitional concept of negative reinforcement is most central to which of the following?

    (A) sitting on a chair following a spanking
    (B) not receiving the praise expected
    (C) walking barefoot from hot sand onto cool grass
    (D) running immediately upon hearing the sound of the school bell
    (E) staying indoors after school

61. Bandura's developmental research

    (A) seriously questions the validity of modeling
    (B) suggests that observation of aggressive models can prompt aggressive behavior by the observer
    (C) suggests that love is a function of "contact comfort"
    (D) suggests that television viewing reduces the incidence of aggressive behavior
    (E) points to the effectiveness of reinforcement in toilet training

62. When a testing organization includes instructions to be read verbatim to each test-taking group, the organization is concentrating upon

    (A) dependent variables   (B) intervening variables
    (C) standardization   (D) reliability   (E) validity

63. During the third through the eighth week of pregnancy, the developing child can be accurately referred to as the

    (A) prenate   (B) zygote   (C) embryo
    (D) fetus   (E) blastocyst

64. Developmental research suggests a possible relationship between anxiety in the expectant mother and

    (A) premature birth
    (B) fetal brain damage
    (C) defective hearing
    (D) color blindness
    (E) the incidence of crying behavior in the newborn

65. Of the following malfunctions, the one not pituitary-based is

    (A) acromegaly   (B) dwarfism   (C) giantism
    (D) disproportionately large hand   (E) cretinism

66. Experiments with Hopi Indian children have suggested that the point at which a child begins to walk is primarily a function of

(A) learning   (B) intelligence   (C) maturation
(D) environment   (E) modeling

67. Which of the following is not associated with the "visual cliff"?

(A) the names Gibson and Walk
(B) the question of depth perception
(C) the suggestion of possible innate capacity
(D) comparison of child and animal performance
(E) the question of retinal disparity and convergence

68. Research evidence suggests highest aggression among boys who come from which of the following settings?

(A) broken   (B) father-absent   (C) father-present
(D) mother-present   (E) parents-deceased

69. According to Paivio's dual-code model of memory, the two types of codes used to store long-term memories are

(A) visual and auditory
(B) semantic and syntactic
(C) semantic and episodic
(D) implicit and explicit
(E) verbal and visual

70. Through test apparatus that, in effect, asks the newborn what she visually prefers, which of the following is found to be most preferred?

(A) bright-colored triangles
(B) bright-colored squares
(C) pictures of toys
(D) pictures of pets
(E) pictures of the human face

71. Checking a newborn male child via EEG, EMG, EOG, and respiration monitoring, would reveal which of the following?

(A) total absence of REM sleep
(B) some irregularities in respiration
(C) no body movement during sleep
(D) no reflex smiles
(E) no penis erection

72. Loftus and her colleagues have found that eyewitness testimony is affected by
   I. Bias in question wording
  II. False information injected into questions
 III. Inferences made to fill memory gaps

(A) I only   (B) III only   (C) I and II only
(D) II and III only   (E) I, II, and III

73. Which of the following would be true of instrumental conditioning?

(A) The response is elicited by the presence of the unconditioned stimulus.
(B) Reinforcement increases the frequency of the response associated with it.
(C) There is trace presentation of CS and UCS.
(D) There is delayed presentation of CS and UCS.
(E) There is simultaneous presentation of CS and UCS.

74. A person who has an IQ score of 60 would be considered

(A) profoundly retarded   (B) severely retarded
(C) moderately retarded   (D) trainable   (E) mildly retarded

75. General knowledge frameworks that help people interpret and remember events are called

(A) chunks   (B) prototypes   (C) episodes
(D) propositions   (E) schemas

76. Which of the following is correct?

(A) The correlation coefficient range is –0.05 to +0.05.
(B) +0.40 is greater correlation than –0.40.
(C) Correlation is related to predictability.
(D) Regression coefficients are essential for factor analysis.
(E) Analysis of covariance is not related to correlation.

77. Which of the following most commonly expresses central tendency and variability, respectively?

(A) mode, range
(B) mean, interval
(C) median, range
(D) median, standard deviation
(E) mean, standard deviation

78. The first two years after birth are critical

(A) to self-concept formation
(B) to aptitude formation
(C) to sensory formation
(D) to formation of secondary sexual characteristics
(E) only in the minds of parents

79. The syllogism is a form appropriate to

(A) deductive thinking
(B) inductive thinking
(C) evaluative thinking
(D) divergent thinking
(E) trial-and-error thinking

80. Which of the following can be anticipated during the first three months after birth?

    (A) shorter periods of wakefulness
    (B) the ability to raise the head slightly to look at something
    (C) a noticeable lack of any effort to attempt an "answer" when an adult talks to the child
    (D) the ability to hold and manipulate a spoon
    (E) masturbation

81. Which of the following would be considered associative—rather than cognitive—learning?

    (A) anxiety when encountering a dangerous situation
    (B) reading a detailed, intricate novel
    (C) writing a letter
    (D) a complex computer-programming task
    (E) solving a complex maze task

82. A conditioned response has been learned to a specific stimulus. When similar stimuli also evoke the conditioned response, the phenomenon is

    (A) stimulus generalization
    (B) response generalization
    (C) successive approximation
    (D) spread-of-effect
    (E) contiguity

83. Learning how to learn is essentially a process of

    (A) establishing learning sets
    (B) operant conditioning
    (C) stimulus generalization
    (D) imprinting
    (E) nonreversal shift

Question 84 is based on the information that follows.

Given the list below, complete the vertical arrangement indicated by the words erase and fate, using words from the group and taking erase as the middle word in the column. (Note that not all words need to be used.)

a, gate, no, i, duty, in , cat, ho, ear,
o, travel, erase, both, get, ho, fate.
erase
fate

84. The preceding information and instructions require a person to engage in a process known as

    (A) interpolation
    (B) extrapolation
    (C) structuring
    (D) modeling
    (E) interposition

85. In social-adjustment terms, early maturity has been found

    (A) advantageous among males
    (B) advantageous among females
    (C) detrimental to males
    (D) detrimental to both males and females
    (E) a source of female prestige and male ridicule

86. The period of the embryo spans the time from the end of

    (A) second week to end of second month
    (B) first week to end of second month
    (C) third week to end of second month
    (D) first week to end of first month
    (E) third week to end of third month

87. In contrast to a dissimilar-items list, a similar-items list is

    (A) more difficult to learn
    (B) easier to learn
    (C) learned with equivalent ease
    (D) more susceptible to the serial position effect
    (E) less susceptible to the serial position effect

88. Which of the following is a cell-type distinction?

    (A) nerve and muscle
    (B) sperm and ova
    (C) chromosome and gene
    (D) amnion and chorion
    (E) germ and body

89. Which of the names listed would be most likely to comment that environment is of central importance?

    (A) Leibnitz   (B) Wundt   (C) Dewey
    (D) Darwin   (E) Watson

90. For classical conditioning, it is essential that

    (A) the subject be informed of desired outcome in advance
    (B) the UCS be inherently rewarding
    (C) the UCS be originally neutral
    (D) the CS be originally neutral
    (E) the CR be identical in strength and intensity to the UCR

91. In which of the following situations would the most classical conditioning be expected?

    (A) UCS preceding CS by one-half second
    (B) CS preceding UCS by two seconds
    (C) UCS preceding CS by two seconds
    (D) CS preceding UCS by one-half second
    (E) CS preceding UCS by five seconds

92. Which of the following *cannot* occur during the germinal stage?

    (A) death of the zygote before implantation
    (B) glandular imbalance preventing implantation
    (C) implantation in a Fallopian tube
    (D) cell division
    (E) cell mass differentiation into three distinct layers

93. Depth of processing theory provides

    (A) an explanation of memory functioning
    (B) the basics of color vision
    (C) the basic link between neurosis and psychosis
    (D) an explanation of pituitary gland function
    (E) the basic theory of emotion

94. The field theorist emphasizes the role of learning in

    (A) S-R associations   (B) drive reduction   (C) reinforcement
    (D) cognitive processes   (E) sensory processes

95. Among the primary effects of anxiety upon learning, one could expect

    (A) removal of mental blocks
    (B) more interference with familiar material than with new material
    (C) reduced ability to discriminate clearly
    (D) heightened motivation leading to proficiency on virtually any task
    (E) proactive facilitation

96. The von Restorff effect applies to

    (A) serial position   (B) task completion   (C) prepotent stimulus
    (D) meaningfulness of learning material   (E) memory span

97. Which of the following is *not* an experimental approach to recall?

    (A) single-trial, free recall
    (B) multi-trial, free recall
    (C) split-half, free recall
    (D) paired associates
    (E) serial presentation

98. Frenkel and Brunswik conclude that the single most important factor distinguishing prejudiced from tolerant adolescents is

    (A) intelligence   (B) aptitude   (C) sexual adjustment
    (D) attitude toward authority   (E) vocational choice

99. Moderate anxiety in a child

    (A) is detrimental to all learning
    (B) may facilitate learning of difficult tasks
    (C) may facilitate learning of simple tasks
    (D) suggests unhealthy defense against Oedipal conflict
    (E) is a function of archetype

100. Which of the following does *not* qualify as a polygenic characteristic?

    (A) intelligence   (B) temperament   (C) schizophrenia
    (D) eye color   (E) violence proneness

101. A man who has normal color vision marries a woman who has normal color vision but who carries a defective color-vision gene. They can expect

    (A) all their offspring to be color-blind
    (B) none of their offspring to be color-blind
    (C) half their sons to be color-blind
    (D) all their daughters and none of their sons to be color-blind
    (E) all their sons and none of their daughters to be color-blind

102. Friends become differentiated from strangers during which of the following young ages?

    (A) twelve months
    (B) six to seven months
    (C) one to two months
    (D) birth
    (E) three to four months

103. Roger Shepard and Steve Kosslyn measured how long people take mentally to rotate or scan visual memories in order to show that

    (A) the duration of iconic memories in the sensory register is very brief
    (B) visual memories are better remembered than verbal memories
    (C) there is a dual-code of both visual and verbal properties of memories
    (D) visual memories are stored as images and not as propositions
    (E) spatial information is stored in the form of mental maps

104. Which of the following is primarily a verbal test?

    (A) WAIS   (B) Stanford-Binet   (C) WISC
    (D) Blacky   (E) WPPSI

105. Within problem-solving processes, the inductive phase encompasses

    (A) information retrieval from memory
    (B) information storage in memory
    (C) information reception and routing
    (D) idea and hypothesis generation
    (E) systematic memory scanning

106. The heights of kindergarten-aged children are

    (A) negatively correlated with comparative adult heights
    (B) positively correlated with comparative adult heights
    (C) in no way related to comparative adult heights
    (D) most strongly correlated with the heights of their mothers
    (E) most strongly correlated with the heights of their fathers

107. Kendler's experimentation suggests that in child maturation

(A) mediational processes precede single-unit S-R cognitive mechanisms

(B) single-unit S-R cognitive mechanisms precede mediational processes

(C) single-unit S-R cognitive mechanisms and mediational processes occur at the same developmental point

(D) neither the single-unit S-R cognitive mechanism nor the mediational process occurs until after age six

(E) single unit S-R cognitive mechanisms never occur

108. In the newborn's second year, the rate of growth

(A) is faster than that of the first year

(B) is slower than that of the first year

(C) parallels that of the first year

(D) is faster than that of the fetal period

(E) is faster than that of the embryonic period

109. Of the following, which group contains the most names foreign to imprinting research?

(A) Hess, Lorenz, Scott

(B) Scott, Hess, Sontag

(C) Lorenz, Hess, Miller

(D) Miller, Hess, Scott

(E) Sontag, Miller, Scott

110. The mouth opens wide and the head turns to the midline in the

(A) Babinski response

(B) Babkin response

(C) plantar response

(D) Moro response

(E) push-back response

111. Maleness in the human is determined by the

(A) Y chromosome   (B) X chromosome   (C) XX zygote
(D) recessive gene   (E) YY genetic transmission

112. In the Guilford model for problem solving, which of the following occurs first?

(A) input   (B) filtering   (C) cognition
(D) production   (E) evaluation

113. The term most closely associated with the work of Tolman is

(A) perceptual learning

(B) sensory preconditioning

(C) reinforcement learning

(D) place learning

(E) contiguity learning

114. The term *fractional anticipatory goal response* refers to

    (A) backward conditioning
    (B) UCR
    (C) CR
    (D) CS
    (E) Mowrer's Two-Factor Theory

115. In the formula $R = H \times D \times K$, if H is very large, D is very large, and reinforcement is zero

    (A) no response occurs
    (B) a small response occurs
    (C) a response may or may not occur
    (D) if a response occurs, it will not be learned
    (E) if a drive occurs, it will be very small

116. In Piaget's classification system, the child learns language and the logic of classification and numbers during which period?

    (A) sensorimotor
    (B) latency
    (C) formal operations
    (D) concrete operations
    (E) assimilation

117. In Hunter's double alternation response, an animal

    (A) gets shocked for incorrect response
    (B) must turn in a circle prior to making the correct response
    (C) must go down the alley twice before making the appropriate T-maze turn
    (D) must remember which direction it turned on the two preceding trials
    (E) must open a small gate at the sound of a buzzer

118. Thinking about the meaning of a word leads to better recall than thinking about the sound or appearance of a word. This is called the

    (A) levels of processing effect
    (B) von Restorff effect
    (C) serial position effect
    (D) forgetting curve
    (E) functional fixedness effect

119. In Dollard and Miller's conceptual terms, infant feeding is not a setting for learning

    (A) future apathy and indifference
    (B) sociability
    (C) fear
    (D) anger-anxiety conflict
    (E) overreaction to minor physical discomfort

120. A curve has its most prominent distribution of scores to the left of center and "tails off" to the right. This information would be sufficient to conclude that the curve showed

(A) negative skew
(B) positive skew
(C) normal distribution
(D) bimodal distribution
(E) platikurtic distribution

121. Fable indicates that a servant once had a problem with a king. Each time it rained, all the cats in the kingdom would walk across the palace floor with their muddy feet and the servant would incur the king's wrath. Tired of receiving the blame for this problem, the servant gathered all the cats and placed them in a bag. The servant then took the cats to the woods and went through a sequence of coughing loudly and then striking the bag with a heavy pole. After repeating this sequence many times the servant set the cats free and assumed that the muddy floor problem had been solved. The assumption was based on

(A) classical conditioning
(B) counterconditioning
(C) backward conditioning
(D) implosion techniques
(E) systematic desensitization

122. Performance of an earlier task is interfered with by the learning of a second, more recent task in

(A) proactive facilitation
(B) proactive inhibition
(C) retroactive facilitation
(D) retroactive inhibition
(E) negative transference

123. *Not* an accurate or frequently mentioned distinction between image and percept is that the

(A) visual image is more labile
(B) visual image is less labile
(C) visual image is less vivid
(D) percept is generally more detailed
(E) visual image may become associated with other objects and images

124. Which of the following developed the "overload theory" of crowding?

(A) Lorenz   (B) Schachter   (C) Aronson
(D) Milgram   (E) Ardrey

125. A person is asked to tell a lie for one of the following sums of money. For which sum would the most dissonance be created?

(A) $1   (B) $10   (C) $20   (D) $25   (E) $50

126. Which of the following is *not* characteristic of the Thurstone-type scale?

    (A) equal-appearing intervals
    (B) a judge expressing his own attitude regarding the statement being judged
    (C) an eleven-category scale
    (D) a large number of judges
    (E) number values assigned to each statement on the scale

127. The most mature view of sex would be evident in which of the following?

    (A) genital stage   (B) phallic stage   (C) anal stage
    (D) puberty   (E) initiative versus guilt

128. "Man's freedom is absolute and it is his own choices which determine what he shall become, since even refusing to choose constitutes a choice." The preceding view is expressed within

    (A) behaviorism   (B) psychoanalysis   (C) ego analysis
    (D) trait theory   (E) existentialism

129. Which of the following is *not* true of attitudes?

    (A) Your own attitudes seem best to you.
    (B) A common defense against differing attitudes is selective attention.
    (C) A common defense against differing attitudes is rationalization.
    (D) Attitudes require an emotional component.
    (E) Attitudes require a stereotype component.

130. A person who judges personality on the basis of facial expression is engaging in

    (A) physiognomy   (B) phrenology   (C) trait analysis
    (D) syntonomy   (E) parataxis

131. In a sequence of measures for creativity, which of the following would be a *least* likely inclusion?

    (A) water jar problems
    (B) Remote Associations Test
    (C) verbal "mind stretchers" such as "What would happen if everyone had three fingers and no thumb?"
    (D) WAIS
    (E) sentence completion

132. An ability that can be expected to continue improving after age thirty-five is

    (A) numerical
    (B) manual
    (C) spatial relations
    (D) verbal comprehension
    (E) associative memory

133. A group of students took a personality test and later were given very general descriptive comments about the test's results. Each student was given the same general description, and the individual students concluded that the description fit their personality very well. This demonstration would be evidence of

    (A) the Freudian effect   (B) the response effect
    (C) the Muller/Lyer effect   (D) the rebound effect
    (E) the Barnum effect

134. Homan's anticipatory socialization refers to

    (A) downward movement in the social system
    (B) upward movement in the social system
    (C) lateral movement in the social system
    (D) preparation for an older age group within one's own social class
    (E) a child's initial preparation for cooperative play

135. Which of the following is unrelated to the 16 PF?

    (A) 16 personality-factor dimensions   (B) Cattell
    (C) standardization on normal subjects   (D) Hathaway
    (E) factor analysis

136. A factor analysis approach to personality would be most positively received within which of the following groups?

    (A) Cattell, Eysenck, Goldstein
    (B) Jung, Freud, Horney
    (C) Rogers, Kelly, Allport
    (D) Skinner, Watson, Bandura
    (E) Sullivan, Erikson, Berne

137. Which of the following makes an accurate distinction between the Strong-Campbell Vocational Interest Blank and the Kuder Preference Record?

    (A) success versus failure
    (B) differences in administration
    (C) occupation emphasis versus broad-area emphasis
    (D) male-female distinctions versus unified format
    (E) an intelligence factor versus an aptitude factor

138. As a corrections officer—other factors being equivalent—which of the following persons would you consider most likely to be rehabilitated successfully?

    (A) person convicted of armed robbery
    (B) person who shot and killed another man found making love to the first man's wife
    (C) person charged with breaking and entering
    (D) person charged with arson
    (E) person who shot and killed another person as part of a profit-making contract

139. Mortimer has worn red shirts for years because he likes them. Now red shirts are the "in" thing with his group and he continues to wear them. In Hollander's terms, he is demonstrating

(A) conformity   (B) anticonformity   (C) dissonance
(D) independence   (E) irrelevance

140. A salesperson makes a call on a retailer who has been buying a competitor's product line. The salesperson compliments the competitor's store display and asks the retailer whether Company X (the competitor) made it. When the retailer responds "Yes," the salesperson says, "You are very fortunate to have such a display made exclusively for you." The retailer then indicates, "Oh no, Company X doesn't give exclusive display lines"—a fact the salesperson knew in advance. This conversation will continue with the salesperson making subsequent absolute statements about Company X with which the retailer will be forced to disagree. The attitude change technique being utilized draws heavily upon

(A) Brehm's theory of reactance
(B) Newcomb's theory of balance
(C) Goffman's theory of consonance
(D) Homan's theory of distributive justice
(E) Adler's theory of superiority striving

141. A major attempt is being launched to change household attitudes toward the use of beef liver as a regular mealtime food. The approach is to have the most influential member of each household (a person who currently dislikes beef liver) design and deliver a talk on the prominent advantages of having beef liver as a regular mealtime food. The theory underlying this approach to attitude change would be

(A) cognitive dissonance
(B) behavior exchange
(C) complementarity
(D) vulnerability
(E) status congruence

142. The *least* likely treatment procedure, virtually extinct in today's psychiatric facilities, is

(A) electroconvulsive shock therapy
(B) chemotherapy
(C) individual psychotherapy
(D) encounter group therapy
(E) prefrontal lobotomy

143. Which of the following was Adler's conceptual substitution for Freud's libido?

(A) superiority striving
(B) social interest
(C) inferiority feeling
(D) organ inferiority
(E) pampering

144. Someone well versed in kinesics would be studying

   (A) the meaning of body movements
   (B) personal, territorial space
   (C) mass communication
   (D) brainwashing
   (E) nonzero sum games

145. Jung cites human infant response to mother-closeness and the adult concept of a power beyond himself as examples of

   (A) anima   (B) animus   (C) archetype
   (D) prototype   (E) intuiting

146. The term *gender schema* refers to

   (A) associating words with people
   (B) preponderance of same-sex children in a family
   (C) intelligence test score distributions
   (D) the "gender design" within DNA
   (E) gender-clustering words in memory storage and retrieval

147. Which of the following is most firmly supported by experimental evidence?

   (A) psychoanalysis   (B) trait theory   (C) behaviorism
   (D) phenomenology   (E) psychodynamic theory

148. The Generalized Thurstone Scales were developed by

   (A) Likert   (B) Bogardus   (C) Osgood
   (D) Remmers   (E) Aronson

149. A nonzero sum game refers to

   (A) a recent development in sociograms
   (B) a game in which both participants may win
   (C) a game in which both participants must lose
   (D) a game in which one participant ends up with zero
   (E) a game in which one participant may win only if the other partici-pant loses

150. Formulation of dissonance theory was initiated by

   (A) Aronson   (B) Thurstone   (C) Festinger
   (D) Heider   (E) Newcomb

151. A therapeutic technique present in the work of Wolpe and not evident within Skinner's method is

   (A) positive reinforcement
   (B) negative reinforcement
   (C) discriminative stimulus
   (D) logotherapy
   (E) response generalization

152. Transvestism would be classified among

    (A) sexual and gender identity disorders
    (B) anxiety disorders
    (C) personality disorders
    (D) somatoform disorders
    (E) dissociative disorders

153. Sixteen different, self-contained personalities within the same individual, manifesting themselves at different times, is a form of

    (A) anxiety disorder
    (B) catatonic schizophrenia
    (C) paranoid psychosis
    (D) dysthymic disorder
    (E) dissociative disorder

154. In stating his view of neurosis as conditioned maladaptive behavior, Eysenck claims that

    (A) extroverts are most likely to become neurotics
    (B) introverts are most likely to develop somatoform disorders
    (C) introverts have greater autonomic reactivity
    (D) phobias persist, once learned, even in the absence of further reinforcement
    (E) parataxic perception must be achieved before therapy can attain significant progress

155. Which of the following distinguishes a sedative from a tranquilizer?

    (A) cost
    (B) drowsiness-inducing characteristics
    (C) speed with which it takes effect
    (D) anxiety-reducing capacity
    (E) mood-elevation properties

156. Which of the following distinguishes anxiety from fear?

    (A) realistic environmental danger
    (B) strength of emotion
    (C) galvanic skin response
    (D) heart rate
    (E) blood pressure

157. A tranquilizer widely used in the treatment of schizophrenia is

    (A) *d*-tubocurarine
    (B) chlorpromazine
    (C) LSD
    (D) mescaline
    (E) Elavil

158. Which one of the following was *not* part of Masserman's experiments?

    (A) conditioned conflict
    (B) air puffs
    (C) electric shock
    (D) rapid increase in room temperature
    (E) sudden lights and sounds

159. The effects of psychotomimetic drugs resemble which one of the following reactions?

    (A) depressive   (B) hypermanic   (C) schizophrenic
    (D) delirium   (E) somatoform

160. Withdrawal reactions do *not* include which of the following elements?

    (A) repression
    (B) fantasy
    (C) regression
    (D) continual wandering—moves without tangible gain
    (E) paranoia

161. A characteristic of schizophrenia is

    (A) heightened awareness of reality
    (B) eidetic imagery
    (C) withdrawal from interpersonal relationships
    (D) psychological "paralysis" in a portion of the body
    (E) the "phantom limb" experience

162. Which of the following would encompass the view that a friend or relative's sympathy may serve to feed the person's depression?

    (A) stress approach
    (B) cognitive approach
    (C) learned helplessness approach
    (D) MAO approach
    (E) reduced-reinforcement approach

163. The simplest, least sophisticated measure of variability is known as the

    (A) range   (B) standard deviation   (C) variance
    (D) stanine   (E) quadrant

164. Intense fear of open places is known as

    (A) ochlophobia   (B) acrophobia   (C) claustrophobia
    (D) triskaidekaphobia   (E) agoraphobia

165. Which one of the following is most likely to set fires?

    (A) pyromaniac   (B) ochlomaniac   (C) kleptomaniac
    (D) aclomaniac   (E) hypomaniac

166. Which of the following is *not* directly related to clinical assessment?

(A) MMPI   (B) 16 PF   (C) Osgood Semantic Differential
(D) Rorschach   (E) TAT

167. Transference and resistance are most common in

(A) psychoanalysis
(B) group therapy
(C) behavior therapy
(D) phenomenological therapy
(E) client-centered therapy

168. Each score in a distribution has been increased by 7 (i.e., 7 has been added to every score). What happens to the standard deviation?

(A) it increases by 7
(B) it remains unchanged from its original value
(C) it triples its current value
(D) it increases by 14
(E) it increases by 3.5

169. The term *mainlining* refers to

(A) use of heroin by the middle class
(B) sniffing heroin
(C) injecting heroin under the skin
(D) smoking heroin
(E) injecting heroin into a vein

170. George has been diagnosed as schizophrenic. Which of the following most likely will be prescribed for him to take?

(A) haloperidol   (B) amphetamines   (C) atropine
(D) LSD   (E) mescaline

171. The procedure of outlining an experimental problem, stating criteria for making observations, describing measuring instruments and their use in observation, and defining procedures to be used in data analysis is

(A) operational definition
(B) hypothetical construct
(C) logical construct
(D) experimental design
(E) hypothesis

172. The function of a theory is to

(A) prove a hypothesis
(B) establish a law
(C) explain and relate observed facts
(D) develop the steps to be used in experimentation
(E) establish significance levels

173. For which of the following forms of sexual deviation would treatment be considered most difficult?

(A) frigidity   (B) impotence   (C) fetishism
(D) pedophilia   (E) coitus interruptus

174. Depression is mild and includes within it no distortions of reality in

(A) sleep disorder   (B) organic disorder   (C) mood disorder
(D) schizophrenic disorder   (E) personality disorder

175. The life-history method is a

(A) laboratory method
(B) field-study method
(C) latitudinal method
(D) longitudinal method
(E) factor-analytical method

176. Michelangelo's frustrated desire for closeness with his mother was expressed in painting. This is an example of

(A) compensation   (B) rationalization   (C) sublimation
(D) projection   (E) reaction formation

177. Which one of the following persons would be most likely to study and analyze drawings by schizophrenic children?

(A) Bandura   (B) Bettelheim   (C) Szasz
(D) Skinner   (E) Adler

178. Which of the following is believed to have an important role in mood disorders?

(A) norepinephrine   (B) estrogen   (C) progesterone
(D) acetylcholine   (E) potassium chloride

179. Assuming a mean of 100 and a standard deviation of 15, what percentage of a group of persons selected randomly can be expected to have IQ scores above 130?

(A) 14 percent   (B) 34 percent   (C) 48 percent
(D) 2 percent   (E) 1 percent

Questions 180 and 181 are based on the following situation.

An experimenter plans to study the effects upon comprehension exerted by differences in sex, age, and hair color. Subjects will be equal numbers of males and females, ages twenty-five and forty-five, and either brown-haired or red-haired.

180. The statistical design is

(A) two-factor   (B) four-factor   (C) one-factor
(D) six-factor   (E) three-factor

181. Assuming that the experimenter can somehow obtain the data in a single test session with one score for each subject, she could use

    (A) a two-factor factorial design
    (B) a three-factor factorial design
    (C) a *t*-test for related measures
    (D) a *t*-test for unrelated measures
    (E) a complex Latin square design

182. *The Psychopathology of Everyday Life* was a prominent work of

    (A) Fromm
    (B) Rank
    (C) Skinner
    (D) Freud
    (E) Adler

183. The moron-imbecile-idiot classification of the mentally retarded was changed because

    (A) the corresponding IQs were inexact
    (B) the categories were not sufficiently inclusive
    (C) four categories were needed instead of three
    (D) unfortunate stereotyping had occurred
    (E) five categories were needed instead of three

184. Human engineering control principles indicate that a system is best in which the operation of the controls imposes a degree of strain on the operator consistent with the required degree of accuracy. This degree is

    (A) below optimum strain
    (B) above optimum strain
    (C) optimal strain
    (D) complete absence of strain
    (E) either above optimum or below optimum, depending on the setting

Questions 185–187 are based on the following information.

Two judges ranked five beauty contestants as follows:

Contestant	Judge 1	Judge 2
A	1	5
B	2	4
C	3	3
D	4	2
E	5	1

185. Which of the following can be concluded from the above?

    (A) A strong positive correlation exists between the judges.
    (B) A strong negative correlation exists between the judges.
    (C) There is no correlation between the judges.
    (D) A moderately positive correlation exists between the judges.
    (E) A moderately negative correlation exists between the judges.

186. Which of the following methods would be used in computation of the correlation?

    (A) Latin Square Design
    (B) Spearman Rank-Order Correlation
    (C) Point-Biserial Correlation
    (D) Simple Analysis of Covariance
    (E) Factorial Analysis of Covariance

187. The correlation coefficient that you would be most likely to find would be

    (A) +0.5   (B) −0.5   (C) 0.0
    (D) −1.0   (E) +1.0

188. In human engineering, the term *shape coding* applies to

    (A) visual discriminations
    (B) dial calibrations
    (C) dial color coding
    (D) traffic flow between work positions
    (E) knob appearance and contour

189. A situation in which trainees are presented with only the "bare bones" of a managerial situation and are told that participants can get additional information only by asking questions is an example of the

    (A) free-association method
    (B) case method
    (C) incident method
    (D) sensitivity-training
    (E) role-playing method

190. A company has a screening test that involves responding to letters, memoranda, telephone messages, and other items typical of the contents of an executive's in-basket. This is an example of

    (A) an aptitude test
    (B) an intelligence test
    (C) an achievement test
    (D) a sociability measure
    (E) an English test

191. Recognizing the difficulty of control in experimental designs, in which of the following could you be assured that variability among subjects has been adequately controlled?

    (A) completely randomized design
    (B) $2 \times 2 \times 2$ factorial design
    (C) point-biserial correlation
    (D) test-retest (repeated measures) design
    (E) *t*-test

192. The measure most meaningful to an industry trying to determine the most popular and fastest selling items would be

    (A) mean
    (B) median
    (C) variance
    (D) standard deviation
    (E) mode

193. In a positively skewed distribution, which of the following will move most noticeably in the direction indicated?

    (A) mean, to the right
    (B) mode, to the left
    (C) mean, to the left
    (D) median, to the right
    (E) median, to the left

194. Given a very limited time (only a few hours) during which to study for a test, a person's best bet would be

    (A) distributed practice
    (B) massed practice
    (C) a combination of distributed/massed/distributed
    (D) a combination of massed/distributed/massed
    (E) a combination of massed/massed/distributed

Questions 195–197 are based on the following choices.

    (1) *t*-test for related measures
    (2) *t*-test for two independent means
    (3) *t*-test for sample and population means
    (4) chi-square
    (5) treatments-by-levels design

195. The experimenter seeks to determine whether one group of eighteen-year-old boys differs significantly in weight from a second group of eighteen-year-old boys. She would use

    (A) 1   (B) 2   (C) 3   (D) 4   (E) 5

196. The experimenter wants to test the effect of child rearing upon identical twins—with one of each pair raised in a foster home and the second of each pair raised in an institution. (IQ scores were obtained for analysis when each group member attained age 15.) Which method would she use?

    (A) 1   (B) 2   (C) 3   (D) 4   (E) 5

197. The experimenter wishes to determine whether the weight of a specific group of eighteen-year-old boys is significantly different from the national average for boys this age. Which method would she use?

    (A) 1   (B) 2   (C) 3   (D) 4   (E) 5

198. Which one of the following could be expected to enhance performance on a vigilance task?

(A) threat of punishment
(B) rest periods
(C) high pay
(D) coworker interaction
(E) background music

199. Most closely associated with the Least Preferred Coworker technique and with task-centered versus people-centered leader distinction is the work of

(A) Newcomb
(B) Asch
(C) Rokeach
(D) Festinger
(E) Fiedler

200. In McLuhan's framework, television is seen as a

(A) hot medium
(B) moderately intense medium
(C) cool medium
(D) political medium
(E) social medium

Test 2: Answer Comments

1. (B) Hess studied imprinting behavior in mallard ducklings at several different time-after-birth intervals.

2. (C) Witkin found the perceptual phenomenon of tilt least prominent among persons relying on bodily cues.

3. (C) Located below the occipital lobe, the cerebellum functions prominently in muscle-movement coordination.

4. (E) Historically, the European and American approaches to comparative psychology differed in the prominence given to naturalistic observation. It was given a very strong emphasis in the European tradition, but the experimental laboratory method took precedence within the American tradition.

5. (D) The table indicates a higher probability of divergent production in the 120–129 IQ range than in the 110–119 range.

6. (B) Interpretations of table data containing IQ or other test scores must rely heavily upon the assumption that standardized testing and scoring procedures were followed.

7. (C) The 120–129 IQ range shows the greatest statistical likelihood for divergent production.

8. (D) In Brady's "executive monkey" experimentation, those animals that developed ulcers had the capacity to control shock onset.

9. (A) The accident severed the connections between the frontal lobe of the cerebral cortex and the limbic system. This alerted scientists to the role of the limbic system in emotions and the moderating influence upon emotional expression exerted by the frontal lobe.

10. (A) The temporal lobe of the brain receives auditory neural impulses.

11. (C) Pitch is the auditory dimension determined by frequency (number of cycles per second).

12. (A) When a stationary spot of light in a darkened room is perceived as moving, the autokinetic effect has occurred.

13. (B) Alcohol consumption lengthens reaction time—one of the driving hazards mentioned in the public media.

14. (D) The all-or-none law, as its name implies, focuses upon the ungraded-spike potential.

15. (B) Alpha waves are associated with the relaxed wakeful state in the older child and the adult but do not appear to be present in the newborn. They become evident at approximately six months of age.

16. (C) Basing his conclusion on rigorous experimentation, Lashley stated that equipotentiality showed that different parts of the cortex are interchangeable in their roles in learning (a finding critical in cases of brain damage).

17. (D) Apraxia refers to disturbances in the memory of bodily motor movements.

18. (B) Gestalt psychologists have most prominently explored perceptual phenomena.

19. (D) Intrinsic to signal detection theory, ROC curves are receiver-operating-characteristic curves. They enable a researcher to plot the basic signal-reception characteristics of a given individual and thereby separate the sensory from the nonsensory variables in signal detection.

20. (E) Sweet, sour, bitter, and salty are the taste primaries.

21. (D) Inability to recognize printed words because of brain damage would be called *alexia*.

22. (A) Such muscle movement following decapitation of a cold-blooded animal occurs because of spinal cord sufficiency for complicated patterns of reflexive behavior.

23. (D) Reciprocal innervation refers to a combination of antagonistic muscle movements such as those present in walking.

24. (E) Sleep interruption during nondreaming periods has no effect upon the incidence of dream attempts in subsequent sleep.

25. (B) The position of the two ears on the head is critical to determinations of sound directionality. Hearing must exist in both ears for the determination of sound direction.

26. (D) The state of consciousness passed through when going from sleeping to waking is called the hypnopompic state.

27. (D) The lowest brain wave frequency is the delta wave, occurring in stage IV (deep) sleep.

28. (A) Broca's area is central to language production, while Wernicke's area is central to language comprehension.

29. (D) The Montreal Foundling Studies indicated that the earliest emotion evident in the newborn is excitement.

30. (E) Although functioning in depth perception, convergence is not a stimulus cue.

31. (C) Tinbergen's fixed-action patterns (e.g., frog's tongue flick when catching flies) are stereotyped action patterns exhibited by all same-sex members of a species and are elicited by simple, specific, external stimuli.

32. (E) The adrenal medulla mobilizes the body by secreting epinephrine in stressful situations.

33. (E) Gustation and olfaction are classified as chemical receptors.

34. (A) Rutherford's frequency theory of audition is best suited to the low frequency range. In the high frequency range, its implementation would be a physical impossibility for the human hearing mechanism.

35. (A) The pituitary gland controls growth and carries responsibilities for stimulating other endocrine glands.

36. (A) Experiments with rats have revealed that sexual behavior survives fairly extensive cortical destruction in males.

37. (C) The study of motivation had its primitive beginnings in the work of Freud and James.

38. (E) Freud did not speak of the manner in which habit combines with drive to express the content of emotion.

39. (C) Thorndike studied animals in puzzle boxes—his major work being *Animal Intelligence*.

40. (B) Consolidation theory expresses Hebb's view that cell assemblies are capable of "self re-exciting" or reverberating to establish memory trace.

41. (E) The quotation most directly constitutes a definition of a species.

42. (D) The normal developmental age range during which a child could be expected to master clock-time concepts would be between five and six years.

43. (C) Reaction time decreases with age up to approximately thirty years, beginning a pattern of increase beyond this age.

44. (D) Ossicles deal with amplification, and actual nerve impulse transformation occurs in the cochlea.

45. (B) Brain stem transections in animals reveal that *organization* of intense emotional responses apparently occurs at a level above the midbrain. Rage response, for instance, becomes bits of response that are disorganized.

46. (D) The terminal point for efferent fibers is muscles or glands.

47. (D) Tolman summarized Watson's definition of emotions in terms of stimuli and responses but, of course, took issue with the Watson definition.

48. (B) The term *effectors* collectively describes muscles and glands.

49. (B) The Ames distorted room was designed to test size constancy.

50. (C) Restricting visual input to a specific point on the retina causes gradual and complete stimulus fading. During normal vision, this phenomenon is avoided by small eye movements made without the viewer's conscious awareness.

51. (D) LSD has been found to produce a cognitive experience similar to psychosis.

52. (C) Turtles, fish, monkeys, and humans provide good evidence of color vision, but rodents are deficient in this area.

53. (B) The abrupt, delineated line "block-out" is characteristic of nerve damage—hearing loss evidenced in specific frequency ranges.

54. (A) Ossification is evidenced by hearing loss throughout all frequency ranges.

55. (C) This curve represents far more acuteness than would be true for humans in either the lower or upper frequency ranges.

56. (A) The effects of aging would be equivalent to the ossification hearing loss.

57. (B) Within the temporal lobe lie cerebral responsibilities for audition.

58. (D) Within the occipital lobe lie cerebral responsibilities for vision.

59. (E) The cerebellum is responsible for muscle coordination.

60. (C) In walking from hot sand onto cool grass, the grass provides negative reinforcement—removal of an aversive stimulus.

61. (B) In his work with children, Bandura has found that observation of aggressive models can prompt aggressive behavior by the observer.

62. (C) A verbatim reading of test-taking instructions is indicative of standardization—the effort to be certain that each test taker has an equivalent testing situation.

63. (C) During the third through eighth week of pregnancy, a developing child would be described as being in the embryo stage.

64. (E) Developmental research has found evidence of a relationship between anxiety in the expectant mother and the incidence of crying behavior in the newborn.

65. (E) Cretinism is a mental-physical disorder resulting from thyroid deficiency at an early age. Children with this problem generally have low intelligence.

66. (C) Hopi Indian children—strapped on their mothers' backs with no opportunity to practice walking skills—were found to walk as early as children who had such practice opportunity. The finding suggested that walking was primarily a function of maturation.

67. (E) Retinal disparity and convergence are not among the questions examined with the visual cliff. Primary emphasis rests with questions regarding the innate capacities for depth perception.

68. (C) Children from father-present home settings have the highest incidence of aggressive behavior—perhaps a function of modeling and paternal discipline.

69. (E) Paivio argued that visual codes are used to store sensory information and concrete verbal information, whereas verbal codes are used to store abstract verbal information.

70. (E) Given a choice among several stimuli, a newborn prefers pictures of the human face.

71. (B) The newborn demonstrates some irregularities in respiration.

72. (E) Loftus and her colleagues found that eyewitness testimony is prominently affected by bias in question wording, false information injected into questions, and inferences made to fill memory gaps. If, for instance, you asked a witness how fast the white sports car was going when it *hit* the red sedan, you will get a very different speed answer than if you ask how fast the white sports car was going when it *smashed* into the red sedan. (Note, too, that this "I only," "I and III only," and so forth, is an answer format you can expect to find on some questions in the GRE exam.)

73. (B) In operant-instrumental conditioning, reinforcement increases the frequency of the response associated with it.

74. (E)   A person with an IQ of 60 is in the mildly retarded classification, which spans the 50 to 70 IQ range.

75. (E)   A schema is a general knowledge framework (or collection of facts) that bias our expectations about objects and events in order to help us interpret, organize, and remember those events.

76. (C)   Correlation is related to predictability. One indication of this relationship is the predictive validity concept.

77. (E)   Mean and standard deviation are the most common expressions of central tendency and variability, respectively.

78. (A)   In developmental psychology, the first two years after birth are critical to self-concept formation.

79. (A)   The syllogism is a form of deductive thinking.

80. (B)   In the first three months after birth, a child can be expected to develop the capacity to raise its head to look at something.

81. (A)   In associative learning our response or feeling is related to the outcome that followed this behavior in the past. Salivation in the knowledge that a good dinner is coming would be associative. Cognitive learning refers to complex reasoning-type tasks. In the answer, the situation was associated with danger in the past, so we feel the anxious expectation of danger in that situation now.

82. (A)   When stimuli similar to the original CS now elicit the CR, stimulus generalization has occurred.

83. (A)   The expression "learning how to learn" refers to the development of learning sets.

84. (B)   The task requires extrapolation, that is, inference from known data.

85. (A)   Jones's studies find early maturity advantageous among males.

86. (A)   The period of the embryo spans the end of the second week to the end of the second month of pregnancy.

87. (A)   A similar-items list is more difficult to learn than a dissimilar-items list because distinctions are more difficult to make.

88. (E)   One of the major distinctions in cytology is between germ cells and body cells.

89. (E)   Watson places primary importance upon environmental influences. He said, in effect, that if you were to give him a child shortly after birth, he would make that child anything you wanted it to be.

90. (D)   Classical conditioning requires that the CS have no innate or original reinforcing qualities in its own right.

91. (D)   Classical conditioning research has found a half-second interval between CS and UCS onset to be most effective.

92. (E)   Cell mass differentiation into three distinct layers occurs during the embryonic period.

93. (A) Posed as an alternative to the dual-process theory of memory, it suggests that the short-term/long-term phenomena can be explained by the level of processing. Initially we analyze information in very surface-characteristic ways (for example, its visual properties). Only later do we analyze its meaning, its relationships, and so on. These deeper-level analyses facilitate its memory retention.

94. (D) The field theorist emphasizes the role of learning in cognitive processes.

95. (C) One of the primary detrimental effects that anxiety can have upon learning is to reduce a person's ability to discriminate clearly.

96. (C) The von Restorff effect suggests a prepotent stimulus—some distinct quality about a particular stimulus in a series that makes that stimulus stand out from the others (e.g., difference in size, a number in the midst of a word list, or a pinup in the midst of a series of automobile pictures).

97. (C) *Split-half* refers to test reliability and has nothing to do with experimental approaches to recall.

98. (D) Frenkel and Brunswik have found attitudes toward authority to be the single most important factor distinguishing prejudiced from tolerant adolescents.

99. (C) Moderate anxiety in a child may facilitate the learning of simple tasks but will prove detrimental to the learning of difficult tasks.

100. (D) Eye color is a singly determined genetic characteristic.

101. (C) Two of the four possible genetic combinations for male children will produce color blindness. Color blindness is a sex-linked genetic characteristic—females act as carriers, but the characteristic itself, when present, appears in males.

102. (B) A child's differentiation and consequent fear of strangers generally develops in the six-to-seventh month age range.

103. (D) Evidence for mental rotation and scanning with the "mind's eye" supports the idea that visual memories, or images, exist and are processed in ways similar to actual perceived objects.

104. (B) The Stanford-Binet Intelligence Test relies heavily on the verbal abilities of the test taker.

105. (D) Idea and hypothesis generation are parts of the inductive phase within problem-solving processes.

106. (B) The heights of kindergarten-aged children are positively correlated with comparative adult heights.

107. (B) Kendler's research suggests that single unit S-R cognitive mechanisms precede mediational processes in a child's conceptual development.

108. (B) In the newborn's second year, rate of growth is slower than in the first year.

109. (E) Among this group, only Scott has conducted imprinting research. All the other groups of names contain at least two research names in imprinting.

110. (B) In the Babkin response, a child's mouth opens wide and its head turns to the midline.

111. (A) Male sex determination is accomplished by the Y chromosome.

112. (A) In the Guilford model for problem solving, input occurs first (followed by filtering, cognition, and production—with evaluation available between steps).

113. (D) Tolman's work is associated with purposive behavior and place learning.

114. (C) The term *fractional anticipatory goal response* is a reference to CR.

115. (A) Hull believed that no response could occur without reinforcement (*K* within the formula, symbolizing response incentive).

116. (D) In Piaget's classification system, the concrete operations period is the point during which the child learns language and the logic of classification.

117. (D) Hunter's double alternation method requires an animal to remember which direction it turned on each of the two preceding trials in order to make the correct current-trial response.

118. (A) Craik and Lockhart demonstrated that memory is superior when it is encoded at a deep (semantic) level than at a surface (physical) level.

119. (D) Dollard and Miller would see anger-anxiety conflict as more likely to occur during the toilet-training period.

120. (B) "Tailing off" to the right would indicate positive skew.

121. (A) The servant was classically conditioning fear to the conditioned stimulus of coughing. Next time it rained he planned to cough quite audibly and watch the cats run.

122. (D) When earlier learning is interfered with by later learning, the direction is retroactive and the effect is inhibition.

123. (B) Compared with percept, a visual image is more labile, less vivid, less detailed, and holds the potential for becoming associated with other objects and images.

124. (D) Stanley Milgram has developed the theory of "overload" and has outlined its implications for human behavior in the urban environment. Among those implications is a tendency not to speak to other persons on a city street nor to pick up trash or offer to help a pedestrian in distress. Each of these settings threatens to overload the individual's "system" and capacity to cope. To avoid such overload, the individual limits and restricts inputs.

125. (A) The greatest dissonance would be created by the one-dollar payment. It is the smallest amount of money available in this situation and gives a person the least external justification for telling a lie.

126. (B) Judges expressing their own personal responses to the statements themselves would be characteristic of the Likert scale.

127. (A) Freud sees a giving-type relationship within the genital stage. At this point, sexual relationships have moved beyond the selfish narcissism characteristic of the phallic stage.

128. (E) Existentialism sees humans as free to make their own choices and, in effect, act as masters of their fates.

129. (E) Attitudes contain cognitive, emotional, and behavioral components. A stereotype component does not constitute a general characteristic of attitudes.

130. (A) Judging personality on the basis of facial expression is an example of physiognomy.

131. (D) Wechsler Scales have no direct relationship to creativity. Although creative expression is generally accompanied by above average intelligence, a person's level of intelligence has not been proven to be an accurate predictor of creativity.

132. (D) Verbal comprehension can be expected to continue improving after age thirty-five while other abilities such as associative memory, spatial relations, and so on, begin gradual declines.

133. (E) When a general description is given—as in astrology—there is an individual tendency to apply the description to oneself. Hence, astrology thrives, as does the Barnum comment that "There's a sucker born every minute."

134. (B) Homans' anticipatory socialization refers to a person's adopting social mores characteristic of a higher social level—toward which that person aspires.

135. (D) McKinley and Hathaway developed the MMPI but had no involvement in the development of the 16 PF scale.

136. (A) Cattell, Eysenck, and Goldstein all espouse factor analytic approaches to the study of personality.

137. (C) The Strong-Campbell interest test makes occupational correlations, and the Kuder preference test puts responses in broad area categories.

138. (B) Persons committing a crime of passion are among those with the least likelihood of committing any subsequent offenses.

139. (D) Mortimer is demonstrating what Hollander calls independence. He wears red shirts when they are both "in" and not "in"—simply because he likes them. Conformity would change systematically in the direction of the "in" style, and anticonformity would change systematically against it.

140. (A) The technique being used was drawing heavily upon Brehm's theory of reactance. In this approach the change agent (salesperson in our example) asserts what the person (e.g., retailer) already agrees with, but the assertion is made in absolute, unqualified-statement terms. Induced to disagree mildly with the unqualified statements, the person is speaking against her own attitude and is weakening support for it. The change agent will then proceed to use the same approach with more strongly held attitudes in the area where change is being sought.

141. (A) The theory underlying this approach to attitude change is cognitive dissonance. In this instance, people who dislike beef liver are being asked to design and deliver a talk on its prominent advantages. Their talk

preparation and the talk itself are very much in contrast with their own beliefs about beef liver. Festinger's theory of cognitive dissonance would indicate that their attitude will move in the direction of their behavior. The people who prepare and deliver the talks will themselves develop a more favorable attitude toward beef liver.

142. (E) Prefrontal lobotomy—excision or removal of parts of the pre-frontal lobes in severe cases of mental disturbance—has long since become extinct in therapeutic practice.

143. (A) Adler replaced Freud's libido concept with his own concept of superiority striving.

144. (A) Kinesics is the study of nonverbal communication within body movements.

145. (C) Jung viewed archetypes as innate concepts being passed from generation to generation within a species. He placed the infant's natural response to mother closeness in this category.

146. (E) Bem found that persons sex-typed on the Bem Sex Role Inventory tended to recall in gender-clusters rather than randomly when recalling a list of words (the list having equal numbers of gender neutral, masculine, and feminine words). Persons androgynous on the Inventory did not recall words in gender-clusters.

147. (C) Among personality approaches, behaviorism is supported by the largest body of research evidence.

148. (D) Developed in the same manner as the Thurstone scale, the Remmers Generalized Thurstone Scale contained a standard grouping of statements that could be used for attitude measurement on virtually any topic.

149. (B) In a nonzero sum game, both participants may win or lose simultaneously.

150. (C) Festinger formulated the theory of cognitive dissonance.

151. (B) Wolpe paired removal of an aversive stimulus with an anxiety-reducing word. He theorized that the word would have calming effects even when the aversive stimulus was no longer present. The word served as negative reinforcement.

152. (A) Classified as a sociopathic personality disturbance, transvestism involves sexual gratification obtained from wearing underclothes of the opposite sex.

153. (E) Sybil is said to have manifested sixteen different personalities—a very rare form of dissociative identity disorder.

154. (C) Eysenck believes introverts have greater autonomic reactivity than extroverts.

155. (B) In contrast to tranquilizers, sedatives have drowsiness-inducing characteristics.

156. (A) Fear relates to realistic environmental danger; anxiety is, in effect, unrealistic fear.

157. (B) Chlorpromazine (Thorazine) is a tranquilizer widely used in the treatment of schizophrenia.

158. (D) Room temperature was not an independent variable within Masserman's experimental designs.

159. (C) Psychotomimetic drugs (hallucinogens) resemble schizophrenic-type reactions.

160. (E) Repression, fantasy, regression, and continual wandering are among withdrawal reactions, but paranoia is not.

161. (C) The schizophrenic exhibits withdrawal from interpersonal relationships.

162. (E) The reduced-reinforcement model of depression (Lewinsohn and others) indicates that depression is related to a reduction of positive reinforcement in one's environment. Sympathy becomes a reinforcement for the depression itself.

163. (A) Range is the simplest and least precise measure of variability.

164. (E) Agoraphobia is a neurotic fear of open places.

165. (A) A pyromaniac has an irresistible impulse to set fires.

166. (C) The Osgood Semantic Differential Scale is used primarily in attitude measurement. It is not an instrument for clinical assessment.

167. (A) Transference and resistance are terms commonly used within psychoanalysis.

168. (B) Though each score in the distribution has been changed through the addition of a constant (the number 7), the variability of the distribution itself is unchanged. Therefore, the standard deviation remains unchanged from its original value.

169. (E) Mainlining heroin—injecting into a vein—leads to prominent and rapid increase in dosages and intense, excruciating pain and discomfort upon withdrawal.

170. (A) Antipsychotic agents—chlorpromazine, haloperidol, clozapine, resperidol—have been shown to be effective in cases of schizophrenia. They are believed to suppress the transmission efficiency of the neurotransmitter called dopamine.

171. (D) An experimental design incorporates all aspects of this description.

172. (C) Within a specific problem area, a theory carries the function of explaining and relating observed facts.

173. (D) Of the forms of sexual deviation listed, pedophilia (in which an adult desires or engages in sexual relations with a child) is the most difficult to treat.

174. (C) Depression of whatever intensity is classified as a mood disorder within DSM-IV.

175. (D) The life-history method is a longitudinal research approach.

176. (C) It could be suggested that Michelangelo's frustrated desire for closeness with his mother was expressed in painting. This would be an example of sublimation—redirection of an unacceptable or ungratified impulse into a higher cultural contribution.

177. (B) Bettelheim worked with schizophrenic children and concentrated much effort on study and analysis of their drawings.

178. (A) Norepinephrine and serotonin are the two neurotransmitters credited with a central role in affective disorders such as depression. Several antidepressant drugs facilitate the activity of these neurotransmitters, most notably the "second generation" serotonin reuptake blockers.

179. (D) The score of 130 is two standard deviations above the mean—a point beyond which only about 2 percent of the scores in a distribution will occur.

180. (E) The experiment has a three-factor design—sex, age, hair color.

181. (B) A three-factor factorial design can be used if only one measure (score) is to be analyzed for each subject. If trials were involved, for instance, a three-factor mixed design with repeated measures on one factor would be needed.

182. (D) Freud wrote *The Psychopathology of Everyday Life* to describe the manner in which apparent accidents, slips of the tongue, and the like betray id impulses.

183. (D) Unfortunate stereotyping became associated with the terms *moron*, *imbecile*, and *idiot*, prompting a change to the educable-trainable-nontrainable categories.

184. (C) Human engineering control principles indicate that a system is best in which the operation of the controls imposes optimal strain on the operator consistent with the required degree of accuracy. Optimal strain is not to be confused with painful stress; rather it involves the degree of stimulation necessary for alertness and accuracy.

185. (B) The fact that the judges' rankings are completely reversed is indicative of strong (in this case, perfect) negative correlation.

186. (B) The example utilizes rank order and therefore would call upon the Spearman Rank-Order Correlation method for analysis.

187. (D) This correlation coefficient would be –1.0—a perfect negative correlation.

188. (E) The human engineering term *shape coding* applies to knob appearance and contour—enabling the operator to locate the correct knob by feel, if necessary.

189. (C) Presenting the "bare bones" of a managerial situation and adding that additional information can only be obtained by asking questions is an example of the incident method in managerial training techniques.

190. (A) A company screening test for executive trainees that involved handling, sorting, and dealing with an array of items in a sample executive in-basket would be an aptitude test.

191. (D)   A test-retest, repeated-measures design contains impressive subject variability control because the subjects, in effect, act as their own controls. This relieves the experimenter of the problem, or possibility, that the subjects' backgrounds may somehow contribute to any differences found.

192. (E)   To spot the fast-moving items in their product line, an industry would concentrate on use of mode—the most frequently occurring score(s).

193. (A)   Of the central tendency measures, the mean moves most noticeably in the direction of the skew.

194. (B)   With only a few hours allotted for test study, massed practice would be the best approach. Given better study planning, distributed practice would be the more effective method.

195. (B)   To determine whether a significant difference in weight exists between two randomly selected groups of eighteen-year-olds, a person would use the *t*-test for independent means.

196. (A)   Matched pairing has occurred in the initial grouping—an indication that the design will utilize a *t*-test for related measures.

197. (C)   Comparison with the national average of the weight found in the specific groups of eighteen-year-old boys would utilize the *t*-test for sample and population means. In this instance, the national average constitutes the population mean.

198. (B)   Researchers have found that rest periods enhance performance on vigilance tasks.

199. (E)   One of the most prominent researchers in the area of leadership, Fiedler has used the Least Preferred Coworker technique to identify task-centered and people-centered leaders.

200. (C)   McLuhan's framework classifies television as a cool medium—not information intensive, a characteristic required for a hot medium.

Test 2: Evaluating Your Score

Abbreviation
Guide for
Quick
Reference
(Translation)

PC:	Physiological/Comparative
SnP:	Sensation/Perception
LM:	Learning/Motivation/Emotion
CHL:	Cognition/Complex Human Learning
D:	Developmental
PrS:	Personality/Social
PyCl:	Psychopathology/Clinical
M:	Methodology
Ap:	Applied

TALLY CHART

- Checkmark to the left of each number you missed.
- In the column to the right of the number note the area your check-marked question is in.
- Move your check mark to the appropriate area column.
- Sum your check marks in each area column.
- Carry these sums to the blanks on the next scaling page.

Q#		PC	SnP	LM	CHL	D	PrS	PyCl	M	Ap
1	PC									
2	SnP									
3	PC									
4	SnP									
5	M									
6	M									
7	M									
8	LM									
9	PC									
10	PC									
11	SnP									
12	SnP									
13	SnP									
14	PC									
15	PC									
16	PC									
17	LM									
18	SnP									
19	SnP									
20	SnP									
21	PC									
22	PC									
23	PC									
24	PC									
25	SnP									
26	PC									
27	PC									

Q#		PC	SnP	LM	CHL	D	PrS	PyCl	M	Ap
28	PC									
29	LM									
30	SnP									
31	LM									
32	PC									
33	SnP									
34	SnP									
35	PC									
36	LM									
37	LM									
38	LM									
39	LM									
40	LM									
41	PC									
42	SnP									
43	SnP									
44	SnP									
45	PC									
46	PC									
47	LM									
48	PC									
49	SnP									
50	SnP									
51	PC									
52	SnP									
53	SnP									
54	SnP									
55	SnP									
56	SnP									
57	PC									
58	PC									
59	PC									
60	LM									
61	D									
62	M									
63	D									
64	D									
65	D									
66	D									
67	D									
68	D									
69	CHL									
70	D									
71	D									

Q#		PC	SnP	LM	CHL	D	PrS	PyCl	M	Ap
72	LM									
73	LM									
74	CHL									
75	CHL									
76	M									
77	M									
78	D									
79	CHL									
80	D									
81	LM									
82	LM									
83	LM									
84	CHL									
85	D									
86	D									
87	CHL									
88	D									
89	LM									
90	LM									
91	LM									
92	D									
93	CHL									
94	CHL									
95	CHL									
96	CHL									
97	CHL									
98	D									
99	D									
100	D									
101	D									
102	D									
103	CHL									
104	CHL									
105	CHL									
106	D									
107	CHL									
108	D									
109	D									
110	D									
111	D									
112	CHL									
113	LM									
114	LM									
115	LM									

Q#		PC	SnP	LM	CHL	D	PrS	PyCl	M	Ap
116	CHL									
117	CHL									
118	CHL									
119	D									
120	M									
121	LM									
122	LM									
123	CHL									
124	PrS									
125	PrS									
126	PrS									
127	PrS									
128	PrS									
129	PrS									
130	PrS									
131	Ap									
132	Ap									
133	PrS									
134	PrS									
135	PrS									
136	PrS									
137	PrS									
138	Ap									
139	PrS									
140	PrS									
141	PrS									
142	Ap									
143	PrS									
144	PrS									
145	PrS									
146	PrS									
147	PrS									
148	PrS									
149	PrS									
150	PrS									
151	PyCl									
152	PyCl									
153	PyCl									
154	PyCl									
155	PyCl									
156	PyCl									
157	PyCl									
158	PyCl									
159	PyCl									

Q#		PC	SnP	LM	CHL	D	PrS	PyCl	M	Ap
160	PyCl									
161	PyCl									
162	PyCl									
163	M									
164	PyCl									
165	PyCl									
166	PyCl									
167	PyCl									
168	M									
169	PyCl									
170	PyCl									
171	M									
172	M									
173	PyCl									
174	PyCl									
175	M									
176	PyCl									
177	PyCl									
178	PyCl									
179	M									
180	M									
181	M									
182	Ap									
183	Ap									
184	Ap									
185	M									
186	M									
187	M									
188	Ap									
189	Ap									
190	Ap									
191	Ap									
192	Ap									
193	M									
194	Ap									
195	M									
196	M									
197	M									
198	Ap									
199	Ap									
200	Ap									
Sum										

Test Score Scaling

Now you have the process down pat. Just bring your tally sums forward from the previous page and tuck them into the blanks below. Then see how you're stacking up with those 75th percentiles.

PC Area: 24 – _____ (your number missed) = _____ // 18 = 75th percentile

SnP Area: 22 – _____ (your number missed) = _____ // 17 = 75th percentile

LM Area: 24 – _____ (your number missed) = _____ // 18 = 75th percentile

CHL Area: 20 – _____ (your number missed) = _____ // 15 = 75th percentile

D Area: 26 – _____ (your number missed) = _____ // 20 = 75th percentile

PrS Area: 23 – _____ (your number missed) = _____ // 17 = 75th percentile

PyCl Area: 23 – _____ (your number missed) = _____ // 17 = 75th percentile

M Area: 22 – _____ (your number missed) = _____ // 17 = 75th percentile

Ap Area: 16 – _____ (your number missed) = _____ // 12 = 75th percentile

Test 3: Answer Grid

1. Ⓐ Ⓑ Ⓒ Ⓓ Ⓔ	51. Ⓐ Ⓑ Ⓒ Ⓓ Ⓔ	101. Ⓐ Ⓑ Ⓒ Ⓓ Ⓔ	151. Ⓐ Ⓑ Ⓒ Ⓓ Ⓔ
2. Ⓐ Ⓑ Ⓒ Ⓓ Ⓔ	52. Ⓐ Ⓑ Ⓒ Ⓓ Ⓔ	102. Ⓐ Ⓑ Ⓒ Ⓓ Ⓔ	152. Ⓐ Ⓑ Ⓒ Ⓓ Ⓔ
3. Ⓐ Ⓑ Ⓒ Ⓓ Ⓔ	53. Ⓐ Ⓑ Ⓒ Ⓓ Ⓔ	103. Ⓐ Ⓑ Ⓒ Ⓓ Ⓔ	153. Ⓐ Ⓑ Ⓒ Ⓓ Ⓔ
4. Ⓐ Ⓑ Ⓒ Ⓓ Ⓔ	54. Ⓐ Ⓑ Ⓒ Ⓓ Ⓔ	104. Ⓐ Ⓑ Ⓒ Ⓓ Ⓔ	154. Ⓐ Ⓑ Ⓒ Ⓓ Ⓔ
5. Ⓐ Ⓑ Ⓒ Ⓓ Ⓔ	55. Ⓐ Ⓑ Ⓒ Ⓓ Ⓔ	105. Ⓐ Ⓑ Ⓒ Ⓓ Ⓔ	155. Ⓐ Ⓑ Ⓒ Ⓓ Ⓔ
6. Ⓐ Ⓑ Ⓒ Ⓓ Ⓔ	56. Ⓐ Ⓑ Ⓒ Ⓓ Ⓔ	106. Ⓐ Ⓑ Ⓒ Ⓓ Ⓔ	156. Ⓐ Ⓑ Ⓒ Ⓓ Ⓔ
7. Ⓐ Ⓑ Ⓒ Ⓓ Ⓔ	57. Ⓐ Ⓑ Ⓒ Ⓓ Ⓔ	107. Ⓐ Ⓑ Ⓒ Ⓓ Ⓔ	157. Ⓐ Ⓑ Ⓒ Ⓓ Ⓔ
8. Ⓐ Ⓑ Ⓒ Ⓓ Ⓔ	58. Ⓐ Ⓑ Ⓒ Ⓓ Ⓔ	108. Ⓐ Ⓑ Ⓒ Ⓓ Ⓔ	158. Ⓐ Ⓑ Ⓒ Ⓓ Ⓔ
9. Ⓐ Ⓑ Ⓒ Ⓓ Ⓔ	59. Ⓐ Ⓑ Ⓒ Ⓓ Ⓔ	109. Ⓐ Ⓑ Ⓒ Ⓓ Ⓔ	159. Ⓐ Ⓑ Ⓒ Ⓓ Ⓔ
10. Ⓐ Ⓑ Ⓒ Ⓓ Ⓔ	60. Ⓐ Ⓑ Ⓒ Ⓓ Ⓔ	110. Ⓐ Ⓑ Ⓒ Ⓓ Ⓔ	160. Ⓐ Ⓑ Ⓒ Ⓓ Ⓔ
11. Ⓐ Ⓑ Ⓒ Ⓓ Ⓔ	61. Ⓐ Ⓑ Ⓒ Ⓓ Ⓔ	111. Ⓐ Ⓑ Ⓒ Ⓓ Ⓔ	161. Ⓐ Ⓑ Ⓒ Ⓓ Ⓔ
12. Ⓐ Ⓑ Ⓒ Ⓓ Ⓔ	62. Ⓐ Ⓑ Ⓒ Ⓓ Ⓔ	112. Ⓐ Ⓑ Ⓒ Ⓓ Ⓔ	162. Ⓐ Ⓑ Ⓒ Ⓓ Ⓔ
13. Ⓐ Ⓑ Ⓒ Ⓓ Ⓔ	63. Ⓐ Ⓑ Ⓒ Ⓓ Ⓔ	113. Ⓐ Ⓑ Ⓒ Ⓓ Ⓔ	163. Ⓐ Ⓑ Ⓒ Ⓓ Ⓔ
14. Ⓐ Ⓑ Ⓒ Ⓓ Ⓔ	64. Ⓐ Ⓑ Ⓒ Ⓓ Ⓔ	114. Ⓐ Ⓑ Ⓒ Ⓓ Ⓔ	164. Ⓐ Ⓑ Ⓒ Ⓓ Ⓔ
15. Ⓐ Ⓑ Ⓒ Ⓓ Ⓔ	65. Ⓐ Ⓑ Ⓒ Ⓓ Ⓔ	115. Ⓐ Ⓑ Ⓒ Ⓓ Ⓔ	165. Ⓐ Ⓑ Ⓒ Ⓓ Ⓔ
16. Ⓐ Ⓑ Ⓒ Ⓓ Ⓔ	66. Ⓐ Ⓑ Ⓒ Ⓓ Ⓔ	116. Ⓐ Ⓑ Ⓒ Ⓓ Ⓔ	166. Ⓐ Ⓑ Ⓒ Ⓓ Ⓔ
17. Ⓐ Ⓑ Ⓒ Ⓓ Ⓔ	67. Ⓐ Ⓑ Ⓒ Ⓓ Ⓔ	117. Ⓐ Ⓑ Ⓒ Ⓓ Ⓔ	167. Ⓐ Ⓑ Ⓒ Ⓓ Ⓔ
18. Ⓐ Ⓑ Ⓒ Ⓓ Ⓔ	68. Ⓐ Ⓑ Ⓒ Ⓓ Ⓔ	118. Ⓐ Ⓑ Ⓒ Ⓓ Ⓔ	168. Ⓐ Ⓑ Ⓒ Ⓓ Ⓔ
19. Ⓐ Ⓑ Ⓒ Ⓓ Ⓔ	69. Ⓐ Ⓑ Ⓒ Ⓓ Ⓔ	119. Ⓐ Ⓑ Ⓒ Ⓓ Ⓔ	169. Ⓐ Ⓑ Ⓒ Ⓓ Ⓔ
20. Ⓐ Ⓑ Ⓒ Ⓓ Ⓔ	70. Ⓐ Ⓑ Ⓒ Ⓓ Ⓔ	120. Ⓐ Ⓑ Ⓒ Ⓓ Ⓔ	170. Ⓐ Ⓑ Ⓒ Ⓓ Ⓔ
21. Ⓐ Ⓑ Ⓒ Ⓓ Ⓔ	71. Ⓐ Ⓑ Ⓒ Ⓓ Ⓔ	121. Ⓐ Ⓑ Ⓒ Ⓓ Ⓔ	171. Ⓐ Ⓑ Ⓒ Ⓓ Ⓔ
22. Ⓐ Ⓑ Ⓒ Ⓓ Ⓔ	72. Ⓐ Ⓑ Ⓒ Ⓓ Ⓔ	122. Ⓐ Ⓑ Ⓒ Ⓓ Ⓔ	172. Ⓐ Ⓑ Ⓒ Ⓓ Ⓔ
23. Ⓐ Ⓑ Ⓒ Ⓓ Ⓔ	73. Ⓐ Ⓑ Ⓒ Ⓓ Ⓔ	123. Ⓐ Ⓑ Ⓒ Ⓓ Ⓔ	173. Ⓐ Ⓑ Ⓒ Ⓓ Ⓔ
24. Ⓐ Ⓑ Ⓒ Ⓓ Ⓔ	74. Ⓐ Ⓑ Ⓒ Ⓓ Ⓔ	124. Ⓐ Ⓑ Ⓒ Ⓓ Ⓔ	174. Ⓐ Ⓑ Ⓒ Ⓓ Ⓔ
25. Ⓐ Ⓑ Ⓒ Ⓓ Ⓔ	75. Ⓐ Ⓑ Ⓒ Ⓓ Ⓔ	125. Ⓐ Ⓑ Ⓒ Ⓓ Ⓔ	175. Ⓐ Ⓑ Ⓒ Ⓓ Ⓔ
26. Ⓐ Ⓑ Ⓒ Ⓓ Ⓔ	76. Ⓐ Ⓑ Ⓒ Ⓓ Ⓔ	126. Ⓐ Ⓑ Ⓒ Ⓓ Ⓔ	176. Ⓐ Ⓑ Ⓒ Ⓓ Ⓔ
27. Ⓐ Ⓑ Ⓒ Ⓓ Ⓔ	77. Ⓐ Ⓑ Ⓒ Ⓓ Ⓔ	127. Ⓐ Ⓑ Ⓒ Ⓓ Ⓔ	177. Ⓐ Ⓑ Ⓒ Ⓓ Ⓔ
28. Ⓐ Ⓑ Ⓒ Ⓓ Ⓔ	78. Ⓐ Ⓑ Ⓒ Ⓓ Ⓔ	128. Ⓐ Ⓑ Ⓒ Ⓓ Ⓔ	178. Ⓐ Ⓑ Ⓒ Ⓓ Ⓔ
29. Ⓐ Ⓑ Ⓒ Ⓓ Ⓔ	79. Ⓐ Ⓑ Ⓒ Ⓓ Ⓔ	129. Ⓐ Ⓑ Ⓒ Ⓓ Ⓔ	179. Ⓐ Ⓑ Ⓒ Ⓓ Ⓔ
30. Ⓐ Ⓑ Ⓒ Ⓓ Ⓔ	80. Ⓐ Ⓑ Ⓒ Ⓓ Ⓔ	130. Ⓐ Ⓑ Ⓒ Ⓓ Ⓔ	180. Ⓐ Ⓑ Ⓒ Ⓓ Ⓔ
31. Ⓐ Ⓑ Ⓒ Ⓓ Ⓔ	81. Ⓐ Ⓑ Ⓒ Ⓓ Ⓔ	131. Ⓐ Ⓑ Ⓒ Ⓓ Ⓔ	181. Ⓐ Ⓑ Ⓒ Ⓓ Ⓔ
32. Ⓐ Ⓑ Ⓒ Ⓓ Ⓔ	82. Ⓐ Ⓑ Ⓒ Ⓓ Ⓔ	132. Ⓐ Ⓑ Ⓒ Ⓓ Ⓔ	182. Ⓐ Ⓑ Ⓒ Ⓓ Ⓔ
33. Ⓐ Ⓑ Ⓒ Ⓓ Ⓔ	83. Ⓐ Ⓑ Ⓒ Ⓓ Ⓔ	133. Ⓐ Ⓑ Ⓒ Ⓓ Ⓔ	183. Ⓐ Ⓑ Ⓒ Ⓓ Ⓔ
34. Ⓐ Ⓑ Ⓒ Ⓓ Ⓔ	84. Ⓐ Ⓑ Ⓒ Ⓓ Ⓔ	134. Ⓐ Ⓑ Ⓒ Ⓓ Ⓔ	184. Ⓐ Ⓑ Ⓒ Ⓓ Ⓔ
35. Ⓐ Ⓑ Ⓒ Ⓓ Ⓔ	85. Ⓐ Ⓑ Ⓒ Ⓓ Ⓔ	135. Ⓐ Ⓑ Ⓒ Ⓓ Ⓔ	185. Ⓐ Ⓑ Ⓒ Ⓓ Ⓔ
36. Ⓐ Ⓑ Ⓒ Ⓓ Ⓔ	86. Ⓐ Ⓑ Ⓒ Ⓓ Ⓔ	136. Ⓐ Ⓑ Ⓒ Ⓓ Ⓔ	186. Ⓐ Ⓑ Ⓒ Ⓓ Ⓔ
37. Ⓐ Ⓑ Ⓒ Ⓓ Ⓔ	87. Ⓐ Ⓑ Ⓒ Ⓓ Ⓔ	137. Ⓐ Ⓑ Ⓒ Ⓓ Ⓔ	187. Ⓐ Ⓑ Ⓒ Ⓓ Ⓔ
38. Ⓐ Ⓑ Ⓒ Ⓓ Ⓔ	88. Ⓐ Ⓑ Ⓒ Ⓓ Ⓔ	138. Ⓐ Ⓑ Ⓒ Ⓓ Ⓔ	188. Ⓐ Ⓑ Ⓒ Ⓓ Ⓔ
39. Ⓐ Ⓑ Ⓒ Ⓓ Ⓔ	89. Ⓐ Ⓑ Ⓒ Ⓓ Ⓔ	139. Ⓐ Ⓑ Ⓒ Ⓓ Ⓔ	189. Ⓐ Ⓑ Ⓒ Ⓓ Ⓔ
40. Ⓐ Ⓑ Ⓒ Ⓓ Ⓔ	90. Ⓐ Ⓑ Ⓒ Ⓓ Ⓔ	140. Ⓐ Ⓑ Ⓒ Ⓓ Ⓔ	190. Ⓐ Ⓑ Ⓒ Ⓓ Ⓔ
41. Ⓐ Ⓑ Ⓒ Ⓓ Ⓔ	91. Ⓐ Ⓑ Ⓒ Ⓓ Ⓔ	141. Ⓐ Ⓑ Ⓒ Ⓓ Ⓔ	191. Ⓐ Ⓑ Ⓒ Ⓓ Ⓔ
42. Ⓐ Ⓑ Ⓒ Ⓓ Ⓔ	92. Ⓐ Ⓑ Ⓒ Ⓓ Ⓔ	142. Ⓐ Ⓑ Ⓒ Ⓓ Ⓔ	192. Ⓐ Ⓑ Ⓒ Ⓓ Ⓔ
43. Ⓐ Ⓑ Ⓒ Ⓓ Ⓔ	93. Ⓐ Ⓑ Ⓒ Ⓓ Ⓔ	143. Ⓐ Ⓑ Ⓒ Ⓓ Ⓔ	193. Ⓐ Ⓑ Ⓒ Ⓓ Ⓔ
44. Ⓐ Ⓑ Ⓒ Ⓓ Ⓔ	94. Ⓐ Ⓑ Ⓒ Ⓓ Ⓔ	144. Ⓐ Ⓑ Ⓒ Ⓓ Ⓔ	194. Ⓐ Ⓑ Ⓒ Ⓓ Ⓔ
45. Ⓐ Ⓑ Ⓒ Ⓓ Ⓔ	95. Ⓐ Ⓑ Ⓒ Ⓓ Ⓔ	145. Ⓐ Ⓑ Ⓒ Ⓓ Ⓔ	195. Ⓐ Ⓑ Ⓒ Ⓓ Ⓔ
46. Ⓐ Ⓑ Ⓒ Ⓓ Ⓔ	96. Ⓐ Ⓑ Ⓒ Ⓓ Ⓔ	146. Ⓐ Ⓑ Ⓒ Ⓓ Ⓔ	196. Ⓐ Ⓑ Ⓒ Ⓓ Ⓔ
47. Ⓐ Ⓑ Ⓒ Ⓓ Ⓔ	97. Ⓐ Ⓑ Ⓒ Ⓓ Ⓕ	147. Ⓐ Ⓑ Ⓒ Ⓓ Ⓔ	197. Ⓐ Ⓑ Ⓒ Ⓓ Ⓔ
48. Ⓐ Ⓑ Ⓒ Ⓓ Ⓔ	98. Ⓐ Ⓑ Ⓒ Ⓓ Ⓔ	148. Ⓐ Ⓑ Ⓒ Ⓓ Ⓔ	198. Ⓐ Ⓑ Ⓒ Ⓓ Ⓔ
49. Ⓐ Ⓑ Ⓒ Ⓓ Ⓔ	99. Ⓐ Ⓑ Ⓒ Ⓓ Ⓔ	149. Ⓐ Ⓑ Ⓒ Ⓓ Ⓔ	199. Ⓐ Ⓑ Ⓒ Ⓓ Ⓔ
50. Ⓐ Ⓑ Ⓒ Ⓓ Ⓔ	100. Ⓐ Ⓑ Ⓒ Ⓓ Ⓔ	150. Ⓐ Ⓑ Ⓒ Ⓓ Ⓔ	200. Ⓐ Ⓑ Ⓒ Ⓓ Ⓔ

Test 3

Time: 170 minutes

Directions: Each of the following questions contains five possible responses. Read the question carefully and select the response that you feel is most appropriate. Then completely darken the oval on your answer grid that corresponds with your choice.

1. Preparing the body "for fight or flight" is the function of the

    (A) pituitary gland
    (B) parathyroid gland
    (C) parasympathetic nervous system
    (D) adrenal medulla
    (E) pancreas

2. Audition encompasses several of the following stimulus dimensions. The entry that should *not* be included among these is

    (A) intensity
    (B) duration
    (C) frequency
    (D) saturation
    (E) locus

3. In Miller's classic black-white straight alley

    (A) successive approximation was observed for the first time
    (B) behavior chaining reached complete development
    (C) the strength of the acquired-fear drive was observed
    (D) the response continued only in the presence of the unconditioned stimulus
    (E) positive reinforcement was given for the correct response

4. Which one of the following is a correct statement?

    (A) Whether a neuron is at rest or conducting is determined by the ionic flux of electrically charged particles (ions).
    (B) An important aspect of excitatory potential is the incremental firing principle.
    (C) Excitatory potential is self-propagating.
    (D) Neural impulse transmission is completely chemical in nature.
    (E) IPSP means Inhibitory Presynaptic Potential.

Questions 5–7 are based on the following information.

The subjects were adult males, ages twenty to twenty-five. For this procedure, each subject was attached to GSR monitoring devices, and a shock electrode was placed on each one's left forefinger. Subjects individually received twenty presentations of a tone. In ten of the presentations, the tone was 700 Hz and was followed by electric shock to the left forefinger. In the remaining ten presentations, the tone was 3,500 Hz and was not followed by shock.

Presentations were randomized for each subject, making it impossible to predict what tone would be presented on any given trial. GSR to each tonal presentation was recorded, and the results are presented in the following table.

AMPLITUDE OF GSR

Trial Block	Tone 1 *700 Hz*	Tone 2 *3,500 Hz*
1	10	10
2	8	13
3	6	15
4	5	18
5	4	20

5. Between Tone 1 and Tone 2, GSR across trials shows

   (A) strong positive correlation
   (B) weak positive correlation
   (C) strong negative correlation
   (D) weak negative correlation
   (E) no correlation

6. The conditioned stimulus in the experiment was

   (A) shock to left forefinger   (B) GSR   (C) age of subjects
   (D) tone   (E) trials

7. Which of the following phenomena was evident across trial blocks?

   (A) stimulus generalization
   (B) stimulus discrimination
   (C) counterconditioning
   (D) reciprocal inhibition
   (E) extinction

8. Which one of the following is included within the parietal lobe of the human brain?

   (A) motor cortex   (B) reticular activating system
   (C) cerebellum   (D) auditory area   (E) somesthetic cortex

9. Depth perception relies heavily on which one of the following binocular cues?

   (A) accommodation   (B) interposition   (C) phi phenomenon
   (D) convergence   (E) movement

10. Schachter and Singer's work with epinephrine demonstrated

    (A) the prevalence of an anger emotion over emotions of happiness
    (B) the validity of the Yerkes-Dodson law
    (C) the importance of external cues
    (D) the predominance of internal cues
    (E) the validity of the Cannon-Washburn theory

11. In contrast with an emotion, a mood is

    (A) more intense and longer in duration
    (B) less intense and shorter in duration
    (C) more intense and shorter in duration
    (D) less intense and longer in duration
    (E) identical in all respects

12. One of the commonly demonstrated effects in strong support of the trichromatic theory has been the

    (A) phi phenomenon
    (B) autokinetic effect
    (C) black-white phenomenon
    (D) negative afterimage
    (E) Muller/Lyer phenomenon

13. Sleep apnea is

    (A) the technical name for sleepwalking
    (B) cessation of breathing during sleep
    (C) non-REM sleep
    (D) narcolepsy
    (E) insomnia

14. Within the cell body of a neuron, a high concentration of positive ions places the neuron in a state described as

    (A) homeostatic
    (B) conducting
    (C) efferent
    (D) afferent
    (E) innervative

15. Striated muscles

    (A) are synonymous with smooth muscles
    (B) produce stomach contractions
    (C) are prominently involved in voluntary muscle activity
    (D) produce heart-rate changes
    (E) supply the viscera

16. An experimenter switches food reinforcement from the right branch to the left branch of a Y-maze, and the rat continues down the nonrein-forced branch for several trials following the switch. Spence believes that this occurs because of

    (A) the rat's low level of intelligence
    (B) the need to extinguish completely right-branch response before left-branch can be effectively learned
    (C) counterconditioning
    (D) functional fixedness
    (E) extreme hunger, which causes irrational behavior in the animal

17. The spinal cord does *not*

    (A) relay nerve impulses
    (B) process sensory impulses
    (C) have any function in reflexive behavior
    (D) contain spinal nerves
    (E) control primitive emotions

18. Walter comes to the clinic with a speech impairment resulting from brain damage. One can be reasonably certain that damage has occurred in the

    (A) left cerebral hemisphere
    (B) right cerebral hemisphere
    (C) reticular formation
    (D) cerebellum
    (E) corpus callosum

19. Which of the following is *not* among stimulus-related perceptual phenomena believed to be generally experienced?

    (A) closure   (B) grouping   (C) divergence
    (D) contrast   (E) phi phenomenon

20. GSR measures

    (A) general synaptic response
    (B) specificity of auditory response
    (C) sweat-gland activity
    (D) kinesthetic reflex
    (E) Down Syndrome

21. Aviators are being briefed on a night bombing mission just prior to flight takeoff. They wear red goggles in the lighted briefing room; they remove the goggles as they head toward their planes. This has permitted them both to see in the briefing and have their eyes dark-adapted as they move out into the night. The goggles-wearing procedure has utilized the principle of

    (A) trichromatic vision
    (B) rod/cone vision
    (C) complementarity
    (D) negative after-effect
    (E) eidetic imagery

22. *Purposive Behavior in Animals and Men* was the major work written by

    (A) Skinner
    (B) Thorndike
    (C) Pavlov
    (D) Tolman
    (E) Woodworth

23. Which one of the following is a function of thyroxine?

    (A) body metabolism-physical growth
    (B) skeletal growth
    (C) sexual arousal
    (D) gamete production
    (E) reticular formation activation

24. Which of the following would enable you to have the Ponzo illusion?

    (A) set of railroad tracks extending off in the distance
    (B) two parallel lines
    (C) center circle surrounded by five smaller circles
    (D) horizontal line intersecting a vertical line
    (E) three-dimensional box

25. Accommodation refers to the activity of

    (A) transmitting binaural sound to the oval windows
    (B) the Meissner corpuscle in pilotropism
    (C) echolocation
    (D) change in lens shape to focus on nearby or distant objects
    (E) perception of object constancy regardless of retinal image size

26. The electroencephalogram relies upon

    (A) signals from a single electrode attached to the forehead
    (B) signals from several pairs of electrodes attached to various parts of
        the scalp
    (C) monitoring of rapid eye movements
    (D) pilograph rhythms
    (E) a frequency rhythm not to exceed six cycles per second

27. In studying bodily reactions to stress, Hans Selye found the initial reaction to be

    (A) resistance
    (B) exhaustion
    (C) alarm
    (D) ulcers
    (E) migraines

28. A subject placed in an elaborate sensory deprivation setting for a remuneration of $100 per day will

    (A) remain in such a setting indefinitely
    (B) usually endure such a setting only one to two weeks
    (C) usually endure such a setting only two to three weeks
    (D) experience motion parallax
    (E) encounter the "phantom limb" phenomenon

29. The adage that a watched pot never boils is given confirmation in the experimental findings that time passage seems

    (A) faster than normal for persons trying hard to complete a task in order to reach a desired goal
    (B) slower than normal for persons trying hard to complete a task in order to reach a desired goal
    (C) faster for younger than for older children
    (D) slower for persons experiencing success than for those experiencing failure
    (E) longer for cooking tasks

30. The Necker cube illusion involves

    (A) a reversible figure
    (B) a square where one line does not reach the corner
    (C) a multicolored cube with each side a different color
    (D) a checkerboard-type design
    (E) a circle within a square

31. The primaries in subtractive color mixing are

    (A) violet, orange, green
    (B) blue, yellow, red
    (C) blue, green, red
    (D) green, orange, red
    (E) green, yellow, red

32. An involuntary response to stress has just occurred involving the digestive and the circulatory systems. Emphasis would center on which of the following parts of the autonomic nervous system?

    (A) central   (B) peripheral   (C) sympathetic
    (D) parasympathetic   (E) somatic

33. "Any response to a situation will, other things being equal, be more strongly connected with the situation in proportion to the number of times it has been connected with that situation and to the average vigor and duration of the connections." The preceding is a quote from

    (A) Thorndike's Law of Exercise
    (B) Lewin's Field Theory
    (C) Skinner's Law of Reinforcement
    (D) Markel's Law of Diminishing Returns
    (E) Watson's Law of Contiguity

34. Hobson and McCarley have advanced which theory of dreams and their origin?

    (A) physiological   (B) Freudian   (C) Gestalt
    (D) phenomenological   (E) structuralist

35. The opponent process theory has been prominent in the field of

    (A) vision   (B) sensory processes   (C) emotion
    (D) learning   (E) neurosis

36. In animal laboratory experiments relating to food intake, it has been found that

    (A) there is no apparent organismic regulation of meal size
    (B) animals have a tendency to keep their caloric intact constant
    (C) animals made artificially fat by insulin injection will maintain their overweight indefinitely
    (D) there is no relationship between animal food intake and the organism's energy requirements
    (E) there is high negative correlation between the amount of food consumed and water intake

37. The glandular system "control center" is the

    (A) thyroid   (B) pancreas   (C) parathyroid
    (D) adrenal cortex   (E) hypothalamus

38. The distinctly male sex hormone is

    (A) estrogen   (B) progesterone   (C) prolactin
    (D) androgen   (E) dextrin

39. By which of the following properties of near and distant objects does motion parallax enable a person to judge distance?

    (A) relative brightness
    (B) texture gradient
    (C) relative movement
    (D) relative closure
    (E) movement illusion

40. Compared with the use of only a starting gun or command, preparatory instructions such as "On your mark, get set, go!"

    (A) have no effect upon reaction time
    (B) shorten reaction time
    (C) lengthen reaction time
    (D) shorten reaction time for the experienced runner while lengthening it for the less-experienced one
    (E) shorten reaction time for the less-experienced runner while lengthening if for the experienced one

41. Visual and thermal reaction time

    (A) are faster when more sensory space is covered by the stimulus
    (B) are slower when more sensory space is covered by the stimulus
    (C) are not affected by more sensory space being covered by the stimulus
    (D) always occur together
    (E) depend heavily upon circadian rhythm

42. The suggestion that the drive concept be replaced with a concept of optimum level of arousal has been advanced by

(A) Hess   (B) Atkinson   (C) Hebb
(D) McDougall   (E) McClelland

43. The group that contains a term not mentioned within Murray's list of needs is

(A) nurturance, autonomy
(B) aggression, abasement
(C) dominance, affiliation
(D) deference, achievement
(E) passivity, destruction

44. In trapezoidal window experimentation, Allport and Pettigrew have found that the illusion is

(A) only present among males
(B) only present among females
(C) only present in Eastern cultures
(D) present among all cultures
(E) present primarily in Western cultures

45. Which of the following most clearly distinguishes perception from sensation?

(A) observation   (B) sensation   (C) learning
(D) sensitivity   (E) threshold

46. The term *low threshold* refers to

(A) very few cycles per second
(B) very low decibel level
(C) low level of sensitivity to an incoming stimulus
(D) high level of sensitivity to an incoming stimulus
(E) virtual loss of any sensitivity to an incoming stimulus

47. A perfectly homogeneous visual environment is technically known as a

(A) Canfield   (B) milieu   (C) Ganzfeld
(D) Bunson field   (E) Gestalt

48. *Mach bands* refer to

(A) a visual stimulus used on the color wheel
(B) an auditory stimulus used on the sound generator
(C) a measurement band on the reaction-time chronoscope
(D) the distasteful auditory reaction obtained when a sound generator reaches a specific frequency level
(E) a means for cumulative measurement of normal street noise

49. William James's theory of emotional experience held that

(A) emotions are primarily a product of learning
(B) the physical reaction causes the emotional response
(C) all responses are preceded by cognitive awareness
(D) emotional patterns are based upon inherited tendencies
(E) emotional patterns are based upon Gestalt tendencies

50. Existing research suggests that the sight of a pleasurable object causes which one of the following measurable effects?

(A) facial tics
(B) blurred vision
(C) pupil dilation
(D) lowered-heart rate
(E) lowered blood pressure

51. A split-brain monkey is taught via his right eye to select triangles but not squares. He is instructed via his left eye to select squares but not triangles. We would expect

(A) complete inability to perform either task
(B) dominance of the right-eye task
(C) dominance of the left-eye task
(D) the equivalence of a short-circuit in motor areas of the brain
(E) in single-eye vision situations, the capacity to perform without confusion the task learned by that eye

52. The concept of instinctive behavior as defined by Lorenz and Tinbergen does *not* refer to behavior patterns that

(A) are innate or develop through maturation
(B) are species-specific, that is, generally found in all members of a species and therefore characteristic of the species
(C) include young bird experience in learning to fly
(D) include bird nestbuilding and migration
(E) are released by certain patterns of stimulation

53. The rod-and-frame test is designed to study

(A) the horizontal-vertical illusion
(B) the Ganzfeld illusion
(C) the Holzman illusion
(D) susceptibility to contextual cues
(E) the Wapner effect

54. *Cannabis sativa* is most commonly known as

(A) LSD
(B) heroin
(C) opium
(D) marijuana
(E) milkweed

Questions 55 and 56 are based on the following diagram.

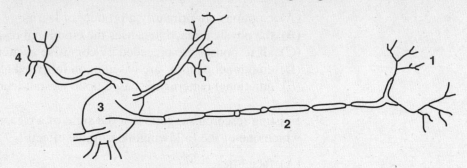

55. The dendrite-to-cell-body connection is correctly represented by which of the following?

    (A) 3–2   (B) 2–1   (C) 1–2   (D) 2–3   (E) 4–3

56. The myelin sheath would be in evidence at

    (A) 1   (B) 4   (C) 3   (D) 2   (E) 4 to 3 connecting point

57. To study and record spike activity within a specific individual fiber, researchers use

    (A) a microelectrode
    (B) a trace-type chemical substance
    (C) an oscilloscope
    (D) an amplifier
    (E) a sonar wave

58. A person performing calculus computations has attained which one of the following stages of cognitive development?

    (A) sensorimotor operations
    (B) formal operations
    (C) preoperational
    (D) concrete operations
    (E) abstract operations

59. Which one of the following terms is not generally used to describe the developmental period from ages two to six?

    (A) pregang age
    (B) age of dominance
    (C) exploration age
    (D) preschool age
    (E) age of solitary, parallel, and associative play

60. Primary work in the area of reversal and nonreversal shift has been conducted by

    (A) Miller   (B) Mowrer   (C) Kagan
    (D) Kaplan   (E) Kendler and Kendler

61. Which one of the following characteristics does an item need to be eligible for inclusion in the Stanford-Binet?

(A) The percentage of test takers getting the item correct is positively correlated with test-taker age.
(B) The percentage of test takers getting the item correct is negatively correlated with test-taker age.
(C) The percentage of test takers getting the item correct is constant across all age levels.
(D) The item has a standard deviation of less than one.
(E) No child below age six can answer the item correctly.

62. A change in the structure of a gene that leads to minor or major changes in an organism's physical constitution is

(A) mitosis (B) meiosis (C) mastation
(D) parthenogenesis (E) mutation

63. According to the tenets of family constellation, which one of the following would be most eager for physical demonstrations of attention?

(A) first-born children
(B) middle children
(C) identical twins
(D) youngest children
(E) fraternal twins

64. Research among institutional children has revealed

(A) strong, normal capacities for deep emotional relationships
(B) lack of normal capacities for deep emotional relationships
(C) easygoing, healthy personalities
(D) a strong sense of responsibility for their actions
(E) strong leadership tendencies

65. Remembering the name of the first president of the United States: Remembering the name of your first teacher :: Semantic memory:

(A) Implicit memory
(B) Episodic memory
(C) Long-term memory
(D) Explicit memory
(E) Procedural memory

66. In the Skinner-box experiments, it has been found that, compared with animals receiving normal extinction trials, animals receiving punishment during extinction trials exhibit

(A) fewer total responses prior to complete extinction
(B) more total responses prior to complete extinction
(C) the same total number of responses prior to extinction
(D) retroactive inhibition
(E) proactive inhibition

67. The relationship between a child's intellectual development and the age at which the child first walks is

    (A) strong
    (B) moderate
    (C) nonexistent
    (D) the subject of current investigation, which will probably form the basis for an established theory
    (E) believed by Wechsler to be important

68. Which one of the following would be most concerned with the development of imagery and verbal systems in the infant, and how they are interwoven?

    (A) Skinner   (B) Bruner   (C) Miller
    (D) Brown   (E) McCandless

69. Acknowledging that some materials are more difficult to learn than others, which of the following would constitute an easy-to-hard spectrum?

    (A) meaningful poetry, nonsense syllables, meaningful prose, digits
    (B) nonsense syllables, meaningful poetry, digits, meaningful prose
    (C) meaningful prose, meaningful poetry, nonsense syllables, digits
    (D) meaningful poetry, meaningful prose, digits, nonsense syllables
    (E) digits, meaningful poetry, meaningful prose, nonsense syllables

70. Damage to the ventromedial hypothalamus of an animal produces:

    (A) blindness   (B) overeating   (C) loss of balance
    (D) taste loss   (E) paralysis

71. The brain of the newborn

    (A) is the least-developed aspect of the child's body
    (B) is fully developed
    (C) will continue to grow in size
    (D) will continue to add brain cells, increasing its total number of cells
    (E) will not permit any reflex activity immediately after birth

72. Which one of the following would most directly affect the development of intelligence?

    (A) diet deficiency in the expectant mother
    (B) smoking by the expectant mother
    (C) premature birth
    (D) Rh factor
    (E) alcoholic beverage intake by the expectant mother

73. One first takes the sum of squared deviations from the mean, divides by the number of scores, and takes the square root to obtain the

    (A) variance   (B) standard deviation   (C) z-score
    (D) t-score   (E) F-score

74. A high SSS score indicates that a person is high in

  (A) sensation seeking
  (B) personality traits found among SS troops in Germany
  (C) likelihood to conform even when it means injury to others
  (D) sensory susceptibility
  (E) satiation sequencing

75. Which one of the following is most likely to enhance learner performance?

  (A) massed practice
  (B) distributed practice
  (C) nonsense syllables
  (D) functional fixedness
  (E) feedback

76. Which of the following types of learning is measured by a matching item on a test?

  (A) savings   (B) relearning   (C) recognition
  (D) recall   (E) reconstruction

77. Which one of the following is characteristic of the fetal period?

  (A) initial indications of sensitivity to stimulation
  (B) human-like physical characteristics beginning to take shape
  (C) highest susceptibility to diseases
  (D) greatest susceptibility to the effects of thalidomide
  (E) initiation of heartbeat

78. Extreme scores in a distribution most prominently affect the

  (A) mean   (B) median   (C) mode
  (D) semi-interquartile range   (E) negative skew

79. Throughout the first three months after birth, there is

  (A) an increase in day sleep and a decrease in night sleep
  (B) a decrease in day sleep and an increase in night sleep
  (C) no change in sleeping schedule
  (D) erratic sleep without identifiable pattern
  (E) increased day sleep for boys, decreased day sleep for girls

80. Menarche refers to the _____ and occurs around _____ years of age.

  (A) appearance of pubic hair; twelve
  (B) acquisition of one's final height; eighteen
  (C) ability to become pregnant; fourteen
  (D) first menstrual period; thirteen
  (E) first incident of secondary sexual characteristics; eleven

81. Memories that are being consciously and actively manipulated, organized, and thought about are part of

(A) the sensory register
(B) long-term memory
(C) working memory
(D) declarative memory
(E) explicit memory

82. Which of the following could you legitimately predict for a person
with an IQ of 50?

(A) fifth-grade level of learning
(B) entire life spent in an institution
(C) need for constant supervision
(D) high-school graduation if given special instruction
(E) no control over basic bodily functions

83. To decide whether a two-digit number is divisible by 9, add the two
digits. If they sum to 9, the number is divisible by 9. This is an example
of a(n)

(A) schema   (B) prototype   (C) syllogism
(D) algorithm   (E) chunk

84. Which of the following deficiencies in a pregnant mother would have
the most direct and marked effect on brain metabolism and development of learning ability in her newborn?

(A) vitamin A   (B) vitamin B   (C) vitamin C
(D) vitamin D   (E) cholesterol

85. Newborns

(A) cannot discriminate differences in tonal pitch
(B) have good eye-muscle coordination
(C) have prominent sphincter-muscle control
(D) can detect color and shape
(E) have keen sensitivity to pain

86. Severe anoxia at birth most likely will result in damage to the

(A) brain   (B) lungs   (C) heart
(D) kidneys   (E) liver

87. In Mowrer's two-factor theory, avoidance responses continue when no
shock is presented because

(A) functional autonomy is operating
(B) fear is reduced by cessation of the CS
(C) fear is reduced by cessation of the UCS
(D) animal drive is sufficiently high to motivate the animal in the
absence of any reinforcement
(E) higher-order conditioning has occurred

88. A continuity theory of learning suggests that learning

(A) is on an all-or-nothing basis
(B) is sudden
(C) is a gradual process
(D) continues throughout one's life
(E) begins at birth

89. *Animal Intelligence* was a major work written by

(A) Hull   (B) Thorndike   (C) Guthrie
(D) Skinner   (E) Watson

90. One boy has brown eyes. His twin brother has blue eyes. This information enables a person to conclude that the two

(A) are identical twins
(B) are fraternal twins
(C) exhibit sex-linked hereditary characteristics
(D) are monozygotic
(E) have blue-eyed parents

91. Developmentally, which of the following refers to reduction division?

(A) mitosis   (B) heterosis   (C) parthenogenesis
(D) morphosis   (E) meiosis

92. Which of the following is a correct developmental sequence?

(A) ovum-sperm, blastocyst, zygote
(B) blastocyst, ovum-sperm, zygote
(C) blastocyst, zygote, ovum-sperm
(D) ovum-sperm, zygote, blastocyst
(E) ovum-sperm, placenta, blastocyst

93. Among the following, the most rigorous type of validity is

(A) face   (B) split-half   (C) content
(D) test-retest   (E) predictive

94. Assuming that the correlation between length of eyelashes and number of dates is +.74, which of the following would apply to the process through which the experimenter seeks to determine the number of dates for a specific girl having a given eyelash length?

(A) correlation   (B) regression   (C) significance level
(D) sampling   (E) hypothesis testing

95. "Period of adolescent sterility" refers to

(A) prepubescence in boys
(B) the time immediately before menarche in girls
(C) the time immediately after menarche in girls
(D) an adolescent male's temporary sterility immediately following the attainment of sexual maturity
(E) the postpubescent period in boys

96. A company wants to utilize an individual intelligence test that (1) will be sensitive to individuals who may do quite well on performance-type tasks but may do poorly on verbal tasks, (2) within its basic formulation evenly represents IQ scores throughout the adulthood age span. Given these guidelines your recommendation would be:

    (A) Draw-a-Person Test
    (B) Wechsler Adult Intelligence Scale
    (C) Stanford-Binet Intelligence Test
    (D) Otis-Lennon Test
    (E) Minnesota Multiphasic Test

97. The smallest meaningful units of a language are

    (A) tacts   (B) morphologies   (C) phonemes
    (D) mands   (E) morphemes

98. During a child's first two years, the child's weight concept is

    (A) highly accurate
    (B) based entirely on stimulus brightness
    (C) based entirely on stimulus shape
    (D) based entirely on stimulus size
    (E) based entirely on stimulus color

99. "One is a bun. Two is a shoe. Three is a tree..." is basic to the mnemonic strategy known as

    (A) method of loci   (B) dual processing model
    (C) chunking   (D) pegword method   (E) visceral method

100. A rule of thumb for solving problems that is generally correct but may be imperfect is called a(n)

    (A) heuristic   (B) syllogism   (C) inference
    (D) script   (E) algorithm

101. Which one of the following is found in newborns?

    (A) identical sleep-wakefulness time proportions
    (B) almost immediate emotional response to their mothers
    (C) fear of strangers
    (D) babbling
    (E) partial taste sensitivity

102. At what point could a newborn be expected to have the capacity for visually tracking a moving object?

    (A) immediately after birth
    (B) within a few days after birth
    (C) during the second week after birth
    (D) at the end of the first month after birth
    (E) only shortly before walking occurs

103. In Bandura's experimental work with children, he has demonstrated that

(A) imitation learning occurs through observation
(B) mimicking occurs through reinforcement
(C) toilet training occurs through modeling
(D) toilet training occurs through judicious use of punishment
(E) aggression does not appear to be learned

104. Schemata are

(A) diagrams of the respiratory system
(B) plans for conducting experiments
(C) basic elements in color vision
(D) cognitive structures in memory
(E) distinctions between dependent and independent variables

105. "It was last spring. I had just studied for the Advanced GRE in Psychology and had done quite well on it." This would be an example of

(A) semantic memory
(B) tip-of-the-tongue phenomenon
(C) acoustical encoding
(D) episodic memory
(E) dual memory

106. Eidetic imagery is

(A) déjà vu
(B) a step in mathematical thought
(C) most prominent among elderly persons
(D) highly correlated with general intelligence
(E) a clear visual memory

107. Research on infant feeding practices indicates that

(A) there is a clear advantage for breast-fed babies
(B) mothers who breast feed actually tend to be rather tense about sexual matters
(C) most women who try breast feeding soon stop for psychological reasons
(D) the particular methods matter relatively little if the mother is sincere and comfortable with the method
(E) there is a lower incidence of smoking among adults who were breast-fed as infants than among their bottle-fed counterparts

108. A ten-year-old child with a mental age of twelve would have an IQ of

(A) 110
(B) 100
(C) 83
(D) 125
(E) 120

109. Which one of the following statements about IQ scores is true?

    (A) There is a strong correlation of IQ test scores throughout the entire life span.
    (B) The highest validity is found in early IQ test scores.
    (C) There is a negative correlation between early and later test scores.
    (D) The highest reliability and lowest validity are found in early test scores.
    (E) There is virtually no predictive validity between scores obtained prior to age two and those obtained at a later age.

110. The implementation of neural networks of cognitive systems that use parallel distributed processing to mimic neural processing has been pioneered by

    (A) Endel Tulving
    (B) Amos Tversky
    (C) George Sperling
    (D) Hermann Ebbinghaus
    (E) David Rumelhart

111. Which one of the following is *not* specifically an aid to retention?

    (A) chunking
    (B) overlearning
    (C) meaningfulness
    (D) knowledge of results
    (E) associating a mental picture or scene with the verbal material

112. In which one of the following areas does an older person have the greatest likelihood of demonstrating increases in intelligence?

    (A) digit span   (B) pursuit rotor   (C) block design
    (D) spatial relations   (E) vocabulary

113. Research evidence suggests that in the final aspects of the fetal stage

    (A) extreme pain sensitivity is present
    (B) capability exists only for reflex movements
    (C) capability exists for learning simple responses
    (D) a "quiet period" sets in during which detectable motor movements are very rare
    (E) the basics of newborn vocal sound can be detected

114. The "savings method" developed by Ebbinghaus to measure memory performance was an early form of measuring

    (A) encoding specificity
    (B) semantic memory
    (C) incidental learning
    (D) deductive reasoning
    (E) implicit memory

115. Childhood accidents are

(A) more prevalent in the second year than in the first year
(B) more prevalent in the first year than in the second year
(C) prevalent with equal incidence in both the first and second years
(D) more frequent among girls than among boys
(E) more prevalent in the first six months after birth than thereafter

116. Which one of the following elements would invariably be present in Type I error?

(A) rejection of a null hypothesis
(B) acceptance of a null hypothesis
(C) one-tailed test
(D) two-tailed test
(E) establishment of a significance level below .05

Questions 117–120 are based on the following diagrams.

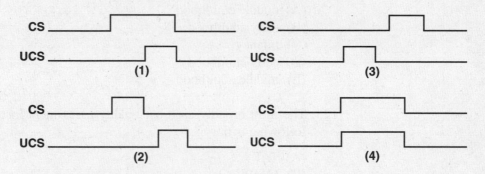

Note: Onset is indicated at the point where the CS and UCS lines move upward from their baselines.

117. The most efficient conditioning paradigm is

(A) 1   (B) 2   (C) 3   (D) 4   (E) 5

118. The least efficient conditioning paradigm is

(A) 1   (B) 2   (C) 3   (D) 4   (E) 5

119. The trace conditioning method is

(A) 1   (B) 2   (C) 3   (D) 4   (E) 5

120. The delayed conditioning method is

(A) 1   (B) 2   (C) 3   (D) 4   (E) 5

121. On a five-item Guttman Scale, a person has a score of 3. To fulfill uni-dimensionality requirements, this person would be in agreement with items

(A) 1, 3, 5   (B) 1, 3, 4   (C) 1, 2, 3
(D) 2, 4, 5   (E) 1, 4, 5

122. Correctional institutions are finding which one of the following to be the most effective rehabilitative device?

    (A) punishment
    (B) isolation
    (C) positive reinforcement
    (D) negative reinforcement
    (E) threat of the electric chair or gas chamber

123. Goldstein's organismic theory is *not* characterized by

    (A) a unified view of the organism
    (B) a nomothetic approach
    (C) the idea of man striving to reach his inherent potential
    (D) development being seen as the unfolding of inherited potential
    (E) Leibnitzian emphasis

124. Erikson's trust-versus-mistrust stage occurs during

    (A) middle childhood
    (B) early adulthood
    (C) infancy
    (D) early childhood
    (E) middle adulthood

125. The most broadly used personality assessment instrument among the following is the

    (A) TAT
    (B) MMPI
    (C) Rorschach
    (D) Draw-a-Man
    (E) Allport-Vernon-Lindzey

126. Circular Dial A contains three equidistant sections labeled *hot*, *safe*, *cold*; Circular dial B contains clockwise calibrations from zero to 500. Human engineering suggests that

    (A) Dial B is easier to interpret
    (B) Dial A is easier to interpret
    (C) Dials A and B are equivalent as far as ease of interpretation
    (D) Dials A and B are both very difficult to interpret
    (E) Such information should not be presented on circular dials

127. Which one of the following criteria would be utilized to differentiate "hot" from "cool" media in McLuhan's definitional framework?

    (A) verbal message combined with pictures
    (B) capacity to present pictures in motion
    (C) amount of information conveyed
    (D) shock potential of the medium
    (E) political potential of the medium

128. Stress-resistant individuals differ from their counterparts on which of the following dimensions?

    (A) social and work involvement
    (B) where they were in their family birth order
    (C) intelligence
    (D) family history of schizophrenia incidence
    (E) creativity

129. Which one of the following pairs contains *unrelated* terms?

    (A) thanatos—eros
    (B) script—contract
    (C) endomorph—ectomorph
    (D) propium—functional autonomy
    (E) parapraxes—anima

130. Which one of the following would be most likely to use the term *ergs* in discussing personality concepts?

    (A) Eysenck
    (B) Cattell
    (C) Jung
    (D) Rogers
    (E) Goldstein

131. When the government first began citing statistics correlating lung cancer with cigarette smoking, which of the following statements was a frequent answer from the cigarette manufacturers?

    (A) The test were biased.
    (B) Representative samples had not been selected.
    (C) The research lacked a control group.
    (D) Correlation does not mean causation.
    (E) Research was performed only on males.

132. A correct sequential or development order is represented by

    (A) ego, superego, id
    (B) anal, oral, phallic
    (C) inferiority feeling, superiority striving
    (D) autonomy versus shame and doubt; trust versus mistrust
    (E) parataxic, prototaxic, syntaxic

133. In a communications diagram, noise is

    (A) any variation in the message received, not predictable at its source
    (B) any variation in the message received, predictable at its source
    (C) only possible at the transmitter
    (D) only possible in channel
    (E) only possible within the receiver

134. According to the concept of coaction,

    (A) Children work faster when another child is present and doing the same task than they would alone.
    (B) Children work more slowly when another child is present and doing the same task than the speed they would work alone.
    (C) Children work faster in the presence of an audience than they do when working alone.
    (D) Children work more slowly in the presence of an audience than they do when working alone.
    (E) Children work most effectively when doing two tasks at the same time.

Questions 135–138 are based on the following questionnaire excerpt.

Under some conditions, war is necessary to maintain justice. (7.5)
The benefits of war rarely pay for its losses even for the victor. (3.5)
War brings out the best qualities in men. (9.7)
There is no conceivable justification for war. (.2)

135. The above items along with their numbers and decimals are part of a (an)

    (A) Likert Scale   (B) Thurstone Scale   (C) Osgood Scale
    (D) Bogardus Scale   (E) Remmers Scale

136. A subject obtaining a high score on a scale of this type (in comparison with a low-scoring subject) would be

    (A) much more pro-war
    (B) much less in favor of war
    (C) essentially the same in war viewpoint
    (D) strongly antiwar
    (E) moderately antiwar

137. To be selected for inclusion in this scale, a statement must meet the criterion of

    (A) high standard deviation in judge ratings
    (B) moderate standard deviation in judge ratings
    (C) low standard deviation in judge ratings
    (D) high mean rating among judges
    (E) low mean rating among judges

138. The numbers in parentheses

    (A) represent the mean of ratings assigned to this statement by a large number of judges
    (B) represent the mode of ratings assigned to this statement by a large number of judges
    (C) represent the average rating assigned to similar statements by a large number of judges
    (D) are determined and assigned by the experimenter
    (E) are determined and assigned by the subject

139. Which one of the following combinations would, by definition, be necessary to have an attitude?

(A) enduring system, feeling component
(B) temporary system, cognitive component
(C) stereotype system, action component
(D) modification system, behavioral component
(E) action system, temporary component

140. According to the findings of Lewin, Lippitt, and White, which of the following leadership styles would create the highest group productivity when the leader is absent?

(A) autocratic
(B) democratic
(C) laissez-faire
(D) laissez-faire or autocratic (equally productive)
(E) laissez-faire or democratic (equally productive)

141. When two people play nonzero-sum games, there is a tendency for

(A) cooperation
(B) competition
(C) high level of trust
(D) matrices renovation
(E) threat potential to enhance cooperation

142. In Sheldon's classification system, the slender, nervous person who is extremely sensitive to pain would come within the category of

(A) endomorph   (B) mesomorph   (C) ectomorph
(D) somatomorph   (E) neuromorph

143. Person A has lied for a $1 payoff while Person B told a similar lie for $20. Person B is

(A) less likely to believe the lie
(B) more likely to believe the lie
(C) equivalent to Person A in belief likelihood
(D) experiencing more cognitive dissonance
(E) experiencing more cognitive irrelevance

144. When pilots must learn to fly a new type of passenger plane, their transfer to the new set of controls is facilitated most when the new panel

(A) is similar to but has subtle functional differences from the old panel
(B) is distinctly different from the old panel in all respects
(C) looks identical but has some functions that are the exact reverse of what they were in the previous setting
(D) is an exact right-left reverse of the previous panel
(E) is an exact copy of the previous panel except that all dial calibrations are reversed

145. Which one of the following lists does *not* contain a name associated with need in personality theory?

    (A) Murray, McClelland, Bandura
    (B) Jung, Murray, Eysenck
    (C) Eysenck, Maslow, Jung
    (D) Maslow, Freud, Bandura
    (E) Freud, Bandura, Jung

146. Which one of the following statements would *not* be a firmly based criticism of psychoanalysis?

    (A) It is heavily based upon subjective, clinical observation.
    (B) It places an overemphasis upon instinctual behavior.
    (C) It places heavy emphasis upon abnormal behavior.
    (D) It stresses intrapsychic, nonobservable emotions.
    (E) It places primary emphasis upon changing the current problem behavior.

147. Which one of the following pairs is incorrect?

    (A) Mowrer—two-factor theory
    (B) Rogers—contract
    (C) Jung—shadow
    (D) Adler—superiority striving
    (E) Sullivan—interpersonal relationships

148. As viewed by phenomenologists, which of the following does *not* affect personality in any tangible way?

    (A) past perceptions
    (B) the length of time a person has been exposed to a given perceptual environment
    (C) the person's perceptual outlook brought to the experiencing of external events
    (D) early childhood relationships to family
    (E) archetypal continuities

149. In Newcomb's theoretical model, which one of the following statements is correct?

    (A) An even number of negative signs indicates balance.
    (B) An odd number of negative signs indicates balance.
    (C) Three negative signs indicate balance.
    (D) Four negative signs indicate balance.
    (E) Two positive signs indicate balance.

150. Emotional problems are treated through role-playing techniques in

    (A) psychodrama
    (B) client-centered therapy
    (C) implosive therapy
    (D) logotherapy
    (E) psychoanalysis

151. Kallmann finds the highest incidence of schizophrenia

(A) between fraternal twins
(B) between identical twins
(C) between siblings
(D) in the southeastern United States
(E) in urban areas

152. Which one of the following name sequences contains no mental hospital reformers?

(A) Clifford Beers, Sigmund Freud
(B) Eric Fromm, Carl Rogers
(C) William Tuke, Hans Hartmann
(D) Dorothea Dix, Alfred Adler
(E) George Miller, Dorothea Dix

153. Relaxation followed by successive approximation to objects formerly feared is

(A) aversive conditioning
(B) fear conditioning
(C) systematic desensitization
(D) implosive therapy
(E) environmental shock therapy

154. A form of group therapy in which the therapist lectures and leads discussions is

(A) inspirational   (B) release   (C) didactic
(D) nondirective   (E) abreaction

155. Long-term follow-up studies of patients treated through behavior modification techniques indicate

(A) high rates of relapse among practically all patients
(B) high rates of relapse among neurotic patients
(C) high rates of relapse among hypochondriacal patients
(D) few relapses
(E) a low, marginal level of effective life functioning

156. Which one of the following constitutes a distinction between conversion disorder and hypochondriasis disorder?

(A) detectable physiological symptoms   (B) learning disability
(C) brain damage   (D) illusions   (E) delusions

157. A process has just been completed in which items were sorted into groups on the basis of color. This sorting process is known as

(A) qualitative classification
(B) quantitative classification
(C) paired comparisons
(D) rank-order correlation
(E) matching

Questions 158 and 159 are based on the following statistical information.

95%—use a z-score of 1.96
99%—use a z-score of 2.58

158. For 100 scores on a given test, the mean is 74 and the standard deviation, 8. The 95% confidence interval for the mean of the population is

(A) 72.4 to 75.6   (B) 71.8 to 75   (C) 70.5 to 73.7
(D) 71 to 74.2   (E) 70 to 73.2

159. The 99% confidence interval for the mean of the population is

(A) 69.8 to 74   (B) 70 to 74.2   (C) 71.9 to 76.1
(D) 72.5 to 76.7   (E) 73 to 77.2

160. A researcher sits beside a playground, carefully observing a small group of children. The method being utilized is

(A) life-history   (B) case-history   (C) laboratory
(D) survey   (E) field-study

161. Enhancing the action of dopamine receptors has what effect on schizophrenic symptoms? Blocking these receptors has what effect on schizophrenic symptoms?

(A) increases/increases
(B) decreases/decreases
(C) increases/decreases
(D) decreases/increases
(E) does not affect/does not affect

162. Which of the following is *not* true of dopamine?

(A) It is a neurotransmitter.
(B) Amphetamines increase its release.
(C) It is implicated as a potential underlying cause in schizophrenia.
(D) It is blocked by antipsychotic drugs.
(E) It is located in the thyroid gland.

163. When a person is secretive about drinking and has occasional "blackouts," that individual is most likely in the

(A) prealcoholic stage
(B) prodromal stage
(C) crucial stage
(D) chronic stage
(E) undifferentiated stage

164. Within the current classification system (DSM-IV), hypochondriasis would be considered what type of disorder?

(A) psychosexual   (B) dissociative   (C) anxiety
(D) affective   (E) somatoform

165. Which one of the following would *not* be categorized among personality disorders?

(A) paranoid   (B) schizoid   (C) antisocial
(D) histrionic   (E) neuroleptic

166. Which one of the following findings has been voiced in the past few years by notable mental health professionals?

(A) Lack of warm social approval is in no way related to disease susceptibility.
(B) Disease prevention is not dependent on diet.
(C) Disease prevention is not dependent on exercise.
(D) Married men have a higher death-rate incidence than their divorced male counterparts.
(E) Geographical locations with the highest heart disease rate also have the highest rates of cancer incidence.

167. A person expressing functional blindness could be experiencing a(n)

(A) dissociative disorder
(B) somatoform disorder
(C) anxiety disorder
(D) mood disorder
(E) cyclothymic disorder

168. Behaviorists would *not* consider counterconditioning an appropriate therapeutic technique for

(A) anxiety reactions   (B) chronic tensions   (C) inhibitions
(D) transvestism   (E) phobias

169. Which of the following substances is/are included within the classification of substance-related disorders?
 I. amphetamine
 II. caffeine
 III. cocaine

(A) I and II only   (B) II and III only   (C) I and III only
(D) I, II, and III   (E) III only

170. A thirsty cat approaches his milk and receives a noxious blast of air. This is most likely an experiment by

(A) Harlow   (B) Scott   (C) Hess
(D) Webb   (E) Masserman

171. Which of the following would *not* characterize any form of personality disorder?

(A) emotional shallowness
(B) antisocial behavior
(C) incapable of group or individual loyalties
(D) depression
(E) rebellion against society

172. Repression : suppression ::

    (A) classical : instrumental
    (B) semiautomatic : automatic
    (C) fixation : regression
    (D) frustration : conflict
    (E) involuntary : voluntary

173. Which of the following is the *most* common disorder?

    (A) anxiety disorder
    (B) somatoform disorder
    (C) dissociative disorder
    (D) factitious disorder
    (E) personality disorder

174. Paraphilias are categorized among the _____ disorders.

    (A) sleep   (B) somatoform   (C) anxiety
    (D) personality   (E) sexual

175. Which of the following would be considered the *least* important factor in a therapist's success rate?

    (A) personality theory orientation
    (B) amount of experience
    (C) capacity for empathy
    (D) genuineness
    (E) warmth

176. The individual is opiate-addicted. The individual is most likely taking which of the following?

    (A) cocaine   (B) morphine   (C) clozapine
    (D) phenobarbital   (E) methaqualone

177. In a positively skewed distribution, the median is

    (A) larger than the mean
    (B) equal to the mean
    (C) equal to the mode
    (D) larger than the mode
    (E) actually negatively skewed

178. Given limited funds and a limited time period, which of the following methods might be recommended for dealing with a phobic reaction?

    (A) psychoanalysis
    (B) transcendental meditation
    (C) systematic desensitization
    (D) logotherapy
    (E) ego analysis

179. As the industrial psychologist deals with physical conditions relating to the work setting, which of the following is of *least* significance?

(A) illumination   (B) heat and humidity   (C) noise
(D) space arrangements   (E) coffee-break intervals

180. In the classic Hawthorne plant study at Western Electric, results pointed to the critical importance of

(A) supervisor dominance
(B) employer's concern toward workers
(C) timing and frequency of coffee breaks
(D) employing only females for work in the plant
(E) employing only highly skilled workers

181. The mean of a group of scores is 50 and the standard deviation, 10. What percentage of the people taking this test will score between 10 and 60?

(A) 16%   (B) 50%   (C) 64%
(D) 84%   (E) 98%

Questions 182 and 183 are based on the following percentile ranks in a normal distribution.

(1) 2nd
(2) 16th
(3) 84th
(4) 98th
(5) none of the above

182. Which one of the above percentile ranks would correspond to a z-score of −1.0?

(A) 1   (B) 2   (C) 3   (D) 4   (E) 5

183. Which one of the above percentile ranks would correspond to a z-score of +3.0?

(A) 1   (B) 2   (C) 3   (D) 4   (E) 5

184. To predict vocational interest you would be well advised to turn to which of the following?

(A) 16 PF   (B) MMPI   (C) Rorschach
(D) Strong-Campbell   (E) Pintner-Patterson

185. A test score that has *not* been converted into a form permitting comparison with scores from other tests is known as a

(A) stanine score   (B) percentile score   (C) raw score
(D) z-score   (E) quartile score

186. Which one of the following has *not* been used as an industrial method at the supervisor-management levels?

    (A) case method
    (B) incident method
    (C) sensitivity-training method
    (D) free-association method
    (E) role-playing method

187. Human engineers estimate that the best room temperature for moderately heavy work extending over two to four hours to be in the range of

    (A) 55–60 degrees
    (B) 80–90 degrees
    (C) 90–95 degrees
    (D) 65–70 degrees
    (E) 75–80 degrees

188. The most reliable public opinion polling is that which

    (A) accompanies census bureau statistics
    (B) was done for the Kinsey report
    (C) private firms conduct prior to a political election
    (D) detergent firms conduct concerning product satisfaction
    (E) gasoline companies conduct to learn about driving habits

189. If the double alternation experimentation is representative of comparative experiments in the learning area, it would be fair to say that

    (A) animals cannot think
    (B) most lower animals can think
    (C) only humans have thought-type mental capacities
    (D) some animals high on the phylogenetic scale demonstrate thought-type mental capacities
    (E) rats have strong capacities for thought-type processes

190. To make a green costume stand out most vividly on stage, which one of the following colors would be the most appropriate for lighting?

    (A) orange   (B) red   (C) violet
    (D) pink   (E) blue

191. The members of the training group each read several pages of description dealing with a managerial dilemma and the way in which it was dealt with by an individual. The method being used with the group is

    (A) case
    (B) incident
    (C) role playing
    (D) sensitivity training
    (E) free association

192. Which one of the following persons could be expected to have the most lasting command of examination material (assuming equal study time and ability)?

    (A) one who engaged solely in rote memory
    (B) one who studied the material in one massed session
    (C) one who studied all the material silently
    (D) one who recited portions of the material periodically
    (E) one who listened to the material on a cassette recorder

193. One of the first steps for a psychologist assigned to develop selection procedures for a specific job would be to

    (A) develop an intelligence test
    (B) develop a test for creativity
    (C) develop a test for musical aptitude
    (D) develop a test for manual dexterity
    (E) examine the tasks of that specific job

194. Human engineering principles indicate that the best type of cockpit display panel

    (A) makes minimum use of shape
    (B) makes minimum use of color
    (C) maximally uses both shape and color
    (D) maximally uses only size, minimizing shape and color
    (E) maximally uses only position, minimizing shape and color

195. To determine the values of a specific group, the best procedure among the following would be the

    (A) Stanford-Binet
    (B) Wechsler
    (C) Otis
    (D) Allport-Vernon-Lindzey
    (E) Doll

196. A company wishes to market a new product and has the natural desire to get large consumer subscription to it. The cognitive dissonance research results of Doob et al. recommend which of the following pricing approaches?

    (A) price initially below the eventual price
    (B) price initially well above the eventual price
    (C) price initially at the eventual price level
    (D) price identically with the largest competitors, regardless of their existing prices
    (E) price regionally rather than nationally set

197. In a randomly selected sample, the following distribution was obtained:

Sex	Democrat	Republican
Male	65	35
Female	30	20

To test the hypothesis that the two discrete variables (sex, political party) are independent in the population that yielded the sample, we should use

(A) a *t*-test
(B) regression statistics
(C) a *z*-test
(D) chi-square
(E) Duncan's multiple-range test

198. Assuming that a multitude of equal-sized, random samples are gathered from the same infinite population, the mean of each sample is computed, and the means of the different samples are put together to form a new distribution; which one of the following statements about the new distribution is true?

(A) The mean would be greater than the median or the mode.
(B) The distribution would be normal.
(C) The distribution would be positively skewed.
(D) The standard deviation would equal 1.0.
(E) The distribution would be negatively skewed.

199. "The mean of the squared differences from the mean of the distribution" is a definition of

(A) mode
(B) platikurtic
(C) chi-square
(D) variance
(E) *t*-distribution

200. According to the research of Janis, Kaye, et al., which one of the following activities would be most likely to establish persuasiveness in a written communication?

(A) reading while in a very relaxed position
(B) reading while watching TV
(C) eating while reading
(D) talking while reading
(E) listening to music while reading

Test 3: Answer Comments

1. (D) The adrenal medulla has this emergency preparatory function for the human body.

2. (D) Saturation is a descriptive term specifically related to color.

3. (C) After shock had been discontinued, rats placed on the former shock side would demonstrate escape behavior indefinitely.

4. (A) Neuron rest or conduction is determined by the ionic flux of electrically charged ions.

5. (C) As the amplitude of GSR increases across trial blocks for tone 2, a corresponding pattern of response decrease across trial blocks is evident for tone 1—events indicative of strong negative correlation.

6. (D) The conditioned stimulus in the experiment was tone.

7. (B) Stimulus discrimination was evident across trial blocks. The pattern described in the explanation accompanying Question 5 gives strong indication that the subjects were making prominent discrimination between the two tones.

8. (E) Within the parietal lobe, the somesthetic cortex is responsible for the skin and kinesthetic senses.

9. (D) Convergence is a very slight crossing of the eyes as they focus upon an object. This focus on the object from two slightly different locations provides depth perception cues.

10. (C) These epinephrine studies vividly demonstrated the potential effects of external suggestion upon experienced emotion.

11. (D) As distinguished from emotions, moods last longer and are less intense.

12. (D) The trichromatic theory suggests that when we view a primary color, those retinal cones become innervated. As we look away from the primary, the retinal cones sensitive to the other two primaries are activated, producing the negative afterimage.

13. (B) In sleep apnea the person stops breathing and must awaken in order to resume it. The exact cause is not known—either windpipe or respiration control functioning within the brain—and it is a fairly prevalent disorder among older people.

14. (B) A high concentration of positive ions in the cell body of a neuron places the neuron in a conducting state.

15. (C) Striated muscles provide skeletal movement. The other two types are smooth muscles (associated with visceral response) and the heart muscle.

16. (B) This is one of the behavioral phenomena in rats for which Spence is best known. There appears to be a need for the rat to extinguish completely his initial response before the second (alternate) response can be learned effectively.

17. (E) Primitive emotion control rests in the hypothalamus.

18. (A) Speech-related functions are localized in the left cerebral hemisphere.

19. (C) Although closure, grouping, contrast, and phi phenomenon are stimulus-related perceptual phenomena, divergence is a "clunker" inserted to trip the uninformed.

20. (C) The letters GSR mean galvanic skin response, a measure of change in the electrical resistance of the skin (a change by sweat-gland activity).

21. (B) This phenomenon is known as the Purkinje shift—daylight vision being predominantly cone vision and night vision being rod vision. Red color wavelengths are beyond the spectrum received by rods and, therefore, do not activate them. By wearing red goggles in the briefing room, the aviators had cone vision to receive their instructions. When they headed out into the night and removed their goggles, their rod vision was activated and they were immediately night-vision-adapted for their mission.

22. (D) *Purposive Behavior in Animals and Men* is Tolman's major work.

23. (B) Secreted by the thyroid gland, thyroxine is integral to the functions of body metabolism and physical growth.

24. (A) Ponzo illusion depends on our experience with objects such as tracks moving off in the distance. Since we know the distance between the tracks remains constant we tend to see a small paper cutout log we put across the distant tracks as being larger than the same size of cutout placed across the near tracks.

25. (D) Muscles stretch the lens for distant-object vision and allow the lens to get "fatter" for near-object vision; this is accommodation.

26. (B) The EEG is a brain wave pattern obtained from electrodes attached to various parts of the scalp.

27. (C) Selye developed the concept of the general adaptation syndrome. The body's reaction under stress occurs in the three major stages—alarm reaction, resistance, and exhaustion.

28. (C) The absence of stimulation has produced within subjects an inability to endure the setting despite appealing remuneration.

29. (B) In contrast with time perception, in which no significant effort is being devoted to task completion, time passage seems much slower where significant effort is being devoted to a completion goal.

30. (A) Necker, in 1832, created the very familiar illusion of two squares—each about two-thirds superimposed on the other. Their edges are connected to resemble a transparent cardboard box. Our tendency is to see the front and back of the box constantly reversing on us.

31. (B) Primaries in subtractive (pigment) color mixing are blue, yellow, and red. For additive (light) color mixing, the primaries are blue, green, and red.

32. (C) The sympathetic nervous system controls bodily response to emergency situations.

33. (A) The number of stimulus-response connections is a concept of Thorndike's Law of Exercise.

34. (A) Hobson and McCarley indicate that dreams are a purely physiological phenomenon caused by neuron activation within the pons. In their view, dreams have no relationship to motivation and originate simply through this spontaneous neural firing. Their hypothesis is very controversial and has been challenged on the grounds of relationship between dream content and predream stimulation.

35. (C) The opponent process theory—principally Solomon's—states that the brain functions to suppress emotional responses. Therefore, when an emotional response occurs (for example, fear) its opposite (sociability) is subsequently experienced—in effect, functioning to counterbalance. In the area of drugs this helps explain why the initial "high" or "rush" that is experienced becomes very minimal with continued use, and its opposite, depression, becomes more pronounced afterward. Stronger dosages are likely to be taken subsequently to counteract this negative experience—a vicious cycle.

36. (B) Animal experiments (Teitelbaum et al.) reveal that animals have a tendency to keep their caloric intake constant.

37. (E) Part of both the endocrine system and the central nervous system, the hypothalamus is generally considered the endocrine system's "control center." In conjunction with the limbic system, it has a major role in the control of emotion and motivation. It has a very close "working relationship" with the pituitary gland, which releases hormones that control the output of other endocrine glands.

38. (D) Among the hormones listed, the distinctly male sex hormone is androgen.

39. (C) Motion parallax enables a person to judge distances by the relative movement of near and distant objects. It is a monocular depth cue.

40. (B) Preparatory instruction serves to shorten reaction time.

41. (A) Visual and thermal reaction times prove faster when more sensory space is covered by the stimulus.

42. (C) It is Hebb's desire to replace the drive concept with an optimum-level-of arousal concept.

43. (E) Murray does not speak of a destruction need.

44. (E) The trapezoidal window illusion has been most evident in Western cultures—perhaps a function of a "carpentered" perceptual world.

45. (C) Perception relates the present sensation to prior perceptual experience.

46. (D) Low threshold suggests a high level of sensitivity to an incoming stimulus.

47. (C) *Ganzfeld* is a perceptual term describing a perfectly homogenous visual environment.

48. (A) The *Mach band* is a three-pointed black stimulus on a white background. When spinning, it produces the perceptual effect of a dark ring midway between the center and the periphery of a disk.

49. (B) The James-Lange theory expresses the view that physical reaction prompts emotional response rather than vice versa.

50. (C) Pupil dilation is a prominent current measure of pleasurable object perception.

51. (E) Whereas two-eye vision can cause performance confusion, single-eye vision preserves the separation necessary to perform without confusion.

52. (C) Lorenz and Tinbergen's concept of instinctive behavior does not include behaviors that are primarily learned.

53. (D) The frame can give a false impression of horizontal-vertical, hindering contextual, cue-dependent persons from accurate vertical rod judgment.

54. (D) *Cannabis sativa* is a technical name for marijuana.

55. (E) 4–3 on the drawing represents the dendrite-to-cell-body connection.

56. (D) The myelin sheath would be in evidence at the axon (2 on the drawing).

57. (A) For research in neuronal physiology, experimenters use microelectrodes to study and record spike activity within a specific individual fiber.

58. (B) In Piaget's system, calculus computations have the cognitive complexity of formal operations.

59. (B) Although the period from ages two to six has been called pregang, preschool, exploration, and the time of solitary-parallel-associative-play sequence, it has not been called a period of dominance.

60. (E) Kendler and Kendler has been the most prominent research team in the investigation of reversal and nonreversal shift.

61. (A) For inclusion in the Stanford-Binet, the percentage of correct responses to a test item must be positively correlated with the ages of the test takers.

62. (E) Gene mutation can produce either minor or major changes in the organism's physical characteristics.

63. (B) In family constellation aspects of personality theory, the middle child is often described as the forgotten child (an Adler concept), therefore the prime candidate for receptiveness to physical demonstrations of attention.

64. (B) Research among institutional children has revealed a lack of normal capacity for deep emotional relationships. Although this finding does not characterize all institutions, it is disturbingly frequent.

65. (B) Tulving distinguished semantic memory of facts, meanings, and general knowledge from episodic memory of personal events tied to specific experiences.

66. (C)   Skinner has found that punishment during extinction trials produces the same total number of responses as are found in extinction trials without punishment—evidence of an immediate but not long-range deterrent effect.

67. (C)   The age of initial walking in no way relates to a child's intelligence.

68. (B)   Bruner is prominently concerned with the development of imagery and verbal systems in the young child, having equal concern for their developmental relationships.

69. (D)   As revealed in a pioneering experiment by Lyon, the most meaningful item is the easiest to learn: meaningful poetry, meaningful prose, digits, nonsense syllables.

70. (B)   The ventromedial hypothalamus inhibits eating. Research has found that damage to this area produces overeating and obesity. Conversely, eating is initiated by the lateral hypothalamus.

71. (C)   Though it will not gain brain cells, the brain of the newborn will continue to grow in size after birth.

72. (A)   Maternal diet deficiency during the embryonic period could be critically detrimental to the development of intelligence.

73. (B)   A standard deviation is obtained by summing deviations from the mean, dividing by the number of scores and taking the square root.

74. (A)   SSS is Zuckerman's Sensation Seeking Scale. It has been found that people differ dramatically in their sensation-seeking tendencies, and the scale has prominent utility in marriage compatibility.

75. (E)   Learner performance is most enhanced by immediate knowledge of results (feedback).

76. (E)   The matching test item deals with ability to reconstruct an association (reconstruction-type learning).

77. (A)   Researchers have found indications of sensitivity to stimulation during the fetal period.

78. (A)   The mean is most dramatically affected by extreme scores because it is, in effect, an average.

79. (B)   During the first three months after birth, the newborn shows a noticeable increase in night sleep and a decrease in day sleep.

80. (D)   Menarche refers to the first menstrual period and occurs around thirteen years of age.

81. (C)   Information transferred to working memory from either the sensory register or long-term memory can be rehearsed, reorganized, and manipulated.

82. (A)   A person with an IQ of 50 (mildly retarded) could be expected to complete a fifth-grade level of learning by adulthood.

83. (D)   An algorithm is a procedure for solving problems that is guaranteed to determine the correct answer.

84. (B) Several B vitamins serve as coenzymes in brain metabolism; vitamin B deficiencies in pregnant women have been found to impair the learning abilities of their children.

85. (D) Stimulus discrimination research with newborns suggests that the infants can detect both color and shape.

86. (A) Severe anoxia at birth (interruption of oxygen supply) could result in brain damage.

87. (B) Fear reduction functions as a negative reinforcement, perpetuating the avoidance response.

88. (C) Continuity theory (in contrast to all-or-none views) suggests that learning is a gradual process. Differences between recognition and recall learning support this position.

89. (B) *Animal Intelligence* was Thorndike's major work.

90. (B) Only two separate zygotes could produce one brown-eyed and one blue-eyed twin (fraternal twins).

91. (E) Meiosis refers to reduction division in which chromosome pairs separate, with one set going to one new cell and the remaining set to the other.

92. (D) Ovum-sperm, zygote, blastocyst is a correct developmental sequence.

93. (E) Predictive validity is the most rigorous form of validity. It is because the GRE has predictive validity that you and your "ancestors" have had to take it.

94. (B) Regression would deal with establishing the best prediction for an individual case based on a known general correlation.

95. (C) Immediately after menarche, a girl is incapable of conception—the time period known as adolescent sterility.

96. (B) The intelligence test that would be suitable to the specifications of performance/verbal distinctions and evenly representative of IQ throughout the adult age span would be the Wechsler Adult Intelligence Scale. It has a separate IQ computation for verbal and for performance, and its standardization process is such that it is not locked in by a formula such as MA/CA × 100, where CA is Chronological Age, which would unfairly lower IQ representation in the older age range.

97. (E) The smallest meaningful units of a language are called morphemes.

98. (D) During the first two years of development, a child bases his weight concept on stimulus size. A large box, therefore, is seen as heavier than a small box.

99. (D) The "One is a bun. Two is a shoe . . ." ten-phrase rhyme is basic to the pegword method of memory recall. It is frequently used to remember ten-item lists over an extended period of time—each item being given a novel picture with its corresponding rhyme phrase.

100. (A) A general problem-solving strategy or rule of thumb is called a heuristic, whereas an algorithm is a methodical recipe for successfully solving a problem.

101. (E) Newborns have a partially developed taste sensitivity and corresponding taste preferences that will change as their sensitivity develops further.

102. (B) The capacity for visually tracking a moving object appears in the newborn a few days after birth.

103. (A) Bandura's research has centered upon observational learning and points to the strength of imitation learning achieved by children through the observation process.

104. (D) Another way to say that you know how to go about driving a car would be to say that you have a schema for driving a car. It is a cognitive structure—an abstract representation of the real-world event of driving a car. The plural of schema is schemata.

105. (D) An incident remembered by time and place is an example of what Tulving characterizes as episodic memory. Semantic memory relates to the billions (likely) bits of knowledge and information we have stored that have no time/place orientation. The episodic/semantic memory distinction is a major contribution by Tulving that has formed the basis for several major research follow-up studies in the field of memory.

106. (E) Eidetic imagery refers to a clear visual memory. In its most extreme form it would be demonstrated by the person described as having a photographic memory.

107. (D) The mother's sincerity and warmth in the child relationship overshadows the feeding method in importance.

108. (E) MA/CA is 12/10, which is then multiplied by 100 to produce 120.

109. (E) Scores obtained prior to age two are most aptly called the Developmental Quotient, which bears no predictive validity for the later Intelligence Quotient.

110. (E) Rumelhart has developed computational models of neural processing based on the principles of neural processing, called connectionist or parallel distributed processing (PDP) models.

111. (D) Knowledge of results is an aid to learning acquisition rather than to retention.

112. (E) The vocabulary or verbal information areas offer the greatest possibility for an older person to demonstrate increases in intelligence.

113. (C) Classical conditioning has been achieved late in the fetal stage, demonstrating that the fetus has a capacity for learning simple responses.

114. (E) Ebbinghaus measured the effect of prior exposure on the amount of time required to relearn a list of words. The effect of past experiences on performance is a measure of implicit memory.

115. (A) Childhood accidents are more prevalent in the second year than in the first—which is at least partially attributable to the youngster's increased mobility.

116. (A) Type I error would be mistaken rejection of a null hypothesis. Type II error is mistaken acceptance of a null hypothesis.

117. (A) Diagram 1 is delayed conditioning, the most efficient classical conditioning method.

118. (C) Diagram 3 is backward conditioning, totally inefficient.

119. (B) Diagram 2 is the trace conditioning method, next in efficiency to delayed conditioning but having the disadvantage of requiring memory of CS onset.

120. (A) As explained in Question 117.

121. (C) Guttman's concept of unidimensionality would require a score of 3 to reflect agreement with items 1, 2, and 3.

122. (C) Positive reinforcement has proved most effective in attaining desired long-range behavioral change. Punishment has been ineffective in attaining this goal.

123. (B) The nomothetic approach involves establishing personality elements (such as id impulse) that are then applied uniformly to all individuals. Goldstein's emphasis on the inherited potential of the organism does not take the nomothetic approach.

124. (C) Erikson's trust versus mistrust stage occurs in the earliest mother-child social interaction related to feeding.

125. (B) The MMPI (Minnesota Multiphasic Personality Inventory) is the most rigorously objective of these personality assessment instruments and the most widely used among them.

126. (B) Human engineers consider a three-section circular dial easier to interpret than the strictly numerical circular dial.

127. (C) The amount of information conveyed distinguishes "hot" from "cool" media in McLuhan's definitional framework. Books and articles are considered "hot" media, but TV is a "cool" medium.

128. (A) Researchers such as Kobasa have found that stress-resistant executives differ from their counterparts on three dimensions—they feel more in control of their life events, have stronger social and work involvement, and have a positive attitude toward challenge and change.

129. (E) *Parapraxes* is a Freudian term relating to slips of the tongue, and *anima* is a Jungian term describing man's bisexual nature.

130. (B) Cattell speaks of instincts and needs in terms of *ergs* and *sentiments*.

131. (D) It was in the cigarette manufacturers' best interests to suggest that correlation does not mean causation but, rather, only shows a relationship between two observed events.

132. (C) Adler believed that inferiority feelings develop early in life through interaction with adults. Superiority striving is the consequence.

133. (A) Generally occurring within channel, *noise* is a communications term referring to any variation in the message received, not predictable at its source.

134. (A) According to the concept of coaction, a child works faster when in the presence of another child performing the same task. This concept—along with the concept of audience effects—is known by the more general term *social facilitation*.

135. (B) These statements are part of a Thurstone Scale designed to measure attitudes toward war.

136. (A) A high-scoring subject would be more pro-war than a low-scoring subject.

137. (C) To be acceptable for inclusion in a Thurstone Scale, an item must have low variability (low standard deviation) in judge ratings.

138. (A) The numbers in parentheses reflect the mean of all judge ratings of this statement.

139. (A) Attitudes are enduring systems that contain both cognitive (knowledge) and affective (feeling) components manifested in behavior.

140. (B) Democratic leadership groups proved most productive in a leader-absent setting.

141. (B) In the nonzero-sum game, where both persons can experience simultaneous gains or losses, there is a tendency for competition to develop.

142. (C) Sheldon's system contains three body-type-related entries: endo-morph (plump), mesomorph (athletic), and ectomorph (very slender).

143. (A) The person receiving $20 is less likely to believe the lie because that person has more external justification ($20) for telling it—and conse-quently, less cognitive dissonance than a person receiving only $1.

144. (B) In contrast to a similar panel with subtle functional differences or identical controls with exact reversal in function, a pilot would experience more success and less interference in learning a new panel that was distinctly different from the old panel in all respects.

145. (E) Murray and Maslow both speak of needs in personality theory. The name grouping of Freud-Bandura-Jung was the only one in which one of those two names did not appear.

146. (E) Psychoanalysis focuses upon the early childhood bases underly-ing personality problems rather than the current behavioral symptoms.

147. (B) Rogers does not speak of a contract. This term is associated with Berne's transactional analysis.

148. (E) Only Jung speaks of archetypal continuities, and concept is totally foreign to phenomenologists.

149. (A) In Newcomb's model, an even number of negative signs indicates balance. You dislike cigarettes, your dad dislikes cigarettes, and you like your dad (two negatives and in balance).

150. (A) Treating emotional problems through role playing is a primary aspect of psychodrama.

151. (B) In Kallmann's studies, the highest incidence of schizophrenia was found in identical twins—evidence frequently cited to prove the disorder's hereditary characteristics.

152. (B) Dorothea Dix, Clifford Beers, and William Tuke were prominent persons dedicated to the reform of mental hospitals.

153. (C) Systematic desensitization in the Wolpe approach involves substituting a relaxation response for fear in the presence of a formerly feared object.

154. (C) Group therapy in which the therapist lectures and leads discussions is classified as didactic.

155. (D) In follow-up studies of patients treated through behavior modification techniques, few relapses to problem behavior have been found.

156. (A) Detectable unexplainable physiological symptoms are present in the conversion disorder but not in hypochondriasis disorder.

157. (A) Sorting items on a dimension such as color is an example of qualitative classification.

158. (A) A basic confidence interval formula determines the lower limit by subtracting the (z-score times the standard deviation/the square root of N) from the mean of the distribution. The upper limit is obtained by adding the same quantity expressed in parentheses to the mean.

159. (C) See Question 158.

160. (E) Such observation of a natural setting is characteristic of the field-study method.

161. (C) Increasing the action of dopamine receptors increases schizophrenic symptoms; blocking the receptors relieves schizophrenic symptoms. This has led researchers to suspect a central role of dopamine in schizophrenia.

162. (E) Dopamine is a neurotransmitter located in the limbic system. Snyder has found that low doses of amphetamines make the schizophrenic symptoms even more obvious. When the release of dopamine is blocked by antipsychotic or neuroleptic drugs, the schizophrenic symptoms are relieved.

163. (B) The prodromal stage is characterized by secretive drinking and possible "blackouts." It is preceded by the prealcoholic stage, which involves social drinking and stress drinking. Crucial and chronic stages follow it.

164. (E) Somatoform disorders have physical symptoms for which no organic basis can be found. For example, the soldier who, in the heat of battle, develops paralysis in his right arm (thereby unable to fire his rifle) would be demonstrating a somatoform disorder.

165. (E) Neuroleptic is a medication-induced movement disorder.

166. (E) Mental health professionals find that the geographical locations with the highest heart-disease rates also have the highest rates of cancer incidence.

167. (B) Functional blindness—not traceable to a physiological cause—could be a somatoform disorder.

168. (D) The pleasure obtained from the problem act itself—transvestism—is too great for counterconditioning to be an effective method for treatment.

169. (D) Amphetamines, caffeine, and cocaine are all included within substance-related disorders.

170. (E) Masserman uses this type of method to achieve conditioned neurotic behavior in cats.

171. (D) Although personality disorders encompass emotional shallowness, antisocial behavior, absence of group or individual loyalties, and rebellion against society, they do not include depression.

172. (E) In Freudian theory, repression constitutes a kind of involuntary absence from consciousness; suppression, on the other hand, involves a voluntary act of removal from consciousness. ("I'm not going to think about that anymore!")

173. (A) Anxiety disorders are the most commonly found disorders, and dissociative disorders are among the most rare.

174. (E) Paraphilias—among them, exhibitionism, fetishism, pedophilia, and sexual sadism—are sexual disorders.

175. (A) The therapist's personal qualities and experience are considered far more important factors in therapeutic success than the therapist's personality theory orientation.

176. (B) The only opiate in this drug listing is morphine.

177. (D) In a skewed distribution, the median moves in the direction of the skew, and the mode occurs at the distribution's high point. The mean moves more exaggeratedly in the tail direction than does the median.

178. (C) Systematic desensitization is the method in this listing used for directly treating problem behavior without concern for its underlying cause.

179. (E) Industrial psychologists find that physical aspects of the work setting itself (noise, illumination, and so on) are more critical than the number of coffee breaks.

180. (B) The Hawthorne plant study at Western Electric launched the human relations movement in American industry. It pointed convincingly to the relationship between supervisory attention and concern for workers and resulting work output.

181. (D) Being four standard deviations below the mean encompasses virtually all scores on that side of the distribution (50%). The score of 60 is one standard deviation above the mean (approximately an additional 34%), resulting in a combined 84%.

182. (B) Approximately 16% of the scores in a distribution would occur beyond a point that is one standard deviation below the mean.

183. (E) For all practical purposes, this point (three standard deviations above the mean) would encompass all distribution scores—essentially a 100th percentile, which is not among your answer choices.

184. (D) A prominent vocational interest test is the Strong-Campbell Vocational Interest Blank.

185. (C) Raw scores are not in a form that permits comparison with performance on other test measures.

186. (D) Although common in psychoanalysis, the free-association method is not used in supervisor-management training within industry.

187. (D) Human engineers have found that 65–70 degrees is the best working temperature for moderately heavy work extending over a two-to four-hour period.

188. (C) The most reliable public opinion polling is that of private organizations conducted prior to a political election. Such firms are heavily staffed for such polling because they know there will be a "day of reckoning" when their findings will be confirmed or disproved.

189. (D) In Hunter's double alternation experimentation, some animals high on the phylogenetic scale have demonstrated thought-type mental capacities.

190. (E) In the subtractive color wheel, green is "next door" to blue. With the probable existence of an "impure" green in the costume, the blue light would best reflect and accentuate the outfit.

191. (A) Having participants read several pages of description relating the problems and dilemmas of a specific manager would be an example of using the case method.

192. (D) Recitation—in effect, an active participation in the material— aids retention.

193. (E) A psychologist assigned to do the screening for a given job must first examine the tasks of that specific job, seeking to approximate their required skills within the testing instrument.

194. (C) Human engineering most firmly underwrites the cockpit display panel that makes maximal use of both shape and color.

195. (D) Among the test groupings presented, the Allport-Vernon-Lindzey Scale would enable you to study the values of a specific group.

196. (C) Research studies indicate that the product should be priced initially at the eventual price level rather than at a discount price. In systematic studies, this recommendation has been demonstrated repeatedly.

197. (D) Determining that two discrete variables are independent within a population on the basis of the sample data would be a mission of chi-square.

198. (B) The distribution of sample means would be a normal distribution.

199. (D) Variance is defined as the average/mean of the squared differences from the mean of the distribution.

200. (C) Eating while reading was found to enhance the persuasiveness of the material being read. Thus, a salesman taking a client to lunch is right on target.

Test 3: Evaluating Your Score

Abbreviation Guide for Quick Reference (Translation)

PC:	Physiological/Comparative
SnP:	Sensation/Perception
LM:	Learning/Motivation/Emotion
CHL:	Cognition/Complex Human Learning
D:	Developmental
PrS:	Personality/Social
PyCl:	Psychopathology/Clinical
M:	Methodology
Ap:	Applied

TALLY CHART

- Checkmark to the left of each number you missed.
- In the column to the right of the number note the area your check-marked question is in.
- Move your check mark to the appropriate area column.
- Sum your check marks in each area column.
- Carry these sums to the blanks on the next scaling page.

Q#		PC	SnP	LM	CHL	D	PrS	PyCl	M	Ap
1	PC									
2	PC									
3	LM									
4	PC									
5	M									
6	M									
7	M									
8	PC									
9	SnP									
10	LM									
11	LM									
12	SnP									
13	PC									
14	PC									
15	PC									
16	LM									
17	PC									
18	PC									
19	SnP									
20	SnP									
21	SnP									
22	LM									
23	PC									
24	SnP									
25	SnP									
26	PC									
27	LM									

	Q#		PC	SnP	LM	CHL	D	PrS	PyCl	M	Ap
	28	SnP									
	29	SnP									
	30	SnP									
	31	SnP									
	32	PC									
	33	LM									
	34	PC									
	35	LM									
	36	PC									
	37	PC									
	38	PC									
	39	SnP									
	40	SnP									
	41	SnP									
	42	LM									
	43	LM									
	44	SnP									
	45	SnP									
	46	SnP									
	47	SnP									
	48	SnP									
	49	LM									
	50	LM									
	51	PC									
	52	PC									
	53	SnP									
	54	PC									
	55	PC									
	56	PC									
	57	PC									
	58	LM									
	59	D									
	60	CHL									
	61	CHL									
	62	D									
	63	D									
	64	D									
	65	CHL									
	66	LM									
	67	D									
	68	CHL									
	69	CHL									
	70	LM									
	71	D									

Q#		PC	SnP	LM	CHL	D	PrS	PyCl	M	Ap
72	D									
73	M									
74	LM									
75	LM									
76	LM									
77	D									
78	M									
79	D									
80	D									
81	CHL									
82	CHL									
83	CHL									
84	D									
85	D									
86	D									
87	LM									
88	LM									
89	LM									
90	D									
91	D									
92	D									
93	M									
94	M									
95	D									
96	CHL									
97	CHL									
98	CHL									
99	CHL									
100	CHL									
101	D									
102	D									
103	D									
104	CHL									
105	CHL									
106	CHL									
107	D									
108	CHL									
109	CHL									
110	CHL									
111	CHL									
112	D									
113	D									
114	CHL									
115	D									

	Q#		PC	SnP	LM	CHL	D	PrS	PyCl	M	Ap
	116	M									
	117	LM									
	118	LM									
	119	LM									
	120	LM									
	121	PrS									
	122	Ap									
	123	PrS									
	124	PrS									
	125	PrS									
	126	Ap									
	127	Ap									
	128	PrS									
	129	PrS									
	130	PrS									
	131	Ap									
	132	PrS									
	133	PrS									
	134	PrS									
	135	PrS									
	136	PrS									
	137	PrS									
	138	PrS									
	139	PrS									
	140	PrS									
	141	PrS									
	142	PrS									
	143	PrS									
	144	Ap									
	145	PrS									
	146	PrS									
	147	PrS									
	148	PrS									
	149	PrS									
	150	PyCl									
	151	PyCl									
	152	PyCl									
	153	PyCl									
	154	PyCl									
	155	PyCl									
	156	PyCl									
	157	M									
	158	M									
	159	M									

Q#		PC	SnP	LM	CHL	D	PrS	PyCl	M	Ap
160	M									
161	PyCl									
162	PyCl									
163	PyCl									
164	PyCl									
165	PyCl									
166	PyCl									
167	PyCl									
168	PyCl									
169	PyCl									
170	PyCl									
171	PyCl									
172	PyCl									
173	PyCl									
174	PyCl									
175	PyCl									
176	PyCl									
177	M									
178	Ap									
179	Ap									
180	Ap									
181	M									
182	M									
183	M									
184	Ap									
185	M									
186	Ap									
187	Ap									
188	Ap									
189	Ap									
190	Ap									
191	Ap									
192	Ap									
193	Ap									
194	Ap									
195	Ap									
196	Ap									
197	M									
198	M									
199	M									
200	Ap									
Sum										

Test Score Scaling

In the groove yet? Same drill as before—just bring your tally sums forward from the previous page and tuck them into the blanks below. Then see how you're stacking up with those 75th percentiles.

PC Area: 22 – _____ (your number missed) = _____ // 17 = 75th percentile

SnP Area: 20 – _____ (your number missed) = _____ // 15 = 75th percentile

LM Area: 25 – _____ (your number missed) = _____ // 19 = 75th percentile

CHL Area: 21 – _____ (your number missed) = _____ // 16 = 75th percentile

D Area: 24 – _____ (your number missed) = _____ // 18 = 75th percentile

PrS Area: 24 – _____ (your number missed) = _____ // 18 = 75th percentile

PyCl Area: 23 – _____ (your number missed) = _____ // 17 = 75th percentile

M Area: 20 – _____ (your number missed) = _____ // 15 = 75th percentile

Ap Area: 21 – _____ (your number missed) = _____ // 16 = 75th percentile

Test 4: Answer Grid

1. Ⓐ Ⓑ Ⓒ Ⓓ Ⓔ	51. Ⓐ Ⓑ Ⓒ Ⓓ Ⓔ	101. Ⓐ Ⓑ Ⓒ Ⓓ Ⓔ	151. Ⓐ Ⓑ Ⓒ Ⓓ Ⓔ
2. Ⓐ Ⓑ Ⓒ Ⓓ Ⓔ	52. Ⓐ Ⓑ Ⓒ Ⓓ Ⓔ	102. Ⓐ Ⓑ Ⓒ Ⓓ Ⓔ	152. Ⓐ Ⓑ Ⓒ Ⓓ Ⓔ
3. Ⓐ Ⓑ Ⓒ Ⓓ Ⓔ	53. Ⓐ Ⓑ Ⓒ Ⓓ Ⓔ	103. Ⓐ Ⓑ Ⓒ Ⓓ Ⓔ	153. Ⓐ Ⓑ Ⓒ Ⓓ Ⓔ
4. Ⓐ Ⓑ Ⓒ Ⓓ Ⓔ	54. Ⓐ Ⓑ Ⓒ Ⓓ Ⓔ	104. Ⓐ Ⓑ Ⓒ Ⓓ Ⓔ	154. Ⓐ Ⓑ Ⓒ Ⓓ Ⓔ
5. Ⓐ Ⓑ Ⓒ Ⓓ Ⓔ	55. Ⓐ Ⓑ Ⓒ Ⓓ Ⓔ	105. Ⓐ Ⓑ Ⓒ Ⓓ Ⓔ	155. Ⓐ Ⓑ Ⓒ Ⓓ Ⓔ
6. Ⓐ Ⓑ Ⓒ Ⓓ Ⓔ	56. Ⓐ Ⓑ Ⓒ Ⓓ Ⓔ	106. Ⓐ Ⓑ Ⓒ Ⓓ Ⓔ	156. Ⓐ Ⓑ Ⓒ Ⓓ Ⓔ
7. Ⓐ Ⓑ Ⓒ Ⓓ Ⓔ	57. Ⓐ Ⓑ Ⓒ Ⓓ Ⓔ	107. Ⓐ Ⓑ Ⓒ Ⓓ Ⓔ	157. Ⓐ Ⓑ Ⓒ Ⓓ Ⓔ
8. Ⓐ Ⓑ Ⓒ Ⓓ Ⓔ	58. Ⓐ Ⓑ Ⓒ Ⓓ Ⓔ	108. Ⓐ Ⓑ Ⓒ Ⓓ Ⓔ	158. Ⓐ Ⓑ Ⓒ Ⓓ Ⓔ
9. Ⓐ Ⓑ Ⓒ Ⓓ Ⓔ	59. Ⓐ Ⓑ Ⓒ Ⓓ Ⓔ	109. Ⓐ Ⓑ Ⓒ Ⓓ Ⓔ	159. Ⓐ Ⓑ Ⓒ Ⓓ Ⓔ
10. Ⓐ Ⓑ Ⓒ Ⓓ Ⓔ	60. Ⓐ Ⓑ Ⓒ Ⓓ Ⓔ	110. Ⓐ Ⓑ Ⓒ Ⓓ Ⓔ	160. Ⓐ Ⓑ Ⓒ Ⓓ Ⓔ
11. Ⓐ Ⓑ Ⓒ Ⓓ Ⓔ	61. Ⓐ Ⓑ Ⓒ Ⓓ Ⓔ	111. Ⓐ Ⓑ Ⓒ Ⓓ Ⓔ	161. Ⓐ Ⓑ Ⓒ Ⓓ Ⓔ
12. Ⓐ Ⓑ Ⓒ Ⓓ Ⓔ	62. Ⓐ Ⓑ Ⓒ Ⓓ Ⓔ	112. Ⓐ Ⓑ Ⓒ Ⓓ Ⓔ	162. Ⓐ Ⓑ Ⓒ Ⓓ Ⓔ
13. Ⓐ Ⓑ Ⓒ Ⓓ Ⓔ	63. Ⓐ Ⓑ Ⓒ Ⓓ Ⓔ	113. Ⓐ Ⓑ Ⓒ Ⓓ Ⓔ	163. Ⓐ Ⓑ Ⓒ Ⓓ Ⓔ
14. Ⓐ Ⓑ Ⓒ Ⓓ Ⓔ	64. Ⓐ Ⓑ Ⓒ Ⓓ Ⓔ	114. Ⓐ Ⓑ Ⓒ Ⓓ Ⓔ	164. Ⓐ Ⓑ Ⓒ Ⓓ Ⓔ
15. Ⓐ Ⓑ Ⓒ Ⓓ Ⓔ	65. Ⓐ Ⓑ Ⓒ Ⓓ Ⓔ	115. Ⓐ Ⓑ Ⓒ Ⓓ Ⓔ	165. Ⓐ Ⓑ Ⓒ Ⓓ Ⓔ
16. Ⓐ Ⓑ Ⓒ Ⓓ Ⓔ	66. Ⓐ Ⓑ Ⓒ Ⓓ Ⓔ	116. Ⓐ Ⓑ Ⓒ Ⓓ Ⓔ	166. Ⓐ Ⓑ Ⓒ Ⓓ Ⓔ
17. Ⓐ Ⓑ Ⓒ Ⓓ Ⓔ	67. Ⓐ Ⓑ Ⓒ Ⓓ Ⓔ	117. Ⓐ Ⓑ Ⓒ Ⓓ Ⓔ	167. Ⓐ Ⓑ Ⓒ Ⓓ Ⓔ
18. Ⓐ Ⓑ Ⓒ Ⓓ Ⓔ	68. Ⓐ Ⓑ Ⓒ Ⓓ Ⓔ	118. Ⓐ Ⓑ Ⓒ Ⓓ Ⓔ	168. Ⓐ Ⓑ Ⓒ Ⓓ Ⓔ
19. Ⓐ Ⓑ Ⓒ Ⓓ Ⓔ	69. Ⓐ Ⓑ Ⓒ Ⓓ Ⓔ	119. Ⓐ Ⓑ Ⓒ Ⓓ Ⓔ	169. Ⓐ Ⓑ Ⓒ Ⓓ Ⓔ
20. Ⓐ Ⓑ Ⓒ Ⓓ Ⓔ	70. Ⓐ Ⓑ Ⓒ Ⓓ Ⓔ	120. Ⓐ Ⓑ Ⓒ Ⓓ Ⓔ	170. Ⓐ Ⓑ Ⓒ Ⓓ Ⓔ
21. Ⓐ Ⓑ Ⓒ Ⓓ Ⓔ	71. Ⓐ Ⓑ Ⓒ Ⓓ Ⓔ	121. Ⓐ Ⓑ Ⓒ Ⓓ Ⓔ	171. Ⓐ Ⓑ Ⓒ Ⓓ Ⓔ
22. Ⓐ Ⓑ Ⓒ Ⓓ Ⓔ	72. Ⓐ Ⓑ Ⓒ Ⓓ Ⓔ	122. Ⓐ Ⓑ Ⓒ Ⓓ Ⓔ	172. Ⓐ Ⓑ Ⓒ Ⓓ Ⓔ
23. Ⓐ Ⓑ Ⓒ Ⓓ Ⓔ	73. Ⓐ Ⓑ Ⓒ Ⓓ Ⓔ	123. Ⓐ Ⓑ Ⓒ Ⓓ Ⓔ	173. Ⓐ Ⓑ Ⓒ Ⓓ Ⓔ
24. Ⓐ Ⓑ Ⓒ Ⓓ Ⓔ	74. Ⓐ Ⓑ Ⓒ Ⓓ Ⓔ	124. Ⓐ Ⓑ Ⓒ Ⓓ Ⓔ	174. Ⓐ Ⓑ Ⓒ Ⓓ Ⓔ
25. Ⓐ Ⓑ Ⓒ Ⓓ Ⓔ	75. Ⓐ Ⓑ Ⓒ Ⓓ Ⓔ	125. Ⓐ Ⓑ Ⓒ Ⓓ Ⓔ	175. Ⓐ Ⓑ Ⓒ Ⓓ Ⓔ
26. Ⓐ Ⓑ Ⓒ Ⓓ Ⓔ	76. Ⓐ Ⓑ Ⓒ Ⓓ Ⓔ	126. Ⓐ Ⓑ Ⓒ Ⓓ Ⓔ	176. Ⓐ Ⓑ Ⓒ Ⓓ Ⓔ
27. Ⓐ Ⓑ Ⓒ Ⓓ Ⓔ	77. Ⓐ Ⓑ Ⓒ Ⓓ Ⓔ	127. Ⓐ Ⓑ Ⓒ Ⓓ Ⓔ	177. Ⓐ Ⓑ Ⓒ Ⓓ Ⓔ
28. Ⓐ Ⓑ Ⓒ Ⓓ Ⓔ	78. Ⓐ Ⓑ Ⓒ Ⓓ Ⓔ	128. Ⓐ Ⓑ Ⓒ Ⓓ Ⓔ	178. Ⓐ Ⓑ Ⓒ Ⓓ Ⓔ
29. Ⓐ Ⓑ Ⓒ Ⓓ Ⓔ	79. Ⓐ Ⓑ Ⓒ Ⓓ Ⓔ	129. Ⓐ Ⓑ Ⓒ Ⓓ Ⓔ	179. Ⓐ Ⓑ Ⓒ Ⓓ Ⓔ
30. Ⓐ Ⓑ Ⓒ Ⓓ Ⓔ	80. Ⓐ Ⓑ Ⓒ Ⓓ Ⓔ	130. Ⓐ Ⓑ Ⓒ Ⓓ Ⓔ	180. Ⓐ Ⓑ Ⓒ Ⓓ Ⓔ
31. Ⓐ Ⓑ Ⓒ Ⓓ Ⓔ	81. Ⓐ Ⓑ Ⓒ Ⓓ Ⓔ	131. Ⓐ Ⓑ Ⓒ Ⓓ Ⓔ	181. Ⓐ Ⓑ Ⓒ Ⓓ Ⓔ
32. Ⓐ Ⓑ Ⓒ Ⓓ Ⓔ	82. Ⓐ Ⓑ Ⓒ Ⓓ Ⓔ	132. Ⓐ Ⓑ Ⓒ Ⓓ Ⓔ	182. Ⓐ Ⓑ Ⓒ Ⓓ Ⓔ
33. Ⓐ Ⓑ Ⓒ Ⓓ Ⓔ	83. Ⓐ Ⓑ Ⓒ Ⓓ Ⓔ	133. Ⓐ Ⓑ Ⓒ Ⓓ Ⓔ	183. Ⓐ Ⓑ Ⓒ Ⓓ Ⓔ
34. Ⓐ Ⓑ Ⓒ Ⓓ Ⓔ	84. Ⓐ Ⓑ Ⓒ Ⓓ Ⓔ	134. Ⓐ Ⓑ Ⓒ Ⓓ Ⓔ	184. Ⓐ Ⓑ Ⓒ Ⓓ Ⓔ
35. Ⓐ Ⓑ Ⓒ Ⓓ Ⓔ	85. Ⓐ Ⓑ Ⓒ Ⓓ Ⓔ	135. Ⓐ Ⓑ Ⓒ Ⓓ Ⓔ	185. Ⓐ Ⓑ Ⓒ Ⓓ Ⓔ
36. Ⓐ Ⓑ Ⓒ Ⓓ Ⓔ	86. Ⓐ Ⓑ Ⓒ Ⓓ Ⓔ	136. Ⓐ Ⓑ Ⓒ Ⓓ Ⓔ	186. Ⓐ Ⓑ Ⓒ Ⓓ Ⓔ
37. Ⓐ Ⓑ Ⓒ Ⓓ Ⓔ	87. Ⓐ Ⓑ Ⓒ Ⓓ Ⓔ	137. Ⓐ Ⓑ Ⓒ Ⓓ Ⓔ	187. Ⓐ Ⓑ Ⓒ Ⓓ Ⓔ
38. Ⓐ Ⓑ Ⓒ Ⓓ Ⓔ	88. Ⓐ Ⓑ Ⓒ Ⓓ Ⓔ	138. Ⓐ Ⓑ Ⓒ Ⓓ Ⓔ	188. Ⓐ Ⓑ Ⓒ Ⓓ Ⓔ
39. Ⓐ Ⓑ Ⓒ Ⓓ Ⓔ	89. Ⓐ Ⓑ Ⓒ Ⓓ Ⓔ	139. Ⓐ Ⓑ Ⓒ Ⓓ Ⓔ	189. Ⓐ Ⓑ Ⓒ Ⓓ Ⓔ
40. Ⓐ Ⓑ Ⓒ Ⓓ Ⓔ	90. Ⓐ Ⓑ Ⓒ Ⓓ Ⓔ	140. Ⓐ Ⓑ Ⓒ Ⓓ Ⓔ	190. Ⓐ Ⓑ Ⓒ Ⓓ Ⓔ
41. Ⓐ Ⓑ Ⓒ Ⓓ Ⓔ	91. Ⓐ Ⓑ Ⓒ Ⓓ Ⓔ	141. Ⓐ Ⓑ Ⓒ Ⓓ Ⓔ	191. Ⓐ Ⓑ Ⓒ Ⓓ Ⓔ
42. Ⓐ Ⓑ Ⓒ Ⓓ Ⓔ	92. Ⓐ Ⓑ Ⓒ Ⓓ Ⓔ	142. Ⓐ Ⓑ Ⓒ Ⓓ Ⓔ	192. Ⓐ Ⓑ Ⓒ Ⓓ Ⓔ
43. Ⓐ Ⓑ Ⓒ Ⓓ Ⓔ	93. Ⓐ Ⓑ Ⓒ Ⓓ Ⓔ	143. Ⓐ Ⓑ Ⓒ Ⓓ Ⓔ	193. Ⓐ Ⓑ Ⓒ Ⓓ Ⓔ
44. Ⓐ Ⓑ Ⓒ Ⓓ Ⓔ	94. Ⓐ Ⓑ Ⓒ Ⓓ Ⓔ	144. Ⓐ Ⓑ Ⓒ Ⓓ Ⓔ	194. Ⓐ Ⓑ Ⓒ Ⓓ Ⓔ
45. Ⓐ Ⓑ Ⓒ Ⓓ Ⓔ	95. Ⓐ Ⓑ Ⓒ Ⓓ Ⓔ	145. Ⓐ Ⓑ Ⓒ Ⓓ Ⓔ	195. Ⓐ Ⓑ Ⓒ Ⓓ Ⓔ
46. Ⓐ Ⓑ Ⓒ Ⓓ Ⓔ	96. Ⓐ Ⓑ Ⓒ Ⓓ Ⓔ	146. Ⓐ Ⓑ Ⓒ Ⓓ Ⓔ	196. Ⓐ Ⓑ Ⓒ Ⓓ Ⓔ
47. Ⓐ Ⓑ Ⓒ Ⓓ Ⓔ	97. Ⓐ Ⓑ Ⓒ Ⓓ Ⓔ	147. Ⓐ Ⓑ Ⓒ Ⓓ Ⓔ	197. Ⓐ Ⓑ Ⓒ Ⓓ Ⓔ
48. Ⓐ Ⓑ Ⓒ Ⓓ Ⓔ	98. Ⓐ Ⓑ Ⓒ Ⓓ Ⓔ	148. Ⓐ Ⓑ Ⓒ Ⓓ Ⓔ	198. Ⓐ Ⓑ Ⓒ Ⓓ Ⓔ
49. Ⓐ Ⓑ Ⓒ Ⓓ Ⓔ	99. Ⓐ Ⓑ Ⓒ Ⓓ Ⓔ	149. Ⓐ Ⓑ Ⓒ Ⓓ Ⓔ	199. Ⓐ Ⓑ Ⓒ Ⓓ Ⓔ
50. Ⓐ Ⓑ Ⓒ Ⓓ Ⓔ	100. Ⓐ Ⓑ Ⓒ Ⓓ Ⓔ	150. Ⓐ Ⓑ Ⓒ Ⓓ Ⓔ	200. Ⓐ Ⓑ Ⓒ Ⓓ Ⓔ

Test 4

Time: 170 minutes

Directions: Each of the following questions contains five possible responses. Read the question carefully and select the response that you feel is most appropriate. Then completely darken the oval on your answer grid that corresponds with your choice.

1. The motion picture depends for its perceptual success upon

   (A) the physiological limitations of the human visual apparatus
   (B) synesthesia
   (C) motion parallax
   (D) the unique capacities of the optic chiasm
   (E) the closure phenomenon

2. Which one of the following statements is *incorrect*?

   (A) Bekesy has done significant research work in the area of audition.
   (B) Olfactory receptors are located within the turbinate bones.
   (C) The work of Hubel and Weisel has been of central importance in the area of visual receptive fields.
   (D) In terms of cortex location, taste and facial somatic functions are closely related.
   (E) Microelectrode techniques have been used in taste research.

3. The area between the eardrum and the oval window is occupied by the

   (A) cochlea   (B) Organ of Corti   (C) cilia
   (D) ossicles   (E) round window

4. Feedback regarding internal organs of the body is obtained through the

   (A) skin senses
   (B) somesthetic senses
   (C) labyrinthine senses
   (D) visceral senses
   (E) striated senses

5. The phenomenon whereby four closely contiguous lines are perceived as a square demonstrates the principle of

   (A) contiguity   (B) closure   (C) continuation
   (D) similarity   (E) contrast

6. In contrast to children who were low in achievement need, McClelland found that children with high achievement need had a

   (A) stronger preference for intermediate-risk tasks
   (B) weaker preference for intermediate-risk tasks
   (C) stronger preference for low-risk tasks
   (D) stronger preference for high-risk tasks
   (E) stronger preference for tasks at all risk levels

7. Given a choice of tasks for which a person can anticipate equal probabilities of success, Atkinson has found that a key factor in determining the strength of the response is the

   (A) size of the achievement
   (B) prepotency of the stimulus
   (C) value that the subject places on the achievement
   (D) value that the experimenter places on the achievement
   (E) UCS nature of the reinforcement

8. Experimental work in perception received its earliest beginnings with

   (A) Restle   (B) Weber   (C) Wertheimer
   (D) Kohler   (E) Koffka

9. Which of the following illusions involves two lines with arrowheads on both ends?

   (A) vertical-horizontal   (B) Ames room
   (C) trapezoidal window   (D) Muller-Lyer   (E) Landolt-C

10. On the basis of existing research, which one of the following influences is found in the childhood backgrounds of adults with a high achievement need?

    (A) encouragement of curiosity
    (B) encouragement of creativity
    (C) encouragement of independence
    (D) frequent frustrations
    (E) encouragement of aggression

11. As Joan walks along the beach, one set of muscles operates antagonistically to another set in achieving the coordination necessary for walking. Coordination of this antagonistic muscle activity is described as

    (A) reciprocal inhibition
    (B) reciprocal innervation
    (C) retroactive innervation
    (D) proprioception
    (E) somatoception

12. Striated muscles are

    (A) known as involuntary
    (B) synonymous with smooth muscles
    (C) the type that produce stomach contractions
    (D) responsible for producing skeletal movement
    (E) responsible for labyrinthine sensitivity

13. Wernicke's center in the brain relates to

    (A) speech
    (B) understanding spoken language
    (C) handedness
    (D) coordination necessary in walking
    (E) sexual arousal

14. Prominent among monocular depth cues is

    (A) accommodation
    (B) texture-density gradient
    (C) retinal disparity
    (D) reciprocal innervation
    (E) retinal polarity

15. Which one of the following statements about the area of vigilance is true?

    (A) The probability of operator detection declines with the amount of vigilance time.
    (B) The probability of operator detection increases with the amount of vigilance time.
    (C) Performance worsens when the operator receives feedback.
    (D) Performance is worsened by the introduction of brief rest periods.
    (E) Performance decline is faster than normal if the position and timing of signals is uncertain.

16. In reaction time settings

    (A) at levels close to threshold, increasing the strength of a stimulus shortens reaction time
    (B) at levels close to threshold, decreasing duration of a stimulus shortens reaction time
    (C) at levels close to threshold, decreasing the strength of a stimulus shortens reaction time
    (D) kinesthesis is generally the sensory modality utilized
    (E) pain sensitivity is generally the sensory modality utilized

17. When two sense organs are stimulated simultaneously, reaction time is

    (A) faster than when only one is stimulated
    (B) slower than when only one is stimulated
    (C) retarded in the second sensory modality being stimulated
    (D) retarded in the first sensory modality being stimulated
    (E) equivalent to reaction time when only one sense organ is being stimulated

18. Perceptually, to "wait 'til Christmas" would be the longest wait for the

    (A) preschool child
    (B) elementary school child
    (C) teenager
    (D) college-age adult
    (E) middle-age adult

19. Between which one of the following pairs of men could basic, conceptual agreement be anticipated?

    (A) Tolman and Lewin
    (B) Lewin and Freud
    (C) Lewin and Skinner
    (D) Tolman and Thorndike
    (E) Tolman and Pavlov

20. Among the following, the most important name in achievement motivation research is

   (A) Miller   (B) Bandura   (C) Mowrer
   (D) Atkinson   (E) Murray

21. Watson identified the three distinct emotional responses in the human infant as

   (A) love, rage, fear
   (B) love, rage, surprise
   (C) surprise, rage, fear
   (D) love, surprise, fear
   (E) love, rage, distress

22. Near the turn of the century, a psychologist named Stratton wore goggles that inverted the retinal image. Which of the following did he experience?

   (A) The world looked upside down while he wore the goggles.
   (B) The world appeared upside down at first, then later became perceptually normal.
   (C) The world looked perceptually normal throughout the time he wore the glasses.
   (D) The world looked perceptually normal immediately after he removed the glasses.
   (E) He was affected by temporary blindness.

23. The orienting reflex

   (A) is a physiological reaction to changes in the perceptual environment
   (B) occurs when the sole of the foot is stimulated
   (C) is equivalent to the child's rooting reflex
   (D) was discovered by Babinski
   (E) relates only to the activity of reading

24. The familiar face-vase picture seen in most introductory and perception sources is an example of

   (A) parallax   (B) closure   (C) figure reversibility
   (D) size constancy   (E) shape constancy

25. The Pacinian corpuscle is related to

   (A) audition   (B) vision   (C) pressure
   (D) taste   (E) smell

26. Which one of the following statements is *not* true of dreaming?

   (A) It is usually accompanied by erection of the penis in males.
   (B) It is reported that about 80% of the subjects awakened during REM periods.
   (C) It occurs in a rhythmic cycle about every ninety minutes.
   (D) It always occurs during beta wave activity.
   (E) It occurs during Stage 1 REM.

27. The Gestalt school of psychology subscribes to the basic principle that

    (A) only overt behavior can be studied scientifically
    (B) behavior or experience equals more than the sum of its parts
    (C) psychology must concern itself only with studying man's adjustment to his environment
    (D) thanatos-eros forms the primary conflict to be studied within psychology
    (E) conscious experience cannot be a legitimate area for scientific investigation

28. Misperception of an illusion: stimulus:: hallucination:

    (A) delusion
    (B) autokinesis
    (C) response in the absence of external stimulus
    (D) accurate perception of an external stimulus
    (E) alpha wave

29. The "moon illusion" relates to the tendency to perceive

    (A) a quarter moon as a half moon
    (B) a three-quarter moon as a full moon
    (C) the moon in the sky as larger than the moon on the horizon
    (D) the moon on the horizon as larger than the moon in the sky
    (E) the Milky Way as a "shadow moon"

30. In the midst of deep sleep, the dominant brain wave is

    (A) alpha   (B) beta   (C) theta
    (D) gamma   (E) delta

31. The basilar membrane plays an important role in

    (A) vision
    (B) hearing
    (C) olfaction
    (D) taste
    (E) kinesthetic sensation

32. William McDougall

    (A) criticized the stimulus-response mode of thought
    (B) criticized the notion of purposive behavior
    (C) aligned himself with the arguments of Thorndike
    (D) initiated the work that eventually led to Pavlov's theories
    (E) differed with the positive valence theory but promoted the views relating to negative valence

33. Tinbergen outlines four major areas of study in animal behavior. *Not* among them is

    (A) development   (B) mechanisms   (C) function
    (D) habits   (E) evolution

34. "The only determinants of behavior at a given time are the properties of the person and his psychological environment at that time." This is a quote from

    (A) Lewin   (B) Skinner   (C) Watson
    (D) Atkinson   (E) McClelland

35. In James's view, habit

    (A) is purely instinctive
    (B) involves instinct in combination with experience
    (C) involves learning in combination with experience
    (D) involves only learning
    (E) is purely emotion-centered

36. Duplicity Theory applies to

    (A) sympathetic and parasympathetic nervous systems
    (B) reciprocal innervation
    (C) bone and nerve conductant elements in audition
    (D) rod-cone vision
    (E) overlapping functions of taste and olfaction

37. The specific-energy-of-nerves concept is directly attributable to

    (A) Mowrer   (B) Magoun   (C) Sherrington
    (D) Meissner   (E) Muller

38. Critical flicker frequency is the rate of light fluctuation

    (A) above which flicker is reported
    (B) above which fusion occurs
    (C) below which fusion occurs
    (D) above which both flicker and fusion occur
    (E) below which both flicker and fusion occur

39. The suggestion that *all* nerves fire constantly and repeatedly to produce the reception of pitch would be an expression of the

    (A) place theory
    (B) frequency theory
    (C) yolley theory
    (D) decibel theory
    (E) amplitude theory

40. The neurotransmitters basic to synaptic transmission are stored in

    (A) vesicles   (B) end plates   (C) cerebellum
    (D) receptors   (E) dendrites

41. Perceptual constancies are primarily a function of

    (A) reflex   (B) tropism   (C) instinct
    (D) learning   (E) convergence

42. The myelin sheath serves to

(A) break down epinephrine
(B) bypass the nodes of Ranvier
(C) depress the reticular activating system
(D) decrease the speed of neural transmission
(E) increase the speed of neural transmission

43. The fact that, during neural transmission, an impulse is sent to the end of the axon without fading or weakening is known as

(A) stimulus constancy
(B) absolute threshold retention
(C) nondecremental property
(D) all-or-none property
(E) activation constancy

44. The alpha wave has a frequency of approximately how many cycles per second?

(A) five   (B) twenty   (C) thirty
(D) ten   (E) two

45. According to the Montreal Studies, the original infant emotion upon which all others are based is

(A) fear   (B) excitement   (C) love
(D) distress   (E) delight

46. Very high anger arousal causes which one of the following bodily responses?

(A) lowered blood pressure
(B) dilation of blood vessels near the skin
(C) heightened visual acuity
(D) lowered activity among the striated muscles
(E) lowered blood sugar

47. Which of the following persons located pleasure centers in the brain via rat experimentation?

(A) Sperry   (B) Krech   (C) Meissner
(D) Olds   (E) Delgado

48. Assuming the analogy of a doorbell, which aspect of the neuron would most closely approximate the button that a visitor would push?

(A) terminal endings
(B) axon
(C) cell body
(D) myelin sheath
(E) dendrites

49. Which one of the following statements can be concluded from dream research?

    (A) Dreaming apparently serves a basic organismic need.
    (B) Dreaming is dispensable and unnecessary.
    (C) Most persons do not dream.
    (D) Dreaming drops markedly in frequency among the elderly.
    (E) No activity suggesting dreaming can be found in EEG sleep research.

50. Which one of the following is an apparent bodily response to the emotions of resentment and hostility?

    (A) lower heart rate
    (B) lower blood pressure
    (C) heightened auditory sensitivity
    (D) lower breathing rate
    (E) increased stomach acidity

51. The Cannon-Bard theory deals with the

    (A) Islets of Langerhans   (B) thalamus and hypothalamus
    (C) corpus callosum   (D) adrenal cortex   (E) pineal gland

52. Axon : dendrite ::

    (A) transmitting information : receiving information
    (B) inhibitory : excitatory
    (C) sympathetic : parasympathetic
    (D) limbic system : hypothalamus
    (E) resting potential : action potential

53. The most appropriate example of the difference-limen method among the following is

    (A) a single tone varied systematically in decibels
    (B) a spot of light continuously presented as a fixed stimulus
    (C) a sequence of light stimuli at different fixed intensities above and below threshold
    (D) two different intensities of light presented simultaneously
    (E) two different decibel levels of tone presented sequentially

54. Which of the following is the formula for Weber's Law?

    (A) Delta $I/K = I$ (B) Delta $I/I = K$ (C) K/I = Delta I
    (D) I/K = Delta I (E) $K/$Delta $I = I$

55. The neural connection pattern between the eyes and the brain

    (A) presents special problems and considerations in split-brain research
    (B) is identical to the auditory pattern
    (C) bears close resemblance to the labyrinthine sensory pattern
    (D) perpetuates the Duplicity Theory concept
    (E) relies heavily on the cerebellum

Questions 56–59 are based on the following drawing.

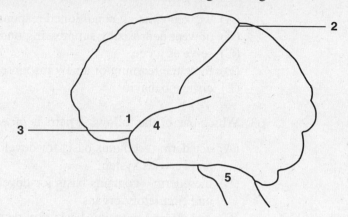

Indicate by the appropriate number:

56. Broca's area

    (A) 1   (B) 2   (C) 3   (D) 4   (E) 5

57. Wernicke's center

    (A) 1   (B) 2   (C) 3   (D) 4   (E) 5

58. Sylvian fissure

    (A) 1   (B) 2   (C) 3   (D) 4   (E) 5

59. Reticular formation

    (A) 1   (B) 2   (C) 3   (D) 4   (E) 5

60. A primary difference between escape and avoidance conditioning is that

    (A) in escape conditioning, the aversive stimulus is always received by the subject
    (B) in escape conditioning, the aversive stimulus is not received by the subject
    (C) in escape conditioning, successive approximation is used
    (D) in escape conditioning, successive approximation is not used
    (E) escape conditioning utilizes response chaining

61. To remember the order of the seven colors of the spectrum, many people learn "ROY" - "G" - "BIV" (Red, Orange, Yellow, Green, Blue, Indigo, Violet). This is easier to learn because

    (A) pictures are easier to remember than words
    (B) semantic encoding results in better memory than physical encoding
    (C) words at the beginning or end of a list are remembered better than words at the middle of a list
    (D) the number of chunks to be learned is reduced from 7 to 3.
    (E) novel, unusual, or emotionally charged events are remembered better than mundane events

62. The principal value of punishment lies in its capacity to

    (A) weaken existing conditioned responses
    (B) prevent neurosis by suppressing undesirable responses
    (C) serve as a cue
    (D) force the learning of a new response
    (E) change behavior

63. Which one of the following pairs is *incorrect*?

    (A) ectoderm—contains basis for development of skin, sensory cells, and nervous system
    (B) mesoderm—contains basis for development of muscles, skeleton, and circulatory organs
    (C) endoderm—contains basis for development of thyroid glands, liver, lungs, and pancreas
    (D) trophoblast—a major substance within the endoderm
    (E) placenta—extends from embryo to the uterus-chorion juncture

Questions 64 and 65 are based upon the following answer choices.

    (1) meat powder
    (2) buzzer
    (3) Skinner box
    (4) fixed-interval reinforcement
    (5) variable-ratio reinforcement

64. Which of the preceding would most accurately characterize the horse-race betting situation?

    (A) 1   (B) 2   (C) 3   (D) 4   (E) 5

65. Which of the above qualifies as an unconditioned stimulus?

    (A) 1   (B) 2   (C) 3   (D) 4   (E) 5

66. Concurrent validity is demonstrated by which one of the following?

    (A) examining of test content by a panel of experts
    (B) correlating scores with a test taker's general performance in other areas
    (C) correlating a current score with a test taker's earlier score on the same instrument
    (D) correlating scores on two halves of the same test
    (E) correlating a given test with other established tests in the field

67. Sternberg found that decision time increases as a direct function of the number of items in short-term memory. This outcome lends support to which process in short-term memory retrieval?

    (A) parallel   (B) chunking   (C) bilateral
    (D) serial   (E) mnemonic

68. A multiple-choice test such as this uses a measure of memory called

   (A) relearning   (B) free recall   (C) cued recall
   (D) recognition   (E) repetition priming

69. In higher-order conditioning, a former

   (A) UCS serves as a CS
   (B) UCR serves as a CR
   (C) CR serves as a UCS
   (D) CR serves as a UCR
   (E) CS serves as a UCS

70. Which one of the following significance levels is most rigorous?

   (A) .05   (B) .02   (C) .01   (D) .005   (E) .1

71. Which one of the following would not be expected in the newborn?

   (A) well-developed temperature sensitivity
   (B) Moro reflex
   (C) Babinski response
   (D) well-developed grasping reflex
   (E) well-developed pain sensitivity

72. Within normal communications, noise

   (A) is nonexistent
   (B) will occur only at the source
   (C) will occur only in encoding
   (D) can occur at any point in the communication process
   (E) occurs only in radio-wave-type transmission

73. In contrast to adolescent gangs, children's gangs

   (A) are formed as a result of social rejection
   (B) are formed on the basis of inferiority feelings
   (C) are not formed with a "get-even" purpose in mind
   (D) are formed on the basis of family similarities
   (E) are formed on the basis of birth order

74. You have been read the sentence "Kathy pounded the nail." Later you are read "Kathy hammered the nail," and you indicate agreement that it is the same sentence you heard originally. This is an example of

   (A) inference   (B) depth of processing theory   (C) déjà vu
   (D) countertransference   (E) dual-process theory

75. Which one of the following is not related closely to the term sickle cell?

   (A) abnormal form of hemoglobin
   (B) possibility of dangerous clotting
   (C) specific race prominence
   (D) a form of cancer
   (E) a form of anemia

76. Tom is blue-eyed (homozygous) and Mary is brown-eyed (heterozygous). Their chances for brown-eyed offspring are

(A) 2 in 4   (B) 1 in 4   (C) 3 in 4
(D) 4 in 4   (E) 0 in 4

77. *Least* likely to succeed in obtaining a balanced diet through self-selection would be a

(A) rat   (B) cat   (C) rabbit
(D) human infant   (E) human adult

78. Genotype : phenotype ::

(A) aptitude : performance
(B) identical : fraternal
(C) recessive : dominant
(D) prenatal : postnatal
(E) heredity : appearance

79. The critical-periods concept of intelligence as it relates to environmental stimulation during early childhood is being challenged by the experimental work of

(A) Scott   (B) Harlow   (C) Kagan
(D) Mussen   (E) McCandless

80. Which one of the following is the Moro response?

(A) sucking
(B) rooting
(C) toes curling upward and outward
(D) grasping reflex
(E) arms and legs stretched outward suddenly

81. In gamete development, the fact that each mature egg or sperm contains only one chromosome from each pair is attributable to a process known as

(A) fertilization
(B) immunization
(C) reduction division
(D) zygotic division
(E) monozygotic division

82. A person has just flipped a coin six times with heads resulting from each toss. The person now predicts with great certainty that the next toss will produce tails. This individual has just fallen prey to

(A) an algorithm error
(B) the conjunction or "gambler's fallacy"
(C) a subgoal analysis error
(D) a reproductive thought error
(E) the deductive error

83. In Harlow's experiments, the surrogate-reared infant monkeys were least fearful in the presence of

    (A) the surrogate mother to which the sucking response had been directed
    (B) the surrogate mother to which the clinging response had been directed
    (C) their siblings
    (D) their natural father
    (E) playmates

84. Which of the following is an *incorrect* pairing?

    (A) duct glands—secretions emptied into body cavities
    (B) ductless glands—secretions made directly into the bloodstream
    (C) gray matter—indicative of cell bodies
    (D) white matter—indicative of myelinated fibers
    (E) cardiac muscle—a nonstriated (smooth) muscle

85. Positive transfer is greatest when a person performs

    (A) new responses to similar stimuli
    (B) old responses to different stimuli
    (C) new responses to different stimuli
    (D) old responses to similar stimuli
    (E) new responses to new stimuli

86. Alan Baddeley is one of the leading figures in research on

    (A) working memory
    (B) implicit memory
    (C) semantic memory
    (D) childhood memory
    (E) procedural memory

87. In Bruner's terms, the three modes of developing a mental world model are

    (A) motor, emotional, cognitive
    (B) enactive, iconic, symbolic
    (C) physical, physiological, psychophysical
    (D) conscious, subconscious, unconscious
    (E) parataxic, prototaxic, syntaxic

88. According to certain learning theories, introduction of a rest interval after massed practice of a motor skill will most likely produce

    (A) spontaneous recovery
    (B) reminiscence
    (C) proactive inhibition
    (D) retroactive inhibition
    (E) chunking

89. Jones's study of early and late maturers indicates that

    (A) early maturation is an advantage for males but a disadvantage for females
    (B) psychological differences between the early and late maturing males disappear when the individuals are in their thirties
    (C) by the late teens, differences in personality traits between early and late maturing girls are at the maximum
    (D) early maturation is advantageous for both sexes
    (E) early maturation is an advantage for girls but a disadvantage for boys

90. Elizabeth Loftus has reported that the testimony given by eyewitnesses in a trial is

    (A) very accurate when the event is highly emotionally charged
    (B) very accurate when the event is surprising or unexpected
    (C) susceptible to errors from post-event misinformation or suggestions
    (D) inaccurate because witnesses fail to pay attention to critical details
    (E) not weighed heavily by jurors in reaching a verdict

91. The most severe conflict situation is likely to be produced by the classification known as

    (A) approach-approach
    (B) simple approach-avoidance
    (C) approach-avoidance
    (D) double approach-approach
    (E) avoidance-avoidance

92. The British associationist school was identified with the

    (A) law of effect
    (B) law of contiguity
    (C) law of psychophysics
    (D) law of continuity
    (E) law of entropy

93. Which one of the following is *not* one of Dollard and Miller's requirements for learning?

    (A) drive   (B) cue   (C) transfer
    (D) response   (E) reinforcement

Questions 94–96 are based on the following answer choices.

    (1) pressing the palms of child's hands while he is lying on his back
    (2) stroking the sole of the neonate's foot
    (3) a loud handclap
    (4) having the baby lie prone with the bottoms of his feet against a vertical surface
    (5) stimulating the baby's palms or fingers

94. Which one of the stimuli is used to obtain the grasping reflex?

    (A) 1   (B) 2   (C) 3   (D) 4   (E) 5

95. The Babkin response is obtained by using which one of the stimuli?

    (A) 1   (B) 2   (C) 3   (D) 4   (E) 5

96. Which one of the stimuli is used to obtain a Babinski response?

    (A) 1   (B) 2   (C) 3   (D) 4   (E) 5

97. That the upper part of the body develops earlier than the lower part is termed

    (A) proximodistal   (B) cephalocaudal   (C) corticodistal
    (D) general to specific   (E) sensorimotor

98. Mitosis refers to

    (A) union of sperm and ovum
    (B) cell division and multiplication
    (C) skeletal muscle tissue development
    (D) nerve tissue development
    (E) intrauterine metabolism

99. Lovaas utilizes behavior modification techniques in the treatment of

    (A) autism   (B) aphasia   (C) acute depression
    (D) alcoholism   (E) drug addiction

100. Which of the following is an *incorrect* pairing?

    (A) Lorenz—aggression
    (B) Bandura—modeling
    (C) Scott—imprinting
    (D) Kagan—intelligence
    (E) Harlow—psycholinguistics

101. In contrast to the Stanford-Binet Scale, the Wechsler Scale

    (A) was developed through trial and error
    (B) was developed through intensive child interviews
    (C) separates verbal from performance IQ
    (D) has a different standard deviation for each age group
    (E) utilizes the MA/CA-type computational formula

102. Adjustment to postnatal environment is accomplished

    (A) more quickly among males than females
    (B) more quickly among females than males
    (C) with equal speed and ease by both males and females
    (D) more quickly among blacks than whites
    (E) more quickly among whites than blacks

103. The term *sham feeding* refers to experiments in which

    (A) food is introduced directly into the stomach
    (B) a brain operation is performed prior to the experiment
    (C) food is eaten in the normal way, without surgical alteration to any portion of the organism
    (D) nonnutritive bulk is fed to the animal
    (E) food is "eaten" and "swallowed" but does not reach the stomach

104. Chomsky includes which one of the following in his explanation of grammar acquisition in children?

    (A) "programmed" nervous system
    (B) learned concept of human language
    (C) learned concept of language specific to one's culture
    (D) archetypal communication
    (E) ITA system

105. Intelligence tests for infants

    (A) correlate with adult tests at +0.85 and above
    (B) sample the same abilities tested at later ages
    (C) provide initial information relating to aptitudes
    (D) require no standardization
    (E) are not accurate predictors of later IQ

106. Memorizing by rote (i.e., repeating something over and over until it is learned) is also called

    (A) declarative rehearsal
    (B) elaborative rehearsal
    (C) maintenance rehearsal
    (D) distributed practice
    (E) massed practice

107. The term *congenital* means

    (A) genetic
    (B) embryonic
    (C) recessive characteristic
    (D) present at birth
    (E) dominant characteristic

108. Which of the following is *not* true of emotion?

    (A) A linkage has been noticed between specific facial expressions and resulting emotions.
    (B) Expecting to experience a given emotion can result in the emotion's actually being experienced.
    (C) Opponent process theory suggests that the opposite of a given emotion may follow its being experienced.
    (D) There appears to be no relationship between ulcers and emotional state.
    (E) The James-Lange theory suggests we are afraid because we run.

109. Which one of the following groups is *not* sequentially correct?

    (A) idiot, imbecile, moron
    (B) trainable, educable, nontrainable
    (C) profoundly, severely, moderately (retarded)
    (D) severely, moderately, mildly (retarded)
    (E) moderately retarded, mildly retarded, dull normal

110. On the basis of Kendler and Kendler's general research findings, one would expect reversal shifts to be accomplished most easily and most rapidly within which one of the following groups?

    (A) rats
    (B) dogs
    (C) two-year-old children
    (D) seven-year-old children
    (E) ten-year-old children

111. Given a Bartlett interpolation sequence such as 2, 4, 6, _____, _____, 12 and a subsequent word sequence such as: a, by, cow, _____, _____, _____, _____, horrible; which one of the following series of words could constitute a correct word sequence?

    (A) gate, no, i, duty
    (B) dog, eagle, from, goat
    (C) ho, get, fate, erase
    (D) drop, event, friend, Germans
    (E) event, friend, drop, Germans

112. If we assume a mean of 100 and a standard deviation of 25, a score of 140 would provide a *z*-score of

    (A) +1.25   (B) +1.50   (C) +1.60
    (D) −1.60   (E) −1.50

113. You perceive the word differently than we because you learned the French language as a young child whereas we learned Swahili. This is an example of

    (A) the Purkinje effect
    (B) the phonemic hypothesis
    (C) the top-down processing model
    (D) the linguistic relativity hypothesis
    (E) the Premack principle

114. Sears's work suggests that a child who has been parentally punished for aggression will demonstrate

    (A) strong prosocial aggression
    (B) strong antisocial aggression
    (C) low anxiety about aggression
    (D) no aggressive behavior
    (E) self-actualization

115. After a night of heavy drinking, alcoholics are unable to remember where they went or what they did. The next time they drink, they suddenly remember everything. This illustrates the effect of

    (A) functional fixedness
    (B) state-dependent memory
    (C) Korsakoff's syndrome
    (D) retroactive interference
    (E) anterograde amnesia

116. If a person has a *z*-score of +2, he or she has scored at approximately which percentile within that specific distribution?

    (A) 75th   (B) 84th   (C) 50th   (D) 98th   (E) 40th

117. A frequency distribution that has two distinct concentrations of scores is

    (A) negatively skewed   (B) positively skewed   (C) normal
    (D) bimodal   (E) bimedial

118. A cryptarithmetic problem widely used in the study of human problem solving has been

    (A) $A + B = C$
    (B) Alpha + Beta = Kappa
    (C) DONALD + GERALD = ROBERT
    (D) MARY + SUSAN = ELIZABETH
    (E) Alpha = Gamma + Beta

119. In the Freudian system, defense mechanisms protect against which one of the following?

    (A) ego   (B) repression   (C) superego
    (D) id   (E) archetype

120. On the basis of Schachter's research, one might conclude that

    (A) misery loves any kind of company
    (B) misery loves any kind of miserable company
    (C) misery loves only miserable company in the same situational circumstances
    (D) familiarity breeds prejudicial contempt
    (E) likes attract, opposites repel

121. In Rogers' view, through interaction with one's environment, a portion of the phenomenal field becomes differentiated and known as the

    (A) archetype
    (B) script
    (C) superego
    (D) frame of orientation
    (E) self-concept

Questions 122 and *123* are based on the following answer choices

(1) same race
(2) same attitudes
(3) same sex
(4) same family-type background
(5) same age

122. In the work of Rokeach and Newcomb, which of the above would seem most critical to social attraction?

(A) 1   (B) 2   (C) 3   (D) 4   (E) 5

123. Rokeach and Mezei's studies combined the most influential social attraction variable with that of _____.

(A) 1   (B) 2   (C) 3   (D) 4   (E) 5

124. When the performance of an individual is enhanced by the mere presence of others, the phenomenon is called

(A) reactive facilitation
(B) cognitive dissonance
(C) conformity
(D) social facilitation
(E) complementarity

125. A person is highly competitive, cannot relax, feels a great sense of time urgency, and frequently becomes impatient or irritated with others. In stress and heart disease terms this person would be characterized as

(A) Type X   (B) Type A   (C) Type Y
(D) Type B   (E) Type H

126. The basic thesis of Newcomb's theory is that

(A) persons with similar orientations are attracted to each other
(B) persons with widely differing backgrounds are attracted to each other
(C) complementarity is essentially predominant except in courtship and marital relationships
(D) cognitive dissonance prevails in interpersonal attraction
(E) the rewards and costs of social exchange are the predominant factors within every interaction

127. "Brotherliness versus incest" is a concern of

(A) Adler   (B) Freud   (C) Jung   (D) Berne   (E) Fromm

128. Sublimation and displacement

(A) are synonymous
(B) differ only in the cultural value of the behavior
(C) refer specifically to the mechanical details of reaction formation
(D) are both identical to projection
(E) speak to the phenomenon of mental compartmentalization

129. Which one of the following combinations is included in Allport's psychodynamic view of prejudice?

    (A) instinctive, scapegoating
    (B) frustration, regression
    (C) regression, aggression
    (D) aggression, exploitation
    (E) reputation, situational response

130. In the psychoanalytic view, childhood negativism can be expected during which one of the following stages?

    (A) oral   (B) anal   (C) phallic
    (D) latent   (E) genital

131. After having been away from the following tasks for several years, a person could be expected to return to which one with least practice?

    (A) a list of nonsense syllables
    (B) a list of digit spans
    (C) verbatim recollection of a story
    (D) tightrope walking
    (E) bicycle riding

132. In Freudian theory, which one of the following is reality oriented?

    (A) id
    (B) ego
    (C) superego
    (D) repression
    (E) reaction formation

133. Which one of the following does *not* refer to attitudes?

    (A) predispositions to respond
    (B) relatively stable
    (C) an emotional component
    (D) unconditioned
    (E) a cognitive component

134. One of the leading researchers in the leadership area has been

    (A) Deutsch   (B) Janis   (C) Dember
    (D) Harlow   (E) Fiedler

135. In psychoanalysis, the castration fear appears

    (A) among pubescent girls
    (B) within both sexes during the genital stage
    (C) among boys during the genital stage
    (D) among girls during the anal sadistic stage
    (E) among boys during the phallic stage

136. Aggression displacement suggests that the farther removed an object or person is from the source of frustration

(A) the lower the frustration
(B) the lower the cooperation
(C) the higher the inhibition
(D) the greater the cooperation
(E) the greater the likelihood of aggressive actions

Questions 137–139 refer to the following experiment.

Fifty children, ages nine and ten, were randomly assigned to two groups, twenty-five children per group. Using a pencil and paper, each subject was given the task of tracing a path around a geometric figure of a star. Normal cues were removed by using a shield between the subject's line of vision and the work area. It was impossible for the subjects to see their hands at work, but they could watch the hands in a mirror that was mounted on the table in front of the immediate work area. A trial began after the subject had been comfortably seated and given the signal to begin work; it concluded when the subject had completed the star-tracing task. A stopwatch monitored the time required for a subject to complete a given trial. Group 1 received one trial per day for seven days; Group 2 received seven trials during a single test session. Comparative tracing time per trial is outlined in the following table.

| | Tracing Time (seconds) | |
Trial	Group 1	Group 2
1	200	200
2	170	190
3	140	170
4	100	165
5	60	150
6	50	130
7	45	120

137. Important to interpretation of the table data would be a determination that the children in the two groups were equivalent in

(A) verbal IQ
(B) motor ability
(C) art proficiency
(D) mechanical aptitude
(E) degree of introversion

138. The mirror serves to

(A) help the child work more quickly than he could if he were directly observing his work
(B) provide immediate, helpful feedback and knowledge of results
(C) promote stimulus generalization
(D) reorient and move the child beyond familiar habits in eye-hand coordination
(E) provide proactive facilitation

139. The results support the statement that

(A) massed practice proved more effective than spaced practice
(B) spaced practice proved more effective than massed practice
(C) practice had no appreciable effect on performance
(D) spaced practice prompted subjects to encounter the effects of forgetting
(E) retroactive aversion operates in star-tracing experiments

140. On the basis of Bryan and Test's experiments, we could expect a person to offer help more readily in which one of the following situations?

(A) where an individual has just seen a situation in which someone was giving help to a person in distress
(B) where an individual comes upon the person in distress without having had any prior example of helping
(C) where the person in distress is injured
(D) where the person in distress is elderly
(E) where several other people are observing the person needing help

141. Adorno's work concludes that

(A) attitudes have no effect on any other aspect of one's personality
(B) no generalizations can be made on the basis of existing research in anti-Semitism
(C) there is slight, low correlation between authoritarian attitudes and distinct personality characteristics
(D) home background has virtually no effect upon the later development of authoritarian attitudes
(E) there is strong correlation between authoritarian attitudes and distinct personality characteristics

142. Phrenology encompasses

(A) free association
(B) systematic behavioral observation
(C) introspection
(D) a primitive, "bumps-on-the-head" approach to personality determination
(E) desensitization

143. A concept *not* associated with Rogers is

(A) ideal self   (B) nondirective therapy   (C) phenomenal field
(D) functional fictionalism   (E) self-actualization

144. Superstition would be most evident within which of the following personality terms?

(A) prototaxic   (B) intuiting mode   (C) syntaxic
(D) thinking mode   (E) parataxic

145. A political candidate wants to get large, ugly-looking signs placed in the front yards of key homes on a major, busy street. For best chance of success in getting the larger signs in yards, the decision is made to approach these households with

(A) a brochure about the political candidate
(B) a briefing on the general campaign strategy
(C) a smaller sign or bumper sticker
(D) an explanation of cognitive dissonance
(E) a strategy for inoculation

146. In Sherif's experimentation on autokinetic effect, individual judgments

(A) remained unchanged in the face of group judgment
(B) changed significantly toward group judgment
(C) changed slightly, but not significantly, toward group judgment
(D) changed slightly in a nonconforming direction
(E) changed dramatically in a nonconforming direction

147. This person is taking Librium (chlordiazepoxide). The disorder being treated is most likely _____ - related.

(A) depression   (B) manic   (C) anxiety
(D) psychotic   (E) terminal cancer

148. Which one of the following is an accurate statement about most sexual offenders?

(A) They are typically homicidal sex fiends.
(B) They progress to more serious types of sex crimes.
(C) They are oversexed.
(D) They are among the least likely to be second offenders.
(E) They suffer from glandular imbalance.

149. On the basis of existing research, which one of the following is an *incorrect* statement relating to suicide?

(A) There is a higher incidence of suicide among churchgoers.
(B) The suicide's family frequently attempts to conceal the cause of death.
(C) The lowest likelihood of suicide is among persons who talk about doing it.
(D) There is a higher incidence of suicide among divorced persons and persons living alone.
(E) There is a higher incidence of suicide among persons believing in life after death.

150. The psychoanalyst becomes the recipient of affection that the patient felt earlier in her life toward her father in

(A) transference   (B) connotation   (C) reaction formation
(D) Oedipus complex   (E) castration fear

151. A person has scored 30 on a test that has a mean of 50 and a standard deviation of 10. The person's score ranks at which of the following percentiles?

(A) 16th   (B) 50th   (C) 2nd   (D) 68th   (E) 84th

152. Which of the following drug classifications would include cocaine?

(A) stimulants   (B) sedative-hypnotics
(C) antipsychotic agents   (D) opiates   (E) psychedelics

153. Frotteurism is a disorder that involves

(A) acute depression   (B) cyclothymia   (C) brief psychosis
(D) rubbing against   (E) pyromania

154. In Roger Brown's terminology, a culture that places great emphasis on the caste system is utilizing which of the following status determinations?

(A) anticipatory socialization
(B) achieved status
(C) ascribed status
(D) status equilibrium
(E) role status

155. Electroconvulsive shock therapy has been most effective in the treatment of

(A) paranoia   (B) schizophrenia   (C) somatoform disorder
(D) hypomania   (E) depression

156. Which of the following has *not* been used in the treatment of alcoholism?

(A) hospital setting   (B) chlorpromazine   (C) Synanon
(D) Alcoholics Anonymous   (E) family support

157. Which one of the following disorders is most likely to lead a person to cover a sizable amount of geographical territory?

(A) amnesia   (B) dysthymia   (C) schizophrenia
(D) somnambulism   (E) fugue

158. A therapeutic technique in which the patient enacts a life situation or experience demonstrating his conflict is called

(A) psychodrama   (B) sociodrama   (C) release therapy
(D) nondirective therapy   (E) Gestalt therapy

159. An experimenter wishes to determine the effects of different shock intensities on GSR. He believes, however, that it will be essential to counterbalance the shock intensities by having one group receive high intensity first, a second group receive medium intensity first, and so on. The statistical design within which he has organized the experiment is

(A) Two Factor Mixed   (B) Pearson Product Moment
(C) *t*-test   (D) point-biserial correlation   (E) Latin Square

160. Hollingshead and Redlich found psychosis most prominent in which of the following social classes?

    (A) upper (B) middle (C) lower
    (D) professional (E) white-collar

161. Which of the following does *not* express a dissociative disorder?

    (A) identity (B) fugue (C) amnesia
    (D) depersonalization (E) somatoform

162. The term *psychosomatic* refers to

    (A) the imagined discomforts of hypochondriacs
    (B) the unique symptoms displayed by psychotics
    (C) a continuous emergency reaction and the resulting tissue damage
    (D) a physical disorder complicated by a neurosis
    (E) malfunction in the Islets of Langerhans

163. Among the following, the most serious phase of alcoholism is

    (A) crucial (B) occasional (C) prodromal
    (D) critical (E) chronic

164. In a psychiatric team, which one of the following would be the exclusive responsibility of the psychiatrist?

    (A) insight therapy (B) group therapy (C) psychodiagnosis
    (D) behavior modification (E) electroconvulsive shock therapy

165. "Driver attention as a function of car radio sound" is a phrase in which the driver attention aspect represents the

    (A) intervening variable
    (B) independent variable
    (C) dependent variable
    (D) irrelevant variable
    (E) divergent variable

166. As one compares the backgrounds of normal and psychotic children, which one of the following is *not* significantly different between the two groups?

    (A) prenatal stress
    (B) abnormal siblings
    (C) destitute home environment
    (D) foster home settings
    (E) difficulty during delivery

167. *X* and *Y* are perfectly positively correlated. It is possible to conclude that

    (A) *A* caused *Y*
    (B) *Y* caused *X*
    (C) *X* and *Y* are caused by still a third variable
    (D) a strong, systematic relationship exists between them
    (E) very little relationship exists between the two

168. Which of the following has *not* been used in the treatment of alcoholism?

    (A) filming the patient's drinking behavior for later viewing by the patient himself
    (B) drinking rules that include taking sips
    (C) drinking rules that include making each drink last at least twenty minutes
    (D) placing electrodes on the patient's drinking hand
    (E) chemoconvulsive shock therapy

169. Which of the following techniques places greatest emphasis upon the goal of making a client aware of the totality of his behavior?

    (A) implosive therapy
    (B) logotherapy
    (C) client-centered therapy
    (D) Gestalt therapy
    (E) ego analysis

170. In electroconvulsive shock therapy

    (A) a muscle relaxant is used to reduce the dangers of the seizure
    (B) a very low voltage current of five to ten volts is applied for ten to twenty seconds
    (C) the resultant seizure lasts for five to ten minutes
    (D) consciousness is retained throughout
    (E) LSD is often administered

171. The patient who is taking lithium carbonate

    (A) has depressive disorder
    (B) has just received an antipsychotic drug
    (C) likely is suffering from depression
    (D) likely is suffering from manic disorder
    (E) is demonstrating sociopathic symptoms

172. If one of a set of monozygotic twins is diagnosed as manic-depressive, there is a 72% chance the other twin will have manic-depression. If one of a set of dizygotic twins is diagnosed as manic-depressive, there is a 14% chance the other twin also will have it. From this information you could conclude that

    (A) Environmental factors have a major role in manic-depression.
    (B) The percentage difference between monozygotic and dizygotic is not significant.
    (C) Concordance rates are higher for dizygotic twins than for monozygotic twins.
    (D) Genetic factors have a major role in manic-depression.
    (E) Seligman's theory has been supported by the data.

173. Which of the following has *not* been found true of schizophrenia?

   (A) Monozygotic twins are both more likely to have it than dizygotic twins.
   (B) The leading biochemical factor identified to date has been norepinephrine.
   (C) Members of families with a history of the disorder are more likely to develop it than members of families without that history.
   (D) Families with a schizophrenic child have trouble focusing attention in a problem-solving task situation.
   (E) Members of the lower class are a higher risk group than members of the middle class.

174. Believing that the CIA and the attorney general are out to get him, a man comes out of his apartment only at night after painstaking efforts to be certain he is not being followed. This is a case of

   (A) paranoid schizophrenia
   (B) paranoid personality disorder
   (C) dissociative reaction
   (D) anxiety reaction
   (E) obsessive-compulsive reaction

175. An IQ of 40 is associated with the classification known as

   (A) educable
   (B) nontrainable
   (C) mildly retarded
   (D) severely retarded
   (E) moderately retarded

176. Industrial screening procedures for given positions rely heavily on

   (A) the intelligence factor
   (B) the creativity factor
   (C) factors correlating with past success in the specific positions
   (D) manual dexterity
   (E) identifiable factors correlating with future success in the specific positions

177. In human engineering, the best display panel

   (A) maximizes operator interpretation and integration of data from several sources
   (B) minimizes operator interpretation and integration of data from several sources
   (C) maximizes time delay between the receipt of information and the behavioral response
   (D) functions adequately in a limited number of ambient conditions
   (E) keeps operator interpretation and integration of data from several sources at an intermediate level

Questions 178–180 are based on the following instructions and answer choices. For each of the following, determine the best definition among the subsequent items.

(1) mean
(2) median
(3) chi-square
(4) *z*-score
(5) mode

178. The average of the scores in a distribution.

(A) 1   (B) 2   (C) 3   (D) 4   (E) 5

179. The score that functions as the midpoint dividing line, i.e., the 50th percentile in a distribution.

(A) 1   (B) 2   (C) 3   (D) 4   (E) 5

180. The most frequently occurring score in a distribution.

(A) 1   (B) 2   (C) 3   (D) 4   (E) 5

181. To utilize the Purkinje effect on a night reconnaissance mission, which of the following should pilots wear in the lighted briefing session just prior to night takeoff?

(A) green goggles   (B) blue goggles   (C) red goggles
(D) yellow goggles   (E) violet goggles

Questions 182–186 are based on the following answer choices. For each of the following situations, determine the most appropriate design among the subsequent items.

(1) *t*-test: related measures
(2) treatments-by-subjects design
(3) completely randomized design
(4) Latin Square design
(5) treatments-by-treatments-by-subjects design

182. Reaction time as a function of distraction level. Group 1—no distraction; group 2—low distraction; group 3—moderate distraction; group 4—high distraction. Equal number of subjects in each group and one score per subject.

(A) 1   (B) 2   (C) 3   (D) 4   (E) 5

183. Children matched initially on the basis of sex and equivalent IQ score. One child in each pair will be assigned to a group that will receive no special instruction. Score recorded for analysis will be IQ score on a second test administered to each group at the end of the instructional period.

(A) 1   (B) 2   (C) 3   (D) 4   (E) 5

184. The effect of drug administration upon learning lists of varying difficulty. Within the drug and no-drug groups, there will be three subdivisions, counterbalancing for order of list learning (e.g., one subgroup—hard, med., easy; a second subgroup—easy, hard, med.; a third subgroup—med., easy, hard). One score for each list learned.

    (A) 1   (B) 2   (C) 3   (D) 4   (E) 5

185. Experimental investigation of short-term and long-term retention of (1) digits and (2) nonsense syllables in a single group of subjects.

    (A) 1   (B) 2   (C) 3   (D) 4   (E) 5

186. An experiment to study the IQ performance of the same group at four different ages.

    (A) 1   (B) 2   (C) 3   (D) 4   (E) 5

187. Human engineering experiments that have involved the comparison of performance by persons who could breathe only warm, "stale" air while their bodies were appropriately cooled with that by persons who breathed cool, dry air while their bodies were exposed to warm, moist air found that the critical factor prompting excellence in performance was

    (A) breathing warm, "stale" air
    (B) breathing cool, dry air
    (C) appropriate exterior body cooling
    (D) body exposure to warm, moist air
    (E) the combination of breathing cool air and having the body exposed to warm, moist air

188. During the past thirty years, industrial psychology has evolved toward

    (A) less reliance on standardized instruments
    (B) more emphasis on human relations
    (C) more emphasis on hierarchy
    (D) more emphasis on organizational structure
    (E) less emphasis on communication

189. In most social settings, the theory of social attraction of which one of the following appears most applicable?

    (A) Newcomb   (B) Winch   (C) Webster
    (D) Finch   (E) Zajonc

190. In which one of the following test setting types might a person be asked to respond to the statement "I would accept him as a close friend?"

    (A) Thurstone
    (B) Osgood
    (C) Bogardus
    (D) Remmers
    (E) Likert

191. If every score in a distribution has been divided by 7, the standard deviation

    (A) decreases by 7
    (B) decreases by 14
    (C) decreases to the quotient obtained when the original standard deviation value is divided by 7
    (D) remains unchanged
    (E) increases to 7 times the original standard deviation value

192. Which test gauges the probability of occupational success by comparing a subject's interests with those reported by persons successfully engaged in various occupational fields?

    (A) Kuder
    (B) 16 PF
    (C) Allport-Vernon-Lindzey
    (D) WAIS
    (E) Strong-Campbell Vocational Interest Blank

193. In designing and arranging work space, human engineering personnel seek to

    (A) build in unnecessary worker movement to reduce boredom
    (B) eliminate all unnecessary movement
    (C) keep workers within close talking distance of each other
    (D) place the most important functions just above the worker's head
    (E) keep as many work settings as possible adjacent to the lounge area

194. Research with industrial workers has found which one of the following to be the most effective motivator?

    (A) money
    (B) prestige
    (C) opportunity for advancement
    (D) frequency of coffee breaks
    (E) laissez-faire supervision

195. The problem encountered with one form of the Stanford-Binet was that

    (A) standard deviations for one age group were not consistent for other age groups
    (B) means for one age group were not consistent for other age groups
    (C) modes for one age group were not consistent for other age groups
    (D) tasks in the test had not been standardized
    (E) no cross-cultural standardization procedures had been used

196. The statistic that deals most prominently with the terms *observed frequency*, *expected frequency*, and *contingency tables* is

    (A) t (B) z (C) chi-square
    (D) analysis of covariance   (E) point-biserial correlation

197. In equipment design, human engineering recommends that the *least* important and *least* frequent tasks on a console be placed

    (A) immediately in front of the person
    (B) immediately above the person
    (C) approximately forty-five degrees to the right of center
    (D) approximately forty-five degrees to the left of center
    (E) approximately ninety to one hundred degrees to the right or left of center

198. Knowledge that two people obtained test scores of 85 in an introductory psychology class is

    (A) sufficient to determine their test performance
    (B) meaningless without knowledge of the mean
    (C) meaningless without knowledge of both the mean and the standard deviation
    (D) meaningless without knowledge of the mode
    (E) meaningless without knowledge of the distribution skew

199. A decision to study bright children intermittently over a period of several years is a decision to conduct a

    (A) cross-cultural study
    (B) latitudinal study
    (C) longitudinal study
    (D) laboratory study
    (E) field study

200. Voters will be heading to the polls tomorrow for an election. Five political candidates will be speaking on a political program this afternoon. One of those candidates—by the luck of the draw—can choose the order of presentation. This candidate would be best advised to speak

    (A) first
    (B) second
    (C) third
    (D) fourth
    (E) fifth

Test 4: Answer Comments

1. (A) The physiological limitations of the human visual apparatus enable the motion picture principle to function effectively. The human eye does not have the capacity to detect individual frames when presented in rapid succession.

2. (B) Olfaction occurs in the roof of the nasal cavity above the turbinate bones.

3. (D) The ossicles—hammer, anvil, and stirrup—occupy the area between the eardrum and the oval window.

4. (D) The visceral senses provide feedback relating to the internal organs of the body.

5. (B) When four closely contiguous lines are perceived as a square, closure (gap fill-in) has occurred.

6. (A) McClelland has found that children with high achievement need seem to demonstrate a preference for intermediate risk tasks.

7. (C) In a situation where winning probabilities are equivalent, Atkinson has found that response strength is also dependent upon the value that the subject places on the achievement.

8. (C) Experimental work in perception was pioneered by Wertheimer, founder of the Gestalt school and approach.

9. (D) Draw two lines of equal length. At either end of one line draw an arrowhead. At either end of the other, draw an inverted arrowhead. You now have the basic ingredients of the Muller-Lyer illusion, which *seems* to show that the two lines are not equal in length.

10. (C) Encouragement of independence has been found in the childhood backgrounds of persons with high achievement need.

11. (B) The term describing coordination of antagonistic muscle activity is *reciprocal innervation*.

12. (D) Striated muscles have skeletal movement responsibility.

13. (B) Wernicke's center, in the left temporal lobe just below the auditory area, relates to the understanding of spoken language.

14. (B) A prominent monocular depth cue is the texture-density gradient.

15. (A) The longer the vigilance time, the lower the likelihood of operator detection.

16. (A) At levels close to threshold, increasing the strength of a stimulus shortens reaction time.

17. (A) When two sense organs are stimulated simultaneously, reaction time is faster than when only one is stimulated.

18. (A) A unit of time (day, month, and so on) seems longest when it is being perceived by a young child.

19. (A) Tolman and Lewin held similar views relating to purposive behavior and field theory.

20. (D) Atkinson's work is among the most important in achievement motivation research.

21. (A) Watson categorized human infant emotional responses as love, rage, and fear.

22. (B) Stratton's "goggle world" was upside-down at first, but within a matter of days surprising visual adaptation occurred, and the world was perceptually normal again, despite the goggles.

23. (A) The orienting reflex is important and self-preservative. It prepares the body to receive critical stimulus information and to respond to it (for example, the quick response within a danger situation). The reflex has been found both in animals and in humans.

24. (C) The familiar face-vase picture is one of the most prominent demonstrations of figure reversibility.

25. (C) The Pacinian corpuscle is related to pressure sensation. Distributed widely in the body, these corpuscles are associated with deep pressure sensitivity.

26. (D) Dreaming occurs in Stage I, rapid-eye-movement sleep, which is characterized by a low-amplitude, fast, irregular rhythm (similar in EEG pattern to that of an active, walking person).

27. (B) A basic Gestalt tenet is that behavior is more than the sum of its parts.

28. (C) Misperception of a stimulus is the definition of illusion, and a response in the absence of an external stimulus defines a basic characteristic of hallucination.

29. (D) In Restle's "moon illusion," the moon on the horizon is perceived as larger than the moon overhead.

30. (E) Deep sleep, Stage IV, is characterized by the delta wave.

31. (B) The basilar membrane is central to the neural transmission aspect of hearing.

32. (A) McDougall was an early, strong proponent of the belief that behavior must be viewed in molar, purposive terms, not in mechanistic S-R terms.

33. (D) Tinbergen considers development, mechanisms, function, and evolution to be the four major areas of study in animal behavior.

34. (A) In his field theory, Lewin expressed the belief that a person responds on the basis of his psychological environment at the moment of action.

35. (B) James expressed the view that habit involves instinct in combination with experience.

36. (D) Duplicity theory relates to rod-cone vision. Early theorists went so far as to postulate a "double retina," later modifying and correcting this theory in terms of rod-cone.

37. (E) Muller's famous "specific energies of nerves" position continues to have a far-reaching effect in sensory theory.

38. (B) Critical flicker frequency is the rate of light fluctuation above which fusion occurs.

39. (B) The suggestion that all auditory nerves fire constantly and repeatedly to produce reception of a given pitch would be the crux of the basic frequency theory.

40. (A) Vesicles store chemical neurotransmitters. As an action potential reaches the axon terminal, the neurotransmitters are released from vesicles into the synaptic cleft. The neurotransmitter then is rapidly diffused across the cleft, causing a slight change in the membrane potential of the receiving neuron. If the neurotransmitter is broken down by the receiving cell, the process is called *inactivation*. If the sending neuron reabsorbs it, the process is called *reuptake*.

41. (D) Perceptual constancies are primarily attributable to learning. A person must learn, for instance, that the train on the distant horizon is a large machine and not a tiny dot.

42. (E) The myelin sheath is an evolutionary development in vertebrates. It is a fatty white covering on some axons that vastly increases the speed of neural transmission.

43. (C) The nondecremental property refers to the neural transmission finding that an impulse is sent to the end of the axon without fading or weakening.

44. (D) Alpha wave frequency is approximately ten cycles per second.

45. (B) The Montreal Studies indicated that the original infant emotion was excitement.

46. (B) Very high anger arousal causes dilation of blood vessels near the skin.

47. (D) By electrical stimulation, Olds located pleasure centers in the rat brain.

48. (E) In comparing the neuron to a doorbell system, the dendrites most closely approximate the button that a visitor would push. They are located at the receiving end of the neuron.

49. (A) Because there is strong evidence of compensation for instances of dream deprivation, it appears that dreaming serves a basic organismic need.

50. (E) There appears to be a relationship between increased stomach acids and the presence of resentment-hostility emotions within a person.

51. (B) The Cannon-Bard theory relates to the thalamus and hypothalamus. Disputing the James-Lange theory of emotion, Cannon and Bard pointed out that different emotions are accompanied by the same visceral state.

52. (A) The axon is a part of the nerve fiber that transmits neural impulses from the nerve cell body to other nerve cells, muscles, and glands. The role of dendrites is to receive impulses. Their branching fibers are located on the receptor end of a neuron.

53. (D) Two different intensities of light presented to a subject simultaneously would be an implementation of the difference-limen method in psychophysics experimentation.

54. (B) Weber's Law is expressed in the formula: (Delta I)$/I = K$. The formula suggests a constant ratio. If, for a weight of twenty-five pounds, you require the addition of five pounds before you can detect that weight has been added, Weber would say that for a fifty-pound weight a ten-pound addition would be required for detection.

55. (A) The left part of each retina is connected to the left occipital lobe, and the right part of each retina is connected to the right occipital lobe—a neural phenomenon creating obvious problems in split-brain research. It is for this reason that split-brain research must be preceded by surgery to the optic chiasm.

56. (A) Broca's area is in the frontal lobe of the left cerebral hemisphere, just above the fissure of Sylvius. It is responsible for speech.

57. (D) Wernicke's center, responsible for understanding spoken language, is an area in the left temporal lobe, just below the auditory area and curving around the end of the fissure of Sylvius.

58. (C) In each cerebral hemisphere, the fissure of Sylvius separates the temporal from the frontal and parietal lobes.

59. (E) Reticular formation refers to neural fibers in the brain stem that have an important telephone-switchboard-type selective arousal function.

60. (A) In escape conditioning, the aversive stimulus (e.g., shock) is always received by the subject. This distinguishes escape conditioning from avoidance conditioning.

61. (D) Although all of the statements are correct about memory performance in general, the one that applies in this case is that the number of chunks is reduced to just three: "ROY," "G," and "BIV." Chunking is a strategy of recoding or regrouping items into larger patterns, to reduce the number of different items to be remembered.

62. (C) Although punishment is generally ineffective in weakening existing conditioned responses and changing long-range behavior patterns, it can have cue value.

63. (D) Trophoblast refers to a group of cells surrounding the blastocyst cavity—cells that will later become the placenta and chorion.

64. (E) A horse-race betting situation illustrates the variable ratio reinforcement setting.

65. (A) Meat powder qualifies as a UCS because of its inherent reinforcing qualities.

66. (E) Concurrent validity is obtained by correlating performances on a new test with the same test taker's performances on an established test in the field.

67. (D) That decision time increases as the number of items in short-term memory increases suggests that the retrieval mechanism is examining them one by one. This is known as the serial process in short-term memory retrieval. Others argue for a parallel process interpretation of Sternberg's data, suggesting that, for example, the more entries in a race (retrieval, in this case) the longer the time required for the last entry to cross the "finish line."

68. (D) Recognition tests require the discrimination of a correct response from any number of incorrect lures (did you correctly recognize this answer?).

69. (E) In higher-order conditioning, a former CS functions as a UCS for further conditioning. The method has limited applicability.

70. (D) The lower the decimal figure, the higher the significance level. In this instance, the lowest figure is .005.

71. (E) The newborn does not have well-developed pain sensitivity, as is evidenced by circumstances that have occurred without anesthesia.

72. (D) One cannot predict at what point in the communication process noise will occur. It has the potential for occurring at virtually any point.

73. (C) Adolescent gangs frequently are formed with "get-even" purposes, but children's gangs are not.

74. (A) Inference suggests drawing assumptions or pulling in information that was not a part of the basic stimulus you were presented. To confuse "Kathy pounded the nail" with "Kathy hammered the nail" means we inferred that Kathy used a hammer when she pounded the nail. Though hammer was nowhere expressed in the original sentence, we inferred it.

75. (D) Sickle cell is a race-prominent form of anemia that involves an abnormal form of hemoglobin and the possibility of dangerous clotting, but it is not a form of cancer.

76. (A) Half the possible combinations could yield brown-eyed children.

77. (E) Balanced diet through self-selection functions most effectively in the absence of learned tastes. The human adult's development of learned taste preferences seriously reduces prospects for success in obtaining a balanced diet via self-selection.

78. (E) A genotype-phenotype relationship is analogous to heredity-appearance.

79. (C) The critical-periods concept of cognitive-intellectual development is being called into question by the research work of Kagan.

80. (E) Moro response is an infantile startle response caused by any sudden, intense stimulus such as a loud noise. The response itself involves the sudden outstretching of arms and legs.

81. (C) The fact that each mature egg or sperm contains only one chromosome from each pair is attributable to the process known as reduction division.

82. (B) Flipping heads six times on a coin toss and then predicting tails with certainty on the next toss is an example of the conjunction or "gambler's fallacy." The seventh coin toss has a 50 percent chance of coming up heads or tails just as each of the preceding coin tosses had.

83. (B) In Harlow's experiments, the surrogate-reared infant monkeys were least fearful in the presence of the surrogate mother to which clinging responses had been directed during early development.

84. (E) The cardiac muscle is a special kind of striated muscle. All striated muscles share the quality of having a striped appearance that is evident through microscopic examination. With the exception of the cardiac muscle, striated muscles have skeletal-movement functions.

85. (D) Positive transfer (proactive facilitation) is greatest where the person is asked to perform an old response to similar stimuli.

86. (A) According to Baddeley, working memory consists of a central executive system that controls a number of slave systems responsible for the maintenance and manipulation of information in working memory.

87. (B) Bruner's terms expressing the three modes of developing a mental world model are *enactive*, *iconic*, and *symbolic*.

88. (B) The rest interval following practice will produce reminiscence—opportunity to "consolidate"—resulting in subsequent performance with an absence of intervening practice.

89. (A) Jones's studies of adolescents indicate that early maturation is an advantage for males but a disadvantage for females.

90. (C) Loftus has repeatedly demonstrated the contamination of memories by subtle suggestions prior to recollection, resulting in memory distortions that could have profound personal, social, and legal implications.

91. (E) The most severe conflict situation is likely to be that of avoidance-avoidance—prompting organismic flight from the conflict situation.

92. (B) The British associationist school was identified with the law of contiguity (the close occurrence in time of two events).

93. (C) Dollard and Miller state the basic requirements for learning to be drive, cue, response, and reinforcement.

94. (E) The grasping reflex in the newborn is obtained by stimulating the palms or fingers.

95. (A) The Babkin response is obtained by pressing the palms of the child's hands while he is lying on his back. The response itself involves head return to midline.

96. (B) Babinski response is obtained by stroking the sole of the neonate's foot. The toes now fan outward, but later in life they will curl inward when such stroking occurs.

97. (B) The term *cephalocaudal* refers to the fact that the upper part of a young child's body develops earlier than the lower part.

98. (B) The developmental term *mitosis* refers to cell division and multiplication. A natural confusion occurs with the term *meiosis*, meaning reduction division.

99. (A) Lovaas has conducted some of the most influential, pioneering behavior modification work with autistic children.

100. (E) Harlow's best-known work deals with primate research relating to emotional development and learning sets. He is not involved in psycholinguistics research.

101. (C) The Wechsler Scale provides separate IQ scores for the verbal and performance sections.

102. (B) In research comparison with male newborns, females have demonstrated more rapid adjustment to the postnatal environment.

103. (E) Sham feeding is an experimental technique of "eating" and "swallowing" food that does not reach the stomach.

104. (A) In Chomsky's explanation of grammar acquisition in children, he speaks of a "programmed" nervous system.

105. (E) Infant intelligence tests are not accurate predictors of later IQ. Instead, they tend to measure DQ (developmental quotient).

106. (C) Repetition of material to keep it in mind longer is called maintenance rehearsal; although it is effective at temporarily maintaining memories, long-term memory typically requires elaborative rehearsal.

107. (D) Congenital refers to presence at birth.

108. (D) There definitely has been a relationship found between ulcers and emotional state—the physical symptoms (ulcers) having been brought on by the psychological state (prolonged stress, for instance).

109. (B) A correct sequence would be nontrainable, trainable, educable.

110. (E) Kendler and Kendler have found that reversal shifts are performed more quickly and more easily among older children than among younger children or animals. The well-known Kendler studies have investigated the phenomenon systematically with children of different ages as well as with laboratory animals.

111. (D) Each subsequent word must both advance by one letter in the alphabetical sequence and increase its total number of letters by one.

112. (C) The score is above the mean by $1^3/_5$ standard deviations, making +1.60 the corresponding *z*-score.

113. (D) The linguistic relativity hypothesis suggests that we differ in thought patterns based on the language we learned in young childhood. One language, for instance, may not have a word to describe a concept integral to another language. This basic premise that language affects thought is known as the Whorfian hypothesis.

114. (A) In his child studies, Sears has found a strong relationship between a child's receiving parental punishment for aggression and that child's expressing strong prosocial aggression.

115. (B) Things that you learn while in one physical or emotional state will be remembered better if you are in the same state, called state-dependent memory. In addition to alcohol, this effect has been observed with marijuana, nicotine, and depression.

116. (D) Two standard deviations above the mean of a normal distribution is a point at which approximately 98% of scores are less than or equal to that point—the 98th percentile.

117. (D) Two distinct concentrations of scores in a frequency distribution means that the distribution is bimodal. It would be possible for such a distribution to be symmetrical, having neither positive nor negative skew.

118. (C) Attributable to Bartlett in England, this cryptarithmetic problem has found wide usage in the study of human problem solving both in this country and abroad.

119. (D) Freudian defense mechanisms carry the function of relieving anxiety associated with the threat of the emergence of the id impulse.

120. (C) Schachter found that persons experiencing fear of an upcoming event preferred the company of others having a similar fear based on their scheduling to experience the same threatening event. If given a choice of associating with other persons not scheduled to experience the event, they preferred to be alone.

121. (E) Rogers emphasizes the self-concept—differentiation of a portion of one's phenomenal field.

122. (B) Similarity in attitudes has proved most critical to social attraction in the work of Rokeach and Newcomb.

123. (A) Rokeach and Mezei found that same attitudes, combined with the same-different race variable, continued to be the most critical variables in social attraction.

124. (D) Social facilitation refers to performance enhancement prompted by the mere presence of others (e.g., "I play better with an audience.").

125. (B) Friedman and Rosenman set out the behavior characteristics of Type A people. These individuals are high-risk in relation to the likelihood of heart attacks. Very competitive, impatient, and time-driven, these individuals cannot relax, and they experience quite a bit of underlying hostility. Their counterpart is Type B behavior characteristics, which encompass relaxing without feelings of guilt, patience, and little evidence of hostility.

126. (A) Newcomb espouses similarity as the basic factor in attraction.

127. (E) Fromm speaks of brotherliness versus incest in his sociopsychoanalytic approach to personality theory.

128. (B) Association with higher cultural value or cultural contribution is related to sublimation.

129. (A) Within his discussion of the psychodynamic view of prejudice, Allport includes the instinctive and scapegoating processes.

130. (B) In psychoanalysis, the anal stage of psychosexual development is seen as carrying a strong likelihood of child negativism.

131. (E)   Motor tasks have the strongest long-term retention.

132. (B)   In Freud's divisions of the psyche, the ego is the reality oriented entry. Id operates on the instinctual, pleasure principle, and superego functions on the social, morality principle.

133. (D)   Attitudes are learned, not unconditioned.

134. (E)   Fiedler has been one of the leading researchers in the area of leadership.

135. (E)   Occurring with the Oedipus complex, the castration fear is experienced by male children and is directed toward the father.

136. (E)   With greater distance from the source of frustration comes lower inhibition and, consequently, greater likelihood of aggressive actions.

137. (B)   It would be essential for the two groups to be equivalent in motor ability. Otherwise, differences in performance would be meaningless.

138. (D)   The child's access only to a mirror to monitor the child's tracing movements means that feedback is reversed from that which the child normally would receive through direct observation. Therefore, the child must reorient himself and move beyond familiar habits in eye-hand coordination.

139. (B)   Group 1 tracing time per trial dropped much more rapidly across trials than tracing time in group 2—a factor in support of spaced practice as more effective than massed practice in this experimental setting.

140. (A)   Models of helping occurring prior to a given potential helping setting increase the likelihood that a person in the latter setting will render help.

141. (E)   Adorno and his associates conclude that there is a strong correlation between authoritarian attitudes and distinct personality characteristics.

142. (D)   Phrenology is the primitive, "bumps-on-the-head" approach to personality determination.

143. (D)   *Functional fictionalism* was a term used by Adler in referring to an individual's perception and interpretation of his environment.

144. (E)   Sullivan's parataxic category—casually associating events occurring in proximity to each other—is tailor-made for superstition.

145. (C)   The political candidate will stand the greatest chance of getting the large, ugly sign placed in a person's yard if that person is approached about making a smaller commitment earlier (e.g., a smaller sign or a bumper sticker for the candidate). Freedman and Fraser have conducted basic research in this area and call the phenomenon the "foot-in-the-door" technique.

146. (B)   Sherif's observed change in individual judgments toward group judgments reflected the strength of group influence upon the judgments of individual members.

147. (C)   Librium—along with Valium (diazepam) and Miltown (meprobamate)—is an antianxiety medication.

148. (D)   Most sexual offenders are among the persons least likely to be second offenders.

149. (C) At one time, talking about suicide was believed to indicate low likelihood of its occurrence. On the basis of research, such a belief is no longer held.

150. (A) Expressing in the psychotherapy setting a strong emotion once held toward a close relative would be transference.

151. (C) The second percentile, two standard deviations below the mean of the distribution.

152. (A) Cocaine is a stimulant. Others in this group include amphetamines, methamphetamines and derivatives of amphetamines, MDMA, caffeine, and nicotine. Alcohol and barbituates are sedative-hypnotics, whereas heroin and morphine are opiates.

153. (D) Frotteurism stems from the French word "frotter," which means "to rub." This sexual disorder involves uninvited rubbing against, touching, or fondling—generally in crowds where people are standing or moving closely together.

154. (C) Ascribed status is a function of birth; achieved status is a function of learning and performance. Caste emphasizes the former.

155. (E) Electroconvulsive shock therapy has proven most effective in the treatment of depression.

156. (C) Synanon is a treatment center for drug addicts—based on the same treatment philosophy employed by Alcoholics Anonymous.

157. (E) The fugue dissociative reaction includes physical flight from the conflict setting.

158. (A) Taking roles and enacting conflict-ridden life situations is characteristic of psychodrama.

159. (E) The Latin Square experimental design sets up controls for the order in which treatments are received.

160. (C) Hollingshead and Redlich found that psychosis was most prominent in the lower social class.

161. (E) Identity, fugue, amnesia, and depersonalization are all expressions of dissociative disorder. Somatoform is not.

162. (C) *Psychosomatic* suggests the presence of a continuous bodily emergency reaction and resulting tissue damage.

163. (E) The most serious phase of alcoholism is the chronic phase—the phase a person generally must reach before being receptive to meaningful rehabilitation efforts.

164. (E) The psychiatrist, as a physician, must take responsibility for the administration of electroconvulsive shock therapy.

165. (C) In this description, car radio sound is the independent variable and driver attention is the dependent variable.

166. (E) Between normal and psychotic children, research has revealed no detectable difference in prevalence of difficulty during delivery.

167. (D) Perfect positive correlation is indicative of the strongest possible systematic relationship between two variables.

168. (E) Chemoconvulsive shock therapy is not used in the treatment of alcoholism.

169. (D) Client awareness of the totality of his behavior is a central emphasis within Gestalt therapy.

170. (A) In electroconvulsive shock therapy, a muscle relaxant is administered to reduce the dangers of the seizure.

171. (D) Lithium carbonate (Eskalith) is prescribed for manic disorder.

172. (D) Since identical twins (developing from the same egg) have the same heritability, this high percentage of manic-depressive incidence in the second of the twin pair lends support to a strong genetic factor in manic-depression. The percentage incidence of the disorder in the second twin is called a concordance rate.

173. (B) The leading biochemical factor identified has been dopamine, but the causes of schizophrenia appear to be complex in a range that includes genetic factors, parent-child relationships, and biochemical functioning.

174. (B) The setting vividly describes a paranoid personality disorder.

175. (E) An IQ of 40 comes in the moderately retarded range, which covers the 30 to 50 span.

176. (C) Industrial screening procedures for a given position rely heavily on factors correlating with past success in that position.

177. (B) In human engineering, the best display is the one that minimizes operator interpretation and integration of data from several sources.

178. (A) The mean is the average of the scores in a distribution.

179. (B) The median functions as the midpoint dividing line for high and low scores in a distribution.

180. (E) The mode is the most frequently occurring score in a distribution.

181. (C) Red goggles would protect the rods so that they could function as soon as the pilot moved out of the briefing room into the darkness.

182. (C) The presence of only one independent variable (distraction level) and one measure (score) per subject suggests a completely randomized design.

183. (A) Initial matching of subjects, with assignment of one member in each pair to the second group and comparison of scores on the same testing instrument, suggests the t-test for related measures (in this case, the related-measure aspect was the initial matching).

184. (D) The built-in control for the order of presentation suggests the Latin Square design.

185. (E) Two treatments for the same group of subjects suggests the treatments-by-treatments-by-subjects design.

186. (B) The same group being tested at four different intervals suggests the treatments-by-subjects design.

187. (C) Human engineering has found performance efficiency more directly related to appropriate exterior body cooling than to breathing cool, dry air.

188. (B) During the past thirty years, industrial psychology has evolved toward more emphasis on human relations, that is, expressed concern for the worker.

189. (A) Newcomb's similarity-in-social-attraction position has proved applicable to the broadest range of settings.

190. (C) The Bogardus-type scale uses several social-distance statements of this kind.

191. (C) Standard deviation will be affected in the same manner as every score in the distribution—in this instance, it will be divided by 7.

192. (E) Comparisons of subjects' interests with the interests of persons successfully engaged in various occupational fields is the basic structure of the Strong-Campbell Vocational Interest Blank.

193. (B) In any given work setting, human engineering seeks to eliminate all unnecessary movement.

194. (C) Among the answer choices, opportunity for advancement has been found to be the most effective work incentive. Contrary to popular belief, money is not the leading work incentive.

195. (A) In the 1937 form, standard deviations were not consistent throughout age ranges. The problem was corrected in the 1960 form.

196. (C) *Observed frequency*, *expected frequency*, and *contingency tables* are terms relating to the chi-square statistic.

197. (E) Human engineering recommends placing the least important and least frequent tasks approximately ninety to one hundred degrees to the right or left of center on a console. Ideally, the most important and frequent tasks should be placed directly in front of the person.

198. (C) Knowledge that two people have obtained a given score is meaningless unless we know both the mean and the standard deviation of the score distribution.

199. (C) The study of bright children intermittently over a period of years would be a longitudinal study.

200. (E) Because the voters will be going to the polls almost immediately after the candidates speak, the candidate who has a choice would be best advised to select the last speaking position. Recency will be the most critical factor in this setting. If, on the other hand, the voting did not occur for another three months, primacy would be most critical (in that instance, the first speaking position).

Test 4: Evaluating Your Score

Abbreviation
Guide for
Quick
Reference
(Translation)

PC: Physiological/Comparative
SnP: Sensation/Perception
LM: Learning/Motivation/Emotion
CHL: Cognition/Complex Human Learning
D: Developmental
PrS: Personality/Social
PyCl: Psychopathology/Clinical
M: Methodology
Ap: Applied

TALLY CHART

- Checkmark to the left of each number you missed.
- In the column to the right of the number note the area your check-marked question is in.
- Move your check mark to the appropriate area column.
- Sum your check marks in each area column.
- Carry these sums to the blanks on the next scaling page.

Q#		PC	SnP	LM	CHL	D	PrS	PyCl	M	Ap
1	SnP									
2	SnP									
3	SnP									
4	SnP									
5	SnP									
6	LM									
7	LM									
8	SnP									
9	SnP									
10	LM									
11	PC									
12	PC									
13	PC									
14	SnP									
15	SnP									
16	SnP									
17	SnP									
18	SnP									
19	LM									
20	LM									
21	LM									
22	SnP									
23	SnP									
24	SnP									
25	PC									
26	PC									
27	SnP									

	Q#		PC	SnP	LM	CHL	D	PrS	PyCl	M	Ap
	28	SnP									
	29	SnP									
	30	PC									
	31	SnP									
	32	LM									
	33	PC									
	34	LM									
	35	LM									
	36	PC									
	37	PC									
	38	SnP									
	39	SnP									
	40	PC									
	41	SnP									
	42	PC									
	43	PC									
	44	PC									
	45	LM									
	46	LM									
	47	PC									
	48	PC									
	49	PC									
	50	LM									
	51	LM									
	52	PC									
	53	SnP									
	54	SnP									
	55	SnP									
	56	PC									
	57	PC									
	58	PC									
	59	PC									
	60	LM									
	61	CHL									
	62	LM									
	63	D									
	64	LM									
	65	LM									
	66	M									
	67	CHL									
	68	CHL									
	69	LM									
	70	M									
	71	D									

Q#		PC	SnP	LM	CHL	D	PrS	PyCl	M	Ap
72	CHL									
73	D									
74	CHL									
75	D									
76	D									
77	PC									
78	D									
79	CHL									
80	D									
81	D									
82	CHL									
83	LM									
84	PC									
85	LM									
86	CHL									
87	D									
88	CHL									
89	D									
90	CHL									
91	LM									
92	CHL									
93	LM									
94	D									
95	D									
96	D									
97	D									
98	D									
99	D									
100	LM									
101	CHL									
102	D									
103	LM									
104	CHL									
105	D									
106	CHL									
107	D									
108	LM									
109	CHL									
110	CHL									
111	CHL									
112	M									
113	D									
114	LM									
115	CHL									

Q#		PC	SnP	LM	CHL	D	PrS	PyCl	M	Ap
116	M									
117	M									
118	CHL									
119	PrS									
120	PrS									
121	PrS									
122	Ap									
123	Ap									
124	PrS									
125	PrS									
126	PrS									
127	PrS									
128	PrS									
129	PrS									
130	PrS									
131	Ap									
132	PrS									
133	PrS									
134	PrS									
135	PrS									
136	PrS									
137	M									
138	M									
139	M									
140	PrS									
141	PrS									
142	PrS									
143	PrS									
144	PrS									
145	PrS									
146	PrS									
147	PyCl									
148	PyCl									
149	PyCl									
150	PyCl									
151	M									
152	PyCl									
153	PyCl									
154	PrS									
155	PyCl									
156	PyCl									
157	PyCl									
158	PyCl									
159	M									

	Q#		PC	SnP	LM	CHL	D	PrS	PyCl	M	Ap
	160	PyCl									
	161	PyCl									
	162	PyCl									
	163	PyCl									
	164	PyCl									
	165	M									
	166	PyCl									
	167	M									
	168	PyCl									
	169	PyCl									
	170	PyCl									
	171	PyCl									
	172	PyCl									
	173	PyCl									
	174	PyCl									
	175	CHL									
	176	Ap									
	177	Ap									
	178	M									
	179	M									
	180	M									
	181	Ap									
	182	M									
	183	M									
	184	M									
	185	M									
	186	M									
	187	Ap									
	188	Ap									
	189	Ap									
	190	Ap									
	191	M									
	192	Ap									
	193	Ap									
	194	Ap									
	195	Ap									
	196	M									
	197	Ap									
	198	Ap									
	199	M									
	200	Ap									
	Sum										

Test Score Scaling

You've made it to the finish line. Now, tuck your last set of tally sums from the previous page into the blanks below.

PC Area: 23 – _____ (your number missed) = _____ // 18 = 75th percentile
SnP Area: 25 – _____ (your number missed) = _____ // 19 = 75th percentile
LM Area: 26 – _____ (your number missed) = _____ // 20 = 75th percentile
CHL Area: 20 – _____ (your number missed) = _____ // 15 = 75th percentile
D Area: 20 – _____ (your number missed) = _____ // 15 = 75th percentile
PrS Area: 23 – _____ (your number missed) = _____ // 18 = 75th percentile
PyCl Area: 23 – _____ (your number missed) = _____ // 18 = 75th percentile
M Area: 23 – _____ (your number missed) = _____ // 18 = 75th percentile
Ap Area: 17 – _____ (your number missed) = _____ // 13 = 75th percentile

You've come a long way and run a great race. Thanks for the privilege of letting us run this distance with you. Test well and travel gently!

Index